The Catholic Church in America:

An Historical Bibliography

Second Edition

by

Edward R. Vollmar, S. J.
Saint Louis University

The Scarecrow Press, Inc.
New York   1963

016.28
V 924 -1

Copyright 1963 by

Edward R. Vollmar, S. J.

L. C. Card No. 63-7466

TABLE OF CONTENTS

INTRODUCTION

The first edition of this bibliography enjoyed an unexpectedly wide circulation. If nothing else, this demonstrates the growing interest in church history, as well as the need for studies of this type. The early edition was generally characterized as the most complete bibliography on the Catholic Church in the United States. In this edition there have been some additions to the earlier years, and a completely integrated supplement of the years 1950 through 1961.

The most interesting addition in this second edition is the inclusion of the titles of unpublished doctoral and master's theses dealing with the history of the Catholic Church in the United States. Coverage of this area was limited to the regular degree granting Catholic colleges. There are many more manuscripts of this nature to be found in the state-supported and other private schools, and some seminaries professing to give a master's degree. The Catholic college group, however, offered a bloc that could be isolated and thoroughly surveyed. These studies vary a great deal in quality. The earlier manuscripts of the nineteen twenties are little better than a present undergraduate term paper. Some of the most recent productions have been worthy of publication in book form. As can be expected, the largest number of theses have been produced by the Catholic University of America. Every effort was made to personally study as many of the theses as possible. The impress of the director of the students was very noticeable, both in the quantity and quality of manuscripts produced at each school. Many interesting topics were studied, but in general it was found that the bibliographies of each study offered more to the scholar than the text. In this day of microfilming, photo-copying, and inter-library loans, a wealth of material has been made much more available.

In order to make the bibliography easier to use, the index has been completely revised along straight alphabetical lines. Several new subject headings have been introduced and the introductory survey has been included.

No new material has been added to the introductory survey. One event of interest was the death of Father Laurence J. Kenny, December 28, 1958. Father Kenny spent some fifty years in the classroom at Saint Louis University.

Publications of the past decade have been characterized by a high degree of scholarship, and less attention to apologetics. Many noteworthy articles and books appeared, but unquestionably the most important were the "Religion in American Life" volumes from the Princeton University Press. Of these volumes the "Critical Bibliography of Religion in America" by Nelson R. Burr stands alone. It is a truly monumental work. One might describe it as a history of American religion in bibliographical form.

Although this new edition includes most of the material in the old, the previous work has not lost is usefulness because of the different indexing and the dropping of many jubilee booklets. The unexpectedly wide circulation and enthusastic reception of the first edition have made the tedious hours of revision seem worth the effort. It is hoped that this revised edition will prove even more helpful.

GENERAL SURVEY

Publications concerning the history of the Catholic Church in the United States follow a definite pattern. During the Colonial period the Catholics of this country were content to have as little attention called to them as possible. Centered, as they were, in Maryland, with a few in Pennsylvania, and a handful in New York there was every reason to take advantage of the toleration offered, and give no occasion for more extensive celebration of "Pope's Day" in America. The Maryland Toleration Act of 1649 has been called the first formal act of religious toleration in any of the British colonies. Others have termed it the beginning of intolerance, because of its specifications. William Penn made anti-Jesuit and anti-popery speeches for political reasons in England, but in the colony of Pennsylvania there was no religious persecution of the Catholics. Except for some personal letters, and the reports of the Maryland Jesuits, we are without source material for the early period.

After Independence, and the appointment of the first Bishop of Baltimore, we find the Catholics a little more outspoken. During these early years of the new nation the best historical efforts were the reports submitted to Propaganda by the various dioceses. These were first-hand accounts, generally prepared by the hierarchy. The first serious effort to write a history of the Church in the United States was made by John Dilhet, who was in this country 1789-1805. His manuscript throws some light on the Church in America, but its value is greatly circumscribed by Dilhet's imagination, personal peculiarities and his prejudice against the German and Irish priests. The next published work of importance was the Notizie Varie of Father John Grassi, S.J., published in 1818. Father Grassi was of Italian extraction, he came to America in 1810 and spent seven years in the United States, mostly at Georgetown, as Rector, and Superior of the Maryland Jesuits. Written by a European for Europeans the Notizie Varie is valuable largely for the picture it gives of the United States, and the work of the Missionaries. It contains little original information. The distinction of being the earliest history of the Catholic Church published in the United States is generally credited to the Laity's Directory for 1822. Bishop John England of Charleston, South Carolina, wrote a brief sketch of the history of the Church in the United States for the Society for the Propagation of the Faith, located at Lyons, France, in 1836, which was published in the Society's Annales. The sketch is particularly valuable for Bishop England's account of the hindrances to the progress of the Church in the United States. Almost twenty years were to elapse before the next publication was to appear. In 1855 Thomas D'Arcy McGee published his Catholic History of North America, the first publication to come within the scope of this study.

Just as the early years were characterized by the work of a few individuals, so the period 1850-1950 can be centered around the efforts of a few great workers. Men such as John Gilmary Shea, Andrew A. Lambing, Martin I. J. Griffin, Gilbert J. Garraghan, S. J., and Peter Keenan Guilday left an impress on the development of Catholic historiography that is indeed memorable. But there is little else to be proud of in American Catholic historiography. In general it has been given to false starts and sudden stops, grandiose announcements and second class results. It is not fair to lay the blame entirely on the shoulders of the historians. Too often their dreams have been frustrated by a lack of money, or a lack of cooperation. This is a severe indictment, but after considering some of the efforts, with a knowledge of the work involved, one is forced to the conclusion that in some cases it looks like the word "facts" has been substituted for the word "evil" in the case of the three little monkeys, leaving the historian looking very much like a monkey, himself. Again it would seem that some writers have too often let imagination take the place of leg work. Incorrect entries, wrong references, careless documentation are all too common.

This lack of professional skill is not entirely of the historians' own making. There is today only one University offering a graduate program in American Church history. That school is the Catholic University of America. And even that program has suffered great loss in the deaths of Guilday and Purcell. Few schools even offer a course in the history of the Catholic Church in America, and even fewer have professors adequately qualified to handle the subject. The few scholars who are trained seldom have the time for further research. Another problem is the discovery of the source material necessary to produce first class works. Much essential material has been lost or destroyed. One venerable missionary of the West when called to task for not keeping records-- even baptismal records--simply shrugged his shoulders and replied that God knew, and that was all that was necessary. Father Howlett once stated that when the move from the old to the new Cathedral was made in Denver much of the archival material was simply taken out in the back yard and burned. And Rothensteiner's great work on the Archdiocese of St. Louis was made possible only by the rescue of the Rosati papers from a hospital basement. Much of the work produced has been the effort of writers, whose interest in history has been only secondary, or has developed from a hobby. The Catholic History of North America, published in 1855 is just such a work.

Thomas D'Arcy McGee was a controversial Irishman who came to the United States in 1842. He was not an historian, but rather a journalist by profession, and an agitator by avocation. His two brief stays in the United States were marked by the founding of the New York Nation, and the American Celt. Both of these news-papers were far more "Irish" than accurate. His Catholic History of North America is a compilation of the lectures he delivered be-tween 1854 and 1855 in various cities in the United States. It is based on second hand sources, and written in a popular journalis-tic style. The one great merit it had was opportuneness. Coming just at the time when "Nativism" and the Know Nothing agitation was at a peak, it provided a compact story of Catholic activity for friend and foe alike. Beyond this little can be said for it.

A work of far more merit, though less well received, was that of De Courcy and Shea issued in 1856 under the title The Catholic Church in the United States. This was a translation of a series of articles appearing under the name of Henri de Courcy de Laroche Heron in several French Catholic periodicals. John Gilmary Shea had helped in the original composition of the articles by supplying De Courcy with information necessary. He revised and edited them in the translation. The work is commonly referred to as the De Courcy-Shea History. A revised edition was published by Shea in 1879, and this is the one generally used. Although free from major errors, the work was not well received. One of its outstanding critics was Orestes Brownson.

In 1868 the Reverend Charles Ignatius White wrote a general account of the church in America as an appendix to the English translation of Joseph E. Darras' General History of the Catholic Church. Father White was a scholar of great erudition, and one of the outstanding literary figures of the American priesthood. From 1834 to 1857 he edited, under variant titles, the United States Catholic Almanac and Laity's Directory. He also founded and edited several short-lived literary magazines. With the assistance of Bernard U. Campbell, Father White collected a mass of source material for a projected history of the Catholic Church in the United States. A sketch of his plan was all that he ever put on paper. This is the appendix published by Darras. However, this little sketch was to have tremendous influence until the appearance of Shea's monumental work some twenty-one years later. Guilday states that the treatment of the first American Bishop John Carroll "has given life to many legends about John Carroll which are still current in American Catholic Circles."

Chronologically the next history of the Church in America is the work, not of a journalist, nor a priest, nor an historian, but the effort of a doctor. John O'Kane Murray was born in Ireland, and came to America with his parents in 1856. He was educated at St. John's College, Fordham, and the University of the City of New York. He practiced medicine in New York until 1880, when he was stricken with tuberculosis, and moved west to Chicago in the hope of relief. He died there in 1885. As an avocation he contributed many literary articles to the various Catholic periodicals of the time. At the suggestion of the Sadlier publishing company he undertook the authorship of a popular history of the Church in the United States. In 1876, as part of the centennial celebration, the company issued Murray's Popular History of the Catholic Church in the United States. The new scientific history was coming into vogue, and there are traces of this approach in Murray's work. However, the book attracted little attention from the historical scholars of the day, who considered it an inferior publication. Though the scholars may not have been impressed, the general public was, as the demand called forth four printings within six months after its first appearance. Today the book is considered of little value because of inaccuracies in the text, though it does contain many references to sources. But, before Murray was born, there was another already gathering sources for a history of the Church in the United States. John Gilmary Shea has been variously styled the "American Bede," or the "Father of American Church History."

John Dawson Shea was born in New York, July 22, 1824. Baptized John Dawson, Shea dropped his middle name and adopted Gilmary (Mary's servant) when he became a novice in the Society of Jesus. Equipped with a frail body and delicate health, his early years were given over to reading and nature study, rather than athletics, leading his father once to facetiously call him "Mary" on the score that he was more like a girl than a boy. He received his early training in the grammar school of the Sisters of Charity, and the Columbia Grammar School, where he was graduated with honors in 1837. He did not enter Columbia College, but engaged in trade for a few years, where his duty of meeting the ships coming into New York from the Spanish ports brought him into intimate contact with that language, which he soon mastered. He soon tired of trade and took up the study of law. In 1846 he was admitted to the New York bar. However, he evidenced an interest in history and was elected a member of the New York Historical Society in 1846. In 1848 he entered the Society of Jesus, and as a novice and scholastic studied at St. John's College, Fordham, 1848 to 1850. In 1850 the move that was to shape his entire career took place. That year he was sent to St. Mary's College, Montreal, where he was to spend the next two years, and acquire a friend and command of the French language. While at Montreal he came under the influence of Father Felix Martin, who had been engaged in accumulating a vast store of material on the history of the Jesuits in New France. During this period of scholastic development also began one of the few intimate friendships of his life. He began correspondence with Edmund Bailey O'Callaghan, the historian of the state of New York. That Shea did not become an historian of the Bancroft school can be largely attributed to O'Callaghan's influence. In 1852 Shea withdrew from the Society of Jesus and entered definitely on his historical career.

In 1852 John Gilmary Shea published the first of a long series of studies, his Discovery and Exploration of the Mississippi River. The volume contained original narratives of the explorers. Perhaps one unfortunate feature was to lead to a controversy many years later, that of the authorship of the Recit of 1673. This account describes the Marquette-Joliet expedition, and Shea's treatment led to an undue glorification of Marquette's place in the history of American exploration. But he wrote with the sources of his time, and if he has since been proven wrong, the very effort is a tribute to Shea. Meanwhile he wrote many articles for the United States Magazine, the American Catholic Quarterly Review, The Catholic World, and Ave Maria. Most of these articles were written in a popular style, but all were based on sound scholarship and did much to enhance Shea's reputation.

The year 1854 marks the appearance of his first great book on the story of the Church in the United States, History of the Catholic Missions Among the Indian Tribes of the United States; 1529-1854. In the preface of this volume we get a glimpse of Shea's historical spirit:

> In writing I have endeavored to be just to all men, to avoid partiality, to take no part in the rivalries which have existed and still exist, all tending to overshadow the truth, and give theories or party views for a real picture of the historical facts.[1]

Even Orestes Brownson, who was not known for his enthusiasm for other's efforts, and particularly was prejudiced against the French work in America, spoke highly of the work. Certainly it was the most valuable study that had been issued by the American Catholic press up to that time, and justly merited several printings before the outbreak of the Civil War. It established Shea's reputation as an historian and brought him into demand by historical societies.

Shea was now thirty years old, and decided to take unto himself a helpmate. Miss Sophie Savage, whom he married, and the two daughters born of this forty year union proved unfailing in their cooperation with the historian's projects. It was a happy marriage, but not blessed with financial security, as Shea was continually in pecuniary straits. His business acumen was in no way commensurate with his historical scholarship. A note from O'Callaghan written in 1855 might be styled typical of the entire lifetime of the historian:

> I do not pity you, working day and night, don't you know that if you let them, these Devilish Booksellers will flay you in order to make a drum afterwards out of your skin to rattle your praise on with your shin bones for drumsticks! What music that will be for Widow Shea! Have a sense, Child, don't be in a hurry to coin your heartstrings into gold. Take some recreation, but don't take it until next month, when, perhaps Providence in its wise dispensations may bring us together.

Over a period of thirty years, beginning in 1857, Shea published some twenty-five little brochures, which are known now as the Shea Cramoisy Series. Only about a hundred copies of each was printed and they are now rare. The burden of the series was the Jesuit Relations of New France--a source he had become acquainted with while at Montreal. The series has been variously evaluated by historians. The fact that he called attention to the material and made an effort to preserve it is of prime importance. At least some, if not most of the imperfections in the reproductions must be blamed on the printer, who showed little reverence for precise scholarship, but was the only one Shea could afford.

The monumental work of the "Father of American Church History" was begun in 1876. In that year he received a letter of recommendation from the Archbishop of Baltimore, James Roosevelt Bayley, which did much to encourage him, and opened many archives in America and Europe. At the Third Plenary Council of Baltimore a committee of four archbishops was appointed to cooperate with Shea in the publication of the projected History of the Catholic

Church in the United States. The first volume appeared in 1886 under the title: The Catholic Church in Colonial Days: 1521-1763. The book was well received. However, the praise was not matched by money, and when Shea totaled up costs and income he found that he had lost 1,500 dollars on the publication. Three more volumes were to make their appearance, sandwiched into Shea's continual battle to make ends meet. The second volume, which covered the life and times of Bishop Carroll proved successful, and secured him the assignment to prepare the centennial history of Georgetown University. The financial plight of the historian at this time can be appreciated by the fact that in 1889 he had written to Archbishop Corrigan of New York asking for a clerkship in the chancery office, or even for the Calvary cemetery. He had hoped to be appointed to the faculty of history of the newly organized Catholic University of America, and his disappointment was bitter when the position was filled by another, not nearly as well qualified. He was able to support his family and continue his History only through the generous help of his friend, Father Corrigan of New York, and by editing the Catholic News of New York City. Twice he had been forced to sell part of his library, and then to insure some security for his family he put up his whole collection for sale. It was purchased by Georgetown University shortly before Shea's death. He died February 13, 1892, while still going over the proof sheets of the fourth volume of the History. The work was never finished, but stops with the Second Council of Baltimore in 1866.

The work of John Gilmary Shea in American Church history is without parallel. A bibliography of his publications prepared by Spillane lists some 247 titles. This includes a great variety of subjects, because, in addition to the history of the Church, Shea was also intrigued by the various Indian languages and tribal histories. Some items are textbooks, prepared and issued with the purpose of making a living, but at the same time acquainting the students with the story of the Church in America. Two criticisms are generally levelled against his writings. The first is that he was excessive in his admiration for the work of the Society of Jesus in America, the second that his volumes lack planning and symmetry. The first objection is probably based more on his short time in the Society and the fact that Georgetown University was to play such an important part in his last few years, than on a careful examination of the evidence. The second criticism can be admitted without yielding anything from his reputation. He failed to solve the problem of reconciling geographical divisions with ecclesiastical provinces and the chronological story--no one since has had any better luck with the problem. During his lifetime Shea complained many times about people who used his material and gave him no credit. Surely his spirit cannot rest in peace, for much of the work done since his time is merely a rehash of Shea's great effort, with no credit given. Since his death many new sources have been brought to light, and some of his work must be redone, the fact that no one, even with all the modern aids of scholarship, has either attempted to re-do any of the volumes, or to continue the story from 1866, is alone sufficient to indicate the magnitude of his accomplishment.

Although the work of Shea overshadows that of the other Church historians of his time, there were other scholars of merit. Martin John Spalding, who became Bishop of Bardstown in 1850 published several studies, the most important being his Sketches of the Life Times and Character of Rev. Benedict Joseph Flaget . . . This work is particularly important because many of the sources used by Spalding are no longer available. Another scholar in the biographical field was John R. G. Hassard, who was a convert to the Church in 1851. His life of Archbishop Hughes is based on personal acquaintance as well as the correspondence of the prelate. It is a well written work, but by no means a definitive biography. A biography of Nerinckx was the book that established the reputation of Paul Camillus Maes as a first-rate historical scholar. He did vast research in the preparation of the book, but there are some who think that he paints too severe a picture of the founder of the Sisters of Loretto. One who thought so, and produced a more favorable biography was William J. Howlett.

The credit of organizing the first Catholic historical society in the United States, of publishing the first Catholic Historical quarterly, and of publishing the first diocesan history according to the new scientific school must be given to Andrew A. Lambing, of the diocese of Pittsburgh. Lambing was born in Pennsylvania in 1842, and devoted almost fifty years to parochial duties in that region. He was not a trained historian, but deserves first rank among the scholars of his day. He had known what work meant as a child and carried over this drive into all his future endeavors. A large man of some two hundred pounds and six feet tall,

> For two generations Monsignor Lambing was one of the most striking characters to be seen on the streets of Pittsburgh, with his enormous and finely chiseled head, crowned by long flowing white hair, and topped with the Mid-Victorian "two gallon stove pipe lid," and his cane. [2]

As early as 1879 he had attempted to organize an historical society in Pittsburgh, but had met with failure. The issue of Saepenumero Considerantes, Pope Leo XIII's letter on the writing of history, served as a spur to bring about his second effort and the organization of the short-lived Ohio Valley Catholic Historical Society in 1884. Lambing began, as a private endeavor, in 1884 the publication of the first Catholic historical quarterly in the United States, which he called Historical Researches in Western Pennsylvania, Principally Catholic, the title was later changed to American Catholic Historical Researches and in 1886 was transferred to the editorship of Martin I. J. Griffin. Like Shea, Lambing lived and died a poor man, and as Shea complained of others using his material without due credit, so did Lambing. In 1915 he was made a Domestic Prelate and the honor pleased him as he looked upon it as an approval of his work. He also published on religious devotional topics as well as in the historical field.

The scholar who took over Lambing's early publication was Martin I. J. Griffin, self-styled iconoclast of American Church history. Griffin was to continue the American Catholic Historical Researches for some twenty-eight volumes, filled with a wealth of information and personal views, so jumbled as to be a scholar's nightmare. When questioned with regard to his method Griffin stated:

> I seek to pull down error and raise up the truth . . . for twenty years . . . I gave no attention to attacking historical errors save by the negative method of relating facts. I saw many awful lies, balderdash, nonsense and ignorant recitals going the rounds as Catholic history . . . In July, 1901, I exposed the lies, yes lies, of Rome Saved America and The Debt America Owes to the Catholic Church . . . I found these and subsequent correction of errors so acceptable to research patrons that I have been pulling down, stamping out and destroying a few of the errors I have happened to meet.[3]

Born in Philadelphia in 1842, Griffin was educated at Philadelphia Central High School and was a special student in the collegiate department of Roth's Academy. It was during his early years in school that an incident happened which was to have profound effect on the historiography of the Church in America. Evidently a rather energetic child in a difficult class, he was to suffer a blow on his knee from a rod wielded by the school teacher, an accident that was to leave him partly crippled for the rest of his life. Because of this handicap he turned his interests to reading. Curiosity aroused by the inscriptions on the tombstones of St. Mary's Cemetery led him to make friends with the Jesuits of St. Joseph's, Willing's Alley. They allowed him access to a number of documents on the history of the parish, and he found that some of the information given out about the Jesuits in Philadelphia was false. The truth about St. Joseph's Church is a favorite topic through the volumes of the Researches.

Griffin spent a short time in business, but soon found that it did not suit his temperament. By the age of twenty-five he was correspondent for twenty-two Catholic newspapers throughout the country. In 1867 he started publishing the Angel Guardian for children. He established and edited for twenty-five years the I.C.B.U. Union, which became Griffin's Journal in 1894. As early as 1882 he had begun publishing in the Journal essays on the history of the Church in Philadelphia. And with the organization in 1884 of the Catholic Historical Society of Philadelphia he became the logical man to take over Lambing's publication in 1886.

During his editorship of the Researches he spared no one. This is not to mean that he was always right, but he did much to correct the errors previous to his time. He ran a column entitled "Errors Corrected," which, although satirical, was very popular. In addition to the Researches he published several books, the material for which had generally appeared previously in the Researches. Two favorite topics were the Catholics in the Revolution, and the life of John Barry. Griffin did much to refute Shea's opinion that the Catholics were all enthusiastic rebels, and to acquire for Barry the title of the "Founder of the American Navy." After his death in 1911 the magazine was issued by his son for a short time, but then merged with the American Catholic Historical Society of Philadelphia Records in 1912. The Researches were indexed, and although not a professional job, the index does make available many items that would otherwise be lost.

One of the persons associated with Griffin in the formation of the Catholic Historical Society of Philadelphia was Thomas Cooke Middleton, O.S.A. He was elected president of the new organization, whose aims were to collect, preserve, and publish all documentary material relating to the history of the Church in America, to investigate the origin and progress of Catholicism in the United States, to form a national Catholic historical library and archives, and to encourage interest in Catholic history in general. How well they have carried out this program can be judged by an examination of the pages of the Records--the only Catholic historical publication to continue in unbroken succession its original object. Thomas Cooke Middleton, the first president of the Society was born in 1842 in Pennsylvania of Quaker parents, but it seems that his father did much shopping around among the various churches, until the whole family was received into the Catholic Church in 1854. The future Augustinian historian began attending Villanova when he was thirteen years old. He was sent to Italy and became a member of the Order in 1858. He studied in Rome, where he was ordained in 1864. The next year he returned to Villanova, where he was to remain the following fifty-eight years. He held several administrative positions until his failing health led to a semi-retirement in 1914, he died at Villanova in 1923. He kept up his interest in the American Catholic Historical Society of Philadelphia during his whole lifetime. At Villanova he kept an irregular record of the community and school life from 1866 to 1923. This record of "Notabilia" was crammed into notebooks, all indexed, and contains much valuable information on the story of the Augustinians in America. He published several studies on the work of the Order, particularly in eastern United States.

Pennsylvania, however, had no monopoly on Catholic Historical Societies. In 1884 an attempt was made to organize a society in New York City. Little was done after the first meeting until, under the editorship of John Gilmary Shea, the group issued the first number of The United States Catholic Historical Magazine on January 1, 1887. From 1888 to 1892 the magazine appeared fairly regularly and contained many well-prepared articles. However, the death of Shea was also the deathblow for the periodical, and it was not until 1898 that the society was reorganized under the presidency of Charles George Herbermann.

Charles Herbermann was born in Westphalia, Prussia, in 1840. In 1850 his family migrated to New York, where they arrived after a long and painful voyage in 1851. The young Herbermann attended school at St. Alphonsus for two years and then entered the Jesuit

College of St. Francis Xavier. In 1858 he received the degree of Bachelor of Arts from St. John's College, Fordham. He became, then, an instructor in St. Francis Xavier College for the next eleven years. True to the Jesuit system of the time he was given the task of teaching just about every course in the curriculum. Meanwhile he also became a very skilled organist, and was a gifted musician. In the classroom he excelled in the classics, and, when the Chair of Latin Language and Literature at the College of the City of New York was offered him in 1869, he was advised to accept, although he was at the time only twenty-nine years old. In 1873 he was appointed college librarian, and he remained as teacher and a member of the library staff until 1914. He edited nine volumes of the United States Catholic Historical Society Records and Studies, as well as some of the early monographs issued by the society. He was a contributor to the Catholic periodicals of his time, particularly the American Catholic Quarterly Review. But his greatest honor was to come when he was chosen editor-in-chief of the Catholic Encyclopedia in 1905. The completion of the work before his death was one of his greatest achievements. He published a number of articles, one long series on the Sulpitians in the United States, which was later issued in book form. His history of the Sulpitians is not free from error as he did it during the last years of his life, when he was able to accomplish a little with the aid of his two faithful daughters, despite his ill health and failing eyesight. He died in 1915.

There were several other historical societies organized around the turn of the century. In 1892 the Long Island Catholic Historical Society was begun, only to change its name to the Brooklyn

Catholic Historical Society in 1894, and soon give up. A short-lived New England Catholic Historical Society was organized in 1900 and by 1904 had issued eight publications, when it ceased to function. Under the leadership of Archbishop Ireland the St. Paul Catholic Historical Society was begun in 1905, and published sporadically Acta et Dicta, a periodical filled with documentary material, particularly on Cretin and Loras, until it ceased publication in 1936. The Maine Catholic Historical Society was begun under the urging of Bishop Walsh of Portland in 1908 and issued a publication called the Maine Catholic Historical Magazine, the first issue appearing in 1913. However, the periodical contributed little to the field of American Catholic historiography.

Before turning our attention exclusively to the twentieth century there are several individuals who merit consideration for the work they accomplished in the latter half of the last century. No story of American Catholic historiography would be complete without mention of Webb, Moosmueller, and Devitt. Benjamin J. Webb was a native of Kentucky and spent practically a lifetime gathering material and publishing the story of the Church in that state. He, more than any other individual, was the answer to the nativistic troubles of the region. He had the advantage of knowing many of the pioneers, and was publisher and editor of the first Catholic newspaper in Kentucky. His great work was The Centenary of Catholicity in Kentucky, which appeared in 1884. It is a poorly organized attempt to put together as many facts as possible, often at the cost of interrupting the story and the confusion of the reader. Despite its defects the book remains an essential source for the study of the Church in the Ohio Valley.

Oswald Moosmueller was the pioneer historian of the Benedictine Order in the United States. He was born in the Bavarian Alps in 1832. As the son of a wealthy family he had the advantage of a good education in the Benedictine College at Metten. He entered the Benedictine Order and in 1852 was sent to finish his novitiate at St. Vincent's Priory at Latrobe, Pennsylvania. He later set out on what seems to be a rather nomadic life for a son of St. Benedict. He served at Carrolltown, Pennsylvania, Brooklyn, New York, Covington, Kentucky, spent some time in Brazil, whence he was transferred to London, Ontario. He was the first Prior of St. Mary's, Newark, New Jersey, serving during the life of the community 1863-1870. After a year as Prior of St. Vincent's we find him in Atchison, Kansas, as Superior. In 1877 he began a period of some ten years of service to the Negroes on Skidway Island, where he attempted to conduct an agricultural school. He was chosen first Abbot of Belmont Abbey in 1885, but after a short term as Superior of the Alabama missions he was recalled to St. Vincent's and again made Prior. In 1892 he founded a new monastery at Wetaug, Illinois, where he died in 1901. Despite all his travel he succeeded in accomplishing much in the literary world. As early as 1867 he published articles on the Catholic school question in the Katholische Volkszeitung of Baltimore, and in 1869 had thirty sketches in the Cincinnati Wahrheitsfreund on America before Columbus. In 1871 he issued a brochure commemorating the silver jubilee of St. Vincent's--a work containing errors later corrected by Shea, and Griffin. His best work was entitled Europaeer in A- merica vor Columbus in which he describes at great length the civilizations of Iceland, Greenland, and Vinland--and even broached the possibility of a Benedictine monastery in New England. This work was used extensively by De Roo. He published for two years Der Geschichtsfreund (1882-1884), a magazine devoted to the history of the American Indian and the apostolic labors of the Spanish and French missionaries among them. It is an unusual coincident that, although he published in German, nearly all his letters to his superiors were written in English. He was proposed for the chair of history at Catholic University, but declined. In 1889 he published his most popular work, Erzabt Bonifaz Wimmer. The last project he undertook was an attempt to form a house of writers at Wetaug, Illinois, to translate into German the work of the Bollandists, and publish the result along with some monthly instructions in a magazine called Legende. Seven volumes of the periodical were issued, although at first popular, it soon lost its appeal and the falling circulation finally led to its cessation and the closing of the monastery in Wetaug two years after Moosmueller's death in 1901. Though he held many posts of honor, Moosmueller's lack of personal magnetism and firmness kept him from ever becoming a great superior. He suffered greatly from swollen limbs, but was known for his practice of punctuality and self-denial. In view of his active life, and personal trials, his accomplishments are all the more great.

Another member of a religious order, whose greatest work was done in the latter part of the past century and early years of the present, was Edward Ignatius Devitt, S.J. He was born at St. John, New Brunswick, in 1840. The family moved to Boston while he was still a boy and it was in the Jesuit parish there that Devitt came under the influence of the famous Father McElroy. He finished Boston High School in 1854, attended Holy Cross College, Worcester, from which he entered the Society of Jesus in 1859. He kept a careful diary for the full sixty years of his religious life, a feat most unusual in Jesuit annals. After his ordination in 1875 he returned to teach for thirty years at Woodstock, Holy Cross, and Georgetown. He held several administrative posts, but showed little ability for governing. He enjoyed teaching, and it was as a professor of philosophy that he showed his greatest skill. He was editor of the Woodstock Letters, 1879-1882, and 1895-1913, and contributed articles to the Philadelphia Records. His great hobby was American Church history and the publication of letters and diaries by him earned him a reputation as a first class research man. He was assigned the task of preparing a history of the Maryland Province of the Society of Jesus, but the results were a disappointment to his friends. Devitt was a great digger and gatherer, but lacked the ability to organize and present his findings. During the later part of his life he was much handicapped by poor hearing and failing eyesight, so that he seldom attended meetings and found further research effort burdensome. His chapters on the history of the Maryland Province appearing in the Woodstock Letters contain much valuable information, but are difficult to follow. He died at Georgetown in 1920.

There was an awakening in Catholic historiography in the midwest at the beginning of the twentieth century. The organization of historical societies and the development of some outstanding scholars is ample evidence of this new movement. Names like Rothensteiner, Garraghan, Holweck, and Souvay remind one of the organization of the St. Louis Catholic Historical Society in 1917.

The next year the Society began publishing its short-lived Review, a periodical containing much archival material on the history of the Church in the middle United States. The year 1918 also saw the formation of the Illinois Catholic Historical Society under the leadership of men such as Seidenberg, Thompson, and Bueckman. The Illinois group published eleven volumes of their Review, before the publication was superseded by Mid-America of Loyola University, Chicago. Another Catholic Historical Society was formed somewhat later in Iowa, and has published since 1928 the Iowa Catholic Historical Review, of which some nine small volumes have appeared. One other historical society was formed at St. Benedict's College, Atchison, Kansas in 1930, but has not been very active.

Although the St. Louis Catholic Historical Society and its Review did not last, the group did bring about the publication of one of the best of the diocesan histories in the work of John E. Rothensteiner on the Archdiocese of St. Louis. Rothensteiner was born in St. Louis, but made his clerical studies at St. Francis Seminary in Milwaukee. He was an active pastor during his entire life, finding time to devote to history and literature only after his parochial obligations were fulfilled. While pastor of Holy Ghost parish in St. Louis from 1907 to 1936 he built there a school, rectory and church, at the same time working on his history of the archdiocese, and publishing some exquisite translations of German poetry. Intensive historical work really began with the establishment in 1915 of the historical Commission of the Catholic Union of Missouri for a study of the German Catholic in Missouri. Together with Holweck, Rothensteiner succeeded in locating and classifying the extensive diocesan collection of documents from the administration of Bishop

Rosati. Many of these documents were published in the St. Louis Catholic Historical Review. In 1925, at the age of sixty-five, he began writing the history of the diocese, a project which he completed after three years. Some idea of the literary tastes, and scholarship of the man can be gathered from the fact that at his death in 1936 he left a personal library of some sixteen thousand volumes.

A man closely associated with Rothensteiner in his work was Gilbert J. Garraghan, S.J. He was born in Chicago in 1871 and entered the Society of Jesus from St. Ignatius College there in 1890. The greater part of his mature years were spent at St. Louis University, either as Socius to the Provincial of the Missouri Province, or as professor of history. His assignments put him in an ideal position to gather material on the history of the Jesuits in the middle United States. Garraghan was known best as a research man, and though his preparations were painstaking, his record as a teacher was not great. He was fortunate in having superiors who recognized his ability, and the value of research. From 1921 to 1925 he was given complete freedom for research and writing, and again from 1932 to 1935 he was Research Professor of History and member of the Institute of Jesuit History at Loyola in Chicago. His books are fundamental works for all adequate study of the history of the Church on the frontier. The earliest volume published by Garraghan was his Catholic Beginnings in Kansas City, Missouri, which appeared in 1920. Built primarily on letters and reports of the pioneer missionaries, it evidences two characteristics which were to be found in his later works--a persevering effort to base his narrative as far as possible on primary sources, and to integrate the story of Catholic activity with the general history of the time and place. During the period 1921 to 1931 he spent most of his effort in research in the history of the Church, and particularly the Jesuits in the mid-west. During the time he published a number of periodical articles, all of superior quality, but no books. He was editor of Mid-America from 1929 to 1934. Garraghan's monumental work, a three volume history entitled, "Jesuits of the Middle United States," was published in 1938. His original intention, he told the present writer, was to take up the story of the history of the Jesuits in America where Hughes had left off, and carry the account down to the Civil War. However, as he progressed in his research he found more than adequate the problem of the Middle United States, and at the urging of Superiors carried the story to the time of publication. He was satisfied with the part down to the Civil War, but stated that he believed the second half should be redone. At the time of his death in 1942 he was preparing for publication a manual on historical method, the book was finished under the editorship of Jean Delanglez, a fellow member of the Institute of Jesuit History.

Jean Delanglez was born in Belgium in 1896, and educated there. He entered the American New Orleans Province of the Society of Jesus in 1921. He received his professional historical training under Guilday at Catholic University, where he chose to present the Jesuit side of the Capuchin-Jesuit troubles of colonial Louisiana for his research problem. He spent a very brief period in the classroom, then was assigned to research at the Institute of Jesuit History in 1936. At first he was of the opinion that there was little left to be done on the history of the Jesuits in early America, and was interested in the story of the development in the Amazon Valley. But he soon developed an interest in the problems of the French regime in the Ohio Valley. His interest blossomed into definite "hates" because of the falsified documents that had been foisted on Francis Parkman, and Delanglez's opinion of Pierre Margry was almost epochal. He could brook no error, and would have made a great partner for Martin I. J. Griffin. He was very severe in his own criticism and research, using all available archives. A command of modern languages greatly facilitated his work, although his English was far from perfect. He published some fifty scholarly articles, and a number of book reviews. At the time of his death he was preparing a biography of Cadillac, much of which had been published as separate articles in Mid-America. Delanglez worked with frenzy and wrote with violence, he will remain a controversial scholar for years to come.

Two other scholars of exceptional merit, who published works on the labors of their religious orders in the United States were Zephyrin Engelhardt, O.F.M., and Victor F. O'Daniel, O.P. Engelhardt was born in Germany in 1851, but was brought to Kentucky as an infant. He became a member of the Franciscans in 1872. From 1879 to 1899 he worked among the Indians of Wisconsin and California. His first book on the Franciscans in California was published in 1897. His monumental four volume work on the Franciscan missions of California was issued 1908 to 1915. It is a very detailed account of the work of the Friars, mostly told by the Friars themselves. Although the set is not well-organized, nor is it unbiased, it has done much to correct the early misrepresentations of historians like H. H. Bancroft. In addition to the four volume set Engelhardt has a number of monographs on individual missions of California, and at the time of his death in 1934 was still preparing a further study. Victor F. O'Daniel, O.P., was born in Kentucky in 1868, and received his training at Louvain in Belgium. He has served as professor of philosophy and theology on the Dominican faculties in Kentucky, California, and Washington, D. C. Most of his writing has been centered around the story of the Dominicans in Kentucky and Tennessee. However, in 1942 he issued a volume which gives a complete and detailed account of the Dominicans throughout the entire United States.

Peter Keenan Guilday has been popularly called the second founder of the field of American Catholic historiography. He was born in Pennsylvania in 1884, and began his clerical studies at Overbrook Seminary in Philadelphia, where he also found time to acquire a proficiency in languages. In 1907 he was sent to Louvain for special studies, and received his degree there in 1912. He was not originally trained for the American history field, and at the outbreak of World War I was engaged in research on the Continent, and in England. However, after his appointment to the faculty of Catholic University, the Rector, Thomas J. Shahan, by gentle prodding convinced Guilday of the enormous field for work. Guilday was the founder of the Catholic Historical Review in 1915, and remained its principal force and guiding spirit until he resigned the management in 1941. The original purpose of the Review was to gather and publish material on the history of the Church in America, and the first six volumes are ample proof of the material available. However, with the formation of the American Catholic Historical Association in 1919, the Review became the Association's publication, and lost its exclusive character. Guilday was also the chief inspiration in the organization of the Association. The publication of his biography of Bishop Carroll won for him a full professorship at Catholic University, and from 1922 until 1943 he directed many dissertations, and the "Studies in American Church History." Most of the work published was an outgrowth of his seminar in American Church History at Catholic University. As happens so many times, he was not a good teacher, and many went away from his classes disappointed, but he did prove an inspiration and guide for the research student. Although he produced several outstanding works in his own right, it is probably that his impact was felt even more in his training of his students. Unfortunately not all the dissertations published under his direction are of even quality, and in some there is a definite shunning of bibliographical technique. In addition he directed some one hundred Master's theses, some of which were printed in learned periodicals of the time. Guilday's influence was very widespread, and did much to promote Catholic scholarship. One unfortunate feature has been that most of the people trained under him have been swallowed up in the teaching schedule, and either do not have the time, or the inclination, to continue research and publication. His death in 1947 left a void in the field that remains unfilled.

The loss of Guilday has already been compensated for to some extent by the activity of John Tracy Ellis, also of Catholic University. Publisher of periodical articles of merit, a bibliography on the Church in America, and definitive biography of Cardinal Gibbons, Ellis needs no introduction to the Church history scholars of today. Although his publications alone merit him a place in the esteem of of all, it is as executive secretary of the American Catholic Historical Association, and managing editor of the Catholic Historical Review, that he has given leadership and inspiration so badly needed in the field of Catholic Church history. Just as Guilday was the originator and organizer, Ellis has been the continuing force.

The death of Richard J. Purcell in 1949 deprived Catholic University of another outstanding member whose work in American Catholic historiography was worthy of note. He was born in Minneapolis, and received his early college training at the University of Minnesota, his Doctorate from Yale in 1916. From 1916 to 1920 he was head of the history department at the College of St. Thomas, but was brought to Catholic University by Bishop Shahan in 1920. He was made a full professor in 1929, and from 1931 until 1943 was co-head of the Department of History with managerial rights. He did considerable publishing, particularly of book reviews, and was chosen to do most of the Catholic biographies in the Dictionary of American Biography. This last appointment was unfortunate because there were others much better qualified to do some of the sketches. Purcell's great interest was in the movement of nativism in the United States, and he directed many doctoral dissertations and Master's theses on that subject. It was here that Purcell was at his best. He always had time and inspiration for the plodding researcher until he well deserved the title "Apostle of Encouragement."

Another recent loss to the field of Catholic Church history was the death in 1950 of Thomas Francis O'Connor. He was born in 1899, received his Bachelor degree from Holy Cross in 1922, and his Master's from Syracuse in 1927. He taught at St. Louis University, Little Rock College, St. Michael's College, Winooski Park, Vermont, at Fordham, and at the time of his sudden death was again on the faculty of St. Louis University. He served for a time after 1941 as historiographer of the Diocese of Syracuse, and from 1944 to 1948 as historiographer of the Archdiocese of New York. O'Connor had a vast store of knowledge of the history of the Church in America, a fund which he kept in his memory, as he left practically no notes. He was the unusual combination of a capable research man, whose classes were extremely interesting and informative. At the time of his death he had just outlined a projected history of the Church in the United States. He did publish a number of periodical articles, but they give no indication of the tremendous potential of which he was capable. From 1944 to 1950 he published in The Americas a bibliography on the writings in Catholic Church history of the United States for each year. Lack of an adequate bibliography in the field was one of his pet peeves, and he was also beginning the preparation of such a tool. The present writer, who received some of his training, and much of his inspiration from O'Connor has continued his yearly bibliography in the May issues of the Historical Bulletin.

Nothing has been said yet about two of the Church historians whose work is considered a turning point in the preparation of Church history, William J. Howlett, and Thomas A. Hughes, S.J. A chronological study of Howlett's work will give the scholar a good example of the development from popular to fundamentally scientific approach. William J. Howlett was born in New York in 1847, but his family migrated westward, eventually to Colorado by 1865. Howlett served in the Diocese of Denver from 1877 to 1913, when he retired to the

Loretto Motherhouse at Nerinckx, Kentucky, where he served as chaplain until his death in 1936. His monumental work was a biography of Bishop Macheboeuf, first Bishop of Denver. He was fortunate in having the relatives of Macheboeuf make available the Bishop's correspondence so that the book forms an essential source on the history of the Church in Ohio, New Mexico, and Colorado.

Termed the progenitor of the modern era of American Church historical scholarship Thomas A. Hughes, S. J., produced only one work, a four volume study of the Jesuits in colonial and federal North America. To Hughes goes the distinction of being the first writer after Shea to display careful and exhaustive scholarship. He was born in England in 1849, and educated at Stonyhurst, but joined the American Missouri Province of the Society of Jesus at the age of seventeen in order to work as a missionary among the Indians. However, he saw little of the Indians as he was assigned to teach in several of the colleges, and in 1893 began a long period of research in preparation for his history. The product of forty years' work, the four volumes are a very complete account of the Jesuit activity in the territory of the United States down to the Restoration. If Hughes at times seems too preoccupied with the problem of the Jesuit property in Maryland, and his dislike for the Calverts, it must be remembered that the period he treats had the same difficulties.

It is impossible to include all the scholars active in Catholic Historiography in 1950, but from the number of publications listed in bibliography special credit must go to scholars such as Marion A. Habig, O.F.M., for his work on the story of the Franciscans, to Benjamin J. Blied and John M. Lenhart, O.M. Cap. for their excellent studies on the German Catholics in the United States, and to Theodore Roemer, O. M. Cap for his treatment of the mission aid societies.

Some years ago an ambitious program was begun at the University of Notre Dame under the title of the Catholic Archives of America. For various reasons this project has not been sufficiently exploited. Nevertheless, the work of Father Thomas T. McAvoy, C.S.C., and Aaron Abel of Notre Dame has been of high caliber, and has contributed several items of importance on the history of the Church in Indiana, and the philosophy of American history.

At present there is no satisfactory general history of the Church in the United States. The Story of American Catholicism by Maynard combines most of the bad features of scholarship with few of the good features of literary history, and is too taken up with the author's own opinions to be considered. Roemer's The Catholic Church in the United States is definitely a step in the right direction, but is so incomplete as to be little better than a guide. It is hoped that this bibliography will bring the appearance of a good general history one step closer.

Footnotes.

1. John Gilmary Shea, History of the Catholic Missions Among the Indian Tribes of the United States, 1529-1854 (New York, D. Dunigan and Bros. 1855), p. 17.

2. Thomas F. Coakley, "Right Rev. Andrew Arnold Lambing," United States Catholic Historical Society Records and Studies, v. 16 (1924), 114.

3. Daniel S. Rankin. "An American Catholic Historian," Sign, v. 16 (1936), 210.

A., S.M. "The Sisters of the Holy Cross," Catholic Educational Review, v. 2 (1911), 627-640. A 1

ABBELEN, PETER M. Venerable Mother M. Carolina Friess. St. Louis, Herder. 1893. 287p. front. (port.), plates. A 2

ABELL, AARON I. American Catholicism and Social Action: A Search for Social Justice, 1865-1950. Garden City. Hanover House. 1960. viii, 306p. A 3

ABELL, AARON. "The Catholic Church and Social Problems in the World War I Era," Mid-America, v. 19 (1948), 139-151. A 4

ABELL, AARON. "The Catholic Factor in Urban Welfare," Review of Politics, v. 14 (1952), 289-324. A 5

ABELL, AARON. "Monsignor John A. Ryan: An Historical Appreciation," Review of Politics, v. 8 (1946), 128-134. A 6

ABELL, AARON. "Origins of Catholic Social Reform in the United States," Review of Politics, v. 11 (1949), 294-309. A 7

ABELL, AARON. "The Reception of Leo XIII's Labor Encyclical in America, 1891-1919," Review of Politics, v. 7 (1945), 464-495. A 8

ABELL, AARON I. "American Catholic Reaction to Industrial Conflict: the Arbitral Process 1885-1900," Catholic Historical Review, v. 41 (1956), 385-407. A 9

ABRAMS, RAY H. Preachers Present Arms. Philadelphia.

University of Pennsylvania Press. 1933. xix, 297p. A doctoral dissertation on the war time attitudes and activities of the Churches and clergy in the United States, 1914-1918. A 10

ABRAHAMSON, WARREN C. "Pio Nono High School, St. Francis, Wis.," Salesianum, v. 35 (1940), 193-199. A 11

"An Account of the Progress of the Catholic Religion in the Western States of North America," American Catholic Historical Researches, v. 10 (1893), 146-159. A 12
    Concerned chiefly with the Ohio region in 1824, contains several letters of Bishop Fenwick of Cincinnati.

ACCURSIA, SISTER MARY. "Poles in Shenandoah, Pennsylvania," Polish-American Studies, v. 6 (1949), 9-13. A 13

ACCURSIA, SISTER MARY. "St. John's Polish College of Pennsylvania," Polish-American Studies, v. 5 (1948), 84-91. A 14

ADAM, J. "Destruction of the Catholic Mission on the Colorado," Historical Society of Southern California Publications, v. 3 pt. 1 (1893). A 15

ADAM, JOSE. "History of the Catholic Church in Los Angeles County," Historical Society of Southern California Publications, v. 1 pt. 5 (1890). A 16

ADAM, M. Life of Ven. Padre Junipero Serra. San Francisco. no pub. 1884. A 17

ADAMS, E. "Penitent Brothers,"

Sunset, v. 38 (1917), 26-28,
illus.   A 18
ADAMS, ELEANOR B. (tr. and
ed.). "Bishop Tamaron's Visitation of New Mexico, 1760,"
New Mexico Historical Re-
view, v. 28 (1953), 81-114,
192-221, 291-315, v. 29
(1954), 41-47.   A 19
  A good translation of the report of the Bishop of Durango on the state of the Church
  in New Mexico. Includes a
  good historical introduction.
ADAMS, ELEANOR B. "The
Chapel and Cofradia of Our
Lady of Light in Santa Fe
(New Mexico)," New Mexico
Historical Review, v. 22 (1947),
327-341.   A 20
ADAMS, ELEANOR B., and J.
E. LONGHURST, "New Mexico
and the Sack of Rome: One
Hundred Years Later," New
Mexico Historical Review,
v. 28 (1953), 243-250.   A 21
  The problem of Church
  and State in New Mexico
  1618-1626, centering around
  Governor Don Juan de
  Eulate.
ADAMS, ELEANOR B. "Two
Colonial New Mexico Li-
braries, 1704, 1776," New
Mexico Historical Review, v.
19 (1944), 135-167.   A 22
ADAMS, WILLIAM F. Ireland
and Irish Immigration to the
New World from 1815 to the
Famine. New Haven. Yale
University Press. 1932.
                         A 23
AGUIRRE, H. JERONIMO. "Mis-
sion de Tejas. Carta del H.
Jeronimo Aguirre al Superior
de Poyanne, Lovaino, 19 de
Marzo de 1875," Cartas de
Poyanne, n. 3 (1879), 101-
107.   A 24
AHERN, ELIZABETH A.
"Sketch of the Roman Catholic
Parish in Danvers," Danvers
Historical Society Collections,
v. 8 (1920), 71-83.   A 25

AHERN, PATRICK HENRY. The
Catholic University of Ameri-
ca, 1887-1896. Washington.
Catholic University of Ameri-
ca Press. 1949. 220p. illus.
                         A 26
AHERN, PATRICK HENRY.
"The First Faculty of the
Catholic University of Ameri-
ca," Catholic Historical Re-
view, v. 33 (1947), 129-157.
                         A 27
AHERN, PATRICK H. The Life
of John J. Keane. Milwaukee.
Bruce. 1954. xi, 396p.
                         A 28
AHERNE, JOHN P., and SISTER
CONSUELO M. AHERN "Some
Additional Notes on the Establishment of St. Gaulus
Mission, Green Lane, Penn-
sylvania," American Catholic
Historical Society of Phila-
delphia Records, v. 65 (1954),
252-256.   A 29
ALBAN OF ST. MARY, BROTHER.
"Century of Service (The
Christian Brothers in the U-
nited States," American Ecclesiastical Review, v. 118
(1948), 28-37.   A 30
ALBANY (DIOCESE) SYNOD,
2nd, 1869. Dioeceseos al-
banensis statuta quae in synodo
albanensi II, A. D. 1869
lata ac promulgata fuere a
Joanne Josepho Conroy ep.
Trojae, A. W. Scribner,
1869.   A 31
  Film reproduction. Positive.
  Collation of the original:
  ix, 25, 2 p.
ALBANY (DIOCESE) SYNOD, 3rd,
1884. Synodus dioecesana al-
banensis tertia quae antecedentium etiam complectitur constitutiones diebus VI et VII
Feb, A. D. 1884, in seminario
S. Josephi Trojae habita a
Francisco McNeirny ep. Neo-
Eboraci, typis Societatis pro
libris catholicis evulgandis
dictae "Catholic publication
society co." 1884.   A 32

Film reproduction. Positive.
Collation of the original:
85p.

ALBANY (DIOCESE) SYNOD, 4th,
1887. Synodus dioecesana al-
banensis quarta, synodos super-
iores mutans et augens, die
XIX Julii, A. D. 1887 in
seminario S. Josephi Trojae
habita a Francisco McNeirny
episcopo Albanensi. Trojae,
excudebat T. J. Hurley, 1887.
               A 33
Film reproduction. Positive.
Collation of the original:
1 p. 1., 3-46p.

ALBANY (DIOCESE) SYNOD, 5th,
1890. Synodus dioecesana al-
banensis quinta quae antecedentium etiam complectitut constitutiones die II. Dec., A.D.,
1890 in seminario S. Josephi
Trojae habita a Francisco
McNeirny ep. Trojae, T. J.
Hurley, 1890.   A 34
Film reproduction. Positive
Collation of the original: 93p.

ALBANY (DIOCESE) SYNOD, 6th,
1895. Statuta diocesis albanen-
sis. Albaniae Week-Parsons.
1895. 108pp.   A 35

ALBANY (DIOCESE) SYNOD, 7th,
1898. Statuta dioecesis alban-
ensis in septima synodo dioecesana die IV Januarii 1898
in ecclesia cathedrali Albaniae
promulgata et edita a Thomas
Martino Aloysio Burke episcopo
albanensi, Albaniae, excudebant
Week-Parsons sociique, typographi, 1898.   A 36
Film reproduction. Positive.
Collation of the original:
2 p.1., 7-30p.

ALBANY (DIOCESE) SYNOD, 8th,
1901. Statuta dioecesis Al-
banensis in octava synodo dioecesana die XVI Januarii 1901
in ecclesia cathedrali Albaniae
promulgata et edita a Thoma
Martino Aloysio Burke episcopo
Albanensi. Albaniae, excudebant Week-Parsons sociique,
typographi, 1901.   A 37

Film reproduction. Positive.
Collation of the original:
2 p. 1., 15p.

ALBRECHT, FIDELIS. With the
Franciscans among the Braceros, Provincial Chronicles, O.
F.M., Cincinnati, v. 28 (1956),
189-191.   A 38

ALDEN, VINCENT A. "Sister
Fanny Allen--A Glory of the
Catholic Sisterhood," Vermon-
ter, v. 45 (1940), 111-113.
               A 39

ALDRICH, VENICE M. "Father
George Anthony Belcourt,
Red River Missionary," North
Dakota Historical Quarterly,
v. 2 (1927), 30-52.   A 40

ALEGRE, FRANCISCO J. His-
toria de la Provincia de la
Compania de Jesus de Nueve
Espana. Nueva edicion por
Ernest J. Burrus, S. J.,
y Felix Zubillaga, S. J. In-
stitutum Historicum S.I.
Rome, 1956-60, 4 v. A 41
Contains much material on
the Southwest.

ALERDING, HERMAN J. The
Diocese of Fort Wayne, 1857-
1907. Fort Wayne. Archer
Printing Co. 1907.   A 42

ALERDING, HERMAN J. The
History of the Church in the
Diocese of Vincennes. In-
dianapolis. Carlon and Hollenbeck. 1883. 636p. front,
ports.   A 43

ALEXANDRIA (DIOCESE) SYNOD,
4th, 1921. Statuta dioecesis
alexandrinae quae in synodo
dioecesana quarta dei 30a Novembris, A.D. 1921, in ecclesia cathedrali S. Francisci
Xaverii in civitate Alexandriae
habita sanxit et promulgavit
Cornelius Van de Ven ep.
Alexandria, "Wall printing co.,"
1922.   A 44
Film reproduction. Positive.
Collation of the original:
52p.

ALEXIUS, P. "St. John's Seminary (Collegeville, Minn.)"

American Ecclesiastical Review, v. 17 (1897), 283-292. A 45

ALL HALLOWS ANNUAL, 1953-1954. Dublin, Ireland. 1954. The section pp. 132-155 treats of certain priest alumni of All Hallows College who worked in various American dioceses and includes excerpts from the correspondence sent back to Ireland from their mission stations in the United States.
A 46

"ALLEGANY FRIARS IN TEXAS," Provincial Annals (Province of the Most Holy Name, O.F.M.), v. 5 (1946), 275-281. A 47

ALLEN, ADRIAN. "Man Against the Wilderness," Sign, v. 32 (October, 1952), 36-38.
A 48

The story of Father Ravalli, S. J., and his mission work in the Northwest during the middle 1880's, particularly at St. Mary's Mission.

ALLEN, CUTHBERT EDWARD. "The Slavery Question in Catholic Newspapers, 1850-1865," United States Catholic Historical Society Records and Studies, v. 26 (1936), 99-179.
A 49

ALLEN, THOMAS JOHN. The Benedictine Fathers of the Swiss-American Congregation as a factor in the educational life of the United States. MA thesis, University of Notre Dame, 1935. 11, 125p. A 50

ALLISON, YOUNG E. "Chapter of Trappist History in Kentucky," Historical Quarterly (Louisville), v. 1 (1926), 68-81. A 51

ALOYSIUS, FR. O.M.CAP. Mission, Garrett Co., Md., 1820-1920. Cumberland, Md. Enterprise Pub. Co. c1921. 95p. A 52

ALOYSIUS, SISTER. "Dominicans in California," Dominicana (San Francisco), v. 1 (1900), 338-346, v. 2 (1901), 9-17,

47-59, 152-158, 295-302, 344-356. A 53

ALTOONA (DIOCESE) SYNOD 1. Synodus Altunensis prima, Lancaster, Pa. Wickersham Printing. 1923. A 54

ALVERINA, SISTER M. "The Franciscan Sisters of Blessed Kunegunda," Polish-American Studies, v. 8 (1951), 92-96.
A 55

AMANDINE, SISTER M. "Seventy-five years of Felician Activity in America," Polish-American Studies, v.6 (1949), 65-79. A 56

AMEDIE, MOTHER M. "Ursulines in Montana," Annals of the Propagation of the Faith, Baltimore, v. 62 (1902), 53, 321-322. A 57

"America in the Consistorial Congregation's 'Acta,' " American Catholic Historical Society of Philadelphia Records, v. 9 (1898), 385-398; v. 10 (1899), 1-16, 129-137, 335-344, 448-456; v. 11 (1900), 61-66, 208-212, 308-313, 455-460. A 58

"AMERICAN CATHOLIC HISTORICAL RESEARCHES: A Note for Bibliographers," American Catholic Historical Society of Philadelphia Records, v. 59 (1948), 257-258. A 59

AMERICAN CATHOLIC HISTORICAL SOCIETY OF PHILADELPHIA RECORDS, Index. vv. 1-31 (1886-1920). A 60

AMERICAN CATHOLIC WHO'S WHO. St. Louis. Herder. 1911-1931. Detroit. Romig. 1934- A 61

"AMERICAN CATHOLICS AND PARTISAN NEWSPAPERS," Catholic World, v. 16 (1873), 756-765. A 62

"AMERICAN CHURCH," Dublin Review, v. 67 (1870), 319-358. A 63

AMERICAN ECCLESIASTICAL REVIEW. Editor. "American Bishops and Polish Catholics,"

American Ecclesiastical Review, v. 29 (1903), 347-352.　　A 64

AMERICAN ECCLESIASTICAL RE-VIEW. Editor. "The Recent Decision of the Holy See in the Case of the Faribault and Stillwater Schools," American Ecclesiastical Review, v. 6 (1892), Supplement, 15p.
　　　　　　　　　　A 65

AMERICAN ECCLESIASTICAL RE-VIEW, v. 121 (1949), October. This issue is devoted to a commemoration of the sixtieth anniversary of the foundation of the periodical. Eight articles, treating of the various aspects of the quarterly re-view, comprise the major por-tion of this number.　　A 66

"AMERICAN RELIGIOUS FOUNDA-TIONS," American Ecclesiasti-cal Review, v. 17 (1897), 269-282 (Congregation of St. Paul), 337-347 (Sisters of Charity); v. 18 (1898), 1-12 (Congrega-tion of the Sisters of the Blessed Sacrament for Indians and Colored People), 484-501 (Sisters of the Divine Com-passion), v. 19 (1898), 15-28 (Sisters of Charity of Nazareth), 259-271, 254-360 (Sisters of Loretto), 601-613 (Institute of Sisters of the Humility of Mary); v. 20 (1899), 254-264, 454-466 (Bishop England's Institute of the Sisters of Mercy); v. 21 (1899), 271-282 (Institute of St. Catherine de Ricci).
　　　　　　　　　　A 67

AMES, JOHN G. Report on Mis-sion Indians of California. Washington, 1873.　　A 68

"ANALYSIS OF THE SERRA CAUSE DOCUMENTS," Pro-vincial Annals (Province of Santa Barbara, O.F.M.), v. 11 (1948), 18-20.　　A 69

ANCILLA, S.M. "Catholic Polish Book Publishing in U.S., 1871-1960," Polish-American Studies, v. 16 (1959),

1-11.　　　　　　　A 70

ANDRESEN, SR. ANITA MARIA, C.S.J. A Brief History of the Sisters of St. Joseph, 1856-1903. M.A. Thesis, St. John's University, N.Y., 1943.　　　　　　　A 71

ANDERSON, FLOYD. "The Pope's U.S. Representative." Ave Maria, v. 81 (1955), 15-17.　　　　　　　　　A 72
　Biographical sketch of Most Rev. Amleto Giovanni Cicognani.

ANDRE, G. Le Catholicisme aux Etats-Unis de l'Amérique du Nord. Paris. Librarie Bloud and Cie. 1905. A 73

ANDRE, G. Luttes pour la Liberté de L'Eglise aux Etats-Unis. Paris. P. Lethielleux. 1907. 128p.　　　A 74

ANDRE, G. Une Page d'His-toire sur les Associations Culturelles, ou un Demi-siècle de Troubles Religieux dans l'Eglise des Etats-Unis par le Fait des Assemblées Laiques Trustees. Paris. Vitte. ca. 1906.　　A 75

ANDRES, SR. ALICIA. The A. P.A. movement in Michigan 1892-1896, M.A. thesis. Catholic University. 1955. 157p.　　　　　　　A 76

ANDREWS, MATTHEW PAGE (ed.) "Unpublished Letter of the First Lord Baltimore," Mary-land Historical Magazine, v. 40 (1945), 90-93.　　A 77

ANDREWS, RENA M. Arch-bishop Hughes and the Civil War. Chicago. University of Chicago Libraries. 1935. 16p.　　　　　　　A 78

"ANFANGE DER BENEDIKTINER-MISSIONEN IN KANSAS TER-RITORIUM (1855-1857)," Cen-tral Blatt and Social Justice, v. 18 (1925), 89-90, 160-162.
　　　　　　　　　　A 79

ANGELA, SISTER M. "The Felician Sisters and Social Service," Polish American

Studies, v. 3 (1946), 21-29.
A 80

ANGELO, MARK V. "America's First," Provincial Annals (N. Y.), v. 15 (1958), 155-57.
A 81

Diomede Cardinal Falconio first American citizen to become a member of the Roman Curia.

ANGELUS, GABRIEL. The Christian Brothers in the United States, 1848-1948. New York. McMullen. 1948. xviii, 700p. illus., ports.
A 82

"ANNALS OF ST. JOSEPH'S CHURCH, PHILADELPHIA," Woodstock Letters, v. 1 (1873), 14-30, 85-108, 172-188; v. 3 (1874), 1-26, 94-111; v. 4 (1875), 30-42, 100-110; v. 5 (1876), 81-98.
A 83

ANNEKEN, SR. MARY GEMMA. A Study of the Growth of Catholicism in Covington, Kentucky, 1830-1868. M.A. Thesis. University of Notre Dame. 1946. iii, 108p.
A 84

ANTICOLI, P. "Carta del P. Anticoli al P. Superior de Poyanne. Tejas, S. Antonio, Diciembre de 1874," Cartas de Poyanne, n. 3 (1879), 107-112.
A 85

"L'APOSTOLAT CATHOLIQUE AUX ETATS-UNIS PENDANT LA GUERRE (DE SECESSION)," Etudes, v. 12, p. 1 (1865), 397.
A 86

"APOSTOLIC COLLEGE OF OUR LADY OF SORROWS, SANTA BARBARA (1853-1885)," Provincial Annals (Province of Santa Barbara, O.F.M.), v. 11 (1948), 54-64, 105-114, 161-167; v. 12 (1949), 1-10, 47-53; v. 13 (1950), 2-5.
A 87

APPLETON, SARAH S. "The Catholic Worker," Jubilee, v. 3 (1955) July, 21-33.
A 88

"APPLICATIONS FOR THE MARYLAND MISSIONS," Woodstock Letters, v. 9 (1880), 73-94.
A 89

"APPOINTMENT OF A GREEK (RUTHENIAN) BISHOP IN THE UNITED STATES," American Ecclesiastical Review, v. 37 (1907), 457-467.
A 90

Gives the principal provisions and regulations made by the Holy See for the spiritual protection of the Ruthenian Catholics in the United States.

"APPOINTMENT OF A SPIRITUAL DIRECTOR OF THE FRENCH SETTLEMENT IN GALLIPOLIS, OHIO," American Catholic Historical Researches, v. 12 (1895), 50-52.
A 91

"APPOINTMENT OF THE FIRST BISHOP OF BALTIMORE," American Catholic Historical Society of Philadelphia, Records, v. 25 (1914), 185-236.
A 92

ARCADIA, SISTER M. "Seventy-five Years of Child Care," Polish American Studies, v. 10 (1953), 13-39.
A 93

Account of child welfare programs under the auspices of the Felician Sisters in Polonia, Wis., Detroit, Mich., Manitowoc, Wis., Buffalo, N. Y., Milwaukee, Wis., Lodi, N.J., Niles, Ill., Jackson, Mich., and Ogleton, Dela.

"ARCHBISHOP JAMES HUGH RYAN," Speculum, v. 23 (1948), 544-545.
A 94

ARCHER, W. B. "First Catholic Church in Ohio," Ohio State Archaeological and Historical Quarterly, v. 24 (1915), 226-230.
A 95

"ARCHIVES AT BALTIMORE," American Catholic Historical Society of Philadelphia Records, v. 25 (1914), 85-95.
A 96

ARENTH, SISTER MARY AURELIA. As a Living Oak: Biography of Mother Baptista Etzel, O.S. F. Milwaukee. Bruce Publish-

ing Co.. 1956. Pp. vi, 133.
$3.00.   A 97
   A biography of the third
   Mother Superior of the
   Sisters of Pittsburgh.
ARETZ, J. M. The History of
   St. Victoria Parish, 1857-
   1957. St. Cloud, Minnesota.
   1957.   A 98
ARIZONA (VICARIATE APOSTOL-
   IC) SYNOD, 1892. Synodus
   dioecesana vicariatus apostol-
   ici arizonensis prima. Die
   29 Jan., 1892 in ecclesia
   pro-cathedrali S. Augustini,
   apud Tucson habita, a Petro
   Bourgade ep. Tucson,
   Citizen printing and pub. co.,
   1892.   A 99
      Film reproduction. Positive.
      Collation of the original:
      5 p. 1., 21p.
ARK, v. 4 (1949), June-July.
   This issue is devoted largely
   to a commemoration of the
   twenty-fifth anniversary in the
   episcopate of the most Reverend Constantine Bohachevsky,
   Apostolic Exarch for Ukranian
   Catholics in the United States.
                          A 100
ARNOLD, JAMES W. "Bracero
   Priest," Ave Maria, LXXXVI
   (1957), 8-12.   A 101
   A sketch of the work of
   Father John Garcia among the
   migrant workers in California.
ARNTZ, THEODORE. "History
   of the Formation of the Province of Santa Barbara," Provincial Annals (Province of
   Santa Barbara, O.F.M.), v. 2
   (1940), Jan., 1-7, April,
   1-4.   A 102
ARTHUIS, P. 'Rocky Mountains.
   Coeur d'Alene Mission. July
   21st, 1884," Woodstock Letters,
   v. 13 (1884), 381-382. A 103
AUDYAITIS, M. TIMOTHY, SR.
   Catholic Action of the Lithuanians in the United States:
   a History of the American
   Lithuanian Roman Catholic
   Federation. Ph.D. Thesis

Loyola Univ. (Chicago) 1958.
643p.   A 104
AUGUSTIN, JAMES M. Sketch
   of the Catholic Church in
   Louisiana. (New Orleans. J.
   M. Augustine and T.H. Ryan),
   1893, 87p. illus., ports.
                          A 105
AUGUSTIN, SR. MARY MILDRED.
   The Territorial Difficulties of
   the Early Dioceses of the Middle West in the Period Between 1784 and 1860. M.A.
   Thesis, University of Notre
   Dame, 1937. iv, 112p.
   maps.   A 106
AULD, HELEN. "The Critical
   Years of the Catholic Church
   in the United States," Ameri-
   can Catholic Historical Society
   of Philadelphia Records, v. 50
   (1939), 1-21.   A 107
"AUS DEM GRUNDUNGSTAGEN
   EINER DEUTSCHEN GEMEINDE
   IN VIRGINIA," Central Blatt
   and Social Justice, v. 16
   (1923), 197-198, 271-272.
                          A 108
AUSTIN, M. "Trail of Blood,"
   Century, v. 108 (1924),
   May, 35-44.   A 109
AUTH, FRANCIS. "First Parish
   Missions Preached in the U. S.,"
   American Ecclesiastical Rev.,
   v. 74 (1926), 251-262.
                          A 110
AVIN, BENJAMIN HERZL. The
   Ku Lux Klan, 1915-1925. Ph.D.
   Thesis. Georgetown Univer-
   sity, 1952. 313p., illus.,
   charts.   A 111
AZARIAS, BROTHER. "The Les-
   sons of a Century of Catholic
   Education," Catholic World,
   v. 50 (1889), 143-154.
                          A 112

            - B -
B., SISTER. 'Reverend Charles
   de la Croix, a Pioneer Missionary in Kentucky, Missouri,
   and Louisiana, 1815-1869,"
   American Catholic Historical
   Researches, v. 24 (1907),

47

59-61. B 1

BABBITT, CATHERINE FRANCES. "Jesuit Influence in the Development of Michigan," Michigan History Magazine, v. 11 (1927), 570-580. B 2

BABO, BEDE. Our Catholic Heritage. New York. Benziger. 1950. 344p. $3.50. B 3

BACA, LUIS. "The Guadalupita Colony of Trinidad (Colorado)," Colorado Magazine, v. 21 (1944), 22-27. B 4

BACHHUBER, C. A. "The Apostle of Four Lakes," Salesianum, v. 32 (1937), 76-79. B 5

"BACKGROUND OF THE CENTRAL VEREIN'S HISTORY," Social Justice Review, v. 33 (1940), 130-131. B 6

BADIN, STEPHEN T. "The Church in Kentucky," American Catholic Historical Researches, v. 29 (1912), 141-174. B 7

BADIN, STEPHEN T. "Father Badin's Account to Bishop Fenwick of the Michigan Indian Missions," American Catholic Historical Researches, v. 20 (1903), 174-176. B 8

BADIN, STEPHEN T. "Father Stephen T. Badin to the U.S. Indian Commissioners, Relates His Labors among the Indians," American Catholic Historical Researches, v. 26 (1911), 197-202. B 9

BADIN, STEPHEN T. Origine et Progrès de la Mission du Kentucky. Paris. 1821. B 10

BAER, SISTER AGNES MARIE. Diary of Reverend Nicholas Point, S. J., 1841-46. M.A. thesis, Saint Louis University, 1952. iv, 159p. B 11

BAER, KURT. The Treasures of Mission Santa Ines. Fresno, California: Academy of California Church History, 1956. Pp. 323; 109 illus. $5.00. A history and catalog of paintings, sculpture, and craft works. B 12

BAESZLER, SISTER SAINT ALFRED OF ROME. The Congregation Notre Dame in Ontario and the United States. Ph.D. thesis, Fordham University, 1944. 251 p. B 13

BAESZLER, SISTER SAINT ALFRED OF ROME. Contribution of the Congregation of Notre Dame of Montreal to Education in the United States. M. A. thesis, Fordham University, 1939. iv., 96p. tables. B 14

BAETS, MAURICE DE. The Apostle of Alaska. Paterson. Saint Anthony Guild Press, 1943, xi, 344p. illus. B 15

BAGLEY, CLARENCE B. (ed.). Early Catholic Missions in Old Oregon. Seattle. Lowman and Hanford Co.. 1932. 2 v. fold plates. B 16

BEHLER, SISTER MARY GABRIEL. Know-nothingism in Cincinnati politics 1855. M.A. thesis, Xavier University (Cincinnati) 1952. 106p. B 17

BAILEY, JAMES H. Century of Catholicism in Historic Petersburg, St. Joseph's Parish, Petersburg, Va. no pl. no pub. 1942. B 18

BAILEY, JAMES HENRY II. A History of the Diocese of Richmond from Its Establishment, 1820, to the Episcopate of Bishop Gibbons, 1872. PhD thesis, Georgetown University, 1952. 246p. B 19

BAILLY DE BARBEREY, HELENE. Elizabeth Seton, New York. Macmillan. 1927. xviii, 594p. front., illus. (incl. ports., facsims.). B 20

BAIRD, HENRY CAREY. "Memoir of Mathew Carey," American-Irish Historical Society, Journal, v. 5 (1905), 124-134. B 21

48

BAISNEE, J. A. "The Catholic
Church in the United States,
1784-1829," American Catholic
Historical Society of Philadelphia Records, v. 56 (1945),
133-162, 245-292.   B 22

BAISNEE, J. A. "France and the
Establishment of the American
Hierarchy," Catholic Historical
Review, v. 24 (1938), 175-
189.   B 23

BAISNEE, JULES A. France and
the Establishment of the American Hierarchy. Baltimore.
Johns Hopkins Press. 1934.
ix, 182p. front. (port). B 24

BAISNEE, JULES A. "The Myth
of the 'French Scheme of the
Enslavement of American
Catholics,' " Catholic Historical Review, v. 19 (1934),
437-459.   B 25

BAKER, O.E. "The Church and
Rural Youth," Catholic Rural
Life Objectives, St. Paul,
Minnesota, 1936. pp. 7-29.
                           B 26

BALDASARRE, RAFFAELE L.
"Lettera XXX," Lettere Edificanti Provincia Napolitana, ser.
1 (1875), 82-85.   B 27

BALDASARRE, RAFFAELE L.
"Mision de Neuvo Mejico,
Residencia de Conejos (Colo-
rado). Carta del Rafael L.
Baldasarre al Superior de
Poyanne, 12 de Noviembre,
1874," Cartas de Poyanne,
n. 3 (1879), 112-115.   B 28

BALDWIN, PERCY M. (tr. and
ed.). "Fray Marcos de
Niza and His Discovery of the
Seven Cities of Cibola," New
Mexico Historical Review, v.
1 (1926), 193-223.   B 29

BALLY, AUGUSTINE. "Historical Sketch of the Mission of
Goshenhoppen, now Church-
ville, Pa.," Woodstock Letters,
v. 5 (1876), 202-213.   B 30

BALMAIN, ALEXANDER
FRANCIS. History of Catholic
Education in the Diocese of
Brooklyn. Ph.D. thesis,

Fordham University, 1935.
iii, 124p.   B 31

BALTIMORE (ECCLESIASTICAL
PROVINCE), COUNCILS.
Concilla Provincialia Baltimori Habita ab Anno 1829
usque ad Annum 1849. Baltimore, Murphy, 1842. 221p.
1d ed. 1851. 307p.   B 32
   Contains the statutes of 1791
   and decrees of the seven
   provincial councils. The
   1852 edition contains the
   decrees of the First Plenary
   Council also.

BALTIMORE (ECCLESIASTICAL
PROVINCE), 1869. Concilii
Provincialis Baltimorensis X
in Metropolitana Baltimorensi
Ecclesia, Dominica quarta post
Pascha, quae Jesto S Marce
Evangelistae incidit ARS 1869
inchoati, et insequenti
Dominica absoluti, Acta et
Decreta. Praeside Illmo. ac
Revmo, Martino Spalding,
Archiepiscopo Baltimorensi.
Baltimore. John Murphy.
1870. 78p.   B 33

BALTIMORE (DIOCESE) SYNOD.
1853. Synodus Dioecesana
Baltimorensis, mense Junio
1853 habita. Baltimore. John
Murphy. 1853. 18p. B 34

BALTIMORE (DIOCESE) SYNOD.
1857. Synodus Dioecesana
Baltimorensis, mense Junio
1857 habita. Baltimore. John
Murphy. 1857. 14pp. B 35

BALTIMORE (DIOCESE) SYNOD.
1855. Concilium Baltimorense
VIII Habitum Anno 1855. Baltimore. John Murphy. 1857.
40 pp.   B 36

BALTIMORE (DIOCESE) SYNOD.
1858. Concilium Baltimorense
Provinciale X. Habitum Anno
1858. Baltimore. John
Murphy. [1858] 42pp.
                           B 37

BALTIMORE (DIOCESE) SYNOD.
1863. Synodus Dioecesana
Baltimorensis, mense Maii
1863 habita. Baltimore. John

Murphy. 1863. n.p. B 38
BALTIMORE (DIOCESE) SYNOD
1865. Acti Synodi Dioecesanae
Baltimorensis Sextae una cum
constiutionibus, ab Illustrissimo ac Reverendissimo Martino Joanne Spalding, Archiepiscopo Baltimorense, latus
ac promulgatus, in feria quarta
Rogationum, die 24 Maii, A.
D. 1865. Baltimore. Kelly
and Piet. 1865. 22pp.
B 39
BALTIMORE (DIOCESE) SYNOD.
1868. Synodus Dioecesana
Baltimorensis Septima, quae
antecedentrum etiam com-
plectitur Constitutiones: die
3 Septembris, AD 1868 in
Ecclesia Collegiali S. Maria
ad Seminarium S. Sulpitii,
Baltimorae habita ab Illustrissimo ac Reverendissimo
Martino Joanne Spalding Archiepiscopo Baltimorensi. Baltimore. John Murphy. 1868.
n.p. B 40
BALTIMORE (DIOCESE) SYNOD.
1875. Synodus Dioecesana
Baltimorensis Octava, quae
antecedentrum complectitur
Constitutiones, die 27 Augusti
1875 ad BMV in Seminario
S. Sulpitii Baltimorae habita ab
Illustrissimo Jacobo Roosevelt
Bayley, Archiepiscopo Balti-
morensi, Baltimore. John
Murphy. 1876. 134pp. B 41
BALTIMORE (DIOCESE) SYNOD.
1886. Synodus Dioecesana
Baltimorensis Nona quae
antecedentrum etiam complec-
titur Constitutiones; die 24
Septembris, AD. 1886 ad BVM
in Seminario S. Sulpitii, Balti-
morae habita ab Eminentissimo
ac Reverendissimo Jacobo
Cardinali Gibbons, Archiepisco-
po Baltimorenai. Baltimore.
Foley Bros. 1886. 136p.
B 42
"'BALTIMORE BREVITIES'
Excerpts from letters in
Cathedral Archives," American

Catholic Historical Society of
Philadelphia Records, v. 22
(1911), 129-153. B 43
BANDELIER, ADOLPH F.
"Fray Juan de Padilla, the
First Catholic Missionary and
Martyr in Eastern Kansas,"
American Catholic Quarterly
Review, v. 15 (1890), 551-
565. B 44
BANDELIER, ADOLPH F.
"Fray Marcos of Niza," in
Hemenway, Southwestern
Archaeological Expedition.
Cambridge. 1890. pp. 106-
178. B 45
BANDINI, A. R. "A Bishop
Comes to California," Amer-
ican Ecclesiastical Review, v.
103 (1940), 253-267. B 46
BANDINI, J. "Montana, St.
Ignatius' Mission. Letter to
the Superior of the Mission,"
Woodstock Letters, v. 11
(1882), 275-279. B 47
BANGERT, WILLIAM. "St.
Andrew through Fifty Years,"
Woodstock Letters, v. 83
(May, 1954), 177-196. plates.
B 48
A documented historical
sketch of the Jesuit Novitiate
at St. Andrews on Hudson in
New York.
BANNON, JOHN FRANCIS.
"Black-Robe Frontiersman:
Gabriel Marest, S.J.," Mis-
souri Historical Society Bulletin, v. 10 (Apr., 1954),
351-366. B 49
A well written and carefully
documented biographical
sketch of this missionary
who died in 1714 after spend-
ing sixteen years laboring
among the Kaskaskia Indians.
BANNON, JOHN FRANCIS. "The
Blackrobes in Americas," Historical Bulletin, v. 17 (1940),
53-54, 65-66. B 50
BANNON, JOHN FRANCIS.
"Kino: Agent for Both Majes-
ties," Historical Bulletin,
v. 25 (1947), 55-56, 62-63.

50

B 51
BANNON, JOHN FRANCIS. "Our
Anniversary Review," His-
torical Bulletin, v. 25
(1947), 83-84.   B 52
BANNON, JOHN F. "Peter M.
Dunne, S.J. (1890-1957),"
Hispanic American Historical
Review, XXXVII (May, 1957),
227-233.   B 53
A good biographical sketch
of this California Jesuit
historian; includes a
bibliography of his writings.
BANNON, JOHN F. "The St.
Louis University Collection
of Jesuitica Americana," His-
panic American Historical Re-
view, XXXVII (Feb., 1957),
82-88.   B 54
BARAGA, FREDERICK. "Extrait
d'une lettre de Mgr. Frederic
Baraga Evêque de Sainte-
Marie (nord du Lac Michigan)"
Annales de la Propagation de
la Foi, v. 33 (1861), 483-
487.   B 55
BARAGA, FREDERICK. "Letter
to Pierz, dated June 13, 1834,"
Social Justice Review, v. 33
(1940), 131-132.   B 56
BARBER, DANIEL. "Conversion
of Rev. Daniel Barber, His
Own Account," American
Catholic Historical Researches,
v. 11 (1894), 81-87.   B 57
BARBER, SISTER MARY JOSE-
PHINE. "First House of the
Sisters of the Visitation at
Kaskaskia, Illinois. A.D.
1833," American Catholic
Historical Society of Philadel-
phia Records, v. 13 (1902),
211-230.   B 58
BARBIAN, JOSEPH. "The Catholic
Normal School of the Holy
Family," Catholic Educational
Review, v. 5 (1913), 123-
131.   B 59
BARBOUR, SISTER RICHARD
MARIE. Joseph Projectus
Machebeuf and the influence
of religion on the development
of the eastern slope of the

Rocky Mountain area. M.A.
thesis, Saint Louis University.
1949. ix, 127pp.   B 60
BARBOUR, SISTER RICHARD
MARIE. Light in Yucca Land.
Santa Fe, N. M. Loretto
Academy of Light. 1952.
166p. illus. $5.00.   B 61
The story of the work of
the Sisters of Loretto in
the Southwest.
BARCELO, G. "Indian Missions.
The Crow Indians. Letter
dated Helena, October 7, 1880,"
Woodstock Letters, v. 10 (1881),
137-139.   B 62
BARCLAY, THOMAS S. "The
Test Oath for the Clergy in
Missouri," Missouri Histori-
cal Review, v. 18 (1924),
345-381.   B 63
BARDSTOWN (DIOCESE) SYNOD.
1850. Constitutiones Dioecesis
Ludovicopolitanae, a Revendis-
simo ac Illustrissimo Domino
Martino Joanne Spalding,
Episcopo Ludicopolitanae in
Synodo Dioecessana prima
habita mense Julii 1850 in
Ecclesia St. Josephi, Bardopoli,
Latae et promulgatae. Louis-
ville. Webb. 1850. 20 pp.
                        B 64
BARKER, SISTER ROSANNA.
Mother Margaret Cecilia
George, first Superior of the
Sisters of Charity of Cincin-
nati, O., M.A. thesis. Saint
Louis University. 1944. 5,
122p.   B 65
BARKER, S. O. "Los Penitentes,"
Overland, v. 82 (1924), 151-
153.   B 66
BARNABA, SISTER MARY. A
Diamond Crown for Christ the
King. Glenn Riddle, Pa.
1930.   B 67
BARNES, JOHN PAUL. Dramatic
Presentation in the Secondary
Schools of the United States.
Ph.D. thesis. Fordham Uni-
versity, 1933. iii, 135p.
                        B 68
BARNES, REGINA GRACE. The

Frontier as Seen in the Letters of Father Gabried Richard. M.A. ND 1943. iii, 119pp.
B 69

BARNUM, FRANCIS. "Development of the Early Jesuit Missions," American Catholic Historical Society of Philadelphia Records, v. 34 (1923), 362-373.
B 70

BARNUM, FRANCIS. "Catholic Missions in Alaska," Historical Records and Studies, v. 13 (1919), 87-100.
B 71

BARNUM, FRANCIS. "Development of the Early Jesuit Missions," Woodstock Letters, v. 52 (1923), 216-225.
B 72

BARNUM, FRANCIS. "The Last of the Indian Missionaries--Father Joseph Joset," Woodstock Letters, v. 30 (1901), 202-214.
B 73

BAROUX, L. "Lettre de M. l'abbe Baroux, missionnaire apostolique du détroit, à M. le President du Conseil Central de Paris. 15 mars, 1863," Annales de la Propagation de la Foi, v. 35 (1863), 287-290.
B 74

BAROUX, L. "Lettre de M. L. Baroux, missionaire apostolique a MM. les Directeurs de l'Oeuvre de la Propagation de la Foi. Dowagiac-Cals County, Michigan, 19 juin, 1863," Annales de la Propagation de la Foi, v. 35 (1863), 483-485.
B 75

BARRE, AIME JOSEPH. History and Present Status of Religious Instruction among Franco-American Population of the Diocese of Fall River. M.A. thesis. Catholic University. 1938. 46p.
B 76

BARRETT, JOHN D. A Comparative Study of the Councils of Baltimore and the Code of Canon Law. Washington. Catholic University of America Press, 1932, x, 223p.
B 77

BARRY, COLMAN J. "Benedictine Pioneers in Minnesota Territory," American Benedictine Review, VI (Winter, 1955-1956), 357-388.
B 78

Based on material in the author's book Worship and Work.

BARRY, COLMAN J. "Boniface Wimmer, Pioneer of the American Benedictines," Catholic Historical Review, v. 41 (1955), Oct. 272-296.
B 79

BARRY, COLEMAN J. Catholic Church and German Americans. Milwaukee, Bruce. 1953. pp. 348. pl. $6.00.
B 80

An excellent study of this problem, might be criticized as being too favorable toward the Germans in some of the controversies.

BARRY, COLMAN J. The Catholic University of America, 1903-1909. Washington. The Catholic University of America Press. 1950. xi, 198p.
B 81

BARRY, COLEMAN J. "The German Triangle of the West," American Benedictine Review, v. 3 (Autumn, 1953), 210-239.
B 82

An interesting account of the German activity in the triangle formed by Milwaukee, St. Louis, and Cincinnati.

BARRY, COLMAN J. "Some Roots of American Nativism," Catholic Historical Review, XLIV (July, 1958), 137-146.
B 83

BARRY, COLMAN J. Worship and Work. Collegeville, Minn.: Saint John's Abbey, 1956. 447p.
B 84

The story of Saint John's Abbey and University 1856-1956, written by one of the outstanding Benedictine scholars of America. Excellent in content and format.

BARRY, JOHN J. "Father Tabb,"
Catholic Educational Review,
v. 42 (1944), 149-155.
B 85

BARRY, JOHN J. "Father Tabb,"
Salesianum, v. 35 (1940),
133-143.
B 86

BARRY, JOHN J. "The Poet-
Priest of the South," Salesian-
um, v. 38 (1943), 147-157.
B 87

BARRY, JOHN M. "Reverend
Matthew Ryan," American
Catholic Historical Society of
Philadelphia Records, v. 36
(1925), 205-208.
B 88

BARRY, JOHN PAUL. Know
Nothing party in the District
of Columbia. M.A. thesis.
Catholic University. 1933.
46p.
B 89

BARRY, T. BYRNES. "Bishop
Richard Vincent Whelan (1841-
1850) and the Reestablishment
of the Richmond Diocese,"
Catholic Virginian, v. (1944),
3-5, 26-27, 47-49.
B 90

BARRY, THOMAS. "The Church
in Albany," American Catholic
Historical Society of Philadelphia Records, v. 21 (1910),
175-178.
B 91

BARRY, THOMAS. "The Church
in Albany," American Catholic
Historical Researches, v. 29
(1912), 175-179.
B 92

BARTELS, BARTHOLOMEW.
"Documents. The First Catholic Settlements of Clinton County, Illinois," Mid-America,
v. 5 (1933), 45-58.
B 93

BARTH, ARTHUR AUGUST.
Guide to materials for the
history of the Indian missions
of the Trans-Mississippi West
(exclusive of De Smetiana) in
the Archives of St. Louis University. M.A. thesis. Saint
Louis University. 1937.
106p.
B 94

BARTH, PIUS J. "Franciscan
Education in French North
America," The Americas, v.

4 (1947), 3-31.
B 95

BARTH, PIUS J. and SISTER
M. MARINELLA GUBOLA.
Franciscan Educational Direc-
tory of the United States.
Chicago, Ill. Franciscan
Herald Press. 1950. 58p.
B 96

BARTH, SILAS. "The Franciscans in Southern Illinois,"
Illinois Catholic Historical Review, v. 1 (1919-1920),
161-174, 328-338, 447-457;
v. 3 (1920-1921), 77-78,
170-175, 260-267.
B 97

BARTLETT, CHESTER J. The
Tenure of Parochial Property
in the United States of America. Washington. Catholic
University of America Press.
1926. v. 108p.
B 98

BARTON, GEORGE. Angels of
the Battlefield. Philadelphia.
1897. Catholic Sisterhoods
and the Civil War.
B 99

BARTON, GEORGE. "A Study
of Self Sacrifice," American
Catholic Historical Society of
Philadelphia Records, v. 37
(1926), 104-192.
B 100
The record of the labors of
the Catholic Sisterhoods in
the Spanish-American War.

BASIL, BROTHER. "Pedro de
Gante, the First Great Educa-
tor and Catechist of America,"
Catholic Educator, v. 19
(1949), 376-377.
B 101

BASKA, SISTER MARY REGINA.
Archbishop Bedini in the U-
nited States: an episode in A-
merican history. M.A. thesis,
Catholic University. 1927.
38p.
B 102

BASKA, SISTER M. REGINA.
The Benedictine Congregation
of Saint Scholastica. Its
Foundation and Development
(1852-1930). Washington.
Catholic University of America
Press. 1935. viii, 154p.
fold. diagr.
B 103

BASKA, SISTER REGINA. "Pioneers and Builders: 1852-

1952," The Benedictine Review, v. 7 (Winter, 1952), 33-42. B 104

A historical sketch of the Benedictine Sisters in the United States, includes a map and diagram showing the development from Eichstatt in the United States for the last century.

BASSETT, J.S. "A North Carolina Monastery," Magazine of American History, v. 29 (1893), 131-135. B 105

Brief sketch of Belmont Abbey, founded by the Benedictines 1876.

BASSO, LEONARD. "Our Martyrology," St. Meinrad Historical Essays, v. 1 (1928), 32-37. B 106

BATTERSBY, SISTER AGNES C. American Public Opinion on the Syllabus Errorum of Pope Pius IX. M. A. thesis. Catholic University. 1953. 77p. B 107

BAUDIER, ROGER. The Catholic Church in Louisiana. New Orleans. A.W. Hyatt Stationery Mfg. Co. 1939. 605, 59p. B 108

BAUDIER, ROGER. "The First Sodality of the Blessed Virgin in New Orleans, 1730," United States Catholic Historical Society Records and Studies, v. 30 (1939), 47-53. B 109

BAUDIER, ROGER. "Marian Devotion in Louisiana," Ave Maria, v. 57 (1943), 687-689. B 110

BAUER, ERVIN L. Father Louis A. Lambert, Catholic Journalist, and his times. M.A. thesis. Catholic University. 1956. 521p. B 111

BAUHS, E. J. "The Renovation of Saint Raphael Cathedral," Wisconsin Magazine of History, v. 39 (Spring 1956), 171-179. B 112

Interesting observations on the structure of the Cathedral at Madison, Wisconsin.

BAUMAN, W. B. Catholic Contributions to Oregon History. Mt. Angel, Oregon. 1959. B 113

BAUMANN, CELESTIN. Diamond Jubilee 1881-1956, St. Anthony Church, Streator, Illinois. Provincial Chronicles O.F.M. (Cincinnati) v. 29 (1957), 124-129. illus. B 114

BAUMGARTNER, APOLLINARIUS W. Catholic Journalism: A Study of Its Development in the United States, 1789-1930. New York. Columbia University Press. 1931. xvi, 113p. B 115

BAUNARD, LOUIS. Histoire de Mme. Duchesne, Paris Poussilgue frères. 1878. xxxii, 563p. B 116

BAUR, A. "Lettre de M.A. Baur, missionnaire à Paulding (Mississippi) à Messieurs les Directeurs de la Propagation de la Foi. Paulding, Mississippi, novembre, 1883," Annales de la Propagation de la Foi, v. 56 (1884), 116-123. B 117

BAX, J. J. "Lettre de R.P. Bax, missionnaire apostolique de la Compagne de Jésus, au R. P. de Smet de la même Société. Village de St. François de Hieronymo parmi les Osages ler juin 1850," Annales de la Propagation de la Foi, v. 24 (1852), 207-219. B 118

BAXTER, M. Pioneers of New France in New England. Albany. no. pub. 1899. unpaged. B 119

BAXTER, MOTHER MARIE MADELEINE. Catholic hierarchy and American Labor Since "Rerum Novarum." M.A. thesis. Fordham University. 1946. vi, 112p. B 120

BAXTER, SISTER M. TERESA CLARE. The Labors of Father Toussaint Mesplie in

Southern Idaho. M.A. thesis. University of Notre Dame. 1937, iii, 66p. B 121

BAYARD, RALPH. Lone Star Vanguard. The Catholic Reoccupation of Texas (1838-1848). St. Louis, Vincentian Press, 1945. xiii, 453p.
B 122

BAYLE, CONSTANTINO. Historia de los Descubrimientos y Colonization de la Baja California por los Padres de la Compania de Jesus. Bilbao, 1933. 230p. B 123

BAYLEY, JAMES ROOSEVELT. A Brief Sketch of the History of the Catholic Church on the Island of New York. New York. E. Dunigan and Brother. 1853. 2d ed. 1869. B 124

BAYLEY, JAMES ROOSEVELT. Memoirs of the Right Reverend Simon W. Gabriel Brute. New York. Catholic Publishing Society. 1876. B 125

BEADLE, H. M. "The Story of Marcus Whitman Refuted," American Catholic Historical Researches, v. 16 (1899), 187-197. B 126

BEATRICE, SISTER. "The Resurrection Sisters--Fifty Years for God and Country," Polish American Studies, v. 6 (1949), 99-105. B 127

BEATTIE, ROBERT F. One Hundred and Fifty Years for Christ. Alexandria, Virginia, 1945. B 128

BEAUCHESNE, ARTHUR. Le Martyr du B. Rasle. Memoires de la Société Royal du Canada. v. (1935), 67-76. B 129

BECK, BERNHARD. Goldenes Jubilaum des Wirkens der Redemptoristevater an der St. Philomena Kirche in Pittsburgh und Umgegend nebst deren ersten Missionen in den Vereinigten Staaten Nord-Amerikas. Pittsburgh. no pub. 1898. unpaged. B 130

BECKER, CAMILLUS. History of St. Benedict the Moor Catholic Colored Mission. Milwaukee, no. pub. 1912.
B 131

BECKER, ROBERT H., "Mission San Jose - de Guadalupe?" California Historical Society Quarterly, v. 34 (1955), Sept. 229-230. B 132
Points out that the addition of de Guadalupe is a misnomer.

BECKER, WILHELM. "(Letter dated Toledo, Aug. 10, 1875), "Die Katholischen Missonen, v. 3 (1875), 258-259. B 133

BECKMAN, PETER. The Catholic Church on the Kansas Frontier, 1850-1877. Washington. Catholic University of America Press. 1943. 168p.
B 134

BECKMAN, PETER. Kansas Monks, A History of St. Benedict's Abbey. Atchison, Kansas. Abbey Student Press, 1957, 362p. B 135

BECKMAN, PETER. "Oswald Moosmueller in Kansas," American Benedictine Review, v. 7 (Autumn and Winter, 1956-1957), 263-280. B 136
A good account of this great Benedictine's activities at Atchison, Kansas, 1857-1877.

BECKMAN, ROBERT E. "Louisville - Monday, August 6, 1855," American Ecclesiastical Review, v. 133 (1955), Oct. 239-252. B 137
A description of the bloody Monday nativism riot.

BEDA-CONNER. "Extrait d'une lettre du R. P. Beda-Conner, religieux benedictin de l'abbaye d'Einsiedeln au T.R.P. Henri Schmidt, abbé du même monastère. St. Ferdinand (?), septembre 1854, Annales de la Propagation de la Foi, v. 27 (1855), 227-232.
B 138

BEDE, BROTHER. Study of the Development of Negro Education under Catholic Auspices in Maryland and the District of Columbia. Baltimore. Johns Hopkins Press. 1935. ix, 125p. B 139

BEDE, MICHAEL. "The Mystery of Wizard Clip," Truth, v. 41 (1937), 10-11. B 140

BEDFORD-JONES, HENRY. The Mission and the Man: the story of San Juan Capistrano. Pasadena. San Pasqual Press, 1939. 50p. incl. front. (port). B 141

BEDIER, J. "Rural Parish in Vermont," Commonweal, v. 60 (Apr. 23, 1954), 64-67. B 142

"BEGINNINGS OF THE CAPUCHIN MISSION IN LOUISIANA," United States Catholic Historical Magazine, v. 2 (1888), 259-300. B 143

BEGNAL, SISTER ST. CALLISTA. American Catholic Opinion on the European Crisis, September 1938 to September 1939. M.A. thesis. Fordham University. 1946. vii, 133p. B 144

BEHM, JOSEPH. Souvenir Magazine of the Assumption Church Rebuilding Fund Bazaar. Syracuse, N.Y. no pub. 1911. Plates, ports., illus. B 145

BEHRMAN, PETER. "The Story of St. Meinrad Abbey," The Grail, v. 10 (1929), 487-516. B 146

BEIERSCHMIDT, JOHN M. "Organized Missions - by Whom Introduced into the United States," American Ecclesiastical Review, v. 83 (1930), 28-36. B 147

BEIERSCHMIDT, JOHN M. "Who Introduced the Forty Hours' Devotion into the United States?" American Ecclesiastical Review, v. 60 (1919), 10-15. B 148

BEISER, J. RYAN. American Secular Newspapers and the Vatican Council, 1869-1870. Washington. Catholic University of America Press. 1942. ix, 327p. front., plate. B 149

BEITING, THOMAS LEO. The History of Federal and State Aid to Private Schools in Ohio. M.A. thesis. Xavier University (Cincinnati), 1954. 100p. B 150

BEITZELL, EDWIN W. "Thomas Copley, Gentleman," Maryland History Magazine, v. 47 (September, 1952), 209-223. B 151

BEIX, JOHN R. St. Francis, Wisconsin, The Chief Educational Center of the Church in Wisconsin, 1856-1946. M.A. thesis Marquette University. 1948. B 152

BEKKERS, B. J. "The Catholic Church in Mississippi during Colonial Times," Mississippi Historical Society Publications, v. 6 (1902), 351-359. B 153

BELCOURT, J. A. "Extrait d'une lettre de M. Belcourt, Missionnaire apostolique à Mgr. Loras, Evêque de Dubuque. Minnesota, 16 février, 1850," Annales de la Propagation de la Foi, v. 23 (1851), 301-319. B 154

BELCOURT, J. A. "Letter dated Minnesota, Feb. 16, 1850." Annals of the Propagation of the Faith (London), v. 12 (1851), 234-247. B 155

BELL, STEPHEN. Rebel, Priest and Prophet, a Biography of Edward McGlynn. New York. Devin-Adair. 1937. xi, 303p. B 156

BELLEVILLE (DIOCESE) SYNOD, 2nd, 1904. Synodus dioecesana bellevillensis secunda habita die 15. Junii, A. D., 1904. a Joanne Janssen ep. no pub. unpaged. 104p. B 157

BELLEVILLE (DIOCESE) SYNOD, 4th, 1920. Synodus dioecesana

bellevillensis quarta habita die 1 Decembris A.D. 1920 in ecclesia cathedrali S. Petri a Henrico Althoff, episcopo bellevillensi. Belleville, Ill., Buechler Printing Co., n.d. 1p. 1, 134p. B 158

BELLEVILLE (DIOCESE) SYNOD, 5th, 1939. Statuta dioecesis bellevillensis lata ac promulgata a Henrico Althoff ep. in synodo dioecesana bellevillensi quinta, die 27 mensis Decembris, A.D. 1939, celebrata in ecclesia cathedrali S. Petri, Belleville, Ill. Belleville, Buechler Printing Co. 1940. 171p. B 159

BELTING, NATALIA MAREE. Kaskaskia under the French Regime. Urbana, Ill. University of Illinois Press, 1948. 140p. B 160

BENAVIDES, FRAY ALONSO DE. Fray Alonso de Benavides' Revised Memorial of 1634. Ed. and tr. by Frederich Webb Hodge, George P. Hammond, and Agapito Rey. Albuquerque. University of New Mexico Press. 1945. xvi, 368p. B 161

BENEDICTA, SISTER M. "Father Joseph Dabrowski: Educator," Polish American Studies, v. 9 (1952), 11-16. B 162
A Sketch of the founder of SS. Cyril and Methodius Seminary in Detroit, Michigan, and of the Congregation of the Felician Sisters in America. Died 1903.

BENEDICTINE SISTER. "Congregation of the Benedictine Sisters of Perpetual Adoration," Benedictine Review, v. 5 (1950), 43-46. B 163

(BENEDICTINE SISTER). "History of St. Mary's Parish Church," American Catholic Historical Researches, v. 22 (1905), 110-115. B 164

[BENEDICTINE SISTERS]. History of the American-Swiss Congregation of the Order of St. Benedict. Cottonwood.

1927. B 165

BENEDICTINE SISTER OF PERPETUAL ADORATION. "The Apostolate of the Press," The Benedictine Review, v. 7 (Summer, 1952), 19. B 166
A brief historical sketch of the printing press at Clyde, Missouri.

BENEDIKTINER IN CONCEPTION, MO. UND IHRE MISSIONTATIGKEIT. Conception, Mo, no pl. no pub. 1885. B 167

"DIE BENEDIKTENER - MISSION UNTER DER INDIANERN DER 'WEISSEN ERDE' " Minnesota, Die Katholischen Missionen v. 9 (1881), 177-179. B 168

BENJAMIN, CLETUS J. "Philadelphia and the North American College, Rome," American Catholic Historical Society of Philadelphia Records, v. 55 (1944), 305-331. B 169

BENNETT, WILLIAM H. Catholic Footsteps in Old New York. New York. Schwartz, Kirwin, and Fauss. 1909. vii, 499p. front, plates, port. B 170

BENSON, NETTIE LEE. "Bishop Marin de Porras and Texas," Southwestern Historical Quarterly, v. 51 (1947), 16-40. B 171

BENT, SISTER MARY ARTHUR. Adrien E. Rouquette: Catholic American Romanist. M.A. thesis. St. John's University, N.Y. 1941. mss. p. B 172

BERCHMANS, FR. Church of Our Lady of Sorrows, Golden Jubilee, New York, 1911. no. pl. no pub. 1911? B 173

BERGER, JOHN A. The Franciscan Missions of California. New York. Putnam's. 1941. xiv. 392p. front. (port.) plates, map on lining papers. B 174

BERGER, JOHN N. Life of the

Right Reverend John N. Neumann. New York. Benziger. 1884. 457p. front. (port). B 175

BERGER, MAX. "The Irish Emigrant and American Nativism as Seen by British Visitors, 1836-1860," Pennsylvania Magazine of History and Biography, v. 70 (1946), 146-160. B 176

BERGHOLD, ALEXANDER, AND SCHLINKERT, ROBERT. Geschichte der Hl. Dreifaltigkeit Gemeinde in New Ulm, Minnesota. New Ulm, Minn. pub. 1919. 238p. plates, ports. B 177

BERNARD, HARRY. "Le Roman Régionaliste en Louisiane," La Revue de L'Université Laval, v. 2 (1948), 888-895. B 178

BERNARD, JOSE ANTONIO (ed.) "Statement on the Virtues of Fray Juan Antonio de Barreneche, O.F.M., Yuma Indian Missionary and Martyr," Provincial Annals (Province of Santa Barbara, O.F.M.), v. 11 (1948), 155. B 179

BERNARD, MOTHER MARY. The Story of the Sisters of Mercy in Mississippi, 1860-1930. New York. Kenedy. 1931. xviii, 281p. front., plates, ports. B 180

BERNARD, RAYMOND. "American Apostolate; a Review with Marginal Notes and Questions on Immaturity," Social Order, v. 3 (Mar., 1953), 318-332. B 181

An extensive and critical review of Ward's American Apostolate (1952), that adds a great deal of information to the subject.

BERNARD, RAYMOND. "Catholic Rural Life Conference," Catholic Mind, v. 47 (1949), 273-279. B 182

BERNARDING, PETER J. "Cath-olic Losses in the United States during 1930," American Ecclesiastical Review, v. 86 (1932), 135-148. B 183

BERRIGAN, SISTER MARY OF ST. ANNE. The Work of the Sisters of the Good Shepherd in Oregon. M.A. thesis. Portland University. 1953. vi, 79p. B 184

BETPOUEY, GWENDOLYN MARIE. History of Catholic Secondary Education in Orleans Parish, Louisiana. M.A. thesis. Catholic University. 1954. 71p. B 185

BETSCHART, ILDEFONS. "Bishop Martin Marty, O.S.B., 1834-1896," American Catholic Historical Society of Philadelphia Records, v. 49 (1938), 97-134, 214-248; v. 50 (1939), 33-64. B 186

BETTEN, FRANCIS S. "Francis Peter Beauprez," Salesianum, v. 37 (1942), 165-170. B 187

BETTEN, FRANCIS S. "The Kensington Stone," Historical Bulletin, v. 12 (1934), 66, 72-73. B 188

BETTEN, FRANCIS S. "Two Obelisk Tombstones in Calvary Cemetery, Milwaukee," Salesianum, v. 36 (1941), 99-105. B 189

BEUCKMAN, FREDERICK. "Catholic Beginnings in Southern Illinois, Shawneetown," Mid-America, v. 3 (1931), 105-126. B 190

BEUCKMAN, FREDERICK. "Civil and Ecclesiastical Jurisdiction in Early Illinois," Illinois Catholic Historical Review, v. 1 (1918), 64-71. B 191

BEUCKMAN, FREDERICK. History of the Diocese of Belleville, 1700-1914. Section One, St. Clair County. Belleville. Beuchler Publishing Co. 1914. 94, 14p. ports., plates. B 192

BEUCKMAN, FREDERICK. "The

Shawneetown-to-Cairo Mission Trail," Mid-America, v. 3 (1932), 253-262.   B 193

BICENTENARY OF JUNIPERO SERRA IN MALLORCA," Provincial Annals (Province of Santa Barbara, O.F.M.), v. 11 (1949), 168-171; v. 12 (1949), 17-21.   B 194

BICHLER, JULIAN J. The Development of Catholic Parochial Grade Schools in the City of Milwaukee. M.A. thesis. Marquette University. 1955.   B 195

BIENVENNE, SISTER MARIE ROSE OF JESUS. History of Catholic Elementary Education in New Hampshire. M.A. thesis. Boston College. 1946. v, 65p.   B 196

BIER, CHARLES J. "Convalescing in Texas," Salesianum, v. 68 (Jan., 1953), 1-9.   B 197
The story of a convalescent's missionary activities in the Pan-handle of Texas 1909-1913.

BIETER, A. J. "The Church in Texas," Columbia, v. 16 (Sept. 1936), 13, 20.   B 198

BIEVER, A. H. Jesuits in New Orleans and the Mississippi Valley, New Orleans, Hauser. 1924. 175p.   B 199

BIGAQUETTE, J. A. "Titular Bishops of the Province of St. Paul," Acta et Dicta, v. 5 (1917), 78-92.   B 200

"BIGGEST U.S. ARCHDIOCESE," Life, v. 39-40 (1955), Dec. 26, 62-69.   B 201
An illustrated sketch of the Archdiocese of Chicago.

BILLINGTON, RAY ALLEN. "Burning of the Charlestown Convent," New England Quarterly, v. 10 (1936), 3-24.   B 202

BILLINGTON, RAY ALLEN. "Maria Monk and Her Influence," Catholic Historical Review, v. 22 (1937), 283-296.   B 203

BILLINGTON, RAY ALLEN. The

Protestant Crusade, 1800-1860. New York. Macmillan. 1938. viii, 514p. incl. maps, plates, port., facsim. Reprinted 1952.   B 204

BILLINGTON, RAY ALLEN. "Tentative Bibliography of anti-Catholic Propaganda in the United States, 1800-1860," Catholic Historical Review, v. 18 (1933), 492-513.   B 205

BINSEE, L. B. "The Catholic Charities of New York," Catholic World, v. 43 (1886), 681-694, 809-821.   B 206

BINSEE, HENRY. "The Church of Saint Vincent de Paul (French Church), New York," United States Catholic Historical Society Records and Studies, v. 12 (1918), 102-114.   B 207

BINSFIELD, EDMUND L. "Church Archives in the United States and Canada," The American Archivist, v. 21 (July, 1958), 311-332.   B 208
The report of the Church Records Committee of the Society of American Archivists.

BINSFELD, EDMUND L. "Francisca Bauer, the Sister of the Woods," Ohio Historical Quarterly, v. 69 (Oct., 1960), 352-366.   B 209

BINSFIELD, E. L. Shrine of the Sorrowful Mother. Maywood, Belleville, Ohio. 1950. 47p.   B 210

BINSFIELD, EDMUND L. The Society of the Precious Blood. Carthegena, Ohio. St. Charles Seminary. 1953. unpaged. front. illus. B 211
Brief account of the beginnings of the Society of the Precious Blood and its work in Ohio and Indiana.

BIOGRAPHIC SKETCH OF THE MOST REVEREND JOHN HUGHES. New York. Metropolitan Record. 1864. 62p.

front. (port.). B 212

BISCHOFF, W.N. and GATES,
C. M. "The Jesuits and the
Coeur d'Alene Treaty of
1858," Pacific Northwest
Quarterly, v. 34 (1943),
169-181. B 213

BISCHOFF, WILLIAM N. The
Jesuits in Old Oregon. Caldwell, Idaho. Caston. 1945.
xvii, 258p. B 214

BISMARK (DIOCESE) SYNOD,
1st, 1924. First diocesan
synod of the diocese of Bismark, held Nov. 12th, 1924
at the St. Mary's pro-cathedral,
by the Right Rev. Vincent
Wehrle, O.S.B. ep. n.p.,
n.d. 32p. B 215

BISPHAM, CLARENCE WYATT.
"Contest for Ecclesiastical
Supremacy in the Valley of
the Mississippi, 1763-1803,"
Louisiana Historical Quarterly,
v. 1 (1917), 158-189. B 216
Of interest only because of
inadequate and prejudiced
treatment of the problem.

BISPHAM, CLARENCE WYATT.
"Fray Antonio de Sedella,"
Louisiana Historical Quarterly,
v. 2 (1918-1919), 24-37, 369-
392. port. B 217

BITTERMIEUS, J. and VAN DER
HEYDEN, J. "The Right
Reverend Camillus P. Maes,
Bishop of Covington," American
Catholic Historical Society of
Philadelphia Records, v. 33
(1922), 97-143. B 218

BITTLE, BERCHMANS. A Herald
of the Great King. Milwaukee.
St. Benedict Moor Mission.
1933. xiii, 197p. B 219
Stephen Eckert, founder of
Negro mission in Milwaukee.

BITTLE, CELESTINE. A Romance
of Lady Poverty. The History
of the Capuchin Province of
St. Joseph of the Capuchin
Order in the United States.
Milwaukee. Bruce. 1933,
xxiv, 600p. front., plates,
ports. B 220

BITTLE, CELESTINE. Soldier-
ing for Cross and Flag. Milwaukee. Bruce. 1929. 6,
531p. front., plates, ports.,
diagr. B 221

BIVEN, EDWARD. "The Kensington
Rune Stone," St. Meinrad Historical Essays, v. 5 (1938),
120-128. B 222

BLAKE, K. R. Minnesota's
Jesuit Martyr (Jean Pierre
Aulneau 18 ?) Jesuit Bulletin, (St. Louis) v. 29
(1950), 3-5, 8. B 223

BLAKE, ST. MARY ANGELUS.
Thomas D'Arcy McGee: An
Analysis of His Political and
Social Principles. M.A.
thesis. St. John's University,
N.Y., 1943. mss. p.
B 224

BLAKE, R. B. "Locations of
the Early Spanish Missions and
Presidios in Nagadoches
County," Southwestern Historical Quarterly, v. 41
(1937), 212-224, map.
B 225

BLAKELY, SISTER MARY DE
CHANTAL. Mother Mary
Odilia and the Sisters of St.
Mary of the Third Order of St.
Francis. M.A. thesis.
Saint Louis University. 1932.
87p. B 226

BLAKELY, PAUL L. "Father of
Catholic Education in Ohio,"
America, v. 47 (1932), 303-
305. B 227
A biographical sketch of
Bishop Edward D. Fenwick,
O.P., first Bishop of Cincin-
nati (1821-1832).

BLANCHARD, CHARLES C. (ed.)
History of the Catholic Church
in Indiana. Logansport. A.W.
Bowne and Co., 1898. 2 v.
B 228

BLANCHARD, PAUL. "The
State and Catholic Power
in the United States," Hibbert
Journal, v. (Apr. 1955).
B 229

BLANCHE, SISTER MARIE. "The

60

Catholic Church in Colonial Pennsylvania," Pennsylvania History, v. 3 (1936), 240-258; v. 4 (1937), 32-46. B 230

BLANCHET, F. N. Dix Ans sur la Côte du Pacifique. Quebec. Leger Brousseau. 1873. 100p. B 231

BLANCHET, F.N. Historical Notes and Reminiscences. Portland. no pub. 1883. unpaged. B 232

BLANCHET, FRANCIS N. Historical Sketches of the Catholic Church in Oregon during the Past Forty Years. Portland. 1878. Washington. 1910. 186p. B 233

BLANCHET, FRANCIS N. Letters of the Most Rev. F.N. Blanchet, D.D. Portland, D.D. Portland, O. Heiman and Atkinson, Catholic Sentinel job print. 1871. 19p. B 234

BLAND, SISTER JOAN. Hibernian Crusade. Washington. The Catholic University of America. 1951. 297p. $3.50. B 235
A well written and documented history of the Catholic Total Abstinence Union of America.

"BLESSING OF THE ACADEMY OF AMERICAN FRANCISCAN HISTORY," Provincial Annals (Province of the Most Holy Name, O.F.M.), v. 7 (1947), 11-15. B 236

BLIED, BENJAMIN J. "After Seventy-five Years," Salesianum. v. 40 (1945), 105-113. B 237
Story of the Catholic normal school and Pio Nono College at Milwaukee.

BLIED, B. J. "American Catholic History," The Salesianum, v. 55 (Oct. 1960), 135-142. B 238

BLIED, B. J. "Archbishop Heiss," Social Justice Review, v. 44 (July-August, 1951), 132-135, (September, 1951), 168-171, 178. B 239

BLIED, B. J. "Archbishop Katzer," Social Justice Review, v. 44 (October, 1951), 203-206, (November, 1951), 240-243, (December, 1951), 274-278. B 240

BLIED, B. J. "Archbishop Messmer," Social Justice Review, v. 45 (June, 1952), 85-89; (July-August), 118-121; (September, 1952), 152-155; (October, 1952), 185-188. B 241

BLIED, BENJAMIN J. Austrian Aid to American Catholics, 1830-1860, Milwaukee. The Author. 1944. 205p. B 242

BLIED, B. J., "Bishop Messmer Comes to Green Bay," Salesianum, v. 50 (Jan., 1955), 1-7. B 243

BLIED, B. J. "Bishop Verot of Savannah," Georgia Review, v. (Summer, 1951). B 244

BLIED, BENJAMIN J. "The Bishops of the North and the Civil War," Salesianum, v. 32 (1937), 174-180. B 245

BLIED, BENJAMIN J. "The Bishops of the South and the Civil War," Salesianum, v. 33 (1938), 57-66. B 246

BLIED, BANJAMIN J. "Catholic Aspects of the American Revolution," Salesianum, v. 44 (1949), 49-58. B 247

BLIED, BENJAMIN J. "Catholic Aspects of the Mexican War, 1846-1848," Social Justice Review, v. 40 (1948), 367-371. B 248

BLIED, BENJAMIN J. "Catholic Aspects of the Spanish-American War," Social Justice Review, v. 39 (1946), 59-60, 96-98. B 249

BLIED, BENJAMIN J. "Catholic Aspects of the War of 1812," Social Justice Review, v. 40 (1947), 75-78, 114-117. B 250

BLIED, BENJAMIN J. "Catholic

Charity in the Army, 1861-
1865," Social Justice Review,
v. 33 (1940), 166-168, 206-
208.   B 251
BLIED, BENJAMIN J. "The
Catholic Knights and the
Seminary," Salesianum, v.
68 (Apr. 1953), 60-67.
                          B 252
The story of the short lived
interest of the Catholic
Knights of America in Wis-
consin in the financial plight
of St. Francis Seminary,
Milwaukee.
BLIED, BENJAMIN J. "The Cath-
olic Press and the Civil War,"
Historical Bulletin, v. 19
(1940), 5-6, 18.   B 253
BLIED, BENJAMIN J. "Catholic
Reaction to the Death of
Lincoln," Salesianum, v. 34
(1939), 82-89.   B 254
BLIED, BENJAMIN J. Catholic
Story of Wisconsin. Milwaukee.
1948. 34p. illus.   B 255
BLIED, BENJAMIN J. "Catholicism
and Abolitionism," Salesianum,
v. 33 (1938), 170-178.
                          B 256
BLIED, BENJAMIN J. Catholics
and the Civil War. Milwaukee.
The Author. 1945. 162p.
                          B 257
BLIED, BENJAMIN J. "Early
Catholic Social Thought in
Wisconsin," Salesianum, v. 59
(Apr. 1954), 62-68.   B 258
Good, but undocumented
survey.
BLIED, BENJAMIN J. "The First
Seminary Rectorate, 1856-
1868," Salesianum, v. 51
(Apr. 1956), 49-56.   B 259
A chapter in the early history
of St. Francis Seminary,
Milwaukee, Wisconsin.
BLIED, BENJAMIN J. Four Es-
says. Milwaukee. The Author.
1949. 69p.   B 260
Treats same matter as B
247, B 250, B 248, B 249.
BLIED, BENJAMIN J. "Francis
Xavier Weninger, 1805-1888,"

American-German Review, v.
15 (Apr., 1949), 25-27.
                          B 261
BLIED, BENJAMIN J. "From
Munich to Milwaukee by Way
of Pennsylvania," American-
German Review, v. 14 (Oct.
1947), 21-23, 27.   B 262
Brief sketch of the travels of
the School Sisters of Notre
Dame.
BLIED, BENJAMIN J. "John
Martin Henni," American-Ger-
man Review, v. 11 (June, 1945)
24-27.   B 263
BLIED, BENJAMIN J. "Michael
Heiss, Seminary Rector.
First Bishop of LaCrosse,"
Salesianum, v. 52 (April,
1957), 55-62.   B 264
BLIED, B. J. "Monsignor Rainer,"
The Salesianum, v. 47 (July,
1952), 105-112.   B 265
BLIED, BENJAMIN J. "The Most
Rev. Otto Zardetti, D.D. (1847-
1902), Salesianum, v. 42
(1947), 54-62.   B 266
BLIED, BENJAMIN J. "Our
Cathedral Curate Wrote a
Book," Salesianum, v. 42
(1947), 158-163.   B 267
The story of William Ma-
honey, author of the Rights
of the Clergy Vindicated,
New York, 1883.
BLIED, BENJAMIN J. "Pioneer
American Ecclesiastical Re-
view," Salesianum, v. 42
(1947), 15-18.   B 268
The story of the German
language review Romana.
BLIED, BENJAMIN J. "Pioneer
Social Reformer, Rev. Peter
E. Dietz," Social Justice Review, v. 46 (July-Aug., 1953),
132-134.   B 269
A biographical sketch of
this champion of social reform, based on personal
acquaintance.
BLIED, BENJAMIN J. "Pre-
cursors of Bishop Henni,"
Salesianum, v. 43 (1948),
148-155.   B 270

BLIED, BENJAMIN J. "Rev. An-
drew E. Breen, D.D. Priest,
Professor, Author," Salesianum,
v. 68 (Oct., 1953), 172-
179.   B 271
A biographical sketch of this
scholar who was born 1863
and died in 1938 after teach-
ing at St. Bernard's,
Rochester, and St. Francis,
Milwaukee.
BLIED, BENJAMIN J. "The Rev.
Chrysostom Verwyst," Sales-
ianum, v. 50 (July, 1959),
91-99.   B 272
This important priest-mis-
sionary died in 1925.
BLIED, BENJAMIN J. "Rev.
John Cebul (1832-1898),"
Salesianum, v. 43 (1948),
99-105.   B 273
BLIED, BENJAMIN J. "Reverend
Anton Gunther, 1783-1863,"
Salesianum, v. 42 (April,
1946).   B 274
BLIED, BENJAMIN J. "Reverend
Francis X. Eschmann (1818-
1896)," Salesianum, v. 42
(1946), 175-183.   B 275
BLIED, BENJAMIN J. St. John
the Baptist Congregation.
Johnsburg, Wisconsin, 1957.
$1.00.   B 276
BLIED, B. J. "Sir John Singen-
berger," Social Justice Review,
v. 43 (January, 1951), 311-
314.   B 277
BLIED. BENJAMIN J. A Survey
of Christian Contributions to
the Catholic Church in the U-
nited States Derived Largely
from the Publications of the
Leopoldine Society, 1830-
1860. Ph.D. thesis. Mar-
quette University. 1943.
                        B 278
BLIED, B. J. Three Archbishops
of Milwaukee. Milwaukee.
The Author. 160p.   B 279
Biographical sketches of
Archbishops Heiss, Katzer,
and Messmer.
BLIED, B. J. "Two Tombstones
Tell a Tale," Salesianum, v.

50 (Oct., 1955), 161-169.
                        B 280
Biographical information
concerning Anthony Keppeler
and Fr. Steiger of Wisconsin.
BLIED, BENJAMIN J. "The Unknown Rector. (Msgr. Augustine
Zeininger, Rector of St.
Francis Seminary, Milwaukee,
1881-1887)," Salesianum, v.
43 (1948), 56-62.   B 281
BLIED, BENJAMIN J. "Wiscon-
sin and the Third Plenary
Council," The Salesianum, v.
53 (Jan., 1958), 1-8. B 282
BLIED, BENJAMIN J. "Wiscon-
sin Catholics and the Civil
War," Social Justice Review,
v. 40 (1945), 23-24, 58-59.
                        B 283
BLIED, BENJAMIN J. "Wisconsin's Catholic Hospitals,"
Salesianum, v. 43 (1948),
10-19.   B 284
BLOOM, LANSING B. "Spain's
Investment in New Mexico
under the Hapsburgs," The
Americas, v. 1 (1944), 3-
14.   B 285
BLUM, SISTER MARIE THOMA-
SINE. History of the Sisters
of the Third Order of St.
Dominic of the Congregation
of the Most Holy Rosary,
Mount St. Mary-on-the-Hud-
son. Newburgh, New York,
M.A. thesis. Catholic Uni-
versity of America. 1938.
128p.   B 286
BLUM, V. C. "Are Catholics
Second Class Citizens?" Cath-
olic World, v. 186 (Mar.,
1958), 418-424.   B 287
BOFFA, CONRAD H. Canonical
Provisions for Catholic
Schools. Washington. Catholic University of America.
1939. x, 211p.   B 288
"BOHEMIA, CECIL COUNTY,
MD.," Woodstock Letters, v.
13 (1884), 333-344; v. 14
(1885), 102-111, 221-231.
                        B 289

BOISE (DIOCESE) SYNOD, 2nd,
1941. Statuta dioecesis
xylopolitanae lata ac promulgata ab Eduardo J. Kelly
ep. in synodo dioecesana
sylopolitana secunda, die
vigesima Junii, A.D. 1941,
celebrata in ecclesia cathedrali Sancti Joannis Evangelistae apud Boise, Idaho.
Boise, Idaho, Syms-York Co.,
n.d.   B 290
BOLAND, FRANK J. The Attitude of the American Hierarchy
toward the Doctrine of Papal
Infallibility at the Vatican
Council. M.A. thesis. University of Detroit. 1948. iv,
78p.   B 291
BOLDRICK, CHARLES C.
"Martin John Spalding, 1810-
1872, Second Bishop of Louisville, 1848-1864," Filson Club
Historical Quarterly (October,
1958).   B 292
BOLGER, WILLIAM M. "A Padre
of the Flames," Columbia, v.
2 (Dec., 1922), 17, 25.
                            B 293
    A biographical sketch of
    Father Vincent de Paul Mc
    Glean of New York City.
BOLLIG, RICHARD J. History
of Catholic Education in Kansas,
1836-1932. Washington. Catholic University of America.
1933. 2, 131p.   B 294
BOLTON, HERBERT EUGENE.
"Beginnings of Mission Nuestra
Senora del Refugio," Southwestern Historical Quarterly, v.
19 (1916), 400-404.   B 295
BOLTON, HERBERT EUGENE.
"Founding of the Missions on
the San Gabriel River, 1745-
1749," Southwestern Historical
Quarterly, v. 17 (1914), 323-
378, map.   B 296
BOLTON, HERBERT EUGENE.
"Founding of the Mission
Rosario," Texas State Historical
Association Quarterly, v. 10
(1906), 113-139.   B 297
BOLTON, HERBERT EUGENE.

"The Mission as a Frontier In-
stitution in the Spanish-Amer-
ican Colonies," American His-
torical Review, v. 23 (1917),
42-61.   B 298
    A very important essay that
    leads to a re-evaluation of
    the importance of the mis-
    sion as a colonizing method.
BOLTON, HERBERT EUGENE.
"Native Tribes about the East
Texas Missions," Texas State
Historical Association Quarter-
ly, v. 11 (1908), 249-276.
                            B 299
BOLTON, HERBERT EUGENE.
Padre on Horseback. San
Francisco. Sonora Press.
1932. 90p.   B 300
BOLTON, HERBERT EUGENE.
Rim of Christendom. A
Biography of Eusebion Fran-
cisco Kino. New York. Mac-
millan. 1936. xiv, 644p.
plates, fold. maps, facsims.
                            B 301
BOLTON, HERBERT EUGENE.
"The Spanish Abandonment
and Re-occupation of East
Texas," Texas State Historical
Association Quarterly, v. 9
(1905), 85-137.   B 302
BOLTON, HERBERT EUGENE.
"Spanish Mission Records at
San Antonio," Texas State
Historical Association Quarter-
ly, v. 10 (1907), 297-307.
                            B 303
BONDER, JAMES B. Life of
Charles Carroll of Carrollton,
M. A. thesis. Villanova Uni-
versity. 1939. 69p.
                            B 304
BONDUEL, FLORIMOND J.
"Letter, dated Prairie du
Chien, August 24, 1844,"
Wisconsin Magazine of History,
v. 20 (1937), 328-336.   B 305
BONDUEL, FLORIMOND J. "Let-
ter to Miss Francis E. Gug-
non, dated Menomonee Bay
Ground, Wisconsin, October
3, 1854," Salesianum v. 43

(1948), 156-157.		B 306
BONENKAMP, S., J. JESSING, AND J. B. MULLER. Schematismus der deutschsprechenden Priester, sowie der deutschen Katholiken-Gemeinden in den Vereinigten Staaten Nord Amerikas. St. Louis. Herder. 1882. xv, 447p. dav. 352-447.		B 307

BONIKOWSKI, SAMUEL. "The Polish Press in Wisconsin," Polish-American Studies, v. 2 (1945), 12-23.		B 308

BONN, JOHN LOUIS. So Falls the Elm Tree. New York. Macmillan. 1940. xviii, 287p.		B 309
The story of Mother Valencia of St. Francis Hospital, Hartford, Connecticut (1855-1936).

BONN, JOHN LOUIS. And Down the Days. New York. Macmillan, 1942. 306p.		B 310

BONN, JOHN L. Gates of Dannemora. New York. Doubleday. 1951. 276p. $3.00		B 311
Biography of Father Ambrose R. Hyland, Catholic Chaplain of Clinton Prison at Dannemora, N.Y. since 1937 and founder of the Good Thief Foundation.

BONNAULT, CLAUDE DE. "Catherin Tegaskuita," Bulletin des Recherches Historiques, v. 45 (July, 1939).		B 312

BONNELL, VICTOR GEORGE. American Liturgical Movement and Its Influence on Catholic Church Art and Architecture. M.A. thesis. Georgetown University. 1956. 103p.		B 313

BONNIKE, FRANCIS J. "Current Expenditures in Catholic High Schools," Catholic Educational Review, v. 50 (January, 1952), 33-39; (February, 1952), 102-113.		B 314

BONZ, Vie de Mgr. Jean Marie Odin, Paris. Dumoulin. 1896. 227p.		B 315

BONZELET, HONORATUS. "Franciscan Home Missions," Franciscan Herald, v. 26 (1938), 233-234, 248, 256.		B 316

BOONE, EDWARD D. "The Chaplaincy of the Maryland Penitentiary," Woodstock Letters, v. 31 (1902), 23-30.		B 317

BORDEN, LUCILLE PAPIN. Francesca Cabrini. Without Staff or Script. New York. Macmillan. 1945. x, 402p.		B 318

BORGMAN, FRANCIS. "Henry Chee Dodge, the Last Chief of the Navaho Indians," New Mexico Historical Review, v. 23 (1948), 81-93.		B 319

BORKY, SISTER MARY OLIVET. Seattle's Pioneer Priest. Right Reverend Francis Xavier Prefontaine. M.A. thesis. Seattle University. 1949. 146p.		B 320

BOSCH, ALOIS. Aus dem Missionsleben in Sud-Dakota. Die Katholische Missionen. v. 23 (1895), 49-55.		B 321

BOSTON (DIOCESE). Constitutiones Dioecesana ab Illmo ac Revmo Domino Joanne Josepho Williams, Episcopo Bostoniensi in Synodo Dioecesana Secunda habita Bostoniae A.D. 1868 latae et promulgatae. 1868. 59p.		B 322

BOSTON (DIOCESE) SYNOD, 1st, 1842. Synodus dioecesana, Bostoniensis I. habita anno 1842. Bostoniae, P. Donahoe n.d. 11p.		B 323

BOSTON (ARCHDIOCESE) SYNOD, 5th, 1909. Constitutiones dioeceseos bostoniensis quae in synodo dioecesana quinta, die 11 Februarii, 1909, habita in ecclesia metropolitana Sanctae Crucis a Gulielmo Henrico O' Connell, archiepiscopo bostoniensi latae et promulgatae fuerunt. Bostoniae, Mass., Ex typis "Washington press," 1910. 58p.		B 324

BOSTON (DIOCESE) SYNOD, 6th,

1919. Constitutiones dioeceseos
bostoniensis quae in synodo
dioecesana sexta die la Aprilis
1919, habita in ecclesia me-
tropolitana Sanctae Crucis a
Gulielmo Cardinale O'Connell,
ep. latae et promulgatae
fuerunt. Bostoniae Ex typis
"Washington press," 1919.
96p.   B 325
BOSTON (ARCHDIOCESE) SYNOD,
7th, 1952. Acta et Statuta
Synodi Bostoniensis Septimae.
Boston. 1953. 144p. facsims.
                                B 326
BOTHE, SISTER BERNALEIN.
History of Saint John's Indian
Mission of Komatke, Arizona.
M.A. thesis. Catholic Uni-
versity. 1953. 103p.
                                B 327
BOUBEE, JOSEPH. "Le Mouve-
ment Religieux hors de France
-- Etats-Unis. Coup d'Oeil sur
la Situation des Catholiques,"
Etudes, v. 135 (1913), 323-
340.   B 328
BOUGIS, P. 'Rocky Mountains,
Letter Dated St. Peter's Mis-
sion P.O., Lewis and Clark
County, Montana Territory,
October 25, 1885," Woodstock
Letters, v. 15 (1886), 77-80.
                                B 329
BOUGIS, P. 'Rocky Mountains,
Montana. Letter Dated St.
Peter's Mission, September
15, 1886," Woodstock Letters,
v. 15 (1886), 318-319.
                                B 330
BOUQUILLON, THOMAS. "The
Apostolic Delegation," Ameri-
can Catholic Quarterly Review,
v. 20 (1895), 112-131. B 331
BOUQUILLON, THOMAS. Educa-
tion: To Whom Does it Be-
long? 2d ed., with a rejoinder.
Baltimore. John Murphy.
1892. 31, 3-42p.   B 332
A pamphlet that set off a
lively discussion among
Catholic theologians on the
issue of the relation of the
state to education.

BOUSCAREN, A. "Catholics in
Intellectualism," Catholic
World, v. 187 (May, 1958),
123-127.   B 333
Includes a good bibliography.
A discussion follows in the
July, 1958 issue.
BOWLER, SISTER M. MARIELLA.
A History of Catholic Colleges
for Women in the United
States of America. Washing-
ton. Catholic University of
America. 1933. vi, 145p.
                                B 334
BOYD, E. Saints and Saint
Makers of New Mexico. Santa
Fe, N.M. Laboratory of
Anthropology. 1946. vi,
139p. illus.   B 335
BOYD, MARK F. (tr. and ed.).
"Enumeration of Florida
Spanish Missions in 1675,"
Florida Historical Quarterly,
v. 26 (1948) 181-185. B 336
BOYD, MARK F. "Further Con-
siderations of the Apalachee
Missions," Americas, v. 9
(Apr., 1953), 459-479.
                                B 337
A supplement to Section
one of Here They Once
Stood (1951). Includes nine
new documents.
BOYD, MARK FREDERICK, ET
AL. Here They Once Stood;
The Tragic End of the Apala-
chee Missions. Gainesville,
Fla. University of Florida
Press. 1951. 218p. maps.
$3.75.   B 338
History and archaeology
of the Franciscan missions
of Florida, concentrating on
the period 1675-1704.
BOYER, ARSENIUS. "Poor Clares
in America," Voice, v. (May,
1935).   B 339
BOYLAN, MARQUERITE T.
"Catholic Charities in the
Diocese of Brooklyn: Fifty
Years of Service, 1899-1949,"
Catholic Charities Review, v.
33 (1949), 88-94.   B 340
BOYLE, SISTER MARY ELECTA.

Mother Seton's Sisters of Charity in Western Pennsylvania. Greensburg, Pa. Sisters of Charity. 1946. x, 251p.
                                        B 341

BOYTON, NEIL. The Cheerful Giver, St. Charles Garnier, S. J. New York. Jesuit Mission Press. 1936. 30p.   B 342

BOZEK, SISTER M. EDWIN. The Early History of SS. Cyril and Methodius Seminary. M.A. thesis. University of Notre Dame. 1943. iv, 104p.
                                        B 343

BRACHT, DONALD F. The Attitude of the Supreme Court on the Question of Religion, 1920-1940. M.A. thesis. Catholic University of America. 1950. 96p.   B 344

BRADLEY, F.J. Brief History of the Diocese of Fall River. New York. 1931. 63p.   B 345

BRADLEY, CYPRIAN, AND BISHOP EDWARD KELLY. History of the Diocese of Boise. Caldwell, Idaho. Caxton. 1953. 481p.   B 346

BRADY, ALEXANDER. Thomas D'Arcy McGee. New York. Macmillan. 1925. 182p. front. (port.).   B 347

BRADY, SISTER ELEANOR MARIE. Anti-Catholic Legislation in Massachusetts Bay Colony. M.A. thesis. Villanova University. 1939. 75 p.
                                        B 348

BRADY, IGNATIUS. "Detroit and the Franciscans," Provincial Chronicle (Province of St. John Baptist, O.F.M.), v. 24 (Fall, 1951), 4-7.
                                        B 349

BRADY, JOSEPH H. (ed.). "One Hundredth Anniversary of the Archdiocese of Newark, N.J.," Supplement to the Advocate (Newark), v. 3 (Oct. 23, 1954), 66p. illus.   B 350

BRADY, JOSEPH H. "St. Mary's Abbey," American Benedictine Review, v. 7 (Spring, 1956),

68-69.   B 351
A reprint of an article in the Newark, N.J., Advocate for Aug. 25, 1956, on the moving of the Abbey from Newark to Morristown, N.J. Includes a short history of the Abbey.

BRANLAGE, SISTER MARY CATHARINE. The Origin, History and Education Activities of the Benedictine Sisters of Covington, Kentucky. M.A. thesis. University of Notre Dame. 1938.   B 352

BRANN, HENRY A. "A Few Chapters in the Church History of the Northwest Part of New York City," United States Catholic Historical Society Records and Studies, v. 6 pt. 1 (1911) 58-72.   B 353

BRANN, HENRY A. History of the North American College. New York. Benziger. 1910. 570p. front., plates, ports.
                                        B 354

BRANN, HENRY A. "Mr. Cahensly and the Church in the United States," Catholic World, v. 54 (1891), 568-581.
                                        B 355

BRANN, HENRY A. Most Reverend John Hughes, First Archbishop of New York. New York. Benziger. 1892. xi, 182p. front. (port.).
                                        B 356

BRANN, HENRY A. "St. Mary's College, Wilmington, Delaware," United States Catholic Historical Society Records and Studies, v. 7 (1914), 81-89.
                                        B 357

BRANN, WILLIAM C. "The A. P.A. Idiocy -- a Retrospect," Columbia, v. 2 (July, 1922), 11, 24.   B 358

BRASSEUR DE BOURBOURG, CHARLES-ETIENNE. Histoire du Canada de Son Eglise et de Ses Missions depuis la Découverte de L'Amérique Jusqu'a Nos Jours.   Paris. Sagnier et Bray, 1852. 2v.   B 359

BRAUN, R. The Most Rev. John
Hughes. New York. no pub.
1892. unpaged.   B 360

BRAUN, SERRAN. Golden Jubilee
Sacred Heart Church. San
Angelo, Texas. Provincial
Chronicles, O.F.M. (Cincin-
nati), v. 29 (1957), 129-135.
illus.   B 361

BRAUTOVICH, C. L. "Fisher-
man's Fiesta," Ave Maria,
v. 77 (June 27, 1953), 21-
22.   B 362
The story of the fiesta of the
fishermen of San Pedro, Los
Angeles Harbor.

BRECK, SAMUEL. "Historical
Sketch of the First Public
Mass in Boston," American
Catholic Historical Researches,
v. 6 (1889), 19-20.   B 363

BREEN, ARTHUR JAMES. Ber-
nard Boil Buil the Just Vicar
Apostolic of the New World,
1493-1495. M. A. thesis.
Catholic University of America. 1920.   B 364

BREGY, KATHRINE. "In Memoriam: Joseph Louis Jerome
Kirlin," American Catholic
Historical Society of Philadelphia Records, v. 38 (1927),
123-131.   B 365

BRENN, HUGO. "The Oldest Catholic Parish in Eire, Pa.,"
Central Blatt and Social Justice
v. 29 (1936), 18-20.   B 366

BRENNAN, THOMAS C. "The
Story of the Seminarians," A-
merican Catholic Historical
Society of Philadelphia Records,
v. 30 (1919), 115-134.
    B 367
Story of the work of the
seminarians during the flu
epidemic in Philadelphia in
1918.

BRENNAN, THOMAS G. "Bishop
William Francis Murphy,
1885-1950," Michigan History,
v. 34 (1950), 249-250.
    B 368

BRENNAN, THOMAS J. "Arch-

bishop Riordan," American
Catholic Historical Society of
Philadelphia Records, v. 26
(1915), 47-54.   B 369

BRENNER, SISTER M. REBEC-
CA.. Church Going Among
Our Italian Immigrants. M.A.
thesis. University of Notre
Dame. 1944. iii, 121p.
    B 370

BRENTANO, SISTER BERNARDA.
"The Early Years of Mount St.
Scholastica Academy," Benedictine Review, v. 4 (1949),
31-33.   B 371

BRENTANO, SISTER BERNARDA.
"Missionary Work of the
Benedictine Sisters in the U-
nited States," Benedictine Review, v. 5 (Summer, 1954),
36-39.   B 372
A brief account beginning in
the 1850's.

BREUNIG, J. "Catholic Revival
in Tennessee," America, v.
88 (March 28, 1953), 704-
705.   B 373
The story of a mission given
in a small town in Tennessee.

"BREVE HISTORIA DE 'REVISTA
CATOLICA' Y SUS FUNDA-
DORES," Revista Catolica, v.
75 (1950), 36-39, 42; 52-53.
    B 374

BREWSTER, S. W. "Rev. Paul
M. Ponziglione," Kansas
State Historical Society Collections, v. 9 (1905-1906),
19-32.   B 375

(BRIC). "Our Fathers at Providence, R.I., 1877-1899,"
Woodstock Letters, v. 29
(1900), 234-238.   B 376

BRIC, JAMES J. "Sketch of
the Abenaquis Mission," A-
merican Catholic Historical
Society of Philadelphia Records, v. 2 (1886-1888), 13-
21.   B 377

BRIDGE, EVERETTE W. Francis
Parkman and the Jesuits. M.
A. thesis. University of
Detroit. 1933. ii, 68p. B 378

BRIDGER, E.A. "The Pioneer Catholic Mission in the Northwest," Catholic World, v. 71 (1900), 842-850. B 379

BRIDGETT, THOMAS E. 'Reverend Thomas Thayer," Irish Monthly, v. 10 (1882), 74-105. B 380

BRIDGETT, THOMAS E. "Saintly Influences: Father Thayer and the Ursulines," Irish Monthly, v. 11 (1883), 625-629. B 381

"BRIEF HISTORY OF ST. PETER'S CHURCH AND COLLEGE, JERSEY CITY, N.J.," Woodstock Letters, v. 14 (1885), 381-383. B 382

"BRIEF SKETCH OF CATHOLICITY IN THE COAL REGIONS OF PENNSYLVANIA," United States Catholic Historical Magazine, v. 1 (1887), 388-391. B 383

A BRIEF STORY OF LOUISIANA. Provincial Chronicles, O.F.M., (Cincinnati), v. 23 (1951), 152-172. illus. B 384 St. Mary of the Angels, New Orleans.

BRINGAZI, M.S. 'Redemptorists in Texas," Extension, v. 26 (1931), 26. B 385

BRISLEN, SISTER M. BERNETTA. The Episcopacy of Archbishop Leonard Neale, the Second Metropolitan of Baltimore. M.A. thesis. Catholic University of America. 1943. 121p. B 386

BRISLEN, SISTER M. BERNETTA. 'The Episcopacy of Leonard Neale, Second Archbishop of Baltimore," United States Historical Society Records and Studies, v. 34 (1945), 20-111. B 387

BRITT, SISTER GERTRUDE MARIE. Catholic Beginnings of the Wheeling Diocese. M.A. thesis. Catholic University of America. 1939. 162p. B 388

BROCKLAND, AUGUST F. 'The Central Verein and the Sale of Papal Bonds in the U.S. in 1867-1868," Central Blatt and Social Justice, v. 26 (1933), 17-19. B 389

BROCKLAND, AUGUST F. 'The Early History of St. Joseph's Orphanage in New York City," Central Blatt and Social Justice, v. 19 (1926), 306-308. B 390

BROCKLAND, AUGUST F. "Fr. Weninger's Encounters with German Atheists," Central Blatt and Social Justice, v. 23 (1931), 347-348. B 391

BROCKLAND, AUGUST F. "Observations of a Visitor to Highland, Ill., in 1850," Central Blatt and Social Justice, v. 26 (1933), 214-215. B 392

BROCKLAND, AUGUST F. "On the Centenary of the German Catholic Colony at Shoal Creek, Ill.," Central Blatt and Social Justice, v. 26 (1933), 249-250, 288, 303, 323, 339. B 393

BROCKLAND, AUGUST F. "One of Father Pierz' Colonization Undertakings in Minnesota," Central Blatt and Social Justice, v. 19 (1926), 197-199. B 394

BROCKLAND, AUGUST F. "Schriftstellerisch oder erziehisch thatig gewesene deutschsprachige Priester Nordamerikas," Central Blatt and Social Justice, v. 13 (1920), 231-233, 276-277. B 395

BROCKLAND, AUGUST F. "Was das U.S. Catholic Magazine 1846 uber deutsche Katholiken Americans zu berichten wuszte," Central Blatt and Justice, v. 13 (1921), 375-376; v. 14 (1921), 50-52. B 396

BRONDEL, JAMES B. 'Rocky Mountains. Letter dated Helena, Montana, November 17, 1883," Woodstock Letters, v. 13 (1884), 150-151. B 397

BROOKLYN (DIOCESE) SYNOD,

1st, 1879. Statuta synodi brooklynensis primae, quae quarto kalendas Sept., anno e Virginis partu MDCCCLXXIX, in ecclesia divo Joanni Baptistae dicata lata sunt, quaeque tulit atque sancivit ... Joannes Loughlin. Neo Eboraci, H.J. Hewitt, 1880. xi, 29p.
B 398

BROOKLYN (DIOCESE) SYNOD 3. Constitutiones diocesanae Brooklynienses Neo-Eboraci typ. Missionis Virginis Immaculatae, 1895. xiii, 134p.
B 399

BROOKLYN (DIOCESE) SYNOD 5. Constitutiones diocesanae Brooklynienses. New York. Loughlin Bros. n. d.   B 400

BROPHY, SISTER M. LIGUORI. The Social Thought of the German Roman Catholic Verein. Washington. Catholic University of America. 1941. x, 102p.
B 401

BROTHERS OF THE CHRISTIAN SCHOOLS. Mississippi Vista; the Brothers of the Christian Schools in the Mid-West, 1849-1949. Winona, Minn. Saint Mary's College Press. 1948. 296p. illus., ports., map.   B 402

BROWN, BEATRICE BRADSHAW. Church of St. Peter the Apostle, 1874-1949. Provincetown, Mass. St. Peter's Church. 1949. 68p.   B 403

BROWN, EDWARD OSGOOD. The Parish Register of the Mission of Michilimackinac. Chicago. Barnard and Gunthrop. 1889?
B 404

BROWN, JOHN. "Collegio del Sacro Cuore in Denver," Lettere Edificanti Provincia Napolitana, ser. 9, n. 11 (1901), 111-114.   B 405

BROWN, SR. MARY BORROMEO The History of the Sisters of Providence of Saint Mary-of-the-Woods. New York. Benziger, 1949. 2v. illus.,

ports.   B 406

BROWN, SISTER RITA MARIE. The History of Immaculate Conception Academy, 1883-1953. M.A. thesis. University of San Francisco. 1953.   B 407

BROWN, W.G. "Historical Sketch of the Diocese of Grand Rapids (Mich.)," Michigan Pioneer and Historical Collection, v. 38 (1912), 509-512.   B 408

BROWN COUNTY URSULINES. Fifty Years in the Brown County Convent. Cincinnati. 1895.   B 409

BROWNE, CLYDE. Cloisters of California. Los Angeles. C. Browne. 1918. 133p. incl. illus., plates, front. (port.).
B 410

BROWNE, HENRY J. "The American Catholic Archival Tradition," American Archivist, v. (April, 1951).   B 411

BROWNE, HENRY J. "American Catholic History: A Progress Report on Research and Study," Church History, v. 26 (Dec., 1957), 372-380.
B 412

BROWNE, HENRY J. "An American Memorial of the Definition of the Immaculate Conception," American Ecclesiastical Review, v. 128 (Apr., 1953), 255-261.
B 413
Archbishop Hughes places the first parish in the United States under the patronage of the Immaculate Conception in 1855.

BROWNE, HENRY J. "Archbishop Hughes and Western Colonization," Catholic Historical Review, v. 36 (1950), 257-285.   B 414

BROWNE, HENRY J. The Catholic Church and the Knights of Labor, Washington. Catholic University of America. 1949. xvi, 415p.   B 415

BROWNE, HENRY J. "The
'Italian Problem' in the Cath-
olic Church of the United States,
1880-1900," United States
Catholic Historical Society
Records and Studies, v. 35
(1946), 46-72.   B 416
BROWNE, HENRY J. The
Diocesan Clergy of New York,
an Historical sketch. no pl.
no pub. 1950? 12p.   B 417
BROWNE, HENRY J. (ed.).
"Letters of Bishop McQuaid from
the Vatican Council," Catholic
Historical Review, v. 41
(Jan., 1956), 408-441.
                      B 418
BROWNE, HENRY J. "Mr.
Maynard and 'Popular' Ameri-
can Catholic History," Ameri-
can Ecclesiastical Review,
v. 130 (May, 1954), 325-329.
                      B 419
    Excellent expose of the
    mistakes in Maynard's
    Catholic Church and the A-
    merican Idea.
BROWNE, HENRY J. "A New
Historical Project: Editing the
Papers of Archbishop Carroll,"
American Ecclesiastical Re-
view, v. 127 (October, 1952),
341-350.   B 420
BROWNE, HENRY J. "New York's
Catholic Heritage in Secondary
Education," Catholic Educational
Review, v. 50 (May, 1952),
330-337.   B 421
BROWNE, HENRY J. "Newly
Published History of the
Catholic University of Ameri-
ca," American Ecclesiastical
Review, v. 121 (1949), 362-
372.   B 422
BROWNE, HENRY J. "Peter E.
Dietz, Pioneer Planner of
Catholic Social Action," Cath-
olic Historical Review, v. 33
(1948), 448-456.   B 423
BROWNE, HENRY J. "Pioneer
Days at the Catholic University
of America," Catholic Educa-
tional Review, v. 48 (1950),
29-38, 96-103.   B 424

BROWNE, HENRY J. "The
Priest and Local History,"
American Ecclesiastical Re-
view, v. 124 (April, 1956),
251-254.   B 425
    A short appreciation of the
    importance of the priest in
    forming and knowing local
    happenings.
BROWNE, HENRY J. "Public
Support of Catholic Education
in New York, 1825-1842;
Some New Aspects," United
States Catholic Historical
Society Records and Studies,
v. 51 (1953), 14-41. B 426
    Includes interesting informa-
    tion on the efforts of Bishop
    Hughes and Governor Seward
    to obtain public funds for
    the Catholic Schools.
BROWNE, HENRY J. "Terrence
V. Powderly and Church Labor
Difficulties of the Early
1880's," Catholic Historical
Review, v. 32 (1946), 1-127.
                      B 427
BROWNE, HENRY J. Terrence
V. Powderly: His Relations
with the Catholic Church,
1879-1888. M.A. thesis.
Catholic University of America.
1945. 130p.   B 428
BROWNE, PATRICK W. "An
Epistle in Quebec-Louisiana
History," Mid-America, v. 11
(1930), 296-305.   B 429
    A study of the episcopal
    character of Louis François
    du Plessis de Mornay, third
    bishop of Quebec--Coadjutor
    1714, Bishop 1728, resigned
    1741.
BROWNE, PATRICK W. "Father
Edmund Burke," Mid-America,
v. 2 (1931), 314-323. B 430
BROWNE, PATRICK W. "John
England," Illinois Catholic
Historical Review, v. 10
(1928), 239-247.   B 431
BROWNE, PATRICK W. "The
National Catholic School of
Social Service," Sign, v. 11
(1932), 726-728, illus. B 432

BROWNE, PATRICK W. "Sala-
manca and the Beginnings of
the Church in Florida," Ameri-
can Ecclesiastical Review, v.
84 (1931), 581-587.　B 433
BROWNSON, HENRY F. Orestes
A. Brownson's Early Life.
Detroit. The Author. 1898.
front., ports.　B 434
BROWNSON, HENRY F. Orestes
A. Brownson's Middle Life.
Detroit. The Author. 1899.
　B 435
BROWNSON, HENRY F. Orestes
A. Brownson's Later Life.
Detroit. The Author. 1900.
　B 436
BROWNSON, ORESTES A. Works.
Ed. by Henry F. Brownson.
Detroit. Henry F. Brownson.
1882-1887. 20v.　B 437
BROWNSON, SARAH. Life of
Demetrius Augustine Gallitzin.
New York. Pustet. 1873.
xv, 444p. front. (port.).
　B 438
BRUCE, WILLIAM G. Holy
Trinity Church, 1850-1925.
Milwaukee. no pub. 1925.
97p.　B 439
BRUCKBERGER, RAYMOND
LEOPOLD. One Sky to Share.
New York. Kenedy. 1952.
248p. illus. $3.00.　B 440
The French and American
journals of Raymond Leopold
Bruckberger, translated and
edited by Dorothy Carr
Howell.
BRUEHL, CHARLES. "In Memori-
am, Dennis Cardinal Dougherty,"
Homiletic and Pastoral Review,
v. 51 (July, 1951), 875-
876, 892.　B 441
BRUEGGEN, SISTER MARY
DOLORES. The Role of the
Franciscans in Bringing
Christianity to the Navajo
Indians. M.A. thesis. Uni-
versity of Notre Dame. 1939.
iv, 89p.　B 442
BRUENER, THEODORE. Katholi-
sche Kirchengeschichte Quincy's
im Staate Illinois mit streitp-

flichten uber ganz Illinois und
die Nachbarstaaten. St. Louis.
Herder. 1887. 362p. illus.,
maps.　B 443
BRUNGS, MARY CARMELITE.
The Church of the Mother of
God. Covington. James
Rolfes. 1941. 64, 26p.
ports. facsims.　B 444
BRUNOWE, MARION J. "The
Catholic Church in Yonkers
on the Hudson, N.Y.," A-
merican Catholic Historical
Society of Philadelphia Rec-
ords, v. 7 (1896), 80-93.
　B 445
BRUNOWE, MARION J. College
of Mount St. Vincent--A
Famous Convent School. New
York. Kenedy, c.1921. ix,
205p.　B 446
BRUNOWE, MARION J. College
of Mount St. Vincent (N.Y.).
New York, Kenedy, 1917.
205p. plates.　B 447
BRUNOWE, MARION J. A
Famous Convent School. New
York. Meany Co. 1897.
153p.　B 448
Story of Mt. St. Vincents-
on-the-Hudson.
BRUTE, SIMON. "Bishop
Bruté's Account of Religion at
Emmitsburg, Md.," American
Catholic Historical Researches,
v. 15 (1898), 88-95. B 449
BRUTE DE REMUR, CHARLES.
Vie de Monseigneur Bruté de
Remur, Rennes et Paris. no
pub. 1887.　B 450
BUCHER, BETTY R. Catholics
and Woodrow Wilson's Mexi-
can Policy. M.A. thesis.
Catholic University of Ameri-
ca. 1954. 112p.　B 451
BUCHER, MARK. "Mission San
Xavier del Bac, Tucson,
Arizona," Hispanic American
Historical Review, v. 16
(1936), 91-93.　B 452
BUCK, WALTER H. "Charles
Joseph Bonaparte: Some
Recollections," Maryland His-
torical Magazine, v. 42

72

(1947), 109-114.   B 453
BUCKLEY, ANNE MAE. "Birth of
a Parish," Ave Maria. v.
184 (Aug. 25, 1956), 8-11.
                       B 454
The story of the beginnings
of the Catholic parish in
Midland Park, N.J.
BUCKNER, SISTER MARY.
History of the Sisters of
Charity of Leavenworth.
Kansas City, Mo. Hudson
Kimberly Pub. Co. 1898.
507p.   B 455
BUDDE, F. H. Jubilee of F.H.
Budde as Pastor of Our Lady
of Mount Carmel Parish, St.
Louis. Amerika Print. 1920.
36p. plates, ports.   B 456
BUDENZ, LOUIS. "A Survey of
Conditions in 'Dago Hill,' St.
Louis," Central Blatt and
Social Justice, v. 8 (1915),
126-128.   B 457
BUDWAY, JOHN F. A History
of the Brooklyn Tablet (1908-
1942). M.A. thesis. St.
John's University, N.Y., 1942.
mss.   p.   B 458
BUEGLER, I. C. Geschichte der
kathol. Kirche Chicago's.
Chicago, Ill. Wilhelm Kuhl-
mann. 1889. 222p. plus ads
illus., ports.   B 459
BUEHLER, SISTER JOHANNITA.
"The Present Status of Catholic
Education in Illinois," Illinois
Catholic Historical Review, v.
6 (1924), 150-167.   B 460
BUENO, STEFANO. "Da una Let-
tera del P. Bueno," Lettere
Edificanti Provincia Napolitana,
ser. 8, n. 1 (1899), 66-68.
                       B 461
Dated "Pueblo, 30 Giugno,
1897." A general report
on the work of the Jesuits
in Pueblo.
BUENO, STEFANO. "Del Norte
(Colo.). Un Vasto Campo
Apostolico," Lettere Edificanti
Provincia Napolitana, ser. 8,
n. 2 (1900), 119-124. B 462

No entry.   B 463

BUFFALO (DIOCESE) SYNOD,
1854. Statuta dioecesis buffalensis lata in synodo
dioecesana A.D. 1854 habita.
Cum decretis emendatis ex
synodis A.D. 1847, 1849,
1851, et 1852 habitis. Buffalo,
Wieckmann & Brandt, 1854.
14p.   B 464
BUFFALO (DIOCESE) SYNOD,
1855. Statuta ... n.p., n.d.
3p.   B 465
BUFFALO (DIOCESE) SYNOD,
1856. Statuta ... n.p., n.d.
24p.   B 466
The 24 pages comprise a
pastoral letter of Stephen
Vincent, Bishop of Buffalo,
to his diocese.
BUFFALO (DIOCESE) SYNOD,
2nd, 1849. Synodus dioecesana
buffalensis secunda, habita
anno MDCCCXLIX. Buffalo,
typis Brunck & Domedion,
1850. 14p.   B 467
BUFFALO (DIOCESE) SYNOD,
Statuta dioeceseos buffalensis
in decretis emandatis ex
synodis A.D. 1847, 1849,
1851, 1852, 1854, 1855, 1856,
1857, 1859, 1860, 1861, 1862,
et 1863 habitis. 38p. B 468
BUFFALO, N.Y. (DIOCESE)
SYNOD, 17th, 1871. Synodus
dioecesana buffalensis decima
septima, quae complectitur
etiam statuta lata in synodis
ab A.D. 1847 usque ad 1866,
die 13a Augusti, A.D. 1871,
in ecclesia cathedrali Sancti
Josephi, in civitate buffalensi
habita, a Stephano Vincentio
Ryan, D.D. episcopo buffalensi.
Buffalensi, 1871. 48p. B 469
BUFFALO, N.Y. (DIOCESE)
SYNOD, 20th, 1886. Synodus
dioecesana buffalensis
vigesima, quae complectitur
etial statuta lata in synodis
ab A.D. 1847 usque ad 1879,
diebus 30a Novembris ac la

et 2a Decembris, A.D. 1886, in ecclesia cathedrali Sancti Joseph, in civitate buffalensi habita, Stephano Vincentio Ryan, S.T.D., episcopo buffalensi. Buffalone, Typis Courier company, 1886. 75p.
B 470

BUFFALO, N.Y. (DIOCESE) SYNOD, 21st, 1891. Synodus dioecesana buffalensis vigesima prima, die 10a Junii, A.D. MDCCXCI, in ecclesia cathedrali Sancti Joseph, in civitate buffalensi habita, a Stephano Vincentio Ryan episcopo buffalensi. Buffalone, N. Eb., typis Soc. Cath. Publ. n.d. 8p. B 471

BUFFALO (DIOCESE) SYNOD, 22nd, 1894. Synodus dioecesana buffalensis vigesima secunda, die VI. Junii, A.D. 1894. in ecclesia cathedrali Sancti Joseph, in civitate Buffalensi habita, a Stephano Vincentio Ryan ep. Buffalone, Soc. Cath. Publ. n.d. 14p. B 472

BUFFALO (DIOCESE) SYNOD, 23rd, 1897. Synodus dioecesana buffalensis vigesima tertia die 30 junii, A.D. 1897 in ecclesia cathedrali Sancti Joseph, in civitate buffalensi habita, a Jacobo Eduardo Quigley ep. Buffalone, Soc. Cath. Publ. n.d. 14p. B 473

BUFFALO, N.Y. (DIOCESE) SYNOD, 24th, 1901. Synodus dioecesana buffalensis vigesima quarta, die 30 Octobris, A.D., MCMI, in civitate buffalensi habita, a Jacobo Eduardo Quigley, S.T.D., episcopo buffalensi. (Buffalone, Typis Soc. Cath. publ., 1901) xi, 78p.
B 474

BUFFALO (DIOCESE) SYNOD, 27th. Synodus dioecesana buffalensis vigesima septima. Buffalo, St. Joseph's Cathedral. 1924. xviii, 147p. B 475

BUFFALO (DIOCESE) SYNOD, 28th, 1938. Synodus dioecesana buffalensis duodetricesima in ecclesia cathedrali titulo S. Joseph die 9 mensis Novembris, anno 1938 celebrata. Praeside Joanne Aloisio Duffy ep. Buffalo, Union and Times Press, n.d. 88p. B 476

BUFFALO CENTENNIAL EUCHARISTIC CONGRESS HISTORICAL COMMITTEE (ed.). Buffalo Centennial Eucharistic Congress. Buffalo. Union and Echo. 1948. 318p. B 477

BUGG, LELIA HARDIN. "Catholicity in the West," Catholic World, v. 66 (1897), 302-318. B 478
West of the Mississippi River, a survey.

"'BULLS OF INDULGENCES' SOLD IN NEW YORK, PHILADELPHIA AND BOSTON, 1743-1748," American Catholic Historical Researches, v. 18 (1901) 26-29. B 479

BUONOCORE, SISTER M. FABIAN. Political Nativism in Syracuse, New York. M.A. thesis. Catholic University of America. 1935. 68p.
B 480

BUOTICH, D.D. Historical Sketch of Sacred Heart Parish and Its Mission in Northwestern Texas. Amarillo, Texas. Rev. J.R. Allard. 1922. 40p. illus. B 481

BURBEY, LOUIS H. "When Was Easter First Celebrated in Michigan?" Michigan History Magazine, v. 33 (1949), 43-46. B 482

BURCH, FRANCIS. "The Apostle of Kentucky," St. Meinrad Historical Essays, v. 1 (1928), 25-31. B 483

BUREAU OF THE CATHOLIC INDIAN MISSIONS. Report of the Catholic Bureau of Indian Missions, 1874-1895. Washington. 1895. B 484

BUREAU OF CATHOLIC INDIAN MISSIONS. Status of the Catholic Indian Missions in the United States in 1876. Balti-

74

more. n.d. B 485
BUREAU OF CATHOLIC INDIAN
MISSIONS. Work of the Decade,
ending December 31, 1883.
Washington. n.d. B 486
BURKE, JOHN J. Trials and
Triumphs. Longfellow Press.
1942. xii, 116p. plates,
ports. B 487
BURKE, JAMES MICHAEL. Diary
of the Potawatomie Mission of
St. Mary's on the Lake by
Father Maurice Gailland, S.J.
Translated and edited with
biography and notes. M.A.
thesis. Saint Louis University,
1951. 287p. B 488
BURKE, JAMES M. (tr.) "Early
Years at St. Mary's Pot-
towatomie Mission, from the
Diary of Father Maurice
Gailland, S.J." Kansas His-
torical Quarterly, v. 20
(Aug., 1953), 500-529. B 489
A translation from the Latin
of the daily mission record
of the mission for the years
1848-1850.
BURKE, THOMAS J. "Catholic
Day, March 25, 1634," A-
merican Catholic Historical
Society of Philadelphia Records,
v. 37 (1926), 203-219. B 490
BURKE, OONA. "Eden Hall,"
Jubilee, v. 5 (Nov., 1957),
29-35; illus. B 491
A good account of this famous
Catholic boarding school of
the Sacred Heart, located
near Philadelphia.
BURLINGTON, VER. (DIOCESE),
SYNOD, 1855 (1907). Statuta
dioecesis burlingtonensis, cum
facultatibus sacerdotibus
ejusdem dioecesis concessis.
Boston, Angel Guardian press,
1907. 2 p.l., 64, 7p. B 492
Statutes of the first synod,
1855, "to which we have
added extracts from our
synods, from letters to our
clergy, and a few decrees
from other sources ..." --
Preface, signed "Joannes

Stephanus, ep. Burlingtonensis."
BURLINGTON (DIOCESE) Statuta
dioecesis burlingtonensis ...
St. Albans, Advertiser printing house, 1878. 14p. B 493
BURLINGTON, VER. (DIOCESE)
SYNOD, 1855, (1886).
Statuta dioecesis burlingtonensis, cum facultatibus sacerdotibus ejusdem dioecesis
concessis.... Burlington, Vt.
1886. 32p., 1 l. B 494
Statutues of the first synod,
1855, "to which we have
added extracts from our
synods, from letters to
our clergy, and a few
decrees from other sources
..."--Preface, signed
"Ludovicus, ep. burlingtonensis."

No entry. B 495

BURNS, ARTHUR J. "New Light
on Mother Seton," United
States Catholic Historical
Society Records and Studies,
v. 22 (1932), 85-100. B 496
BURNS, C.A. Glory of SS.
Peter and Paul's, Detroit.
Detroit. SS. Peter and Paul's.
1948. 77p. front. (port.).
plates. B 497
BURNS, FRANCIS P. "Notes on
the Legislation and Litigation
Affecting the Title of St.
Louis Cathedral," Louisiana
Historical Quarterly, v. 18
(1935), 362-376. B 498
St. Louis Cathedral, New

Orleans, Louisiana.

BURNS, JAMES A. Catholic
Colonial Schools in Philadelphia. Philadelphia, Dolphin.
1908. 31p.   B 499

BURNS, JAMES A. The Catholic
School System in the United
States. New York. Benziger.
1908. 415p.   B 500

BURNS, JAMES A. "Catholic
Schools in the Immigration
Period," Catholic Educational
Review, v. 1 (1911), 430-
437.   B 501

BURNS, JAMES A. The Growth
and Development of the Catholic School System in the U-
nited States. New York.
Benziger. 1912. 421p.
incl. maps, tables.   B 502

BURNS, JAMES A. "A History of
the Catholic Parochial Schools
in the United States," Catholic
University Bulletin, v. 12
(1906), 434-453.   B 503

BURNS, JAMES A. 'Report of
the Committee on High
Schools," National Catholic
Educational Association Bulletin, v. 8 (1911), 45-73; v.
8 (1912), 5-48.   B 504
A study of the number,
location, and character of
Catholic boys' high schools in
the United States.

BURNS, JAMES A. AND BERNARD
J. KOHLBRENNER. A History
of Catholic Education in the U-
nited States. New York. Benziger. 1937. xi, 295p. illus.
(incl. ports., facsims.),
diagrams.   B 505

BURNS, SISTER MARY ANNE.
Materials for the Study of the
Life and Works of Reverend A.
B.C. Dunne. M.A. thesis.
Marquette University. 1935.
                                B 506

BURNS, SISTER MARY HELENE.
The Historical Continuity Between the Old Missions and the
Early Churches of the Northwest. M.A. thesis. University
of Notre Dame. 1936.   B 507

BURNS, SISTER M. STEPHANIE.
The Role of Catholics in the
Early History of Utah, M.A.
thesis. Portland University.
1956. vi, 119p.   B 508

BURNS, R. IGNATIUS (ed.).
"Coeur d'Alene diplomacy in
the Nez Perce War of 1877,"
American Catholic Historical
Society of Philadelphia Records, v. 63 (March, 1952),
37-60.   B 509

BURNS, R. IGNATIUS. "Descriptive Calendar of the Joset
Papers in Jesuit Historical
Archives of the Oregon Province. Affixed to Père Joset's
Account of the Indian War of
1858," Pacific Northwest
Quarterly, v. 38 (1947), 307-
314.   B 510

BURNS, R. IGNATIUS. "A Jesuit
at the Hell Gate Treaty of
1855," Mid-America, v. 34
(April, 1952), 87-114. B 511

BURNS, R. IGNATIUS. "A
Jesuit in the War Against the
Northern Indians," American
Catholic Historical Society of
Philadelphia Records, v. 61
(1950), 9-54.   B 512

BURNS, R. IGNATIUS. 'The
Jesuits and the Spokane Council
of 1877," Pacific Historical
Review, v. 21 (February,
1952), 65-110.   B 513

BURNS, R. IGNATIUS. 'The
Jesuits, the Northern Indian
and the Nez Perce War of
1877," Pacific Northwest
Quarterly, v. 42 (January,
1951), 40-76.   B 514

BURNS, R. IGNATIUS (ed.).
"Père Joset's Account of the
Indian War of 1858." Pacific
Northwest Quarterly, v. 38
(1947), 285-314.   B 515

BURR, NELSON R. 'Religious
History of New Jersey
Roman Catholics," New Jersey
Historical Society Proceedings,
v. 56 (1938), 54-56. B 516

BURR, NELSON R. A Critical
Bibliography of Religion in

America. Princeton, N.J.
Princeton University Press.
1961. 1219p. $17.50.
B 517

BURRUS, ERNEST J. "Father
Jacques Marquette, S.J. His
Priesthood in the Light of the
Jesuit Roman Archives," Cath-
olic Historical Review, v. 41
(October., 1955), 257-271.
B 518
An excellent scholarly study
of the problem of the priest-
hood of Marquette, concludes
that Marquette was unques-
tionably a priest.

BURRUS, E. J. "Georgetown and
Catholic University," Woodstock
Letters, v. 83 (Feb., 1954),
77-101. B 519
Based on the notes of Father
Joseph H. Richard, Rector
of Georgetown, 1888-1898.
Gives an interesting picture
of the cooperation between
the officials of the two
schools.

BURTON, EDWIN H. The Life
and Times of Bishop Challoner
(1691-1781). New York. Longmans, Green and Co. 1909.
2v. front., plates, ports.,
map, facsims. B 520

BURTON, KATHERINE. According
to the Pattern. New York.
Longmans, Green and Co.
1946. 252p. B 521
A popular account of the efforts of the Edinburgh
physician, Agnes McLaren,
to promote Catholic medical
mission work, and of her
disciple, Dr. Anna Dengel,
who in 1925 established in
Washington, D.C., the Society
of Catholic Medical Missionaries.

BURTON, KATHERINE. Celestial
Homespun. The Life of Isaac
Thomas Hecker. New York.
Longmans, Green and Co.
1943. 393p. B 522

BURTON, KATHERINE. The Dream
Lives Forever: the Story of St.

Patrick's Cathedral. New York.
Longmans, Green, 1960. xiii,
238p. $4.50. B 523

BURTON, KATHERINE. The
Golden Door. The Life of
Katherine Drexel. New York.
Kenedy, 1957, xi, 329p.
$3.75. B 524

BURTON, KATHERINE. His
Dear Persuasion. New York.
1940. Elizabeth Seton.
B 525

BURTON, KATHERINE. Mightily
and Sweetly. Paterson, N.J.
St. Anthony Guild Press.
1948. 292p. B 526
Popular biographical account
of Mother Josephine of the
Sacred Heart, one-time
Provincial Superior of the
Hartford Community of the
Sisters of St. Joseph.

BURTON, KATHERINE. Mother
Butler of Marymount. New
York, Longmans, Green and
Co., 1944. xi, 290p. B 527

BURTON, KATHERINE. No
Shadow of Turning, the Life of
James Kent Stone, Father
Fidelis of the Cross. New
York. Longmans, Green and
Co. 1944. 243p. B 528

BURTON, KATHERINE. Sorrow
Built a Bridge. New York.
Longmans, Green and Co.
1937. 288p. front. (port.).
B 529
A popular life of Mother
Alphonsa Hawthorne Lathrop,
foundress of the Servants of
Relief for Incurable Cancer.

BURTSELL, R. L. Canonical
Status of Priests in the United
States. New York. O'Brien.
1887. 106p. B 530

BUSCH, WILLIAM. "The Diocesan
Seminary Project in St. Paul,"
Acta et Dicta, v. 7 (1935),
56-82. B 531

BUTLER, J.D. "Fr. Samuel Mazzuchelli," Wisconsin Historical
Collections, v. 14 (1898),
155-161 port. B 532

BUTLER, JOHN J. AND O'HERN,

EDNA M. "Medical Education and Research in Catholic Medical Schools and Hospitals," American Catholic Sociological Review, v. 19 (Oct., 1958), 224-237. B 533

BUTLER, SISTER MARY BERTRAND. The "Annales" as a Source for American Catholic History, 1822-1832. M.A. thesis. Catholic University of America. 1936. 78p. B 534

BUTLER, SISTER MARY WERI. The Beginnings of the Church in Lower Maumee Valley. M.A. thesis. University of Notre Dame. 1942. iv, 78p. B 535

BUTCHER, HAROLD. "Lily of the Mohawks," Mary, v. 14 (Nov.-Dec.,1953), 47-51. B 536

An illustrated article giving a brief life and the development of the cause of beatification of Katherin Tekakwitha.

BUTLER, THADEUS. The Catholic Church in America. 1869. B 537

BUTSCH, JOSEPH. "Negro Catholics in the United States," Catholic Historical Review, v. 3 (1917), 33-51. B 538

BYRNE, EDWARD JOHN. Anti-Catholicism in National Politics. M.A. thesis. Catholic University of America. 1928. 63p. B 539

BYRNE, JOHN F. The Glories of Mary in Boston. Boston, Mission Church Press. 1921. 584p. front., plates, ports. B 540

BYRNE, JOHN F. Golden Memories. New York. no pub. 1937. 98p. front., illus., incl. ports. B 541

Story of Our Lady of Perpetual Help Church, New York City, 1887-1937.

BYRNE, JOHN F. The Redemptorist Centenaries, 1732-1932. Philadelphia. Dolphin. 1932.

xvi, 628p. front. B 542

BYRNE, JOHN F. "The Redemptorists in America," American Catholic Historical Society of Philadelphia Records, v. 41 (1930), 263-288 (The Pioneer Days, 1832-1839), 353-384 (Baltimore and Rochester, N. Y.); v. 42 (1931), 55-90, 155-190 (Pennsylvania and Michigan), 247-282 (Buffalo, New Orleans), 379-400 (Missions); v. 43 (1932), 34-61 (Bishop Neumann). B 543

BYRNE, JOHN T. A Study of Student Problems in Catholic Men's Colleges. Washington: Catholic University of America. 1957. 116p. B 544

This is volume twenty of the Educational Research Monographs published by Catholic University.

BYRNE, SISTER MARY COLMAN. History of the Sisters of Mercy in Camden. M.A. thesis. Villanova University. 1951. 200p. B 545

BYRNE, PATRICK JAMES. Father Price of Maryknoll. Maryknoll, N.Y. Catholic Foreign Mission Society of America. 1923. xv, 93p. front., plates, ports. B 546

BYRNE, PAUL RYAN. "American Catholic Bibliography: In Retrospect and a Preview," Catholic Library World, v. 20 (1948), 8-11. B 547

- C -

C., M.A. "The Church of the Attakapas, 1750-1889," American Catholic Quarterly Review, v. 14 (1889), 462-486. C 1

CACHIA, THEOPHILUS. "St. Paul of the Shipwreck Parish, San Francisco," Provincial Annals (Province of Santa Barbara, O.F.M.), v. 2 (April, 1940), 9-12. C 2

CADDEN, JOHN JOSEPH. Father Jeremiah O'Callaghan; Economist and Pioneer Missionary,

1780-1861. M.A. Thesis, Catholic University, 1936. 89p. C 3

CADDEN, JOHN PAUL. The Historiography of the American Catholic Church, 1785-1943. Washington. Catholic University of America. 1944. xi, 122p. C 4

CAHENSLY, PETER PAUL. "Cahensly über seine Reise nach den Vereinigten Staaten im Jahre 1883," Central Blatt and Social Justice, v. 16 (1917), 136-137. C 5

CAHENSLY, PETER PAUL. "P. P. Cahensly über die Noth der Deutschen Auswanderer," Central Blatt and Social Justice, v. 16 (1923), 376-379, 412-415. C 6

CAILLY, LOUIS DE. Memoirs of Bishop Loras. New York. Christian Press Association Publishing Co. 1897. C 7

CAIN, H. EDWARD. "The National Center of Catholic Education," Sign, v. 11 (1931), 169-173, illus. C 8
A general appreciation of Washington, D.C., and Catholic University.

CALAHAN, JAMES. "History of St. Mary's Parish, Marshal, Mich.," Michigan History Magazine, v. 1 (1917). C 9

CALDERON, IGNATIO. "Letter in Prevision of the Episcopal Visitation of the Missions by Tamaron, Bishop of Durango, April 8, 1755," Americas, v. 4 (1947), 257-258. C 10

CALLAGHAN, BRIAN L. "Fifty Years in Louisiana," The Colored Harvest, (1948), 8-11. C 11

CALLAGHAN, EMILY A. Memoirs and Writings of the Very Reverend James F. Callaghan. Cincinnati. Clarke. 1903. 568p. C 12

CALLAHAN, ADALBERT. "Death Comes to Archbishop Robinson," Provincial Annals (Province of the Most Holy Name, O.F.M.), v. 8 (1948), 397-424. C 13

CALLAHAN, ADALBERT. "The Early Years of Our Seraphic Seminary," Provincial Annals (Province of the Most Holy Name, O.F.M.), v. 8 (1948), 272-283, 312-321, 374-381. C 14

CALLAHAN, ADALBERT. "Manhattan's Franciscan Centenary," Provincial Annals (Province of the Most Holy Name, O.F.M.), v. 5 (1945), 71-77, 123-128, 172-176. C 15

CALLAHAN, ADALBERT J. Medieval Francis in Modern America; the Story of Eighty Years, 1855-1935. New York. Macmillan, 1936. xiv, 494p. front., plates, ports. C 16
History of the Province of the Most Holy Name of Jesus (New York), O.F.M.

CALLAHAN, JEROME R. American Opinion on Pius X and the Election of Benedict XV. M.A. Thesis. Catholic University. 1955. 55p. C 17

CALLAHAN, SISTER MARY GENEROSA. History of the Sisters of Divine Providence San Antonio Texas. Milwaukee, Bruce, 1955. xv, 304p. C 18

CALLAN, LOUISE. "Patriot Priest," Missouri Historical Society Bulletin, v. 5 (1949), 266-288. C 19

CALLAN, LOUISE. Philippine Duchesne. Westminster, Maryland: Newman, 1957. xiii, 805p. C 20

CALLAN, SISTER MARY ANNA ROSE. Sisters of Charity of the Blessed Virgin and Their Schools in Chicago, 1867-1940. M.A. Thesis. Chicago Loyola University. 1941. C 21

CALLAN, LOUISE. The Society of the Sacred Heart in North America. New York. Longmans, Green and Co. 1937. xvii,

809p. plates, map. C 22

"THE CAMALDOLESE COME TO AMERICA," Jubilee, v. 6 (December, 1958), 37-41. illus. C 23

The story of the first foundation in North America at Lucia Ranch, California.

CAMERON, SISTER MARY DAVID. The College of Notre Dame of Maryland, 1895-1945. New York. McMullen. 1947. xiv, 219p. illus. C 24

CAMPBELL, B. U. "Early Missions Among the Indians in Maryland," Maryland Historical Magazine, v. 1 (1906), 293-316. C 25

CAMPBELL, HENRY COLEN. Père René Ménard, the Predecessor of Allonez in the Lake Superior Mission. Milwaukee. 1897. np. C 26

CAMPBELL, THOMAS J. "Dr. John McLoughlin," United States Catholic Historical Society Records and Studies, v. 8 (1915), 83-115. C 27

CAMPBELL, THOMAS J. "Eusebio Kino, 1644-1711," Catholic Historical Review, v. 5 (1920), 353-376. C 28

CAMPBELL, THOMAS J. "Father Louis Jouin," United States Historical Records and Studies, v. 2 (1900), 163-171. C 29

CAMPBELL, THOMAS J. "The First Mass in New York State," United States Catholic Historical Society Records and Studies, v. 11 (1917), 31-46. C 30

CAMPBELL, THOMAS J. "Fordham University," Woodstock Letters, v. 45 (1916), 349-370. C 31

CAMPBELL, THOMAS J. Pioneer Laymen of North America. New York. America Press. 1915. 2v. front., plates, ports., maps. C 32

Limited to the pioneers of New France.

CAMPBELL, THOMAS J. Pioneer Priests of America, 1642-1710. New York. Fordham University.

1908-1919. 3v. C 33

Limited to the Jesuit missionaries to the Indians of New York, 1642-1710.

CAMPION, DONALD R. "Pioneer Social Catholics," Historical Bulletin, v. 24 (1946), 57-58, 67-68. C 34

CANAVAN, MARY ELIZABETH. The Appeal of Catholic Mysticism to New England Protestants of the Early Nineteenth Century and the Conversions It Inspired. MA thesis. Boston College. 1932. 55p. C 35

CANEVIN, J. F. REGIS. Catholic Growth in the United States. Pittsburgh. C.T.S. 1923. C 36

CANEVIN, J.F. REGIS. "Loss and Gain in the Catholic Church in the United States, 1800-1916," Catholic Historical Review, v. 2 (1917), 377-385. C 37

CARAYON, AUGUSTE. Bannissement des Jésuites de la Louisiane; Relation et Lettres Inédites. Paris. 1865. C 38

CAREW, PAUL T. Story of a Mother Church. St. John's, Orange, N.J., 1851-1934. Orange, N.J. The Author. ca. 1934. 164p. front., plates, ports. C 39

CAREY, SISTER MARY HELEN. The Irish Element in Iowa up to 1865. M.A. thesis. Catholic University. 1944. 109p. C 40

CAREY, MATTHEW. Matthew Carey Autobiography. Brooklyn. Eugene L. Schwab. 1941. ix, 134p. incl. front. (port.) C 41

CARLIER, AUGUSTE. La République Américaine, Etats-Unis. Paris. Guillaumier. 1890. 4v. fold map. C 42

CARLIN, SISTER MARY ANGELA. The Attitude of the Republican Party toward Religious Schools, 1875-1880. M.A.

thesis. Catholic University, 1948. 98p. C 43

CARMEL, SISTER JOSEPH. "Early Parish Libraries in Conewago Valley," Catholic Library World, v. 20 (1949), 171-174. C 44

CARMEL ON THE MISSISSIPPI. Davenport, Ia. Our Lady of Mount Carmel. 1926. 62p. plates. C 45
Story of the Carmelite monastery Regina Coeli, Davenport, Ia.

CARMEN, J. NEALE. "The Bishop East of the Rockies Views His Diocesans," Kansas Historical Quarterly, v. 21 (Summer, 1954), 81-86. C 46
Deals with Bishop Miege of Leavenworth and his diocese in the 1850s.

CARR, MICHAEL W. A History of Catholicity in Richmond and Wayne Co., Indiana. Indianapolis. Carlton and Hollenbeck. 1889. 74p. incl. plates, ports. C 47

CARRIERE, G. "Une Mission Tragique aux Illinois-Chinug Oblats," Revue d'histoire de l'Amérique Française, v. (Mar. 1955). C 48

CARROLL, MOTHER AUSTIN. The Ursulines in Louisiana, 1727-1823. New Orleans. 1886. C 49

CARROLL, CHARLES. Unpublished Letters of Charles Carroll of Carrollton, and of His Father, Charles Carroll of Doughoregan. New York. United States Catholic Historical Society. 1902. 250p. front., port., facsim., geneal. table. C 50

CARROLL, JOHN. "Letter of Rt. Rev. John Carroll, D.D. to Hon. Sam Dexter, Esq., Secretary of War, on the Indian Missions," United States Catholic Historical Magazine, v. 2 (1888), 217. C 51

CARROLL, JOHN. "Letter to Fr.

Marmaduke Stone, dated Baltimore, 1805," Woodstock Letters, v. 15 (1886), 194-195. C 52

CARROLL, JOHN. "Letters of Bishop Carroll to Archbishop Troy of Dublin," American Catholic Historical Researches, v. 13 (1896), 156-166; v. 14 (1897), 17-26; v. 15 (1898), 129. C 53

CARROLL, JOHN. "Two Letters from Archbishop Carroll Concerning the Restoration of the Society. Dated Baltimore, July 14, 1805, and Baltimore, October 22, 1805," Woodstock Letters, v. 12 (1883), 288-291. C 54

CARROLL, KENNETH L. "Religious Influences on the Manumission of Slaves," Maryland Historical Magazine, v. 56 (June, 1961), 176-197. C 55

CARROLL, MARY TERESA AUSTIN. A Catholic History of the Alabamas and the Floridas. New York. Kenedy. 1908. C 56

CARROLL, MARY TERESA AUSTIN. Leaves from the Annals of the Sisters of Mercy. New York. Shea. 1895. 4v. C 57

CARROZZINI, VITO. "Lettera XXV," Lettere Edificanti Provincia Napolitana, ser. 1 (1875), 70-71. C 58
Dated "Ottobre, 1874," A description of the work of the missionaries at Fort Union, New Mexico.

CARTER, CHARLES FRANKLIN. The Missions of Neuva California. San Francisco. Whitaker and Ray. 1900. xv, 189p. incl. front. (port.) illus., plates. C 59

CARTER, CHARLES FRANKLIN. Stories of the Old Missions of California. San Francisco. P. Elder and Co. 1917. vii, 184p. illus. C 60

CARTHY, MOTHER MARY PETER. English Influences on Early American Catholicism. Washington, D.C. Catholic University, 1959. 155p. C 61

CARTHY, MOTHER MARY PETER. Old St. Patrick's, New York's Oldest Cathedral. M.A. thesis. Catholic University. 1948. 108p. C 62

CARTHY, MOTHER MARY PETER. Old St. Patrick's, New York's First Cathedral. Monograph Series, v. 23. New York. United States Catholic Historical Society. 1947. 111p. C 63

CARTWRIGHT, JOHN K. "The American Catholic Historical Association," Catholic Historical Review, v. 30 (1945), 382-393. C 64

CARTWRIGHT, JOHN K. "Thoughts of Our Twenty-Fifth Anniversary," Catholic University Bulletin, v. (1945), 4, 11-12. C 65

CARUANA, J. M. "Indian Missions. The Rocky Mountains, Letter to Superior General of the Mission," Woodstock Letters, v. 11 (1882), 269-275. C 66

CARUANA, J. M. "Indian Missions. Letter dated Colville, W. T., Jan. 21, 1882," Woodstock Letters, v. 12 (1883), 43-49. C 67

CARUANA, J. M. "Indian Missions. Letter dated Colville, W.T., April 17, 1882," Woodstock Letters, v. (1883), 49-51. C 68

CASAS, AUGUSTO. Fray Junipero Serra. El Apostel de California. Barcelona. Luis Miracle. 1949. 271p. illus., photos. C 69

CASE, SHIRLEY JACKSON, ET AL. A Bibliographical Guide to the History of Christianity. Chicago. University of Chicago. 1931. xi, 265p. Reprinted 1951. C 70

CASEY, SISTER CELESTINE, AND SISTER M. EDMOND FERN. Loretto in the Rockies. Denver. Loretto Heights College. 1943. xv, 314p. plates, ports., diagr. C 71

CASEY, JOHN. "The First Priest of Bishop Brute," St. Meinrad Historical Essays, v. 3 (1934), 118-125. C 72

CASEY, JOHN. "Mission Work Among the Negroes," St. Meinrad Historical Essays, v. 1 (1932), 216-223. C 73

[CASEY, PATRICK ed.]. 1841-1941: A Century of Catholicity in Montana: Souvenir Centenary Edition. The Register. Diocese of Helena. v. 17 (Aug. 27, 1941), 35. C 74

CASPER, HENRY W. History of the Catholic Church in Nebraska. Omaha. True Voice Publishing Co. Projected 3v. v. 1 published 1961. C 74a

CASSIDY, FRANCIS P. Catholic College Foundations in the United States, 1667-1850. Washington. Catholic University of America. 1924. 103p. C 75

A slight dissertation presented at Catholic University--based principally on secondary sources; of little value.

CASSIDY, FRANCIS P. "Catholic Education in the Third Plenary Council of Baltimore," Catholic Historical Review, v. 34 (1948-1949), 257-305, 414-436. C 76

CASSILLY, FRANCIS. The Old Jesuit Mission in Council Bluffs. 12p. illus., plates, map. C 77

CASTANEDA, CARLOS E. "Earliest Catholic Activities in Texas," Catholic Historical Review, v. 17 (1931), 278-295. C 78

CASTANEDA, CARLOS E. Earliest Catholic Activities in

Texas, Austin, Texas. Texas Catholic Historical Society. 1931. C 79

CASTANEDA, CARLOS E. "Pioneers in Sackcloth," Catholic Historical Review, v. 25 (1939), 309-327. C 80

CASTANEDA, CARLOS E. "The Sons of St. Francis in Texas," Americas, v. 1 (1945), 289-302. C 81
See also K 184.

CATALDO, JOSEPH M. "The Nez Perce Indian Mission," The Lewiston Catholic Monthly, v. 5 (1922), Jan. 16-20, 24; Feb. 19-21; Mar. 18-20; Apr. 13-14; May 12-16; June 15-16, 23. C 82

"CATALOGUE OF OUR MISSIONARY FATHERS, 1634-1805," Woodstock Letters, v. 15 (1886), 89-100. C 83

CATHER, WILLA. Death Comes for the Archbishop. New York. Knopf. 1927. 343p. illus. C 84

CATHERINE, SISTER FRANCIS. The Convent Schools of French Origin in the United States, 1727-1843. Philadelphia. University of Pennsylvania. 1936. 246p. C 85

"CATHOLIC AND ANTI-CATHOLIC ITEMS IN AMERICAN COLONIAL PAPERS," United States Catholic Historical Magazine, v. 1 (1887), 81-91, 203-214, 316-318, 442-443. variant title. C 86

CATHOLIC BUILDERS OF THE NATION. Ed. by Constantine E. Maguire. Boston. Continental Press. 1923. 5v. front., plates, ports. C 87

CATHOLIC CHURCH. Congregatio de propaganda fide. Relatio collationum quas Romae coram S. C. de P.F. praefecto habuerunt archiepiscopi pluresque episcopi Statuum Foederatorum Americae. 1883. C 88

CATHOLIC CHURCH. Pope. Pontificia Americana: A Docu-

mentary History of the Catholic Church in the United States (1784-1884). Comp. and ed. by Donald C. Shearer. Washington, Catholic University of America. 1933. xi, 413p. C 89

"CATHOLIC CHURCH IN BELFAST (MAINE)," Maine Catholic Historical Review, v. 7 (1917), 227-237. C 90

"CATHOLIC CHURCH IN DETROIT," Michigan History Magazine, v. 2 (1918), 121-123. C 91

"CATHOLIC CHURCH IN MAINE, EARLY HISTORY," Maine Catholic Historical Magazine, v. 3 (1914), July, 40-46, Aug. 39-43, Sept., 43-48, Oct., 39-48, Nov., 42-48. C 92

"CATHOLIC CHURCH IN MAINE," Maine Catholic Historical Magazine, v. 7 (1916), 158-166. C 93

CATHOLIC CHURCH IN THE UNITED STATES OF AMERICA. New York. Catholic Editing Co. 1912. 3v. C 94

CATHOLIC CHURCH IN THE UNITED STATES. Bishops. The National Pastorals of the American Hierarchy. 1792-1919. Westminster, Md. Newman. 1954. xi, 358p. C 95

CATHOLIC CHURCH IN THE UNITED STATES. Bishops. Our Bishops Speak. Edited by Raphael M. Huber. Milwaukee. Bruce. 1952. xxxiii, 402p. C 96
A companion volume to the National Pastorals of the American Hierarchy 1791-1919.

"CATHOLIC CHURCH IN THE UNITED STATES, 1776-1876," Catholic World, v. 23 (1876), 434-452. C 97

CATHOLIC CHURCH IN THE UNITED STATES. (Diocesan Synods: a microfilm collection of 17 reels made by Woodstock

College, Woodstock, Maryland).
C 98
CATHOLIC CHURCH IN THE
UNITED STATES. Plenary
Council. 1st. Baltimore.
1852. Concilium Plenarium
Totius Americae Septentrio-
nales Foederatae Baltimori
Habitum Anno 1852. Baltimore.
Murphy. 1853. 72p.   C 99
CATHOLIC CHURCH IN THE
UNITED STATES. Plenary
Council. 2d. Baltimore.
1866. Concilii Plenarii Balti-
morensis II. Acta et Decreta.
Baltimore. Murphy. 1868.
cliv, 346, xxviii, xxvip.
C 100
CATHOLIC CHURCH IN THE
UNITED STATES. Plenary
Council. 2d. Baltimore. 1866.
Concilii Plenarii Baltimorensis
II. Acta et Decreta. E itio
altera mendis expurgata.
Baltimore, Murphy. 1877.
lxxv, 311, xxviiip.   C 101
CATHOLIC CHURCH IN THE
UNITED STATES. Plenary
Council, 3d. Baltimore. 1884.
Acta et Decreta Concilii
Plenarii Baltimorensis Tertii
IX Novembris usque ad diem
VII Decembris, A.D.
MDCCCLXXXIV. Baltimore.
Murphy. 1884.   C 102
CATHOLIC CHURCH IN THE
UNITED STATES. Plenary
Council. 3d. Baltimore. 1884.
Acta et Decreta Concilii Plen-
arii Baltimorensis Tertii, A.D.
MDCCCLXXXIV. Baltimore.
Murphy. 1886. vii-cix, 821p.
C 103
CATHOLIC CHURCH IN THE
UNITED STATES. Plenary
Council. 3d Baltimore. 1884.
Decreta Concilii Plenarii Bal-
timorensis Tertii. Baltimore.
Murphy. 1894. vii, 3-189p.
C 104
CATHOLIC CHURCH IN WEST
TENNESSEE. (Published by the
West Tennessee Deanery Coun-
cil of the Diocesan Council of

Catholic Women). 1951. 46p.
illus.   C 105
CATHOLIC COLONIZATION
BUREAU. Catholic Coloniza-
tion in Minnesota. St. Paul,
Minn.   C 106
CATHOLIC COLONIZATION
BUREAU. Catholic Coloniza-
tion in Minnesota. Colony of
Avoca, Murray County, South-
western Minnesota. St. Paul,
Minn. Pioneer Press. 1880.
32p.   C 107
CATHOLIC CONFERENCE OF
THE SOUTH. Report of Pro-
ceedings and Addresses. 3d
Annual Meeting, 1942. Rich-
mond, Va. Executive Head-
quarters. 1943.   C 108
On the state of the Catholic
Church in the Southern
states.
CATHOLIC EDUCATIONAL RE-
VIEW. Advisory Board. "The
condition of Catholic Secondary
Education in the United States,"
Catholic Educational Review, v.
10 (1915), 204-223. C 109
CATHOLIC EDUCATIONAL RE-
VIEW. v. 43 (1944),
September. This issue is
devoted largely to a com-
memmoration of the late
Monsignor George Johnson,
leader in the field of American
Catholic Education.   C 110
CATHOLIC ENCYCLOPEDIA.
New York. Robert Appleton
Co. 1907-1912. 15v. C 111
In addition to the matter
carried in the regular
volumes under the names of
dioceses and individuals, the
Supplement, published in
1922 contains some brief
items, chiefly biographical,
on the Church in the United
States. The index volume is
handy in locating material
contained in other articles.
CATHOLIC ENCYCLOPEDIA AND
ITS MAKERS. New York.
Encyclopedia Press, 1917. vii,
192p. groups of ports.C 112

The most useful biographical guide to American Catholic scholarship available for the period prior to its publication.

"CATHOLIC ENCYCLOPEDIA DIOCESAN BIBLIOGRAPHY," Catholic Historical Review, v. 4 (1918), 264-273, 389-392.
C 113

"CATHOLIC GERMANS OF NORTH AMERICA," Tablet, v. 180 (1942), 165-166, 178-179.
C 114

CATHOLIC HISTORICAL BOOK OF DELAWARE...Centenary of St. Peter's Cathedral, Wilmington, Delaware. Wilmington. Mercantile Printing Co. c1916. 47p. illus., ports., incl. ads.
C 115

CATHOLIC HISTORY AND DIRECTORY FOR THE DIOCESE OF SIOUX FALLS. Sioux Falls, La. 1915.
C 116

[CATHOLIC HOSPITAL ASSOCIATION]. "C.H.A. Grows!," Hospital Progress, v. 34 (1953), 43-45.
C 117
Gives a brief history of the growth of the Catholic Hospital Association.

[CATHOLIC HOSPITAL ASSOCIATION]. "Important Dates in the Life of the Association," Hospital Progress, v. 34 (1953), 14.
C 118

"CATHOLIC LOSSES IN AMERICA," United States Catholic Historical Magazine, v. 4 (1891-1892), 70-90.
C 119

[CATHOLIC MEDICAL MISSION BOARD]. "Twenty-five Years of Medical Missions," America, v. 88 (1953), 640.
C 120
Brief story of the work of the Medical Missions.

CATHOLIC MEMOIRS OF VERMONT AND NEW HAMPSHIRE, ETC. New York, Benziger. 1886?
C 121

[CATHOLIC MIND]. The Catholic Mind Through Fifty Years, 1903-1953. New York. America. 1953. pp. xii, 681.
C 122
Selection from this publication during the past fifty years - selected and edited by Father Benjamin Masse.

CATHOLIC MIRROR. Springfield, Mass. A Century of Catholicism in Western Massachusetts. Springfield, Mass. Catholic Mirror, c. 1931. 350p. cxxxiip. illus., incl. ports., map, ads. iii-cxxxii.
C 123

"CATHOLIC MISSIONS IN EMMETT COUNTY, MICH.," Michigan History Magazine, v. 2 (1918), 324-329.
C 124

"CATHOLIC MISSIONS IN SOUTHERN MICHIGAN," Michigan History Magazine, v. 1 (1917), 23-25.
C 125

CATHOLIC PITTSBURGH'S 100 YEARS. Chicago, Loyola University. 1943. xvi, 271p. front., plate, ports.
C 126

"CATHOLIC SURVEY IN BUFFALO," Catholic Charities Review, v. 3 (1919), 56-57.
C 127

CATHOLIC UNIVERSITY OF AMERICA. Dissertations in American Church History (1889-1932) Washington. Privately Printed. 1922. 27p.
C 128
List of those printed by students of Catholic University.

CATHOLIC UNIVERSITY OF AMERICA. Vital Problems of Catholic Education in the United States. Washington. Catholic University of America. 1939. x, 231p.
C 129

CATHOLIC UNIVERSITY OF AMERICA. Workshop on the Curriculum of the Catholic College, 1951. The Curriculum of the Catholic College, Integration and Concentration. Ed. by Roy J. Deferrari. Washing-

ton. Catholic University.
1952. viii, 236p. illus.
paper. C 130

CATHOLIC YOUTH ORGANIZA-
TION. Diocese of Galveston.
Houston District. Centennial.
The Story of the Development
of the Kingdom of God on
Earth in that Portion of the
Vineyard Which for One
Hundred Years has been the
Diocese of Galveston. Houston,
Texas. Catholic Youth
Organization, Centennial Book
Committee. 1947. 174p. illus.,
ports., maps. C 131

"CATHOLICISM AND THE
NEGRO," Jubilee, v. 3 (1955).
C 132

"CATHOLICITY IN EASTERN
PENNSYLVANIA FROM 1800
to 1836," Catholic Record, v.
13 (1877), 129-141. C 133

"CATHOLICITY IN EASTERN
PENNSYLVANIA FROM 1835
to 1845," Catholic Record, v.
13 (1877), 210-223. C 134

"CATHOLICITY IN MONTANA,"
American Catholic Historical
Researches, v. 9 (1892), 183-
184. C 135

"CATHOLICITY IN TWO TEXAS
COMMUNITIES IN 1850,"
Central Blatt and Social Justice,
v. 26 (1933), 55. C 136

CAVANAUGH, SISTER MARY
AUGUSTINE. The Influence
of Father Pierre Jean de Smet
on the Indians. MA thesis.
Villanova. 1948. 103p.
port. C 137

CAVANAGH, WILLIAM. The
Hospital Activities of the
Sisters during the Civil War
and Their Influence on the
Catholic Hospitalization Move-
ment up to 1875. Washington.
Catholic University of America.
1931. C 138

CAZAYOUS, SISTER MARY
EUGENE. Schools of the
Dominican Sisters in Louisiana.
MA thesis. Catholic University.
1943. 81p. C 139

CECILIA, SISTER. "Mother
Seton and the Priests of
Pioneer America," Ave Maria,
v. 79 (1954), 17-19. C 140
A popular article.

CELESTINE, SISTER M. 'Rt.
Rev. Msgr. Frank A. O'
Brien," Michigan History
Magazine, v. 6 (1922), 611-
629. C 141

"CENTENARY IN ST. BERNARD
(OHIO)," Provincial
Chronicle (St. John Baptist
Province, O.F.M.), v. 23
(Winter, 1950-1951), 96-108.
C 142

"CENTENARY OF EDEN HALL,
1847-1947," American Catholic Historical Society of
Philadelphia Records, v. 57
(1946), 145-149. C 143

CENTENARY OF THE CONVENT
OF THE VISITATION, Freder-
ick, Maryland, 1846-1946.
Frederick, Md. Convent of the
Visitation, 1946. 99p. C 144

CENTENARY OF THE CONVENT
OF THE VISITATION, Mount
de Chantal, 1848-1948. Mount
de Chantal. Library. 1948.
n.p. ports., plates. C 145

CENTRAL BLATT AND SOCIAL
JUSTICE. "Blätter für die
Geschichte der deutschen
Katholiken Americas," Central
Blatt and Social Justice, v.
10 (1917). C 146
Under this title a number of
small items of interest in
the history of the German
Catholics in America appear
in this and succeeding issues. Many of the items
are of little interest, many
of much more importance
German-wise than Church-
wise. The series began as
a project of Father Holweck.

CENTRAL VEREIN. "Die 17.
General-Versammlung der
Kath.-Vereine Deutschlands
u.d. Auswandererfrage (ein
Beitrag zum Cahensly-Streit),
Central Blatt and Social

Justice, v. 14 (1922), 83-87.
C 147

CESTELLO, BOSCO D. "Catholics in American Commerce and Industry, 1925-1945," American Catholic Sociological Review, v. 17 (1956), 219-233.
C 148
A statistical study of the position of American Catholics in commerce and industry as determined by their number in executive positions and other influential elements. Biographies of 869 individuals were examined.

CHABOT, FREDERICK C. Mission La Purissima Concepcion (Texas). San Antonio. Naylor Co. 1935. x, 51p. front., illus., map.
C 149

CHALLONER, RICHARD. "Letter of Bishop Challoner to the Propaganda in 1763 Giving an Account of the American Missions under His Jurisdiction," American Catholic Historical Researches, v. 12 (1895), 44-45.
C 150

CHALLONER, RICHARD. "The State of Religion in America," American Catholic Historical Researches, v. 13 (1896), 35-37.
C 151

"CHAPLAINS DURING THE CIVIL WAR," Woodstock Letters, v. 14 (1885), 375-380; v. 15 (1886), 111-114.
C 152

CHAMBON, CELESTIN M. In and Around the Old St. Louis Cathedral of New Orleans. New Orleans, Phillipe's Printery. 1908. 181p. incl. front., illus., facsim., ports.
C 153

CHAPMAN, CHARLES E. "A Great Franciscan in California: Fermin Francisco de Lasuen," Catholic Historical Review, v.5 (1919), 131-155.
C 154

CHANCELLOR, LOREN E., and THOMAS P. MONAHAN, 'Religious Preferences and Interreligious Mixtures in Marriages and Divorces in Iowa," American Journal of Sociology, v. 61 (1955), 233-239.
C 155

CHAPMAN, JOHN. "Monseigneur Le Berger: Bishop Odin's Labors in Early Texas," Southwest Review, v. 21 (1935), 65-82.
C 156

CHARACTER GLIMPSES OF THE MOST REVEREND WILLIAM HENRY ELDER, SECOND ARCHBISHOP OF CINCINNATI. New York. Pustet. 1911. 181p. ports.
C 157

CHARITY, SISTER OF. "The Educational Work of New York Sisters of Charity," Catholic Educational Review, v. 2 (1911), 793-798.
C 158

CHARLES, ANTHONY. "The Church in Savannah Early in This Century," United States Catholic Historical Magazine, v. 4 (1891-1892), 109.
C 159

CHARLESTON (DIOCESE). The constitution of the Roman Catholic churches of the states of North Carolina, South Carolina and Georgia, which are comprised in the diocese (!) of Charleston, and province of Baltimore, U.S.A. as fully agreed to, and accepted; after repeated discussion, by the clergy and the several congregations, and regularly confirmed by the bishop, and subsequently amended according to the form proscribed. Second edition. Charleston, printed by Burges & James, 1840. vii [1] 48p.
C 160

CHARLESTON (DIOCESE) SYNOD, 16th. Statuta quae in synodo carolopolitana XVI. lata ac promulgata fuere a Henrico P. Northrop [ep.] Carolopoli, Walker, Evans & Cogswell et socii [n.d.] 47p.
C 161

CHARLESTON (DIOCESE) SYNOD, 17th, 1925. Constitutiones

dioecesanae carolopolitanae, quas in synodo dioecesanae septima decima, die 21. Aprilis, A.D., 1925, in ecclesia cathedrali S. Ioannis Baptistae, Carolopoli habita. Confirmavit et auxit Gulielmus T. Russell [ep.] [n.p., n.d.]. 72p.								C 162

CHARLEVOIX, PIERRE F.S. History and General Description of New France. Tr. and ed. by John Gilmary Shea. New York. J.G. Shea. 1866-1872. 6v.								C 163

CHARTIER, R. "Michigan, Letter Dated Sault Ste. Marie, Mich., February 1st, 1887," Woodstock Letters, v. 16 (1887), 139-144.								C 164

CHARTIER, R. "Michigan, Letter Dated Sault Ste. Marie, July 7, 1889," Woodstock Letters, v. 18 (1889), 364-367. C 165

CHARTIER, R. "Sault Ste. Marie, Michigan. Letter Dated Saulte Ste. Marie, Mich., April 11, 1881," Woodstock Letters, v. 10 (1881), 204-205.				C 166

CHATARD, FRANCIS SILAS. "Dr. Bouqillon on the School Question," American Ecclesiastical Review, v. 6 (1892), 98-103.				C 167

CHAVEZ, ANGELICO. Archives of the Archdiocese of Santa Fe, 1678-1900. Washington, D.C.: Academy of American Franciscan History, 1957. 283p. map on end papers.
								C 168

CHAVEZ, ANGELICO. The Cathedral of the Royal City of the Holy Faith of Saint Francis. Santa Fe, N.M. Cathedral of St. Francis. 1948. 50p. illus.				C 169

CHAVEZ, ANGELICO. "La Conquistadora," New Mexico Historical Review, v. 23 (1948), 94-128, 177-216. illus.				C 170
A good study of the origin and nature of the cultus and

its "hermanidad." A history of the confraternity beginning 1692, and description of the statue, chapels, fiestas and processions.

CHAVEZ, FRAY ANGELICO. La Conquistadora. Paterson, N.J. St. Anthony Guild. 1954. 134p.				C 171
Concerned principally with the devotional aspect of the statue.

CHAVEZ, ANGELICO. "The Gallegos Relacion Reconsidered," New Mexico Historical Review, v. 23 (1948), 1-21.				C 172

CHAVEZ, ANGELICO. "Oldest Marian Shrine in the United States," American Ecclesiastical Review, CXXXVI (1957), 371-375.				C 173
Defends the cause of La Conquistadora.

CHAVEZ, ANGELICO. Our Lady of the Conquest. Santa Fe, N.M. New Mexico Historical Society. 1948. 94p.				C 174

CHAVEZ, FRAY ANGELICO. "The Penitents of New Mexico," New Mexico Historical Review, v. 29 (1954), 97-123. C 175
The best article which has been written on the Penitentes.

CHAVEZ, ANGELICO. "A Resume of Ecclesiastical History in New Mexico," Provincial Chronicle (Province of St. John Baptist, O.F.M.), v. 20 (1948), 137-143.				C 176

CHAVEZ, ANGELICO. "Saints Names in New Mexico Geography," El Palacio, v. (1949), 323-335. Nov.				C 177

CHAVEZ, ANGELICO. "Santa Fe Church and Convent Sites in the Seventeenth and Eighteenth Centuries," New Mexico Historical Review, v. 24 (1949), 85-93, map.				C 178

CHAVEZ, ANGELICO. A sequel to "The Mystery of Father Padilla," El Palacio, v. 54 no. 11 (1952). 251-268.

C 179
CHAVEZ, ANGELICO. A sequel to "The Mystery of Father Padilla," Prov. Chron. O.F.M. (Cincinnati) 25 (1953) 268-270. illus.　　C 180

CHESTER, JOHN J. "New Mexico. Holy Week at San Miguel," Woodstock Letters, v. 10 (1881), 274-280.　C 181

CHEVERUS, JOHN. "Correspondence between Bishop Cheverus of Boston and Bishop Plessis of Quebec," American Catholic Historical Researches, v. 29 (1912), 10-20.　　C 182

CHEVERUS, JOHN. "Letters Describing First Visit to the Indians of Maine," American Catholic Historical Researches, v. 23 (1906), 125-133.　C 183

CHEYENNE (DIOCESE) SYNOD, 1st., 1913. Statuta dioecesana (ex synodis dioeceseos omahensis sumpta) lata in synodo prima cheyennensi, in oratorio ecclesiae cathedralis Sanctae Mariae habita die 17 Aprilis A.D. 1913, praeside Patritio A. M'Govern, D.C. Omahae, Swartz print co. [n.d.] 96p.
　　C 184

"CHEYENNE INDIANS," Woodstock Letters, v. 19 (1890), 50-55.
　　C 185

CHICAGO, ILL. (DIOCESE) SYNOD, 1860. Synodus dioecesana chicagensis, mense Augusti 1860 habita. Chicagiae, Apud Tobey fratres typographos, 1860. 14p.　　C 186

CHICAGO (DIOCESE) SYNOD, 1st, 1887. Synodus dioecesana chicagiensis prima, juxta normam a conc. Balt. III, praestitutam, habita in ecclesia metropolitana Ss. Dominis, a Patritio Augustino Feehan [abp.] die 13 decembris, A.D. 1887. Chicagiae, Cameron Amberg, 1887. xxv, 65p.　　C 187

CHICAGO (DIOCESE) SYNOD, 2nd, 1902. Synodus dioecesana

chicagiensis secunda, juxta normam a conc. Balt. III, praestitutam habita in ecclesia metropolitana Ss. Dominis. A Patrictio Augustino Feehan ep. Die III. Junii, A.D. MCMII. Chicagiae, Cameron, Amberg et sociorum 1902. xv, 2p.　　C 188

CHICAGO (DIOCESE) SYNOD, 3rd, 1905. Synodus dioecesana chicagiensis post concilium baltimorense III. tertia, die 14 Dec., 1905, in civitate chicagiensi habita a Jacobo Eduardo Quigley ep. Chicagine, typis mundarunt Cameron, Amberg sociique, 1906. xvii, 81p.　　C 189

"CHIESA DEL NORTE (COLORADO)," Lettere Edificanti Provincia Napolitana, ser. 8, n. 2 (1900), 123-130.
　　C 190

CHIMINELLI, PIESO. Missionari Italiani nella storia nordamericana dei secoli XVIII-XIX. II Pensiero Missionario, 1940, 113-119.　　C 191

CHINQUY, CHARLES P.T. Fifty Years in the Church of Rome. Chicago, Craig and Barlow. 1885. 7, lx-xvi, 9-382p. front. (port.).　C 192

CHINQUY, CHARLES P.T. Forty Years in the Church of Christ. Chicago. Fleming H. Revell Co. 1900. 498p. front. (port.).　　C 193
These two volumes are by an apostate priest who brought on a schism among some of the French-speaking people of the Diocese of Chicago in the 1850s.

CHIROUSE, E.C. "Lettre du R.P. Chirouse, de la Congregation des Oblats de Marie-Immacule, à Mgr. Blanchet, évêque de Nesqually. Mission de Santi-Anne le 25 Août 1877," Annales de la Propagation de la Foi, v. 50 (1878), 283-290.
　　C 194

CHMIELIEWSKI, EDWARD A.
"The Founding of Holy Cross
Parish in Minneapolis," Polish
American Studies, v. 17
(1960), 82-92; v. 18 (1961),
1-18.   C 195
"CHOOSING A CATHOLIC COL-
LEGE," The Catholic Educator,
v. 27 (1957).   C 196
   A series runs through the
   entire volume describing the
   current offerings of the
   various Catholic Colleges of
   the United States.
CHRIST IN OKLAHOMA. Tulsa.
Jubilee Book Co., 1956. 120p.
illus.   C 197
   Fifty years of the Church in
   Oklahoma.
CHRISTIE, F.A. "An Historical
Footnote to Cardinal O'Connell's
Recollections," New England
Quarterly, v. 8 (1935), 258-
262.   C 198
"CHURCH IN AMERICA," Jubilee,
v. 2 (1955) 9-11.   C 199
   A brief general illustrated
   article.
CIANGETTI, PAUL P. "A Diocesan
Chronology of the Catholic
Church in the United States,"
Catholic Historical Review,
v. 28 (1942), 57-70.   C 200
CICOGNANI, A.G. "Assumption
and Devotion to Mary in A-
merica," Thomist, v. 14 (1951),
22-30.   C 201
CICOGNANI, AMLETO G.
Sanctity in America. rev. ed.
Paterson, N.J. St. Anthony
Guild Press. 1941. xix, 228p.
illus (incl. ports.).   C 202
CINCINNATI (ECCLESIASTICAL
PROVINCE) COUNCIL, 1st.
Concilium cincinnatense
provinciale I, habitum anno
1855. Cincinnati, J.P. Walsh,
[n.d.] 1p. 1., 50p.   C 203
CINCINNATI (ECCLESIASTICAL
PROVINCE) COUNCIL, 2nd.
Concilium cincinnatense
provinciale II. habitim anno
1858. Cincinnati, J.P. Walsh
[n.d.] 32p.   C 204

CINCINNATI (ECCLESIASTICAL
PROVINCE) COUNCIL, 1861.
Concilium cincinnatense
provinciale III. habitum anno
1861. Cincinnati et New York
Sumptibus fratrum Benziger
[n.d.] 144p.   C 205
CINCINNATI (ARCHDIOCESE)
SYNOD. Statuta dioecesana a
Joanne Baptista Purcell, ep.
in variis synodis, quae huc
usque in ecclesia sua cathedrali
...celebratae sunt, lata et
promulgata. Una cum decretis conciliorum provincialium
et plenarii baltimorensium,
quibus interfuerunt omnes
Statuum Foederatorum episcopi
et decretis conciliorum trium
cincinnatensium. Nunc primum
in unum collecta et publici
juris facta. Cincinnati, J.P.
Walsh 1865. iv, 69, x, 15p.
                          C 206

   Includes pastoral letter of
   the Archbishop, dated Sept.
   8, 1853.
CINCINNATI (DIOCESE) SYNOD,
2nd, 1886. Synodus dioecesana
cincinnatensis secunda, diebus
19, 20, 21 Octobris, A.D.
1886 in ecclesia metropolitana
St. Petri in vinculis Cincinnati habita, a Gulielmo Henrico Elder. [n.p., n.d.]
xviii, 82p.   C 207
CINCINNATI (ARCHDIOCESE)
PROVINCIAL COUNCIL, 5th,
1889. Concilium cincinnatense
provinciale V habitum anno
1889 a die 19 ad diem Maii.
Cincinnati, Keating & Co.,
1893, 1., 54p.   C 208
   Includes an English translation of the Pastoral letter
   of William Henry, Archbishop of Cincinnati.
CINCINNATI (DIOCESE) SYNOD,
3rd, 1898. Synodus dioecesana
cincinnatensis tertia, habita
die 9a novembris, 1898, in
ecclesia metropolitana St.

Petri in vinculis a Gulielmo Henrico Elder [abp.] [n.p., n.d.] xx, 161p.   C 209

Cirigliano see C 341

CIZON, FRANCIS A. "Interethnic and Interreligious Marriage Problems in Parish X, " American Catholic Sociological Rev., v. 15 (1954), 244-255.   C 210
A study of a Polish ethnic group in a midwestern city of 60,000 people.

CLARK,E.C. "Catholic Elementary Education in the Past Fifty Years and Now," Catholic School Journal, v. 51 (1951), 111-113.   C 211

CLARK, SISTER MARY EDWARD. Contribution of the Irish Immigrant to the Early Growth and Development of Ohio, 1758-1860. MA thesis. Catholic University 1945. 63p.   C 212

CLANCY, RAYMOND J. "American Prelates at the Vatican Council," United States Catholic Historical Society Records and Studies, v. 28 (1937), 7-135.   C 213

CLANCY, RAYMOND JOSEPH. Francis Patrick Kenrick and the Oxford Movement in America. MA thesis. University of Notre Dame. 1932. 24p.   C 214

CLARKE, ISABEL C. "Elizabeth Ann Seton," Studies, v. 38 (1949), 90-100.   C 215

CLARKE, R.C. "Beginnings of Texas," Texas State Historical Association Quarterly, v. 5 (1901-1902), 171-205; v. 6 (1902-1903), 1-26.   C 216

CLARKE, RICHARD. "Our Converts," American Catholic Quarterly Review, v. 18 (1893), 539-561.   C 217

CLARKE, RICHARD H. Lives of Deceased Bishops of the Catholic Church in the United States. New York. Richard H. Clarke. 1888. 3v. ports.   C 218

CLARKE, THOMAS. "Simon Bruté

de Rémur," St. Meinrad Historical Essays, v. 3 (1934), 126-133.   C 219

CLAVREUL, H. "Lettre de M. Clavreul, Missionnaire en Florida, à MM. les Membres des Conseils Centraus de l'Ouevre de la Propagation de la Foi, Paris, 19 août, 1872," Annales de la Propagation de la Foi, v. 44 (1872), 427-438.   C 220

CLAVREUL, H.P. Notes on the Catholic Church in Florida. St. Leo, Florida. The Abbey Press.   C 221

CLEARY, JOHN J. "Catholic Pioneers of Trenton, New Jersey," United States Catholic Historical Society Records and Studies, v. 11 (1917), 55-71.   C 222

CLEARY, THOMAS F. The History of the Catholic Church in Illinois from 1763-1844. Urbana, Ill. 1932. 14p.   C 223

CLEARY, THOMAS F. "Huet de la Valinière," Mid-America, v. 4 (1933), 213-228. C 224

CLEARY, THOMAS F. "The Organization of the Catholic Church in Central Illinois," Mid-America, v. 6 (1935), 105-124, 185-190, map.   C 225

CLELAND, ROBERT G. (ed.). "The Gabriel Moraga Expedition of 1806; The Diary of Fray Pedro Munoz," Huntington Library Quarterly, v. 9 (1946), 223-248.   C 226

CLEMENS, A.H. The Cana Movement in the United States. Washington. Catholic University of America. 1953. 54p.   C 227
A survey of the movement during the past ten years.

CLEVELAND (DIOCESE) SYNOD, 1857. Statuta dioecesis clevelandensis lata in synodo dioecesana habita A.D. 1852 et in aliis synodis A.D. 1854 et

A.D. 1857. Aucta et emen-
data. Clevelandi, Apud H.
Kramer, 1857. 8p.   C 228
CLEVELAND (DIOCESE) SYNOD.
Constitutiones dioecesis
clevelandensis quae in synodis
dioecesanis A.D. 1852, 1854,
1857, 1868 habitis edictae sunt
ab Amadeo Rappe [ep.] Clevelandi, 1869. 8p.   C 229
CLEVELAND (DIOCESE) SYNOD,
1882. Statuta dioecesis
clevelandensis, in synodis
dioecesanis, habitis annis
domini 1852, 1854, 1857,
1868, 1872, lata et, prout
nunc prostant, edita in synodo,
die 27 mensis Maii, A.D.
1882, a Riccardo Gilmour,
episcopo clevelandensi.
Clevelandi, M.E. M'Cabe,
1882. xiii, [1], 58p., 1 1.,
24p.   C 230
Bibliographical footnotes.
CLEVELAND (DIOCESE). Rules
and directions for the administration of the temporal and
spiritual affairs of churches,
schools, &c., in the diocese
of Cleveland. Compiled from
the "Statuta dioecesana" for
the use of the laity. Cleveland,
O., M.E. M'Cabe, 1882.
23p.   C 231
CLEVELAND (DIOCESE) SYNOD,
1852-(1908). Statuta dioecesis
clevelandensis, in synodis
dioecesanis, habitis annis
domini 1852, 1854, 1857,
1868, 1872, 1882, 1889, lata
et, prout nunc prostant, edita
a Riccardo Gilmour, episcopo
Clevelandensi. Editio tertia
et emendata. Clevelandiae,
Ward et Shaw, 1908. xiv, 62,
31p.   C 232
CLINE, CATHERINE ANN.
"Priest in the Coal Fields: the
Story of Father Curran," A-
merican Catholic Historical
Society of Philadelphia Records,
v. 63 (1952), 67-84.   C 233
The story of Father John
Joseph Curran of Wilkes

Barre, Pennsylvania, 1868-
1936.
CLINCH, BRYAN J. California
and Its Missions, Their History to the Treaty of Guadalupe Hidalgo. San Francisco.
Whitaker and Ray. 1904.
2v.   C 234
CLINCH, BRYAN J. "Jesuit Missions in American California,"
American Catholic Historical
Society of Philadelphia Re-
cords, v. 17 (1906), 48-66,
125-143, 312-321, 445-456.
        C 235
CLINCH, BRYAN J. "Spanish
Friars in California," Ameri-
can Catholic Quarterly Review,
v. 27 (1902), 760-781.
        C 236
CLINCHY, EVERETT R. All in
the Name of God. New York.
Day. 1934. 194p.   C 237
A study in anti-Catholic
prejudice.
(CLOTILDE, SISTER ANGELICA).
The Ursulines of the West,
1535-1935; 1880-1935, by an
Ursuline of the Roman Union.
(Everett, Wash.) no pub.
1935? 72p. illus.   C 238
CLOISTERED LIFE. Cleveland.
Catholic Universe Pub. Co.
1909.   C 239
CLYNE, JAMES BARTLEY.
Catholic Attitude toward Fed-
eral Aid to Education in the
United States, 1870-1892. MA
thesis. Catholic University.
1952. 93p.   C 240
COAKLEY, THOMAS F. 'Right
Rev. Andrew Arnold Lambing,"
United States Catholic His-
torical Society Records and
Studies, v. 16 (1924), 112-
118.   C 241
CODE, J.B. "American Catholic
History and the Librarian,"
Catholic Library World, v. 24
(1953), 155-162.   C 242
CODE, JOSEPH B. The Catholic
Hierarchy and United States
Culture. Thought, v. 16
(1941), 224-240.   C 243

CODE, JOSEPH B. "Colored Catholic Educator before the Civil War," Catholic World, v. 146 (1938), 437-443. C 244
A biographical sketch of Mother Mary Lange of the Oblates of Providence (Maryland), who was born 1793 and died 1882.

CODE, JOSEPH B. Dictionary of the American Hierarchy. New York. Longmans, Green and Co. 1940. xxii, 425p. C 245
Must be used with caution because of inaccuracies.

CODE, JOSEPH B. "Grajal in Leon and Its American Carmelite," Catholic World, v. 144 (1937), 552-558.
C 246

CODE, JOSEPH B. Great American Foundresses. New York. Macmillan, 1929. xviii, 512p. ports. C 247

CODE, JOSEPH B. "Mother Elizabeth Seton," Studies, v. 28 (1941), 397-414. C 248

CODE, JOSEPH B. "Negro Sisterhoods in the United States," America, v. 58 (1938), 318-319. C 249

CODE, JOSEPH B. "A Selected Bibliography of the Religious Orders and Congregations of Women Founded within the Boundaries of the United States, 1727-1850," Catholic Historical Review, v. 23 (1937), 331-351; v. 26 (1940), 222-245. C 250

CODY, EDMUND R. History of the Coeur d'Alene Mission of the Sacred Heart. Caldwell, Ida, Caxton. 1930. 45p. illus. (incl. ports.). C 251

COFFEE, REGINALD M. "The Very Reverend Walter Farrell, O.P., S.T.M.," American Ecclesiastical Review, v. 126 (1952), 271-278. C 252

COFFREY, SISTER M. AQUINAS, C.S.J. Sisters of St. Joseph and Their Foundation in America...1650-1950. MA thesis.

Loyola University (Chicago), 1935. C 253

COLE, GEORGE W. "Missions and Mission Pictures: a Contribution towards an Iconography of the Franciscan Missions of California," California Library Assoc. Publications, no. 11 (1910), 44-66. C 254

COGHLAN, FRANCIS ANTHONY. The Impact of the Spanish American War on the Catholic Church in the United States, 1898-1903. MA thesis. University of Notre Dame, 1956. 111p. C 255

COLEMAN, A. I. du P. "The Foundation of the Dominican Province in the United States," United States Catholic Historical Society Records and Studies, v. 2 (1900), 36-81, 227-267. C 256

COLEMAN, JAMES WALTER. Labor Disturbances in Pennsylvania, 1850-1880. Washington. Catholic University of America. 1936. vii, 189p. incl. front. (map). Published also without thesis note under title: Molly Maguire Riots.
C 257

"COLLEGIO DEL SACRO CUORE IN DENVER," Lettere Edificanti Provincia Napolitana, ser. 8, n. 1 (1899), 48-53.
C 258

COLLIARD, B. "Historical Sketch of the Parish of Opelousas, Louisiana," St. Louis Catholic Historical Review, v. 3 (1921), 14-38.
C 259

COLLIGAN, JAMES A. Some Facts About Santa Barbara Mission. San Francisco. The Author. 1932. 45p. C 260

COLLINS, JOSEPH B. "Catechitics in the United States and the American Ecclesiastical Review," American Ecclesiastical Review, v. 121 (1949), 322-331. C 261

COLLINS, JOSEPH B. The

Confraternity of Christian Doctrine in the United States of America. Washington. Confraternity of Christian Doctrine. 1945. 24p. C 262

COLLINS, JOSEPH B. "Spiritual Formation in the CCD," American Ecclesiastical Review, v. 127 (1952), 87-116. C 263

Contains a brief sketch of the beginning of the Confraternity of Christian Doctrine in the United States.

COLUMBUS, O. DIOCESE. Diocese of Columbus. The Story of Fifty Years, 1868-1918. Cleveland. 1918. 611p. front., plates. C 264

COLUMBUS (DIOCESE) SYNOD, 2nd, 1873. Record of the second diocesan synod of Columbus, held in St. Joseph's cathedral August 27, 1873, and episcopal approbation of synodal acts. Columbus, Ohio, Nevins & Myers, 1873. 12p. C 265

COLUMBUS (DIOCESE) SYNOD, 4th, 1902. Synodus dioecesana columbensis quarta, habita Columbi, die 16 Julii, 1902, in ecclesia cathedrali Sancti Joseph, a Henrico Moeller ep. n.p., n.d. xiv, 168p. C 266

COMEAN, BRO. ALFONSO. Study of the Trustee Problem of St. Louis Cathedral, New Orleans, Louisiana, 1842-1844. MA thesis. University of Notre Dame, 1947. viii, 120p. C 267

COMERFORD, SISTER BERNADINE MIRIAM. A Century of Educational Contributions by the Sisters of Charity of New York. MA thesis. Fordham University, 1935. vi, 138p. C 268

"COMING OF BISHOP GRACE," Acta et Dicta, v. 7 (1936), 174-202. C 269

"COMING OF THE FRANCISCANS TO ILLINOIS, 1858," Annals of the Franciscan Province of the Sacred Heart, O.F.M. (Chicago), no. 1 (1929), 3-17, no. 2, 65-83; no. 3, 130-158; no. 4, 194-234; no. 5, 257-297; no. 6 337-375; no. 7, 419-443; no. 8, 497-545; no. 9, 570-596; no. 10, 633-655; no. 11, 681-699; no. 12, 737-768; no. 13, 797-822; no. 14, 853-882; no. 15, 911-931; no. 16, 965-984. C 270

CONCANNON, HELENA. "Canon John O'Hanlon (1821-1905): His Early Days in St. Louis," Irish Ecclesiastical Record, v. 69 (1947), 11-19. C 271

CONCANNON, HELENA. "The Making of a Parish," Irish Ecclesiastical Record, v. 70 (1948), 229-240. C 272

CONDON, PETER. "Archbishop Bedini's Visit to the United States: Official Correspondence," United States Catholic Historical Society Records and Studies, v. 3, pt. 1 (1903), 149-154. C 273

CONDON, PETER. "Charles George Herbermann," United States Catholic Historical Society Records and Studies, v. 10 (1917), 8-25. C 274

CONDON, PETER. "Constitutional Freedom of Religion and Survivals of Religious Intolerance," United States Catholic Historical Society Records and Studies, v. 2, pt. 2 (1901), 401-431; v. 3, pt. 1 (1903), 92-114; v. 4 (1904), 145-217; v. 5 (1909), 426-462. C 275

CONEN, CYRIL JOHN. Politico-Religious Disturbances in Indiana, 1922-1926. MA thesis. Catholic University. 1938. 78p. C 276

CONGREGATION OF THE SISTERS OF THE THIRD ORDER OF ST. FRANCIS OF THE PERPETUAL ADORATION. Our Community. The Origin and

Development through Seventy
Years ... La Crosse, Wis. St.
Rose Convent. 1922. 287p.
illus., plates, ports.   C 277
"CONEWAGO MISSION," Wood-
stock Letters, v. 9 (1880),
35-43.   C 278
CONGIATO, P. Lettre du P.
Congrato Mau R.P. Beckx
[sur la mort du P. Jean
Nobili]. Santa Clara,
Calif. 19 III 1856, in Collec-
tion de Précis Historiques
VII [Bruxelles 1856] n 108,
p. 293-297.   C 279
CONLON, JAMES. "Catholic
College Education of the
Pacific Coast," National Cath-
olic Educational Association
Bulletin, v. 5 (1919), 187-
203.   C 280
CONLON, JOHN THOMAS. The
Beginnings of Catholicism in
New Netherlands. MA thesis.
Catholic University. 1933.
94p.   C 281
CONLON, JOHN THOMAS. "The
Beginnings of Catholicism in
New Netherlands (1609-1664),"
United States Catholic Historical
Society Records and Studies,
v. 23 (1933), 171-246. C 282
CONNAUGHTON, EDWARD A.
A History of the Educational
Legislation and Administra-
tion in the Archdioceses of
Cincinnati. Washington.
Catholic University. 1946.
ix, 213p.   C 283
CONNAUGHTON, SISTER M.
STANISLAUS. The Editorial
Opinion of the Catholic Tele-
graph of Cincinnati on Con-
temporary Affairs and Politics,
1871-1921. Washington.
Catholic University. 1943.
xxvii, 309p.   C 284
CONNELL, FRANCIS J. "Dogmatic
Theology in the American Ec-
clesiastical Review," American
Ecclesiastical Review, v. 121
(1949), 312-321.   C 285
CONNELLY, JAMES F. The Visit
of Archbishop Gaetano Bedini

to the United States of Ameri-
ca (June, 1853-February,
1854). [Analecta Gregoriana,
v. 109.] Rome. Gregorian
University. 1960. xiii, 308p.
                          C 286
CONNELLY, SISTER MARY
HENRIETTA. History of the
Sisters of Mercy of Philadel-
phia, 1861-1916. MA thesis.
Villanova University. 1953.
126p.   C 287
CONNER, PHILIP S.P. "Early
Church Registers of Penn-
sylvania," American Catholic
Historical Society of Philadel-
phia Records, v. 2 (1886-
1888), 22-28.   C 288
CONNOLLY, ANDREW A. Begin-
nings of the St. Francis
Xavier Mission Colony for the
Iroquois. MA thesis. Loyola
University (Chicago). 1957.
123p.   C 289
CONNOLLY, ARTHUR T. "His-
torical Sketch of the Rev.
John Thayer, Boston's First
Native Born Priest," United
States Catholic Historical
Magazine, v. 2 (1888), 261.
                          C 290
CONNOLLY, DONALD F. X.
"A Chronology of New England
Catholicism before the May-
flower Landing," American
Catholic Historical Society of
Philadelphia Records, LXX
(1959), 3-17.   C 291
CONNOLLY, DONALD F. X. "A
Chronology of New England
Catholicism before the Landing
of the Mayflower," Part II,
American Catholic Historical
Society of Philadelphia Records,
LXX (1960), 88-108. C 292
CONNOLLY, JOHN. "Letters of
Rt. Rev. John Connolly, O.P.,
D.D.," United States Catholic
Historical Magazine, v. 4
(1891-1892), 58-61, 186-198.
                          C 293
CONNOR, JEANNETTE T.
Colonial Records of Spanish
Florida. Deland, Fla. Florida

State Historical Society. 1925.
2v. front., facsim. C 294

CONNORS, DANIEL J. "Archbishop Troy and the American Church (1800-1823)," United States Historical Society Records and Studies, v. 22 (1932), 168-183. C 295

CONNORS, EDWARD M. Church-State Relationships in Education in the State of New York. Washington. Catholic University. 1951. xviii, 187p. C 296

CONNORS, FRANCIS JOHN. Samuel Finley Breese Morse and the Anti-Catholic Political Movements in the United States, 1791-1872. MA thesis. Catholic University. 1927. 71p. C 297

CONNORS, FRANCIS J. "Samuel Finley Breese Morse and the Anti-Catholic Political Movement in the United States (1791-1872)," Illinois Catholic Historical Review, v. 12 (1918) 83-122. C 298

CONROY, JOSEPH P. Arnold Damen, S.J., a Chapter in the Making of Chicago. New York. Benziger. 1930. ix, 329p. front. (port.). C 299

CONROY, JOSEPH P. "Father Coffee at Mingo," American Ecclesiastical Review, v. 64 (1921), 152-60. C 300

CONROY, THOMAS M. "The Ku Klux Klan and the American Clergy," American Ecclesiastical Review, v. 70 (1924), 47-58. C 301

CONROY, THOMAS P. St. Michael's Church, Madison, Indiana. Madison, Ind. no pub. 1937. C 302

CONSIDINE, JOHN J. History of Canonical Legislation in the Diocese and Province of New York, 1842-1861. MA thesis. Catholic University. 1937. vii, 77p. C 303

CONSIDINE, M. J. Brief Chronological Account of the Catholic Educational Institutions of the Archdiocese of New York. New York. Benziger. 1894. 59p. C 304

CONSIDINE, MICHAEL J. "History of a Parochial School," United States Catholic Historical Society Records and Studies, v. 4 (1906), 232-242. C 305

CONTROVERSY BETWEEN SENATOR BROOKS AND 'JOHN' ARCHBISHOP OF NEW YORK. New York. n.d. ca. 1855. C 306

CONWAY, BERTRAND L. "Father Hecker and the Paulists," Month, v. 161 (1933), 233-241. C 307.

CONWAY, JAMES J. The Beginnings of Ecclesiastical Jurisdiction in the Archdiocese of St. Louis, 1765-1776. St. Louis. Missouri Historical Society. 1897. 40p. illus. (incl. ports., map). C 308

CONWAY, JAMES J. Historical Sketch of the Church and Parish of St. Charles Borromeo, St. Charles, Mo. no pl. no pub. 1892. 56p. C 309

CONWAY, JAMES J. The State Last. A Study of Doctor Bouqillon's Pamphlet. 2d rev. ed. New York. Pustet. 1892. 116p. C 310

CONWAY, JAMES. "Wisconsin. Letter Dated College of the Sacred Heart, Prairie du Chien, Wis., Aug. 25th, 1884," Woodstock Letters, v. 13 (1884), 376-380. C 311

CONWAY, JOHN. "Cahenslyism vs. Americanism," Review of Reviews, v. 6 (1892), 43-48. C 312

CONWAY, JOSEPH P. The Question of the Hour: A Survey of the Position and Influence of the Catholic Church in the United States. New York. John McBride Co. 1909. 241p. C 313

CONWAY, R.V. St. Mary's

Church, Pittsburgh...1853-
1950. Westminster, Md.
Newman. 1950. xviii, 259p.
front., ports. C 314
COOGAN, JOHN E. "Father
James J. Daly," Woodstock
Letters, v. 83 (1954), 204-
209. port., plates. C 315
COOKE, SISTER FRANCIS. His-
tory of the Hospital Sisters
of the Third Order of St.
Francis. Ph.D. thesis.
Marquette University. 1943.
C 316
COOKSEY, RITA. History of St.
Peter's Parish [Washington,
D. C.] MA thesis. Catholic
University. 1940. 103p.
C 317
COOLEY, LAWRENCE J. Father
Mathew and the Catholic Tem-
perance Movement in the U-
nited States. MA thesis. St.
John's University, N.Y. 1940.
mss. pp. C 318
COOLEY, LEO P. Bishop
England's Solution of the Negro
Problem, MA thesis. St.
John's University. N.Y.
1940. mss. pp. C 319
COONEY, J. M. "In Catholic
Kentucky," Ave Maria, v. 32
(1930), 737-742. C 320
COONEY, PAUL. "War Letters
of Father Paul Cooney of the
Congregation of the Holy
Cross," American Catholic His-
torical Society of Philadelphia
Records, v. 44 (1943), 47-69,
151-169, 220-237. C 321
COPPENS, CHARLES. "Father
Coppens' Recollections of
Notable Pioneers," Illinois
Catholic Historical Review, v.
2 (1920), 389-395. C 322
Scattered recollections,
mostly dealing with the
period 1853-1867.
COOPER, JOHN M. "The National
Catholic War Council," American
Ecclesiastical Review, v. 59
(1918), 607-617. C 323
CORBETT, JAMES A. "The First
Printing Press of the University

of Notre Dame," Indiana
Magazine of History, v. 41
(1945), 50-56. C 324
CORBY, WILLIAM. Memoirs of
Chaplain Life. Chicago.
Lamonte. 1893. 391p. C 325
Three years chaplain in the
famous Irish brigade,
Army of the Potomac.
CORCORAN, JAMES A. "The
Decrees of the Third Plenary
Council," American Catholic
Quarterly Review, v. 11
(1886), 344-355. C 326
CORCORAN, SISTER MARY A'
KEMPIS. American Catholic
Opinion in Response to Free
Thought, 1865-1895. MA
thesis. Catholic University,
1953. 170p. C 327
CORCORAN, MARY STANISLAUS.
"Mission San Juan Bautista,"
Mid-America, v. 1 (1930),
246. C 328
CORKERY, JOSEPH JOHN.
Catholic Culture in Colonial
North America. MA thesis.
Boston College. 1938. iv,
144p. C 329
CORMICAN, P.J. "Golden Jubilee
of the Catholic Church on
Ward's Island, New York,"
Woodstock Letters, v. 53
(1924), 64-74, 217-243.
C 330
CORNELL, THOMAS C. The
Beginnings of the Roman Cath-
olic Church in Yonkers.
Yonkers. The Gazette Press.
1883. 24p. C 331
CORNELL, THOMAS C. "Catholic
Beginnings in Yonkers," United
States Catholic Historical
Society Records and Studies,
v. 58 (1947), 68-96. C 332
CORPUS CHRISTI (DIOCESE)
SYNOD, 1934. Hic prospectus
est dioeceseos Corporis
Christi Texas facta in adminis-
tratione episcopi Pauli Joseph
Nussbaum ...cum additione
paucarum regulationum admoni-
tionumque datarum in letteris
episcopi praesentis Emmanuel

B. Ledvina ...[n.p. 1934?]
60p.   C 333
CORREALE, FRANCES M. The
New York Draft Riots of July,
1863. MA thesis, St. John's
University, N.Y. 1939. mss.
                              C 334
"CORRESPONDENCE BETWEEN
BISHOP CHEVERUS OF BOS-
TON AND BISHOP PLESSIS
OF QUEBEC," American
Catholic Historical Researches,
v. 29 (1912), 10-20.   C 335
CORRIGAN, ANTHONY BARRETT.
Financial Support of Roman
Catholic Colleges and Uni-
versities in the United States.
Ph.D. thesis. Fordham Uni-
versity, 1954, xv, 297p.
                              C 336
CORRIGAN, JOSEPH A. "The
Catholic Industrial School of
Minnesota," Acta et Dicta,
v. 7 (1935), 3-25.   C 337
CORRIGAN, JOSEPH M. "Peter
De Smet--Mighty Sower,
1801-1873," American Catholic
Historical Society of Philadelphia Records, v. 27 (1916),95-
112, 259-274.   C 338
CORRIGAN, MICHAEL AUGUS-
TINE. "Register of Clergy
Laboring in the Archdiocese of
New York from Early Mis-
sionary Times to 1885," United
States Catholic Historical
Society Records and Studies,
v. 1, pt. 1 (1899), 18-44;
v. 1 pt. 2 (1900), 191-217;
v. 2, pt. 2 (1900), 36-81;
v. 2 pt. 2 (1901), 227-267;
v. 3, pt. 2 (1904), 288-319;
v. 4 (1906), 96-138; v. 5
(1907), 148-185; v. 5, pt. 2
(1909), 392-413; v. 6, pt. 1
(1911), 36-57; v. 6, pt. 2
(1912), 166-201; v. 7 (1914),
198-205; v. 8 (1915) 228-244;
v. 9 (1916), 200-202. C 339
CORRIGAN, OWEN B. "Catholicity
in Allegeny and Garrett Counties,
Maryland," American Catholic
Historical Society of Philadelphia
Records, v. 36 (1925), 113-115,

209-253.   C 340
CIRIGLIANO, DOMINIC A. "The
Social Background of Jesuit
Work in the Bowery District,"
Woodstock Letters, v. 73
(1944), 8-27; v. 74 (1945),
96-110.   C 341
CORRIGAN, OWEN B. "Chronological List Showing the Dates
of Appointment of the Bishops
of the United States," American Catholic Historical
Society of Philadelphia Records, v. 35 (1924), 295-
324.   C 342
CORRIGAN, OWEN B. "Chronol-
ogy of the Catholic Hier-
archy of the United States,"
Catholic Historical Review,
v. 1 (1916), 267-388, v. 2
(1917), 127-145, 283-301; v.
3 (1917), 22-52, 151-164.
variant title.   C 343
CORRIGAN, OWEN B. "A Model
Country Parish," American
Catholic Historical Society of
Philadelphia Records, v. 35
(1924), 197-241.   C 344
CORRIGAN, RAYMOND. "The
Jesuit Relations," Historical
Bulletin, v. 9 (1931), 69-71.
                              C 345
CORRIGAN, RAYMOND. Die
Kongregation de Propaganda
und ihre Tätigkeit in Nord-A-
merica. München. Druckerei
Studentenhaus München, Uni-
versität. 1928. 183p. C 346
CORRIGAN, RAYMOND. "Mission
Aid Societies," Thought, v.
10 (1935), 286-297.   C 347
CORTESI, SALVATORE. My
Thirty Years of Friendships.
New York. Harpers. 1927.
296p. front., plates, ports.
                              C 348
COSTELLO, CHARLES AUGUS-
TINE. The Episcopacy of the
Right Reverend Josue M.
Young. Bishop of Erie, 1845-
1866. MA thesis, University
of Notre Dame, v. 11, 190p.
                              C 349
COSTELLO, FRANK B. "Kohl-

98

man and Fenwick. Two New York Jesuits and a Treatise on Penance," Archivum Historicum Societatis Jesu. v. 23 (1954) 334-344. C 350
Treats of the 1813 trial of Kohlman regarding the seal of confession; states that the treatise is the work of Kohlman, not Fenwick.

COSTELLO, SISTER MARY LORETTO. The Sisters of Mercy of Maryland, 1855-1930. St. Louis. Herder. 1931. xvi, 249p. front. (port.). plates. C 351

COSTELLOE, JOSEPH. "Church History in American Colleges and Universities," Journal of Higher Education, v. 32 (Feb., 1961), 70-76. C 352
Report on findings of a questionnaire survey.

COSTELLOE, JOSEPH. "The Reverend James A. Kleist, S.J.--In Memoriam," Catholic Biblical Quarterly, v. 11 (1949), 323-324. C 353

COUHIG, SISTER MARY HOPE. "St. Lucy's Priory: Our California Daughterhouse," Benedictine Review, XI (1956), 19-22. C 354
Story of the founding of a new Benedictine convent under the sponsorship of Mt. St. Scholastica, Atchison, Kansas.

COURCY DE LAROCHE-HERON, HENRI DE. The Catholic Church in the United States; Pages of its History. Tr. and enlarged by John Gilmary Shea. 2d ed. New York. E. Dinigand and Brother. 1856. 591p. C 355

"COURT SUMMONS FOR 'ONE RAYMOND, WHO PRETENDS HIMSELF A PAPIST PRIEST,'" Virginia Magazine of History and Biography, v. 5 (1897-98), 153. C 356

COVINGTON, KY. (Diocese) Synod, 1st, 1879. Acta et constitu-

tiones synodi dioecesanae covingtonensis primae, quam habuit diebus 10, 11, 12 Septembris, 1879 Augustus Maria Toebbe, episcopus covingtonensis. Cincinnati, O., Fr. Pustet & Co., 1880. 48p. Bibliographical foot-notes. C 357

COVINGTON (DIOCESE) SYNOD, 2nd, 1886. Acta et decreta synodi dioecesanae covingtonensis secundae, quam diebus 28, 29, et 30 Sept., A.D. 1886 habuit Camillus Paulus Maes [ep.] Cincinnati, Braunwart & Brockhoff, 1886. 40p. C 358

COVINGTON (DIOCESE) SYNOD, 3rd, 1934. Acta et decreta synodi dioecesanae covingtonensis tertiae quam die 20 mensis Martii 1934 habuit Franciscus Gulielmus Howard [ep.] [Covington, The Messenger press, 1934] 87p. C 359

COX, I. J. "Father John Peter Schmitt," Texas State Historical Association Quarterly, v. 5 (1902), 206-211. C 360

COX, SISTER IGNATIUS LOYOLA. "Notes on the Early History of the Sisters of St. Joseph in Minnesota," Acta et Dicta, v. 3 (1914), 253-289. C 361

COXE, RT. REV. A. CLEVELAND. Jesuit Party in American Politics: Letters to Monsignor Satolli, Boston, American Citizen Co. 1894. C 362

COYLE, JOHN G. "Catholic Signers of the Constitution," United States Catholic Historical Society Records and Studies, v. 11 (1917), 47-54. C 363

COYNE, JOSEPH A. "Vocational Education in Catholic Secondary Schools," Catholic School Journal, v. 52 (1952), 237-239. C 364
A brief survey of the efforts

at vocational guidance in the secondary schools, includes a good table of the findings of the survey.

CRATZ, SIGMUND. History of St. Mary's Church, Herman, Pennsylvania. 75th Anniversary, 1916. no pl. no pub. 1916? 90p. illus., plates, ports.   C 365

CRAWFORD, EUGENE JOSEPH. The Daughters of Dominic on Long Island. New York. Benziger, 1938. xxi, 389p. front., plates, ports., diagr.   C 366

CREHAN, J. H. "Catholic Toleration in Maryland (1649)," Month, v. 185 (1948), 205-215.   C 367

CREPEAU, SISTER ROSEMARY. Un Aporte Dominicain aux Etats-Unis. Paris. J. de Gigord. 1932. xvi, 352p. incl. front. (port.), illus., maps.   C 368
Biography of Father Mazzuchelli, missionary of the upper Mississippi Valley.

CRESPI, JUAN. Fray Juan Crespi, Missionary Explorer on the Pacific Coast, 1769-1774. Berkeley. University of California. 1927. lxiv, 402p. front., plates, maps, facsim.   C 369

"CRETIN COLLECTION," Acta et Dicta, v. 2 (1909-1910), 1-41, 183-205; v. 3 (1911-1914), 1-21, 226-235.   C 370
A collection of the correspondence to and from Bishop Joseph Cretin, first Bishop of St. Paul (1850-1857) between the years 1812 and 1836.

CRETIN, JOSEPH. "Diary of Bishop Cretin," Acta et Dicta, v. 1 (1907), 39-42.   C 371

CRETIN, JOSEPH. "Letter of Rev. J. Cretin," Acta et Dicta, v. 1 (1907), 24-38.   C 372

CROGHAN, SISTER M. EDMUND. The Sisters of Mercy in Nebraska, 1864-1910. Washington. Catholic University of America. 1942. vii, 158p.   C 373

CRONIN, BERNARD C. Father Yorke and the Labor Movement in San Francisco, 1900-1910. Washington. Catholic University of America. 1944. ix, 239p.   C 374

CRONIN, PATRICK. Memorial on the Life and Labors of Right Rev. Stephen Vincent Ryan, D.D., C.M., Second Bishop of Buffalo, N.Y. Buffalo Catholic Publication Co. 1896. xi, 141p. front., illus. (incl. ports.)   C 375

CROOKSTON (DIOCESE) SYNOD, 1921. Statutes of the diocese of Crookston, promulgated at the diocesan synod held Sept. 20, 1921 by Timothy Corbett [bp.] St. Louis, B. Herder, 1923. vii, 191p.   C 376

CROSS, JOSEPH L. "The American Protective Association: A Sociological Analysis of the Periodic Literature of the Period 1890-1900," American Catholic Sociological Review, v. 10 (1949), 172-187.   C 377

CROSS, ROBERT D. The Emergence of Liberal Catholicism in America. Cambridge, Mass. Harvard University, 1958. Pp. xi, 328.   C 378
An interesting study by a non-Catholic author.

CROWLEY, DOROTHY. "Benedictines in Nursing," The Benedictine Review, v. 7 (1952), 16-18.   C 379

CROWLEY, FRANCIS M. "American Catholic Universities," United States Catholic Historical Society Records and Studies, v. 29 (1939), 79-106.   C 380

CROWLEY, FRANCIS M. "Catholic Education in 1948," Catholic School Journal, v. 49 (1949), 1-3.   C 381

CROWLEY, FRANCIS M. "The Catholic School," Columbia,

v. 6 (Feb., 1927), 16-17, 42.
C 382
CRUMP, SISTER THOMAS
FRANCIS. The History of the
Bardstown Diocese, 1785-
1815. MA thesis. Xavier Uni-
versity (Cincinnati). 1953.
103p.   C 383
CRUZAT, HELOISE HULSE.
"Marriage Contract between Pre.
Lemoine D'Iberville and Marie
Thérèse Pollet de La Combe,
October 8, 1693," Louisiana
Historical Quarterly, v. 17
(1934), 247-   C 384
CRUZAT, HELOISE HULSE. "The
Ursulines of Louisiana,"
Louisiana Historical Quarterly,
v. 2 (1919), 5-23.   C 385
CUDAHY, SISTER EUTROPIA.
Religious Liberty in Maryland
Prior to the Act of 1649.
MA thesis. Marquette Uni-
versity. 1948.   C 386
CUDDY, BROTHER HENRY. The
Life and Works of John Ireland,
Archbishop of St. Paul. MA
thesis, St. John's University,
N.Y., 1943 mss.   pp. C 387
CUEVAS, MARIANO. Historica de
la Iglesia en Mexico, Tlalpam,
D. F., Mexico. 1921, v. 1-4;
El Paso, Texas.   C 388
CULEMANS, J.B. "Catholic
Explorers and Pioneers of
Illinois," Catholic Historical
Review, v. 4 (1918), 141-169.
C 389
CULEMANS, J.B. "Father de la
Valinière, 'Rebel' and Illinois
Missionary," Illinois Catholic
Historical Review, v. 1 (1919),
339-351.   C 390
CULEMANS, J.B. "A Great Illinois
Pioneer--the Rev. John George
Alleman, O.P.," Illinois Cath-
olic Historical Review, v. 2
(1919), 208-222.   C 391
CULEMANS, J.B. "John Lancaster
Spalding--Early Years in the
Priesthood," Illinois Catholic
Historical Review, v. 4 (1922),
397-404.   C 392
CULEMANS, J.B. "Missionary

Adventures among the Peorias,"
Illinois Catholic Historical
Review, v. 5 (1922), 27-40.
C 393
CULLEN, JAMES BERNARD.
The Story of the Irish in
Boston. Boston. Jas. B.
Cullen and Co. 1889. 443p.
C 394
CULLEN, THOMAS F. The
Catholic Church in Rhode
Island. North Providence.
Franciscan Missionaries of
Mary. 1936. 482p. front.,
plate, ports.   C 395
CULLEN, THOMAS FRANCIS.
The Spirit of Serra. New
York. Spiritual Book Associ-
ates. 1935. 202p. front.,
plates, ports., facsim.
C 396
CULLETON, JAMES. Indians
and pioneers of Old Monterey,
Fresno. Academy of Califor-
nia Church History. 1950.
286p.   C 397
CULLIGAN, JOHN M., AND H.J.
PRENDERGAST. "St.
Joseph's Hospital in St. Paul,"
Acta et Dicta, v. 6 (1934),
195-211.   C 398
CUMMINGS, SISTER AGNES
MARION. Vatican and A-
merican Relations: Two World
Wars. MA thesis, St. John's
University, N.Y., 1945 mss.
pp.   C 399
CUMMINGS, SISTER M. WIL-
LIAM. The Development
and Organization of Secondary
Education for Catholic Girls
in the Archdiocese of Phila-
delphia. MA thesis, Villanova
University, 1946, 110pp.
C 400
CUMMINS, DAMIAN. Catholic
Beginnings in Nodaway County;
Missouri. MA thesis, Saint
Louis University, 1930, iii,
100p.   C 401
CUMMINS, DAMIAN L. Catholic
in the Early Platte Purchase
(to 1845), and in Nodaway
County (to 1930). St. Joseph,

Mo. Lawlor Print Co. 1934.
49p.   C 402
CUMMINS, DAMIAN L. "The
Founding of Conception Abbey,"
Benedictine Review, v. 4
(1949), 18-21, 28.   C 403
CUMMINS, DAMIAN L. "Pioneer
Catholic of Nodaway County,
Missouri, 1846-1873," Mid-
America, v. 2 (1931), 207-
224.   C 404
CUNNINGHAM, R.J. "Yankee
Catholic Church," America,
XCIX (July 12, 1948), 408-
410.   C 405
CURLEY, EDWARD P. Origin and
Progress of the Catholic
Church in Montana. MA
thesis, Catholic University,
1926. 101p.   C 406
CURLEY, EDWARD P. "Origin
and Progress of the Catholic
Church in Montana," American
Catholic Historical Society of
Philadelphia Records, v. 38
(1927), 47-96, 98-122.   C 407
CURLEY, MICHAEL J. Church
and State in the Spanish
Floridas, 1783-1822. Washing-
ton. Catholic University of
America. 1940. xi, 380p.
illus., port., map.   C 408
CURLEY, MICHAEL. "A Deeper
Study of Catholic Immigration
Needed," American Catholic
Historical Society of Philadel-
phia Records, LXIX (1958),
56-62.   C 409
CURLEY, MICHAEL J. "Personal
Characteristics of Bishop
Neumann," American Catholic
Historical Society of Phil-
adelphia Records, v. 63
(1952), 3-20.   C 410
CURRAN, ATHANASIUS. History
of Elementary Education in
the Archdiocese of St. Paul.
MA thesis, Catholic Uni-
versity, 1956. 147p.   C 411
CURLEY, MICHAEL J. Venerable
John Neumann. Washington.
Catholic University, 1952. 547p.
illus.   C 412
CURRAN, F.X. Andrew White

Apostle of Maryland (1579-
1636) Month n.s. 12 (London
1954) 222-232.   C 413
CURRAN, FRANCIS X. "Father
Pierre Chazelle, 1789-1845,"
Catholic Historical Review,
v. 41 (1955), 1-17.   C 414
First superior of the French
mission and founder of St.
Mary's College, Bardstown,
Ky.
CURRAN, F.X. "The Founding
of Fordham University and
of the New York Mission,"
Archivum Historicum Societa-
tis Jesu, XXVI (1957), 285-
294.   C 415
CURRAN, F.X. "The Jesuit
Colony in New York, 1808-
1817," United States Catholic
Historical Records and Studies, v. 42 (1954), 51-97.
                          C 416
Father Kohlmann and five
companions go to New York
at the request of Bishop
Carroll to administer a
parish and consider founding a college. Mostly concerned with the work of
Kohlmann and the New York
Literary Institute.
CURRAN, FRANCIS X. "The
Jesuits in Kentucky, 1831-
1846," Mid-America, v. 35
(1953), 223-246.   C 417
A well documented study of
the Jesuit administration
of St. Mary's College,
1833-1846, and of the work
of Father Peter Chazelle,
S.J.
CURRAN, FRANCIS X. Major
Trends in American Church
History. New York. Ameri-
ca Press. 1946. xviii,
198p.   C 418
A brief survey, compiled
from secondary sources,
of the religious history of
the United States. Mostly
on non-Catholic sects, incomplete, but helpful.
CURRAN, FRANCIS X. "The

Mystery of Andrew White,"
Woodstock Letters, LXXXV
(1956), 375-380.   C 419
Father Curran points out
some unanswered problems
about Maryland's first Jesuit
missioner.

CURRAN, JANEMARIE. "I Went
to a Catholic College,"
Catholic World, v. 182
(1956), 271-274.   C 420

CURRIER, CHARLES WARREN.
Carmel in America. Baltimore,
Murphy, 1890.   C 421

CURRIER, CHARLES W. "History
of the Church of Our Lady of
Perpetual Succor in Boston,"
American Catholic Historical
Society of Philadelphia Records, v. 2 (1886-1888), 206-
224.   C 422

CURRY, CORA C. Records of the
Roman Catholic Church in the
United States. Washington.
National Genealogical Society.
1935. Pub. no. 5. 41p. C 423

CURTI, MERLE. The Growth of
American Thought. New York.
Harpers. 1943. xx, 848p.
plates.   C 424
Good picture of the intellectual milieu in which
Catholicism took its rise
in the United States. The
Catholic historian cannot
always agree with all the
author's interpretations.

CURTI, MERLE D. The Social
Ideas of American Educators.
New York. Scribners. 1935.
xxii, 613p.   C 425

CURTIN, GEORGE. "Apostles in
the Greenwood, 1907-" Provincial Annals (Province of the Most
Holy Name, O.F.M.), v. 2
(1929), 19-24.   C 426

CURTIN, J. R. Attitudes of
Parents toward Catholic
Education. Washington. Cath-
olic University. 1954. 52p.
                         C 427

CURTIS, GEORGINA P. "Early
Conversions to the Catholic
Church in America," Catholic

Historical Review, v. 1 (1916),
271-281.   C 428
Among both White and
Indians 1521-1820.

CYRIL, BROTHER V. "St.
Mary's College," Catholic
Educational Review, v. 6
(1913), 406-413.   C 429
The story of this college
founded at Oakland, California, 1863; the Christian
Brothers took over the
administration in 1868.

- D -

DABBS, J. AUTREY (tr. and
ed.). "Texas Missions in
1785. Document. Report of
Father President of the Mission, 1785," Mid-America,
v. 11 (1940), 38-58. Translation only.   D 1

DABLON, CLAUDE. "Account
of the Second Voyage and
the Death of Father Jacques
Marquette," Illinois Catholic
Historical Review, v. 7
(1925), 291-301.   D 2

DAIGNAULT, ELPHEGE J.
Le Vrai Mouvement Sentinel-
liste en Nouvelle Angleterre,
1923-1929, et l'affaire du
Rhode Island. Montreal.
Libraire Deon Frère. 246p.
                         D 3

DAKOSKI, RUPERT A. "Father
Richard's Journalistic
Effort," Salesianum, v. 17
(July-Nov., 1922), 29-38.
                         D 4

DALEY, JOHN M. "Pioneer
Missionary, S.J.: 1720-
1786," Woodstock Letters,
v. 75 (1946), 103-115, 207-
231, 311-321.   D 5

DALLAS (DIOCESE) SYNOD,
2nd, 1934. Synodus dioecesana dallasensis secunda a
Josepho Patritio Lynch [ep.]
celebrata dallasii in ecclesia
cathedrali Ss. Cordis Iesu
die 20 Iunii, A.D. 1934.
[n.p., n.d.] xvi, 181p. D 6

DALTON, W.J. Life of Father

103

Donnelly, with Historical
Sketches of Kansas City, St.
Louis, and Independence,
Missouri. Kansas City, Mo.
Grimes-Joyce, 1921. 197p.
incl. front. (port.), illus.
D 7
DALY, JAMES J. "Campion Col-
lege, Prairie du Chien," Wood-
stock Letters,v. 45 (1916),
188-196. D 8
DALY, JOHN M. Georgetown
University: Origin and Early
Years. Washington, D.C.;
Georgetown University, 1957.
Pp. xxi, 324. D 9
DALY, LOWRIE J. "The Story of
St. Stephen's Mission," Jesuit
Bulletin, v. 39 (1960), 3-6,
18. Wyoming. D 10
DAMIANI, P. "Indian Missions.
Mission of the Rocky Mountains,
Letter to Superior General of
the Mission," Woodstock Let-
ters, v. 11 (1882), 179-183.
D 11
DANIEL, BROTHER. "The Old
Franciscan Library at Mission
San Juan Bautista," California
Historical Society Quarterly,
v. 25 (1946), 133-138. D 12
D'APONTE, GIOVANNI. "Da
alcune Lettere del P. Giovanni
D'Aponte al R.P. Provinciale,"
Lettere Edificanti Provincia
Napolitana, ser. 8, n. 1
(1899), 61-63. D 13
D'APONTE, GIOVANNI. "El Paso,
Texas," Lettere Edificanti
Provincia Napolitana, ser. 9,
n. 1 (1901), 127-128. D 14
D'APONTE, GIOVANNI. "Lettere
VII," Lettere Edificanti Pro-
vincia Napolitana, ser. 1 (1875),
11-13. D 15
D'APONTE, JOHN. "New Mexico.
Letter to Very Rev. Fr. D.
Palomba, Provincial of the
Neapolitan Province, dated
Las Vegas, April, 1874,"
Woodstock Letters, v. 4 (1875),
75-78. D 16
(D'APONTE), J. "Indian Missions
St. Mary's, Montana Ty., Dec.

30th, 1878," Woodstock
Letters, v. 8 (1879), 87-
89. D 17
(D'APONTE), J. "Indian Missions.
Letter dated St. Mary's,
Montana Ty., May 6th, 1878,"
Woodstock Letters, v. 7
(1878), 179-184. D 18
D'ARCY, WILLIAM. The Fenian
Movement in the United States,
1858-1886. Washington. Cath-
olic University of America.
1947. xii, 453p. D 19
DAVENPORT (DIOCESE) SYNOD,
2nd, 1904. Synodus dioecesana
davenportensis secunda, die
22a Junii, A.D. 1904 in
capella collegii Sancti Ambrosii
Davenportus habita. A.
Henrico Cosgrove, episcopo
Davenportensi. [n.p.,n.d.] xi
p., 1 1., 104p. D 20
DAVENPORT (DIOCESE) SYNOD,
3rd, 1932. Statutes; third
synod. Diocese of Davenport.
June 7, 1932. [n.p., n.d.]
78p. D 21
DAVID, ALOYSIUS, AND
GEFFREY BENILDE, BROS.,
"Pius X and the Church in the
United States," American Cath-
olic Historical Society of
Philadelphia Records, v. 65
(1954), 193-215. D 22
A general survey of the
activity of the Pope who
granted full maturity to the
Church in the United States.
DAVID, BROTHER. American
Catholic Convert Authors: a
Bio-Bibliography. Detroit.
Romig. 1944. 15-259p. D 23
DAVIS, SISTER MARY SAMUEL.
E.T.A. Hoffmann and the
Catholic Church. MA thesis.
Catholic University, 1940. 52p.
D 24
DAVIS, NOLAN. The Old Mis-
sions of California: the Story
of the Peaceful Conquest of
the State. Oakland. Clare-
mont Press. 1926. 118p.
incl. illus., plates. D 25
DAVIS, WILLIAM L. History of

St. Ignatius Mission. Spokane.
W. L. Davis. 1954. x, 147p.
D 26
An excellent history of this
early Jesuit mission of the
Northwest.

DAVIS, WILLIAM L. "Peter
John De Smet: The Journey
of 1840," Pacific Northwest
Quarterly, v. 35 (1944),
121-142. D 27

DAVIS, WILLIAM L. "Peter John
De Smet: The years of Preparation, 1801-1837," Pacific Northwest Quarterly, v. 32 (1941),
167-196. D 28

DAVIS, WILLIAM L. "Peter John
De Smet: Missionary to the
Potawatomi, 1837-1841,"
Pacific Northwest Quarterly,
v. 33 (1942), 123-152. D 29

DAVIS, WILLIAM L. A Short
History of the Beginnings of
the Catholic Church in Prosser,
Washington, 1899-1949.
Prosser, Washington. Sacred
Heart Church, 1949. 11p.
D 30

DAXACHER, JOHN. "[Character
of first German Catholic
Settlers at West Point and St.
Helena, Nebraska]," Central
Blatt and Social Justice, v.
23 (1931), 384. D 31

DAY, DOROTHY. House of
Hospitality. New York: Sheed
and Ward, 1939. xxxvi, 275p.
D 32

DAY, DOROTHY. "Peter Maurin,
Agitator," Blackfriars, v. 30
(1949), 409-415. D 33

DAY, DOROTHY. From Union
Square to Rome, Silver
Spring, Md. Preservation
Press. 1939. x, 173p.
D 34
Autobiography of a leading
Catholic social reformer
and convert.

DAY, EDWARD. "They Came to
St. Michael's," Social Justice
Review, v. 54 (1961), 25-30,
59-64, 95-100. D 35
Redemptorist beginnings in

Chicago.

DAY, VICTOR. The Cathedral of
Saint Helena. Anaconda,
Montana. Standard Publishing
Co. 1938. 180p. (?). front.
illus., incl. ports., plan,
diagr. D 36

DeCOSTA, BENJAMIN F. The
Pre-Columbian Discovery of
America. 2d ed. Albany:
J. Munsell. 1890., 196p.
D 37

DeCOSTA, BENJAMIN F. The
Story of Mt. Benedict.
Sommerville, Mass. Citizen
Press. 1893. 14p. D 38

DeCOURCY, HENRY. "The
Sisters of the Visitation of
Our Lady," Metropolitan
Monthly Magazine, v. 33
(1855), 649-656. D 39

DeFOE, SISTER CONSTANCE
MARIE. History of the Catholic Social Welfare Agencies in
the Archdiocese of Saint Paul.
MA thesis, Catholic University,
1946. 81p. D 40

DeHUFF, ELIZABETH WILLIS.
Say the Bells of Old Missions.
176p. illus. D 41
Legends of old New Mexico
Churches.

De la RONCIÈRE, CH. Au Fin
du Mississippi avec Père
Marquette. Paris. Bloud &
Gay 1935. 191p. D 42

De la RONCIÈRE, CH. Le
Troisième centenaire du P.
Marquette," Etudes v. 231
(1937) 204-215. D 43

DeLAMY, SISTER MARY DOLORA.
The Religious Issue of the
Campaign of 1928 as Reflected
in the Wisconsin Press. MA
thesis. Catholic University.
1949. 77p. D 44

DeMARSH, ETHEL M. Some
Principles of Religious and
Civil Liberty Developed by
Maryland Catholics, 1632-
1789. MA thesis. Marquette
University. 1941. D 45

DeMATO, SISTER MARY ASSUNTA.
Catholic Attitudes and Patriot-

ism in the Civil War. MA thesis. Loyola University (Chicago). 1953. 115p. D 46

DeMONTIGNY, De ST. COSME, et Thamur de la Source. Relation de la Mission du Mississippi au Séminaire de Québec in 1700. New York. 1861. D 47

DeSANTIS, VINCENT. "Catholicism and Presidential Elections, 1865-1900," Mid-America, V. 42 (1960), 67-79. D 48

DEANE, CHARLES J. "Fordham-- the First Century," Sign v. 20 (1940), 87-88. D 49

"DEATH OF FATHER JOHN Mc ELROY," Woodstock Letters, v. 6 (1887), 178-186. D 50

"DEATH OF VENERABLE HISTORIAN OF AMERICAN MISSIONS," Catholic World, v. 139 (1934), 361-362. D 51
Obituary of the historian of the Franciscan missions of California, Father Zepherin Engelhardt, who was born in Germany 1851, came to the United States 1852, died 1934.

DeBEURME, TH. "Our New Residence at Ybor, Florida," Woodstock Letters, v. 30 (1901), 62-66. D 52

DEDEAUX, SISTER MARY LIBERATA. The Influence of Saint Frances Academy on Negro Catholic Education in the Nineteenth Century. MA thesis. Villanova University. 1944. 53p. D 53

DEEDY, JOHN G. "Operation Crossroads," Ave Maria, V. 184 (1956), 11-13. D 54
An account of the movement to place wayside shrines in Massachusetts.

DeFERRARI, ROY J. (ed.). Essays on Catholic Education in the United States. Washington. Catholic University of America Press. 1942. xi, 556p. D 55

DEFOURI, JAMES H. Historical Sketch of the Catholic Church in New Mexico. San Francisco. McCormick Bros. 1887. 164p. D 56

DEFOURI, JAMES H. "Lettre de M. Defouri, vicaire général du Kansas à MM. Membres des Conseils centraux de l'Oeuvre de la Propagation de la Foi. avril, 1866," Annales de la Propagation de la Foi, v. 39 (1867), 48-54. D 57

DEFOURI, JAMES H. The Martyrs of New Mexico. Las Vegas, N.M. Revista Catholic Press. 1893. 78p. D 58

DEGNAN, WILLIAM E. The Golden Jubilee of Saint Agnes Parish, New York City. New York, no pub. c1923. 171p. D 59

DEHEY, ELINOR TONG. Religious Orders of Women in the United States. rev. ed. Hammond, Ind. W.B. Conkey Co. 1930. xxxi, 908p. incl. front., illus. (incl. ports.). D 60

DEHNER, SISTER M. XAVIER. The Know Nothing Party in Virginia, 1852-1860. MA thesis. Catholic University. 1942. 85p. D 61

DEILER, J. HANNO. The Settlement of the German Coast of Louisiana. Philadelphia. American Germanica Press. 1909. 136p. illus., plates. D 62

DEILER, J. HANNO. Zur Geschichte der deutschen Kirchegemeinden in Staate Louisiana. New Orleans. The Author. 1894. 144p. text. p. 145-168 ads. D 63

DEJEAN, J. "The Church in Michigan in 1825," American Md. Preservation Press. 1939. x, 173p. D 64

DEJEAN, J. "A Missionary in Michigan," American Catholic Historical Researches, v. 3 (1887), 27-29. D 65

DELAHOYDE, LOUIS J. "Catholicism among the Yankton Sioux Indians," St. Meinrad Historical Essays, v. 6 (1943), 123-136. D 66

DE LANEY, HOWARD L. All Our Yesterdays. The Story of St. Mary Parish, Walsenburg, Colo. Walsenburg, Consolidated Publishing Co. 1944. 72p. illus., plates, ports. D 67

DE LANEY, JOHN BERNARD. The Life and Writings of the Right Reverend John Bernard Delany, D. D., Second Bishop of Manchester, N.H. Lowell, Mass. Lawler Printing Co. 1911. 452p. front. (port.). col. plate. D 68

DE LANGLEZ, JEAN. "Antoine Loumet, alias Cadillac, Commandant at Michilmackinac: 1694-1697," Mid-America, v. 16 (1945), 108-112, 188-216, 232-256. D 69

DE LANGLEZ, JEAN. "Cadillac at Detroit," Mid-America, v. 19 (1948), 152-176. D 70

DE LANGLEZ, JEAN. "Cadillac's Early Years in America," Mid-America, v. 15 (1944), 3-39. D 71

DE LANGLEZ, JEAN. "Cadillac Proprietor at Detroit," Mid-America, v. 21 (1950), 226-258. D 72

DE LANGLEZ, JEAN. "Claude Dablon, S.J., 1619-1697," Mid-America, v. 15 (1944), 91-110. D 73

DE LANGLEZ, JEAN. The French Jesuits in Lower Louisiana (1700-1763). Washington. Catholic University of America. 1935. iii-xxvi, 547p. D 74
Presents the Jesuit side of the differences between certain Capuchins and Jesuits in early Louisiana. For the Capuchin account cf. Vogel.

DE LANGLEZ, JEAN (ed.). "The Journal of Pierre Vitry, S.J." Mid-America, v. 17 (1946), 23-29. D 75

DE LANGLEZ, JEAN. Life and Voyages of Louis Jolliet (1645-1700). Chicago, Institute of Jesuit History, Loyola University. 1948. vii, 289p. D 76

DE LANGLEZ, JEAN. "Le Récit des Voyages et des Découverts du Père Jacques Marquette," Mid-America, v. 17 (1946), 173-194, 211, 258. D 77

DE LANGLEZ, JEAN. El Rio del Espiritu Santo. Monograph Series, XXI. New York. United States Catholic Historical Society. 1945. xiii, 182p. D 78

DE LANGLEZ, JEAN. "The Voyages of Tonti in North America," Mid-America, v. 15 (1944), 255-300. D 79

DE LATRE, A.J. Un Catholicisme Américain. Namur. A. Godenne. 1898. D 80

DE LAUNEY, GREGORY F.X. "Catholic Teachers at Secular Colleges," Catholic World, v. 182 (1956), 347-351. D 81

"DELAWARE [N. J.] Mission Observes Silver Jubilee (1914-1939)," Provincial Annals (Province of the Most Holy Name, O.F.M.), v. 2 (1941-42), 92-96, D 82

DELPLACE, L. "Les Missionnaires Belges et Hollandais aux Etats-Unis d'Amérique, 1773-1850," Revue Générale, Brussels, v. 95 (19), 51-78. D 83

DEMERS, MODEST. Mission De l'Orégon. Notice Sur Les Travaux Apostoliques. Paris. 1851. D 84

DENEHIE, ELIZABETH. "Catholic Education in Indiana, Past and Present," Indiana Magazine of History, v. 12 (1916), 337-350. D 85

DENGEL, ANNA. Mission for Samaritans. A Survey of Achievements and Opportunities in the Field of Catholic Mis-

sions, Milwaukee. Bruce.
1945. v. 126p. plates,
port.   D 86
DENNIS, ALFRED PEARCE.
"Lord Baltimore's Struggle
with the Jesuits, 1643-1649,"
American Historical Association Annual Report, v. 1
(1900), 107-125.   D 87
Unfriendly, inaccurate and
not based on facts.
DENNIS, FRANCIS L. Most
Rev. James Frederick Wood,
1813-1883, the Fifth Bishop
and First Archbishop of
Philadelphia. MA thesis.
Catholic University. 1932.
39p.   D 88
DENVER, COL. (DIOCESE)
SYNOD, 1st, 1889. Synodus
dioecesana denverensis prima,
juxta normam a conc. Balt.
III praestitutam, habita in
collegio Ss. Cordis, Highlands,
a Nicolao Chrysostomo Matz,
episcopo denverensi, die II
Augusti, a.d. MDCCLXXXIX.
Las Vegas, ex typis Societatis
Jesu, 1889. 59p.   D 89
DENVER, COL. (DIOCESE)
SYNOD, 2nd, 1891. Synodus
dioecesana denverensis secunda,
habita in collegio Ss. Cordis,
Denver, a Nicolao Chrysostomo
Matz, episcopo denverensi die
XXXI Julii, a.d. MDCCCXCI.
Las Vegas, ex typis Societatis
Jesu, 1891. 39p.   D 90
DENVER, COL. (DIOCESE)
SYNOD I., II., III., 1889,
1891, 1893. Synodus dioecesana
denverensis I. II. III. a
Nicolao Chrysostomo Matz,
episcopo denverensi habitae die 2
Augusti, A.D. MDCCCLXXXIX,
die 31 Julii A.D. MDCCCXCI,
die 4 Augusti A.D. MDCCCXCIII.
Las Vegas, Ex typis Societatis
Jesu, 1894. 59p.   D 91
DES MOINES (DIOCESE) SYNOD,
1923. The code of the diocese
of Des Moines decreed in
diocesan synod held June 15th,
1923 in the chapel of Des

Moines Catholic College and
promulgated Sept. 8th, 1923,
by Thomas W. Drumm [bp.]
[n.p., n.d.] 2 p.l., 110p.
                                D 92
DES MOINES (DIOCESE) SYNOD,
3rd, 1933. Dioecesis des
moinensis synodus dioecesana
tertia celebrata Des Moini
in ecclesia cathedrali Sancti
Ambrosii die 16, mensis
Junii, 1933 a Thoma G.
Drumm [ep.] [Des Moines] ex
Cancellaria dioecesana, 1933.
11p.   D 93
DESGEORGE, R. (verfasser).
Monseigneur Flaget Evêgne de
Bardstown et Louisville.
Paris. Jacques Lecoffre.
1851. 328p.   D 94
DESJARDINS, PAUL. "Jacques
Marquette, S.J., était-il
prêtre?" La Revue de l'Uni-
versité Laval, v. 3 (1949),
634-639.   D 95
DESJARDINS, PAUL. Le projet
de mission du P. Aulneau
chez les Mandanes. Report
of the Canadian Catholic His-
torical Association. 1949.
                                D 96
DESMOND, HUMPHREY J. The
A.P.A. Movement. Washing-
ton. New Century Press. 1921.
102p.   D 97
DESMOND, HUMPHREY, J. The
Know-Nothing Party. Washing-
ton. New Century Press.
1905. 159p.   D 98
"DESTRUCTION OF THE CHARLES-
TOWN CONVENT," United
States Catholic Historical
Society Records and Studies,
v. 12 (1918), 66-75.   D 99
"DESTRUCTION OF THE CHARLES-
TOWN CONVENT," United
States Catholic Historical
Society Records and Studies,
v. 13 (1919), 106-119.
                                D 100
DETROIT (DIOCESE) Petrus
Paulus Levevere episcopus
Zelanus, coadjutor et adminis-
trator detroitensis. Universo

dilecto suae dioecesis clero
salutem et benedictionem.
Quanquam Christus Dominus...
[n. p., 1851?] 15p.   D 101
DETROIT, MICH. (DIOCESE)
SYNOD, 1st, 1859. Constitutiones synodi dioecesanae
detroitensis primae, habitae
mense Octobri, A.D. 1859.
Detroiti, Ex typis J. Slater,
1859. 44p.   D 102
DETROIT (DIOCESE) SYNOD,
2nd, 1862. Synodus dioecesana
detroitensis secunda habita
mense Septembri, A.D.
MDCCCLXII. Detroiti, J.
Slater, 1862. 9p.   D 103
DETROIT (DIOCESE) Rules and
directions for the administration of the temporal affairs
of the church in the diocese
of Detroit, wherever the
bishop may deem it necessary
or advantageous. Detroit, J.
Slater, 1862. 8p.   D 104
DETROIT (DIOCESE) SYNOD, 4th
1878. Acta et constitutiones
synodi dioecesanae detroitensis
quartae quam diebus 15, 16,
17 et 18 Oct., A.D. 1878,
habuit ... Caspar Henricus
Borgess [ep.] Detroiti, Free
press book and job printing
house, 1878. 52p.   D 105
DETROIT (DIOCESE) SYNOD, 5th
1881. Acta et constitutiones
synodi dioecesanae detroitensis
quintae, habitae in collegio
Assumptionis B.M.V. sand-
wichensi, diebus 16, 18, 19
mensis Julii, A.D. 1881,
praeside Casparo Henrico
Borgess [ep.] Detroiti, Typis M'
Cormack & Co., 1881. 36p.
                          D 106
DETROIT (DIOCESE) SYNOD, 6th
1885. Acta et constitutiones
synodi dioecesanae detroitensis
sextae, habitae in collegio
Assumptionis B.M.V. sand-
wichensi diebus 20 et 21 mensis
Julii, A.D., 1885. Praeside
Casparo Henrico Borgess [ep.]
Detroiti, Kilroy et Brennan,

1881 (!) 17p.   D 107
DETROIT (DIOCESE) SYNOD,
7th, 1886. A.M.D.G. Synodus
dioecesana detroitensis septima;
quae antecedentium etiam
complectitur constitutiones; die
XIX. M. Augusti, A.D. 1886,
in collegio Assumptionis B.M.
V. sandwichensi habita: a
Casparo Henrico Borgess
[ep.] Marshall, Mich., Marshall publ. co., 1886. x, 24
11p.   D 108
DETROIT (DIOCESE) SYNOD,
8th, 1944. Synodi detroitensis
octavae statuta. 1944. [n.p.,
n.d.] [14] xiv, 116p. D 109
DEUSTER, LOUIS. Account of
the Origin of Rhineland Colony
and St. Joseph's Parish at
Rhineland. Rhineland, Munday,
P.O., Texas. The Parish.
1945. 159p.   D 110
DEUTHER, CHARLES G. Life
and Times of the Right
Reverend John Timon. D.D.
Buffalo. The Author. 1870.
xiv, (17)-338p. front., port.
                       D 111
DEUTHER, CHARLES G. 'Rev.
Charles Smith," American
Catholic Historical Researches,
v. 6 (1889), 88-92.   D 112
"DEUTSCHEN KATHOLIKEN IN
DEN VEREINIGTEN STAATEN,"
Die Katholischen Missionen,
v. 6 (1878), 86-87.   D 113
DEVER, DANIEL J. "The Church
in Hawaii," Ave Maria, XC
(July 25, 1959), 5-9, illus.
                       D 114
DEVITT, EDWARD I. "Axacan.
The Martyrs of the Rappa-
hannock," American Catholic
Historical Society of Philadel-
phia Records, v. 19 (1909),
1-17.   D 115
DEVITT, EDWARD I. "Bohemia,"
American Catholic Historical
Society of Philadelphia Re-
cords, v. 23 (1913), 97-139.
                       D 116
DEVITT, EDWARD I. "The
Clergy List of 1819, Diocese

of Baltimore," American Catholic Historical Society of Philadelphia Records, v. 22 (1911), 238-267. D 117

DEVITT, EDWARD I. "A Dark Chapter in the Catholic History of Maryland," United States Catholic Historical Magazine, v. 1 (1887), 121-149. D 118

DEVITT, EDWARD I. "Father Andrew White," American Catholic Historical Researches, v. 19 (1902), 72-74. D 119

DEVITT, EDWARD I. "Georgetown College in the Early Days," Columbia (D.C.) Historical Society Records, v. 12 (1909), 21-37. D 120

DEVITT, EDWARD I. "History of the Maryland-New York Province," Woodstock Letters, v. 60 (1931), 199-226 (St. Inigoes), 346-376 (St. Thomas), v. 61 (1932), 11-25 (Newton-Leonardtown), 175-191 (same), 335-374 (Conewago), v. 62 (1933), 3-15 (Goshenhoppen), 171-187 (White Marsh-Lancaster), v. 63 (1934), 1-38 (Bohemia), 213-230 (St. Joseph's Church), 400-420 (Deer Creek-Novitiate), v. 64 (1935), 24-41 (Holy Trinity, Washington), 41-57 (Gonzaga and St. Aloysius), 399-421 (Boston College and Immaculate Conception), v. 65 (1936), 6-32 (Fordham), 189-223 (College and Church of St. Francis Xavier). D 121

DEVITT, EDWARD I. "Letters from the Baltimore Archives," American Catholic Historical Society of Philadelphia Records, v. 19 (1908), 214-238, 243-275, 455-482; v. 20 (1909), 49-74, 193-208, 250-289, 431-436. variant title. D 122

DEVITT, EDWARD I. (ed.) "Letters of Father Joseph Mosley, 1757-1786," Woodstock Letters, v. 35 (1906), 35-55, 226-245. D 123

DEVITT, EDWARD I. (comp. and ed.) "Letters of Father Mosley, S.J., and Extracts from His Diary," American Catholic Historical Society of Philadelphia Records, v. 17 (1906), 180-210, 289-311. D 124

DEVITT, EDWARD I. (ed.). "Letters of Father Mosley, S.J., and Some Extracts from His Diary," American Catholic Historical Society of Philadelphia Records, v. 17 (1906), 180-210, 289-311. D 125

DEVITT, EDWARD I. "Miscellaneous Letters to Bishop Carroll, 1784-1815," American Catholic Historical Society of Philadelphia Records, v. 19 (1908), 385-415. D 126

DEVITT, EDWARD I. "Mission of St. Francis Xavier, Cecil County, Maryland," American Catholic Historical Society of Philadelphia Records, v. 23 (1913), 97-139. D 127

DEVITT, EDWARD I. (ed.). "Papers Relating to the Early History of the Maryland Mission," Woodstock Letters, v. 9 (1880), 157-180, v. 10 (1881), 3-28, 89-120, 209-224; v. 11 (1882), 3-24 117-140. D 128

DEVITT, EDWARD I. "The Planting of the Faith in America," American Catholic Historical Society of Philadelphia Records, v. 6 (1895), 137-179. D 129

DEVITT, EDWARD I. (ed.). "Some Old Letters from the Archives of Georgetown College," American Catholic Historical Society of Philadelphia Records, v. 18 (1907), 389-396. D 130

DEVITT, EDWARD I. "The Suppression and Restoration of the Society in Maryland," Woodstock Letters, v. 33

(1904), 371-381. D 131

DEVITT, EDWARD I. "Trinity Church, Georgetown, An Historical Discourse," Woodstock Letters, v. 23 (1904), 302-324; v. 34 (1905), 113-130, 203-235. D 132

DEVITT, EDWARD I. "Who Was Father Smith of Talbot County Md., 1693?" American Catholic Historical Researches, v. 15 (1898), 65-68. D 133

DEWEY, RALPH E.S. "Letter from a Scholastic in Texas, dated San Antonio, Texas, Oct. 16th, 1873," Woodstock Letters, v. 3 (1874), 64-68. D 134

DEWEY, RALPH E.S. "Letter from a Scholastic in Texas, dated San Antonio, Jan. 28th, 1874," Woodstock Letters, v. 3 (1874), 133-134. D 135

DEYE, ANTHONY H. Archbishop John Baptist Purcell of Cincinnati, Pre-Civil War Years, Ph.D. thesis. University of Notre Dame. 1959. iii, 122p. D 136

DEYNCODT, FRANCOIS. L. Rev. Père P. J. de Smet, S.J. Missionaire Belge aux Etats-Unis. Brussels. 1878. D 137

D'HERBOMEZ, J. "Lettre du R.P. d'Herbomez, Missionaire Oblat de Marie, à son frère. Saint Joseph d'Olympia 6 décembre, 1855," Annales de la Propagation de la Foi, v. 28 (1856), 247-254. D 138

D'HEROUVILLE, PIERRE. "Un Apotre du Far West Americain. Le Père Georges le Fer de la Motte," Etudes, v. 157 (1918), 193-202. D 139
A biographical sketch of this Jesuit missionary of Montana and Idaho, who died 1918.

DI MATTEO, N. "Uno Sguardo alla Nostra Missione," Lettere Edificanti Provincia Napolitana, (1912-1914), 171-180. D 140
A general survey of the New

Mexico Colorado Mission of the Neapolitan Jesuits.

DIAMARE, GIACOMO. "Lettera XXXV," Lettere Edificanti Provincia Napolitana, ser. 1 (1876-1877), 114-116. D 141

DIAMOND, MALCOLM L. "Catholicism in America: an Emerging Dialogue," Judaism, IX (1960), 307-318. D 142

DICKEY, ROLAND F. "St. Francis and the Birds," Arizona Quarterly, v. 3 (1947), 338-350. D 143

DICKEY, ROLAND F. "Saints and New Mexico," New Mexico Quarterly Review, v. 17 (1947), 311-321. D 144

DICTIONARY OF AMERICAN BIOGRAPHY. New York. Scribners. 1926-1944. 21v., index, supplement. D 145
Contains many biographies of important figures in the history of the Catholic Church in the United States. Unfortunately the sketches are of uneven workmanship, and many times the choice of biographer is poor.

DICTIONARY OF AMERICAN HISTORY. New York, Scribners. 1940. 5v. D 146

DIDAS, JAMES F. Six Years of Josephite Development," Colored Harvest, v. (1948), 8-11. D 147

DIECKMAN, VINCENT. Oldenburg House of Theology: Retrospect. Provincial Chronicles O.F.M. (Cincinnati), 30 (1958), 271-278 illus., 471-474. D 148

DIETSCHE, W. "A Great University," Christian Family, 53 (1958), 18-21. D 149
A popular sketch of Catholic University.

DIFFLEY, JEROME E. Catholic Reaction to American Public Education, 1792-1852. Ph.D. thesis. University of Notre Dame, 1959. D 150

DIGGINS, JOHN ANTHONY.

Reverend William Gleeson (1827-1903). Historiographer of the Catholic Church in California. MA thesis. University of San Francisco. 1951. viii, 104p. plates. D 151

DIGMANN, FLORENTINE. "Mission of Our German Fathers among the Dakota Indians. Letter dated St. Ignatius, Chicago, September 19, 1902," Woodstock Letters, v. 31 (1902), 352-359. D 152

DIGMANN, P.F. "Pictures from the German Sioux Missions," Central Blatt and Social Justice, v. 26 (1933), 89-90. D 153

DIGNAN, PATRICK J. A History of the Legal Incorporation of Catholic Church Property in the United States 1784-1932. Washington. Catholic University of America. 1933; and New York. Kenedy. 1935. vi, 288p. D 154

DIGNAN, PATRICK J. Peter Anthony Malou, Patriot and Priest, 1753-1827. MA thesis. Catholic University. 1931. 91p. D 155

DIGNAN, PATRICK J. "Peter Anthony Malou, Patriot and Priest (1753-1827)," American Catholic Historical Society of Philadelphia Records and Studies, v. 42 (1931), 305-343; v. 43 (1932), 62-96. D 156

DILHET, JEAN. Etat de l'Eglise Catholique aux Diocèse des Etats-Unis de l'Amérique Septentrionale. Tr. and annotated by Patrick W. Browne. Washington. Salve Regina Press. 1922. xxii, xx-xii, 140-140 (141)-261p. D 157
French and English on opposite pages.

DILLINGHAM, WILLIAM C. The Franciscan Missions of California. Los Angeles, W.D. Dillingham. 1908. 31 mounted plates on 16 leaves. Map on verso of t.p. D 158

DILLON, JOHN J. The Historic Story of St. Mary's Albany N.Y. New York. Kenedy. 1933. viii, 270p. plates. D 159

DILLON, JORDAN MARIE. A Dominican Influence in the Discovery of America. MA thesis. Catholic University. 1930. 51p. D 160

DILLON, RICHARD A. (ed. and tr.). "Father Payeras at San Rafael California," Americas, v. 11 (1954), 79-86. D 161
An estimation of the prospects of San Rafael in either 1818 or 1819--not very enthusiastic.

DIMMITT, L.M. "Reverend Father Blanchet, 1818-1906," Washington Historical Quarterly, v. 25 (1934), 294-296. D 162

DINEEN, M.F. "Historical Sketch of St. Mary's Seminary of St. Sulpice, Baltimore, Md.," American Ecclesiastical Review, v. 16 (1897), 225-240, illus. D 163

"DIOCESE SIOUX FALLS, Süd Dakota," Die Katholischen Missionen, v. 24 (1896), 67-68. D 164

DIOMEDI, A. "Diozese Nesqualy," Die Katholischen Missionen, v. 7 (1879), 107-109. D 165

DIOMEDI, A. "Indian Missions. Letter dated Fort Colville, Wash. Ty., July 20th, 1878," Woodstock Letters, v. 8 (1879), 32-41. D 166

DIOMEDI, A. "Sketches of Modern Indian Life," Woodstock Letters, v. 22 (1893), 231-265, 353-378; v. 23 (1894), 23-49. D 167

DIONNE, NARCISSE E. Hennepin, Ses Voyages et Ses Oeuvres. Quebec. R. Renault. 1897. 40p. D 168

DIONNE, NARCISSE E. Gabriel

Richard. Laflamme and Proulx. 1911. 191p. D 169

DIONNE, N.E. Le Pere Sebastian Râle. Ottawa. Hope et Fils. 1903. n.p. D 170

DITLINGER, ANDREW. "Father De Seille," St. Meinrad Historical Essays, v. 2 (1932), 205-215. D 171

DIVINEY, T.J. "American Catholic Action," Month, v. 166 (1935), 221-226. D 172

DIX ANS SUR LA COTE DU PACIFIQUE. Québec. Léger Brousseau. 1873. D 173

DOCKLER, PANCRATIUS. Souvenir of Golden Jubilee of SS. Peter and Paul's Church, Cumberland, Md., 1848-1898. no pl. no pub. 1898? 141p. ports. D 174

"UN DOCUMENT CURIEUX. L'épitaphe du Père Rasle," Bulletin des Recherches Historiques, v. 59 (1953), 131-136. D 175
An interesting verse telling of the virtues of the missionary of Maine who was martyred by the English in 1724. The author is unknown.

"DOCUMENTS--A BISHOP FOR THE INDIANS IN 1790," Catholic Historical Review, v. 3 (1917), 79-89. D 176

"DOCUMENTS--RAGGUAGLIO DELLO STATO DELLA RELIGIONE CATTOLICA NELLE COLONE INGLESI D'AMERICA," Catholic Historical Review, v. 6 (1921), 517-524. D 177

"DOCUMENTS RELATING TO THE CATHOLIC CHURCH IN GREEN BAY AND THE MISSION AT LITTLE CHUTE, 1825-1840," Wisconsin Historical Collections, v. 14 (1898), 162-205. D 178

"DOCUMENTS RELATIVE TO THE ADJUSTMENT OF THE ROMAN CATHOLIC ORGANIZATION IN THE UNITED STATES," Ameri-

can Historical Review, v. 15 (1910), 800-829. D 179

"DOCUMENTS. SELECTED LETTERS FROM THE ROUX CORRESPONDENCE (1833-1834);" Catholic Historical Review, v. 4 (1918), 84-100. D 180
French and English translations of the earliest account of the exercise of the Catholic Ministry in Kansas City.

DODD, WILLIAM H. (ed.). "A Confederate Chaplain's War Journal," United States Catholic Historical Society Records and Studies, v. 32 (1941), 94-103. D 181
Some extracts from the journal of Father James Sheeran.

DOHERTY, DAVID J. "Kaskaskia, the Ancient," United States Catholic Historical Magazine, v. 4 (1891-1892), 31-45. D 182

DOHERTY, MARTIN W. "Oregon Catholics Celebrate," Columbia, v. 18 (May, 1939), 17. illus., ports. D 183

"DOKUMENTE ZUM CAHENSLY-STREIT," Central Blatt and Social Justice, v. 16 (1923), 91-92. D 184

DOLAN, REGINA. "Matthew Carey, Citizen and Publisher," American Catholic Historical Society of Philadelphia Records, v. 65 (1954), 116-128. D 185

D'OLIVER, NICHOLAU. "Comments on the Evangelization of the New World," The Americas, 14 (1958), 399-410. D 186

DOLL, LOUIS W. The History of St. Thomas Parish, Ann Arbor. Ann Arbor, Mich., Saint Thomas Parish. 1941. vi, 291p. illus., plates, ports., facsim. D 187

DOLLE, ELIZABETH L. Glenmary or a History of the Home Missioners of America.

113

MA thesis. Xavier University
(Cincinnati), 1951. 142p.
D 188
DOMENECH, EMMANUEL HENRI
DIEUDONNE. Journal d'un
Missionaire au Texas et au
Mexique., 1846-1852. Paris.
Gaumé freres, 1857. xii,
477p. map. D 189
Also published in English
translation under the title:
Missionary Adventures in
Texas and Mexico. London.
1858.
DOMINGUEZ, FRAY FRANCISCO
ATANASIO. The Missions of
New Mexico, 1776. Albuquerque,
N.M.: University of New
Mexico, 1956. Pp. xxi, 387.
D 190
An excellent translation of
this classic by Eleanor B.
Adams and Fray Angelico
Chavez.
DOMINICAN SISTERS. Congrega-
tion of Our Lady of the
Rosary, Sparkhill, New York.
Fifty Years in Retrospect.
New York. Privately printed.
1926. 318p. C 191
DONAHUE, WILLIAM H. "The
Missionary Activities of Fray
Margil de Jesús in Texas,
1716-1722," The Americas,
14 (1957), 45-56. D 192
DONATO, PIETRO DI. Immigrant
Saint. New York: McGraw-
Hill, 1960. Pp. 246. D 193
Popular life of Mother
Cabrini.
DONLON, HUGH P. "The Shrine
at Auriesville," Columbia,
v. 10 (Jan. 1931), 17-33,
illus. D 194
DONNELLY, CHRYSOSTOM.
'Right Reverend Edward
Dominick Fenwick, O.P.,"
Dominicana, v. 17 (1932),
169-178. D 195
DONNELLY, ELEANOR C. Life
of Father Barbelin, S.J.
Philadelphia, F. A. Fasey.
1886. D 196
DONNELLY, JOHN JOSEPH.

History of the Christian
Brothers of Ireland in the
Pacific Northwest. MA thesis.
Seattle University. 1947.
53p. D 197
DONNELLY, JOSEPH P. "Nine-
teenth Century Jesuit Reduc-
tions in the United States,"
Mid-America, v. 6 (1935),
69-83. D 198
A story of the attempts in
Missouri and Montana.
Erroneously credited to W.
Patrick Donnelly.
DONNELLY, JOSEPH P. "The
Parish of the Holy Family,
Cahokia, Illinois, 1699-1949.
East St. Louis. Cahokia
250th Anniversary Associa-
tion. 1949. 62p. D 199
DONNELLY, JOSEPH P. "A
Silver Crown for the Statue
of the Virgin," Missouri His-
torical Society Bulletin, v. 5
(1949), 207-210. D 200
An account of the crown
placed on the Statue of the
Blessed Virgin by the
students of St. Louis Uni-
versity in thanksgiving for
preservation from the
cholera of 1849.
DONNELLY, JOSEPH P. (ed.).
"Burial Records of the Holy
Family Church," in McDermott,
Old Cahokia, 255-285. D 201
DONNELLY, JOSEPH P. "The
Cahokia Anniversary," His-
torical Bulletin, v. 27 (1949),
75-76, 83. D 202
DONNELLY, JOSEPH P.
"Cahokia's 250th Birthday,"
America, v. 81 (1949), 257-
258. D 203
DONNELLY, JOSEPH P. "Colonel
John Fitzgerald," Historical
Bulletin, v. 7 (1928), 61-63.
D 204
DONNELLY, JOSEPH P. (ed.).
'The Founding of the Holy
Family Mission and Its His-
tory in the Eighteenth Century:
Documents," in John Francis
McDermott (ed.), Old Cahokia.

A Narrative and Documents Illustrating the First Century of Its History, 55-92. D 205

DONNELLY, JOSEPH P. (ed.). "Letters from Monk's Mound: the Correspondence of Dom Urban Guillet with Bishop Plessis of Quebec, 1809-1812," in McDermott, Old Cahokia, 286-320. D 206

DONNELLY, W. PATRICK. Father Pierre-Jean De Smet: United States Ambassador to the Indians. MA thesis. Saint Louis University. 1934. v, 138p. D 207

DONNELLY, W. PATRICK. "Father Pierre-Jean De Smet: United States Ambassador to the Indians," United States Catholic Historical Society Records and Studies, v. 24 (1934), 7-142, illus. D 208

DONNELLY, W. PATRICK. "Catholic Giant of the Northwest," Historical Bulletin, v. 17 (1939), 23-24, 35-36. D 209

DONNELLY, W. PATRICK. "Father De Smet, a Review," Historical Bulletin, v. 19 (1941), 57-59. D 210

DONOHUE, ARTHUR D. "Financing a Catholic College in Kansas in 1850," Illinois Catholic Historical Review, v. 11 (1929), 291-298. D 211

DONOHUE, J. AUGUSTINE. "The Unlucky Jesuit Mission of Bac, 1732-1767," Arizona and the West. v. 2 (1960), 127-139. D 212

DONOHUE, SISTER JOAN MARIE. The Irish Catholic Benevolent Union. Washington. Catholic University. 1953. xi, 229. D 213

DONOHUE, THOMAS. History of the Diocese of Buffalo. Buffalo. Catholic Publication Co. 1929. 391p. D 214

DONOHUE, THOMAS A. Iroquois and the Jesuits. Buffalo. Catholic Publication Society.

1895. 276p. D 215

DONOHUE, WILLIAM H. "Mary of Agreda and the Southwest United States," Americas, v. 9 (1953), 291-314. D 216 A documented study of the story of the conversion of the Jumano Indians and other Southwest tribes stemming from the miraculous appearances of the Spanish nun.

DONOVAN, C.F. The Story of the Twenty-eighth International Eucharistic Congress. Chicago. Eucharistic Congress Committee. 1927. D 217

DONOVAN, GEORGE F. The Pre-Revolutionary Irish in Massachusetts, 1620-1775. Menasha, Wisconsin. George Banta Publishing Co. 1932. 158p. D 218

DONOVAN, JOHN D. "American Catholic Hierarchy--a Social Profile," American Catholic Sociological Review, 19 (1958), 98-112. D 219

DONOVAN, JOHN D. "American Catholic Sociologists and the Sociology of Religion," American Catholic Sociological Review, v. 15 (1954), 104-114. D 220 Includes a good bibliography of works on this subject.

DONOVAN, JOHN T. The Catholic Church in Paducah, Kentucky. Paducah, Ky. Young Print Co. 1934. 2 v. in 1, 171p. D 221

DONOVAN, SISTER MARY MARK. The Episcopate of the Most Reverend Otto Zardetti, First Bishop of Saint Cloud, Minnesota, 1889-94. MA thesis. Saint Louis University. 1954. v, 97p. D 222

DONOVAN, NELLE CATHERINE. Fifty Golden Years in Central Illinois; an Epic in Purple. New York. Paulist Press. 1935. vii, 141p. front., plates, port. D 223

DONOVAN, VINCENT JOSEPH.
First American Catholic Lay
Congress, Held at Baltimore,
November 10-11, 1889. MA
thesis. Catholic University.
1940. 94p.   D 224

DOOLEY, P.J. "Woodstock and
Its Makers," Woodstock Letters,
v. 56 (1927), 1-112, 113-224,
245-273. illus., ports. D 225

DORAN, SISTER MARY LAMBER-
TINE. In the Early Days:
Pages from the Annals of the
Sisters of Charity of the
Blessed Virgin Mary. St. Louis.
1912.   D 226

DORAN, WILLIAM T. "Historical
Sketch of the University of
Detroit," Michigan History
Magazine, v. 2 (1918), 154-
164. illus.   D 227

DORAN, WILLIAM T. "Historical
Sketch of the University of
Detroit," Woodstock Letters,
v. 50 (1921), 303-310. D 228

DORCHESTER, DANIEL. Christianity in the United States
from the First Settlement
down to the Present Time.
New York. Phillips and Hunt.
1888. 795p. incl. tables,
front. (port.)., 3 maps
(2 double), col. charts, xi
diagr.   D 229

DORSEY, ELVIRA, MOTHER.
Catholics of Illinois in the Civil
War. MA thesis. Loyola Uni-
versity (Chicago).   D 230

DORSEY, KATHERINE (COSTIGAN).
Life of Father Thomas Copley.
Woodstock, Md. 1885. 75p.
                              D 231

DORSEY, KATHERINE C. "The
Life of Father Thomas Copley,"
Woodstock Letters, v. 13
(1884), 249-264; v. 14 (1885),
29-61, 197-223.   D 232

DOSCH, DELMAR R. Father
Pierre-Jean De Smet, S. J.,
Ambassador Extraordinary to
the Sioux Indians 1862-1868.
MA thesis. Loyola University
(Chicago). 1947.   D 233

DOSTAL, W.A. "Bohemian (Czech)

Catholics in Iowa," Iowa Catholic Historical Review, v. 5
(Oct., 1932), 3-10.   D 234

DOUGHTY, ARTHUR G. "Sources
for the History of the Catholic
Church in the Public Archives
of Canada," Catholic Historical
Review, v. 19 (1933), 148-
166.   D 235
A bibliographical essay
pointing out the location of
material and a survey of
holdings.

DOUGLAS, MARIAN. Mission to
Navaho Land. World Mission
4 (N.Y. 1953), 219-227.
                              D 236

DOWLING, AUSTIN. "The
National Catholic Welfare
Conference," American Ec-
clesiastical Review, v. 79
(1928), 337-354.   D 237

DOWLING, MICHAEL P.
Creighton University. Reminiscences of the First Twenty-
five Years. Omaha. Burkley
Printing Co. 1903. 272p.
front., plates, ports., plan,
diagrs.   D 238

DOWNING, MARGARET B.
Chronicles of Loretto.
Chicago. McBride. 1897.
127p. plates.   D 239

DOWNING, MARGARET B. "De-
velopment of the Catholic
Church in the District of
Columbia from Colonial Times
to the Present," Columbia
(D.C.) Historical Society Records, v. 15 (1912), 23-53.
                              D 240

DOYLE, JOHN. History of
Holy Rosary Parish, Galveston,
Texas, 1938. no pl. no pub.
1938?   D 241

DOYLE, JOHN T. "Brief History
of the 'Pius Fund' of
California. Right of the R.
C. Church of California to Its
Portion Thereof," Woodstock
Letters, v. 31 (1902), 223-
234.   D 242

DOYLE, SISTER MARGARET
MARIE. The Curriculum of

the Catholic Women's College. Ph.D. thesis. University of Notre Dame. 1932. 144p.
D 243

DOYON, BERNARD. Cavalry of Christ on the Rio Grande. Milwaukee. Bruce. 1956. Pp. xiii, 252.
D 244

DREANE, A. "Dal Collegio di Denver," Lettere Edificanti Provincia Napolitana, (1905), 89-94.
D 245

DRENNAN, M.A. "The Early History of the 'Congregation of the Mission,' in Philadelphia," American Catholic Historical Society of Philadelphia Records, v. 20 (1909), 4-21.
D 246

DRESSMAN, ALOYSIUS. St. Leo Golden Jubilee, 1890-1940. St. Leo, Fla. Abbey Press. 1940. xiv, 126p. plates, ports.
D 247

DREWRY, ELIZABETH B. "Material in the National Archives Relating to Florida, 1789-1870," Florida Historical Quarterly, v. 22 (1944), 97-115.
D 248

DREXLER, L.G. Reverend Pierre Gibault and the Old Northwest. MA thesis. Loyola University (Chicago). 1936.
D 249

DRAYER, ADAM M. A History of Catholic Secondary Education in the Diocese of Scranton, Pennsylvania. Ph.D. thesis. Fordham University. 1953. vi, 252p.
D 250

DRISCOLL, MAURICE A. "A Martyr of Charity: the Reverend Francis X. Seelos, C.SS.R.," Central Blatt and Social Justice, v. 21 (1929), 356-358, 392-394; v. 22 (1929), 52-54, 95-97, 141-143, 176-178.
D 251

DRISCOLL, MAURICE A. "The Reverend Joseph Wissel, C.SS. R., Redemptorist Missionary," Central Blatt and Social Justice, v. 20 (1927), 284-286, 358-359, 394-395; v. 21 (1927), 52-

53, 88-89, 130-134, 177-179, 249-250.
D 252

DRURY, CLIFFORD M. "Nez Perce 'Delegation' of 1831," Oregon Historical Quarterly, v. 36 (1930), 283-287.
D 253

DUBOIS, JOHN. "Bishop Dubois on New York in 1836," United States Catholic Historical Society Records and Studies, v. 10 (1917), 124-129.
D 254

DUBOURG, WILLIAM. "Correspondence with Propaganda," St. Louis Catholic Historical Review, v. 1 (1918), 73-80, 127-145, 184-198, 300-311; v. 2 (1920), 43-52, 130-150, 210-224; v. 3 (1921), 106-150, 191-222.
D 255

DUBOURG, WILLIAM. "Rt. Rev. Bishop DuBourg to Rev. S. Bruté, St. Mary's College, Baltimore, Md.," American Catholic Historical Researches, v. 4 (1887), 137-138. D 256

DUBUISSON, E.L. "Mission of Rev. Father E.L. Dubuisson in Northern Pennsylvania, U.S.A. in January, 1835," American Catholic Historical Researches, v. 4 (1887), 169-178.
D 257

DUBUISSON, E.L. "St. Joseph's Church, Philadelphia in 1836," American Catholic Historical Researches, v. 4 (1887), 179-180.
D 258

DUBUISSON, STEPHEN L. "Short Account of the Maryland Province Forty-three Years Ago," Woodstock Letters, v. 13 (1884), 119-122.
D 259

DUBUISSON, STEPHEN L. "A Sketch of the Maryland Province Written a Hundred Years Ago," Woodstock Letters, v. 70 (1941), 375-382.
D 260

DUBUQUE (DIOCESE) SYNOD, 1st, 1871. Statuta lata et promulgata a Clementi Smyth [ep.] in synodo prima dioecesana. Dubuquii, mense Maii, A.D.

1871, habita. Dubuquii, Rich
& Ryan, 1871. 19p. D 261
DUBUQUE (DIOCESE) SYNOD,
2nd, 1901. [Statutes of the
second diocesan synod] xiv,
140, [6] p. D 262
DUBUQUE, IOWA (ARCHDIOCESE)
SYNOD, 3rd, 1905. Synodus
dioecesana dubuquensis tertia,
die 4a mensis Aprilis A.D.
1905, in ecclesia cathedrali
Sancti Raphaelis Archangeli
dubuquensi habita. A Joanne
Joseph Keane, archiepiscopo
dubuquensi. [n.p., n.d.]
xiii, 1 1., 3p. D 263
DUBUQUE (DIOCESE) SYNOD,
4th, 1908. Synodus dioecesana
dubuquensis quarta die 31
Martii 1908 in ecclesia cathedrali Sancti Raphaelis Archangeli dubuquensi habita.
A Joanne Joseph Keane, [ep.]
[n.p., n.d.] xiv, 7p. D 264
DUBUQUE (DIOCESE) SYNOD,
5th, 1911. Synodus dioecesana
dubuquensis quinta die 16 Nov.
1911 in ecclesia cathedrali
Sancti Raphaelis Archangeli
dubuquensis habita a Jacobo Joanne Keane [ep.1 [n.p., n.d.]
xiv, [2], 8p. D 265
DUERINCK, J.B. Une année
de séjour chez les Pottowa-
tomies 1850. Lettre du P.J.B.
Duerinck S.J. au R.P. De
Smet S.J. in Collection de
Précis Historiques IX [Bruxelles
1858] in 168 p. 577/586.
D 266
DUERR, HELEN. "Benedictines
of Logan County," Arkansas
History Quarterly, v. (1955).
D 267
DUFFEE, F. HAROLD. 'Reminis-
cences of the Rev. Wm. Hogan,
Rev. William V. Harold, and
the Memorial Vow of Father
Cartier," American Catholic
Historical Researches, v. 8
(1891), 76-80. D 268
DUFFEE, PETER BAPTIST.
Your Portiuncula, 1844-1944;
History of St. Francis Church,

New York City. New York.
St. Francis Rectory. 1944.
46p. D 269
DUFFY, J.A. "Coming of Age of
the Catholic Trade Book,"
Publisher's Weekly, v. 157
(1950), 978-986. D 270
DUFOUR, CHARLES L. (ed.).
St. Patrick's of New Orleans,
1833-1958. New Orleans:
St. Patrick's Parish, 1958.
xiii, 137. D 271
DUGAN, FRANCIS XAVIER.
English Catholic Refugee Inter-
prises [sic] in the American
Colonies, 1558-1632. MA
thesis. Catholic University.
1925. 69p. D 272
DUGGAN, THOMAS C. The
Catholic Church in Connecticut,
New York. State History Co.
1930. xx, 622p. D 273
DUGGAR, SISTER ANNA CLARE.
Catholic Institutions of the
Walla Walla Valley, 1847-
1950. MA thesis. Seattle
University. 1953. 310p.
D 274
DUHIGG, T.S. "Most Rev.
Francis Satolli, D.D.," Cath-
olic World, v. 58 (1893),
306-320. port. D 275
DULUTH, MINN. (DIOCESE).
Statutes of the diocese of
Duluth, Collegeville, Minn.,
Record press, St. John's Uni-
versity [1912]. 160p. D 276
DUNIGAN, DAVID R. A History
of Boston College. Milwaukee.
Bruce. 1947. xviii, 362p.
D 277
DUNN, JACOB PRATT. Missions
to the Quabache. Indianapolis.
Bowen-Merrill Co. 1902.
Indiana Historical Society
Publication, v. 3, no. 4, 255-
330. D 278
DUNN, JAMES J. "Scenes of the
Huron Mission," American
Catholic Historical Researches,
v. 5 (1888), 105, 121.
D 279
DUNN, JOSEPH. The Brendan
Problem. Catholic Historical

Review, v. 1 (1921), 395-477.
D 280

DUNN, J. P. "Father Gibault: the Patriot Priest of the Northwest," Illinois State Historical Society. Transactions, v. 10 (1905), 15-35. D 281

DUNN, LOUIS V. Catholic Church in Clinton County (Iowa). Clinton?, Iowa. 1907. 114p. incl. front., illus., plates, ports. D 282

DUNN, WILLIAM E. "Apache Mission on the San Saba River," Southwest Historical Quarterly, v. 17 (1914), 379-414. D 283

DUNN, WILLIAM E. "Missionary activities among the Eastern Apaches Previous to the Founding of San Saba Mission," Texas State Historical Association Quarterly, v. 15 (1912), 186-200. D 284

DUNNE, PETER MASTEN. "Jesuits begin the West Coast Missions," Pacific Historical Review, v. 4 (1935), 131-142. D 285

DUNNE, PETER MASTEN. Pioneer Black Robes on the West Coast, Berkeley. University of California Press. 1940. xiii, 286p. illus., maps. D 286

DUNNE, PETER MASTEN. Pioneer Jesuits in Northern Mexico. Berkeley. University of California Press. 1944. vii-x, 277p., front., ports., fold. map. D 287

DUNNE, PETER MASTEN. "Salvatierra's Legacy to Lower California," The Americas, v. 7 (1950), 31-50. D 288

DURANQUET, H. "The Prisons and Hospitals of New York," Letter dated New York, Nov. 5, 1882, Woodstock Letters, v. 12 (1883), 183-185. D 289

DURATSCHEK, SISTER M. CLAUDIA. The Beginnings of Catholicism in South Dakota. Washington. Catholic University. 1943. xiii, 271p. port., map. D 290

DURATSCHEK, SISTER M. CLAUDIA. Crusading Along Sioux Trails. St. Meinrad, Ind. The Grail. 1947. xii, 334p. illus. D 291

DURIEU, PAUL. "Letter dated Inshomish, Oregon, July 1, 1859," Annals of the Propagation of the Faith, Baltimore, v. 21 (1860), 211-223.
D 292

DURIEU, PAUL. "Lettre de M. Paul Durieu, Oblat de Marie Immaculée à ses parents. Orégon des Inshomish le 1er juillet, 1859," Annales de la Propagation de la Foi, v. 32 (1860), 262-279. D 293

DURKIN, JOSEPH T. "The Case of the Pontifical Consul at New York in 1876," Catholic Historical Review, v. 28 (1943), 499-503. D 294

DURKIN, JOSEPH T. "Catholic Training for Maryland Catholics, 1773-1786," United States Catholic Historical Society Records and Studies, v. 32 (1941), 70-82. D 295

DURKIN, JOSEPH T. "The First Catholic Chaplains in the United States Army," Thought, v. 16 (1941), 421-432.
D 296
The story of the commissioning of Fathers John McElroy and Anthony Roy in 1848.

DURKIN, JOSEPH T. General Sherman's Son: The Life of Thomas Ewing Sherman, S.J. New York. Farrar, Straus and Cudahy, 1959. ix, 276p.
D 297

DURKIN, JOSEPH T. (ed.). John Dooley, Confederate Soldier; His War Journal. Washington. Georgetown University. 1945. xiii, 244p.
D 298

DURKIN, JOSEPH T. (ed.). "Journal of the Rev. Adam Marshall, Schoolmaster, USS North Carolina, 1824-1825," American Catholic Historical Society of Philadelphia Records,

119

v. 53 (1942), 152-168; v. 54
(1943), 44-65.   D 299
DUROCHER, AURELE A. "Mark
Twain and the Roman Catholic
Church," Journal of the Central
Mississippi Valley American
Studies Association, v. 1
(1960), 32-43.   D 300
DUTTO, L.A. "Father Luis
[Cancer dé] Barbastro,"
American Ecclesiastical Review,
v. 27 (1902), 59-71, 160-173.
                        D 301
DUVAL, SISTER MARY FERDINAND.
The Development of Catholic
Education in North Dakota.
MA thesis. University of
Notre Dame. vi, 52p. D 302
DWORACSYK, EDWARD J.
(comp.). Church Records of
Panna Maria, Texas. Chicago.
Polish Roman Catholic Union
of America. 1945. 64p.
                        D 303
DWORACZYK, EDWARD J. The
First Polish Colonies of A-
merica in Texas. San Antonio,
Texas. Naylor Co. 1936. xix,
291p. incl. front., illus.,
ports., plan.   D 304
DWYER, JOHN T. One Hundred
Years an Orphan. St.
Vincent's Home for Boys at San
Rafael, 1855-1955. Fresno.
Academy Library Guild. 1955.
160p.   D 305
DWYER, R.J. "American Laity,"
Commonweal, v. 60 (Aug. 27,
1954), 503-506.   D 306
DWYER, ROBERT J. "Pioneer
Bishop: Lawrence Scanlan,
1843-1915," Utah Historical
Quarterly, v. 20 (1952).
                        D 307
DYMPNA, SISTER. Mother
Caroline and the School
Sisters of Notre Dame in North
America. St. Louis. Wood-
ward and Tiernan. 1928. 2v.
front., plates, ports. D 308

- E -
EARLEY, THOMAS J. Padres and
People of Salinas (Calif.).

Fresno. Academy Library
Guild. 1955. 98p.   E 1
"EARLY ANNALS OF CATHOLIC-
ITY IN NEW JERSEY," Cath-
olic World, v. 21 (1875),
565-570.   E 2
"EARLY HISTORY OF THE CATH-
OLIC CHURCH ON THE
ISLAND OF NEW YORK," Cath-
olic World, v. 10 (1869),
413-420.   E 3
"EARLY MISSIONS ON THE
MENOMINEE RIVER," Wiscon-
sin Magazine of History, v. 3
(1920), 237.   E 4
"EARLY PASTORS OF EAST
RUTHERFORD," Provincial
Annals (Province of the Most
Holy Name, O.F.M.), v. 7
(1947), 37-44.   E 5
EASBY-SMITH, JAMES S.
Georgetown University ...
1789-1907. New York. Lewis
Publishing Co. 1907. 2 v.
illus., plates, ports., facsims.
                      E 6
EAST TENNESSEE DEANERY
COUNCIL OF THE NASHVILLE
DIOCESAN COUNCIL OF CATH-
OLIC WOMEN. East Tennessee
Deanery Handbook. unp. 1952.
n.p. illus., map.   E 7
Has some brief historical
sketches of the churches of
eastern Tennessee.
EASTERLY, FREDERICK J.
Foundations of the Vincentians
in the United States, 1816-
1835. MA thesis. Catholic
University. 1938. 104p.
                      E 8
EASTERLY, FREDERICK J. The
Life of the Rt. Rev. Joseph
Rosati, First Bishop of St.
Louis, 1789-1843. Washington.
Catholic University. 1942.
xi, 203p.   E 9
"EASTERN CATHOLICS IN AMER-
ICA," The Lamp, v. 47
(1949), 9-11 (Ruthenians),
77-79 (Ukranians), 139-141
(Roumanian), 198-200 (Italo-
Greeks), 357-359 (Melkites).
                      E 10

120

EASTMAN, SISTER AUGUSTINE.
A Study of the Release-time
Religious Education Program
in the Diocese of Syracuse.
MA thesis. Villanova. 1946.
94p.   E 11
EBERSCHWEILER, FREDERIK.
"An Indian Clergy Impossible,"
Catholic World, v. 65 (1897),
815-824.   E 12
EBERSCHWEILER, FREDERIK.
"Eine neue Mission in Gernen
Nordwesten. Die Katholischen
Missionen." XV (1887), 137p.
Gros Ventres & Assiniboines.
                              E 13
ECCLESTON, SAMUEL. "State of
Religion in the Diocese of
Baltimore, 1838," American
Catholic Historical Researches,
v. 9 (1892), 138-142.   E 14
ECHELE, CYRIL T. "An Ameri-
can Povrello (1877-1949),"
Social Justice Review, v. 42
(1949), 117-119.   E 15
Peter Maurin.
"AN ECHO OF THE OLD ORDER
OF CHURCH AND STATE IN
LOUISIANA," American Catholic
Historical Society of Phila-
delphia Records, v. 24 (1914),
288-295.   E 16
ECKERT, R.P. "A Missionary in
the Wilderness," Catholic
World, v. 144 (1937), 590-
595.   E 17
A biographical sketch of
Mazzuchelli, based on his
Memoirs.
ECKHART, ADALBERT. "The
Thuringian Friars in the New
World," Provincial Annals
(Province of the Most Holy
Name, O.F.M.), v. 5
(1946), 330-341.   E 18
EDWARDS, LAWRENCE E. The
Desmetiana of Saint Louis Uni-
versity. MA thesis. Saint
Louis University. 1937. 138p.
                              E 19
EDWARDS, MARTHA L. "A
Problem of Church and State
in the 1870's," Mississippi Val-
ley Historical Review, v. 11

(1924) 37-53.   E 20
A good treatment of the
experiment of appointing
Indian agents from a list of
candidates submitted by
religious organizations.
EDWINA, SISTER M. "The
Franciscan Sisters of St.
Joseph," Polish American
Studies, v. 5 (1948), 8-13.
                              E 21
EGAN, SISTER M. FRANCIS
LORETTA. The Defeat of
Rufus King - His Racial and
Religious Prejudices. MA
thesis. St. John's University,
N.Y., 1941. mss.   E 22
EGAN, MAURICE FRANCIS.
The Hierarchy of the Roman
Catholic Church in the United
States. Philadelphia. George
Barrie. 1888. 2v. illus.,
plates.   E 23
EGAN, MAURICE FRANCIS.
Recollections of a Happy Life.
New York. George H. Doran
Co. 1924. xi, 17-374p.
front., plate, ports.   E 24
EGAN, MAURICE FRANCIS. Ten
Years Near the German
Frontier. New York. George
H. Doran Co. 1919. xiii,
17-364p. front., plate, ports.
                              E 25
EGAN, MAURICE FRANCIS. "The
U.S. and the Vatican," Colum-
bia, v. 1 (Aug., 1921), 5.
                              E 26
EGLER, RAYMOND OTTMAN.
The Rule of St. Benedict as
Adapted to American Conditions.
MA thesis. University of
Notre Dame. 1936. vi, 110p.
                              E 27
EL PASO (DIOCESE) SYNOD,
1st., 1930. Synodus dioecesana
elpasensis prima ab Antonio
J. Schuler, S.J. [ep.] cele-
brata El Paso in ecclesia
cathedrali S. Patritii, die
3a junii A.D. 1930. [El Paso,
Typis "Revista catolica", 1930]
xviii, 31, [2] p.   E 28
ELDER, DAVID PAUL. The Old

121

Spanish Missions of Calif-
ornia. San Francisco. 1913.
v, 89p. mounted front.,
mounted illus., mounted
plates.   E 29
ELDER, WILLIAM HENRY.
Character Glimpses of the Rt.
Rev. William Henry Elder,
Second Archbishop of Cincin-
nati. Cincinnati, Pustet. 1911.
181p.   E 30
ELEANORE, SISTER MARY.
Mother Mary Ignatius of the
Holy Child Jesus. Philadelphia.
Peter Reilly Co. 1949. vii,
200p.   E 31
ELEANORE, SISTER MARY. On
the King's Highway. New York.
Appleton. 1931. xi, 347p.
front., plates, ports.   E 32
  Well written history of the
  Sisters of the Holy Cross of
  the Immaculate Conception,
  Notre Dame, Indiana.
ELEANORE, SISTER MARY. "Por-
trait of a Valiant Woman,"
American Catholic Historical
Society of Philadelphia Re-
cords, v. 57 (1946), 201-
218.   E 33
  Cornelia Connelly, born
  1809, died 1897, convert and
  foundress of the Society of
  the Holy Child Jesus.
ELIZABETH MARIE, SISTER.
Academy for a Century. St.
Paul. Central Publishing Com-
pany. 1951. 89p.   E 34
  The history of St. Joseph's
  Academy, St. Paul, Minnesota,
  the first school of the Sisters
  of St. Joseph in Minnesota.
ELLARD, GERALD. "The American Scene, 1926-1951," Orate
Fratres, v. 25 (1951) 500-
508.   E 35
  A brief survey of twenty-five
  years development of the
  liturgical apostolate.
ELLIOTT, RICHARD R. "The
Apostolate of Father Baraga
among the Chippewas and Whites
of Lake Superior," American
Catholic Quarterly Review, v.

21 (1896), 596-617.   E 36
ELLIOTT, RICHARD R. "The
Bones and Ashes of the
Martyred Recollect Father
Constantin Delhalle, Who Was
the Founder and First Pastor
of St. Anne's Church, Detroit,"
American Catholic Historical
Researches, v. 13 (1896) 17-
22.   E 37
ELLIOTT, RICHARD R. "Cath-
olicity in Detroit," American
Catholic Historical Researches,
v. 13 (1896), 98-110. E 38
ELLIOTT, RICHARD R. "The
Chippewas and Ottawas:
Father Baraga's Books in
Their Language," American
Catholic Quarterly Review, v.
22 (1897), 18-46.   E 39
ELLIOTT, RICHARD R. "The
Chippewas of Lake Superior,"
American Catholic Quarterly
Review, v. 21 (1896), 354-
373.   E 40
ELLIOTT, RICHARD R. "The
Classical Academy of St.
Anne's of Detroit during the
'thirties' under Bishop Rese,"
American Catholic Historical
Researches, v. 14 (1897),
146-155.   E 41
ELLIOTT, RICHARD R. "The
Episcopate of Bishop Baraga,"
American Catholic Quarterly
Review, v. 11 (1897), 465-
492.   E 42
ELLIOTT, RICHARD R. "First
Irish Catholic Parochial Or-
ganization Established in the
Western States," American
Catholic Historical Researches,
v. 12 (1895), 128-139. E 43
ELLIOTT, RICHARD R. "Frederick
Baraga among the Ottawas,"
American Catholic Quarterly
Review, v. 21 (1896) 106-
129.   E 44
ELLIOTT, RICHARD R. "The
Glorious Record of an Illus-
trious Priest of the Diocese of
Detroit. The Septuagenarian,
Father Amandus Van Den
Driessche," American Catholic

Historical Researches, v. 19 (1902), 160-168. E 45

ELLIOTT, RICHARD R. "The Interdict of the Côte du Nord Est, Suburban Church of Detroit by Bishop Flaget, February 17th, 1817," American Catholic Historical Researches, v. 13 (1896), 81-90. E 46

ELLIOTT, RICHARD R. (ed.). "The Jesuit Manuscript," United States Catholic Historical Magazine," v. 4 (1891-1892), 141-164, 290-327, 440-453. E 47
An account book of the Huron mission of Detroit 1733-1751, written by Father Portier.

ELLIOTT, RICHARD R. "The Jesuit Missionaries who Labored in the Lake Superior Region during the 17th and 18th Centuries," Michigan Pioneer and Historical Collections, v. 33 (1903), 22-35. port. (of Richard R. Elliott). E 48

ELLIOTT, RICHARD R. "The Last of the Huron Missions," American Catholic Quarterly Review, v. 23 (1898), 526-549. E 49

ELLIOTT, RICHARD R. "The Recollects at Detroit during nearly all the Eighteenth Century," American Catholic Quarterly Review, v. 23 (1898), 759-778. E 50

ELLIOTT, RICHARD R. "The Relations of the Catholic Church with the Indians in North America," American Catholic Quarterly Review, v. 23 (1898), 45-70. E 51

ELLIOTT, RICHARD R. "Rev. Thomas Cullen, Pioneer Catholic Priest of Detroit, 1833-1862," American Catholic Historical Researches, v. 13 (1896), 177-185. E 52

ELLIOTT, RICHARD R. "Secularization of Catholic Indian Education," American Catholic Quarterly Review, v. 25 (1900) 148-168. E 53

ELLIOTT, RICHARD R. "Sketch of the Life and Times of Rev. Gabriel Richard of Detroit, Michigan," American Catholic Historical Researches, v. 14 (1897), 50-61. E 54
Biographical sketch of Father St. Michael Edgar Evelyn Shawe, first pastor of the Cathedral of Sts. Peter and Paul, Detroit, Michigan, born 1792, died 1853.

ELLIOTT, RICHARD R. "The Sulpitians at the Cradle of the American Hierarchy," American Catholic Quarterly Review, v. 24 (1899), 99-123. E 55

ELLIOTT, RICHARD R. "Two Centuries of Catholicity in Detroit," American Catholic Quarterly Review, v. 26 (1901), 499-523. E 56

ELLIOTT, RICHARD R. "Very Reverend Martin Kundig, the Apostle of Charity in Detroit," American Catholic Historical Researches, v. 15 (1898), 6-10. E 57

ELLIOTT, WALTER. "Bishop Baraga," American Catholic Quarterly Review, v. 21 (1896), 106-130, 354-374, 596-618; v. 22 (1897), 18-46, 465-492. E 58

ELLIOTT, WALTER. "Bishop Baraga, The Apostle of the Chippewas," Catholic World, v. 73 (1901), 78-87. E 59

ELLIOTT, WALTER. The Life of Father Hecker. New York. Columbus Press. 1891. 427p. 3 ports., incl. front. E 60

ELLIOTT, WALTER. "Father Walworth, a Character Sketch," Catholic World, v. 73 (1901), 320-337. E 61

ELLIS, FLORENCE HAWLEY, AND EDWIN BACA. "The Apuntes of Father J. B. Ralliere," New Mexico Historical Review, XXXII (1957), 10-35, 259-273. E 62
A good edition of the notes

on the history of the Catholic Church in New Mexico as seen by one of the famous secular priests of the Southwest.

ELLIS, FLORENCE H. "Tomé and Father J.B.R.," New Mexico Historical Review, v. 30 (1955), 82-114; July, 195-220. port. E 63
An account of the activity of Father Ralliere.

ELLIS, JOHN T. American Catholicism. Chicago: University of Chicago, 1956. xiii, 208p. E 64
A collection of four essays on the general history of the Church in the United States. An excellent introductory survey.

ELLIS, JOHN TRACY. "American Catholicism in 1906: An Historical Perspective," American Benedictine Review, V. 11 (1960), 1-20. E 65

ELLIS, JOHN T. American Catholics and the Intellectual Life. Chicago: Heritage Foundation, 1956. 63p. E 66
This essay has stirred up much discussion. The validity of some assumptions and conclusions have been seriously questioned.

ELLIS, JOHN T. "American Catholics and the Intellectual Life-- Some Reactions," National Catholic Educational Association Bulletin. v. 53 (1956), 105-112. E 67

ELLIS, JOHN TRACY. "Archbishop Carroll and the Liturgy in the Vernacular," Worship, v. 24 (1952), 245-252. E 68

ELLIS, JOHN TRACY. "Can We Have a History of the Church in the United States?" Catholic University Bulletin. v. 13 (March, 1945), 2-3, 11. E 69

ELLIS, JOHN TRACY. "Cardinal Gibbons and Philadelphia," American Catholic Historical Society of Philadelphia Records, v. 58 (1947), 87-102. E 70

ELLIS, JOHN T. "Cardinal Gibbons and New York," United States Catholic Historical Society Records and Studies, v. 39-40 (1952), 5-32. E 71

ELLIS, JOHN TRACY (ed.). "Cardinal Gibbons' Assistance to Pastor's History of the Popes," Catholic Historical Review, v. 34 (1948), 306-318. E 72

ELLIS, JOHN TRACY. "The Centennial of the First Plenary Council of Baltimore," American Ecclesiastical Review, v. 126 (1952), 321-350. E 73

ELLIS, JOHN TRACY. "A Challenge to the American Church on its One Hundredth Birthday," Catholic Historical Review, v. 30 (1944), 290-298. E 74

ELLIS, JOHN TRACY, "Catholics in Colonial America," American Ecclesiastical Review, CXXXVI (1957), 11-27, 100-119, 184-196, 265-276, 304-307. E 75

ELLIS, JOHN TRACY. "Church and State: An American Catholic Tradition," Harper's Magazine, v. 207 (1953), 63-67. E 76
Contains a number of statements of American Catholic Bishops on the stand for separation of Church and State.

ELLIS, JOHN T. (ed.). Documents of American Catholic History. Milwaukee. Bruce, 1956. xxiv, 677p. E 77
The term "Catholic History" is taken in a very wide sense, and does not mean that the contents are limited to the history of the Church.

ELLIS, JOHN TRACY. The Formative Years of the Catholic University of America. Washington. American Catholic Historical Association. 1946. xiv, 415p.   E 78

ELLIS, JOHN T. A Guide to American Catholic History. Milwaukee. Bruce, 1959. viii, 147p.   E 79
Classified annotated bibliography.

ELLIS, JOHN TRACY. "A Guide to the Baltimore Cathedral Archives," Catholic Historical Review, v. 32 (1946), 341-360.   E 80

ELLIS, JOHN TRACY. "Half Century of Financial Support," Catholic University of America Bulletin, v. 21 (1953), 10-12, table.   E 81
A study of the collection for Catholic University taken each year throughout the United States.

ELLIS, JOHN TRACY. The Life of Cardinal Gibbons, Archbishop of Baltimore, 1834-1921. Milwaukee. Bruce. 1952. 2v. illus.   E 82

ELLIS, JOHN TRACY (comp.). "Old Catholic Newspapers in Some Eastern Catholic Libraries," Catholic Historical Review, v. 33 (1947), 302-305.   E 83

ELLIS, JOHN TRACY. "Peter Guilday," Catholic Historical Review, v. 33 (1947), 257-268.   E 84

ELLIS, JOHN T. "Saint Patrick in America," American Benedictine Review, v. 12 (1961), 415-430.   E 85

ELLIS, JOHN TRACY (comp.). A Select Bibliography of the History of the Catholic Church in the United States. New York. McMullen. 1947. 96p.   E 86

ELLIS, JOHN TRACY. "The Sixtieth Birthday of the American Ecclesiastical Review," American Ecclesiastical Review, v. 121 (1949), 261-280.   E 87

ELLIS, JOHN TRACY (ed.). "Some Newman Letters from the Baltimore Archives," Catholic Historical Review, v. 31 (1946), 437-445.   E 88

ELLIS, JOHN TRACY. "A Venerable Church of Maryland," Woodstock Letters, v. 78 (1949), 133-139.   E 89

ELLIS, H.D. "The Russian Catholic Center in San Francisco, California," Eastern Churches Quarterly, v. 13 (1959) 75-80.   E 90

ELZNIC, WILLIAM H. "Bohemians in Richland County," North Dakota Historical Society Collections, v. 4 (1915), 62-80.   E 91

EMERICK, A.J. "The Colored Mission of Our Lady of the Blessed Sacrament," Woodstock Letters, v. 42 (1913), 69-82, 175-188, 352-362; v. 43 (1914), 10-23, 181-194.   E 92

EMERICK, A.J. "The Jesuits in Florida," Woodstock Letters, v. 55 (1926), 215-225.   E 93

EMERY, SUSAN L. A Catholic Stronghold and Its Making. Boston. Geo. H. Ellis. ca. 1910. 12, 95p. plates, ports.   E 94

ENGLEBERT, OMER. Last of the Conquistadors: Junipero Serra (1713-1784). New York. Harcourt, Brace, 1956. ix, 368p.   E 95

ENGELHARDT, ZEPHYRIN. "Die deutsche Franziskanermission unter den Menominee Indianern," Die Katholischen Missionen, v. 13 (1885), 137-139, 157-160, 181-183, 201-203, 225-227.   E 96

ENGELHARDT, ZEPHYRIN. "Florida's First Bishop," Catholic Historical Review, v. 4 (1918), 479-485.   E 97

ENGELHARDT, ZEPHYRIN. The Franciscans in Arizona. Harbor Springs, Mich. Holy Childhood Indian School. 1899.

236p. front., illus., ports.,
fold map.   E 98
ENGELHARDT, ZEPHYRIN. The
Franciscans in California.
Harbor Springs, Mich. Holy
Childhood Indian School. 1897.
xvi, 516p. front., illus.
(incl. map).   E 99
ENGELHARDT, ZEPHYRIN. The
Holy Man of Santa Clara. San
Francisco. James H. Barry
Co. 1909. 199p. front.,
illus., plates, port.   E 100
Biography of Magin Catala,
1761-1830.
ENGELHARDT, ZEPHYRIN. Mis-
sion la Concepcion Purisima
de Maria Santisima. Santa
Barbara, Calif. Mission
Santa Clara. 1932. ix, 131p.
incl. front., illus., maps,
plan, diagr.   E 101
Bound with Mission Santa
Ines.
ENGELHARDT, ZEPHYRIN. Mis-
sion Nuestra Senor de la
Soledad. Santa Barbara,
Calif. Mission Santa Barbara.
1929. v, 88p. front., illus.
(incl. map, facsim.).   E 102
ENGELHARDT, ZEPHYRIN. Mis-
sion San Carlos Borromeo
(Caremlo). Santa Barbara,
Calif. Mission Santa Barbara,
1934. xxi, 264p. incl. front.
(port.), illus.   E 103
ENGELHARDT, ZEPHYRIN. Mis-
sion San Juan Bautista. Santa
Barbara, Calif. Mission Santa
Barbara. 1931. viii, 148p.
incl. front., illus., ports.,
maps, facsims.   E 104
ENGELHARDT, ZEPHYRIN. Mis-
sion San Luis Obispo in the
Valley of the Bears. Santa
Barbara, Calif. Mission Santa
Barbara. 1933. x, 213p. incl.
front., illus., ports., maps.
                         E 105
ENGELHARDT, ZEPHYRIN. Mission Santa Ines. Santa Barbara,
Calif. Mission Santa Barbara.
1932. ix, 194p. incl. front.,
illus., ports., map, plans.

                              E 106
ENGELHARDT, ZEPHYRIN.
Missionary Labors of the
Franciscans in the Early
Days. Chicago. Franciscan
Herald Press. 1913-1914. 2v.
                         E 107
ENGELHARDT, ZEPHYRIN. The
Missions and Missionaries of
California. San Francisco.
James H. Barry Co. 1908-1915.
4v. front., illus. (incl.
facsims.), plates, ports.,
maps (part fold.), tables.
                         E 108
ENGELHARDT, ZEPHYRIN. San
Antonio de Padua, the Mission
in the Sierras. Santa Barbara,
Calif. Mission Santa Barbara.
1929. 140p. front., illus.
                         E 109
ENGELHARDT, ZEPHYRIN. San
Buenaventura, the Mission by
the Sea. Santa Barbara,
Calif. Mission Santa Barbara,
1930. ix, 166p. incl. front.,
illus., ports., map, plan,
facsims.   E 110
ENGELHARDT, ZEPHYRIN. San
Francisco. James H. Barry
Co. 1920. xiv, 358p. front.,
illus. (incl. port.), maps,
plans, facsims.   E 111
ENGELHARDT, ZEPHYRIN. San
Fernando Rey, the Mission of
the Valley. Chicago, Fran-
ciscan Herald Press. 1927.
xi, 160p. incl. front., illus.
                         E 112
ENGELHARDT, ZEPHYRIN.
San Francisco, or Mission
Dolores. Chicago. Franciscan
Herald Press. 1924. xv, 432p.
incl. front., illus., fold.
plan.   E 113
ENGELHARDT, ZEPHYRIN. San
Gabriel Mission and the Begin-
nings of Los Angeles. San
Gabriel, Calif. Mission San
Gabriel. 1927. xiv, 369p.
incl. front., illus.   E 114
ENGELHARDT, ZEPHYRIN. San
Juan Capistrano Mission. Los
Angeles, (Standard Printing Co.)

126

1922. xii, 259p. incl front.,
illus.   E 115
ENGELHARDT, ZEPHYRIN. San
Luis Rey Mission. San Fran-
cisco. James H. Barry Co.
1921. x, 265p. incl. front.,
illus.   E 116
ENGELHARDT, ZEPHYRIN. San
Miguel Arcangel, the Mission
on the Highway. Santa
Barbara, Calif. Mission Santa
Barbara, 1929. 92p. front.,
illus.   E 117
ENGELHARDT, ZEPHYRIN. Santa
Barbara Mission. San Fran-
cisco. James H. Barry Co.
1923. xviii, 470p. incl. front.,
illus.   E 118
ENGELHARDT, ZEPHYRIN. "The
Writing of History," Franciscan
Educational Conference Report,
v. 4 (1922), 73-90.   E 119
ENGELHART, SISTER GONZAGA.
"The Daughters of St. Walburg
Cross the Ocean," The Bene-
dictine Review, v. 7 (1952),
29-32.   E 120
ENGLAND, JOHN. "American
Missions. Michigan and the
Northwest Territory," American
Catholic Historical Researches,
v. 11 (1894), 113-117. E 121
ENGLAND, JOHN. "Diurnal of the
Rt. Rev. John England, 1820-
1823," American Catholic
Historical Society of Philadelphia
Records, v. 6 (1895), 29-55,
184-224.   E 122
[ENGLAND, JOHN]. "Letters of
Bishop England to Hon. William
Gaston," United States Catholic
Historical Magazine, v. 4
(1891-1892), 55-58, 101-102,
165-185.   E 123
[ENGLAND, JOHN]. "Memoirs
of the Roman Catholic Church
in America (North Carolina),"
American Catholic Historical
Researches, v. 11 (1894), 119-
122.   E 124
ENGLAND, JOHN. The Works of
the Right Reverend John England,
ed. by Sebastian Messmer et
al. Cleveland. Arthur H.

Clark Co. 1908. 7v. E 125
ENGLISH, ADRIAN T. "The
Historiography of American
Catholic History," Catholic
Historical Review, v. 11
(1926), 561-597.   E 126
A discussion of only general
accounts or histories, e.g.
reports of Carroll (1785),
Flaget (1815), and Marechal
(1818) to Propaganda; also
the pamphlet of Patric Smyth
(1788); Claude Florent
Bouchard de la Poterie
(1789); John Dilhet, S.S.
(1810); John Grassi, S.J.
(1818); Laity's Directory
(1822); John England's Let-
ter of 1836; and general
works such as those of
Thomas D'Arcy McGee (1855);
Henry DeCourcey, John Gil-
mary Shea (1856); Charles
White (1868), and John O'
Kane Murray (1876).
ENGLISH, ADRIAN T. Historiog-
raphy of American Catholic
Church History, 1783-1884.
MA thesis. Catholic Uni-
versity. 1925. 48p.   E 127
ENNIS, SISTER MARY CLARE.
Mary Virginia Merrick and the
History of the Christ Child
Society. MA thesis. Xavier
University (Cincinnati). 1960.
88p.   E 128
EPPICH, SISTER MARY GEORGE.
History of St. Bridget of
Erin Parish, Saint Louis,
1853-1917. MA thesis, Saint
Louis University. 1951. 110p.
                          E 129
EPSTEIN, FRANCIS JAMES.
Decet Meminisse Fratrum; A
Necrology of the Diocesan
Priests of the Chicago Arch-
diocese, 1844-1936. Chicago.
J. F. Higgins ptg. co. 1937.
109p. front.   E 130
EPSTEIN, FRANCIS J. "History
in the Annals of the Leopoldine
Association," Illinois Catholic
Historical Review, v. 1
(1918), 225-233, (1919), 372-

378. E 131
ERBACHER, SEBASTIAN A. Catholic Higher Education for Men in the United States, 1850-1866. Washington. Catholic University of America. 1931. 143p. E 132

ERIE (DIOCESE) SYNOD, 1855, 1868. Statuta dioecesis eriensis lata in synodo dioecesana celebrata A.D. 1855 et in alia synodo A.D. 1868. Erie, Ex Officinis "Observatoris," 1869. 32p. E 133

ERIE, PA. (DIOCESE) SYNOD, 6th, 1912. Statuta dioeceseos eriensis in synodis dioecesanis lata, aucta et emendata et prout nunc prostant promulgata in synodo dioecesana sexta die 9. mensis Maii, 1912 habita. A Joanne Edmundo Fitzmaurice, episcopo eriensi. [n.p., n.d.] 72p. E 134

ERSKINE, MARJORY. Mother Philippine Duchesne. London. Longmans, Green and Co. 1926. xiii, 400p. front., port., plates. E 135

"ERSTE CONGRESS KATHOLISCHER SIOUX-INDIANER," Die Katholischen Missionen, v. 20 (1892), 16-19. E 136

"ERSTE KATHOLISCHE KIRCHE IN BROWN CO., MINN.," Central Blatt and Social Justice, v. 12 (1919), 149-150. E 137

"ERSTE PRIESTER AUS DEM STAMME DER CHIPPEWA INDIANER," Die Katholischen Missionen, v. 42 (1914), 212. E 138

"ERSTE DEUTSCHEN KATHOLIKEN IN NEW JERSEY," Central Blatt and Social Justice, v. 14 (1922), 367-368, 403-404. E 139

ESCHMANN, C.J. (tr. and ed.). "Kaskaskia Church Records," Illinois State Historical Society Transactions, v. 9 (1904), 394-413. E 140

ESCHMANN, C. J. (tr. and ed.). "Prairie du Rocher Church Records," Illinois State Historical Society Transactions, v. 8 (1903), 129-149. E 141

ESLING, C.H.A. "Catholicity in the Three Lower Counties," American Catholic Historical Society of Philadelphia Records, v. 1 (1884), 117-160. E 142

ESPERANZA, . "Oldest Church in the United States," American Catholic Historical Researches, v. 20 (1903), 133. E 143

ESPERANZA, . 'Right Rev. Juan Suarez, O.S.F., First Bishop of Florida," American Catholic Historical Researches, v. 16 (1899), 142-144. E 144

ESPINOSA, GILBERT. "New Mexico Santos," New Mexico Quarterly, v. 6 (1936), 181-189. E 145

ESPINOSA, JOSE E. Saints of the Valley: Christian Sacred Images in the History, Life and Folk Art of Spanish New Mexico. Albuquerque, N.M. University of New Mexico, 1960. 122p. E 146

ESPINOSA, J. MANUEL (tr. and ed.). "Documents; Account of the First Jesuit Missionary Journey across the Plains to Santa Fe," Mid-America, v. 9 (1938), 51-62. E 147

ESPINOSA, J. MANUEL. "Francisco de Florencia, S.J., 1619-1695, Our First Native Born Priest," Historical Bulletin, v. 13 (1935), 65-66. E 148

ESPINOSA, J. MANUEL. "Neapolitan Jesuits in the Colorado Frontier," Colorado Magazine, v. 15 (1938), 64-73. E 149

ESPINOSA, J. MANUEL. "New Mexico as a Historical Laboratory of the Good Neighbor Policy: With Special Reference to the Hispano-American Cul-

tural Contribution," The Americas, v. 2 (1945), 211-219.
E 150

ESPINOSA, J. MANUEL. "The Opening of the First Jesuit Mission in Colorado," Mid-America, v. 8 (1936), 272-275.
E 151

ESPINOSA, J. MANUEL. "Our Debt to the Franciscan Missionaries of New Mexico," The Americas, v. 1 (1944), 79-87.
E 152

ESPINOSA, J. MANUEL. "The Virgin in the Reconquest of New Mexico," Mid-America, v. 7 (1936), 79-87.
E 153

EUGENE, BROTHER ANGELUS. "Christian Brothers in Boy Welfare Work. A Century of Faith, Zeal and Service, 1848-1948," Social Justice Review, v. 41 (1948), 41-43, 79-82.
E 154

EVANS, JANE BROOKE. "Irish Priests in Early Florida," American-Irish Historical Society Journal, v. 32 (1941), 74-78.
E 155

EVANS, JOHN WHITNEY, "Catholics and the Blair Education Bill," Catholic Historical Review, v. 46 (1960), 273-298.
E 156
Bill for federal support of education proposed by Senator Blair of New Hampshire during 1880's.

EVANS, MARY ELLEN. The Spirit in Mercy. The Sisters of Mercy in the Archdiocese of Cincinnati: 1859-1958. Westminster, Md. Newman, 1959. xi, 346p.
E 157

EVANSVILLE (DIOCESE) SYNOD 1st. Statuta diocesis Evan-evicensis. Evansville, Moser Printing Co. 1948. xvi, 56p.
E 158

EVERETT, LAWRENCE P. "Our Lady in the American Ecclesiastical Review,"American Ecclesiastical Review, v. 121 (1949), 286-300.
E 159

EWING, RUSSELL C. "The First Histories and Historians of the Southwest (Texas, Arizona, New Mexico)," Arizona Quarterly, v. 2 (1946), 66-76.
E 160

EWING, RUSSELL C. "Modern Histories and Historians of the Spanish Southwest," Arizona Quarterly, v. 3 (1947), 71-82.
E 161

"EXPULSION OF THE JESUITS FROM LOUISIANA IN 1763," Woodstock Letters, v. 4 (1875), 88-100; v. 5 (1876), 161-173; v. 6 (1877), 19-30.
E 162

EXTENSION MAGAZINE. God on the Open Road. Extension Magazine. Chicago. 1953. 63p.
E 163
A booklet giving the times of Masses, Sundays, Holy days, and week days, Novenas, and other devotions in resort areas, large cities, and Catholic towns of North America.

"EXTRACT FROM A LETTER OF A JESUIT CHAPLAIN WITH THE CONFEDERATE ARMY DESCRIBING THE WORK OF THE SISTERS," Etudes, v. 19 (1867), 424-427.
E 164

"EXTRACT FROM A REPORT OF THE FATHER GENERAL OF THE JESUITS," Annals of the Propagation of the Faith, Baltimore, v. 19 (1950), 297-300.
E 165

EYRAUD, JEAN M. AND DONALD J. MILLET. History of St. John the Baptist Parish with Biographical Sketches. Marrero, La. Hope Haven Press. 1939. 144p. incl. ads, plates, ports., illus. E 166

- F -

FABER, SISTER MARY DE PAUL. The Luxemburger Gazette. A Catholic German Language Paper of the Middle West, 1872-1918. MA thesis. Catholic University. 1948. 74p. F 1

FAHERTY, W. B. "The First English-speaking Parish in Illinois," Mid-America, v. 9 (1938), 164-169. F 2

FAHEY, FRANK JOSEPH. The Sociological Analysis of a Negro Catholic Parish. Ph.D. thesis. University of Notre Dame. 1959. 216p. chart, table. F 3

FALL RIVER (DIOCESE) SYNOD, 1st, 1905. Statuta dioecesis riverormensis quae in synodo dioecesana prima die 28a Junii, A.D. 1905, in ecclesia pro-cathedrali beatissimae Mariae Virginis in Coelum Assumptae dicata in civitate Fall River habita sanxit et promulgavit Guilielmus Stang [ep.] Phila-delphia, The Dolphin press, 1905. 90p. F 4

FALLON, CHARLES D. All Hallows College: its Contribu-tion to the Church in the U-nited States, 1834-1865. MA thesis. Catholic University. 1935. 77p. F 5

FALLON, SISTER MARY LEO CLEMENT. Early New England Nuns. Ph.D. thesis. Boston College. 1936. 223p. F 6

FALLS, THOMAS B. "Develop-ment of the Diocese and Prov-ince of Philadelphia," Ameri-can Catholic Historical Society of Philadelphia Records, v. 64 (1953), 50-56. Maps, tables, statistics. F 7

FANNING, WILLIAM. Historical Sketch of St. Louis University. St. Louis, Mo. St. Louis University. 1908. 64p. illus. (incl. port.). F 8

FARGO (DIOCESE) SYNOD 1. Synodus diocesana Fargensis prima Milwauchiae. Bruce. 1941. xiv, 303p. F 9

FARGO, N. D. (DIOCESE) SYNOD, 2d, 1951. Synodus Diocesana Fargensis Secunda, e mandato

speciali, Aloisii Joseph Muench. Milwauchiae. Bruce. 1951. (c1952). xviii, 332p. F 10

FARLEY, JOHN M. "History of St. Patrick's Cathedral, New York. New York. Society of the Propagation of the Faith. 1908. 262p. plates, ports. F 11

FARLEY, JOHN MURPHY. The Life of John Cardinal Mc-Closkey, First Prince of the Church in America, 1810-1885. New York. Longmans, Green and Co. 1918. xiii, 401p. plates, 2 ports. (incl. front.). facsim. F 12

[FARMER, FERDINAND]. "Let-ters of Father Farmer," American Catholic Historical Researches, v. 5 (1888), 28-33. F 13

FARMER, FERDINAND. "(Why There Were No Bishops in Colonial Times) An Unpub-lished Letter dated Philadelphia, April 22, 1773," Woodstock Letters, v. 28 (1899), 173-178. F 14

FARRELL, ALLAN P. "The School Controversy (1891-1893)," Catholic Educational Review, v. 43 (1945), 203-207. F 15

FARRELL, JOHN T. "Arch-bishop Ireland and Manifest Destiny," Catholic Historical Review. v. 33 (1947), 269-301. F 16

FARRELL, JOHN T. "Background of the Taft Mission to Rome, Catholic Historical Review, v. 36 (1950), 1-32; v. 37 (1951), 1-22. F 17

FARRELLY, CLARENCE E. "The Foundation of the Catholic Church in Pocahontas County," Iowa Catholic Historical Re-view, v. 7 (June, 1934), 12-22. F 18

FARRELLY, SISTER M. NATALENA. Thomas Francis Meehan (1854-1943). New York.

FEDE, LORENZO M. "Lettera XL," Lettere Edificanti Provincia Napolitana, ser. 2 (1876-1877), 125-126.　F 43

FEDE, LORENZO M. "Lettera XX," Lettere Edificanti Provincia Napolitana, ser. 7 (1895), 50-52.　F 44

FEDE, LORENZO M. "Trinidad (Colorado) Conversione ed Abiure," Lettere Edificanti Provincia Napolitana, ser. 8, n. 2 (1900), 130-132.　F 45

"FEDERNAMEN DEUTSCHSPRACHIGER KATHOLIKEN AMERIKAS," Central Blatt and Social Justice, v. 11 (1918), 254.　F 46

FEENEY, LEONARD. "A Neglected Chapter of Catholic History: Our Poets," United States Catholic Historical Society Records and Studies, v. 27 (1937), 7-27.　F 47

FEIERTAG, SISTER LORETTA CLARE. American Public Opinion on the Diplomatic Relations between the United States and the Papal States (1847-1867). Washington. Catholic University. 1933. vii, 188p.　F 48

FEIKERT, SISTER M. OF ST. JOSEPH. The History of the Tidings, Official Organ of the Archdiocese of Los Angeles, 1895-1945. MA thesis. Catholic University. 1951. 154p.　F 49

FELIX, FATHER. "Bishop England's Institute of the Sisters of Mercy," American Ecclesiastical Review, v. 20 (1899), 254-264, 454-467.　F 50

FELL, SISTER MARIE LEONORE. Bishop Hughes and the Common School Controversy. MA thesis. Catholic University. 1936. 100p.　F 51

FELL, SISTER MARIE LEÓNORE. The Foundations of Nativism in American Textbooks. 1783-1860. Washington. Catholic University. 1941. ix, 259p.

FELLNER, FELIX. "Archabbot Boniface Wimmer and Historical Sources," American Catholic Historical Society of Philadelphia Records, v. 37 (1926), 299-304.　F 53

FELLNER, FELIX. "Erzabt Bonifaz Wimmer, O.S.B., und die Anfänge der St. Benedicti Abtei, Atchison, Kansas," Central Blatt and Social Justice, v. 21 (1928), 53-54, 89-91.　F 54

FELLNER, FELIX. "Father Oswald Moosmueller, the Pioneer Benedictine Historian of the United States," American Catholic Historical Society of Philadelphia Records, v. 34 (1923), 1-16.　F 55

FELLNER, FELIX. Phases of Catholicity in Western Pennsylvania during the Eighteenth Century. Latrobe, Archabbey Press. 1942. 30p.　F 56

FELLNER, FELIX. "The Rev. Theodore Brouwers, O.F.M.," American Catholic Historical Society of Philadelphia Records, v. 24 (1914), 356-363.　F 57

FELLNER, FELIX. "Trials and Triumphs of Catholic Pioneers in Western Pennsylvania," American Catholic Historical Society of Philadelphia Records, v. 34 (1923), 195-261, 287-343.　F 58

FENCL, LEONARD J. (tr. and ed.). "The Death of Father Jacques Marquette," Illinois Catholic Historical Review, v. 11 (1928), 147.　F 59

FENNELLY, CATHERINE. "Father Claude Jean Allouez, S.J.," American Catholic Historical Society of Philadelphia Records, v. 52 (1941), 12-24.　F 60

FENNER, SISTER GERTRUDE. The Daughters of Charity of St. Vincent de Paul in the Spanish American War. MA thesis. Villanova University. 1949. 68p. F 61

FENTON, JOHN H. The Catholic Vote. New Orleans. Hauser Press. 1960. xiii, 146p. F 62

FENTON, JOSEPH CLIFFORD. "The Councils of Baltimore and the Catholic Press," American Ecclesiastical Review, v. 136 (1957), 120-131. F 63

FENTON, JOSEPH CLIFFORD. "Devotion to the Holy Ghost and its American Advocates," American Ecclesiastical Review, v. 121 (1949), 486-501. F 64

FENTON, JOSEPH C. "Intellectual Standards among American Catholics," American Ecclesiastical Review, v. 135 (1956), 323-336. F 65
An excellent critical review of American Catholics and the Intellectual Life.

FENTON, JOSEPH CLIFFORD. "The Teaching of the Testem Benevolentiae," American Ecclesiastical Review, v. 129 (1953), 124-133. F 66
A theological discussion of the problem of Americanism, which questions the accuracy of the appellation "phantom heresy."

FENTON, JOSEPH CLIFFORD. "A Statement of Policy," American Ecclesiastical Review, v. 121 (1949), 332-340. F 67

FENTON, W.D. "Father Wilbur and His Work," Oregon Historical Society Quarterly, v. 10 (1909), 16-30. F 68

[FENWICK, BENEDICT]. "P. Anton Kohlman, S.J. am Sterbett Thomas Paine," Central Blatt and Social Justice, v. 14 (1922), 402-403. F 69

FERSTLER, INNOCENT. History of Our Lady of Angels Parish, East 113th St., New York. F 70

FESTENBERG-PAKISCH, WILHELM

VON. Die St. Peter und Paul's Gemeinde in Mankato, Minnesota. Mankato. 1899. 242p. plates, port. F 71

FERLAND, DAVID J. Plenary, Provincial and Synodal Legislation Concerning Liturgical Music in the United States as Causative and Resultant of the Enactments of the Third Council of Baltimore. Washington, 1955. F 72

FETH, SISTER VINCENT. A History of the Sisters of Notre Dame in Columbus: the First Fifty Years, 1855-1905. MA thesis. Xavier University (Cincinnati) 1957. ix, 117p. F 73

FICHTER, JOSEPH H. "The Profile of Catholic Religious Life," American Journal of Sociology, v. 58 (1952), 145-149. F 74

FICHTER, JOSEPH H., AND P. W. FACEY, "Social Attitudes of Catholic High School Students," American Catholic Sociological Review, v. 14 (1953), 94-105. F 75

FICHTER, JOSEPH H. Social Relations in the Urban Parish. Chicago. University of Chicago. 1954. 270p. F 76

FICHTER, JOSEPH. Southern Parish: the Dynamics of a City Church. Chicago. University of Chicago Press. 1951. ix, 283p. F 77

FIELD, MARIA A. Chimes of Mission Bells, and Historical Sketch of California and Her Missions. San Francisco. 1914. F 78

FIFTIETH ANNIVERSARY OF MURDER OF FR. LEO [HEINRICHS] MARKED IN DENVER. Provincial Annals, O.F.M. (New York) 15 (1958), 72-75 ports. F 79

FILLEY, SISTER MARY ROSELDA. Settlement and Growth of Clinton County, Illinois, with Special Reference to the Cath-

olic Church, 1825-1880. MA
thesis. University of Notre
Dame. 1955. 98p. F 80
FINCK, SISTER M. HELENA.
The Congregation of the Sisters
of Charity of the Incarnate
Word of San Antonio, Texas.
A Brief Account of Its Origin
and Its Work. Washington.
Catholic University. 1925.
vii, 232p. F 81
FINK, LEO GREGORY. Bally,
a Brief History of Goshen-
hoppen, Later Known as Church-
ville and Today as Bally.
Philadelphia. Jeffries and
Mainz Co. 1932. 16p.
plates. F 82
FINK, LEO GREGORY. "Father
Stommel, 'Church Builder,' "
American Historical Society of
Philadelphia Records, v. 48
(1937), 399. F 83
FINK, LEO GREGORY. "Monsignor
Heinen, Diocesan Missionary,"
American Catholic Historical
Society of Philadelphia Records,
v. 48 (1937), 147-203. F 84
FINK, LEO GREGORY. Monsignor
Heinen, Militant Missionary.
Philadelphia. Dolphin Press.
1937. 75p. F 85
FINK, LEO GREGORY. Old
Jesuit Trails in Penn's Forest.
New York. Paulist Press. 1936.
xv, 270p. incl. front., illus.
(incl. ports., map, facsims.).
F 86
FINK, LEO GREGORY. "Tradi-
tions of Bally," American
Catholic Historical Society of
Philadelphia Records, v. 54
(1943), 82-109. F 87
FINK, LEO GREGORY. "Tradi-
tions of Bally," Woodstock
Letters, v. 70 (1941), 350-
362; v. 71 (1942), 56-68.
F 88
FINN, BRENDAN A. "John Boyle
O'Reilly, 1844-1944," Catholic
World, v. 159 (1944), 410-
416. F 89
FINN, BRENDAN A. Twenty-Four
American Cardinals. Boston.

Bruce Humphries, Inc. 1948.
475p. F 90
FINN, FRANCIS. Story of His
Life as Told by Himself. New
York. Benziger. 1929. 236p.
F 91
FINN, WILLIAM J. Sharps and
Flats in Five Decades. New
York, Harper and Bros.
1947. x, 342p. F 92
The autobiography of the
former director of the fa-
mous Paulist Choristers.
FINNEGAN, DARRELL F. X.
Function of the Academic
Dean in American Catholic
Higher Education. Washington.
Catholic University. 1951.
x, 120p. diagrm, tables.
F 93
FINOTTI, JOSEPH M. Biblio-
graphia Catholica Americana.
New York. Catholic Publica-
tions House. 1872. 318p.
F 94
Subtitle: "A list of works
written by Catholic authors
and published in the United
States, Part I from 1784
to 1820 inclusive."
FINOTTI, J.M. "Chronology of
Catholicity in Massachusetts,"
United States Catholic His-
torical Magazine, v. 1
(1867), 314-315. F 95
FINOTTI, JOSEPH M. The
Mystery of the Wizard Clip.
Baltimore. Kelly, Piet and
Co. 1879. xi, 143p. front.,
plates, port. F 96
"FIRST AMERICAN APOSTATE
PRIEST," American Catholic
Historical Researches, v. 6
(1889), 22-29. F 97
The story of Charles
Henry Wharton, born in
Maryland 1784, died 1833.
"FIRST CATHOLIC CELEBRA-
TION OF THE FOURTH OF
JULY," American Catholic
Historical Researches, v. 17
(1900), 60-67. F 98
"FIRST DIOCESAN SYNOD OF
BALTIMORE," United States

Catholic Historical Magazine, v. 2 (1868), 218-219.   F 99

"FIRST EPISCOPAL VISITATION IN THE UNITED STATES," Catholic Historical Review, v. 2 (1917), 442-459.   F 100

THE FIRST FIFTEEN YEARS OF THE COLLEGE OF ST. SCHOLASTICA. New York. McMullen. 1947. xii, 184p.   F 101

"FIRST RELIGIOUS MINISTRA-TIONS ON THE SITE OF THE PRESENT CITY OF SIOUX CITY," Iowa Catholic Historical Review, v. 1 (1930), 26-28.   F 102

"FIRST ROMAN CATHOLIC PRIEST," William and Mary College Quarterly Historical Papers, v. 1 (1892), 46-47.   F 103

FISCHER, SISTER MARY ALEXANDRINE. Illinois Editorial Opinion on the Alfred E. Smith Campaign. MA thesis. Catholic University. 1950. 89p.   F 104

FISCHER, MAX A. "A Key Problem of Prince Gallitzin's Biography," Historical Bulletin, v. 24 (1945), 7-8, 18. F 105

FISH, CARL RUSSELL (ed.). "Documents Relative to the Adjustment of the Roman Catholic Organization to the Conditions of National Indepen-dence," American Historical Review, v. 15 (1910), 800-829.   F 106

FISH, CARL RUSSELL. Guide to the Materials for American History in Rome and other Italian Archives. Washington. Carnegie Institution of Wash-ington. 1911. ix, 289p.   F 107

[FISHER, DANIEL J.]. "Letters of Daniel J. Fisher, a Seminarian in St. Paul," Acta et Dicta, v. 1 (1907), 43-51.   F 108

FISHER, J. HARDING. "In Memoriam, Father Pardow," American Catholic Historical Society of Philadelphia Re-cords, v. 26 (1915), 21-24.   F 109

FISHER, HENRY P. "The Early Days of The Saint Paul Guild," The Epistle, v. 15 (1949), 25-28.   F 110

FISHER, W. D. History of St. Mary's Training School at Des Plaines, Illinois (1882-1942). MA thesis. Loyola University (Chicago). 1942.   F 111

FITCH, ABIGAIL H. Junipero Serra: The Man and His Work. Chicago. McClurg. 1914. xii, 364p. front., (port.), plates, fold. map, plan.   F 112

FITTON, JAMES. Sketches of the Establishment of the Church in New England. Boston. P. Donohoe. 1872. 346p. front., ports., table.   F 113

FITZGERALD, BERNARD M. History of Religious Dis-qualifications for Office in New Hampshire. MA thesis. Catholic University. 1923. 23p.   F 114

FITZGERALD, SISTER CATHER-INE ANITA. A Union List of Catholic Periodicals in Cath-olic Institutions on the Pacific Coast. MA thesis. Portland University. 1952. iii, 97p.   F 115

FITZGERALD, FREDERICK E. Politico-Religious Discrimina-tion Against Catholics in the Early Constitutions of the Southland, 1776-1835. MA thesis. Catholic University. 1928. 129p.   F 116

FITZGERALD, J.A. "Saint John the Baptist Church of Hay-cock (Pa.)," Bucks County Historical Society Papers, v. 4 (1917), 118-125.   F 117

FITZGERALD, SISTER MARY CLEMENT. Bishop Marty and His Sioux Missions from 1876-1896. MA thesis. Uni-

versity of Notre Dame. 1933.
iv, 47p.   F 118

FITZGERALD, MARY CLEMENT.
"Bishop Marty and His Sioux
Missions, 1876-1896," South
Dakota Historical Collections,
v. 20 (1940), 523-558.
                                  F 119

FITZGERALD, SISTER MARY
INNOCENTIA. Historical
Sketch of the Sisters of Mercy
in the Diocese of Buffalo.
Buffalo. Mount Mercy
Academy. 1942. xx, 132p.
                                  F 120

FITZGERALD, SISTER MARY
PAUL. Beacon on the Plains.
Leavenworth, Kansas. St.
Mary College. 1939. 297p.
front., ports., map.   F 121

FITZGERALD, SISTER MARY
PAUL, "A Jesuit Circuit
Rider," Mid-America, v. 6
(1936), 182-198.   F 122

FITZGERALD, SISTER MARY
PAUL. "John Baptist Miége,
S.J. (1815-1884), A Study
in Frontier History," United
States Catholic Historical
Society Records and Studies,
v. 24 (1934), 284-362. F 123

FITZGERALD, SISTER MARY
PAUL. The Osage Mission; a
Factor in the Making of Kansas.
Ph.D. thesis. Saint Louis
University. 1937. iv, 312p.
                                  F 124

FITZGERALD, SISTER MARY
PAUL. "Osage Mission, a
Factor in the Making of Kansas,"
Mid-America, v. 8 (1937),
182-196.   F 125

FITZGERALD, WILLIAM A.
"Sister Reparata," Catholic
Library World, v. 26 (1954),
10.   F 126
Biographical obituary of
this pioneer in the Catholic
Library Association, who
was born 1889, died 1954.

FITZMORRIS, SISTER M.
ANGELA. Four Decades of
Catholicism in Texas, 1820-
1860. Washington. Catholic

University. 1926. vii, 109p.
                                  F 127

FITZPATRICK, E.A. "American
Hierarchy and Education,"
Catholic School Journal, v.
51 (1951), 107-111.   F 128

FITZMORRIS, T.J. "The Pioneer
of Religion and the First
Church and Cathedral in
Omaha and Nebraska," American Catholic Historical Society
of Philadelphia Records, v. 3
(1888), 111-120.   F 129

FITZPATRICK, JOSEPH P.
"Catholic and the Scientific
Knowledge of Society," A-
merican Catholic Sociological
Review, v. 15 (1954), 2-5.
                                  F 130

FITZPATRICK, EDWARD A.
"The Catholic School Journal,
1929-1949," Catholic School
Journal, v. 49 (1949), 179-
184.   F 131

FITZPATRICK, EDWARD A.
"William George Bruce: a
Maker of History," Wisconsin
Magazine of History, v. 33
(1949), 184-187. port.
                                  F 132

FITZPATRICK, J.P. "Mexicans
and Puerto Ricans Build a
Bridge; Role of Spanish
Speaking Catholic Church,"
America, v. 94 (1955), 373-
375.   F 133

FITZPATRICK, THOMAS J. The
Colonial Administration of
James II in the Colony of New
York. MA thesis. St. John's
University, N.Y., 1940. mss.
                                  F 134

FLAGET, BENEDICT J. "Bishop
Flaget Applies for Two of Ours
to be Bishops," Woodstock
Letters, v. 28 (1899), 73-77.
                                  F 135
Some unpublished letters
dated Bardstown, Ky.,
March 17, 1820, and Louisville, Oct. 19, 1847. Flaget
wants Fr. Fenwick for
Detroit and Fr. McElroy for
his own coadjutor.

136

[FLAGET, BENEDICT JOSEPH]. "Erection of the See of St. Louis, Missouri," American Catholic Historical Researches, v. 19 (1902), 108-109. F 136
A letter dated June 26th, 1816, from Loretto, addressed to Rev. Archb. Neale, Georgetown, Md. Gives Flaget's views on the erection of the diocese and his opposition to being transferred there.

FLAGET, BENEDICT JOSEPH. "An Interdict of Bishop Flaget," American Catholic Historical Researches, v. 13 (1896), 81-90. F 137
Against Côte du Nord Est. Suburban Church of Detroit, February 27, 1817. An incident of Trusteeism.

FLAGET, BENEDICT JOSEPH. "Letter to Henry Clay, dated September 21, 1825," ed. by Bernard Mayo, Catholic Historical Review, v. 27 (1941), 210-213. F 138

[FLAGET, BENEDICT JOSEPH]. "The See of St. Louis," American Catholic Historical Researches, v. 21 (1904), 158-160. F 139

FLAHERTY, FREDERICK ROBERT. The Role of the Catholic Church in the Spanish-American War. MA thesis. Boston College. 1960. 112p. F 140

FLANAGAN, SISTER MARY CALLISTA. Jesuit Education in the Archdiocese of Cincinnati in the Last Hundred Years. MA thesis. University of Notre Dame. 1940. x, 131p. graph. F 141

FLANAGAN, SISTER MARY RITA. Work of the Sisters of St. Dominic of the Congregation of St. Thomas Aquinas in the Diocese of Seattle, 1888-1951. MA thesis. Seattle University. 1951. iv, 146p. F 142

FLANIGEN, GEORGE J. Catholicity in Tennessee, 1541-1937. Nashville. Ambrose Printing Co. 1937. 176p. illus., incl. ports. F 143

FLANIGEN, GEORGE J. The Centenary of Sts. Peter and Paul's Parish, Chattanooga, Tennessee. Chattanooga. Sts. Peter and Paul's Parish. 1952. n.p. F 144
Here is a carefully written and beautifully printed booklet that could well serve as a model for parishes contemplating similar publications.

FLANNERY, HARRY W. "N.C.W.C.-Voice of America's Bishops," Ave Maria, v. 87 (June 7, 1958), 5-8. F 145

FLEEGE, URBAN H. "Expansion in Catholic Higher Education in the Past Decade and in the Next," Catholic Educational Review, v. 51 (1953), 434-441. F 146

FLEMING, SISTER M. SAINT AGNES. The Influence of Father Abram Ryan, Civil War Chaplain. MA thesis. Villanova University. 1944. 66p. F 147

FLEMING, MOTHER STANISLAUS. Life of the Right Reverend Mathias Loras, D.D. New York. Kenedy. c1933. 216p. front. (port.), plates. F 148

FLICK, ELLA M.E. Chaplain Duffy of the Sixty-Ninth Regiment, New York. Philadelphia. Dolphin Press. 1935. xii, 203p. front., plate, ports. F 149

FLICK, ELLA M. E. Beloved Crusader, Lawrence F. Flick, Physician. Philadelphia. Dorance and Co. 1944. 390p. F 150

FLICK, ELLA M. E. "Bishop Curtis," Catholic World, v. 133 (1931), 411-421. F 151

FLICK, ELLA M.E. (tr. and ed.). "Epistle or Diary of the Reverend Marie Joseph

Dunand," American Catholic Historical Society of Philadelphia Records, v. 26 (1915), 328-346; v. 27 (1916), 45-64.   F 152

FLICK, ELLA M.E. "Father Duffy," Catholic World, v. 137 (1933), 385-394.   F 153

FLICK, ELLA M.E. "The First Bishop of Buffalo," Catholic World, v. 131 (1930), 524-533.   F 154

FLICK, ELLA M. E. "Founding the Faith in Philadelphia," Catholic World, v. 125 (1927), 740-747.   F 155

FLICK, ELLA M.E. "John England," American Catholic Historical Society of Philadelphia Records, v. 38 (1927), 355-376.   F 156

FLICK, ELLA M.E. The Life of Bishop McDevitt. Philadelphia. Dorance and Co. 1940. 357p. front., plates, port.   F 157

FLICK, ELLA M.E. "The Rev. Charles Ignatius Hamilton Carter, V. G. (1803-1879)," American Catholic Historical Society of Philadelphia Records, v. 23 (1922), 193-215.   F 158

FLICK, ELLA M.E. "The Rev. Samuel Southerland Cooper (1796-1843)," American Catholic Historical Society of Philadelphia Records, v. 23 (1922), 300-316.   F 159

FLICK, ELLA M.E. "The Right Reverend Edward W. Barron, D. D., 1801-1854," American Catholic Historical Society of Philadelphia Records, v. 34 (1923), 99-112.   F 160

FLICK, LAWRENCE F. "Biographical Sketch of Rev. Peter Lemke, O.S.B., 1796-1882," American Catholic Historical Society of Philadelphia Records, v. 9 (1897), 129-192.   F 161

FLICK, LAWRENCE. "The French Refugee Trappists in the United States," American Catholic Historical Society of Philadelphia Records, v. 1 (1884-1886), 86-116.   F 162

FLICK, LAWRENCE F,"Gallitzin," Catholic Historical Review, v. 13 (1927), 394-496.   F 163

FLICK, LAWRENCE F. (ed.). "Minute Book of St. Mary's Church, Philadelphia, Pa., 1782-1811," American Catholic Historical Society of Philadelphia Records, v. 4 (1893), 245-459.   F 164

FLICK, LAWRENCE F. "The Papago Indians and Their Church," American Catholic Historical Society of Philadelphia Records, v. 5 (1894), 385-416.   F 165

FLICK, LAWRENCE F. "What the American Has Got Out of the Melting Pot from the Catholics," Catholic Historical Review, v. 11 (1925), 407-430.   F 166
    Concerned mostly with colonial contributions.

FLINTHAM, LYDIA STIRLING. "Franciscan Tertiaries, First Established in the United States at Philadelphia, Pa., 1855." American Catholic Historical Society of Philadelphia Records, v. 15 (1904), 125-128.   F 167

FLINTHAM, LYDIA STIRLING. "Leaves from the Annals of the Ursulines," Catholic World, v. 66 (1897), 319-339.   F 168

FLINTHAM, LYDIA STIRLING. "Sisters of Charity of the B.V.M. A Philadelphia Foundation of A.D. 1833," American Catholic Historical Society of Philadelphia Records, v. 15 (1904), 45-68. F 169

FLUSCHE, EMIL. "A Group of Colonies Founded by Three Brothers," Central Blatt and Social Justice, v. 25 (1932), 276-277.   F 170
    Westphalia, Shelby Co.,

Iowa (1872); Westphalia, Anderson Co., Kansas (1880); Olpe, Lyon Co., Kansas (1885); Muenster, Cooke Co., Texas (1889); Lindsay, Cooke Co., Texas (1847); Pilot Point, Denton Co., Texas (1891); Mt. Carmel, near Electra, Wichita Co., Texas (1907).

FLYNN, SISTER M. AGNES FRANCIS. Growth and Development of the Diocesan Organization of the Oregon Diocese. MA thesis. Villanova University. 1951. 129p.　　　　　　　　　F 171

FLYNN, D. J. 'Holy Week with the Penitentes," Harper's Weekly, v. 38 (1894), 489-490. illus.　　　　F 172

FLYNN, FRANCIS C. Origin, Growth, and Development of the Catholic Schools in Yonkers, New York. MA thesis. Fordham University. 1935. ix, 100p.　　　　　　F 173

FLYNN, JOSEPH M. The Catholic Church in New Jersey. Morristown. The Author. 1904. xiii, 695p. illus.　　　　　　　　　　F 174

FLYNN, JOSEPH M. The Story of a Parish, 1847-1892. New York. Columbia Press. 1892. vii, 327p. front., plates, ports.　　　　　F 175
Assumption parish, Morristown, New Jersey.

FLYNN, JOSEPH P. Early Years of Augustine F. Hewitt, C.S.P. 1820-1846. MA thesis. Catholic University. 1945. 95p.　　　　　　F 176

FLYNN, ROBERT. L'Eglise Catholique et les Noirs en Amérique. Nouvelle Revue Théologique, v. 83 (1951), 833-845.　　　　　　F 177

FOELLER, K. ELIZABETH. A Study of Four Catholic Periodicals in the Problem of Peace. MA thesis. Marquette University. 1949.　　　F 178

FOERSTER, ROBERT F. The Italian Emigration of Our Times. Cambridge, Mass. Harvard University. 1919. xv, 556p.　　　　　　F 179

FOIK, PAUL J. "Anti-Catholic Parties in American Politics, 1776-1860," American Catholic Historical Society of Philadelphia Records, v. 36 (1925), 41-69.　　　F 180

FOIK, PAUL J. Fray Juan de Padilla. Austin, Texas. Texas Catholic Historical Society. 1930. Preliminary Studies, v. 1, no. 5. F 181

FOIK, PAUL J. "Fray Juan de Padilla," Mid-America, v. 2 (1930), 132-140.　　　F 182

FOIK, PAUL J. "The Martyrs of the Southwest," Illinois Catholic Historical Review, v. 11 (1928), 27-55.　　　F 183

FOIK, PAUL J. "Pioneer Efforts in Catholic Journalism in the United States (1809-1840)," Catholic Historical Review, v. 1 (1915), 258-270.　　　F 184

FOIK, PAUL J. Pioneer Catholic Journalism. New York. United States Catholic Historical Society. 1930. x, 221p.　　　　　　　　F 185

FOIK, PAUL J. "Survey of Source Materials for the Catholic History of the Southwest," Catholic Historical Review, v. 15 (1929), 275-281. F 186

FOIN, JULES C., 'Rev. Louis Barth," American Catholic Historical Society of Philadelphia Records, v. 2 (1886-1888). 29-37.　　　　　F 186a

FOISY, J. ALBERT. The Sentinellist Agitation in New England, 1925-1928. Providence. Providence Visitor Press. 1930. vi, 234p.　　　F 187

FOLEY, ALBERT S. Bishop Healy and the Colored Catholic Congress," Interracial Review, v. 28 (1954), 79-80. F 188

FOLEY, ALBERT S. Bishop Healy: Beloved Outcast. New

York. Farrar Strauss and Young. 1954. 243p. F 189
An excellent biography of this son of an Irish immigrant and Georgia slave, who became the second Bishop of Portland in Maine.

FOLEY, ALBERT J. God's Men of Color. New York. Farrar Strauss. 1955. 322p. F 190
Biographical information on some forty-five colored priests in the United States between the years 1854 and 1954.

FOLEY, ALBERT S. "St. Elizabeth's Full Circle," Interracial Review, v. 24 (1951), 120-122. F 191
A brief appreciation of the St. Louis parish which was the center of Negro Catholic activity for forty years.

FOLEY, ALBERT S. "Status and Role of the Negro Priest in the American Catholic Church," American Catholic Sociological Review, v. 16 (June, 1955), 83-92. F 192

FOLEY, ALBERT S., "U.S. Colored Priests: Hundred Years' Survey," America, v. 89 (June 13, 1953), 295-297. F 193

FOLEY, JOSEPH B. "St. Charles College," Catholic World, v. 168 (1948), 61-67. F 194

"FORANEUS." "The Catholic Census of the United States," American Ecclesiastical Review, v. 53 (1915), 1-14. F 195

FORBES. "L'Eglise Catholique aux États-Unis depuis un siècle." Revue Catholique des Institutions et du Droit. 2d Sér. 30 (1903), 481 sqq. F 196

FORBES, A.S.C. California Missions and Landmarks, El Camino Real. 8th ed. Los Angeles. no pub. 1925. 392p. illus. F 197

FORD, SISTER CONSUELA MARIA. St. James Mission Claim, Vancouver, Washington. MA thesis. Seattle University. 1946. viii, 106p. F 198

FORD, FRANCIS X. Stone in the King's Highway. New York, McMullen. 1953. 297p. F 199
Selection from the writings of Bishop F.X. Ford (1892-1953) with an introductory memoir by Raymond A. Lane.

FORD, HENRY CHAPMAN. "Some Detached Notes by Henry Chapman Ford on the Missions of California [1888]," California Historical Society Quarterly, v. 3 (1924), 238-244. F 200

FORD, LAWRENCE C. The Triangular Struggle for Spanish Pensacola, 1689-1739. Washington. Catholic University. 1939. vii, 185p. F 201
The struggle between France, Spain and England, a diplomatic study, only occasional reference to the Church.

FORDHAM MONTHLY, v. 34 (1916), June. F 202
Diamond Jubilee issue contains articles on the history of Fordham University.

FORESTAL, PETER P. (tr. and ed.). "Pena Diary of the Aguayo Expedition," United States Catholic Historical Society Records and Studies, v. 24 (1934), 143-208. F 203

FORMICA, GERMANO. Cardinal Hayes, A Treasury of Wisdom and Knowledge. New York. N.F. Hobson and Co. 1933. F 204

FORREST, EARLE R. Missions and Pueblos of the Old Southwest. Cleveland. Arthur H. Clark Co. 1929. 386p. plates. F 205

FORREST, E. R. "Sanguinary Passion Play of the Penitentes," Travel, v. 50 (Dec., 1927),

29-32. illus. F 206

FORRESTER, DONALD F. A
Study of the Migration of
Catholics to the Tennessee
Valley Region from 1769-
1810. MA thesis. Catholic
University. 1934. 69p.
F 207

FORT WAYNE (DIOCESE) SYNOD,
1863. Statutes for the administration of the temporal
affairs of the congregations
within the diocese of Fort
Wayne. Promulgated in
synod, August 26, 1863.
Cincinnati, J.P. Walsh, 1863.
18p. F 208

FORT WAYNE (DIOCESE) SYNOD,
1874. Statuta dioecesis wayne
castrensis, in synodo dioecesana,
1874 promulgata a Joseph
Dwenger. Fort Wayne, Sentinel
steam printing house, 1875.
23p. F 209

FORT WAYNE (DIOCESE) SYNOD,
1903. Synodus dioecesana
Wayne-castrensis habita die
llmo Novembris, 1903, Wayne-
castris, in ecclesia cathedrali
Immaculatae Conceptionis a
Hermanno Iosepho Alerding
[ep.] Nostrae Dominae,
Indiana, Typis universitatis [n.d.]
168p. F 210

FORT WAYNE (DIOCESE) SYNOD.
Synodi Wayne-castrensis appendix XVIII [-XX] Decretum
S. Congregationis Concilii de
observandis et evitandis in
missarum manualium satis-
factione. Ut debita ... [n.p.,
1907?] 169-192p. F 211

FORT WAYNE (DIOCESE) SYNOD,
1926. Synodus dioecesana
Wayne Castrensis habita die
19 Aug., 1926, in ecclesia
Ssmi Cordis Jesu, apud Uni-
versitatem Notre Dame, a
Joanne Francisco Noll [ep.]
[n.p., n.d.] 7p. 1., 151p.
F 212

FORTIER, ALCEE. History of
Louisiana. New York.
Goupil and Co. 1904. 4v.

F 213
This is not a diocesan history, as it is classified
in several bibliographies,
but rather a general history
of Louisiana which contains
much information on the
story of the Church.

FORTIER, E. J. "The Establishment of the Tamarois Mission,"
Illinois State Historical Society.
Transactions, v. 13 (1908),
233-239. F 214

FOSSELMAN, D. H. Transitions
in the Development of a
Downtown Parish. Washington.
Catholic University. 1952.
F 215

FOX, SISTER M. COLUMBA.
The Life of the Right Reverend
John Baptist Mary David
(1761-1841). New York.
United States Catholic Histori-
cal Society. 1925. F 216

FOX, MARY M. Peter E.
Dietz, Labor Priest. Notre
Dame. University of Notre
Dame. 1953. 294p. F 217

FRANCIS, SISTER CATHERINE.
Convent Schools of French
Origin in the United States,
1727-1843. Philadelphia. 1936.
246p. F 218

FRANCIS, E. K. "Padre
Martinez: a New Mexican
Myth," New Mexico Historical
Review, v. 31 (Oct. 1956),
265-289. F 219

"FRANCIS NORBERT BLANCHET,
APOSTLE OF OREGON AND
FIRST ARCHBISHOP OF THE
GREAT WEST," Catholic Re-
cord, v. 10 (1876), 355-359.
F 220

"FRANCISCAN ANNIVERSARY IN
OBERNBURG, 50 YEARS,"
Provincial Annals (Province of
the Most Holy Name, O.F.M.),
v. 5 (1946), 217-227, 282-289.
F 221

"FRANCISCAN DIOCESE OF
TEXAS," Provincial Chronicle
(St. John Baptist Province,
O.F.M.), v. 22 (1950), 29-

56, 72, 90-107. F 222
FRANCISCAN HISTORY OF
NORTH AMERICA. Washington.
Capuchin College. 1937. 385p.
illus. F 223
(FRANCISCAN FATHER). Friars
Minor in the United States.
Chicago, Ill. 1926. 365p.
illus., plates, ports. F 224
(FRANCISCAN FATHER). L'
Opera dei Franciscani in A-
merica. New York. Franciscan
Father, 150 Thompson Street,
New York. 1925. F 225
"FRANCISCANS IN EAST RUTHER-
FORD," Provincial Annals
(Province of the Most Holy
Name, O.F.M.), v. 7
(1947), 121-129. F 226
"FRANCISCANS IN PAJARO VAL-
LEY (1874-1919)," Provincial
Annals (Province of Santa
Barbara, O.F.M.), v. 5
(Jan., 1943), 7-21. F 227
"FRANCISCAN MISSIONS AMONG
THE INDIANS OF WISCON-
SIN," Franciscan Herald.
v. (1935), 297-298, 322,
348, 371, 395, 420, 443, 466,
491, 514. F 228
"FRANCISCANS OF THE OREGON
FRONTIER, 1907-1923," Pro-
vincial Annals, (Province of
Santa Barbara, O.F.M.), v.
2 (Apr., 1940), 16-21.
F 229
FRANZISKANER PROVINZ,
HEILIGSTEN HERZEN JESU,
1858-1908. no pub., 1908?
222p. illus., plates, ports.
F 230
FRAWLEY, SISTER M. ALPHON-
SINE. Patrick Donahoe.
Washington. Catholic Univer-
sity. 1946. xiii, 327. F 231
v. 34 of Catholic University
Studies in American Church
History.
FREDERICK, J.A. "Old St.
Peter's, or the Beginnings of
Catholicity in Baltimore,"
United States Catholic His-
torical Society Records and
Studies, v. 5, pt. 2 (1909),

354-391. F 232
FREESE, H. (comp.). Histori-
cal Sketches of the Town of
Martinsburg, Missouri and Its
Institutions. Martinsburg, Mo.
Monitor. 1926. 112p. illus.,
plates, ports. F 233
FREGAULT, GUY. "Jean De-
langlez, S.J. (1896-1949),"
Revue d'Histoire de l'Améri-
que française, v. 3 (1949),
165-171. F 233a
[FRERI, JOSEPH]. Society of
the Propagation of the Faith
and Catholic Missions. Balti-
more. 1902. F 234
FRESE, JOSEPH R. Catholic
Public Opinion and Secession,
1860-1861. MA thesis.
Georgetown University. 1939.
73, xxii, p. F 235
FRESE, JOSEPH R. "Some Notes
on the 'United States Catholic
Miscellany,' " American
Catholic Historical Society of
Philadelphia Records, v. 55
(1944), 388-400. F 236
FRESE, JOSEPH R. "Pioneer
Catholic Weeklies," United
States Catholic Historical
Society Records and Studies,
v. 30 (1939), 140-144.
F 237
FREY, BONAVENTURE. Erin-
nerungen über die Uranfänger
der Kapuzinerprovinz zum Hl.
Josef in Amerika. New York.
1904. F 238
FRIEND, A.B. "Alabama.
Letter Dated Selma, Alabama,
June 7th, 1887," Woodstock
Letters, v. 17 (1888), 52-72.
F 239
FRIES, L. J. One Hundred and
Fifty Years of Catholicity in
Utah. Salt Lake City, Utah.
Intermountain Catholic Press.
1942. illus., ports. F 240
FRIESENHAM, SISTER M.
CLARENCE. Catholic Second-
ary Education in the Province
of San Antonio. Washington.
Catholic University. 1930.
viii, 97p. F 241

FRITZ, SISTER M. IRMINGRAD.
John Lancaster Spalding, Cath-
olic Social Educator. MA
thesis. Catholic University.
1945. 115p.   F 242
"FROM PENSACOLA TO ST.
AUGUSTINE IN 1827," Florida
Historical Quarterly, v. 25
(1947), 135-166.   F 243
FRONCEK, SISTER M. ZYMUNTA.
Blaine and the Irish. MA
thesis. Catholic University.
1932. 35p.   F 244
FRY, C. LUTHER. U.S. Looks
at Its Churches. New York.
Institute of Social and Religious
Research. 1930. 183p.
                                F 245
FRYE, VIRGINIA K. "St. Patrick's
--First Catholic Church of
the Federal City," Columbia
(D.C.) Historical Society
Records, v. 23 (1920), 26-51.
                                F 246
FUERST, ADRIAN. "The Cate-
chism in the United States,"
St. Meinrad Historical Essays,
v. 5 (1941), 325-344.   F 247
   Good historical survey of the
   development of printing and
   use of the Catechism in the
   United States.
FUERTGES, THEODORE. The
History of St. Bede College
and Abbey, Peru, Illinois,
1889-1941. MA thesis. Cath-
olic University. 1941. 104p.
                                F 248
FUHRMANN, JOSEPH P. A
Golden Jubilee History of the
Sacred Heart Parish, 1889-
1939, Muenster, Texas. San
Antonio, Texas. Standard Print.
Co. 1939. 170p. illus.
                                F 249
FUHRMANN, JOSEPH. Souvenir
of the Diamond Jubilee of St.
Mary's Church, Iowa City,
Iowa, 1840-1916. no pl. The
Author. 1916. 176p. plates,
ports.   F 250
FUREY, FRANCIS T. "The
Charleston, S.C. Schism of
1815-1818," American Catholic

Historical Society of Philadelphia Records, v. 4 (1887),
184-188.   F 251
FURFEY, PAUL H. "The Sociology of a Southern Parish,"
American Ecclesiastical Review, v. 127 (1952), 182-
193.   F 252
   A very detailed, critical and
   unfavorable review of
   Fichter's Southern Parish
   v. 1 (1951).
FURLAN, LEWIS. "Father Paul
of Greymoor," The Lamp,
v. 46 (1948), 10-14, 41-44,
76-80, 105-108, 137-140,
172-174, 201-205, 233-236,
267-270, 293-296, 327-331,
359-360; v. 47 (1949), 12-15,
40-44, 72-74, 111-114, 136-
138, 143, 171-174.   F 253
FURLAN, WILLIAM P. In
Charity Unfeigned. Paterson,
N.J. St. Anthony Guild Press.
1952. 280p.   F 254
   Biography of the pioneer
   Minnesota missionary Father
   Francis Xavier Pierz.
FUSCO, NICOLA. Mount St.
Peter. Pittsburgh. St.
Joseph's Protectory. 1944.
xiv, 140p. plates, ports.
                                F 255
   Story of St. Peter's Church
   in New Kensington, Pa.

            - G -
GABEL, RICHARD J. Public
Funds for Church and Private
Schools. Washington. Catholic
University. 1937. xiv, 858p.
                                 G 1
GABRIEL, RALPH H. The
Course of American Democratic
Thought. New York. Ronald
Press. 1940. xi, 452p.
                                 G 2
GABRIELS, HENRY. Histori-
cal Sketch of St. Joseph's
Provincial Seminary, Troy,
New York. New York. United
States Catholic Historical
Society, 1905. 188p. front.,
illus., ports.   G 3

GACHE, L.H. "Our College at
Baton Rouge, Louisiana.
Letter dated St. Joseph's
Church, Philadelphia, Oct. 1,
1897," Woodstock Letters,
v. 27 (1898), 1-7.   G 4
Story of the attempt to found
Sts. Peter and Paul College,
Baton Rouge, 1849-1855.
GACHET, ANTOINE MARIA.
Cinq Ans en Amérique. Fri-
bourg. Catholique Suisse. 1890.
120p.   G 5
GACHET, ANTOINE MARIA.
"Five Years in America,"
Wisconsin Magazine of History,
(1934-1935), 66-84, 191-204,
345-359.   G 6
GAGE, GEORGE. "Letter to
Bishop Richard Smith, dated
July 21, 1642," Maryland
History Magazine, v. 4 (1910),
262-265.   G 7
On the subject of faculties
for America.
GAILLAND, MAURICE. "Lettre
du R.P. Gailland de la
Compagnie de Jésus à MM.
les Membres des Conseils
centraux de Lyon et Paris.
Sainte-Marie, Mission des
Potowatomies le 13 novembre,
1851," Annales de la Propaga-
tion de la Foi, v. 24 (1852),
227-235.   G 8
GALBALLY, EDWARD J. "The
Reverend Herman J. Heuser,
Founder of the Ecclesiastical
Review," American Ecclesiasti-
cal Review, v. 89 (1933), 337-
360. port.   G 9
GALINDO, NASARIO. "Early
Days at Mission Santa Clara,"
California Historical Society
Quarterly, v. 38 (1959), 101-
112.   G 10
GALL, LOUIS. Jesuit Missions
among the Sioux. St. Francis,
South Dakota. St. Francis
Mission. 1940. 70p.   G 11
GALLAGHER, H.S. "Bishop
Baraga," Ave Maria, v. 36
(1932), 744-749.   G 12
GALLAGHER, JOHN JOSEPH.

"Theodore Roosevelt Letters to
Cardinal Gibbons, (1901-1916),"
Catholic Historical Review, v.
44 (1959), 440-456.   G 13
GALLAGHER, LOUIS J. "Father
Edmund A. Walsh," Woodstock
Letters, v. 86 (1957), 21-
70; port.   G 14
A biographical sketch of
this famous Jesuit member
of the faculty of Georgetown
University who was a lead-
ing authority on Communist
Russia.
[GALLITZIN, DEMETRIUS.]
"Letters of Father Gallitzin,
the Prince-Priest of the Al-
leghanies," American Catholic
Historical Researches, v. 20
(1903), 15-18.   G 15
[GALTIER, L.] "Letter of Rev.
L. Galtier to Rt. Rev.
Thomas L. Grace, Bishop of
St. Paul," Acta et Dicta, v. 1
(1908), 184-190.   G 16
GALUS, WALTER J. History of
the Catholic Italians in Saint
Louis, MA thesis. Saint
Louis University. 1936. v.,
194p.   G 17
GALVESTON (DIOCESE) SYNOD,
1st, 1858. Synodus dioecesana
galvestonensis prima, habita a
Joanne Maria Odin [ep.] mense
Junio anno 1858. Neo Aureliae,
Ex typis Propagatoris Catholici
1858, 22p.   G 18
GALVESTON (DIOCESE) SYNOD,
2nd, 1869. Synodus gemina
dioecesana galvestonensis
secunda, a Claudio Maria
Dubuis, episcopo galvestonensi,
in civitate galvestonensi mense
Decembri MDCCCLXIX habita.
New Aureliae, Ex typis Propagatoris Catholici, 1869. 43p.
                          G 19
GALVESTON (DIOCESE) SYNOD,
1882 (1910). The statutes
and regulations in force in
the diocese of Galveston as
published in different synods and
retreats since 1882. 6p.
                          G 20

GALVESTON (DIOCESE) SYNOD,
7th, 1930. Synodus dioecesana
galvestonensis septima a
Christophero Eduardo Byrne [ep.]
habita seminario Stae Mariae,
La Porte, Texas, die 23a
Aprilis A.D. 1930. 64p.
G 21
GALWAY, BERNARD BENIGNUS.
Cardinal Gibbons and the
Labor Movement in the United
States. MA thesis. Fordham
University. 1939. iii, 78, xip.
G 22
GAMBLE, ANNA DILL. "An
Ancient Mission Among a Great
People," American Catholic
Historical Society of Phila-
delphia Records, v. 60
(1949), 125-143. G 23
Mission among the Sus-
quehannock Indians of Penn-
sylvania, the background of
the beginnings of Conewago
Mission.
GAMBLE, RICHARD D. "Army
Chaplains at Frontier Posts,
1830-1860," Historical Mag-
azine of the Protestant Epis-
copal Church, v. 27 (1958),
286-307. G 24
A good general article cover-
ing all faiths.
GANNON, DAVID. Father Paul
of Greymoor. New York. Mac-
millan. 1951. x, 372p. illus.
G 25
GANNON, ROBERT I. "The
Centenary of the California
Province," San Francisco
Quarterly, v. 16 (1949), 23-
28. G 26
GANSS, H. C. "Indian Mission
Problem, Past and Present,"
Catholic Mind, v. 2 (1904),
325-344. G 27
GANSS, HENRY G. History of
St. Patrick's Church, Carlisle,
Pennsylvania. Philadelphia.
D. J. Gallagher. 1895.
215p. G 28
GANSS, H. G. "History of St.
Patrick's Church, Pennsylvania,"
American Catholic Historical

Society of Philadelphia Re-
cords, v. 6 (1895), 266-350,
353-422.
G 29
GARESCHE, EDWARD F. "Cath-
olic Centers for Youth," Cath-
olic Educational Review, v.
50 (April, 1952), 257-263.
G 30
Contains some interesting
information of the history
of Catholic youth work and
the Y.M.C.A., and Y.W.
C.A.
GARESCHE, EDWARD F. "Cath-
olic Medical Mission Board
Inc. and the Daughters of
Mary, Health of the Sick,"
Woodstock Letters, v. 69
(1940), 25-39. G 31
GARESCHE, EDWARD. "The
Rise and Progress of the
Queen's Work," Woodstock
Letters, v. 47 (1918), 1-18;
v. 48 (1919), 54-71; v. 49
(1920), 209-215. variant
title. G 32
GARESCHE, FERDINAND P.
"Texas. Letter dated Seguin,
Texas, July 10, 1881," Wood-
stock Letters, v. 10 (1881),
281-285. G 33
GARESCHE, FERDINAND P.
"Texas. Letter dated Seguin,
Texas, Oct. 3, 1882," Wood-
stock Letters, v. 12 (1882),
60-65. G 34
GARESCHE, FERDINAND P. "Tex-
as. Letter dated Seguin,
Texas," Woodstock Letters, v.
11 (1882), 185-190. G 35
GARESCHE, FERDINAND P.
"Texas. Letter dated Gonzales,
Jan. 31st, 1887," Woodstock
Letters, v. 16 (1887), 136-
139. G 36
GARESCHE, FERDINAND P. "Tex-
as. Letter dated Gonzales,
Texas, March 12th, 1888,"
Woodstock Letters, v. 17
(1888), 202-204. G 37
GARESCHE, MARIE LOUISE.
Biography of Father James
Conway of the Society of Jesus.

St. Louis. Herder. 1911.
ix, 245p. plates, ports.
(incl. front.). G 38

GARGAN, EDWARD. 'Reply to 'American Catholics and the Intellectual Life,' " Books, v. 15 (1956), 169-170. G 39

GARIN, CHANOINE JACQUES. Notices Biographiques sur Mgr. J. B. Miége, Premier Vicaire Apostolique de Kansas. Moutiers. Cane Soeurs. 1886. iii, 504p. G 40

GARLAND, SISTER MARY ANNELLA. The Work of Bishop John Lancaster Spalding, Diocese of Peoria, 1877-1908. MA thesis., University of Notre Dame. 1954. 147p. G 41

GARRAGHAN, GILBERT J. "Beginnings of the Holy Family Parish, Chicago, 1857-1871," Illinois Catholic Historical Review, v. 1 (1919), 436-458. illus. G 42

GARRAGHAN, GILBERT J. 'The Beginnings of St. Louis University," St. Louis Catholic Historical Review, v. 1 (1918), 85-102. G 43

GARRAGHAN, GILBERT J. "Bishop Bruté and the Mission of Chicago," Saint Louis Catholic Historical Review, v. 1 (1918), 201-214. G 44

GARRAGHAN, GILBERT J. "Bishop Bruté of Vincennes, 1779-1839," Mid-America, v. 4 (1933), 151-165. G 45

GARRAGHAN, GILBERT J. "Catholic Beginnings in Chicago," Mid-America, v. 5 (1933), 33-44. G 46

GARRAGHAN, GILBERT J. Catholic Beginnings in Kansas City, Missouri, Chicago. Loyola University. 1920. 137p. plates, ports., maps, facsims. G 47

GARRAGHAN, GILBERT J. "Catholic Beginnings in Maryland," Thought, v. 9 (1934), 5-31, 261-285. G 48

GARRAGHAN, GILBERT J. The Catholic Church in Chicago, 1673-1871. Chicago. Loyola University. 1921. xi, 236p. plates, ports., facsims. G 49

GARRAGHAN, GILBERT J. "Catholic First Things in the United States," Mid-America, v. 10 (1939), 110-186. G 50

GARRAGHAN, GILBERT J. Chapters in Frontier History. Milwaukee. Bruce. 1934. xv, 188p. front., ports., map. G 51

GARRAGHAN, GILBERT J. "Chicago's Catholic Century of Progress," Catholic World, v. 137 (1933), 454-462. G 52

GARRAGHAN, GILBERT J. "Documents: James Bouchard, S.J., French-Delaware Indiana," Mid-America, v. 8 (1937), 265-284. G 53

GARRAGHAN, GILBERT J. 'Earliest Settlements of the Illinois Country," Catholic Historical Review, v. 15 (1930), 351-362. G 54

GARRAGHAN, GILBERT J. 'Early Catholicity in Chicago," Illinois Catholic Historical Review, v. 1 (1918), 8-28, 147-172. illus., port. G 55

GARRAGHAN, GILBERT J. 'Ecclesiastical Rule of Old Quebec in Mid-America," Catholic Historical Review, v. 19 (1933), 17-32. G 56

GARRAGHAN, GILBERT J. "Father De Smet--History Maker," Illinois Catholic Historical Review, v. 6 (1924), 174-178. G 57

GARRAGHAN, GILBERT J. 'The First Settlement on the Site of St. Louis," Illinois Catholic Historical Review, v. 9 (1927), 342-347. G 58

GARRAGHAN, GILBERT J. "Fordham's Jesuit Beginnings," Thought, v. 16 (1941), 17-39. G 59

GARRAGHAN, GILBERT J.

"George Washington and the Catholics," Historical Bulletin, v. 20 (1942), 51-52, 62-66, 77-79, 81-82. G 60

GARRAGHAN, GILBERT J. "A Jesuit Westward Movement," Mid-America, v. 6 (1936), 165-181. G 61

The story of the beginnings of the Missouri Province, 1823.

GARRAGHAN, GILBERT J. The Jesuits of the Middle United States. New York. America Press. 1938. 3v. plates, ports., maps, facsims. G 62

GARRAGHAN, GILBERT J. "John Anthony Grassi, S.J., 1775-1849," Catholic Historical Review, v. 23 (1938), 273-292. G 63

GARRAGHAN, GILBERT J. "The Joliet-Marquette Expedition of 1673," Thought, v. 4 (1929), 32-71. G 64

GARRAGHAN, GILBERT J. "The Kickapoo Mission," St. Louis Catholic Historical Review, v. 4 (1922), 25-50. G 65

GARRAGHAN, GILBERT J. Marquette. New York. America Press. 1937. 48p. G 66

GARRAGHAN, GILBERT J. "Marquette University in the Making," Illinois Catholic Historical Review, v. 2 (1920), 417-446. G 67

GARRAGHAN, GILBERT J. "Marquette's Titles to Fame," Mid-America, v. 9 (1938), 30-36. G 68

GARRAGHAN, GILBERT J. "The Mission of Central Missouri," St. Louis Catholic Historical Review, v. 2 (1920), 157-182. G 69

GARRAGHAN, GILBERT J. "New Light on old Cahokia," Illinois Catholic Historical Review, v. 11 (1928), 99-146. G 70

GARRAGHAN, GILBERT J. "Old Vincennes: A Chapter in the Ecclesiastical History of the West," Mid-America, v. 2 (1931), 324-340. G 71

GARRAGHAN, GILBERT J. "Origins of Boston College, 1842-1869," Thought, v. 17 (1942), 627-658. G 72

GARRAGHAN, GILBERT J. "The Potawatomi Mission of Council Bluffs," St. Louis Catholic Historical Review, v. 3 (1921), 155-173. G 73

GARRAGHAN, GILBERT J. St. Ferdinand de Florissant. The Story of an Ancient Parish. Chicago. Loyola University. 1923. 271p. plates, ports., maps, fascims. G 74

GARRAGHAN, GILBERT J. "St. Regis Seminary--First Catholic Indian School (1823-1831)," Catholic Historical Review, v. 4 (1919), 452-478. G 75

GARRAGHAN, GILBERT J. "Samuel Charles Mazzuchelli, Dominican of the Frontier," Mid-America, v. 9 (1938), 253-262. G 76

GARRAGHAN, GILBERT J. "The Society of Jesus in America, 1566-1940," Historical Bulletin, v. 18 (1940), 59-60. G 77

GARRAGHAN, GILBERT J. "Some Early Chapters in the History of St. Louis University," St. Louis Catholic Historical Review, v. 5 (1923), 99-128. G 78

GARRAGHAN, G. J. Some Newly Discovered Marquette and La Salle Letters. Archivum Historicum S.J. v. 4 (1935), 268-290. G 79

GARRAGHAN, GILBERT J. "The Trappists of Monks Mound," Illinois Catholic Historical Review, v. 8 (1925), 106-136. G 80

GARRAGHAN, GILBERT J. "The Trappists of Monks Mound," American Catholic Historical Society of Philadelphia Records, v. 36 (1925), 70-110. G 81

GARRAND, VICTOR. "The Rocky Mountains. Letter dated North Yakima, April 4th, 1888," Woodstock Letters, v. 17 (1888), 196-198. G 82

GARRAND, VICTOR. "The Rocky Mountains. Extract from a letter dated North Yakima, Dec. 9th, 1888," Woodstock Letters, v. 17 (1888), 192-193. G 83

GARTNER, JOHANN MARIA. "The First Slavic Mission Institute under the Protection of the Sacred Heart in the United States," Central Blatt and Social Justice, v. 32 (1940), 381. G 84

GARVEY, JOHN W. The Residence and Mission of Ste. Marie 1639-1649, a Thrilling Chapter in the History of Huronia. MA thesis. Loyola University (Chicago). 1952. 128p. G 85

GARVEY, SISTER MARIA GRATIANA. Ku Klux Klan, Its Origins, Its Traditions, Its Character. MA thesis. Villanova. 1941. 79, xxii, vp. G 86

GASNICK, ROY M. "The Catholic Interracial Council of New York," St. Meinrad Essays, v. 12 (1959), 71-86. G 87

GASPARRI, DONATO M. "Lettera II," Lettere Edificanti Provincia Napolitana, ser. 1 (1875), 1-2. G 88
Dated Albuquerque, Feb., 1874. A description of the beginning of the New Mexico-Colorado Mission of the Neapolitan Jesuits, by the founder of the mission.

GASPARRI, DONATO M. "Lettere XI," Lettere Edificanti Provincia Napolitana, ser. 1 (1875), 17-18. G 89
Dated "Albuquerque, N. M., Guigno, 1874." An account of the acquisition of San Felippo Church in Albuquerque.

GASS, DAVID A. The Founding of the First Catholic Parish on Lake Superior. MA thesis. Marquette University. 1955. G 90

GASSLER, LEON F. Dedication. St. Joseph's Church. Baton Rouge, La. 1924. 18p. front., port. G 91

GASTON, WILLIAM. "Judge Gaston's Plea for Toleration," United States Catholic Historical Society Records and Studies, v. 17 (1926), 189-249. G 92

GATELY, SISTER FRANCIS MAGDALEN. Religious Conditions in Early Colonial Maryland (1634-1655). MA thesis. Boston College. 1941. ii, 57p. G 93

GATELY, SISTER MARY JOSEPHINE. The Sisters of Mercy; Historical Sketches, 1831-1931. New York. Macmillan. 1931. xix, 503p. front., ports. G 94

GAZEAU, F. (ed.). "L'Apostolat Catholique aux Etats-Unis Pendant la Guerre," Etudes, v. 7 (1862), 807-830. G 95

GEARY, GERALD J. The Transference of Ecclesiastical Jurisdiction in California, 1840-1853. MA thesis. Catholic University. n.d. 89p. G 96

GEARY, GERALD J. The Secularization of the California Missions (1810-1846). Washington. Catholic University. 1934. x, 204p. G 97

GEARY, GERALD J. "Transfer of Ecclesiastical Jurisdiction in California (1840-1853)," United States Catholic Historical Society Records and Studies, v. 22 (1932), 101-167. G 98

GEBHARDT, DANIEL FRANCIS. A History of the Catholic Daily Tribune. MA thesis. Marquette University. 1953. G 99

GEBLER, SISTER MARY MACRINA. History and Present Organization of the Diocesan High Schools in the Archdiocese of Philadelphia. MA thesis. Catholic University. 1955.
G 100

GEIGER, SISTER MARY VIRGINIA. Daniel Carroll. A Framer of the Constitution. Washington. Catholic University. 1943. x, 210p. incl. 2 fold. geneal. tables.
G 101

GEIGER, MAYNARD. "The Apostolic College of Our Lady of Sorrows, 1853-1885," Provincial Annals (Province of Santa Barbara, O.F.M.), v. 11 (1949), 105-114, 161-167; v. 12 (1949), 1-10, 47-53.
G 102

GEIGER, MAYNARD. Biographical Dictionary of the Franciscans in Spanish Florida and Cuba (1528-1841). Paterson, N.J. St. Anthony Guild Press. 1940. xii, 140p. Franciscan Studies, v. 21.
G 103

GEIGER, MAYNARD. Apostolic College of Our Lady of Sorrows, Santa Barbara, 1853-1885. Province Annals (Santa Barbara, California), v. 12 (1949), 163-171; v. 13 (1950-51), 2-5, 29-33, 53-58, 81-85; v. 14 (1951-52), 3-10, 21-25, 41-49, 65-67; v. 15 (1952-53) 1-6, 21-24, 41-48, 69-74; v. 16 (1953-54), 1-5, 29-36, 61-73, 93-97; v. 17 (1954-55), 1-5, 71-75, 130-133, 167-171; v. 18 (1955-56), 27-29, 45-50, 223-229; v. 19 (1956-57), 62-64, 144-150, 207-211. G 104

GEIGER, MAYNARD. (ed.). "The Arrival of the Franciscans in the Californias -- 1768-1769," The Americas, v. 8 (October, 1951), 209-218.
G 105

GEIGER, MAYNARD. Calendar of Documents in the Santa Barbara Mission Archives. Washington. Academy of American Franciscan History. 1947. xiv, 291p.
G 106

GEIGER, MAYNARD. "Dates of Palou's Death and Lasuen's Birth Determined," California Historical Society Quarterly, v. 28 (1949), 19-22.
G 107

GEIGER, MAYNARD. Early Franciscans in Florida and Their Relation to Spain's Colonial Effort. Paterson, N. J. St. Anthony Guild Press. 1936. 22p. G 108

GEIGER, MAYNARD. The Franciscan Conquest of Florida (1573-1618). Washington. Catholic University. 1937. xii, 319p. G 109

GEIGER, MAYNARD. "The Franciscan Historian and History Writing," Franciscan Educational Conference Annual Report, v. 18 (1936), 359-378. G 110

GEIGER, MAYNARD. "Important California Missionary Dates Determined," Americas, v. 4 (1948), 287-293. G 111

GEIGER, MAYNARD. "In Quest of Serrana," Americas, v. 1 (1944), 97-103. G 112

GEIGER, MAYNARD. "Junipero Serra, O.F.M. in the Light of Chronology and Geography (1713-1784)," Americas, v. 6 (1950), 291-233. map.
G 113

GEIGER, MAYNARD. Kingdom of St. Francis in Arizona, 1539-1949. Santa Barbara, Calif. The Author. 1939. 56p. G 114

GEIGER, MAYNARD. "The Mallorcan Contribution to Franciscan California," Americas, v. 4 (1947), 141-150. G 115

GEIGER, MAYNARD J. The Life and Times of Fray Junipero Serra, O.F.M.; or the Man Who Never Turned Back (1713-1784). G 116
Publications of the Academy

of American Franciscan
History, Monograph Series,
Volumes Five and Six. Wash-
ington, D.C. Academy of
American Franciscan History,
1959. 2 vols.

GEIGER, MAYNARD. "The Opening of the Cause of Fray
Junipero Serra, O.F.M.,"
Provincial Annals (Province
of Santa Barbara, O.F.M.),
v. 11 (1949), 114-117. G 117

GEIGER, MAYNARD. "Our Lady
in Franciscan California,"
Franciscan Studies, v. 23
(1942), 99-112.   G 118

GEIGER, MAYNARD. Palou's Life
of Junipero Serra. Washington.
Academy of American Franciscan History. 1955. xxx, 547p.
                        G 119
A new edition and translation
of a standard reference for
the early work of Serra, by
one of the leading authorities
on Serrana.

GEIGER, MAYNARD (ed.). "Questionnaire of the Spanish Government in 1812 concerning
the Native Culture of the
California Mission Indians.
Reply of Mission San Diego."
Americas, v. 6 (1949), 474-
490.   G 120

GEIGER, MAYNARD (ed. and
tr.). "Reply of Mission San
Antonio to the questionnaire
of the Spanish Government
in 1812 concerning the
Native Culture of the California
Mission Indians," Americas, v.
10 (Oct. 1953), 211-227.
                        G 121
Both Spanish text and translation are given. The report
was written by Father Pedro
Cabot, O.F.M. after ten
years' experience on the
mission.

GEIGER, MAYNARD (tr. and ed.).
"Reply of Mission San Carlos
Borromeo to the Questionnaire
of the Spanish Government in
1812 concerning the Native

Culture of the Mission
Indians," Americas, v. 6
(1950), 467-486.   G 122

GEIGER, MAYNARD (ed.). "The
Royal Presidio Chapel of San
Carlos, Monterey, Capital of
Colonial California," The
Americas, v. 9 (October,
1952), 207-211.   G 123
A documentary study of the
efforts made to ensure the
erection of a suitable build-
ing.

GEIGER, MAYNARD. "The
Scholastic Career and Preach-
ing Apostolate of Fray Junipero Serra, O.F.M., S.T.D.,
1730-1749," Americas, v. 4
(1947), 65-82.   G 124

GENTILE, LUIGI. "Cenni
Biografici del P. Giacomo
Diamare," Lettere Edificanti
Provincia Napolitana, ser. 4
(1882-1883), 6-9.   G 125

GENTILE, LUIGI M. "Lettera
XXVIII," Lettere Edificanti
Provincia Napolitana, ser. 2
(1876-1877), 97-110.   G 126

GENTILE, LUIGI M. "Lettera
LXXVI," Lettere Edificanti
Provincia Napolitana, ser. 3
(1879-1880), 181-182.   G 127

GENTILE, LUIGI M. "Lettera
XXXVIII," Lettere Edificanti
Provincia Napolitana, ser. 4
(1882-1883), 87-88.   G 128
Description of the fire that
destroyed the Church and
residence in Pueblo, Colorado, 1882.

GENTILE, LUIGI M. "Lettera
V," Lettere Edificanti Provincia Napolitana, ser. 5
(1886-1887), 24-27.   G 129

GENTILE, LUIGI M. "Lettera
XXVI," Lettere Edificanti
Provincia Napolitana ser. 7
(1895), 60-61.   G 130
Dated "Albuquerque, N.M.,
19 Luglio, 1897," Describes
a mission given at Silver
City, New Mexico beginning
May 14th.

GENTILE, LUIGI M. "Albuquer-

que (Nuovo Messico)," Lettere
Edificanti Provincia Napolitana,
ser. 9, n. 1 (1901), 106-112.
G 131
    Two letters dated "Albuquer-
que 8 Maggio, 9 Maggio,
1900." Treats of the new
church for the Mexicans of
Albuquerque and a mission
given in Chihuahua, Mexico.
[GENTILE, LUIGI M.] "Lettera
del medesimo Gentile del 22
Settembre, 1898," Lettere
Edificanti Provincia Napolitana, ser. 8, nn. 1 (1899),
79-83. G 132
GENTILE, LUIGI M. "Lettera del
P. Gentile," Lettere Edificanti
Provincia Napolitana, ser. 8,
n. 1 (1899), 72-73. G 133
    Dated "Albuquerque, 29 Genn.
1897," Mentions missions
given at Clifton, Morenci,
Solomonville.
GENTILE, LUIGI M. "Lettera
dello stesso (Gentile) Padre
del 30 Agosto, 1898,"
Lettere Edificanti Provincia
Napolitana, ser. 8, n. 1
(1899), 73-78. G 134
"GEORGETOWN COLLEGE. Its
Early History, with a Bio-
graphical Sketch of Its Founder
and Extracts from His Cor-
respondence," Woodstock
Letters, v. 7 (1878), 3-14,
69-86, 135-144; v. 8 (1879),
3-13; v. 9 (1880), 3-15.
G 135
GERARD, H. L. "Notre-Dame
des Victoires, San Francisco,
California," French American
Review, v. 1 (1948), 36-46.
G 136
GERARD, BROTHER HUBERT
(ed.). Mississippi Vista: the
Brothers of the Christian Schools
in the Midwest, 1849-1949.
Winona, Minn. St. Mary's
College, 1948. 296p. G 137
GEREND, M. M. "Archbishop
Heiss," Salesianum, v. 29
(Oct. 1934), 1-7. G 138
GEREND, M.M. "Memories of

By-gone Days," Salesianum, v.
6 (Apr., 1911), 1-9 (July,
1911), 1-11; v. 7 (Oct. 1911),
1-8 (Jan., 1912), 1-9, (Apr.,
1912), 1-13, (July, 1912),
1-11; v. 8 (Oct. 1912), 1-7
(Jan., 1913), 1-10 (Apr.,
1913), 1-14 (July, 1913), 1-
10; v. 9 (Oct., 1913), 4-12,
(July, 1914), 12-19, (Apr.,
1914), 1-5; v. 10 (Oct.,
1914), 1-9, (Jan., 1915), 7-13,
(Apr., 1915), 9-16, (July,
1915), 1-9; v. 10 (?) (Oct.,
1915), 7-16, (Apr., 1916),
7-17, (July, 1916), 7-13; v.
12 (Oct., 1916), 15-21, (Jan.
1917), 14-25, (July, 1917),
18-32, (Jan., 1918), 34-49,
(Apr., 1918), 28-39, (July,
1918), 35-44; v. 14 (Oct.,
1918), 23-29, (Jan., 1919),
25-33, (Apr., 1919), 32-41;
v. 15 (Oct., 1919), 29-40,
(Jan., 1920), 25-34, (Nov.,
1920), 13-22; v. 16 (Jan.,
1921), 35-42, (Apr., 1921),
39-48, (Aug., 1921), 31-39.
G 139
GEREND, M.M. "Twenty-five
Years with the Deaf," Salesianum, v. 9 (July, 1914), 1-14.
G 140
GERLACH, DOMINIC B. A
History of St. Joseph Parish,
Victoria, Ohio. MA thesis.
Saint University. 1952. vii,
112p. G 141
GERMAIN, AIDAN H. Catholic
Military and Naval Chaplains,
1776-1917. Washington.
Catholic University. 1929.
vii, 165p. G 142
    Concerned with "official"
chaplains. Includes the
Confederacy. Largely a list
of names.
GERMAIN, AIDAN H. "Catholic
Military and Naval Chaplains,
1776-1917," Catholic Histori-
cal Review, v. 15 (1929),
171-178. G 143
"GERMAN VOLKSVEREIN," Cen-
tral Blatt and Social Justice,

v. 2 (1909), 6-9.　　　G 144
GEROW, RICHARD O. Catholicity in Mississippi. Natchez, Miss. The Author. 1939. xvii, 492p. incl. front. (facsim.), plates, ports.　　　G 145
GEROW, RICHARD O. Cradle Days of St. Mary's at Natchez. Natchez, Miss. The Author. 1941. xiii, 302p. incl. front., plates, ports.　　　G 146
GERTRUDE, SISTER M. AGNES. "Italian Immigration into Philadelphia," American Catholic Historical Society of Philadelphia Records, v. 58 (1947), 133-143, 189-208, 256-267.　　　G 147
GESCHICHTE DER FRANZISKANER SCHWESTER DER PROVINZ ZUR HL. CLARA IN NORD AMERIKA, 1873-1915. no pl. no pub. 1915? 200p. illus., ports.　　　G 148
GETHSEMANI MAGNIFICAT. Trappist, Ky. 1949. unpaged. illus., plates.　　　G 149
GETLEIN, FRANK. "Marquette (University)," Jubilee, IV (Jul.-Aug. 1956), 58-65.　　　G 150
A good, popular, illustrated account of one of America's largest and most progressive Jesuit universities.
GIANNOTTA, ROSARIO. Contributions of Italians to the Development of American Culture in the Eighteenth Century. MA thesis. St. John's University, N.Y., 1942. mss.　　　G 151
GIBBONS, JAMES CARDINAL. Retrospect of Fifty Years. Baltimore. John Murphy. 1916. 2v.　　　G 152
GIBBONS, JAMES JOSEPH. In the San Juan. Chicago. Calument Book and Engraving Co. 1898. 194p. plates.　　　G 153
GIBBONS, JAMES JOSEPH. Notes of a Missionary Priest in the Rocky Mountains. New York. Christian Press Association Publishing Co. 1900?

illus.　　　G 154
GIBSON, SISTER LAURITA. Catholic Women of Colonial Maryland. MA thesis. Catholic University. 1939. 122p.　　　G 155
GIBSON, SISTER LAURITA. Some Anglo-American Converts to Catholicism Prior to 1829. Washington. Catholic University. 1943. xi, 259p.　　　G 156
GIGLINGER, GEORGE. "Rt. Rev. Henry Cosgrove, D.D., Bishop of Davenport, Iowa," Acta et Dicta, v. 2 (1910), 211-218. port.　　　G 157
GILBERT, MATTHEW JOSEPH. Archdiocese of San Antonio, 1874-1949. San Antonio. The Author. 1949. xx, 304p. illus., plates, ports., maps.　　　G 158
GILES, SISTER MARY BERNADETTE. A Changing Urban Parish; A study of Mobility in St. Agnew Parish, San Francisco, California. MA thesis. Gonzaga University. 1959. 144p.　　　G 159
GILLARD, JOHN T. The Catholic Church and the American Negro. Baltimore. St. Joseph's Society Press. 1929. xv, 324p. illus. (map), tables, diagr.　　　G 160
GILLARD, JOHN T. Colored Catholics in the United States. Baltimore. Josephite Press. 1941. x, 298p. incl. tables.　　　G 161
GILLARD, JOHN T. "First Negro Parish in the United States," America, v. 50 (1934), 370-372.　　　G 162
GILLARD, JOHN T. The Negro American, A Mission Investigation. Cincinnati. Catholic Student Mission Crusade. 1935. 69p.　　　G 163
GILLIS, JAMES M. "Americanism: Fifty Years After," Catholic World, v. 169 (1949), 246-253.　　　G 164
GILLIS, JAMES M. "Father

Hecker and His Friends," American Benedictine Review, v. 4 (Spring, 1953), 47-64. G 165
A lengthy review of the book by the same name that adds to the information concerning the founding of the Paulists.

GILLIS, JAMES M. The Paulists. New York. Macmillan. 1932. vi, 67p. G 166

GILLOGLY, ILDEFONSE. "Thirtieth Anniversary," Provincial Annals (Province of the Most Holy Name, O.F.M.), v. 2 (1941), 135-145. G 167

GILMAN, RICHARD. "Carthusians in Vermont," Jubilee, v. 2 (1955), Apr., 49-55. illus. G 168

GILMAN, RICHARD. "Spain in America," Jubilee, v. 3 (1955), June, 17-39. G 169
A well written and illustrated article on the origins of the Church in the Southwest.

GILMARTIN, THOMAS V. "A Partial Appraisal of the Character and Works of Archbishop William Henry Elder from His Letters of 1887-1888," St. Meinrad Essays, v. 12 (1959), 53-70. G 170

GILMORE, SISTER JULIA. Come North. New York. McMullen. 1951. 310p. illus. G 171
The life story of Mother Xavier Ross, foundress of the Sisters of Charity of Leavenworth.

GILMORE, SISTER JULIA. "Mother Xavier Ross," Review for Religious, v. 15 (1956), 113-127. G 172
A brief, pious biographical sketch of the foundress of the Sisters of Charity of Leavenworth.

GILSDORF, GORDON. Wisconsin's Catholic Heritage. Madison, Wisconsin. Holy Name Society Office. 1948. 50p. G 173

GIMPL, SISTER M. CAROLINE ANN. Immaculate Conception Mission, Steilacoom, Washington. MA thesis. Seattle University, 1951. 128p. maps, tables. G 174

GIORDA, F. "Indian Missions, Washington Territory. Extracts from a Letter dated De Smet, Pine Creek P.O., W.T., October 21, 1879," Woodstock Letters, v. 9 (1880), 27-28. G 175

GISRIEL, SISTER FRANCIS. Mother Seton and the Philosophy of Catholic Education. MA thesis. Villanova University. 1948. 103p. G 176

GLEASON, SISTER MIRIAM THERESA. Archbishop O'-Hara, a Pioneer in Social Welfare Legislation for Women," Catholic Charities Review, v. 40 (1956), 8-10. G 177

GLEASON, PHILIP. "From Free Love to Catholicism: Dr. and Mrs. Thomas L. Nichols at Yellow Springs," Ohio Historical Quarterly, v. 70 (Oct. 1961), 283-307. G 178
Utopian Colony in Southwestern Ohio - lasted one year 1856-1857.

GLEESON, WILLIAM. History of the Catholic Church in California. San Francisco, A. L. Bancrofts and Co. 1872. 2v. in 1. front., plates, ports., maps. G 179

GLEISS, PAUL G. "German Jesuit Missionaries in 18th Century Maryland," Woodstock Letters, v. 75 (1946), 199-206. G 180
Theodore Schneider, Wilhelm Wapoler, Mathias Sittenberger (Mr. Manners), Ferdinand Steinmeyer, Jacob Frambach.

GLIEBE, JULIUS. "Coming of the Friars to the Inland Empire of the Great Northwest," Provincial Annals (Province of Santa Barbara, O.F.M.), v.

1 (Apr. 1939), 7-12.
G 181
Franciscan arrival in Spokane, 1915.
GLODEN, SISTER MARY CORTONA. Sisters of Saint Francis of the Holy Family, Jesus, Mary and Joseph. St. Louis Herder. 1928. 278p. illus., ports.
G 182
GLODT, JOHN T. "Our Florida Martyr Priests," American Ecclesiastical Review, v. 69 (1923), 498-513, 614-631.
G 183
GODECKER, SISTER M. SALESIA. History of Catholic Education in Indiana. Washington. no pub. 1925. 80p.
G 184
GODECKER, SISTER M. SALESIA. Simon Bruté de Remur, First Bishop of Vincennes. St. Meinrad. St. Meinrad Abbey Press, Ind. 1931. xliii, 441p. front., plates, map, facsims.
G 185
GOEB, CUTHBERT ALOYSIUS. Journey of Father Theobald Mathew to America, 1849-1851. MA thesis. Catholic University. 1922. 66p.
G 186
GOEBEL, EDMUND J. A Study of Catholic Secondary Education during the Colonial Period up to the First Plenary Council of Baltimore, 1852. Washington. Catholic University. 1938. x, 269p.
G 187
GOELZ, CHRISTOPHER. Fifty Golden Years. no pub. 1938.
G 188
GOELZ, CHRISTOPHER. History of the Diocese of Belleville. (Belleville). The Messenger. 1939. 100p. illus.
G 189
GOESBRIAND, LOUIS DE. Catholic Memoirs of Vermont and New Hampshire. Burlington. The Author. 1886. 167p.
G 190
GOHMANN, SISTER MARY DE LOURDES. Political Nativism in Tennessee to 1860. Washington. Catholic University. 1938. vii, 192p.
G 191

GOLDEN, SISTER MARY CONSTANCE. "Catholic Eastern Churches in New York City," United States Historical Society Records and Studies, v. 34 (1945), 112-136.
G 192
"GOLDEN JUBILEE," Provincial Annals (Province of the Most Holy Name, O.F.M.), v. 7 (1947), 44-52.
G 193
"GOLDEN JUBILEE OF THE ARRIVAL OF THE FRANCISCANS IN ARIZONA IN MODERN TIMES," Provincial Annals (Province of Santa Barbara, O.F.M.), v. 10 (1948), 109-115.
G 194
"GOLDEN JUBILEE OF THE PASSIONIST FATHERS. FIFTY YEARS IN THE UNITED STATES," Catholic World, v. 76 (1903), 502-515. G 195
GOLDMAN, ERIC F. Charles J. Bonaparte, Patricial Reformer. His Earlier Career. Baltimore. Johns Hopkins. 1943. 150p. G 196
GOLDSTEIN, DAVID. Autobiography of a Campaigner for Christ. Boston. Catholic Campaigners for Christ. 1936. xi, 146p.
G 197
GOLITSYN, DMITRII DMITRIEVICH. Gallitzin's Letters. A Collection of the Polemical Works, ed. by Grace Murphy. Loretto, Pa. Angelmodde Press. 1940. 302p. G 198
GOLL, LOUIS J. Jesuit Missions among the Sioux. St. Francis, S.D. 1940. 70p. G 199
GONNER, SISTER LAWRENCE. History of the First Fifty Years of the Sisters of Providence in the United States. MA thesis. Loyola University (Chicago). 1933. G 200
"GONZAGA COLLEGE, A SKETCH OF SOME OF ITS PRESIDENTS, PROFESSORS, STUDENTS," Woodstock Letters, v. 18 (1889), 269-284; v. 19 (1890), 7-22, 163-178; v. 20

(1891), 228-237.　　G 201
GOOD SHEPHERD SISTERS ON
EIGHTH STREET, LOUISVILLE
CENTENNIAL SOUVENIR,
1843-1943. (Louisville.
Schuhmann Printing Co.). 1943.
86p. ports.　　G 202
GOODALL, FRANCIS P. "The
Society of Catholic Medical Mis-
sionaries of Philadelphia,"
American Catholic Historical
Society of Philadelphia Records,
v. 61 (1950), 237-247. G 203
GOODROW, SISTER ESTHER
MARIE. Catholic Participation
in the Diplomacy of the Ameri-
can Civil War. Ph.D. thesis.
Saint Louis University. 1954.
371p.　　G 204
GOOSENS, VICTOR L. "John
Francis Rivet," St. Meinrad
Historical Essays, v. 1 (1928),
213-226.　　G 205
GOOSENS, VICTOR L. "Pierre
Gibault," St. Meinrad Histori-
cal Essays, v. 1 (1928), 7-15.
　　G 206
GORAYEB, JOSEPH. Life and
Letters of Walter Drum, S.J.
New York. America Press.
1928. 313p. front., (port.).
　　G 207
GORMAN, SISTER M. JANE
THOMAS. Tertiary Franciscan
Missionary Sisters of the Sacred
Heart and Catholic Education in
the United States. Ph.D. thesis.
Fordham University. 1946.
vii, 383p.　　G 208
GORMALY, MOTHER ST. WIL-
LIAM. History of the Founda-
tions of the Institute of the
Blessed Virgin Mary in North
America. MA thesis. Loyola
University. (Chicago). 1934.
　　G 209
GORMAN, ROBERT. Catholic
Apologetical Literature in the
United States (1784-1858).
Washington. Catholic University.
1939. x, 192p.　　G 210
GORMAN, ROBERT. "Indiana
Historiography and the Founding
of Vincennes," American Cath-

olic Historical Society of
Philadelphia Records, v. 50
(1949), 41-52.　　G 211
GORMAN, THOMAS K. Seventy-
Five Years of Catholic Life
in Nevada. (Reno? 1935).
131p. illus., ports.　　G 212
GORMLEY, SISTER GERTRUDE.
An Inquiry into the Attitude of
the American Catholic Press
toward the League of Nations,
1918-1919. MA thesis. Cath-
olic University. 1946. xxxv,
100p.　　G 213
GORRELL, J.J. Earliest Francis-
can Missionary Labors in
Texas. St. Francis Home
Journal. v. (1936), 76-78,
108-111.　　G 214
GORRELL, JOHN J. Early
Franciscan Missions in Texas.
St. Francis Home Journal. v.
(1933), 333-334, 345.
　　G 215
GORRELL, JOHN JOS. First
Missionary Days in Texas,"
Mary Immaculate. v. (1934),
228-230, 291-293, 313, 330-
333, (1935), 27-28.　　G 216
GORRELL, J. J.　NEVILLE.
"The Lay Apostolate in the
U.S.A.," Month, v. 165
(1935), 511-518.　　G 217
"THE GOSHENHOPPEN REGIS-
TERS: FIFTH SERIES,
BAPTISMS, 1815-1918," Tr.
and ed. by John R. Dunne.
Records of the American Cath-
olic Historical Society of
Philadelphia, v. 61 (December,
1950), 248-262.　　G 218
GOSS, EDWARD F. "The Taft
Commission to the Vatican,
1902," American Catholic His-
torical Society of Philadelphia
Records, v. 46 (1935), 184-
201.　　G 219
GOSSELIN, AUGUSTE H.
L'Eglise du Canada. Québec.
Laflamme. 1911-1916. 4v.
　　G 220
GOSSELIN, A.　Les Sauvages du
Mississippi (1698-1705)
d'après la Correspondence des

Missionaires des Missions.
Etrangères de Québec. XV
Congrès International des A-
méricanistes. Québec, 1906
(Québec, 1907), p. 31-51.
G 221
GOSSELIN, AUGUSTE H. Vie
de Mgr. de Laval, Premier
Evêque de Québec et Apôtre
du Canada, 1622-1708. Québec.
L.-J. Demers and Frère.
1890. G 222
GOUGH, FANNY C. "Fort St.
Inigoes," Maryland Historical
Magazine, v. 40 (1945), 54-59.
G 223
GOUGH, JOHN F. St. Mary's in
Jersey City, 1859-1938. New
York. Burr Printing House.
1938. 256p. front., plates,
ports. G 224
GOUGHAN, J. H. "The Catholic
Church in Goodhue County,
Minn." Acta et Dicta, v. 4
(1916), 241-252. G 225
GOWEN, MARGUERITE H., AND
SISTER MARY MERCEDES.
"Sisters of Notre Dame de
Namur--Philadelphia 1856-
1956," American Catholic His-
torical Society of Philadelphia
Records, v. 48 (1957), 29-45.
G 226
GOYAN, GEORGES. Un Apôtre aux
États-Unis. Le P. Samuel
Mazzuchelli. RHM 1933, 184-
206. G 227
GRACE, THOMAS L. "Journal
of Trip to Red River, August
and September, 1861,"
Acta et Dicta, v. 1 (1908),
166-183. G 228
GRACE, WILLIAM J. "Inquiry
Forum and Convert Guild of
the Church of the Gesu, Milwau-
kee," Woodstock Letters, v.
81 (February, 1952), 3-12.
G 229
GRAESSEL, LAWRENCE. A
Pioneer Priest, Bishop Elect,
to His Parents in Bavaria,"
Central Blatt and Social
Justice, v. 20 (1927), 53-54.
G 230

GRADY, SISTER MARY CYRILLUS.
A Survey of the Catholic Girls'
Academies of Pennsylvania.
MA thesis. Villanova Univer-
sity. 1943. 96p. G 231
GRAF, HIERONYMUS, O.M.I.
"Die Kapuzinermission zum
heiligen Benedikt dem Mohren
in Milwaukee," Seraphisches
Weltapostolate, v. (1935),
162-172. G 232
GRAHAM, EDWARD P. History
of St. John's Parish, Canton,
Ohio. Canton, Ohio. The
Author. 1925. G 233
GRAHAM, FRANK. Al Smith,
American. New York. Putnam's
1945. ix, 242p. G 234
GRAHAM, HUGH. "Catholic
Missionary Schools among the
Indians of Minnesota," Mid-
America, v. 2 (1931), 199-
206. G 235
GRAHAM, HUGH. "St. Genevieve
Academy: Missouri's First
Secondary School," Mid-
America, v. 4 (1932), 67-
79. G 236
GRAHAM, JAMES M. "Catholic
Heroes of Illinois," Illinois
Catholic Historical Review, v.
1 (1919), 294-302. G 237
GRAND RAPIDS (DIOCESE)
SYNOD, 1903. Synodus dioe-
cesana grandormensis prima
habita die 18 Septembris,
1903 in aedibus nosocomii a
Misericordia nuncupati in urbe
big Rapids a Henrico Josepho
Richter [ep.] [n.p., n.d.]
201p. G 238
GRANT, DOROTHY.John England,
American Christopher. Mil-
waukee. Bruce. 1949. xvi,
167p. G 239
GRASSI, JOHN. "The Catholic
Church in the United States
in 1818," American Catholic
Historical Researches, v. 8
(1891), 98-111. G 240
GRASSI, JOHN. "The Catholic
Religion in the United States
in 1818," Woodstock Letters,
v. 11 (1882), 229-246. G 241

GRASSI, URBAN. "Indian Missions --the Sinpesquensi. Letter dated Washington Territory, Yokama County, Oct. 4th, 1873," Woodstock Letters, v. 3 (1874), 68-73.   G 242

GRASSI, URBAN. "Indian Missions. Letter dated Fort Colville, Wash. Ty., April 23rd, 1878," Woodstock Letters, v. 7 (1878), 174-178.   G 243

GRASSI, URBAN. "Indian Missions. Washington Territory. Letter," Woodstock Letters, v. 11 (1882), 65-70.   G 244

GRATTAN, ANN. An Examination of the Politics and Practices of the Commonweal with Regard to Its Catholic Character. MA thesis. Marquette University. 1956.   G 245

GRAVES, WILLIAM WHITE. The Legend of Greenbush; The Story of a Pioneer Country Church. St. Paul, Kansas. Journal Press. 1937. 78p. illus. (incl. ports.).   G 246

GRAVES, WILLIAM WHITE. Life and Letters of Father John Schoenmakers, S.J., Apostle to the Osages. Parsons, Kansas. Commercial Publishers. 1928. 144p. illus., port.   G 247

GRAVES, WILLIAM WHITE. Life and Letters of Fathers Ponziglione, Schoenmakers, and Other Early Jesuits at Osage Mission; Sketch of St. Francis' Church; Life of Mother Bridget. St. Paul, Kansas. 1916. 287p. illus., ports.   G 248

GRAY, SISTER GERTRUDE MARY. A Preliminary Survey of the Life of the Most Rev. Joseph Sadoc Alemany, O. P. First Archbishop of San Francisco. MA thesis. Catholic University. 1942. 125p.   G 249

GRAY, LOUIS HERBERT. A History of the Parish of St. Ignatius in the City of New York, 1871-1946. New York.

no pub. 1946. 40p. illus., plates.   G 250

GREAT FALLS (DIOCESE) SYNOD, 1st, 1935. Synodus dioecesana greatormensis prima celebrata die 21 mensis iunii anno Domini 1935, praeside Eduino Vincentio O'Hara [ep.] [Portland, Ore., Sentinel printery, n.d.] 61, [1] p.   G 251

GREEN, JAMES J. "American Catholics and the Irish Land League, 1879-1882," Catholic Historical Review, v. 35 (1949), 19-42.   G 252

GREEN, JAMES J. "The Organization of the Catholic Total Abstinence Union of America, 1866-1884," American Catholic Historical Society of Philadelphia Records, v. 61 (1950), 71-97.   G 253

GREEN, JAMES JEREMIAH. Impact of the Henry George Agitation on Catholics. MA thesis. University of Notre Dame. 1948. 192p.   G 254

GREEN, JAMES JEREMIAH. The Impact of the Henry George Theories on American Catholics. Ph.D. thesis. University of Notre Dame. 1956. 366p.   G 255

GREEN BAY, WIS. (DIOCESES). Constitutiones Dioeceseos Sinus Vindus. Milwaukee. P. V. Deuster. 1869. 12p.   G 256

GREEN BAY, WIS. (DIOCESE) SYNOD, 1st, 1876. Decreta edita in synoda dioecesana lma celebrata Sinu Viridi a Francisco Xaverio Krautbauer, [ep.] diebus 11mo et 12mo Julii, A.D. 1876. Sinu Viridi, Wis., Robinson Bros., & Clark, 1877. 30p.   G 257

GREEN BAY, WIS. (DIOCESE) SYNOD, 2nd, 1889. Statuta synodi dioecesanae Sinus Viridis secundae, habitae diebus XXI, XXII, et XXIII Maji, a.d. 1889, in ecclesia cathedrali, praeside Friderico

Xaverio, episcopo Sinus Viridis tertio. Green Bay, Wis., Landsmann, 1890. 74, 15, 13p. 2 1.   G 258
Separate pagings include: Revised by-laws of incorporated congregations of the diocese of Green Bay. March 31st, 1890. [15p.] Constitution and revised by-laws (Revised Feb. 18, 1890) of Leo's benevolent association of the R.C. priests of the diocese of Green Bay. Incorporated December 3d, 1879. [13p. 2 1].

GREEN BAY, WIS. (DIOCESE) SYNOD, 1895. Statuta dioecesis Sinus Viridis. Green Bay, Wis., Ex typographia Landsmann, 1898. 3p. 1., 108p.   G 259
Contains statutes of the 1st, 2nd, and 3rd diocesan synods: July 11, 12 under Franciscus Xaverius Krautbauer; May 21-23 under Fredericus Xaverius Katzer; Aug. 1895, under Sebastianus Gebhardus. -- cf. Introduction.

GREEN BAY, WIS. (DIOCESE). Notae ad statuta dioecesana. [n.p., n.d.] 12p.   G 260
Document signed: Sebastianus Gebhardus; dated 1898.

GREEN BAY, WIS. (DIOCESE) SYNOD, 4th, 1920. Constitutiones dioeceseos Sinus Viridis (Green Bay, Wis.) quae in synodo dioecesana quarta, die 14, 15, 16 Dec., 1920 A.D. habita in ecclesia Sti. Francisci Xav., cathedral. A Paulo Petro Rhode, D.D. latae et promulgatae fuerunt. Pulaski, Wisc., Typis Franciscanae typog. [1921.] xxix, 173p.   G 261

GREENE, EVARTS BOUTELL. Religion and the State. The Making and Testing of An American Tradition. New York. New York University Press.

1941. 172p.   G 262

GREENE, JOHN H. "A Brief History of the Catholic Church in Newport," Newport Historical Society Bulletin, no. 101, (January, 1940), 19-25.   G 263

GREENLY, A.H. "Father Louis Hennepin: His Travels and His Books," Papers of the Bibliographical Society of America, v. 51 (1957), 38-60.   G 264

GREENWELL, SISTER BERENICE. Nazareth's Contribution to Education. Ph.D. thesis. Fordham University. 1933. xvi, 638p.   G 265

GREGOROVICH, JOSEPH. The Apostle of the Chippewas. The Life Story of the Most Reverend Frederick Baraga. Lemont, Illinois. Franciscan Fathers. 1932. 103p. G 266

GRELICHE, HENRY. Essai Sur la Vie et Les Travaux De Mgr. Flaget Évêque de Bardstown Et De Louis-Ville. Aux États-Unis D'Amérique. Paris-Lyon,Librairie Catholique De Périsse Frères. 1851. 192p.   G 267

GRETEMAN, JAMES B. "The Church in Carroll County," Iowa Catholic Historical Review, v. 2 (Nov., 1930), 3-21.   G 268

GRIFFIN, CLIFFORD S. "Converting the Catholics: American Benevolent Societies and the Ante-Bellum Crusade against the Church," Catholic Historical Review, v. 47 (1961), 325-341.   G 269

GRIFFIN, JOSEPH A. The Contribution of Belgium to the Catholic Church in America (1523-1857). Washington. Catholic University. 1932. xvi, 235p. incl. geneal. tab.   G 270

GRIFFIN, MARTIN I.J. "The Anti-Catholic Spirit of the Revolution," American Catholic

Historical Researches, v. 6 (1889), 140-178. G 271

GRIFFIN, MARTIN I.J. "Archives of 'Old' St. Joseph's--Philadelphia--List of Deeds and Documents from 1689-1851," American Catholic Historical Researches, v. 14 (1897), 161-170. G 272

GRIFFIN, MARTIN I.J. "Asylum: A Colony of French Catholics in Bradford County, Pennsylvania, 1794-1800," American Catholic Historical Society of Philadelphia Records, v. 18 (1907), 245-261, 421-433. G 273

[GRIFFIN, MARTIN I.J.]. "The Beginning of the Hierarchy in the United States," American Catholic Historical Researches, v. 19 (1902), 155-159. G 274

[GRIFFIN, MARTIN I.J.]. "Catholic Annals of St. Louis," American Catholic Historical Researches, v. 4 (1887), 135-136. G 275

[GRIFFIN, MARTIN I.J.]. "The Catholic Indians and the American Revolution," American Catholic Historical Researches, v. 25 (1908), 195-230. G 276 The story of the Indians of Maine and their attempt to obtain a priest.

GRIFFIN, MARTIN I.J. "Catholic Lies in American History," American Catholic Historical Researches, v. 18 (1901), 163-165. G 277

GRIFFIN, MARTIN I.J. "Catholic Loyalist Highlanders of the Mohawk Valley," American Catholic Historical Researches, v. 25 (1908), 231-249. G 278

GRIFFIN, MARTIN I.J. "Catholic Loyalists of the Revolution," American Catholic Historical Researches, v. 6 (1889), 77-88. G 279

[GRIFFIN, MARTIN I.J.] "Catholic Loyalists of the Revolution," American Catholic Historical

Researches, v. 25 (1908), 289-312. G 280

[GRIFFIN, MARTIN I.J.]. "Catholic Officers in the Revolutionary Army," American Catholic Historical Researches, v. 25 (1908), 313-344. G 281

GRIFFIN, MARTIN I.J. Catholics and the American Revolution. Ridley Park. The Author. 1907-1911. 3v. G 282

GRIFFIN, MARTIN I.J. "Catholics in Colonial Maryland, American Catholic Historical Society of Philadelphia Records, v. 22 (1911), 84-100. G 283

[GRIFFIN, MARTIN I.J.]. "Catholics in the American Revolution," American Catholic Historical Researches, v. 23 (1906), 1-40, 97-120, 193-239, 289-331; v. 24 (1907), 1-31, 97-153, 193-258; v. 25 (1908), 1-21. G 284

[GRIFFIN, MARTIN I.J.]. "The 'Cessation' at St. Mary's (Phila.)," American Catholic Historical Researches, v. 3 (1887), 83-89. G 285

[GRIFFIN, MARTIN I.J.]. "Chaplains of the French in the American Revolution," American Catholic Historical Researches, v. 21 (1904), 2-10. G 286

GRIFFIN, MARTIN I.J. "The Church of the Holy Trinity, Philadelphia," American Catholic Historical Society of Philadelphia Records, v. 2 (1910), 249-261, v. 25 (1914), 1-45. G 287

GRIFFIN, MARTIN I.J. Commodore John Barry. Philadelphia. The Author. 1903. xi, 424p. incl. map. front., plate, port., facsim. G 288

GRIFFIN, MARTIN I. J. "Doctor John Michael, The Alleged

Priest of Colonial Philadelphia: Dr. Thaddeus Murphy,
Also Reputed a Priest," A-
merican Catholic Historical
Society of Philadelphia Records, v. 16 (1905), 266-
313, 391-415.   G 289

[GRIFFIN, MARTIN I.J. (ed.)].
"Documents of Probable
Catholic American Historical
Value," American Catholic
Historical Researches, v.
18 (1901), 178-182.   G 290
  A selection from reports of
  the English Historical
  Manuscripts Commission and
  appendices.

GRIFFIN, MARTIN I.J. "Early
Catholics in Bucks County,"
Bucks County Historical
Society Collections, v. 1
(1908), 489-495.   G 291

GRIFFIN, MARTIN I.J. "Excerpts
from Letters in the Archives of
Baltimore," American Catholic
Historical Researches, v. 18
(1907), 416-420.   G 292

GRIFFIN, MARTIN I.J. "Father
Peter Huet de la Valinière
the 'Fiery, Factious, and
Turbulent Rebel,' " American
Catholic Historical Researches,
v. 23 (1906), 203-239. G 293

GRIFFIN, MARTIN I.J. "Father
Smith of Talbot County, Maryland," 1683-1693," American
Catholic Historical Researches,
v. 15 (1898), 50-54.   G 294

[GRIFFIN, MARTIN I.J.]. "The
First American Catholic
Bible," American Catholic
Historical Researches, v. 3
(1887), 64-68.   G 295

GRIFFIN, MARTIN I.J. "The
First American 'Mission to Non-
Catholics,' " American Catholic
Historical Researches, v. 18
(1901), 41-43.   G 296

GRIFFIN, MARTIN I.J. "The
First Mass in Philadelphia,"
American Catholic Historical
Researches, v. 12 (1895),
39-43.   G 297

GRIFFIN, MARTIN I.J. "The First

Parish Sodality," American
Catholic Historical Researches,
v. 18 (1901), 60-63. G 298

No entry   G 299

[GRIFFIN, MARTIN I.J.]. "The
Founding of the Faith in Philadelphia," American Catholic
Historical Researches, v. 15
(1898), 177-184.   G 300

GRIFFIN, MARTIN I.J. "Historical Notes of St. Ann's
Church and Mission, Philadelphia (1845-1895)," American Catholic Historical Researches, v. 6 (1895), 426-
449.   G 301

GRIFFIN, MARTIN I.J. "History of Rt. Rev. Michael
Egan, D.D.," American
Catholic Historical Researches,
v. 9 (1892), 65-80, 113-128,
161-176; v. 10 (1893), 17-
32, 81-96, 113-128, 161-192.
                        G 302

GRIFFIN, MARTIN I.J. History
of "Old St. Joseph's" Philadelphia. Philadelphia. I.C.B.
U. Journal Print. 1882.
16p.   G 303

GRIFFIN, MARTIN I.J. "History
of the Church of Saint John
the Evangelist, Philadelphia,"
American Catholic Historical
Researches, v. 20 (1909),
350-405.   G 304

GRIFFIN, MARTIN I.J. "History
of the Church of St. John the
Evangelist, Philadelphia from
1845-1853," American Catholic
Historical Society of Philadelphia Records, v. 25 (1914),
129-138.   G 305

GRIFFIN, MARTIN I.J. "Penn-
sylvania's First Catholic
Convert," American Catholic
Historical Researches, v. 7
(1890), 50-66.   G 306
  The story of Lionell Brittin,
  probably received into the
  Church in 1707.

GRIFFIN, MARTIN I.J. History of the Rt. Rev. Michael Egan, D.D., First Bishop of Philadelphia. The Author. 1893. 128p. front., illus. (incl. port.).   G 307

GRIFFIN, MARTIN I.J. History of St. John's Church, Philadelphia. Philadelphia. I.C.B. U. Journal Print. 1882. 16p.   G 308

GRIFFIN, MARTIN I.J. "Life of Bishop Conwell of Philadelphia," American Catholic Historical Society of Philadelphia Records, v. 23 (1913), 16-42, 162-178, 217-250, 238-361; v. 24 (1914), 52-67, 146-178, 217-248, 296-341; v. 26 (1915), 64-88, 131-165, 227-249; v. 27 (1916), 74-87, 145-160, 275-283, 359-378; v. 28 (1917), 64-84, 150-183, 244-265, 310-347; v. 29 (1918), 170-182, 250-261, 360-384.
                                       G 309

GRIFFIN, MARTIN I.J. Stephen Moylan, Muster Master General, Secretary and Aide-de-Camp to Washington. Philadelphia. The Author. 1909. 142p. col. front.   G 310

[GRIFFIN, MARTIN I.J.]. "Philadelphia's Two Masonic Priests," American Catholic Historical Researches, v. 17 (1900), 29-32.   G 311

[GRIFFIN, MARTIN I.J. (ED.)]. "Popery in Maryland," American Catholic Historical Researches, v. 25 (1908), 258-276.   G 312

[GRIFFIN, MARTIN I.J.]. "Proposed Jesuit College in Philadelphia in 1808," American Catholic Historical Researches, v. 18 (1901), 168-170.
                                       G 313

[GRIFFIN, MARTIN I.J.]. "The Return of the Jesuits to Old St. Joseph's," American Catholic Historical Researches, v. 3 (1887), 53-57.   G 314

GRIFFIN, MARTIN I. J. 'Rev.

Ferdinand Farmer, S.J. of Philadelphia, 1758-1786," American Catholic Historical Researches, v. 14 (1897), 2-5.   G 315

GRIFFIN, MARTIN I.J. 'Rev. Francis A. Fleming, Pastor of St. Mary's, Philadelphia," American Catholic Historical Researches, v. 8 (1891), 16-24.   G 316

[GRIFFIN, MARTIN I.J.]. 'Rev. James Harold, the Botany Bay Irish Convict Priest of Philadelphia, 'the Cause' of the Direful Dissension at St. Mary's Church, 1812-1813," American Catholic Historical Researches, v. 17 (1900), 17-28.   G 317

GRIFFIN, MARTIN I.J. 'The Reverend John Nepomucene Goetz, Third Pastor and William Elling, Assistant, of Holy Trinity Church, Philadelphia," American Catholic Historical Society of Philadelphia Records, v. 21 (1910), 94-124.
                                       G 318

GRIFFIN, MARTIN I.J. 'Rev. Joseph Greaton, S.J.," American Catholic Historical Researches, v. 16 (1899), 59-106.   G 319

GRIFFIN, MARTIN I.J. 'The Rev. Peter Helbron, Second Pastor of Holy Trinity Church, Philadelphia," American Catholic Historical Society of Philadelphia Records, v. 21 (1910), 1-21.   G 320

GRIFFIN, MARTIN I.J. 'Rev. Robert Harding," American Catholic Historical Researches, v. 7 (1890), 82-92.   G 321

[GRIFFIN, MARTIN I.J.]. "Revolutionary Catholic Notes," American Catholic Historical Researches, v. 26 (1909), 332-347, v. 27 (1910), 217-232, 297-311.
                                       G 322

[GRIFFIN, MARTIN I.J.]. "The Right of Patronage to St.

Mary's," American Catholic Historical Researches, v. 3 (1887), 58-63.   G 323

GRIFFIN, MARTIN I.J. "St. Joseph's Orphan Asylum, Philadelphia," American Catholic Historical Researches, v. 14 (1897), 9-12.   G 324

GRIFFIN, MARTIN I.J. "The Sir John James Fund," American Catholic Historical Society of Philadelphia Records, v. 9 (1898), 195-209.   G 325
An account of the establishment of the fund and its founder. Also called the German fund, and the Lancastrian Fund.

[GRIFFIN, MARTIN I.J.]. "Some Errors of Catholic History," American Catholic Historical Researches, v. 19 (1902), 49-52.   G 326

GRIFFIN, MARTIN I.J. "The Story of St. Mary's," American Catholic Historical Researches, v. 10 (1893), 2-16, 50-72.   G 327

GRIFFIN, MARTIN I.J. "Thomas FitzSimmons," American Catholic Historical Society of Philadelphia Records, v. 2 (1886-1888), 45-111.   G 328

GRIFFIN, MARTIN I.J. "The Toothless Priest, Rev. Samuel Sutherland Cooper," American Catholic Historical Researches, v. 15 (1898), 17-32.   G 329

[GRIFFIN, MARTIN I.J.]. "Where Did Colonial Priests Get Faculties?" American Catholic Historical Researches, v. 22 (1905), 9-10.   G 330

GRIFFIN, MARTIN I.J. "Why Old St. Joseph's, Philadelphia, Was Not Founded Until 1733......." American Catholic Historical Researches, v. 9 (1892), 17-27.   G 331

GRIFFIN, MARTIN I.J. "William Penn, the Friend of Catholics," American Catholic Historical Society of Philadelphia Records,

v. 1 (1884), 71-85.   G 332

GRIFFIN, MARTIN I.J. AND JOSEPH WILLCOX (eds.). "Extracts from a Diary of Rev. Patrick Kenny," American Catholic Historical Society of Philadelphia Records, v. 7 (1896), 94-137, v. 9 (1898), 62-128, 223-256, 305-342, 422-458.   G 333

GRIFFIN, ROSEMARY RING. "Rogel, Padre of the Ports," Mid-America, v. 19 (1948), 3-43.   G 334

GRIFFITH, CHARLES F. "Catholic Beginnings in Southeastern Iowa, 1832-44," Mid-America, v. 1 (1930), 311-338.   G 335

GRIFFITH, CHARLES F. "Erection of the Diocese of Davenport," Mid-America, v. 3 (1933), 335-343.   G 336

GRIFFITH, C.F. "H.V. Gildea, Pioneer Church Builder," Iowa Catholic Historical Review, v. 1 (1930), 14-52.   G 337

GRIFFITH, C.F. Saint Matthias Parish, Muscatine, Iowa, a History. Muscatine, Iowa. no pub. 1928.   G 338

GRIFFITH, C.F. "St. Peter's Parish, Keokuk, Iowa, 1832-1929," Iowa Catholic Historical Society Collections, no. 2 (1929), 80p. plates, ports.   G 339

GRIFFITH, MARTHA E. "The Czechs in Cedar Rapids, Iowa," Iowa Journal of History and Politics, v. 42 (1944), 115-161, 266-315.   G 340

GRIVEL, FIDELIUS DE. "Letter of Fidelius de Grivel, S.J. to Rev. Joseph Tristram, S.J. Worcester, England," American Catholic Historical Society of Philadelphia Records, v. 16 (1905), 48-52.   G 341

GRIVEL, F. "Some Letters of Father F. Grivel," Woodstock Letters, v. 10 (1881), 245-260.   G 342

GROESSEL, WILLIAM V. "Most Rev. Albert G. Meyer, S.T.D.,

S.S.L., Archbishop of Milwaukee," Salesianum, v. 68 (Oct., 1953), 165-171. G 343
A biographical sketch of the recently appointed Archbishop of Milwaukee.

GROLLIG, FRANCIS X. Father Sebastian Rale, S.J., incendiary or martyr? MA thesis. Loyola University (Chicago) 1925. 103p. G 344

GROSS, MARK S. "Lettre de Mgr. Gross, Vicaire Apostolique de la Caroline Septentrionale à M.M. les Membres des Conseils Centraux de l'Oeuvre de la Propagation de la Foi. Wilmington, 20 mai, 1880," Annales de la Propagation de la Foi, v. 52 (1880), 448-454. G 345

GROSS, N.L. One Hundred Years of Mackville, 1849-1949. Mackville. The Author. 1949. x, 94p. G 346

GROSS, R. D. "Changing Image of Catholicism in America," Yale Review, v. 48 (June, 1959), 562-575. G 347

GROTENRATH, THOMAS H. The Right Reverend Dwenger, C.P. P.S., D.D. The Second Bishop of Fort Wayne, a Biographical Sketch. MA thesis. Catholic University. 1938. 97p. G 348

GROVER, FRANK REED. "Father Pierre Francis Pinet, S.J., and His Mission of the Guardian Angel of Chicago, 1696-1699," Chicago Historical Society Proceedings, v. 3 (1905), 153-180. G 349

GRUBB, SISTER MARY ANSELMA. The Establishment of Contemplative Life in the United States. MA thesis. Villanova University. 1947. 208p. tables, map. G 350

GRYNKIEWICZ, SISTER M. AGNES. The Beginnings and Organization of the Roman Catholic Church in Connecticut. MA thesis. Villanova University. 1956. 90p. G 351

GUEMES Y HORCASITAS. "Letter to the Bishop of Guadalajara concerning the Foundation of Jesuits' Missions among the Moqui Indians," Americas, v. 4 (1947), 256. G 352

GUENTHER, FRANCIS J. "In Memoriam: Father James A. Kleist, S.J., 1873-1949," Classical Bulletin, v. 25 (1949), 6-7. G 353

GUERIN, M. Le Martyr de la Charité, ou Notice sur Gabriel Richard, Missionaire. Lille, Lefort. 1850. 106p. G 354

GUERIN, MOTHER THEODORE. Journals and Letters of Mother Theodore Guerin, ed. by Sister M. Theodosia Mug. St. Mary of the Woods, Ind. Providence Press. 1937. xxviii, 452p. front., plates, ports., facsim. G 355

GUERRIERI, MOTHER DORA. Catholic Thought in the Age of Jackson. Ph.D. thesis. Boston College. 1960. ii, 355p. G 356

GUIDE TO CATHOLIC LITERATURE, ed. by Walter Romig, Detroit. Walter Romig Co. v. 1 (1940), v. 2 (1944), v. 3 (1948), v. 4 (1952), v. 5 (1955), v. 6 (1959), Catholic Library Association, v. 7 (1961). G 357

GUIDE TO THE CATHOLIC SISTERHOODS IN THE UNITED STATES. Compiled by Thomas P. McCarthy. Washington. Catholic University. 1952. viii, 280p. G 358
Includes pictures and short accounts of nearly all the Sisterhoods active in the United States. An excellent work, worthy of more than paper binding.

GUIDI, J. "Indian Missions. Letter dated Pend' Oreilles, St. Ignatius Mission, December 27, 1881," Woodstock Letters, v. 12 (1883), 51-53. G 359

GUIDI, J. "Missionen unter den

Indianern," Die Katholischen Missionen, v. 5 (1877), 40-42. G 360

GUIDI, J. "Washington Territory; Letter to Fr. A. Romano, S.J., dated Colville, W.T., January 22nd, 1875," Woodstock Letters, v. 4 (1875), 178-180. G 361

GUILDAY, PETER K. "American Catholic Historical Association," Catholic Mind, v. 18 (1920), 227-236. G 362

GUILDAY, PETER K. "The Catholic Church in the United States, 1776-1926," Thought, v. 1 (1926), 3-20. G 363

GUILDAY, PETER K. The Catholic Church in Virginia (1815-1822). New York. United States Catholic Historical Society. 1924. xxxv, 159p. G 364

GUILDAY, PETER K. "Catholic Historical Societies," Official Catholic Year Book for 1928 (New York, 1928), 639-644. G 365

GUILDAY, PETER K. "Catholic Lay Writers of American Catholic History," Catholic Historical Review, v. 23 (1937), 52-62. G 366

GUILDAY, PETER K. "Catholic Laymen of Action: Daniel Carroll of Maryland," Sign, v. 15 (1935), 49-50. G 367

GUILDAY, PETER K. "Catholic Laymen of Action: General Charles Ewing," Sign, v. 15 (1937), 495. G 368

GUILDAY, PETER K. "Catholic Laymen of Action: James Campbell of Pennsylvania," Sign, v. 14 (1935), 693-694. G 369

GUILDAY, PETER K. "Catholic Laymen of Action: William Gaston of North Carolina," Sign, v. 14 (1935), 634. G 370

GUILDAY, PETER K. "Church Reconstruction under Bishop England, 1822-1842," American Ecclesiastical Review, v. 68 (1923), 135-146. G 371

GUILDAY, PETER K. (ed.). "Documents. The Appointment of John Carroll as Prefect Apostolic of the Church in the New Republic (1783-1785)," Catholic Historical Review, v. 6 (1921), 204-248. G 372

GUILDAY, PETER K. (ed.). "Documents. Guide to Materials for American Church History in the Westminster Archives, 1675-1798," Catholic Historical Review, v. 5 (1920), 382-401. G 373

GUILDAY, PETER K. (ed.). "Documents. Our Earliest Printed Church History of the United States," Catholic Historical Review, v. 6 (1920), 343-357. G 374

GUILDAY, PETER K. "Father John McKenna: a Loyalist Catholic Priest," Catholic World, v. 133 (1931), 21-27. G 375

GUILDAY, PETER K. "The Founding of the Catholic University of America," American Ecclesiastical Review, v. 110 (1944), 2-16. G 376

GUILDAY, PETER K. "Four Early Ecclesiastical Observers in America," American Ecclesiastical Review, v. 85 (1931), 226-254. G 377 Bishop Plessis, Bishop de Forbin Janson, Cardinal Bedini, Canon Slazbacher.

GUILDAY, PETER K. "Gaetano Bedini," United States Catholic Historical Society Records and Studies, v. 23 (1933), 87-170. G 378

GUILDAY, PETER K. "Guide to the Bibliographical Sources of the American Hierarchy. Bibliography," Catholic Historical Review, v. 5 (1919), 120-128, 290-296; v. 6 (1919-1920), 128-132, 267-271, 548-552. G 379

GUILDAY, PETER K. 'Historians in the American Hierarchy," American Ecclesiastical Review, v. 93 (1935), 113-122. G 380

GUILDAY, PETER K. A History of the Councils of Baltimore, (1791-1884). New York. Macmillan. 1932. x, 291p. G 381

GUILDAY, PETER K. An Introduction to Church History. St. Louis. Herder. 1925. vii, 350p. G 382

GUILDAY, PETER K. "John Gilmary Shea," United States Catholic Historical Society Records and Studies, v. 17 (1926), 1-171. illus., ports. G 383

GUILDAY, PETER K. John Gilmary Shea. New York. United States Catholic Historical Society. 1926. 171p. front., plates, ports., facsim. G 384

GUILDAY, PETER K. "Lambing, Historian of Pittsburgh," America, v. 50 (1933), 251-252. G 385

GUILDAY, PETER K. The Leopoldine Foundation Reports," Catholic Historical Review, v. 23 (1938), 467-476. G 386

GUILDAY, PETER K. The Life and Times of John Carroll, Archbishop of Baltimore (1735-1815). New York. Encyclopedia Press. 1922. xiv, 864p. front., plates, ports., maps, geneal. chart. G 387

GUILDAY, PETER. The Life and Times of John England, 1786-1842. New York. America Press. 1927. 2v. front. G 388

GUILDAY, PETER K. "Notes and Comment. The Church in the United States (1870-1920)," Catholic Historical Review, v. 6 (1921), 533-547. G 389

GUILDAY, PETER K. Outline of an Introduction to the Study of American Church History. Washington. Privately printed. 1919. 13p. G 390

GUILDAY, PETER K. "The Popes and the United States," Commonweal, v. 13 (1931), 573-574. G 391

GUILDAY, PETER K. "The Priesthood of Colonial Maryland (1634-1773)," American Ecclesiastical Review, v. 90 (1934), 14-31. G 392

GUILDAY, PETER K. "Proceedings of the Ninth Annual Meeting, American Catholic Historical Association," Catholic Historical Review, v. 15 (1929), 3-22. G 393

GUILDAY, PETER K. "Proceedings of the Seventh Annual Meeting, American Catholic Historical Association ...," Catholic Historical Review, v. 13 (1927), 3-28. G 394

GUILDAY, PETER K. 'Recent Studies in American Catholic History," American Ecclesiastical Review, v. 84 (1931), 528-546. G 395

GUILDAY, PETER K. 'Restoration of the Society of Jesus in the United States, 1806-1815," American Catholic Historical Society of Philadelphia Records, v. 32 (1921), 177-232. G 396

GUILDAY, PETER K. "Sesquicentennial of the American Hierarchy, 1784-1924," America, v. 51 (1934), 510-511. G 397

GUILDAY, PETER K. "Trusteeism," United States Catholic Historical Society Records and Studies, v. 18 (1928), 7-73. G 398
Treats only Philadelphia and New York.

GUILDAY, PETER K. 'The Writing of Parish Histories," American Ecclesiastical Review, v. 93 (1935), 236-257. G 399

GURIAN, W. AND M.A. FITZSIMMONS (eds.). The Catholic Church in World Affairs. Notre Dame, Ind. University of Notre Dame. 1954. ix,

420p.   G 400

GURN, JOSEPH. "A Big Day in
'Thirty-five,' " Columbia, v.
14 (Sept., 1934), 7-8, 23.
                              G 401

GURN, JOSEPH. "Bishop Lynch's
Vindication," Columbia, v. 17
(Dec., 1927), 18-19, 40.
                              G 402

GURN, JOSEPH. "Boston's First
Bishop," Sign, v. 15 (1936),
720-722. port.   G 403
A popular biographical
sketch of Bishop John Cheverus, who was born 1768, came
to the United States 1796,
was Bishop of Boston 1810-
1823, died 1836.

GURN, JOSEPH. "The Catholic
Stake in the Constitutional
Crisis," Sign, v. 15 (1935),
138-140.   G 404

GURN, JOSEPH. Charles Carroll
of Carrollton, 1737-1832. New
York. Kenedy. 1932. viii, 312p.
front., plate, ports.   G 405

GURN, JOSEPH. Commander
John Barry, Father of the A-
merican Navy. New York.
Kenedy. 1933. x, 318p.
plates, 2 ports., facsim.
                              G 406

GURN, JOSEPH. "The Faith in
Connecticut," Columbia, v. 14
(June, 1935).   G 407

GURN, JOSEPH. "Navy Sons of
Flag and Faith," Columbia,
v. 7 (June, 1928), 18-19, 44.
ports.   G 408

GURN, JOSEPH. "Papal-American
Relations," Columbia, v. 14
(July, 1934), 11, 26. ports.
                              G 409

GURN, JOSEPH. "A Priest Goes
with Franklin," Columbia, v.
7 (Sept., 1927), 18-19, 42.
                              G 410
The story of the expedition
to Quebec to enlist the aid
of the Canadians in the A-
merican Revolution, John
Carroll was the priest who
accompanied the expedition.

GURN, JOSEPH. "They Solved a
Big Problem," Columbia, v.
9 (Oct., 1929), 10-11, 47.
ports.   G 411
American notables who
joined the Church, e.g. P.
H. Burnett, Joel Chandler
Harris, General Thomas
Kilby Smith, etc.

GURN, JOSEPH. "Who Was John
Gilmary Shea?" Columbia,
v. 12 (June, 1933), 9-10.
port.   G 412

GUY, FRANCIS JOSEPH. The
Catholic Church in Arkansas,
1541-1843. MA thesis. Catholic University. 1932. 57p.
                              G 413

GUY, FRANCIS S. Edmund
Bailey O'Callaghan. A Study
in American Historiography
(1797-1880). Washington.
Catholic University. 1934.
x, 93p.   G 414

GWYNN, DENIS. "Dr. Wiseman
as Roman Agent for Baltimore,"
Homiletic and Pastoral Review, v. 41 (1940), 11-18.
                              G 415

- H -

H.F. "The Franciscans Seek the
Maryland Mission in 1642,"
American Catholic Historical
Researches, v. 22 (1905),
289-291.   H 1

HAAS, FRANCIS. Berichte über
die Kapuzinerprovinz des
Heiligen Joseph in Nord A-
merika. 1886.   H 2

HAAS, FRANCIS. Geschichte
der Herz Jesu Gemeinde in
Indianapolis, Indiana. 1875-
1900. no pl. no pub. 1900?
64p. plates, ports.   H 3

HABIG, MARION A. "The Builders
of San Xavier del Bac," Southwest Historical Quarterly, v.
41 (1937), 154-166.   H 4

HABIG, MARION A. "Father
Gabriel de la Riboude, O.F.
M.," Mid-America, v. 2
(1930-31), 103-120, 225-235.
                              H 5

HABIG, M.A. Father Zénobe

Membrê, O.F.M., La Salle's
Chaplain and Missionary
Companion 1645 (?)-1689, MA
thesis. Loyola University
(Chicago) 1933.   H 6
HABIG, MARION. "The First
Immaculate Conception Mission,"
American Ecclesiastical Review,
v. 131 (Aug., 1954), 73-80.
                                   H 7
    Locates the mission in New
    Mexico in 1629.
HABIG, MARION H. "First
Marian Shrine in the United
States," American Ecclesiastical
Review, v. 134 (1957), 81-89.
                                   H 8
    Identifies it as the Shrine of
    Nuestra Señora de la Leche
    about 1602-1620, located in
    the stone church of Nombre
    de Dios north of St. Augus-
    tine, Florida.
HABIG, MARION A. "The Fran-
ciscan Martyrs of North Amer-
ica," Franciscan Educational
Conference Annual Report,
v. 18 (1936), 274-330. map.
table.   H 9
HABIG, MARION A. The Franciscan Père Marquette. Franciscan Studies, v. 13. New
York. Wagner. xiii, 301p.
front., plates, map.   H 10
    A critical biography of Father
    Zénobe Membré, O.F.M.,
    La Salle's chaplain and mis-
    sionary companion, 1645-
    c1689.
HABIG, MARION A. "The Franciscan Provinces of Spanish
North America," Americas,
v. 1 (1944), 88-103, 215-229.
map.   H 11
HABIG, MARION A. Heroes of
the Cross; the Franciscan
Martyrs of North America.
New York. Fortuny's. 1939.
175p. front., plates, ports.,
map.   H 12
HABIG, MARION A. "Land of
Mary Immaculate," American
Ecclesiastical Review, v. 130
(June, 1954), 376-383. H 13

An excellent study of the
title of Mary Immaculate in
the United States.
HABIG, MARION. "Our First
Church of Mary Immaculate,"
American Ecclesiastical Re-
view, v. 131 (Nov., 1954),
313-319.   H 14
    Sets forth the claim for the
    chapel of the Franciscan
    Friary at St. Augustine,
    Florida, established 1584.
HABIG, MARION A. "Our Oldest
Church of Mary Immaculate,"
American Ecclesiastical Re-
view, v. 134 (Jan. 1956), 5-
9.   H 15
    La Purísima Concepción
    Mission two and one-half
    miles south of San Antonio's
    Alamo. This church was
    completed in 1762.
HACKETT, JAMES DOMINICK.
Bishops of the United States
of Irish Birth or Descent.
New York. American Irish
Historical Society. 1936. 86p.
                                   H 16
HAFERD, MARGARET. "The
Shrine of Our Lady of Consola-
tion, Carey, Ohio," American
Catholic Historical Society of
Philadelphia Records, v. 48
(1937), 204-214.   H 17
HAGAN, SISTER M. THOMA-
SINA. Monsignor Frank A.
O'Brien of Kalamazoo. MA
thesis. University of Detroit.
1953. v, 78p.   H 18
HAGEDORN, EUGENE. Beiträge
zur Geschichte von Teutopolis
und Umgegend. St. Louis.
Amerika Print. 1902. plates,
ports.   H 19
HAGEDORN, EUGENE. The
Franciscans in Nebraska.
Norfolk, Nebraska. Printed by
the Humphrey Democrat, and
the Norfolk Daily News. 1931.
572p. incl. illus., plates,
ports., maps.   H 20
HAGEDORN, EUGENE. Histori-
cal Sketch of Teutopolis and
of St. Francis Parish...

Diamond Jubilee, 1851-1926. no
pl. no pub. 145p. plates,
ports.   H 21
HAGEDORN, EUGENE. History
of St. Peter's Parish, Chicago,
Ill. Chicago. no pub. 1925.
                            H 22
HAGGERSON, SISTER MARY
ELIZABETH. The History of
the Diocese of Mobile from 1826
to 1859. MA thesis. Univer-
sity of Notre Dame. 1942. vii,
170p.   H 23
HAILE, BERNARD. "Some Navaho
History: The Story of the
Ethnologic Dictionary," Pro-
vincial Chronicle (Province of
St. John Baptist, O.F.M.),
v. 20 (1948), 195-199.   H 24
HAILE, HERBERT. Catholic
Women of Tennessee, 1937-
1956. Nashville, Tenn.
Printers Service Co., Marshall
and Bruce, 1956. 417p.
                            H 25
HAIMAN, MIECISLAUS. The Polish
Past in America, 1608-1865.
Chicago. Polish Roman Cath-
olic Union Archives. 1939.
89p. incl. front., illus.
(facsims.).   H 26
HAIMAN, MIECISLAUS (comp.).
"A Tentative Bibliography of
the Writings of Msgr. Syske,"
Polish American Studies, v. 2
(1945), 107-113.   H 27
HALBACH, ARTHUR A. Dyers-
ville, Its History and Its
People. Milwaukee. St.
Joseph Press. 1939. xiv,
495p. incl. front., illus.
(incl. map), ports.   H 28
HALBACH, ARTHUR ANTHONY.
The German Catholic Settlement Idea in the Leopoldine
Letters, 1830-1870. MA
thesis. Catholic University.
1932. 80p.   H 29
HALL, THOMAS C. Religious
Background of American Culture. Boston. Little, Brown
and Co. 1930. xiv, 348p.
                            H 30
HALL, TROWBRIDGE. California

Trails. New York. Macmillan.
1920. 243p. front., plates.
                            H 31
HALLAHAN, JOHN. "St.
Joseph's Cathedral, Bardstown,
Kentucky," St. Meinrad His-
torical Essays, v. 1 (1930),
321-330.   H 32
HALLENBECK, CLEVE (ed.).
The Journey of Fray Marcos
de Niza. Dallas. Southern
Methodist University Press.
1949. 115p.   H 33
HAMILTON, RAPHAEL N.
"Father James Marquette, S.
J., Priest," La Revue de l'
Université Laval, v. 3
(1949), 640-642.   H 34
HAMILTON, RAPHAEL N. (ed.).
"The Journey of the Bishop of
Walla Walla," Illinois Catholic
Historical Review, v. 9
(1927), 208-222.   H 35
HAMILTON, RAPHAEL N.
"Location of the Mission of
St. Ignace from 1670-1673,"
Michigan History, v. 42
(1958), 260-266.   H 36
HAMILTON, RAPHAEL. "Mar-
quette University Building
Program, 1948-1952," Wood-
stock Letters, v. 81 (Novem-
ber, 1952), 373-378.   H 37
HAMILTON, RAPHAEL N.
"Significance of the Frontier
to the Historian of the Cath-
olic Church in the United
States," Catholic Historical
Review, v. 25 (1939), 160-
178.   H 38
HAMILTON, RAPHAEL N. The
Story of Marquette University.
Milwaukee. Marquette Uni-
versity Press. 1953. xi, 434p.
plates, maps on end papers.
                            H 39
HAMMER, B. Die katholische
Kirche in den Vereinigten
Staaten Nordamerikas. N.Y.
Wildermann. 1897. 438p.
                            H 40
HAMMER, BONAVENTURA. Die
Franziskaner in den Vereinig-
ten Staaten Nord-Amerika.

Köln. J.B. Bachen. 1884, 1892. 141p. plates. H 41

HAMMER, BONAVENTURA. Der Apostel von Ohio. Freiburg. Herder. 1890. ix, 168p. incl. front., port. H 42

Biography of Bishop Edward Dominic Fenwick, O.P., first Bishop of Cincinnati (1821-1832).

HAMMER, BONAVENTURA. Unsere Bischöfe. Louisville, Ky. Katholischen Glaubensboten. 1872. 146p. H 43

HAMMON, WALTER. The First Bonaventure Men. Paterson, N.J. St. Anthony Guild Press, 1958. xii, 249p. H 44

HAMMON, WALTER. New Page in an Old Diary. Provincial Annals (New York) 11 (1954), 87-90. H 45

Concerns Franciscan activity in Virginia.

HAMON, EDOUARD. Les Canadiens Français de la Nouvelle-Angleterre. Québec. N.S. Hardy. 1891. xv, 483p. H 46

HAMON, EDOUARD. "French Canadians in New England," Woodstock Letters, v. 17 (1888), 335-339. H 47

HAMY, ALFRED. Au Mississippi. Paris. Honoré Champion Librairie. 1903. 329p. incl., illus., plates, port., map, front., fold tab. H 48

Biography of Father Marquette (1637-1675).

HANDLIN, OSCAR. Boston's Immigrant, 1790-1865. Cambridge, Harvard University. 1941. xviii, 287p. incl. illus. (incl. maps, plans), tables, diagrs. H 49

HANEY, SISTER MARIE IMMACULATE. The John W. Hallahan Catholic Girls' High School. MA thesis. Villanova University. 1951. 97p. H 50

HANLEY, THOMAS O. "Catholic Political Thought in Colonial Maryland Government," Historical Bulletin, v. 32 (Nov.,

1953), 27-34. H 51

A well-written and documented study of Maryland colonial government up to the Toleration Act of 1649 with emphasis on the work of the Assembly of 1640.

HANLEY, THOMAS O. "The Catholic Tradition of Freedom in America," American Ecclesiastical Review, v. 145 (1961), 307-318. H 52

HANLEY, THOMAS O. "Church and State in the Maryland Ordinance of 1639," Church History, v. 26 (1957), 325-341. H 53

HANLEY, THOMAS O'BRIEN. Church-State Concepts in the Maryland Ordinance of 1639. MA thesis. Marquette University. 1955. H 54

HANNAN, JEROME D. "Initial American Discrimination against Charitable Trusts," Jurist, v. 8 (1948), 287-305. H 55

HANNAN, JEROME D. "Prince Gallitzin's Experience with a Quasi-spiritualistic Phenomenon," United States Catholic Historical Society Records and Studies, v. 15 (1921), 35-44. H 56

The story of the voice at the Livingston place in Cliptown, Virginia; cf. Brownson's Gallitzin.

HANNON, W.B. "A Saintly American Bishop," American Catholic Quarterly Review, v. 45 (1920), 55-72. H 57

Biographical sketch of Simon Bruté, Bishop of Vincennes (1834-39).

HANNON, WILLIAM B. "An Historic Church in Our Southland," American Ecclesiastical Review, v. 38 (1908), 40-51. ports. H 58

HANOUSEK, SISTER MARY EUNICE. The Life and Labors of Mother Mary Thecla Thren, O.S.F. of the Congregation of the Third Order of St. Francis of Assisi, Sisters of Penance and Charity, St. Francis, Wisconsin, 1868-1930. MA thesis. Marquette University. 1942. H 59

HANOUSEK, SISTER MARY EUNICE. A New Assisi. The First Hundred Years of the Sisters of St. Francis of Assisi, Milwaukee, Wisconsin, 1849-1949. Milwaukee. Bruce, 1948. xiv, 231p. H 60

HANOUSEK, SISTER MARY EUNICE. "An Adventure in Education," Wisconsin Magazine of History, v. 32 (1949), 284-289. H 61
Beginnings of work at Nojoshing (St. Francis) Wisconsin, 1849, and the work of the Sisters of St. Francis of Assisi.

HANSEN, SISTER MARY URBAN. "The American Cassinese Keep a Centenary," Benedictine Review, v. 10 (1955) Summer, 46-48. H 62
Contains a list of the sixteen American Cassinese Benedictine Abbeys with statistics and summary.

HARBUTT, CHARLES. "Chicago, the Country's Biggest Diocese, Fathers a New Approach to Contemporary Problems," Jubilee, v. 4 (Sept., 1956), 8-15. H 63

HARDON, JOHN A. "The Polish National Catholic Church," Homiletic and Pastoral Review, v. 56 (Apr., 1956), 552-560. H 64
An excellent brief history of this movement.

HARDY, SISTER MARY ANTONELLA (ed.). "Loretto, Bishop Flaget and Sister Eulalia Flaget," American Catholic Historical Society of Philadelphia Records, v. 36 (1925), 188-201. H 65

HARKINS, GEWALD PATRICK. Christian Brothers and Their Work in the United States. MA thesis. Villanova University. 1935. 33p. H 66

HARKINS, ROBERT J.J. "The First Catholic Churches in Zanesville, Ohio," American Catholic Historical Society of Philadelphia Records, v. 24 (1914), 194-216. H 67

HARNEY, SISTER LOYOLA. The Defensive Action of the Rt. Rev. Benedict J. Fenwick, S.J. to Anti-Catholicism in New England, 1829-1845. Ph.D. thesis. 1936. ix, 180, xv p. H 68

HARNEY, MARIN P. "The Traditions of Boston College," Woodstock Letters, v. 78 (1949), 140-156. H 69

HARNEY, SISTER MARY CARMEL. The History of Catholic Education in South Dakota from 1880 to 1931. MA thesis. University of Notre Dame. 1933. 33p. H 70

HARPER, MRS. LIZZIE (ST. JOHN) ECKEL. Maria Monk's Daughter. An Autobiography. New York. United States Pub. Co. 1874. xvi, (5)-604p. front., plate, ports. H 71

HARRINGTON, BERTIN. "Los Cerrillos Mission," Provincial Chronicle (St. John Baptist Province, O.F.M.), v. 5 (1933), 111-115. H 72

HARRINGTON, EDWARD THOMAS. A History of the Diocese of Boston from 1788 to 1792. MA thesis. Boston College. 1933. 198p. H 73

HARRIS, W. R. The Catholic Church in the Magra Peninsula, 1626-1895. Toronto. Wm. Biggs. 1895. n.p. H 74

HARRIS, W. R. The Catholic Church in Utah. Salt Lake City. Intermountain Catholic Press. 1909. 350p. illus., plates, ports., map. H 75

HARRISBURG (DIOCESE) SYNOD,

6th, 1911. Statuta dioecesis harrisburgensis quae in synodo dioecesana sexta, die 28 Septembris, 1911 in ecclesia cathedrali Sancti Patritii in civitate Harrisburg habita sanxit et promulgavit Joannes G. Shanahan, episcopus harrisburgensis. Philadelphia, Pa., Ex typis The Dolphin press, 1911. iv, 103p. H 76

HARRISBURG (DIOCESE) SYNOD, 8th, 1928. Synodus dioecesana harrisburgensis octava in ecclesia cathedrali S. Patritii a Philippo Richardo McDevitt [ep.] habita die XVII mensis Januarii 1928. Philadelphia, Dolphin press, 1928. xxviii, 170p. H 77

HARRISBURG (DIOCESE) SYNOD, 9. Ninth Synod of the Diocese of Harrisburg. Harrisburg. St. Patrick's Cathedral. n.d. H 78

HARTE, THOMAS J. "The Use of Parish Records in Social Research," American Catholic Sociological Review. v. 19 (1958), 113-123. H 79

HARTFORD (DIOCESE) SYNOD, 1st, 1854. Decreta synodi hartfordiensis primae mense Octobris, A. MDCCCLIV. celebratae. Providentiae, B. T. Albro, 1855. 20p. H 80

HARTFORD (DIOCESE) SYNOD, 2nd, 1878. Constitutiones synodi hartfordiensis II. Mense Septembri an. MDCCCLXXVIII habitae. Hartford, Conn., Ex typis The Case, Lockwood et Brainard Co. 1878. 40p. H 81

HARTFORD, CONN. (DIOCESE) SYNOD, 4th 1886. Constitutiones synodi hartfordiensis IV. a Laurentio Stephano McMahon, episcopo hartfordiensi, mense Augusti an. MDCCCLXXXVI. habitae. Hartford, Conn., Ex typis 'The Case, Lockwood et Brainard company," 1887. 2p. 1., 61p. H 82

HARTLEY, JAMES J. Diocese of Columbus. The History of Fifty Years, 1868-1918. Columbus. The Author. 1918. H 83

HARTMANN, B. Geschichte der St. Josephsgemeinde zu Logansport, Ind. St. Louis. Bechtold and Co. 1895. port., plates. H 84

HARTNETT, ROBERT C. Feature X; Trip to Visit Jesuit Communities," America, v. 93 (June 4, 1955), 268-270. H 85

HASQUE, URBAN DE. Early Catholic History of Oklahoma. Oklahoma City. Southwest Courier. 1928. 90p. H 86

HASQUE, URBAN DE. St. Patrick's Indian Mission of Anadarko, Okla., 1891-1915. St. Joseph's Orphanage. n.d. 26p. H 87

[HASSARD], JOHN R.G. Life of the Most Reverend John Hughes, First Archbishop of New York. New York. D. Appleton. 1866. 519p. front. (port.), fold. facsim. H 88

HASSETT, MAURICE M. "Historical Sketch of the Diocese of Harrisburg," American Catholic Historical Society of Philadelphia Records, v. 29 (1918), 193-218. H 89

HASSETT, MAURICE M. "Organizing a Parish in Central Pennsylvania," American Ecclesiastical Review, v. 63 (1920), 373-388. H 90

HASSETT, MAURICE M. 'Right Rev. John W. Shanahan," American Catholic Historical Society of Philadelphia Records, v. 28 (1917), 28-42. H 91

HASTING, MARTIN F. "Our American Martyrs: A Tercentenary Commemoration," Historical Bulletin, v. 25 (1946), 11-12. H 92

HASTING, MARTIN F. Parochial Beginnings in Colorado to

1889. MA thesis. Saint Louis
University. 1941. viii, 264p.
                    H 93
HASTING, MARTIN. "United
States-Vatican Relations,"
American Catholic Historical
Society of Philadelphia Records,
v. 69 (1958), 20-55.   H 94
HAUBER, ULRICH. "Catholic
Education for Rural Living in
Iowa," The Catholic Educator,
v. 22 (1952), 299-302, 322,
                    H 95
  The story of the work done
at St. Ambrose College dur-
ing the past five years.
HAUBER, U.A. Oaks and Acorns
from the College Campus.
Davenport, Iowa. The Author.
St. Ambrose College. n.d.
71p. ports.   H 96
  Jottings about the history
of St. Ambrose College,
1882-1905.
HAUGHEY, SISTER M. CATHER-
INE JOSEPH. "A Candle
Lighted: A Capsule Biography
of Margaret Gaffney Haughery,"
American Catholic Historical
Society of Philadelphia Records,
v. 64 (1953), 113-120. H 97
  A brief account of this great
apostle of charity, who was
called the "Bread Woman of
New Orleans." Born 1835,
died 1882.
HAWES, HORACE. The Missions
in California and the Rights
of the Catholic Church to the
Property Pertaining to Them.
San Francisco. Daily Evening
News. 1856. 46p.   H 98
HAWKS, EDWARD. History of
the Parish of St. Joan of Arc.
Harrowgate, Philadelphia.
Philadelphia. Peter Reilly Co.
1937. vii, 172p. plates,
maps.   H 99
HAWKS, EDWARD. "Philadelphia
and the Open Pulpit Controversy,"
American Catholic Historical
Society of Philadelphia Records,
v. 52 (1941), 3-11. H 100
HAWKS, EDWARD. William Mc-

Garvey and the Open Pulpit.
Philadelphia. Dolphin Press.
1935. vii, 258p.   H 101
HAWLEY, CHARLES. "Jesuit
Missions among the Senecas,"
Cayuga Co. (N.Y.) Historical
Society Collections, no. 3
(1884), 9-89.   H 102
HAWTHORNE, HILDEGARD.
California's Missions, Their
Romance, and Beauty. New
York. D. Appleton-Century.
1942. viii, 237p. front.,
plates.   H 103
HAYDEN, E.R. "Forgotten
Monastery: Mount Carmel,
First Convent Home of Religious
Women in the United States,"
Commonweal, v. 13 (1930),
65-66.   H 104
  An account of the Carmelite
foundation at Port Tobacco,
Md., 1790-1831.
HAYES, JAMES M. Bon Secours
Sisters in the U.S. Washing-
ton. National Capital Press.
1931. 285p. front., plates,
ports.   H 105
HAYES, JOHN E. The Francis-
can Missions of California.
Los Angeles. 1897. H 106
HAYES, LUCY AGNES. Compara-
tive Study of Public and Paro-
chial Elementary Education in
the Nineteenth Century in New
York City. Ph.D. thesis.
Fordham University. 1936.
243p.   H 107
HAYES, SISTER MARY FRANCIS
ANN. The Years Beginning;
a History of the Third Regular
Order of St. Francis of the
Congregation of Our Lady of
Lourdes, Rochester, Minn.
1877-1902. MA thesis.
Catholic University. 1957. 88p.
                    H 108
HAYES, P.J. "John Cardinal
Farley, Archbishop of New
York," United States Catholic
Historical Society Records and
Studies, v. 6, pt. 1 (1912),
5-68. port.   H 109
HAYES, T. W. "Church of the

Sacred Heart. Historically
Known as Conewago Chapel.
Letter dated Edgrove, Pa.,
April 23, 1892," Woodstock
Letters, v. 21 (1892), 189-
193, 289-297; v. 22 (1893),
8-15, 191-203.　　　H 110

HAYES, T. W. "Some Records of
Archbishop Carroll's Relations
with the Jesuits of Maryland,"
American Catholic Historical
Society of Philadelphia Re-
cords, v. 28 (1917), 28-42.
　　　　　　　　　　H 111

HAYNES, GEORGE H. "Causes
of Know-nothing Success in
Massachusetts," American
Historical Review, v. 3 (1897),
67-83.　　　　　　　H 112

HEALY, GEORGE P. A. Reminiscences of a Portrait Painter.
Chicago. A.C. McClurg and
Co. 1894. ix, 221p. 21 ports.
(incl. front.).　　　H 113

HEALY, KILIAN J. "The Spiritual
Life of the Priest in the A-
merican Ecclesiastical Review,"
American Ecclesiastical Review,
v. 121 (1949), 301-311.
　　　　　　　　　　H 114

HEALEY, ROBERT C. A Catholic
Book Chronicle. New York.
Kenedy. 1951. 56p.　　H 115
An attractive and well written
story of the publishing firm
of J.P. Kenedy and Sons,
1826-1951.

HEANEY, SISTER JANE FRANCIS.
A Century of Pioneering; a
History of the Ursuline Nuns
in New Orleans (1727-1827)
Ph.D. dissertation. Saint
Louis University. 1949. xii,
543p.　　　　　　　　H 116

HECK, NICHOLAS H. "The Jesuit
Contribution to Seismology in
the U.S.A.," Thought, v. 19
(1944), 221-228.　　　H 117

HECK, THEODORE. "Pioneer
Benedictine in Indiana," St.
Meinrad Historical Essays, v.
1 (1928), 58-64.　　　H 118
Father Bede (James O'Con-
nor), who was born 1826,

came to the United States
1852, died 1875.

HECK, THEODORE. "Very Rev.
Isidore Hobi, O.S.B., First
Rector of St. Meinrad
Seminary," St. Meinrad His-
torical Essays, v. 1 (1928),
79-89.　　　　　　　H 119

(HECKER, I.T.?). "The Next
Phase of Catholicity in the
United States," Catholic
World, v. 23 (1876), 577-592.
　　　　　　　　　　H 120

HEDGES, S.B. "Father Hecker
and the Establishment of the
Poor Clares in the United
States," Catholic World, v.
61 (1895), 380-386.　H 121

HEFFERNAN, ARTHUR J. A
History of Catholic Education
in Connecticut. Washington.
Catholic University of America. 1937. 186p. Catholic
University Educational Research Monographs, v. 10
no. 1.　　　　　　　H 122

HEFFERNAN, BERNARD L.
Some Cross-Bearers of the
Finger Lakes Region. Chicago.
John Anderson Publishing
Company. 1925.　　　H 123
A painstaking history of St.
Patrick's Parish, Aurora,
Cayuga Co., New York.

HEFFRON, EDWARD J. "Ten
Years of the Catholic Hour,"
American Ecclesiastical Re-
view, v. 102 (1940), 238-249.
　　　　　　　　　　H 124

HEGNER, A. Ein Schwyzerischer
Indianerapostel P. Balthasar
Fensi, S.J. (1854-1936). Lu-
zern. Raber. n.d. 212p.
　　　　　　　　　　H 125

HEINEMAN, JOHN L. The
Early Days of St. Gabriel's,
Connersville, Indiana, 1884-
1934. 2d ed. Connersville,
Ind. J.L. Heineman. 1937.
130p. illus. (incl. ports.,
facsim.).　　　　　　H 126

HEISS, MICHAEL, ET AL. "A
Historical Pronouncement.
Wisconsin Bishops Protest the

Bennett Law," Social Justice Review, v. 33 (1940), 282-284, 318-320. H 127

HELEN LOUISE, SISTER. Sister Louise (Josephine van der Schrieck) American Foundress of the Sisters of Notre Dame de Namur. New York. Benziger. 1931. xlii, 336p. front. (port.), illus., plates. H 128

HELEN LOUISE, SISTER. Sister Julia (Susan McGroarty). New York. Benziger. 1928. xii, 375p. front., plates, ports. H 129

HELM, M. Fray Junípero Serra: the Great Walker. Stanford University: Stanford University Press, 1956. 86p. H 130

HELMES, JOSEPH W. Thomas M. Mulry: A Volunteer's Contribution to Social Work. Washington. Catholic University. 1938. 132p. H 131

HEMING, HARRY H. The Catholic Church in Wisconsin. Milwaukee. Catholic Historical Publishing Co. 1895-1898. lv. or lv. in 1. xiv, 1181p. front., illus. (incl. ports.). H 132

HEMKER, JOHN F. "Catholic Missionaries in Early Iowa," Annals of Iowa, 3d series, v. 10 (1911), 54-62. H 133

HEMPHILL, BASIL. "The Vicar Apostolic of England," Clergy Review, v. 31 (1949), 35-41, 99-106, 165-173, 247-254, 394-400; v. 32 (1949), 180-187, 249-256, 323-330. H 134

HENCKEN, HUGH. "The North Salem 'Irish Monastery,' " New England Quarterly, v. 12 (1939), 427-442. H 135

HENDEE, J. KIRBY. "Newspaper Coverage in New England of the Illness and Death of Pope Leo XIII," American Catholic Historical Society of Philadelphia Records, v. 68 (1957), 71-95. H 136

HENDERSON, ALICE CORBIN. Brothers of Light. New York. Harcourt Brace. 1937. 126p. illus., plates. H 137
A sympathetic account of the Penitentes of New Mexico, but neither complete nor scholarly.

HENDERSON, ALICE CORBIN. "Calvary in New Mexico," Reader's Digest, v. 36 (1940), 109-112. H 138

HENDERSON, GERTRUDE. "An Epic of Early Iowa: Father Trecy's Colonization Scheme," Iowa Catholic Historical Review, v. 3 (Oct., 1931), 3-13. H 139

HENNESSEY, JAMES J. "Canisius High School," Woodstock Letters, v. 83 (Nov., 1954), 352-364. plates. H 140
A historical sketch of this Jesuit school of Buffalo, New York, begun 1855.

HENNESSEY, JAMES J. "Jesuit Provinces in North America, 1805-1955," Woodstock Letters, v. 84 (Feb., 1955), 155-159. H 141
An excellent factual survey.

HENNESSY, MOTHER MARY CYPRIAN. The Catholic Sentinal of Portland, Oregon. MA thesis. Villanova University. 1948. 94p. H 142

[HENNI, JOHN M.]. "Milwaukee in the Year 1851," United States Catholic Historical Society Records and Studies, v. 9 (1916), 214-217; v. 10 (1917), 162-163. H 143

HENNRICH, KILIAN. Diamond Jubilee of the Church of St. John the Baptist (West 31st St., New York). no pl. no pub. 1915. H 144

HENRY, HUGH T. (ed.). "Papers Relating to the Church in America from the Portfolio of the Irish College at Rome," American Catholic Historical Society of Philadelphia Records,

v. 7 (1896), 283-388, 454-
492; v. 8 (1897), 195-240,
294-329, 450-611, v. 9
(1898), 1-34.   H 145
HENRY, SISTER MARY GERTRUDE.
The Life of the Most Reverend
Clement Smyth. Peosta, Ia.
New Melleray Abbey. 1937.
259p. front., plates, ports.
                         H 146
HENTHORNE, SISTER MARY
EVANGELA. "Foundations of
Catholic Secondary Education
in Illinois," Mid-America, v.
6 (1935), 145-171.   H 147
HENTHORNE, SISTER MARY
EVANGELA. The Irish Cath-
olic Colonization Association of
the United States. Champaign,
Ill. Twin City Printing Co.
1932. front. (port.), illus.
(incl. maps).   H 148
HERBERG, WILL. "Religious
Communities in Present-Day
America," Review of Politics,
v. 16 (Apr., 1954), 155-
177.   H 149
A general survey on the
various religious groups in
America. Not of great value
for the Catholic Church
historian.
[HERBERMANN, CHARLES G.]
"A Catholic German Colony in
Ohio," United States Catholic
Historical Magazine, v. 4 (1891-
1892), 125-133.   H 150
HERBERMANN, CHARLES G.
(tr. and ed.). "Letter of Rt.
Rev. Lawrence Graessel," U-
nited States Catholic Historical
Magazine, v. 1 (1887), 68-70.
                         H 151
HERBERMANN, CHARLES G.
"Reverend Charles Hypolite de
Luynes, S.J.," United States
Catholic Historical Society
Records and Studies, v. 10
(1916), 130-151.   H 152
HERBERMANN, CHARLES
GEORGE. "Rt. Rev. John Du
Bois, Third Bishop of New
York," United States Historical
Society Records and Studies, v.

1, pt. 2 (1900), 278-355.
                         H 153
HERBERMANN, CHARLES
GEORGE. "Rt. Rev. Winand
Michael Wigger, D.D., Third
Bishop of Newark," United
States Catholic Historical
Society Records and Studies,
v. 2 (1900), 292-320. H 154
HERBERMANN, CHARLES
GEORGE. The Sulpicians in
the United States. New York.
Encyclopedia Press. 1916.
xi, 360p. front., plates,
ports.   H 155
HERBERMANN, CHARLES
GEORGE. "The Sulpicians in
the United States," United
States Catholic Historical
Society Records and Studies,
v. 7 (1914), 7-50; v. 8
(1915), 7-82; v. 9 (1916),
9-100; v. 10 (1917), 38-116.
                         H 156
HERBERMANN, CHARLES
GEORGE. "The Very Rev.
Pierre Gibault, V.G.," United
States Historical Society Re-
cords and Studies, v. 6, pt.
2 (1912), 130-165.   H 157
HERBERMANN, HENRY F.
"The Reverend Lawrence
Graessel," United States
Catholic Historical Society Re-
cords and Studies, v. 8
(1915), 209-222.   H 158
HERLIHY, DAVID JOSEPH.
"Battle against Bigotry:
Father Peter C. Yorke and
the American Protective As-
sociation in San Francisco,
1893-1897," Records of the
American Catholic Historical
Society of Philadelphia, v.
62 (June, 1951), 95-120.
                         H 159
HERMAN, SISTER AGATHA OF
JESUS. Growth of Catholicity
in Yakima Valley. MA thesis.
Seattle University. 1937.
46p.   H 160
HERNAEZ, FRANCISCO J.
Coleccion de Bulas, Breves,
y Otras Documentos Relativos

a la Iglesia de America y
Filipinas. Brussels. Impr.
de A. Vronmant. 1879. 2v.
H 161
HERRON, SISTER M. EULALIA.
The Sisters of Mercy in the
United States. New York. Macmillan. 1929. xvii, 434p.
front., (port.).   H 162
HERRON, SISTER EULALIA.
"The Work of the Sisters of
Mercy in the United States,"
American Catholic Historical
Society of Philadelphia Records, v. 32 (1921), 161-176
(Pittsburgh, 1843-1921), 314-
343 (Diocese of Chicago,
1846-1921); v. 33 (1922), 144-
192 (Hartford, 1851-1872, Providence Diocese, 1872-1921),
216-237 (Diocese of New York,
1846-1921), 317-337 (Diocese
of Little Rock, 1851-1921);
v. 34 (1923); 50-78 (Archdiocese of Baltimore, 1852-
1921), 113-150 (Archdiocese
of San Francisco, 1854-1921),
262-281 (Archdiocese of St.
Louis, 1856-1921), 344-361
(Archdiocese of Cincinnati,
1858-1921); v. 35 (1924), 56-
100 (Diocese of Portland, Me.
1858-1921, Diocese of Manchester, 1884-1921), 267-293
(Diocese of Philadelphia, 1861-
1875, Archdiocese, 1875-1921,
and in Dioceses of Altoona,
Brooklyn, Albany, and Ogdensburg), 357-402 (Scranton
Diocese, 1874-1921); v. 36
(1925), 155-187 (The South),
254-384 (South, Southeast, and
elsewhere, Toledo, Peoria,
Michigan, Omaha, Wichita),
372-395 (Colorado, Milwaukee,
Oklahoma); v. 37 (1926), 73-96
(Iowa), 193-202 (general).
H 163
HERSCHER, IRENAEUS. "St.
Bonaventure College, St. Bonaventure, N.Y.," American
Catholic Historical Society of
Philadelphia Records, v. 57
(1946), 165-168.   H 164

HERSCHER, IRENAEUS. "Arch-
bishop Paschal Robinson,
O.F.M., 1870-1948," Fran-
ciscan Studies, v. 29 (1948),
317-320.   H 165
HERSCHER, IRENAEUS. "Fran-
ciscan Bibliography for 1946,"
Franciscan Studies, v. 28
(1947), 439-507.   H 166
HERSCHER, IRENAEUS. "Our
Forgotten Cardinal," The
Priest, v. 4 (1948), 282-
284.   H 167
HERSCHER, IRENAEUS. "St.
Bona's First Librarian,"
Provincial Annals (Province of
the Most Holy Name, O.F.M.),
v. 9 (1949), 129-132. H 168
HERSCHER, IRENAEUS. "St.
Bonaventure College and
Seminary," United States Cath-
olic Historical Society Re-
cords and Studies, v. 33
(1941), 77-100.   H 169
HERSCHER, IRENAEUS. "The
Franciscans and New York's
Year of History," American
Catholic Historical Society of
Philadelphia Records, v. 71
(1960), 14-22.   H 170
Some of the associations
which the sons of St.
Francis have had with New
York during past centuries.
HERSCHER, IRENAEUS. "The
History of St. Bonaventure
University," Franciscan
Studies, v. 11 (September-
December, 1951), 365-424.
H 171
HERTLING, LUDWIG. Geschichte
der katholischen Kirche in
den Vereinigten Staaten. Berlin.
Morus-Verlag. 1954. ix, 333p.
illus., ports., maps.
H 172
HESS, LUKE, AND VINCENT
ONTH. New Subiaco Abbey,
A Retrospect. 1917. 125p.
incl. front. (port.), illus.
(incl. ports.).   H 173
HESS, M. WHITCOMB. "Portrait
of an Early American." Ave.
Maria, v. 78 (Aug. 1, 1953),

15-18. H 174
A popular biographical sketch of Bishop Jean Baptiste Miege, Vicar Apostolic of the Indian Territory (Kansas), 1850-1874.

HESTER, SISTER M. Canticle of the Harvest. New York. Kenedy. 1951. 196p. H 175
Story of one hundred years of the School Sisters of Notre Dame in the United States.

HESTON, EDWARD L. The Alienation of Church Property in the United States. Washington. Catholic University. 1941. xv, 222p. H 176

HEUSER, HEIMAN J. "Establishment of the First Vicariate of America, A.D. 1493," American Catholic Historical Society of Philadelphia Records, v. 7 (1896), 141-154. H 177

HEUSER, H.J. "Mother Mary Patricia Waldron," American Catholic Historical Society of Philadelphia Records, v. 30 (1919), 64-74. H 178

HEUSER, HERMAN J. Mother Mary Veronica. New York. Kenedy. 1915. 140p. front., plates, ports. H 179

HEUSER, HERMAN J. Pastor Halloft; a Story of Clerical Life. New York. Longmans, Green and Co. 1918. ix, 291p. H 180

HEUSINGER, EDWARD. Early Explorations and Mission Establishments in Texas. San Antonio. Naylor Co. 1936. xvi, 222p. H 181

HEWETT, EDGAR L. AND REGINALD G. FISHER. Mission Monuments of New Mexico. Albuquerque. University of New Mexico. 1943. 269p. front., illus. H 182

HEWIT, A.F. "Acta Concilii Neo-Eboracensis, IV," Catholic World, v. 44 (1887), 543-551. H 183

HEWIT, A. F. "Cardinal Mc-Closkey, Archbishop of New York," Catholic World, v. 42 (1885), 367-381. H 184

HEWITT, WILLIAM P.H. History of the Diocese of Syracuse. Syracuse. W.O.H. Hewitt. 1909. 367p. H 185

HEYDEN, JOSEPH VAN DER. Louvain American College, 1857-1907. Louvain. Fr. and R. Ceutrick. 1909. v., 412p. incl. illus., ports., plates. H 186

HEYDEN, THOMAS. A Memoir on the Life and Character of the Rev. Prince Demetrius A. de Gallitzin. Baltimore. John Murphy. 1869. viii, 200p. front. (port.). H 187

HICKEY, EDWARD JOHN. St. Anne's Parish: One Hundred Years of Detroit History. Detroit. Wayne University Press. 1951. 22p. illus. H 188

HICKEY, EDWARD J. The Society for the Propagation of the Faith. Its Foundation, Organization, and Success (1822-1922), Washington. Catholic University. 1922. x, 195p. incl. tables. H 189

HICKEY, SISTER ZOE. The Daughters of Charity of St. Vincent de Paul in the Civil War. MA thesis. Catholic University. 1946. 90p. H 190

HICKS, L. "Jesuits of the Middle United States: Work among the Indians," The Month, v. 177 (1941), 256-269. H 191

HIGGINS, JAMES J. John Mullanphy and His Contribution to St. Louis. MA thesis. Catholic University. 1940. 63p. H 192

HIGHAM, JOHN. "Another Look at Nativism," Catholic Historical Review, v. 44 (1958), 147-158. H 193

HILBERT, SISTER MIRIAM CECILIA. The Development

of Catholic Social Thought as
Contained in the National
Pastoral Letters Issued by the
Hierarchy of the United States
from 1791 to 1938. MA thesis.
St. John's University, N.Y.,
1943. mss. H 194

HILBURGER, SISTER M.
CHARITINA. "The Writings of
the Felician Sisters in the
United States," Polish American
Studies, v. 3 (1946), 65-97.
H 195

HILDNER, GEORG J. One Hundred Years for God and
Country. Washington, Mo.
Washington Missourian. 1940.
128p. H 196

HILDRUP, JESSE S. The Missions
of California and the Old
Southwest. Chicago. McClurg.
1907. H 197

HILFERTY, SISTER JOSEPH
LEONA. The Catholic Theatre
in the United States. MA thesis.
Villanova University. 1954.
182p. H 198

HILGER, SISTER M. AGNES.
"Letters and Documents of
Bishop Baraga Extant in the
Chippewa Country," American
Catholic Historical Society of
Philadelphia Records, v. 47
(1936), 292-302. H 199

HILL, CHARLES F. 'Roman
Catholic Indian Relics in the
Possessions of the Wyoming
[Pa.] Historical and Geological
Society," Wyoming Historical
and Geological Society Pro-
ceedings, v. 9 (1905), 171-
174. illus. H 200

HILL, EDMUND. "Passionist
Foundations in the United
States, 1852-1894," American
Catholic Historical Society of
Philadelphia Records, v. 10
(1899), 90-96. H 201

HILL, PETER J. (ed.). 'Reports
of Two Ecclesiastical Investiga-
tions of the Grave of Padre
Padilla in the Church of St.
Augustine, Isleta, New Mexico,"
New Mexico Historical Review,

v. 23 (1948), 58-65. H 202

HILL, ROSCOE R. American
Missions in European Archives.
Mexico, D.F. Comisión de
historia del instituto pana-
mericano. 1951. 138p.
H 203

HILL, VALENTINE. 'Historical
Briefs on American Bigotry,"
Sign, v. 11 (1931), 39-41.
H 204

HILL, WALTER H. "Death of
Fr. Van Assche, S.J.,"
Woodstock Letters, v. 6 (1877),
172-178. H 205

HILL, WALTER H. 'Early
Missions of Our Society in
St. Charles Co., Mo.," Woodstock Letters, v. 4 (1875),
79-87. H 206

HILL, WALTER H. 'Fr. Adrian
Hoecken, a Sketch," Woodstock
Letters, v. 26 (1897), 364-
368. H 207

HILL, WALTER H. "Father
Felix L. Verreydt," Woodstock
Letters, v. 12 (1883), 193-
200. H 208

HILL, WALTER H. 'Fr. Paul
M. Ponziglione, S.J., a
Sketch," Woodstock Letters,
v. 30 (1901), 50-56. H 209

HILL, WALTER H. "Father
Peter J. Verhaegen, S.J.
An Historical Sketch," Woodstock Letters, v. 27 (1898),
191-202. H 210

HILL, WALTER H. Historical
Sketch of the St. Louis Uni-
versity. St. Louis. Patrick
Fox. 1879. x, 260p. front.
H 211

HILL, WALTER H. 'The
Origin of St. Mary's College,
Kansas. Letter dated St.
Louis University, St. Louis,
Mo. Sept. 11, 1897," Wood-
stock Letters, v. 26 (1897),
421-426. H 212

HILL, WALTER H. "Pottowattomy
Indians," Woodstock Letters,
v. 4 (1875), 42-56.
H 213

HILL, WALTER H. "Pottowattomy

Indians, the Mission of Our Fathers among Them from 1846 to the Present Time," Woodstock Letters, v. 6 (1876), 2-18, 73-84.　H 214

HILL, WALTER H. "A Short Biographical Sketch of James Oliver Van de Velde," Woodstock Letters, v. 8 (1879), 65-73, 129-137.　H 215

HILL, WALTER H. "Some Facts and Incidents Relating to St. Joseph's College, Bardstown, Kentucky," Woodstock Letters, v. 26 (1897), 90-105.
　　　　　　　　　　　　　H 216

HILL, W. H. "Some Reminiscences of St. Mary's College, Kentucky, (1833-1846)," Woodstock Letters, v. 20 (1891), 25-38.　　　　　　　　H 217

HILTENBEITEL, PAUL H. Franciscan Mission Colleges in Mexico. MA thesis. Xavier University (Cincinnati). 1949. 115p.　　　　　　　　　H 218

HINSSEN, H. Die St. Peters Gemeinde in Belleville, Ills. Belleville, Ill. No pub. 1882. 155p. front., plates.　H 219

HIRSCH, EDWARD L. "The 'Anti-Jesuit' Law of 1647," Historical Bulletin, v. 23 (1944), 9-10, 18.　　　H 220

"HIS EXCELLENCY THE MOST REV. ALBERT T. DAEGER, O.F.M., D.D., ARCHBISHOP OF SANTA FE," Provincial Chronicle (St. John Baptist Province, O.F.M.), v. 5 (1933), 50-54.　　　H 221

[HISTORICAL BULLETIN.] "A Symposium, the Maryland Centenary," Historical Bulletin, v. 12 (1934), 21-38.　H 222

HISTORICAL RECORDS SURVEY. DISTRICT OF COLUMBIA. A Directory of Churches and Religious Organizations in the District of Columbia. Washington. Historical Records Survey. 1939. 188n. leaves (mimeographed).　　　H 223

HISTORICAL RECORDS SURVEY.

Florida. Preliminary List of Religious Bodies in Florida. Jacksonville, Fla. Historical Records Survey. 1939. 239n. leaves (mimeographed).
　　　　　　　　　　　　　H 224

HISTORICAL RECORDS SURVEY. Idaho. Directory of Churches and Religious Organizations of Idaho. Boise, Ida. Historical Records Survey. 1940. 129 n. leaves, map. reproduced from type-written copy.
　　　　　　　　　　　　　H 225

HISTORICAL RECORDS SURVEY. Maine. Directory of Churches and Religious Organizations in Maine. Portland, Me. The Maine Historical Records Survey Project. 1940. iii, 166 n. leaves.　　　　　　　H 226

HISTORICAL RECORDS SURVEY. New Mexico. Directory of Churches and Religious Organizations in New Mexico. Albuquerque, N.M. New Mexico Historical Records Survey, v. 15 1940. xi, 385p. illus. reproduced from typewritten copy.　　H 227

HISTORICAL RECORDS SURVEY. Oregon. Directory of Churches and Religious Organizations, State of Oregon. Portland, Ore. Oregon Historical Records Survey. 1945. 304p. reproduced from typewritten copy.　　　　　　　H 228

HISTORICAL RECORDS SURVEY. Vermont. Directory of Churches and Religious Organizations in the State of Vermont. Montpelier, Vt. Historical Records Survey. 1939. 3-122p. mimeographed. H 229

HISTORICAL RECORDS SURVEY. Wisconsin. Directory of Catholic Churches in Wisconsin. Madison, Wis. Historical Records Survey. 1942. x, 213p. illus., maps.　H 230

HISTORICAL RECORDS SURVEY. Wyoming. A Directory of Churches and Religious Organi-

zations in the State of
Wyoming. Cheyenne, Wyo.
Historical Records Survey.
1939. 64 n. leaves. mimeo-
graphed.   H 231
"HISTORICAL SKETCH OF ST.
ELIZABETH'S PARISH, ST.
LOUIS," Chronicle, v. 4 (1931),
561-565.   H 232
HISTORICAL SKETCH OF THE
CONVENT AND ACADEMY OF
THE SISTERS OF ST. FRANCIS
IN OLDENBURG, INDIANA,
AND THE WORK OF THEIR
COMMUNITY IN THE UNITED
STATES. Oldenburg, Ind. The
Community. 1901. 290p.
illus., plates, ports.   H 233
"HISTORY OF OLD MISSION SANTA
BARBARA," Provincial Annals
(Province of Santa Barbara, O.
F.M.), v. 5 (Apr., 1943),
3-16.   H 234
"HISTORY OF ST. ANTHONY'S
PARISH, SAN FRANCISCO,
CALIF.," Provincial Annals
(Province of Santa Barbara,
O.F.M.), v. 3 (Apr., 1941),
10-17.   H 235
"HISTORY OF ST. ANTHONY'S
PARISH, TIGARD, OREGON,"
Provincial Annals (Province
of Santa Barbara, O.F.M.),
v. 2 (Apr., 1940), 5-9.
                        H 236
"HISTORY OF ST. FRANCIS
PARISH, SACRAMENTO
CALIF.," Provincial Annals
(Province of Santa Barbara,
O.F.M.), v. 3 (Oct., 1940),
11-17.   H 237
"HISTORY OF ST. MARY'S
PARISH, PHOENIX, DEDICA-
TION OF THE HIGH SCHOOL,"
Provincial Annals (Province of
Santa Barbara, O.F.M.), v.
1 (Jan., 1939), 1-8.   H 238
"HISTORY OF ST. TURBIUS
MISSION AND ST. MARY'S
PARISH LAKEPORT, LAKE
COUNTY, CALIFORNIA,"
Provincial Annals (Province of
Santa Barbara, O.F.M.), v.
3 (July, 1941), 1-9.   H 239

"HISTORY OF THE ESTABLISH-
MENT OF THE CARMELITES
IN MARYLAND," United States
Catholic Historical Magazine,
v. 3 (1890), 65-71.   H 240
"HISTORY OF THE FRANCISCAN
ARIZONA INDIAN MISSIONS
AS REFLECTED IN THE
FRANCISCAN HERALD (1913-
1940)," Provincial Annals
(Province of Santa Barbara,
O.F.M.), v. 11 (1948), 73-
79.   H 241
HISTORY OF THE SISTERS OF
ST. JOSEPH OF CARONDOLET
IN THE TROY PROVINCE.
Troy, N. Y. [Albany. The
Argus Press.]. n.d. 404p.
illus.   H 242
"HISTORY OF THE SOCIETY OF
ST. VINCENT DE PAUL IN
THE ARCH-DIOCESE OF
PHILADELPHIA," American
Catholic Historical Society of
Philadelphia Records, v. 47
(1936), 198-207.   H 243
HITCHCOCK, JAMES R. A
History of Catholic Secondary
Education in the Diocese of
Nashville, 1837-1953. MA
thesis. Catholic University.
1953. 92p.   H 244
HOARE, SISTER MARY REGIS.
Virgin Soil: Mother Seton
from a Different Point of
View. Boston. Christopher
Publishing House. 1942.
176p. incl. geneal. tables, diagr.,
plates.   H 245
HOECKEN, ADRIEN. Lettres du
P. Adrien Hoecken au R.P.
de Smet, in Précis Historiques
[1856] p. 522-532, 537, 543.
                        H 246
HOEHN, MATTHEW (ed.). Cath-
olic Authors: Contemporary
Biographical Sketches, 1930-
1947. Newark, N.J. St.
Mary's Abbey Press. 2v. 1948-
1952.   H 247
HOEY, JOSEPH L. The Church
in the Metropolis, a Chronological Compendium from St.
Peter's, Barclay Street, 1785,

to St. Francis De Sales,
East 96th Street, 1896. Rectory
of St. Francis De Sales,
1452 Lexington Avenue. New
York. 1896. 2d ed.   H 248
HOEY, SISTER MARY LIOBA.
The Sisters of Saint Joseph in
St. Louis, 1836-1896. MA
thesis. Saint Louis University.
1935. v, 143p.   H 249
HOFFERER, M. J. "St. Stephen's
Mission, Wyoming," Woodstock
Letters, v. 54 (1925), 40-
49.   H 250
HOFFMAN, M. M. Arms and the
Monk. The Trappist Saga in
Mid-America. Dubuque. Wm.
C. Brown Co. 1952. ix, 233p.
                        H 251
HOFFMANN, MATHIAS, M.
Ancient Dubuque, 1673-1833.
Dubuque. Telegraph-Herald
Press. 1930. x, 219p.
front., illus., maps, plates.
                        H 252
HOFFMANN, MATHIAS M. Cen-
tennial History of the Arch-
diocese of Dubuque. Dubuque.
Columbia College Press. 1938.
lxxx, 733p. incl. illus., ports.
                        H 253
HOFFMANN, MATHIAS M. The
Church Founders of the North-
west, Loras and Cretin, and
Other Captains of Christ.
Milwaukee. Bruce. 1937. xiii,
387p. ports., facsim.   H 254
HOFFMANN, MATHIAS M. "Cle-
ment Smith; the Second Bishop
of Iowa," Iowa Catholic His-
torical Review, v. 9 (1936),
3-20.   H 255
HOFFMANN, MATHIAS M.
"Davenport's 'First Cross,' "
Iowa Catholic Historical Re-
view, v. 3 (Oct., 1931), 30-
34.   H 256
HOFFMANN, MATHIAS M.
"Europe's Pennies and Iowa's
Missions," Iowa Catholic His-
torical Review, v. 5 (1932), 39-
48.   H 257
HOFFMANN, MATHIAS M. "First
Native Iowans of the Catholic

Priesthood," Iowa Catholic
Historical Review, v. 2
(Nov., 1932), 22-26. H 258
HOFFMANN, MATHIAS M. "From
Early Iowa to Boston," Iowa
Catholic Historical Review,
v. 1 (1930), 6-13.   H 259
HOFFMANN, MATHIAS M.
"Letters and Documents,"
Iowa Catholic Historical Re-
view, v. 9 (Jan., 1936), 42-
51.   H 260
HOFFMANN, MATHIAS M.
"Loras in Alabama," Iowa
Catholic Historical Review,
v. 6 (Apr., 1933), 29-37;
v. 7 (June, 1934), 31-40.
                        H 261
HOFFMANN, MATHIAS M. "New
Light on Old St. Peter's
and Early St. Paul," Min-
nesota History, v. 8 (1927),
27-51.   H 262
HOFFMANN, MATHIAS M. "The
Oldest College in Iowa,"
Iowa Catholic Historical Re-
view, v. 8 (May, 1935),
3-14.   H 263
HOFFMANN, MATHIAS M. "The
Roman Catholic Church in
Iowa," Palimpsest, v. 24
(1953), 337-400. illus., maps,
ports.   H 264
    This entire issue of the
    Palimpsest is devoted to
    the history of the Catholic
    Church in Iowa.
HOFFMANN, MATHIAS M. (ed.).
"Some Unpublished Lorian Docu-
ments," Mid-America, v. 1
(1929), 103-121.   H 265
HOFFMANN, MATHIAS M. "The
Winnebago Mission--a Cause
Célèbre," Mid-America, v. 2
(1930), 26-52.   H 266
HOFFMANN, ROSS J. "The
American Republic and Western
Christendom," American Cath-
olic Historical Society of
Philadelphia Records, v. 35
(1946), 3-17.   H 267
HOGAN, ALOYSIUS. "Published
Works of the Woodstock Profes-
sors, 1897-1922," Woodstock

Letters, v. 51 (1922), 25-
34.   H 268
HOGAN, JAMES A. The Story
of a Hundred Years. St.
Mary's Rectory, Medina, N.Y.
1940. 120p. plates.   H 269
HOGAN, JOHN A. "Church
Work among the Negroes. Letter dated Galveston, Texas,
August 3, 1901," Woodstock
Letters, v. 30 (1901), 223-
230.   H 270
HOGAN, JOHN A. "Reminiscences
of the Galveston Storm. Letter
dated Galveston, Texas, Nov.,
1900," Woodstock Letters, v.
29 (1900), 428-447.   H 271
HOGAN, JOHN JOSEPH. Fifty
Years Ago, A Memoir, Written
in 1898. Kansas City, Mo.
Hudson Publishing Co. 1907.
108p.   H 272
HOGAN, JOHN J. On the Mis-
sions in Missouri. Kansas
City, Mo. The Author.
1892. 205, ccvii-ccxxxi p.
                             H 273
HOGAN, PETER E. "Americanism
and the Catholic University of
America," Catholic Historical
Review, v. 33 (1947), 158-
190.   H 274
HOGAN, PETER E. The Catholic
University of America, 1896-
1903. Washington. Catholic
University. 1949. xi, 212p.
                             H 275
HOLAIND, R. J. "A Last Word
(on Dr. Bouquillon,)" American
Ecclesiastical Review, v. 6
(1892), 455-464.   H 276
HOLAIND, RENE I. The Parent
First. An Answer to Dr.
Bouquillon's Query. New York.
Benziger. 1891. 34p.   H 277
HOLAND, HJALMAR R. "Claude
Allouez, the Indomitable Mis-
sionary," Salesianum, v. 50
(Apr., 1955), 64-75.   H 278
HOLAND, HJALMAR RUED.
"The First Mission in Wiscon-
sin," Salesianum, v. 49
(July, 1954), 107-115. H 279
Story of the Jesuit mission

in Door County Peninsula.
HOLAND, HJALMAR RUED.
"A Review of the Kensington
Stone Research," Wisconsin
Magazine of History, v. 36
(Summer, 1953), 235-240,
273-276. illus.   H 280
A documented answer to the
critics by the early
champion of the genuinity
of the stone.
HOLAND, H. R. "St. Michael,
the First Mission of the West,"
Mid-America, v. 5 (1934),
157-164.   H 281
HOLAND, HJALMAR R. "The
Sign of the Cross," Wisconsin
Magazine of History, v. 17
(1933), 155-167.   H 282
HOLDEN, BENEDICT M.
"Gabriel Druillettes, S.J.--
Diplomat," American Catholic
Historical Society of Phila-
delphia Records, v. 68 (1957)
51-58.   H 283
A well documented article
on the envoy of the
Governor of New France to
the New England Colonies in
the 1650's.
HOLDEN, VINCENT F. The
Early Years of Isaac Thomas
Hecker (1819-1844). Washing-
ton. Catholic University.
1939. ix, 257p.   H 284
HOLDEN, VINCENT F. "A
Myth in L'Américanisme,"
Catholic Historical Review, v.
31 (1945), 154-170.   H 285
HOLKEN, JOSEPH. The Mission
Church. St. Nicholas Church,
St. Louis, Mo. no pl. no pub.
n.d. 26p.   H 286
HOLLAND, SISTER MARY
ILDEPHONSE. Lengthened
Shadows. A History of the
Sisters of Mercy, Cedar Rapids,
Iowa. New York. Bookman
Associates. 1952. 337p.
illus.   H 287
HOLLAND, TIMOTHY J. Catholic
Church and the Negro in the
United States Prior to the
Civil War. Ph.D. thesis.

Fordham University. 1950. vi,
149p. H 288
HOLTE, RAYMOND. Golden
Jubilee of St. Bernard's Church,
St. Bernard, Nebraska.
no pl. no pub. 1928. unpaged.
H 289
HOLUBOWICZ, BILL. "A Univer-
sity in Print," Sign, v. 21
(1941), 281-282, illus. H 290
A popular article on Father
Husslein and the tenth
anniversary of the Science
and Culture Series of the
Bruce Pub. Co.
HOLWECK, FREDERICK G. "Abbé
Joseph Anthony Lutz," St.
Louis Catholic Historical Re-
view, v. 5 (1923), 183-204.
H 291
HOLWECK, FREDERICK G.
"Der älteste Bericht über den
Stand der deutschen Seelsorge
in der damaligen Diözese St.
Louis," Central Blatt and
Social Justice, v. 10 (1917),
163. H 292
HOLWECK, FREDERICK G.
"Ammerkungen über die
Anfänge der katholischen Kirche
zu Evansville, Ind., special
unter den Deutschen," Central
Blatt and Social Justice, v. 15
(1922), 91-92, 163-164.
H 293
HOLWECK, FREDERICK G. "Die
Anfänge der deutschen Gemeinden
in und um St. Louis nach den
Annalen der Leopoldinen
Stiftung," Central Blatt and
Social Justice, v. 16 (1923),
269-270. H 294
HOLWECK, FREDERICK G. "Die
Anfänge der ersten deutschen
Pfarrgemeinde am Mississippi,"
Central Blatt and Social
Justice, v. 10 (1917), 43-44.
H 295
HOLWECK, FREDERICK G.
"The Arkansas Mission under
Rosati," St. Louis Catholic
Historical Review, v. 1
(1918), 243-267. H 296
HOLWECK, FREDERICK G.

"Beginning of the Church in
Little Rock," Catholic His-
torical Review, v. 6 (1920),
156-171. H 297
HOLWECK, FREDERICK G.
(ed.). "Bittschrift der
Katholiken von Chicago an
Bischof Rosati, 1833," Central
Blatt and Social Justice, v.
11 (1919), 388-389. H 298
HOLWECK, FREDERICK G.
"Briefe eines deutschen Ein-
wanderers an Bishop Rosati,"
Central Blatt and Social Jus-
tice, v. 10 (1918), 325-326.
H 299
HOLWECK, FREDERICK G.
"Briefe eines schwergeprüften
Priesters der Pionierzeit,"
Central Blatt and Social Jus-
tice, v. 14 (1922), 261-263,
294-297, 354-367. H 300
HOLWECK, FREDERICK G.
"Contribution to the 'Inglesi
Affair," St. Louis Catholic
Historical Review, v. 5
(1923), 14-39. H 301
HOLWECK, FREDERICK G.
"Côte des Allemands, La.,"
Central Blatt and Social
Justice, v. 10 (1917), 235-
236. H 302
[HOLWECK, FREDERICK G.]
"Deutsche unter den 'Trustees
of the Roman Catholic In-
habitants of St. Louis' in J.
1884," Central Blatt and
Social Justice, v. 10 (1918),
254. H 303
HOLWECK, FREDERICK G.
"Father Edward Saulinier," St.
Louis Catholic Historical Re-
view, v. 4 (1922), 189-206.
H 304
HOLWECK, FREDERICK G.
"The Historical Archives of St.
Louis," Catholic Historical
Review, v. 1 (1918), 24-39.
H 305
HOLWECK, FREDERICK G.
Kirchen Geschichte von St.
Louis 62 General-Versammlung
der deutschen römisch-katholi-
schen Central Verein. 1917.

154p. H 306
HOLWECK, FREDERICK G. "The Language Question in the Old Cathedral of St. Louis," St. Louis Catholic Historical Review, v. 2 (1920), 5-17. H 307

HOLWECK, FREDERICK G. "Miscellany-An American Martyrology," Catholic Historical Review, v. 6 (1921), 495-516. H 308

HOLWECK, FREDERICK G. "Monsignore Jos. Andr. Stephan," Central Blatt and Social Justice, v. 12 (1919), 181-185. H 309

[HOLWECK, FREDERICK G.]. "Die Petition der deutschen Katholischen von Shoal Creek, Ill.," Central Blatt and Social Justice, v. 11 (1918), 47. H 310

HOLWECK, FREDERICK G. "Public Worship in St. Louis; before Palm Sunday, 1843," St. Louis Catholic Historical Review, v. 4 (1922), 5-12. H 311

HOLWECK, FREDERICK G. "Reverend Gaspar Henry Ostangenberg," Illinois Catholic Historical Review, v. 3 (1920), 43-60. H 312

HOLWECK, FREDERICK G. "Rev. Jos. Hamion, der erste deutsche Seelsorger von Fort Wayne, Ind.," Central Blatt and Social Justice, v. 15 (1922), 55-56. H 313

HOLWECK, FREDERICK G. "Die St. Marienkapelle und der erste deutsche Gottesdienst in St. Louis, Mo.," Central Blatt and Social Justice, v. 11 (1918), 183. H 314

HOLWECK, FREDERICK G. "Two Pioneer Indiana Priests," Mid-America, v. 1 (1929), 63-81. H 315
Biographical sketches of Joseph Kundeck, who died 1857, and Joseph Ferneding, who died 1866.

HOLWECK, FREDERICK G. "Vater Alexander Pax," Central Blatt and Social Justice, v. 13 (1920), 49-50. H 316

HOLWECK, FREDERICK G. "Vater Nikolaus Mertz," Central Blatt and Social Justice, v. 12 (1920), 355-357, 389-391. H 317

HOLWECK, FREDERICK G. "Zur Vorgeschichte der ersten deutschen Kirche in St. Louis," Central Blatt and Social Justice, v. 10 (1917), 235. H 318

HOLWECK, FREDERICK G. Zur Vorgeschichte der Gründung der ersten deutschen Gemeinde in St. Louis," Central Blatt and Social Justice, v. 11 (1918), 251. H 319

HOLWORTHY, SISTER MARY XAVIER. Diamonds for the King. Corpus Christi, Texas. Incarnate Word Academy. 1945. xi, 129p. H 320
Story of the Incarnate Word Sisters in Texas since 1852.

HOLY TRINITY CHURCH, BOSTON," Woodstock Letters, v. 16 (1887), 260-265. H 321

HOLZMEISTER, DE PAUL. The Catholic Church in the Oklahoma Panhandle. Provincial Chronicles, O.F.M. (Cincinnati) v. 28 (1956), 265-271. illus. H 322

HOLZNECHT, J.J. "Footprints of the Saintly Father Marquette," American Catholic Historical Researches, v. 12 (1895), 76-80. H 323

HOLZNECHT, J.J. "The Relics of Père Marquette," American Catholic Historical Researches, v. 12 (1895), 30-34. H 324

HOMERA, SISTER MARY CAEDMON. Years of Vision, 1903-1928, a Study of the Third Regular Order of St. Francis of the Congregation of Our Lady of Lourdes, Rochester, Minn. MA thesis. Catholic University. 1957. H 325

HOPCRAFT, M. L. "Blandina Segale, Sister of Charity," Ave Maria, v. 79 (May 8, 1954), 8-11. H 326
A slight sketch based on The End of the Santa Fe Trail.

HOPE, ARTHUR J. "Father Petit, Apostle of the Pottowattomies," Ave Maria, v. 44 (1936), 545-549. H 327

HOPE, ARTHUR J. Notre Dame. One Hundred Years. Notre Dame, Ind. Notre Dame University Press. 1942. xii, 482p. plates, ports. H 328

HOPKINS, J. G. E. Black Robe Peacemaker. New York: Kenedy, 1958. 188p. illus. H 329
A biography of Father De Smet in the American Background Books series.

HOPKINS, THOMAS F. St. Mary's Church, Charleston, S.C., Charleston, S.C. no pub. 1898. H 330

HORGAN, PAUL. "Churchman of the Desert," American Heritage, v. 7 (1957), 30-35, 99-101; illus. H 331
Popular sketch of the first Catholic Bishop of Santa Fe, John B. Lamy.

HORTON, LOUISE C. "Friar-prophet of the Seaway," Ave Maria, v. 81 (June 4, 1955), 16-18. map. H 332
Friar Hennepin and the Soo Canal.

HOUCK, F. A. A Biography of St. Ann's Parish, Toledo, O. Toledo. The Author. 1945. 118p. plates. H 333

HOUCK, GEORGE F. The Church in Northern Ohio and in the Diocese of Cleveland, 1817-1887. New York. Benziger. 1887. iv, 266p. front., plates, ports., tables. H 334

HOUCK, GEORGE F. "Historical Sketch of Early Catholicity

and the First Catholic Church in Cleveland, Ohio," American Catholic Historical Society in Philadelphia Records, v. 3 (1888-1891), 129-141. H 335

HOUCK, GEORGE F. AND MICHAEL W. CARR. A History of Catholicity in Northern Ohio and in the Diocese of Cleveland from 1747 to 1900. Cleveland. J.B. Savage. 1903. 2v. plates, ports. H 336

HOUCK, GEORGE F. Die Kirche in Nord Ohio und in der Diocese Cleveland, 1749-1890. Cleveland. Harts Bros. 1890. 300 p. plates, ports. H 337

HOUCK, GEORGE F. "A Memoir of the Life and Labors of the Right Rev. Amadeus Rappe, D.D., First Bishop of Cleveland," United States Catholic Historical Magazine, v. 2 (1888), 225-260. H 338

"HOUSE OF GOOD SHEPHERD IN ST. PAUL, A RETROSPECT OF FIFTY YEARS," Acta et Dicta, v. 5 (1918), 206-229. H 339

HOUSER, SISTER M. SYLVANA. The Catholic Church in East St. Louis to 1900. MA thesis. Saint Louis University. 1937. 270p. H 340

HOUTART, FRANCOIS. Aspects Sociologiques du Catholicisme Américain. Paris. Éditions Ouvrières, 1957. 340p. illus. H 341
Confined to the Catholic Church in Chicago.

HOUTIN, ALBERT. L'Américanisme. Paris. E. Nourry. 1904. vii, 497p. H 342

"HOW THE BENEDICTINES CAME TO ENTER TEXAS," Central Blatt and Social Justice, v. 24 (1931), 132. H 343

HOWARD, BRICE J. A History of St. Joseph (Minn.), 1856-1956. St. Joseph, Minn.: St. Joseph's Rectory, 1957. 80p. H 344

185

The centennial of Minnesota's
first consecrated Catholic
Church.
HOWARD, V. J. St. Bridget
Parish, Detroit. no pl. no
pub. n.d. 72p. plate, ports.
                              H 345
HOWARD, HELEN ADDISON.
"Padre Ravalli: Versatile
Missionary," Historical
Bulletin, v. 18 (1940), 33-
35.   H 346
HOWELL, C. "Pastoral Practices
in the U.S.A.," Clergy Review,
n.s. v. 34 (October, 1950),
245-257; v. 35 (May, 1951),
311-323.   H 347
Observations of an English
visitor on American Catholic
life.
HOWLETT, WILLIAM J. (ed.).
"Diary of Bishop Flaget," A-
merican Catholic Historical
Society of Philadelphia Re-
cords, v. 29 (1918), 37-59,
153-169.   H 348
HOWLETT, WILLIAM J. "The
Early Days of St. Joseph's
College, Bardstown, Ky.,"
Illinois Catholic Historical
Review, v. 4 (1922), 372-
380.   H 349
HOWLETT, WILLIAM J. His-
torical Tribute to St. Thomas
Seminary at Popular Neck near
Bardstown, Kentucky. St. Louis,
Herder. 1906. 197p. ports.,
illus.   H 350
HOWLETT, WILLIAM J. Life
of Rev. Charles Nerinckx, 2d
ed. Techny, Ill. Mission
Press. 1940. 439p.   H 351
HOWLETT, WILLIAM J. Life
of the Right Reverend Joseph
P. Macheboeuf, D.D. Pueblo,
Colo. Franklin Press. 1908.
419p. front., plates, ports.
                              H 352
HOWLETT, WILLIAM J. A Re-
view of Father O'Daniel's
Estimate of the Early Secular
Missionaries of Kentucky. no
pl. no pub. 24p.   H 353
HOWLETT, WILLIAM J. "St.

Joseph's, the Cathedral Church
of the Diocese of Bardstown,
Kentucky," Illinois Catholic
Historical Review, v. 4
(1922), 278-285.   H 354
HOWLETT, WILLIAM J. "The
Very Rev. Stephen Theodore
Badin," United States Catholic
Historical Society Records and
Studies, v. 9 (1916), 101-
146. port.   H 355
HREN, SISTER MARY LOUISE.
Trends in Educational Adminis-
tration in the Diocese of
Brooklyn, 1929-1939. MA
thesis. St. John's University,
N.Y. 1940. mss.   H 356
HUBER, RAPHAEL M. "Pre-
Columban Devotion to Mary in
America: Testimony of the
Kensington Stone," American
Ecclesiastical Review, v. 117
(1947), 7-21.   H 357
HUBER, VINCENT. "Sportsman's
Hall," American Catholic His-
torical Society of Philadelphia
Records, v. 3 (1888), 142-
173.   H 358
HUCKENBECK, JUNIPER. "Mis-
sions of Keweenaw County
(Michigan)," Provincial
Chronicle (St. John Baptist
Province, O.F.M.), v. 12
(1940), 119-128.   H 359
HUDSON, WILLIAM HENRY
(1862-1918). The Famous
Missions of California. New
York. Dodge. 1901. 70p. incl.
map, front., plates.   H 360
HUELLER, FRANCIS. Archbishop
John Hughes and the New York
Press during the Civil War.
MA thesis. Catholic Univer-
sity. 1954. 68p.   H 361
HUESMAN, HENRY JOSEPH.
Catholic Schools and the Allen-
town Tax Rate. MA thesis.
Villanova University. 1942.
60p.   H 362
HUGER, GREGORY CHARLES.
The Catholic Missions and the
Fur Trade in the Trans-Mis-
sissippi West, 1838-1864. MA
thesis. Saint Louis University.

1939. 125p.　　　　H 363
HUGER, GREGORY CHARLES.
The Catholic Press of the United
States on Church and State Re-
lationship, 1865-95. Ph.D.
thesis. Saint Louis University.
1950. v, 324p.　　　H 364
HUGH. "Tampa, Fla. Letter
dated Tampa, Fla. Church of
St. Louis, Diocese of St.
Augustine, Jan. 5, 1890,"
Woodstock Letters, v. 19
(1890), 82-85.　　　H 365
HUGHES, ARTHUR J. The
Influence of the Catholic Church
and Her People upon the History
of Illinois. Notre Dame, Ind.
University Press. 1917. 40p.
　　　　　　　　　　H 366
HUGHES, ELIZABETH. The
California of the Padres; or,
Footprints of Ancient Commu-
nism. San Francisco. I. N.
Choynski. 1875. 41p. H 367
HUGHES, JOHN J. "The Arch-
diocese of New York a Century
Ago: A Memoir of Archbishop
Hughes, 1838-1858," edited by
Henry J. Browne. United
States Catholic Historical Socie-
ty Records and Studies, v.
39-40 (1952), 129-190.
　　　　　　　　　　H 368
[HUGHES, JOHN.]. "Archbishop
Hughes to Governor Seward on
the School Question, 1842,"
American Catholic Historical
Society of Philadelphia Records,
v. 21 (1910), 36-40. H 369
HUGHES, JOHN. Complete Works
of the Most Reverend John
Hughes, First Archbishop of
New York, ed. by Lawrence
Keohoe. New York. Catholic
Publishing House. 1864. 2v.
　　　　　　　　　　H 370
HUGHES, MICHAEL. "Labors of
Ours in Albuquerque, Letter
dated Albuquerque, New Mexico,
January, 1898," Woodstock
Letters, v. 27 (1898), 49-52.
　　　　　　　　　　H 371
HUGHES, MICHAEL. "Missionary
Work in New Mexico. Letter

dated Trinidad, Colorado,
June 21, 1898," Woodstock
Letters, v. 27 (1898), 320-
322.　　　　　　　H 372
HUGHES, MICHAEL. "New
Mexico, Letter dated Las
Vegas, N.M., March 28th,
1880," Woodstock Letters, v.
9 (1880), 134-141.　H 373
A description of Las Vegas
College, opened 1877,
closed 1888.
[HUGHES, MICHAEL]. "New
Mexico. Letter dated Las
Vegas. N.M.," Woodstock
Letters, v. 12 (1883), 299-
305.　　　　　　　H 374
A summary of the history
of the New Mexico-Colorado
Mission of the Neapolitan
Province of the Society of
Jesus from its founding
1867 to 1878.
[HUGHES, MICHAEL]. "New
Mexico. Letter," Woodstock
Letters, v. 13 (1884), 42-
50.　　　　　　　H 375
Continues the history of the
Mission begun, H 374.
HUGHES, THOMAS. "An Alleged
Popish Plot in Pennsylvania,
1756-1757," American Catholic
Historical Society of Philadel-
phia Records, v. 10 (1909),
208-221.　　　　　H 376
HUGHES, THOMAS. "Educational
Convoys to Europe in the Olden
Times,"American Ecclesiastical
Review, v. 29 (1903), 24-39.
　　　　　　　　　　H 377
HUGHES, THOMAS. The History
of the Society of Jesus in North
America Colonial and Federal.
New York. Longmans, Green
and Co. 1908-1917. 4v.
　　　　　　　　　　H 378
HUGHES, THOMAS. "The Journal
of a Western Missionary,
Letter dated St. Louis Univer-
sity, April, 1892," Woodstock
Letters, v. 21 (1892), 155-
160.　　　　　　　H 379
HUGHES, THOMAS. "London
Vicariate Apostolic and the

West Indies," Dublin Review, v. 134 (1904), 66-93. H 380

HUGHES, THOMAS. "Notes from the West. Letter dated Chicago, College of St. Ignatius, Christmas, 1889," Woodstock Letters, v. 19 (1890), 41-50. H 381

HUGHES, THOMAS. "Notes from the West, Letter dated St. Louis, Mo., June 29, 1890," Woodstock Letters, v. 19 (1890), 291-301. H 382

HUGHES, THOMAS. "Properties of the Jesuits in Pennsylvania; 1730-1830," American Catholic Historical Society of Philadelphia Records, v. 11 (1900), 177-195, 281-294. H 383

HUGHES, THOMAS. The Sacrament of Confirmation in the Old Colonies," American Ecclesiastical Review, v. 27 (1903), 23-41. H 384

HUGHES, VINCENT R. The Right Reverend Richard Luke Concanen, O.P., First Bishop of New York (1747-1810), Freiburg. Studia Friburgensia. 1926. H 385

HUGHES, WILLIAM. Souvenir Volume Illustrated. Detroit, Mich. W.H. Hughes. 1890? xvi, 114p. front., illus., incl. ports. H 386
Commemorates three great events in the history of the Catholic Church in the U.S.: (1) the centenary celebrations, (2) proceedings of the first American Catholic Congress, (3) dedication of the Catholic University.

HUNTER, SISTER MARY CONSTANCE. The Life of Bishop James J. Schwebach, D.D., Bishop of LaCrosse, Wisconsin. MA thesis. Marquette University. 1934. H 387

HURD AND EVARTS. History of the Catholic Church in New England. Boston. n.p. 1899. H 388

HURLEY, SISTER HELEN ANGELA.

"John Shanley, Bishop of Fargo," Acta et Dicta, v. 7 (1936), 141-146. H 389

HURLEY, SISTER HELEN ANGELA. "The Sisters of St. Joseph and the Minnesota Frontier," Minnesota History, v. 30 (1949), 1-13. map. H 390

HURLEY, SISTER HELEN ANGELA. On Good Ground. Minneapolis. Univ. of Minnesota Press. 1951. 325p. illus. map. H 391
Story of the Sisters of St. Joseph in St. Paul, Minn.

HURLEY, JAMES M. The Political Status of Roman Catholics in North Carolina. MA thesis. Catholic University. 1927. 74p. H 392

HURLEY, JAMES MICHAEL. "Political Status of Roman Catholics in North Carolina," American Catholic Historical Society of Philadelphia Records, v. 38 (1927), 237-296. H 393

HURLEY, NEIL P. "The Catholic Evidence Guild of New York City," Woodstock Letters, v. 82 (Nov., 1953), 301-316. H 394
A history of twenty-five years of the organization of Catholic Action begun in 1918.

HURLEY, MARK J. Church-State Relationships in Education in California. Washington. Catholic University of America. 1949. xx, 183p. H 395

HURLEY, PHILIP S. "Father Robert Molyneux, 1738-1808," Woodstock Letters, v. 67 (1938), 271-292. H 396
Biographical sketch of the first Superior of the restored Society of Jesus in America. The proper pronunciation of the name is Molinux.

HUSTON, SISTER MARY ALBERTINA. The Educational Endeavors of the Most Reverend Edward Dominic Fenwick, O.P. MA thesis. University of Notre Dame. 1932. 60p. H 397

HUTTING, ALBERT M. St. Peter's Parish, Mount Clemens, Mich., 1843-1943. The Author, 1943. 28p. plates, ports. H 398

HYACINTH, BERNARD, BROTHER. "Church Problems in 19th Century America," La Salle Catechist, v. 26 (1960), 21-27. H 399

HYDE, B. B., AND M. V. BREWINGTON. "New Light on the Ark and Dove," Maryland Historical Magazine, v. 48 (Sept., 1953), 185-190. illus. H 400
Information on the description of the ships gathered from carvings.

HYDE, DOUGLAS. "British Impressions of U.S. Catholics," America. v. 90 (Dec. 26, 1953), 337-338. H 401
A sympathetic treatment-- a welcome relief after the bitterness of some other travellers.

HYLAND, F. E. "Church in Georgia," Extension, v. 48 (Oct., 1953), 24-25. H 402

HYLAND, M. Progress of the Catholic Church in America. Chicago. n.p. 1897. H 403

HYNES, EMERSON MERTON. The Catholic Church and Rural Life. MA thesis. University of Notre Dame. 1939. ii, 142p. H 404

HYNES, SISTER MARY CALLISTA. History of the American Protective Association in Minnesota. MA thesis. Catholic University. 1940. 135p. 3 facsims. H 405

HYNES, M. J. History of the Diocese of Cleveland. Cleveland. Diocese of Cleveland. 1953. 544p. illus. H 406
Omits many pertinent items.

- I -

IGNOTUS (pseud.). Avremo un Papa Americano. (Roma). Edizioni della Bussola. (1945), 173p. I 1

ILG, JOHN. San Jose, Queen of the Missions. San Antonio. The Author. 1936. 64p. 30 photos. I 2

IMHOFF, MAURICE. "Notes on the Early History of St. Joseph's Parish at Utica, N.Y.," Central Blatt and Social Justice, v. 30 (1938), 349-350. I 3

"IMPOSTOR 'BISHOP' IN ILLINOIS AND KENTUCKY IN 1827," American Catholic Historical Researches, v. 9 (1892), 81-83. I 4

"IN MEMORIAM. CHARLES EWING." By his youngest corporal. Philadelphia. J. B. Lippincott. 1888. 123p. front. (port.). I 5

"IN MEMORIAM, LAVAL LAUREN, O.F.M.," Americas, v. 1 (1944), 231-232. I 6

"IN MEMORIAM--RIGHT REVEREND JAMES McGOLDRICK," Acta et Dicta, v. 5 (1918), 153-169. I 7

[INAMA, ADELBERT]. "Ein Schreiben des Missionärs Inama aus dem Jahre 1853," Central Blatt and Social Justice, v. 17 (1924), 305-306. I 8

INAMA, ADELBERT. "Letters," Wisconsin Magazine of History, v. 11 (1927-1928), 77-95, 197-217, 328-354, 437-438, v. 12 (1928), 58-96. I 9

INAMA, ADELBERT. "Missionberichte des Praemonstatensers Inama," Central Blatt and Social Justice, v. 15 (1922-1923), 53-55, 89-91, 162-163, 205, 208, 277-280, 314-316, 329, 386-387, 420-424; v. 16 (1923), 54-56, 90-91,

162-164, 198-200.   I 10
INAMA, ADELBERT. "(Ein)
Schreiben des Missionärs
Inama aus dem Jahre 1853,"
Central Blatt and Social Justice,
v. 17 (1924), 305-306. I 11
"INDIAN MISSION. ST. JOSEPH
MISSION, YAKIMA. EXTRACT
FROM A LETTER TO THE
SUPERIOR OF THE MISSION,"
Woodstock Letters, v. 12
(1883), 58-59.   I 12
INDIANAPOLIS (ARCHDIOCESE)
SYNOD, 1st [i.e. 7th, 1947.]
Statuta archdioeceseos indiana-
politanae lata ac promulgata a
Paulo Schulte [ep.] in synodo
archdiocesana (I) septima die
21 mensis Maii 1947 habita
in ecclesia cathedrali Sanctorum
Apostolorum Petri et Pauli
civitatis indianapolitanse in
Indiana. [Indianapolis, Standard
printing co., n.d.] xx, 134p.
  I 13
INDIANAPOLIS (DIOCESE) SYNOD,
1-5. Acta et decreta quinque
synodorum dioceseos Vincennopolitanae, 1844-1891. Indianapoli, Carlon, 1891. 18,
17, 12, 22, 10p.   I 14
INDIANAPOLIS (DIOCESE) SYNOD
6th, 1937. Statuta dioecesis
indianapolitanae lata ac promulgata a Josepho Elmero
Ritter [ep.] in synodo dioecesana
sexta, die 20 mensis Maii
1937 habita in ecclesia cathedrali Sanctorum Apostolorum
Petri et Pauli, civitatis Indianapolitanae in Indiana.
Indianapolis, Harrington &
Folger [n.d.] xx, 128p. I 15
"INDIAN ERMISSION IN DAKOTA,"
Die Katholischen Missionen,
v. 16 (1888), 258.   I 16
"INDIAN ERMISSION IN KANSAS,"
Die Katholischen Missionen, v.
12 (1884), 86-90.   I 17
"INSTANCE OF BIGOTRY IN
1842," Central Blatt and Social
Justice, v. 19 (1926), 269-
271.   I 18
"INSTRUCTION FOR THE GOVERN-

MENT OF THE PAROCHIAL
CLERGY OF THE DIOCESE OF
LOUISIANA," United States
Catholic Historical Magazine,
v. 1 (1887), 418-442. I 19
Latin and English of the in-
struction of 1795 issued by
Bishop Penalver y Gardenas.
"INTERESTING DECISION," Salesianum, v. 11 (Apr., 1916),
32-36.   I 20
The State Supreme Court of
Wisconsin affirms an order
that the Civil Courts have
no right to inquire into the
reasons and motives of the
issuance of a pastoral letter
by Archbishop Messmer, who
was being sued by the
Kuryer Publishing Company
for 100,000 dollars.
IRELAND, JOHN. "The Catholic
Church and the Saloon," North
American Review, v. 159
(1894), 498-505.   I 21
IRELAND, JOHN. The Church
and Modern Society. Lectures
and Addresses. Chicago. D.
H. McBride and Co. 1897.
v. 1; St. Paul. Pioneer
Press. 1904. v. 2 front.
(port. v. 2).   I 22
IRELAND, JOHN. "Life of the
Rt. Rev. Joseph Cretin, First
Bishop of the Diocese of St.
Paul," Acta et Dicta, v. 4
(1916), 187-219; v. 5 (1917),
3-67; 170-205.   I 23
IRELAND, JOHN. 'Right Rev.
Mathias Loras, First Bishop
of Dubuque," Catholic World,
v. 67 (1898), 721-723; v.
68 (1898), 1-12.   I 24
IRELAND, JOHN. "Memoir of
Rev. Lucian Galtier; The
First Catholic Priest of Saint
Paul," in Minnesota Historical
Collections, v. 3 (1880), 222-
230.   I 25
IRELAND, JOHN. "Very Rev-
erend Samuel Charles Maz-
zuchelli, O.P.," Acta et Dicta,
v. 4 (1915), 7-22.   I 26
IRICK, SISTER MARY AUSTIN.

Catholicity in the Sandusky Region Prior to 1847. MA thesis. University of Notre Dame. 1939. iv, 133p.
I 27

IRISH CATHOLIC COLONIZATION ASSOCIATION OF THE UNITED STATES. 3d Annual Report. Reprint from the Chicago Daily News, May 4, 1882.
I 28

IRISH EMIGRATION TO THE UNITED STATES. Catholic Publication Society. 1873.
I 29

IRISH FAITH IN AMERICA. Recollections of a Missionary. Translated from the French by Miss Ella McMahon. New York. Benziger. c1881.   I 30

IVES, JOHN MOSS. The Ark and the Dove. New York. Longmans, Green and Co. 1936. xi, 435p. front., plate, ports.
I 31

IVES, L. SILLIMAN. The Trials of a Mind in Its Progress to Catholicism. London. Richardson and Son. 1854. 233p.
I 32

IVES, RONALD L. "Herbert Eugene Bolton, 1870-1953," American Catholic Historical Society of Philadelphia Records, v. 65 (1954), 40-55.   I 33
A biographical sketch of this great historian of the Southwest; includes a bibliography of his publications.

IVORY, BERTHA MAY. Fifty Years a Bishop. St. Louis. The Author. 1891. 43p. front., illus. (incl. ports.).
I 34
Peter Richard Kenrick, St. Louis.

- J -

JACKER, EDWARD. "Catholic Indians in Michigan and Wisconsin," American Catholic Quarterly Review, v. 1 (1876), 404-435.   J 1

JACKER, EDWARD. "Father Henry Nouvel, S.J.," United States Catholic Historical Magazine, v. 1 (1887), 258-280.   J 2

JACKER, EDWARD. "Father Marquette, S.J., Discovery of His Remains," Woodstock Letters, v. 6 (1877), 159-172.
J 3

JACKER, EDWARD. "La Salle and the Jesuits," American Catholic Quarterly Review, v. 3 (1878), 404-426.   J 4

JACKS, L. V. Claude DuBois, Bishop of Galveston. St. Louis. Herder. 1946. ix, 268p.
J 5

JACKSON, HELEN HUNT. Father Junípero and the Mission Indians of California. Boston. Little, Brown. 1902. xii, 159p. incl. illus., plate, front.   J 6

JACKSON, HELEN HUNT. Glimpses of California and the Missions. Boston. Little, Brown. 1902. xii, 292p. incl. front., illus., plate, facsims.   J 7

JACKSON, HELEN HUNT. Report on the Condition and Needs of the Mission Indians of California. Washington. Government Printing Office. 1883.   J 8

JACKSON, JOSEPH. "Admiral William Shepherd Benson, U.S.N.," American Catholic Historical Society of Philadelphia Records, v. 56 (1945), 36-43.
J 9

JACKSON, JOSEPH. "Building Philadelphia's Cathedral," American Catholic Historical Society of Philadelphia Records, v. 56 (1945), 163-176.
J 10

JACKSON, JOSEPH. "Catholic Burial Grounds in Philadelphia," American Catholic Historical Society of Philadelphia Records, v. 56 (1945), 69-81.   J 11

JACKSON, JOSEPH. "The Catholic Church in Southwark, Philadelphia," American Catholic Historical Society of Philadelphia Records, v. 55 (1944), 283-300. J 12

JACKSON, JOSEPH. "First Catholic Bible Printed in America," American Catholic Historical Society of Philadelphia Records, v. 56 (1943), 19-25. J 13

JACKSON, JOSEPH. "Old St. John's and Its Neighborhood," American Catholic Historical Society of Philadelphia Records, v. 54 (1943), 189-204. J 14

JACKSON, SAMUEL M. A Bibliography of American Church History. New York. Christian Literature Co. 1894. J 15

JACOBS, HUBERT. "The Potawatomi Mission 1854," Mid-America, v. 36 (1954), 220-248. J 16
An account of the activities at the Kansas mission based on a letter by Father Gailland dated St. Mary's, Kansas, June 5, 1854. Original text with a translation by Father Jerome V. Jacobsen is included. Notes to the translation are by Jacobs.

JACOBS, SISTER MARY CORNELIA. The History of the Catholic Church in the Diocese of Cleveland before 1847. MA thesis. University of Notre Dame. 1936. iv, 104p. J 17

JACOBS, T. Geschichte der Gründung und Arbeitung der deutschen katholischen St. Sebastians-Gemeinde von Burlington, Racine O., Wis., no pl. no pub. 1898. 12p. J 18

JACOBSEN, JEROME V. "Attempted Mayhem on Père Marquette," Mid-America, v. 20 (1949), 109-115. J 19

JACOBSEN, JEROME V. "Jean Delanglez, S.J.--In Memoriam," Mid-America, v. 20 (1949), 209-212. J 20

JACQUET, A. "Spokane Mission. Letter dated Spokane Falls, St. Michael's Mission, June 8th, 1883," Woodstock Letters, v. 12 (1883), 332-333. J 21

JACQUET, DAVID. "Bishop Gilmour and the Third Plenary Council of Baltimore," St. Meinrad Essays, v. 12 (1959), 49-59. J 22

JAEGER, LEO A. The Administration of Vacant and Quasi-Vacant Dioceses in the United States. Washington. Catholic University of America. 1941. xi, 236p. J 23

JAILLET, C. "Sketches of Catholicity in Texas," American Catholic Historical Society of Philadelphia Records, v. 2 (1889), 143-153. J 24
The Vicariate Apostolic of Brownsville.

JAMES, GEORGE WHARTON. In and Out of the Old Missions. Boston. Little, Brown. 1905. xx, 392p. lxvi plates, incl. front. J 25

JAMES, GEORGE WHARTON. Old Missions and Mission Indians of California. Los Angeles. Baumgarat. 1895. 124p. illus. J 26

JAMES, GEORGE WHARTON. The Old Franciscan Missions of California. Boston. Little, Brown. 1913. xvi, 287p. front., plates, port., map. J 27

JAMES, GEORGE WHARTON. Picturesque Pala. Pasadena, Calif. Radiant Life Press. 1916. 82p. incl. front. (port.) plates. J 28

JAMES, JAMES A. Oliver Pollock, the Life and Times of an Unknown Patriot. New York. D. Appleton-Century Co. 1937. xii, 376p. illus. (map, facsim.). J 29

JAMES, SISTER MARY. An American Pioneer in Retreat Work, Mother Catherine de Ricci (1845-1894). Elkins Park, Pa. Dominican Retreat House. 1949. 32p. J 30

JAMISON, JAMES K. By Cross and Anchor: The Story of Frederick Baraga on Lake Superior. Paterson, N.J. St. Anthony Guild Press. 1946. xi, 225p.   J 31

JAMMES, J.M., AND H. MENDRAS. "Religious Sociology in the United States," Lumen, v. 6 (1951), 133-146.   J 32
Includes good bibliography.

JANDOLI, RUSSELL J. "The Other Governor," Ave Maria, v. 81 (January 22, 1955), 15-17. port.   J 33
Biographical sketch of Edward Kavanaugh, first Catholic governor of Maine, who died 1844.

JANELLE, P. "Catholic Organization in the United States," Tablet, v. 199 (1952), 472-473.   J 34

JANSEN, J.L. Ein Apostel van Noord Amerika (Neumann). Amsterdam. n.p. 1899. viii, 324p.   J 35

JANSSEN, HANS. Bishop Martin Marty in the Dakotas. American-German Review, v. 27 (1961), 24-26, port., illus.
J 36

JANSSENS, FRANCIS. Sketches of the Catholic Church in the City of Natchez, Mississippi. Natchez. no pub. 1886.
J 37

JAVOR, EGON AND CHRISTOPHER HITES. "Hungarian Benedictines in California," American Benedictine Review, v. 12 (1961), 310-323.   J 38

"JEFFERSONVILLE (N.Y.). CELEBRATES CENTENNIAL," Provincial Annals (Province of the Most Holy Name, O.F.M.), v. 4 (1944), 196-204.   J 39

JENKINS, R.R. "Edmund Quincy Schaefe Waldron, 1812-1888," American Ecclesiastical Review, v. 94 (1936), 33-46.   J 40

JENKINS, THOMAS J. "Know-Nothingism in Kentucky and its Destroyer," Catholic World,

v. 57 (1893), 511-522. J 41
A study of the labors of Benjamin J. Webb.

JENKINS, THOMAS J. Six Seasons on Our Prairies and Six Weeks in Our Rockies. Louisville, Ky. C.A. Rogers. 1884. 218p.   J 42

JEREMIAH, S.M. "Father Drabrowski and the Felicians," Polish American Studies, v. 16 (1959), 12-23.   J 43
Greatest supporter of Felician Sisterhood in America, died 1903.

JEROME, SISTER FRANCIS. This is Mother Pauline. Notre Dame, Ind. Sisters of the Holy Cross. 1945. x, 250p.
J 44

JERON, OTTO. "The Capuchins in America," United States Catholic Historical Society Records and Studies, v. 5 (1907), 274-437.   J 45

"JESUIT AND MORMON. History of the First Printing Press in the Northwest Territory, Imported from France by Jesuits nearly 150 Years Ago." Detroit Free Press. July 31, 1890.   J 46

JESUIT FATHERS IN DENVER. Denver. James Phelan Cuddy. 1924. 112p. incl. ads, illus. plates, ports.   J 47

JESUITS. Letters from Missions. (North America). "Extracts from the Annual Letters of the English Province of the Society of Jesus, 1634, 1638, 1640, 1642, 1654, 1656, 1681," in Narratives of Early Maryland, 1633-1684. New York. 1910. pp. 113-144.   J 48

JESUITS. Letters from the Missions. (North America). Jesuit Relations and Allied Documents. Cleveland. Burrows Bros. 1896-1901. 73v.
J 49

JESUITS. Letters from the Missions (North America). Jesuit Relations and Allied Documents.

New York. Albert and Charles Boni. 1925. liv, 527p. front. plates, ports., maps. J 50

"JESUIT MISSION OF CALIFORNIA (1849-   )," Woodstock Letters, v. 20 (1891), 347-368. J 51

"JESUITS IN CINCINNATI," Woodstock Letters, v. 5 (1876), 115-125, 188-220; v. 6 (1877), 53-69. J 52

JEZIERSKI, B.A. 'Father Alexander Syski: a Tribute to His Memory," Polish American Studies, v. 2 (1945), 95-107. J 53

JOCHUM, WILLIAM A. St. Mary's Congregation. New Albany, Indiana, 1858-1933. no pl. no pub. 1933? 57p. plates, ports. J 54

"JOHANN BAPTIST BAPST, S.J." Die Katholischen Missionen, v. 42 (1914), 170-171, 199-203. J 55

JOHANNEMANN, SISTER MARY THOMAS. Apostle of the Valley; the Life of Daniel Francis Dade, Pioneer Priest of the San Francisco Valley. Fresno, Calif. Academy of California Church History. 1947. 137p. J 56

"JOHN F. O'HARA, C.S.C. MILITARY DELEGATE (1939-1945)," American Catholic Historical Society of Philadelphia Records, v. 64 (1953), 23-28. J 57
    The March issue of the Records is devoted to a series of articles comprising a biography of Archbishop O'Hara.

JOHNSON, C.T. 'The Evolution of a Lament," Washington Historical Quarterly, v. 2 (1908), 193-208. J 58
    An account of the 1831 Indian trip to St. Louis for Black Robes and how it grew to such a major historical problem.

JOHNSON, GEORGE. 'Thomas

Edward Shields; 1862-1921," Catholic Educational Review, v. 27 (1929), 3-7. J 59

JOHNSON, PETER LEO. 'The American Odyssey of the Irish Brigidines," Salesianum, v. 39 (1944), 61-67. J 60

JOHNSON, PETER LEO. "Antecedents of St. Francis Seminary in Milwaukee," Wisconsin Magazine of History, v. 40 (1956), 39-44. J 61

JOHNSON, PETER LEO. "Bartholomites in Wisconsin," Salesianum, v. 45 (1950), 9-15. J 62

JOHNSON, PETER LEO. Crossier of the Frontier. Madison, Wis. State Historical Society of Wisconsin, 1959. xiii, 240p. J 63
    An excellent biography of John Martin Henni, first Archbishop of Milwaukee (1805-1881). He spent fifty years in Mid-America.

JOHNSON, PETER LEO. Centennial Essays for the Milwaukee Archdiocese, 1843-1943. Milwaukee. The Author. 1943. vii, 177p. plates, ports. J 64

JOHNSON, PETER LEO. "Churches of Yesterday," Salesianum, v. 34 (1939), 28-30 (St. Ambrose), 129-131 (St. Michael's), 174-178 (St. Andrew's Yorkville). J 65

JOHNSON, PETER LEO. The Daughters of Charity in Milwaukee, 1846-1946. Milwaukee. Daughters of Charity, St. Mary's Hospital. 1946. x, 235p. J 66

JOHNSON, PETER LEO (ed.) "Documents," Salesianum, v. 68 (1953), 180-182. J 67
    A letter of Sister Gabriella Eardly, O.S.B., to Mother Josephine, Tullow, Ireland, dated June 23, 1927. The letter deals with the two final episodes of the Brigi-

dines in America--Wisconsin, 1851-1855, Grand Rapids, Michigan, 1861.

JOHNSON, PETER LEO, (ed.) "Documents," Salesianum, v. 54 (1959), 107-112 (three letters); (1959), 163-168 (four letters).

J 68

These seven letters deal with the early Catholic school activities among the Indians of Wisconsin.

JOHNSON, PETER LEO. (tr. and ed.) "Documents--Letters to Bishop Henni," Salesianum, v. 25 (July, 1930), 34-42, (Oct., 1930), 42-47; v. 26 (July, 1931), 12-20, (Oct., 1931), 14-22; v. 27 (Jan., 1932), 43-49, (April, 1932), 29-33, (July, 1932), 32-37; v. 28 (Jan., 1933), 33-36; (Apr. 1933), 58-60, (July, 1933), 28-29, (Oct., 1933), 44-48; v. 29 (Jan., 1934), 31-36, (Apr., 1934), 41-46, (July, 1934), 43-47; v. 30 (Jan., 1935), 35-42, (Apr., 1935), 40-46, (July, 1935), 34-36, (Oct., 1935), 29-32; v. 31 (1936), 30-35, 81-84, 134-140, 189-192; v. 32 (1937), 34-37, 80-81; v. 34 (1939), 31-32; v. 40 (1945), 24, 75-77, 116-123; v. 43 (1948), 63-65; v. 49 (1954), 18-21, 69-73; v. 50 (1955), 15-21, 77-83, 129, 180-187; v. 51 (1956), 17-21, 65-70, 120-125, 179-182; v. 52 (1957), -29, 69-74.

J 69

The arrangement of letters is explained in the installment of April, 1934. Gives a good many sidelights on the history of the Church in Wisconsin. The first letter is dated 1848.

JOHNSON, PETER LEO (tr. and ed.) "Documents (Forty-two letters received by Bishop Henni from the Ludwig Missions-verein, Munich, 1844-1873)," Salesianum, v. 37

(1942), 26-30, 82-86, 135-139, 184-191; v. 38 (1943), 25-29, 67-76, 117-121, 166-170; v. 39 (1944), 24-28, 68-72, 116-118, 171-177; v. 40 (1945), 21-29, 75-80, 120-129, 168-180.

J 70

Although announced as letters to Bishop Henni, the collection also includes five more letters for Rev. Michael Heiss, and one by Rev. Joseph Salzmann. Tell the story of the Society's aid to the Church in Wisconsin.

JOHNSON, PETER LEO (ed.) "Documents," Salesianum, v. 68 (Apr., 1953), 68-74.

J 71

Letter of Mrs. M.A. Law begun October 22d and resumed later in 1842 at Milwaukee to Miss Gertrude Green, Washington, Virginia. Contains sidelights on early Milwaukee and brief notices of Bishop Lefevre, Father Kundig, Solomon Juneau and his wife Josette.

JOHNSON, PETER LEO (tr. and ed.). "Documents," Salesianum, v. 52 (1957), 116-120.

J 72

Letter of Mazzuchelli, dated Fort Crawford, Prairie du Chien, Wis., May 2, 1835; summary of the report of Francis Haetocher on Catholic mission school at Green Bay, dated Sept. 14, 1836. This installment begins a series of documents pertaining to early Catholic school activities among the Wisconsin Indians.

JOHNSON, PETER LEO (ed.) "Documents," Six letters to Frederick Rese, dated Canton, Ohio, variously 1832-1834. Salesianum, v. 49 (1954), 123-125, 178-183.

J 73

JOHNSON, PETER LEO (ed.) "Documents," Salesianum, v. 53 (1958), 19-24; (Apr.,

1958), 63-69; (Oct., 1958),
160-169.   J 74
    Fourteen items pertaining
    to early Catholic school
    activities among Wisconsin
    Indians, mostly concerning
    Father Theodore J. Van
    den Broed at Little Chute
    in the 1840's.
JOHNSON, PETER LEO. 'Early
Catholic Church Property in
the Archdiocese of Milwaukee,"
Catholic Historical Review,
v. 28 (1942), 247-250.   J 75
JOHNSON, PETER LEO. "An
Experiment in Adult Education,
White Water, Wisconsin,"
Salesianum, v. 45 (1950),
149-158.   J 76
JOHNSON, PETER LEO. "The
Federal Marine Hospital," Wis-
consin Magazine of History,
v. 30 (1946), 192-199.
                            J 77
JOHNSON, PETER LEO. "First
Catholic Church in Milwaukee,
St. Peter's, 1839," Salesianum,
v. 33 (1938), 123-131. J 78
JOHNSON, PETER LEO. "'Ghost
Churches," Salesianum, v. 35
(1940), 200-206.   J 79
JOHNSON, PETER LEO. Golden
Jubilee Book of Monsignor
Edward J. Blackwell. no pl.
no pub. 1937. 154p. plates,
ports.   J 80
JOHNSON, PETER LEO. Halcyon
Days: Story of St. Francis
Seminary, Milwaukee, 1856-
1956. Milwaukee: Bruce,
1956. xiv, 416p.   J 81
    An excellent history of this
    great Catholic seminary
    by an outstanding scholar.
JOHNSON, PETER LEO. 'The
Historical Antecedents of St.
Francis Seminary," Salesianum,
v. 24 (Oct., 1929), 8-21; v.
25 (Jan., 1930), 17-29, (Apr.,
1930), 29-51, (July, 1930),
15-23, (Oct., 1930), 19-41;
v. 26 (Jan. 1931), 24-45,
(Apr., 1931), 1-20; v. 28
(Apr., 1933), 12-27, (July,

1933), 16-27, (Oct., 1933), 32-
43; v. 29 (Jan., 1934), 17-
30; v. 31 (Jan., 1936), 15-
29. variant title.   J 82
JOHNSON, PETER LEO. (tr.
and ed.) "Letters of Rev.
Michael Heiss to the Board of
Directors of the Ludwig Missionsverein," Salesianum, v.
39 (1944), 68-72, 116-118;
v. 40 (1945), 21-29, 80, 169-
180; v. 43 (1948), 20-23.
                            J 83
    The letters were written
    between 1855 and 1861.
    They give many interesting
    sidelights on mission work
    in the middle United States.
JOHNSON, PETER LEO. "Mil-
waukee's First Mass,"
Salesianum, v. 31 (1936),
74-80.   J 84
JOHNSON, PETER LEO. 'The
Organization of the Catholic
Church in the United States
1880-1882," Salesianum, v.
15 (Apr., 1920), 18-65.
                            J 85
JOHNSON, PETER LEO. 'Rev-
erend Patrick O'Kelley, First
Resident Catholic Pastor of
Milwaukee," Salesianum, v.
45 (1950), 108-113.   J 86
JOHNSON, PETER LEO. "Review
of Baisnee's France and the
Establishment of the American
Catholic Hierarchy," Catholic
Historical Review, v. 21
(1935), 88-93.   J 87
JOHNSON, PETER LEO. "Samuel
Charles Mazzuchelli, Inter-
preter of Catholic Action,"
Salesianum, v. 30 (Jan.,
1935), 29-34.   J 88
JOHNSON, PETER LEO.
"Seminary Projects for the
Missions among Catholic Ger-
mans in the United States,
1835-1855," Salesianum, v.
27 (Jan., 1932), 23-32.
                            J 89
JOHNSON, PETER LEO. 'The
Sisters of Charity and the
Immigrant Hospital on Jones

Island, Wisconsin," Salesianum,
v. 40 (1945), 162-168. J 90

JOHNSON, PETER LEO. "Site
of Milwaukee's First Hospital,"
Salesianum, v. 40 (1945),
15-20. J 91

JOHNSON, PETER LEO. "Some
Ghost Churches," Salesianum,
v. 33 (1938), 179-181. map.
J 92

JOHNSON, PETER LEO. Stuffed
Saddlebags: The Life of
Martin Kundig, Priest, 1805-
1879. Milwaukee. Bruce.
1942. vii, 297p. front.
(port.). J 93

JOHNSON, PETER LEO. "Unofficial
Beginnings of the Milwaukee
Catholic Diocese," Wisconsin
Magazine of History, v. 23
(1939), 3-16. J 94

JOHNSON, ROBERT C. John
McLoughlin: Patriarch of the
Northwest. Portland, Ore.
Metropolitan Press. 1935.
302p. front., illus. (incl.
maps), plates, ports. J 95

JOHNSTON, ROBERT S. Mar-
quette College: A Quarter
Century, 1881-1906, Milwaukee.
no pl. no pub. 1906. J 96

JOLLY, ELLEN RYAN. The Nuns
of the Battlefield. 4th ed.
Providence. Providence Visitor
Press. 1930. ix, 336p. incl.
front. J 97

JONES, CARMITA DE SOLMS.
"Acadia in Maine," American
Catholic Historical Society
of Philadelphia Records, v.
36 (1925), 359-371. J 98

JONES, CARMITA DE SOLMS.
"Black Gowns among the
Abnakis," American Catholic
Historical Society of Phila-
delphia Records, v. 33 (1922),
276-299. J 99

JONES, CARMITA DE SOLMS.
"Missions in Lincoln County,
Maine," American Catholic His-
torical Society of Philadelphia
Records, v. 36 (1925), 396-
400. J 100

JONES, CARMITA DE SOLMS.

'Right Reverend Michael John
Hoban, D.D., Bishop of
Scranton," American Catholic
Historical Society of Philadel-
phia Records, v. 37 (1926),
372-375. J 101

JONES, CARMITA DE SOLMS.
"St. Peter's, Point Pleasant,
New Jersey," American Cath-
olic Historical Society of
Philadelphia Records, v. 37
(1926), 230-241. J 102

JONES, HOWARD MUMFORD.
"The Idea of a Franciscan
Academy," Americas, v. 1
(1944), 160-165. J 103

JONES, SISTER MARY BENE-
DICTA. History of the Sisters
of St. Joseph in Catholic Education in the Ogdensburg
Diocese of New York. MA
thesis. Villanova University.
1948. 48p. J 104

JONES, WILLIAM H. History of
Catholic Education in the State
of Colorado. Washington.
Catholic University. 1955.
xl, 574p. J 105
A very detailed and well
documented history of the
Catholic schools of
Colorado.

"JOSEPH M. MARA," Woodstock
Letters, v. 44 (1915), 389-
392. J 106

JOSET, JOSEPH. Histoire de la
Mission de Colville, d'Après
les Notes du P. Joset. n.p.
n.d. J 107

JOSET, JOSEPH. "Vereinigten
Staaten von Nordamerika," Die
Katholischen Missionen, v. 5
(1877), 130-131. J 108

JOSET, JOSEPH. "Washington
Territory. Then and Now.
Letter dated Spokane Falls,
June 14th, 1882," Woodstock
Letters, v. 12 (1883), 172-
180. J 109

"JOURNAL OF MISSIONS IN
KENTUCKY," Woodstock
Letters, v. 8 (1879), 74-80.
J 110

JOUVE, R. "Les Catholiques et

197

le Problème Noir aux États-Unis," Etudes, v. 265 (1950), 354-364. J 111

"JUBILEE AT YONKERS (NEW YORK) UKRANIAN CATHOLIC PARISH," The Ark, v. 4 (1949), 172-176. J 112

"JUBILEE MISSIONS IN NEBRAS-KA," Woodstock Letters, v. 11 (1882), 78-90, 169-179. J 113

"JUBILEE OF THE PROVINCE [MARYLAND, S.J.], 1833-1883," Woodstock Letters, v. 12 (1883), 205-257, 278-283. J 114

JUDGE, ANN. "Fra Junipero Serra and the California Missions," United States Catholic Historical Society Records and Studies, v. 7 (1914), 168-182. illus. J 115

JUDGE, CHARLES JOSEPH. An American Missionary: A Record of the Work of Rev. William H. Judge, S.J. 4th ed. Boston. Catholic Foreign Mission Bureau. 1907. xix, 308p. front., illus., plates, ports., map., facsim. J 116

JUDGE, RAYMOND J. "The First Bishop of the West: a Sketch of Flaget," The Priest, v. 5 (1949), 422-429. J 117

JUDGE, ROBERT K. "Foundation and First Administration of the Jesuits of the Maryland Province," St. Meinrad Essays, v. 12 (1959), 13-21. J 118

JUDSON, PAUL M. "Sketch of the Life of Father Gabriel Richard," American Catholic Historical Society of Philadelphia Records, v. 37 (1926), 250-297. J 119

JUENEMAN, DEMETRIUS AND RUTH SEBASTIAN. Between the Years 1895-1945. St. Martin's College. Lacey. n.p. 1945. J 120

JUJAT, L'ABBE. Mission de l'Oregon. Notice sur les travaux apostoliques de Mgr. Demers. Paris. Varyet de

Surcy. 1851. 16p. J 121

JULIA AGNES, SISTER. The Development of Catholicity in Massachusetts. MA thesis. Boston College. 1930. 69p. J 122

JULIAN, BROTHER. Men and Deeds, the Xavier Brothers in America. New York. Macmillan. 1930. xx, 539p. J 123

JUNG, A.M. Jesuit Missions among the American Tribes of the Rocky Mountain Indians. Spokane. Gonzaga Univ. 1925. plate. J 124

JUNG, MARGETTA P. "Texas' First Catholic Mission," Ave Maria, v. 43 (1936), 430-433. J 125

JUSMAC, B. "Letter of B. Jusmac, Secretary General of Haiti, to Mr. Joseph L. Smith, Maryland, 1829," Americas, v. 2 (1945), 226-J 126

JUSTIN, BROTHER. An Epitome of the Important Historical Events in the Educational Activities of the Xaverian Brothers in the United States, 1854-1925. MA thesis. University of Notre Dame. 1926. 112p. J 127

JUTZ. "Die jüngsten Indianer-wirren und deren Ursachen." Die Katholischen Missionen. v. 19 (1891), 157p. J 128

JUTZ, JOHN. "Historic Data on the Causes of the Dissatisfaction among the Sioux Indians in 1890," Woodstock Letters, v. 47 (1918), 313-372. J 129

JUTZ, JOHN. "Recollections of an Old Indian Missionary," Woodstock Letters, v. 50 (1921), 310-318; v. 51 (1922), 361-369. J 130

- K -

K., M. "Galveston. Letter dated St. Mary's University, Galveston, Texas. New Year's Day, 1890," Woodstock Letters,

v. 19 (1890), 75-80.   K 1

K., M. "Our New Church at
Galveston. Letter dated St.
Mary's University, Galveston,
Texas. March 5, 1892,"
Woodstock Letters, v. 21
(1892), 181-184.   K 2

K., P.J. "Louisiana. A Short
Account of the Society in New
Orleans," Woodstock Letters,
v. 14 (1885), 317-326; v. 15
(1886), 33-44, 144-150; v.
17 (1887), 42-48.   K 3

KAISER, E. G.   History of St.
John's Parish, Whiting, 1897-
1947. Whiting, Indiana. The
Pastor. 1948. 162p. illus.,
ports.   K 4

KAISER, SISTER M. LAURINA.
Development of the Concept
and Function of the Catholic
Elementary School in the
American Parish. Washington.
Catholic University. 1955.
ix, 149p.   K 5

KALINOWSKI, MARY THEOPHANIA.
The First Decade of the Sisters
of Saint Felix in America,
1874-1884. Chicago. Loyola
University, 1956. 102p.
thesis.   K 6

KALMER, LEO. Stronger than
Death. Quincy, Ill. Quincy
College. 1929. 49p.   K 7
Subtitled "Historical notes
on the heroic sacrifices of
Catholic priests and religious
during the yellow fever
epidemic in Memphis in
1873, 1878, 1879."

KALSTATTER, MAXIMILIAN.
"Deutsche Volksmissionen in
den Vereinigten Staaten von
Nordamerika," Die Katholischen
Missionen, v. 8 (1880), 29-
36.   K 8

KALT, ILDEPHONS. Das
Benedektinerinnen Kloster. St.
Scholastika zu Arkansas, Nord
America, 1879-1904. Little
Rock. 153p. illus.   K 9

KALT, ILDEPHONS. Die
Deutsche Katholische Gemeinde
St. Scholastica zu Shoal Creek,

Logan County, Arkansas.1903.
34p. illus., ports.   K 10

KALVELAGE, F.L. The Annals
of St. Boniface Parish, 1862-
1926. Chicago, Ill. no pub.
1926. 241p. plates, ports.
   K 11

KAMMER, ALCUIN. "Franciscan
Return to Louisiana," Province
Chronicle (St. John Baptist
Province, O.F.M.), v. 10
(1938), April.   K 12

KANE, JOHN J.   Catholic-
Protestant Conflicts in America. Chicago. Regnery. 1955.
244p.   K 13

KANE, JOHN J.   "Church and the
Laity among Catholics," Annals
of the American Academy of
Political and Social Science,
no. 332 (1960), 50-59.
   K 14

KANE, JOHN J.   "Social Structure of American Catholics,"
American Sociological Review,
v. 16 (Mar. 1955), 23-30.
   K 15

KANE, SISTER M. ZITA MARIA.
The Sisters, Servants of the
Immaculate Heart of Mary
(Scranton, Pennsylvania) in the
Northwest, 1897-1947. MA
thesis. Villanova University.
1948. 165p.   K 16

KANSAS (VICARIATE APOSTOLIC).
Pastoral instruction of the
Vicar apostolic of Kansas,
[Louis Maria Fink, O.S.B.]
to the clergy, secular and
regular, the religious communities, and the faithful of
his vicariate. Issued March
21, 1876. [n.p.] vi, [7]-
158p.   K 17

KANSAS CITY, KANSAS.
(DIOCESE) SYNOD, 2nd.
[Synodus dioecesana leaven-
worthensis II.] xxii, 125p.
   K 18

KANSAS CITY, MISSOURI.
(DIOCESE) SYNOD, 3rd-4th,
1920, 1928. Statuta dioecesana;
decreta synodi dioecesanae
kansanopolitanae tertiae, die

20 mensis Aprilis 1920 in ecclesia cathedrali Immaculatae Conceptionis B.M.V. habitae a Thoma Francisco Lillis [ep.] [et synodus ... quarta ... celebrata ... 30 Octobris, A. D. 1928]. [n.p., n.d.] xvii, 176p.   K 19

KANSAS CITY, (DIOCESE) SYNOD, 1st, 1887. Synodus dioecesna kansanopolitana prima, diebus 14, 15, et 16. Junii, A.D., 1887, in cathedrali Immaculatae Conceptionis, Kansanurbi habita a Joanne Josepho Hogan [ep.] Baltimorae, Foley fratres, 1887. 34p.   K 20

KANSAS CITY, MISSOURI. (DIOCESE) SYNOD, 2nd, 1912. Decreta synodi dioecesanae kansanipolitanae secundae, die IX., mensis Aprilis, 1912, in ecclesia cathedrali kansanopoli habitae a Joanne Josepho Hogan, D. D., episcopo kansanopolitano, et a Thoma Francisco Lillis, D. D., episcopo coadjutore. [Atchison, Kans., Abbey student press, St. Benedict's college, 1912]. xxiii, 121p.   K 21

KAROL, JOSEPH. "America's Only Blessed," Priest, v. 9 (July, 1953), 518-522. K 22
Brief popular biographical sketch of Blessed Philippine Duchesne.

KAROL, JOSEPH S. Bishop of the Great American Desert," Jesuit Bulletin, v. 35 (1956), 9-12.   K 23
A brief illustrated sketch of Bishop Miege; of little scholarly value.

KAROL, JOSEPH. "The First Hoosier Jesuits," Woodstock Letters, v. 79 (1950), 155-156.   K 24

KAROL, JOSEPH. "What Happened to the Potawatomi," American Ecclesiastical Review, v. 129 (1953), 361-367.   K 25

An undocumented account of the wandering migrations of the Indian tribe and the missionary efforts among them.

KAROLCZAK, SISTER MARY VALENTIA. Some Aspects of Polish Immigration to the United States with Special Reference to the Period 1870-1905. MA thesis. Marquette University. 1942.   K 26

KARSON, MARC. "The Catholic Church and the Political Development of American Trade Unionism (1900-1918)," Industrial and Labor Relations Review, v. 4 (1951), 527-542.   K 27

"KATHOLISCHE PRESSE IN DEN U. S. A.," Stimmen der Zeit, v. 152 (1953), 377-378.   K 28

DIE KATHOLISCHEN MISSIONEN IM NORDÖSTLICHEN ARKANSAS UND DAS BENEDIKTENER FRAUENKLOSTER MARIA STEIN BEI POCAHONTAS. Randolph City, Arkansas. 1893. n.p.   K 29

KAUSLER, ALOYSIUS. History of St. Stephen's and St. Anne's Missions, Garrett, Maryland. Cumberland, Md. no pub. 1920.   K 30

(KAUSLER, EMMERAM). Some Early History of the Pioneer Catholic Settlers and Parishes of Northwestern Kansas. Herndon, Kansas. Capuchin Fathers. 1913. [42p.] plates.   K 31

KAVANAUGH, DENNIS JOHN. The Holy Family Sisters of San Francisco... 1872-1922. San Francisco, Calif. Gilmartin Co. 1922. 328p. front., plates, ports. K 32

KEANE, JAMES PATRICK. Status of Catholics in Maryland. 1689-1760. MA thesis. Catholic University. 1950. 76p.   K 33

KEANE, JOHN J. "Father Hecker,"

Catholic World, v. 49 (1889),
1-19. K 34
KEARNEY, . "The Padre of
the Rains," Columbia, v. 41
(1924), 13. port. K 35
KEEFE, SISTER ST. THOMAS
AQUINAS. Bishop Wadhams
and the Diocese of Ogdensburg.
MA thesis. Catholic Univer-
sity. 1940. 50p. K 36
KEEFE, SISTER ST. THOMAS
AQUINAS. The Congregation
of the Grey Nuns (1737-1910).
Washington. Catholic Univer-
sity. 1942. x, 373p. K 37
KEEHAN, SISTER MARTHA
JULIE. The Irish Catholic
Beneficial Societies Founded
between 1818-1869. MA thesis.
Catholic University. 1953. 77p.
K 38
KEELER, SISTER JEROME. "The
Most Reverend George Donnel-
ly," Benedictine Review, v.
6 (Winter, 1951), 5-8. K 39
Obituary of the late Bishop
of Kansas City, Kansas,
includes portrait.
KEENAN, SISTER MARY ELLEN.
French Teaching Communities
and Early Convent Education
in the United States, 1727-
1850. MA thesis. Catholic
University. 1934. 74p. K 40
KEENAGHAN, SISTER HONORIA.
The Efforts of the Hierarchy
of San Antonio to Put into
Effect the Recommendations
of the Third Council of Balti-
more with Regard to Catholic
Education. MA thesis. Cath-
olic University. 1953. 103p.
K 41
KEHOE, SISTER MARY URBAN.
"The Educational Activities
of Distinguished Catholic
Missionaries among the Five
Civilized Tribes," Chronicles
of Oklahoma, v. 24 (1946),
166-182. K 42
KEIM, JOHN H. Saint Cecilia's
Parish, Bartelso, Illinois,
1885-1935. Bartelso, Clinton
County, Illinois. no pub.

1935. 60p. plates, ports.
K 43
KEKAN, JOSEPH F. James
Cardinal Gibbons and the
Press. MA thesis. Catholic
University. 1949. 144p.
K 44
KELEHER, JULIA, AND ELSIE
RUTH CHANT. The Padre of
Isleta. Santa Fe. Rydal
Press. 1940. K 45
(KELLER, PH. L.). "Die
Negermission in Galveston,"
Die Katholischen Missionen,
v. 30 (1902), 280-283. K 46
KELLEY, FRANCIS CLEMENT.
The Bishop Jots It Down. New
York. Harper and Bros.
1939. vii, 333p. front.,
plates, ports. K 47
KELLEY, FRANCIS CLEMENT.
First American Catholic Mis-
sionary Congress. Chicago.
J.S. Hyland. 1909. K 48
KELLEY, FRANCIS CLEMENT.
The Story of Extension.
Chicago. Extension Press.
1922. 302p. front. (port.),
illus. K 49
KELLEY, MARY DE SALES. A
Study of the Osage Mission
Schools Based on United States
Archival Material, 1847-1870.
MA thesis. Catholic Univer-
sity. 1955. 92p. K 50
KELLOGG, LOUISE P. "Father
Jacques Marquette: A Tercen-
tenary Tribute," Catholic
World, v. 145 (1937), 266-
273. K 51
KELLOGG, LOUISE P. "First
Missionary in Wisconsin,"
Wisconsin Magazine of History,
v. 4 (1921), 417-425. K 52
KELLY, GEORGE A. Catholics
and the Practice of the Faith.
A Census Study of the Diocese
of Saint Augustine. Washing-
ton. Catholic University.
1946. viii, 224p. K 53
KELLY, GEORGE A., AND
THOMAS COOGAN. "What is
Our Real Catholic Population,"
American Ecclesiastical Re-

view, v. 110 (1944), 368-377. K 54

KELLY, GERALD. The Life of Mother Hieronymo. Rochester, N. Y. The Author, Nazareth College. 1948. 30p. K 55

KELLY, HENRY W. "Franciscan Missions of New Mexico, 1740-1760," New Mexico Historical Review, v. 15 (1940), 345-368; v. 16 (1941), 41-69, 148-183. maps. K 56

KELLY, HENRY W. Franciscan Missions of New Mexico 1740-1760. Albuquerque. University of New Mexico Press. 1941. 94p. maps. K 57

KELLY, J. P. History of St. Mary's Parish, Glens Falls, N.Y., 1848-1949. Glens Falls post Co. 1950. 223p. illus.; ports. K 58

KELLY, LAURENCE J. "Father Charles Neale and the Jesuit Restoration in America," Woodstock Letters, v. 71 (1942), 255-290; v. 72 (1943), 21-33, 116-147, 242-263. K 59

KELLY, LAURENCE J. History of Holy Trinity Parish, Washington, D.C., 1795-1945. Washington. Holy Trinity Church. 1946. 137p. K 60

KELLY, LAURENCE J. "Negro Missions in Maryland," Woodstock Letters, v. 38 (1909), 239-244. K 61

KELLY, LAURENCE J. "Southern Maryland Shrine," Woodstock Letters, v. 69 (1940), 157-172, plate. K 62
The Carmelite convent of Port Tobacco, founded 1790.

KELLY, SISTER MARGARET JEAN. American Catholics in the War of 1812. MA thesis. Catholic University. 1938. 71p. K 63

KELLY, SISTER MARGARET JEAN. The Career of Joseph Lane, Frontier Politician. Washington. Catholic University. 1942. ix, 107p. K 64

KELLY, SISTER M. GILBERT. A History of Catholic Immigrant Colonization Projects in the United States, 1815-1860. New York. United States Catholic Historical Society. 1939. ix, 209p. K 65

KELLY, SISTER MARY JAMES. Two Decades of Catholic Church History in the South Dakota Country from 1839 to 1859. MA thesis. University of Notre Dame. 1933. 52p. K 66

KELLY, M. T. "Eucharistic Devotion on an American Frontier of 1800," American Ecclesiastical Review, v. 101 (1939), 346-353. K 67

KELLY, M. V. "The Recent (1920) Census and Catholic Growth," American Ecclesiastical Review, v. 73 (1925), 392-396. K 68

KELLY, MATTHEW P. The Society of St. Vincent de Paul in the Diocese of Brooklyn. MA thesis. Catholic University. 1932. 121p. K 69

KEMPKER, JOHN F. "Catholic Missionaries in the Early and in the Territorial Days of Iowa," Annals of Iowa, 3d series, v. 10 (1910), 54-62. K 70

KEMPKER, JOHN F. "Catholicity in Southeastern (Lee County) Iowa," American Catholic Historical Society of Philadelphia Records, v. 2 (1886-1888), 128-142. K 71

KEMPKER, JOHN F. "Decennium of the Catholic Church in Lee Co., Iowa," American Catholic Historical Researches, v. 2 (1886), 128-131. K 72

KEMPKER, JOHN F. "The Early Catholic Clergy of Iowa," American Catholic Researches, v. 12 (1885), 81-85. K 73

KEMPKER, JOHN F. "The First

Priests in Iowa," Iowa Historical Record, v. 4 (1888), 17-21.　　　　　　　　　K 74

KEMPKER, JOHN F. The Golden Jubilee of Our Lady of Mt. Carmel, Iowa, 1869-1919. St. Louis.Amerika Print. 1919. 38p. plates, ports., diagrs., illus.　K 75

KEMPKER, JOHN F. History of the Catholic Church in Iowa. Iowa City. Republican Pub. Co. 1887. 64p.　　　K 76

KEMPKER, JOHN F. 'Rt. Rev. Dr. Mathias Loras," Iowa Historical Record, v. 3 (1887), 555-560.　　　　　　　K 77

(KENKEL, F.P.) "A Benedictine Agricultural School for Negroes," Central Blatt and Social Justice, v. 30 (1938), 348.　　　　　　　　　K 78

(KENKEL, F.P.) "The Chronicle of a Pioneer Parish (St. Francis, Teutopolis)," Central Blatt and Social Justice, v. 19 (1926), 160-161.　K 79

(KENKEL, F.P.) "Die Einladung des Missionärs Pierz an deutsche Katholiken, sich in Minnesota niederzulassen," Central Blatt and Social Justice, v. 11 (1910), 288-290.
　　　　　　　　　　　K 80

(KENKEL, F.P.) "Die erste deutsche Katholische Gemeinde in New Orleans, La.," Central Blatt and Social Justice, v. 12 (1919), 44-46.　　　K 81

KENKEL, F.P. "Die Einladung des Missionärs Pierz an deutsche Katholiken, sich in Minnesota niederzulassen," Central Blatt and Social Justice, v. 11 (1918), 289-290.　K 82

(KENKEL, F.P.) "An Extraordinary Project," Central Blatt and Social Justice, v. 18 (1925), 305-308, 377-378.
　　　　　　　　　　　K 83

American German Catholic University.

(KENKEL, F.P.) "Fr. F.X. Weninger in Texas," Central Blatt and Social Justice, v. 29 (1936), 20-21.　　　K 84

KENKEL, F.P. "Geschichte und Organisation des katholischen Instituts zu Cincinnati, O.," Central Blatt and Social Justice, v. 12 (1919), 146-149.
　　　　　　　　　　　K 85

(KENKEL, F.P.) "A Tribute to Ludwig I of Bavaria, Patron of Catholic Missions in the U.S.," Central Blatt and Social Justice, v. 17 (1925), 413-414.　　　　　　　K 86

(KENKEL, F.P.) "Urtheile der Gegner uber den Chicagoer Katholikentag des Jahres 1887," Central Blatt and Social Justice, v. 14 (1921), 49-50.
　　　　　　　　　　　K 87

KENNEALLY, FINBAR. "The Catholic Seminaries of California as Educational Institutions, 1940-1950," Catholic Educational Review, v. 55 (1957), 1-18.
　　　　　　　　　　　K 88

KENNEDY, AMBROSE. Quebec to New England. Boston. Bruce Humphries Inc. 1948. 244p. illus., ports.　K 89

KENNEDY, J. H. Jesuit and Savage in New France. New Haven. Yale University Press. 206p.　　　　　　　　　K 90

KENNEDY, J. S. "After Fifty Years," Columbia, v. 38 (1958), 6-9.　　　　　　K 91

KENNEDY, JOHN H. Thomas Dongan, Governor of New York (1682-1688). Washington. Catholic University. 1930. ix, 131p.　　　　　　K 92

KENNEDY, SISTER MALACHY. "Thomas Francis Lillis: Second Bishop of Leavenworth," Benedictine Review, v. 5 (1950), 24-28.　　　K 93

KENNEDY, SISTER M. NATALIE. A Pioneer Religious Venture in Ohio. MA thesis. University of Notre Dame. 1936. ii, 81p.　　　　　　K 94

KENNEDY, PHILIP WAYNE. Bishop M.J. Spalding and the

Know-nothing Movement in
Kentucky. MA thesis. Mar-
quette University. 1957. K 95
KENNEDY, THOMAS. Father
Ryan, the Irish-American Poet-
Priest of the Southern States.
Dublin. J. J. Lalor, n.d.
K 96
KENNEDY, WILLIAM H. "Cath-
olics in Massachusetts before
1750," Catholic Historical Re-
view, v. 17 (1931), 10-28.
K 97
KENNEY, I. L. "CrossBearers
of New Mexico," Overland,
n.s. v. 56 (1910), 292-295.
K 98
KENNEY, JAMES F. "The
Public Records of the Province
of Quebec, 1763-1791," Royal
Society of Canada Transactions,
3d series, sec. 2, 34 (1940).
K 99
KENNY, LAURENCE. "The First
American Nun in This Country,"
Illinois Catholic Historical Re-
view, v. 1 (1919), 495-499.
K 100
KENNY, LAURENCE. "The
Gallipolis Colony (1790)," Cath-
olic Historical Review, v. 4
(1919), 415-451.   K 101
KENNY, LAURENCE. "The
Indians at St. Ignatius Mission,
Montana," Woodstock Letters,
v. 27 (1898), 82-84.   K 102
KENNY, LAURENCE. "Missouri's
Earliest Settlement, and Its
Name," Illinois Catholic His-
torical Review, v. 1 (1919),
151-156.   K 103
KENNY, LAURENCE. "The Mul-
lanphys of St. Louis," United
States Catholic Historical
Society Records and Studies,
v. 14 (1920), 70-111.   K 104
KENNY, LAURENCE. "Pioneer
Catholic Universities," United
States Catholic Historical
Society Records and Studies,
v. 31 (1940), 145-148.   K 105
KENNY, LAURENCE. "Old
Jamestown's Catholic Memo-
ries," Historical Bulletin, v.

7 (1928), 3-4.   K 106
KENNY, LAURENCE. "Points
in Illinois History--a Symposium," Illinois Catholic Historical Review, v. 4 (1922),
355-371.   K 107
KENNY, LAURENCE J. "The
'Jesuit College' at Kaskaskia,
Illinois, 1718-1763," Wood-
stock Letters, v. 81 (1952),
58-62.   K 108
KENNY, LAURENCE J. "Recol-
lections of Father Helias,"
Jesuit Bulletin, v. 35 (1956),
12-14.   K 109
This brief sketch forcefully
points up the need of a
major bit of research con-
cerning the activities of
Father Helias d'Huddeghem
in central Missouri.
KENNY, MICHAEL. Catholic
Culture in Alabama. Cen-
tenary Story of Spring Hill
College, 1830-1930. New
York. America Press. 1931.
400p. front., plates, ports.
K 110
KENNY, MICHAEL. "The First
Jesuit Mission in Florida,"
United States Catholic His-
torical Society Records and
Studies, v. 33 (1941), 42.
K 111
KENNY, MICHAEL. Romance of
the Floridas. Milwaukee.
Bruce. 1934. xxiii, 395p.
front., plate, illus., fold. map.
map on end papers.   K 112
KENNY, MICHAEL. "What His-
tory Says of Florida's Begin-
nings," Catholic World, v. 162
(1945), 232-237.   K 113
KENRICK, FRANCIS PATRICK.
Diary and Visitation Record.
tr. and ed. by Francis E.
Tourscher. Lancaster, Pa.
Wickersham Printing Co.
1916. 298p. front., port.
K 114
KENRICK, FRANCIS PATRICK.
"The Diocese of Philadelphia
at the Opening of the Year
1834," American Catholic His-

torical Researches, v. 8 (1891), 136-142. K 115

KENRICK, FRANCIS PATRICK. "Report on the Condition of the Church of Philadelphia Made to Our Holy Father Pope Gregory XVI June 1, 1838," American Catholic Historical Society of Philadelphia Records, v. 38, (1927), 207-217. K 116

KENRICK, PETER RICHARD. "Report of the Situation and Condition of the Diocese of Philadelphia ... 1838," American Catholic Historical Researches, v. 22 (1915), 144-146. K 117

KENTON, EDNA (ed.) The Jesuit Relations and Allied Documents. New York. Vanguard. 1954. 581p. map. K 118
Selections from the 73 volume set.

KEPPEL, LADY LEOPOLDINE OLIVIA. Blessed Rose Philippine Duchesne. London. Longmans. 1940. vii, 188p. K 119

KERNAN, JULIE. "American Catholic Writing, a Publisher's View," Catholic Library World, v. 24 (1952), 14-17. K 120

KERSCHEN, SISTER MARY DONATA. Father Mazzuchelli's Influence on the Frontier Prior to His Appointment as Provincial. MA thesis. Marquette University. 1946. K 121

KERWIN, JEROME G. "Catholics and Civil Life," Ave Maria, v. 86 (October 12, 1957), 8-12. K 122
Believes Catholics have not taken advantage of the opportunities they have had for participation in secular society.

KESSLER, W. G. "Sources in Early Iowa Catholic Church History," Iowa Catholic Historical Review, v. 2 (Nov., 1930), 27-34; v. 3 (1931), 25-29. K 123

KEYES, J. M. Misiones Españoles de California. Madrid.

C.S.I.C. Instituto Juan Sebastian Elcano. 1950. 244p. illus., ports. K 124

KIEFER, SISTER MONICA. The History of the Catholic Church in Coshocton County, Ohio. MA thesis. University of Notre Dame. 1933. vi, 110p. ports. K 125

KIELEY, . Memoranda. Norfolk, Va. 1874. K 126

KIELY, . "Rapport de M. Kiely, Missionnaire a Salt Lake City à M.M. Les Directeurs de l Oeuvre de la Propagation de la Foi," Annales de la Propagation de la Foi, v. 55 (1883), 274-280. K 127

KIENAN, MATHIAS C. "In Memoriam: Carlos Eduardo Castañeda," The Americas, v. 15 (1958), 61-62. K 128

KIENTZ, SISTER FLORENCE. Alverno: Story of the Franciscan Sisters of Alverno, Wis., 1866-1919. Washington. Catholic Educ. Press. c1919. 146p. plates, ports. K 129

KING, JOSEPH EDWARD. "The Real Quebec Act," Mid-America, v. 34 (1952), 14-41. K 130

KING, TERENCE, "A Confederate Chaplain at Frederick, 1862-1864," Woodstock Letters, v. 58 (1929), 566-578. K 131

KING, TERENCE S. "Letters of Civil War Chaplains," Woodstock Letters, v. 43 (1914), 24-34, 168-180. K 132

KING, WILLIAM. "Lord Baltimore and His Freedom in Granting Religious Toleration," American Catholic Historical Society of Philadelphia Records, v. 32 (1921), 295-313. K 133

KINGSLEY, H.C.'Roman Catholic Contributions and Missions," New Englander, v. 17 (1859), 93-110. K 134

KINO, EUSEBIO FRANCISCO. Kino's Historical Memoirs of

Primeria Alta, 1683-1711. ed.
by Herber Bolton. Cleveland.
Arthur H. Clark Co. 1919.
2v. front., maps, plan,
facsim. Offset reprint issued
by University of California
Press, 1948, 2v. in 1, pp.
379 and 329.   K 135
KINO, EUSEBIO FRANCISCO.
Las Missiones de Sonora y
Arizona. Mexico. Editorial
"Cultura." 1913-1922. lxxix,
413p. incl. facsim.   K 136
KINSELLA, THOMAS H. A
Century of Catholicity in Kan-
sas, 1822-1922. Catholic
Indian Missions and Mission-
aries of Kansas. The Pioneers
of the Prairies. Kansas City.
1921.   K 137
KINSELLA, THOMAS H. The
History of Our Cradle Land.
Kansas City. 1921.   K 138
Popular account of early
missions to Indians and
Whites in Kansas. Incor-
porates considerable source
material.
KINSMAN, FREDERICK J. A-
mericanism and Catholicism.
New York. Longmans, Green
and Co. 1924. ix, 250p.
                      K 139
KINSMAN, FREDERICK J. Salve
Mater. New York. Long-
mans, Green and Co. 1920.
vii, 302p.   K 140
KINTZ, LAWRENCE. "Demetrius
Augustine Gallitzin," Salesi-
anum, v. 17 (May, 1922),
12-36.   K 141
KINZER, DONALD L. "Political
Uses of Anti-Catholicism:
Michigan and Wisconsin, 1890-
1894," Michigan History,
v. 39 (1955), 312-326. K 142
KIP, WILLIAM J. Early Jesuit
Missions in North America.
2d ed. Albany, N.Y. Peace
and Prentice. 1866. iv,
325p.   K 143
KIP, WILLIAM J. Historical
Scenes from the Old Jesuit
Missions. N.Y. Anso D.F.

Randolph. c1875. 375p.
                      K 144
KIRKFLEET, C. J. History of
the Parish of St. John the
Baptist, Somonauk, Ill.
Somonauk, Ill. no pub. 1929.
                      K 145
KIRKFLEET, CORNELIUS. Life
of Patrick Augustus Feehan...
Chicago. Matre and Co.
1922. xix, 381p.   K 146
KIRKFLEET, CORNELIUS. "The
Premonstatention Centenary,"
American Catholic Historical
Society of Philadelphia Re-
cords, v. 53 (1942), 11-20.
                      K 147
KIRKFLEET, CORNELIUS J.
The White Canons of St. Nor-
bert. A History of the Pre-
monstatensian Order in the
British Isles and America.
West De Pere, Wis. St. Nor-
bert Abbey. 1943. xxvi,
307p. front. (map), plates,
ports., plan.   K 148
KIRLIN, JOSEPH J.L. Cath-
olicity in Philadelphia. Phila-
delphia. J. J. McVey.
1909. xv, 546p. incl. front.,
ports.   K 149
KIRLIN, JOSEPH J. L. "An
English Benefactor of Colonial
Times," American Catholic
Historical Society of Phila-
delphia Records, v. 26 (1915),
78-88.   K 150
The origin of the Sir John
James Fund.
KIRRANE, JOHN PHILIP. The
Establishment of Negro
Parishes and the Coming of
the Josephites, 1863-1871. MA
thesis. Catholic University.
1932. 59p.   K 151
KIRST, ADOLPH. Centenary of
St. Francis Seminary. Prov-
ince Chronicles, O.F.M.,
(Cincinnati), 31 (1959), 161-
166. illus.   K 152
KIRWIN, JAMES MARTIN (ed.)
Diamond Jubilee, 1847-1922
of the Diocese of Galveston.
Galveston, Texas. Knapp,

1922. 131p. front., plates, ports. K 153
KIRWIN, JAMES M. Memoirs of Monsignor J.M. Kirwin. Houston, Texas. Standard Printing and Lithographing Co. 1928. 236p. illus., ports. K 154
KISSLING, THOMAS E. "The Burning of the Convent," Columbia, v. 14 (Aug., 1934), 6, 20. K 155
KISSLING, T. E. "The Pope's Stone," Columbia, v. 12 (Feb., 1933), 9, 17. K 156
The story of the stone given by the Pope for the Washington Monument and what happened to it.
KITE, ELIZABETH S. "Antoinette Margot and Clara Barton," American Catholic Historical Society of Philadelphia Records, v. 55 (1944), 30-50. K 157
KITE, ELIZABETH S. The Catholic Part in the Making of America, 1656-1850. Philadelphia. Dolphin Press. 1936. 105p. K 158
KITE, ELIZABETH S. "Charles-Armoand Tuffin, Marquis de la Rouërie," American Catholic Historical Society of Philadelphia Records, v. 59 (1948), 1-34. K 159
KITE, ELIZABETH S."Establishment of the American Hierarchy: Diplomatic Sidelights," American Ecclesiastical Review, v. 87 (1932), 495-501. K 160
KITE, ELIZABETH S. "The Franco-American Alliance and Its Relation to Catholic Emancipation in English-Speaking Countries," American Catholic Historical Society of Philadelphia Records, v. 60 (1949), 65-69. K 161
KITE, ST. ALBAN. "William Penn and the Catholic Church in America," Catholic Historical Review, v. 13 (1927),

480-496. K 162
KITTELL, FERDINAND. Souvenir of Loretto Centenary, 1799-1899. Loretto, Cambria Co., Cresson, Pa. Swope Bros. 1899. xi, 405p. illus., plates, ports., facsims. K 163
KITTLER, GLENN D. "Brooklyn's Chaplain of the Sea," Sign v. 32 (1952), 46-47. K 164
The story of Father William J. Farrell and the Catholic Seaman's Institute of Brooklyn.
KJELGAARD, JAMES A. The Exploration of Père Marquette, N.Y. Random House. Landmark book, no. 17. 1951. x, 181p. K 165
KLEBER, ALBERT. "The Founding of St. Meinrad's Abbey," Benedictine Review, v. 5 (1950), 14-18. K 166
KLEBER, ALBERT. "The Naming of Troy, Indiana," Indiana Magazine of History, v. 44 (1948), 178-180. K 167
KLEBER, ALBERT. St. Joseph's Parish, Jasper, Indiana (1837-1937). St. Meinrad, Ind. 1937. K 168
KLEBER, ALBERT. History of St. Meinrad Archabbey, 1854-1954. St. Meinrad, Ind. The Grail. 1954. 552p. K 169
KLEBER, ALBERT."A Seminary is Born," St. Meinrad Essays, v. 9 (1951), 2-19. The founding of St. Meinrad Seminary. K 170
KLEIN, AB FELIX. Americanism: a Phantom Heresy. Atchison, Kansas. Aquin Book Shop. 1951. xxx, 345p. K 171
An English translation of the French of 1949.
KLEIN, FELIX. La Route du Petit Morvandian. Souvenirs. v. 5 Paris. Librairie Plon. 1949. 346p. K 172
KLEIN, FELIX. La Séparation aux Etats-Unis. Histoire, Lois, Coutumes, Documents.

Paris. Bloud. 1908. 126p.
K 173
KLEIN, FELIX. Une Hérésie
Fantome, L'Américanisme.
Souvenirs. v. 4. Paris. Li-
brairie Plon. 1949. 447p.
K 174
KLEIN, IGNATIUS A. Geschichte
der St. Joseph's Gemeinde von
East Bristol, Wisconsin, 1847-
1907. no pl. no pub. 1907?
184p. illus., ports. K 175
KLEIN, JAMES. History of St.
Mary's of the Purification,
Scott County, Minnesota. no
pl. no pub. 1930? 62p.
plates. K 176
KLEIN, JAMES. "The Church
in Spanish American History,"
Catholic Historical Review,
v. 3 (1917), 290-307. K 177
KLINKHAMER, SISTER MARIE
CAROLYN. "The Catholic Uni-
versity of America, 1889-
1905; Ideological Foundations,"
Catholic Educational Review, v.
52 (1954), 162-182. K 178
KLINKHAMER, SISTER MARIE
CAROLYN. Edward Douglas
White, Chief Justice of the
United States. Washington.
Catholic University. 1943.
viii, 308p. K 179
KLINKHAMER, SISTER MARIE
CAROLYN. "The Family
Background of Chief Justice
White," Catholic Historical
Review, v. 33 (1947), 191-
205. K 180
KLINKHAMER, SISTER MARIE
CAROLYN. "Historical
Reason for Inception of Paro-
chial School System," Catholic
Educational Review, v. 52
(1954), 73-94. K 181
KLOPPER, STEPHEN. "The
First Conference of the Society
of St. Vincent de Paul in Mil-
waukee," Salesianum, v. 29
(Apr., 1934), 23-32, (July,
1934), 8-17, (Oct., 1934),
39-44. K 182
KNAB, RAYMOND. "Father
Joseph Prost, Pioneer Redemp-

torist in the United States,"
United States Catholic His-
torical Society Records and
Studies, v. 22 (1932), 32-
84. K 183
KNAB, RAYMOND. Father
Prost. Pioneer Redemptorist
in the United States. MA
thesis. Catholic University.
1932. 75p. K 184
KNIGHTS OF COLUMBUS. Texas.
State Council. Historical
Commission. Our Catholic
Heritage in Texas. Austin,
Texas. Von Boeckmann-Jones
Co. 1936- K 185
A definitive, scholarly
history of the Catholic de-
velopment in Texas from
the missionary times.
Started in cooperative pro-
ject, first six volumes pro-
duced by Carlos E. Cas-
tañeda.
KOELZER, NICHOLAS J. The
Development and Educational
Contribution of the Sisters of
the Visitation in the United
States. MA thesis. Villanova
University. 1951. 163p.
K 186
KOERBER, LEONARD G. Anti-
Catholic Agitation in Milwau-
kee, 1834-1860. MA thesis.
Marquette University. 1960.
K 187
KOESTER, LEONARD. "Louis-
ville's 'Bloody Monday'--
August 6, 1855," Historical
Bulletin, v. 26 (1948), 53-
54, 62-64. K 188
KOHLBRENNER, BERNARD J.
"Catholic Education in Colonial
Maryland," Historical Bulletin,
v. 12 (1934), 35-36. K 189
KOHLER, SISTER MARY
HORTENSE. The Genesis and
Early History of the Congrega-
tion of St. Catherine of
Sienna, Racine, Wisconsin. MA
thesis. Marquette University.
1936. K 190
KOHLMANN, ANTHONY. "Letter
to Father William Strickland,

Poland Street, London, dated
Georgetown, Feb. 23, 1807,"
Woodstock Letters, v. 12
(1883), 86-89.   K 191
KOHLMANN, ANTHONY. "Letter
to Father William Strickland,
Poland Street, London, dated
Philadelphia April 23, 1807,"
Woodstock Letters, v. 12
(1883), 89.   K 192
KOHLMANN, ANTHONY. "Letter
to Father William Strickland,
Poland Street, London, dated
Georgetown, March 9, 1908,"
Woodstock Letters, v. 12
(1883), 88.   K 193
Report on progress of Jesuit
restoration in America. 10
Novices in second year, 8
in first year; 11 Fathers (3
of them novices).
KOHLMANN, JOHN A. St. Peter's
Church, Franklin County,
Indiana, First Official Year-
book, 1919. no pl. no pub.
1919?   K 194
KOHN, SISTER MARY LAUREN-
TINE. The Catholicity of
Manitowoc County with Back-
ground of Wisconsin. MA
thesis. University of Notre
Dame. 1942. v, 103p. K 195
KOLASH, BERNARD. "The
Padre of the Poor," Ave Maria,
v. 72 (1950), 583-586. K 196
Biographical sketch of Msgr.
Nelson H. Baker, born in
Buffalo, N.Y. 1841, died
1936, founder of Father
Baker's Homes of Charity
in Rackawana, N.Y., 1890-
1926.
KORTENDICK, JAMES J.
"Contemporary Catholic Authors:
Monsignor Peter K. Guilday,
Historian of the American Cath-
olic Church," Catholic Library
World, v. 12 (1941), 263-269,
282.   K 197
KOTWOSKI, LEONARD J. "A
History of Polish Periodicals at
the Polish Seminary," Polish-
American Studies, v. 6 (1949),
87-98.   K 198

KRAKE, GERARD HENRY.
"Haycock, Its First Catholic
Settlers, Churches, etc.,"
American Catholic Historical
Researchss, v. 4 (1887),
98-106.   K 199
KRAMER, F.J. "Catholicity in the
Silver San Juan, " Catholic World,
v. 68 (1898), 173-184. illus. K200
Krammer see K 209
KRAUTBAUER, F. X. "Short
Sketch of the History of the
Menominee Indians of Wiscon-
sin and the Catholic Missions
among Them," American Cath-
olic Historical Researches,
v. 4 (1887), 152-158. K 201
KREBS, ALBERT. Les décou-
verts de Jolliet et de Marquette.
Le Monde Française, v. 19
(1950), 243-262.   K 202
KREINER, SISTER MARIE
BERNADETTE. Henry Francis
Brownson As a Lay Catholic
Leader. MA thesis. Univer-
sity of Notre Dame. 1944. iv,
98p.   K 203
KREMER, MICHAEL N. Church
Support in the United States.
Washington. Catholic Univer-
sity. 1930. vi, 136p.
          K 204
KREY, AUGUST CHARLES.
"Monte Cassino, Metten, and
Minnesota," Minnesota History,
v. 8 (1927), 217-231. illus.
          K 205
KRIER, P. A. "Missouri.
Letter dated Westphalia, Osage
Co., Mo., July 15th, 1882,"
Woodstock Letters, v. 11
(1882), 295-297.   K 206
KROHA, JOSEPH F. "St.
Aemilian's Orphan Asylum,"
Salesianum, v. 31 (1936),
164-173.   K 207
KRUMERL, CARL F. "Cath-
olicism, Americanism,
Democracy and Orestes Brown-
son," American Quarterly,
(1954).   K 208
KRAMMER, SISTER MARY
MECHTILDE. Archbishop
Purcell in the Years between

1830 and 1860. MA thesis.
University of Notre Dame.
1940. vii, 137p. plates,
ports. K 209
KRUG, SISTER MARY BENIGNA.
Relations of Mission San
Gabriel to the Beginning of
Diocesan Organization in
Southern California. MA thesis.
Catholic University. 1942. 66p.
K 210
KUBLER, GEORGE. The Religious
Architecture of New Mexico,
in the Colonial Period and
since the American Occupation.
Colorado Springs. Taylor
Museum. 1940. 232p.
K 211
KUHLS, A. A Few Reminis-
cences of Forty Years in
Wyandotte County, Kansas. no
pl. no pub. 1904. 45p.
plates, port. K 212
KUKULA, SISTER MARY FUL-
GINETTA. Career of James
Roosevelt Bayley, First
Bishop of Newark, Eighth
Bishop of Baltimore. MA
thesis. Catholic University.
1942. 81p. K 213
KUNDECK, JOSEPH. "Letters to
Archbishop of Vienna," St.
Meinrad Historical Essays,
v. 3 (1935), 261-266; v. 4
(1936), 62-70, 168-173, 253-
258, 364-368; v. 5 (1938),
61-64; v. 5 (1939), 159-162.
K 214
KUNKEL, FRANCIS W. "Balti-
more's First Church," Voice,
v. (1941), Mar. K 215
KUPPENS, FRANCIS XAVIER.
"Christmas Day, 1865,
Virginia City, Montana,"
Illinois Catholic Historical
Review, v. 10 (1927), 48-53.
K 216
KUPPENS, FRANCIS XAVIER.
"Indian Missions, Extract
from a letter of Father F.X.
Kuppens, S.J. (Grand River,
Dakota Territory, June 18,
1871)," Woodstock Letters,
v. 1 (1872), 106-110. K 217

KURTH, PAULA. "Forgotten
Page in Mission History,"
Magnificat, v. 44 (1929),
164-169, 219-224. K 218
KUZMA, GEORGE. History of
St. Joseph's Parish. Joliet,
Illinois. (1891-1941). Joliet.
The Author. 1941. 146p.
plates, ports. K 219

- L -

LA BOULE, JOSEPH S. Claude
Jean Allouez. Milwaukee,
Wis. Parkman Club Pub.
No. 17. 1897. Part 1,
Early life...and labors in the
Lake Superior Region, pp.
181-209, map. L 1
LA BUDDA, BROTHER HENRY
CASIMIR. The History of the
Brothers of the Christian
Schools in the St. Louis
District in the Years between
1849 and 1941. MA thesis.
University of Notre Dame.
1941. vi, 133p. L 2
LA CROSSE, WIS. (DIOCESE).
Constitutiones dioeceseos
crossensis. Milwauchiae,
Typis P. V. Deutster, 1869.
12p. "Decreta synodi Milwauch-
iensis primae etiam in dioe-
cesibus Sinus Viridi et Cros-
sensi obligatoria." p. [3]
I. Milwaukee (Diocese) Synod,
1st. L 3
LA CROSSE, WIS. (DIOCESE)
SYNOD, 1871. Decreta synodi
dioecesanae crossensis I.
habitae die 25. et 26. mensis
Julii A.D. 1871, in oppido
pratocanensi. Milwauchiae,
Excudebat P. V. Deutster,
1871. 10p. L 4
LA FARGE, JOHN. "East and
West Praise the Queen of
Heaven," America, v. 92
(1954), 179-181. L 5
A popular account of the
National Eucharistic Marian
Congress of the Oriental
Rites.
LA FARGE, JOHN. "Father

Talbot, S.J.," America, v. 90 (1953), 317-318.   L 6
A biographical sketch of a great journalist and author, who was editor of the magazine America, and who was an authority on the North American Martyrs.

LA FARGE, JOHN. "Father Wilfrid Parsons," Woodstock Letters, v. 90 (1961), 195-217.   L 7
A good biographical sketch of one of the outstanding modern Jesuit scholars, and militant editor of America during the 1920's.

LA FARGE, JOHN. "The Jesuit-Baltimore Controversy," Historical Bulletin, v. 12 (1934), 23-24.   L 8

LA FARGE, JOHN. The Manner is Ordinary. New York. Harcourt Brace and Co. 1953. viii, 408p.   L 9
The autobiography of a former editor of the magazine America, and advocate of interracial justice.

LA FARGE, JOHN. "The Missions of Old Maryland," America, v. 50 (1934), 586-587.   L 10

LA FARGE, JOHN. A Report on the American Jesuits. New York: Farrar, Straus, and Cudahy, 1956. 236p.   L 11
A popular and very sketchy picture of the work of the Society of Jesus in the United States. This is not a scholarly publication.

LA FARGE, JOHN. "Some Aspects of the Jesuit-Baltimore controversy," Thought, v. 4 (1930), 638-666.   L 12

LA FARGE, JOHN. "The Survival of the Catholic Faith in Southern Maryland," Catholic Historical Review, v. 21 (1935), 1-20.   L 13

LA SALLE CATECHIST, v. (1948), Spring.   L 14
This number is devoted largely to the Centenary of the Christian Brothers in the United States. It contains historical and statistical accounts of the various provinces and types of activity, and brief sketches of some famous Brothers.

LACY, JOHN J. "The New Ecclesiastical Province of Kansas," Benedictine Review, (1953), 9-11.   L 15
A very brief history of the development of the Church in the state of Kansas to the establishment of the Archdiocese of Kansas City, Kansas.

LAING, FRANCIS S. Father Felix M. Kirsch, O.F.M. Cap.: A Sketch of His Life and Activities. Pittsburgh. Catholic Home Journal. 1946. 101p.   L 16

LA FARGUE, ANDRE. "A Man of God and a Servant of Humanity: The Reverend Marie Arthur Guillaume le Mercier du Quesnay," Louisiana Historical Quarterly, v. 20 (1937), 680-689.   L 17

LAFAYETTE (DIOCESE) SYNOD, 1st, 1923. Constitutiones dioeceseos lafayettensis in synodo dioecesana prima a Julio Benjamin Jeanmard [ep.] latae et promulgatae die XVI Julii MCMXXIII. 134, [5] p.   L 18

LAFAYETTE (DIOCESE) SYNOD, 2nd, 1933. Constitutions of the diocese of Lafayette promulgated by Jules Jeanmard bp. at the second diocesan synod held October 18, 1933 in the cathedral of St. John the Evangelist. [n.p., n.d.] 102, [2] p.   L 19

LAFAYETTE (DIOCESE) SYNOD, 3rd, 1943. Constitutions of the diocese of Lafayette promulgated by Jules B. Jeanmard bp. at the third diocesan synod held October 8, 1943 in the church of the Sacred Heart of Jesus, Grand Coteau, Louisiana...[n.p., n.d.] xiii, 144p.   L 20

LALLOU, WILLIAM J. "The Apostolic Delegation at Washington," American Ecclesiastical Review, v. 65 (1922), 447-462.   L 21

LALLOU, WILLIAM J. The Fifty Years of the Apostolic Delegation. Paterson, N.J. St. Anthony Guild Press. 1943. vi, 41p. plates, 2 ports. (incl. front.)   L 22

LALLOU, WILLIAM J. "Herman J. Heuser, Founder of the American Ecclesiastical Review," American Ecclesiastical Review, v. 121 (1949), 381-385.   L 23

LALLOU, WILLIAM J. "Monsignor Guilday," American Ecclesiastical Review, v. 118 (1948), 1-11.   L 24

LALLOU, WILLIAM J. "Sermon Preached at the 125th Anniversary of St. John the Evangelist Parish, Philadelphia," American Catholic Historical Society of Philadelphia Records. v. 67 (1956), 61-64.   L 25

Includes an historical sketch of the parish.

LALLY, F. J. "State of the Catholic Press," Commonweal, v. 57 (Feb. 6, 1953), 443-445.   L 26

An interesting evaluative article that stirred up considerable controversy.

LAMB, HUGH L. "Catholicism in Philadelphia," Records of the American Catholic Historical Society of Philadelphia, v. 62 (1951), 5-14.   L 27

LAMBERT, AGNELLUS. "Mission at Old Laguna," New Mexico Magazine, v. (1949), 24, 52-53.   L 28

[LAMBING, ANDREW A.] "A Century of Catholicity in Greene County, Pa.," American Catholic Historical Researches,

v. 2 (1886), 148-153. L 29

[LAMBING, ANDREW A.] "Detroit in Early Times--Very Rev. Gabriel Richard," American Catholic Historical Researches, v. 3 (1886), 41-58.   L 30

[LAMBING, ANDREW A.] "The Early Days of Catholicity in Pittsburgh," American Catholic Historical Researches, v. 1 (1884-1885), 32-36, 76-80, 156-160.   L 31

LAMBING, ANDREW A. "The Establishment of the Catholic Hierarchy in the United States," American Catholic Historical Researches, v. 1 (1885), 121-130.   L 32

[LAMBING, ANDREW A.] "The Establishment of the See of Pittsburg [sic]," American Catholic Historical Researches, v. 2 (1885), 3-14.   L 33

LAMBING, ANDREW A. Foundation Stones of a Great Diocese, Vol. 1, 1749-1860. Pittsburgh. The Author. 1914.   L 34

LAMBING, ANDREW A. A History of the Catholic Church in the Diocese of Pittsburgh and Allegheny. New York. Benziger. 1880. 531p. front., ports.   L 35

[LAMBING, ANDREW A.] "Very Rev. Andrew White, S.J., The Apostle of Maryland," American Catholic Historical Researches, v. 3 (1886), 13-20.   L 36

[LAMBING, ANDREW A.] "Very Rev. Pierre Gibault, the Patriot Priest," American Catholic Historical Researches, v. 2 (1885-1886), 54-60, 117-119.   L 37

[LAMBING, ANDREW A.] "Very Reverend Stephen Theodore Badin, the Proto-priest of the United States," American Catholic Historical Researches, v. 3 (1886), 1-13.   L 38

LAMBING, ANDREW A. "Who Was the Apostle of the Indians?"

American Catholic Historical Researches, v. 4 (1889), 124-132. L 39

[LAMBING, ANDREW A.] "Necrology of the Diocese of Pittsburgh," American Catholic Historical Researches, v. 2 (1886), 88-102. L 40

[LAMBING, ANDREW A.] "Reflections on the Life and Work of Very Rev. D. A. Gallitzin," American Catholic Historical Researches, v. 3 (1886), 58-68. L 41

LAMBING, ANDREW A. "Scenes from the Texas Mission of Half a Century Ago," American Catholic Historical Researches, v. 3 (1887), 2-11. L 42

LAMBING, ANDREW A. "A Sketch of Catholicity in the City of Pittsburgh, Pa.," American Catholic Historical Society of Philadelphia Records, v. 9 (1898), 293-304. L 43

LAMMERS, HERMAN JOSEPH. History of the St. Vincent de Paul Society: the Particular Council of Louisville, Kentucky, 1854-1932. MA thesis. Catholic University. n. d. 87p. L 44

LAMOTT, JOHN H. History of the Archdiocese of Cincinnati, 1821-1921. New York. Pustet. 1921. xxiii, 430p. front., plates, ports., map. L 45

LAMY, JOHN B. "Archbishop Lamy's Visitation of New Mexico, 1851-1852," American Catholic Historical Researches, v. 15 (1898), 136-137. L 46

LAMY, JOHN B. "Catholicity in New Mexico," Ave Maria, v. 3 (1867), 613-616. L 47

LAMY, JOHN B. "Lettre de Mgr. J. B. Lamy, évêque de Sante Fé (Nouveau-Mexique), à MM les Membres des Conseils Centraux de l' Oeuvre de la Propagation de la Foi. Santa Fé 25 août 1866," Annales de la Propagation de la Foi, v. 39 (1867), 318-329.

L 48
LAMY, JOHN B. "Letter dated Santa Fe, Aug. 25, 1866," Annales of the Propagation of the Faith, Baltimore, v. 28 (1867), 216-222. L 49

LAMY, JOHN B. "Lettre de Mgr. J. B. Lamy, évêque de Santa Fé (Nouveau-Mexique), à MM les Directeurs de l'Oeuvre de la Propagation de la Foi. Paris, le 1er maio, 1870," Annales de la Propagation de la Foi, v. 42 (1870), 385-397. L 50

LAMY, JOHN B. "Short History of the Pueblo Indians of New Mexico," American Catholic Historical Society of Philadelphia Records, v. 12 (1901), 169-192. L 51

LAMY MEMORIAL: Centenary of the Archdiocese of Santa Fe. Santa Fe Chancery Office. 1950. 103p. L 52
Pictorial brochure of the Diocese of Santa Fe. Good factual summary of the "two hundred and fifty years before Lamy," also contains sketches and photographs of each parish and institution.

LAMP, v. 47 (1949), October. L 53
This issue is devoted largely to the Golden Jubilee of the Society of the Atonement.

LANCTÔT, GUSTAVE (ed.) Les Canadiens Français et leurs Voisins du Sud. New Haven. Yale University Press. 1941. iv, 322p. incl. tables. L 54

LANE, RAYMOND A. The Early Days of Maryknoll. New York. David McKay Co., 1951. viii, 311p. L 55

LANG, ELFRIEDA. "German Influence in the Churches and Schools of Dubois County, Indiana," Indiana Magazine of History, v. 42 (1946), 151-172. L 56

LANGAN, SISTER MARY MAR-

213

TIN. General John O' Neill, Soldier, Fenian and Leader of Catholic Colonization in America. MA thesis. University of Notre Dame. 1937. iii, 45p. L 57

LANGEN, RICHARD. "Joseph Chartrand," St. Meinrad Historical Essays, v. 3 (1934), 164-172. L 58

LANGIES, LOUIS A. "The Marcus Whitman Myth and Missionary History of Oregon," United States Catholic Historical Society Records and Studies, v. 11 (1917), 72-85. L 59

LANHAM, BROTHER LEO. The Missionary Confraternity of Christian Doctrine in the Diocese of Pittsburgh. Washington. Catholic University. 1945. xii, 384p. L 60

LANNING, JOHN TATE. The Spanish Missions of Georgia. Chapel Hill. University of North Carolina Press. 1935. xiii, 321p. illus., map. L 61

LANSING, MICHAEL. "The Founding of New Subiaco Abbey," Arkansas Historical Quarterly, v. 3 (1944), 193-210. L 62

LAPATI, AMENCO D. A History of Catholic Education in Rhode Island. Ph.D. thesis. Boston College. 1958. iii, 267p. L 63

LARACY, JOHN. "Sacred Heart Mission and Abbey," Chronicles of Oklahoma, v. 5 (1927), 234-250. plates, illus. L 64

LARIOS, FELIPE. "Franciscan College, Santa Barbara, California, 1869-1874," Provincial Annals (Province of Santa Barbara, O.F.M.), v. 3 (Jan., 1941), 63-74, (Apr., 1941), 57-61, (Apr., 1942), 61-67. L 65

LARKIN, HELEN M. "Catholic Education in Illinois," Illinois Catholic Historical Review, v. 4 (1922), 339-354. L 66

LARMER, JOHN. Epitome of the Catholic Church in Illinois. Chicago. Adair. c1907. 31p. L 67

LARMER, M. Lives of Early Catholic Missionaries of the Nineteenth Century in Illinois. Chicago. n.p. 1898. L 68

"LAS VEGAS," Lettere Edificanti Provincia Napolitana, ser. 8, n. 1 (1899), 59-60. L 69
A description of the work of the Revista Catolica.

"LAS VEGAS COLLEGE, NEW MEXICO. (Veto of Act of Incorporation by Governor Axtell)," Woodstock Letters, v. 7 (1888), 40-43. L 70

LATHROP, GEORGE PARSONS. A Story of Courage. Annals of the Georgetown Convent of the Visitation. Boston. Houghton Mifflin and Co. 1895. xii, 380p. front., plates, ports., double facsim. L 71

LATONDRESS, CASSIAN. "Apostle of California," Round Table of Franciscan Research, v. 15 (1950), 137-141. L 72

LATOURETTE, KENNETH SCOTT. "The Contribution of the Religion of the Colonial Period to the Ideals and Life of the United States," The Americas, v. 14 (1958), 340-355. L 73

LATOURETTE, KENNETH SCOTT. The Great Century, A. D. 1800-A.D. 1914. New York. Harper and Bros. 1941. L 74

LAUER, ALOYSIUS. "Pages from the Diary of Fr. Aloysius Lauer," Provincial Annals (Province of the Most Holy Name, O.F.M.), v. 9 (1949), 87-92, 132-134, 170-173. L 75

LAUER, R. "Mission to Cheraw," Catholic World, v. 181 (1955), June, 173-179. L 76
Interesting account of Catholic propaganda work around Cheraw, South Carolina.

LAURENCE, SISTER M. "A
Trip to Quapaw in 1903,"
Chronicles of Oklahoma, v.
31 (1953), 142-167.   L 77
The story of a visit of
Carmelite nuns to St. Mary's
on the Quapaw in 1903, an-
notated by Velma Nieberding.
LAURENT, LAVAL. Québec et
l'Eglise aux Etats-Unis sous
Mgr. Briand et Mgr. Plessis.
Washington. Catholic Uni-
versity. 1945. xxviii,
258p.   L 78
LAURI, ACHILLE. "Mons.
Giuseppe-Rosati (1789-1843),
Primo Vescovo della Diocesi
di St. Louis (Missouri) negli
Stati Uniti d'Amerique Roma."
Annali della Missione (1949),
15p.   L 79
LAVEILLE, E. The Life of
Father de Smet, S.J. New
York. Kenedy, 1916. xxii,
400p. front., plates, ports.,
map.   L 80
LAVELLE, M. J. "John Cardinal
Farley, Archbishop of New
York," American Ecclesiastical
Review, v. 60 (1919), 113-125.
                         L 81
LAWLER, JUSTUS GEORGE.
"Mission of Catholic Scholar-
ship," Catholic World, v. 183
(1956), 262-269.   L 82
Points out that the first
loyalty is to the truth as the
scholars see it.
LAWLER, LORETTO R. Full
Circle. The Story of the
National Catholic School of
Social Service, 1918-1947.
Washington. Catholic Univer-
sity. 1951. xi, 243p.
                         L 83
LAWLESS, D. C. "Worthy of
Immortality," Columbia, v. 13
(June, 1934), 8-9, 25.   L 84
"LAYING OF THE CORNER-
STONE OF BROPHY COLLEGE,
PHOENIX, ARIZONA," Wood-
stock Letters, v. 57 (1928),
539-540.   L 85
LE FEVRE, EFFIE DE COURSEY.

The Manor Chapel, or St.
Augustine Church ... Cecil
County, Maryland. (St. Augus-
tine, Me.?) no pub. 1932.
34p. plates.   L 86
LEAHY, WALTER T. The
Catholic Church in the Diocese
of Trenton. Princeton. St.
Michael's House. 1907. 441p.
illus. (incl. ports.)   L 87
LEAHY, WILLIAM ET AL. His-
tory of the Catholic Church in
the New England States. Bos-
ton. 1889. 2v.   L 88
LEAMY, EDMUND. Holy Cross
Church, New York City. New
York. The Author. 1939.
                         L 89
LEARY, JOHN P. I Lift My
Lamp. Westminster. New-
man. 1955. xv, 383p.
                         L 90
Biographical sketches of
some well known Jesuits in
the United States.
LEAVENWORTH (DIOCESE)
SYNOD, 1st, 1880. Statuta a
Ludovico Maria Fink, O.S.B.
[ep.] in synodo dioecesana
prima in cathedrali diebus 17,
18, 19 Octobris Anno Domini
1880 habita, lata et promulgata. Leavenworth, Ketcheson,
1881. 61p.   L 91
LEAVENWORTH (DIOCESE)
SYNOD, 2nd, 1887. Decreta
synodi dioecesanae leavenworthensis secundae, diebus X. et
XI., mensis Augusti, 1887, in
ecclesia cathedrali leaven-
worthii habitae a Ludovico
Maria Fink, O.S.B. ... cum
aliquot mutationibus et emen-
dationibus factis a Thoma
Francisco Lillis, D.D., episcopo leavenworthensi. [n.p.,
n.d.] xi, 98, 25p.   L 92
LEAVENWORTH (DIOCESE)
SYNOD, 2. Synodus dioecesana
Leavenworthensis secunda.
Laurentii Kan. P.T. Foley,
1887. xix, 125p.   L 93
LEAVENWORTH (DIOCESE)
SYNOD, 3rd, 1922. Statuta

215

dioecesana; decreta synodi dioecesanae leavenworthensis tertiae, die VI mensis Junii, 1922, in ecclesia S. Mariae in civitate Kansas City, Kansas habitae a Joanne Ward [ep.] promulgata 1922. [n.p., n.d.] xxxi, 128p. L 94

LEAVENWORTH (DIOCESE) SYNOD, 4th, 1938. Synodus dioecesana leavenworthensis quarta a Paulo C. Schulte [ep.] convocata in ecclesia S. Benedicti apud Atchison, Kansas, die 16 Iunii, 1938. celebrata. [n.p., n.d.] 21p. L 95

"LEAVES FROM AN OLD DIARY-- THE JESUITS IN BUFFALO, 1867-1870," Woodstock Letters, v. 48 (1919), 330-340. L 96

"LEAVES FROM THE HISTORY OF A BUFFALO PARISH," Provincial Annals (Province of the Most Holy Name, O.F.M.), v. 2 (1941-1942), 193-201, 239-243. L 97

LEBEN UND WIRKEN DES HOCHWÜRDIGEN P. FRANZ SALES BRUNNER, APOSTOLISCHEN MISSIONÄRS UND GRÜNDERS DER KLÖSTER DER CONGREGATION VON KOST-BAREN BLUTE IN NORDAMERICA. Carthage. Charles Boromeo Seminary. 1882. v, 204p. L 98

LEBRETON, DAGMAR RENSHAW. Chata-Ima; The Life of Adrien-Emmanuel Rouquette. Baton Route, La. Louisiana State University Press. 1947. xix, 442p. L 99

LEBROCQUY, AUGUSTE. Le Fondateur des Missions du Missouri Central; Vie du R.P. Helias d'Huddeghem de la Compagnie de Jésus. Gand. C. Poleman. 1878. vii, 324p. front. (port.) L 100

LECHNER, PETER. Bericht einer Missionsreise nach den Vereinigten Staaten Nord Amerika's. Augsburg. K.

Kohlmann'schen. 1851. 58p. L 101

Beginnings of St. Vincents, Pa. LECOMPTE, EDOUARD. Glory of the Mohawks. Milwaukee. Bruce. 1944. ix, 164p. incl. front., illus. L 102

LEDOCHOWSKI, WLODIMURUS. "La Separazione della Missione del Nuovo Messico e Colorado dalla Provincia Napolitana. Documenti," Lettere Edificanti Provincia Napolitana, (1914-1920), 155-158. L 103

LEE, LAURENCE F. Los Hermanos Penitentes. Printed privately in El Palacio, Santa Fe, January 31, 1920. L 104

LEE, SISTER M. FORITA. Efforts of the Archbishop of New Orleans to Put into Effect the Recommendations of the Second Council of Baltimore with Regard to Catholic Education. MA thesis. Catholic University. 1940. 150p. L 105

LEE, SISTER ROSANA. History of Catholic Education in the Diocese of Amarillo. MA thesis. Catholic University, 1954. 92p. L 106

LEE, S. R. "The Maryland Influence on American Catholicism," American Catholic Historical Society of Philadelphia Records, v. 41 (1930), 328-352. L 107

LEGER, SISTER M. CELESTE. The Catholic Indian Missions in Maine (1611-1820). Washington. Catholic University. 1929. x, 184p. incl. facsim., maps. L 108

LEITERMANN, CLARENCE DUKE. History of St. Luke the Evangelist Church, Antigo, Wisconsin, Golden Jubilee, 1880-1930. Antigo, Wis. Berner Bros., 1930. 139p. illus., front. (plate, fold). L 109

LEMANSKA, SISTER M.
ADELINE. The Catholic
Negroes in the Diocese of
Brooklyn. MA thesis. Villa-
nova University. 1951. 126p.
L 110
LEMAY, HUGOLIN. "The Friars
Minor in French and British
North America," Franciscan
Educational Conference, Annual
Report, v. 18 (1936), 151-
182.   L 111
LEMCKE, MARTIN. "Brief des
hochw. P. Martin Lemcke an
den Redakteur des Katholiken,"
Central Blatt and Social Jus-
tice, v. 16 (1923), 304-305,
379-380, 394, 415-416, 429;
v. 17 (1924), 54-55.   L 112
LEMCKE, PETER HENRY. Life
and Work of Prince Demetrius
Augustine Gallitzin. tr. by
Joseph C. Plumpe. New York.
Longmans, Green and Co.
1940. xxi, 257p.   L 113
LENHART, JOHN M., tr. and ed.
"Address of Peter Paul
Cahensly on the Care of Emi-
grants, Delivered at the
General Meeting of the German
Societies in Trier, Sept. 11,
1865," Social Justice Review,
v. 51 (1959), 22-27, 59-60.
L 114
   One of the most important
   contributions to the problem
   of language in the American
   Church.
LENHART, JOHN M. "Beginnings
of Catholicity in the City of
Columbus, Ohio (1833-1849),"
Social Justice Review, v. 38
(1945), 129-131.   L 115
LENHART, JOHN M. "Beginnings
of German Congregations in and
around St. Louis, 1838-1884,"
Social Justice Review, v. 54
(1961), 163-165, 202-208.
L 116
LENHART, JOHN M. "Beginnings
of the German Colony of St.
Mary's, Elk Co., Pa. (1842-
1843), Central Blatt and
Social Justice, v. 25 (1933),

313-315.   L 117
LENHART, JOHN M. "Bishop
Neumann's German Catechism"
Social Justice Review, v. 39
(1946), 131.   L 118
LENHART, JOHN M. "The
Capuchin Prefecture of New
England (1630-1656)," Fran-
ciscan Studies, v. 24 (1943),
21-46, 180-195, 306-313.
L 119
LENHART, JOHN. "The Capuchin
in Acadia and Northern Maine
(1632-1655)," American Cath-
olic Historical Society of
Philadelphia Records, v. 27
(1916), 191-229, 300-327;
v. 28 (1917), 47-63.   L 120
LENHART, JOHN M. "Catholic
Action in the German Congre-
gation of Wheeling, West
Virginia, 1865-1955," Social
Justice Review, v. 50
(1957), 96-99.   L 121
LENHART, JOHN M. "The
Catholic Church in the State
of Virginia, 1785-1843," Social
Justice Review, v. 49 (1956),
274-278.   L 122
LENHART, JOHN M. "The Cath-
olic Church in the U.S. in
1869," Central Blatt and Social
Justice, v. 35 (1942), 22-23.
L 123
LENHART, JOHN M. Catholics
and the American Declaration
of Independence. (1774-1776).
St. Louis. Central Bureau,
C.C.V. of A. 1934. 71p.
L 124
LENHART, JOHN M. "Conditions
among German Catholics in
the United States in 1847,"
Social Justice Review, v. 37
(1944), 207-208, 244-245.
L 125
LENHART, JOHN M. "Contribu-
tions to the Life of Charles
Whelan, O.M. Cap. (D. 1806),"
American Catholic Historical
Society of Philadelphia Re-
cords, v. 37 (1926), 242-
249.   L 126
LENHART, JOHN M. "The

Double Jurisdiction in French Louisiana, (1722-1766)," Franciscan Studies, v. 28 (1947), 344-347. L 127

LENHART, JOHN M. "Early German Settlements in America," Social Justice Review, v. 52 (1960), 510-513, Stallotown, Ohio c. 1832, the upper Mississippi, 1833-1850; 348-352, St. Louis, Mo., 1831-1844. L 128

LENHART, JOHN M. "Economic Valuation of the German Catholic Congregation in Wheeling, W. Va., 1856-1955," Social Justice Review, v. 49 (1956), 240-243. L 129

LENHART, JOHN M. "Ethnic Groups of the German Congregation of the Wheeling District, 1820-1949," Social Justice Review, v. 49 (1956), 130-133. L 130

LENHART, JOHN M. "Fr. Ambrose Oschwald's Defense," Social Justice Review, v. 38 (1945), 94-95. L 131

LENHART, JOHN M. "Father Francis Xavier Tschemens, C.SS.R., A Pioneer Priest, 1832-1877," Social Justice Review, v. 41 (1948-1949), 204-207, 244-246, 280-283, 317-320. L 132

LENHART, JOHN M. "Father Helias D'Huddeghem, S.J., Pioneer Missioner among the Germans (1796-1874)," Central Blatt and Social Justice, v. 26 (1933), 177-178, 212-214. L 133

LENHART, JOHN M. "Father John Geo. Alleman, O.P., German Pioneer Priest in Ohio and Iowa," Social Justice Review, v. 38 (1945), 206-208, 242-243, 278-280. L 134

LENHART, JOHN M. "Father John Nicholas Mertz, Pioneer Priest (1764-1844)," Central Blatt and Social Justice, v. 28 (1935), 18-20, 54-56, 91-92, 129-130, 180. L 135

LENHART, JOHN M. "Father Joseph Anthony Lutz, Pioneer Priest (1801-1861)," Central Blatt and Social Justice, v. 31 (1938), 17-20, 53-56, 89-92, 125-127, 161-163, 177. L 136

LENHART, JOHN M. "Father Rudolph Etthofen, Pioneer Priest, 1849-1855," Social Justice Review, v. 50 (1957), 99-100. L 137

LENHART, JOHN M. "The First Catholic Mission in Ohio," Central Blatt and Social Justice, v. 25 (1932), 205. L 138

LENHART, JOHN. "Francis Xavier Haetscher, C. SS.R.," Social Justice Review, v. 44 (1952), 308-311; 340-342; 366-368; v. 45 (1952), 19-22, 49-53. L 139
The biography of an Indian missionary and pioneer priest, 1832-1837.

LENHART, JOHN M. "Franciscan Historians of North America," Franciscan Educational Conference Annual Report, v. 18 (1936), 1-53. L 140

LENHART, JOHN M. "German - American Catholics in Boston, 1846," Social Justice Review, v. 36 (1943), 167-168, 206-208. L 141

LENHART, JOHN M. "German Catholic Aid to the Church in America," Central Blatt and Social Justice, v. 32 (1939), 237-238, 273-274. L 142

LENHART, JOHN M. "German Catholic Congregation in the Wheeling, W. Va., District 1820-1955. Statistics," Social Justice Review, v.49 (1956), 96-99. L 143

LENHART, JOHN M. "The German Catholic Orphanage in Wheeling, West Virginia, 1886-1954," Social Justice Review, v. 49 (1956), 204-207. L 144

LENHART, JOHN M. "German
Catholic School in Wheeling,
West Virginia, 1846-1955,"
Social Justice Review, v. 49
(1956), 168-169.   L 145

LENHART, JOHN M. "German
Catholic Settlements in Ohio,
1834-1844," Social Justice
Review, v. (1946), 167-170,
208-210, 244-246, 280-283,
(1947), 316-318.   L 146

LENHART, JOHN M. "German
Catholic Settlers in Colonial
New York (1639-1683),"
Central Blatt and Social Justice,
v. 26 (1933), 52-54.   L 147

LENHART, JOHN M. "German
Catholic Soldiers and Their
Chaplain in the Revolutionary
War," Central Blatt and Social
Justice, v. 24 (1931), 17-18,
55-56.   L 148

LENHART, JOHN M. "German
Catholics in Colonial Louisiana
(1721-1803)," Central Blatt and
Social Justice, v. 25 (1932),
17-19, 53-55, 88-91, 126-
129.   L 149

LENHART, JOHN M. "German
Catholics in the Diocese of
Philadelphia in 1846," Central
Blatt and Social Justice, v. 26
(1933), 128-132.   L 150

LENHART, JOHN M. "A Guide
for Catholic German Immi-
grants, 1869," Social Justice
Review, v. 52 (1959), 132-
135, 166-168.   L 151
    Concerns E. A. Reiter, S.J.,
    Schematismus der katholis-
    chen deutschen Geistlichkeit.

LENHART, JOHN M. "Historical
Library at the Central Bureau
of the Catholic Central
Verein in St. Louis, Mo.," Social Justice Review, v. 49
(1957), 348-352, 384-387, v.
50 (1957), 24-27.   L 152

LENHART, JOHN M. Historical
Notes on Sacred Heart Church,
Charleston, West Virginia.
no pl. no pub. 1941.   L 153

LENHART, JOHN M. "History
of St. Wendelin's Church at

Carbon Centre, Pa., 1845-
1953," Social Justice Review,
v. 47 (1954), 60-63; 96-100;
132-136; 168-171; 202-206,
240-242; 278-279.   L 154

LENHART, JOHN M. "History
of the Parochial School at
Carbon Centre, Pa., 1845-
1937," Social Justice Review,
v. 47 (1955), 312-314; 348-
350.   L 155

LENHART, JOHN M. "An
Important Chapter in American
Church History (1625-1650),"
Catholic Historical Review, v.
14 (1929), 500-524.   L 156

LENHART, JOHN M. (ed.) "The
Letters of Fr. Adalbert
Inama," Social Justice Review,
v. 54 (1961), 237-242, 276-
278.   L 157
    Dated variously 1842-1843.

LENHART, JOHN M. "The
Miraculous Cures by Prince
Hohenlohe in the U.S. in
1824," Central Blatt and
Social Justice, v. 25 (1932),
240-242.   L 158

LENHART, JOHN M. "Missionary
Correspondence from Philadelphia in 1835," Central Blatt
and Social Justice, v. 32
(1940), 309-310, 345-347.
                          L 159

LENHART, JOHN M. "The
Missionary Journey of Rev.
Frederick Rese to Wisconsin
and in Michigan in 1830,"
Central Blatt and Social Jus-
tice, v. 25 (1933), 348-350.
                          L 160

LENHART, JOHN M. "Notes
on the Biography of Paul de
Saint Pierre," Catholic Historical Review, v. 21 (1935),
322-329.   L 161

LENHART, JOHN M. "On the
Trail of Father Weninger in
1869," Social Justice Review,
v. 51 (1958), 96-101, 128-
132, 164-168.   L 162

LENHART, JOHN M. "Order
of Services in German Congregation in Wheeling, W. V.,

1858-1956," Social Justice Review, v. 49 (1957), 312-314.   L 163

LENHART, JOHN M. "Origin of the St. Raphael's Verein," Social Justice Review, v. 37 (1944), 282-284, 318-320, 354-356.   L 164

LENHART, JOHN M. "Pioneer German Priests," Social Justice Review, v. 53 (1960), 26-28, New York City, 1782-1835; 61-64, 94-96; Philadelphia, 1833-1835; 132-134, Philadelphia (Cont.); 164-167, St. Louis, 1828-1837; 200-203, Indiana, 1834-1840; 234-240, Indiana (Cont.); 272-275, Indiana (Concl.)   L 165

LENHART, JOHN M. "Projected German Missionary Seminaries for America," Social Justice Review, v. 34 (1941), 58-59, 95-96.   L 166

LENHART, JOHN M. (tr. and ed.) 'Report of Bishop Heiss of La Crosse to the Ludwig Mission Society, 1872," Social Justice Review, v. 50 (1957), 153-155.   L 167

LENHART, JOHN M. (tr. and ed.) 'Report of Rev. Francis Xavier Paulhuber, Missionary, on His Labors in the United States, 1851-1856," Social Justice Review, v. 50 (1957), 276-279.   L 168

LENHART, JOHN M. 'Rev. Simon Saenderl, C.SS.R., Indian Missionary," Central Blatt and Social Justice, v. 34 (1941), 130- , 166-168, 206-207, 242-244, 278-280, 314-316, 350-353, 386-388.   L 169

LENHART, JOHN M. 'Rev. Valentine Sommereisen, Pioneer Priest of the West," Central Blatt and Social Justice, v. 29 (1936), 164-166, 204-207, 240-243, 276-279, 312-315, 348-350.   L 170

LENHART, JOHN M. "St. Augustine's Aid Society of Lawrenceville, Pa.," Social Justice Review, v. 37 (1945), 319-320.   L 171

LENHART, JOHN M. "The Short Lived American College at Muenster in Westphalia," Social Justice Review, v. 35 (1942), 58-60, 94-96, 130-131, 280.   L 172

LENHART, JOHN M. "Statistics of Pastoral Functions of the German Speaking Congregation at Wheeling, W. Va.," Social Justice Review, v. 50 (1957), 61-63.   L 173

LENNON, SISTER MARY ISIDORE. Milestones of Mercy. Story of the Sisters of Mercy in St. Louis, 1856-1956. Milwaukee. Bruce, 1957, x, 323p.   L 174

LENNON, SISTER MARY ISIDORE. Social History of the Sisters of Mercy in St. Louis, MA thesis. Saint Louis University, 1934. 161p. L 175

LENSING, MICHAEL. "New Subiaco Abbey, 1878-1953," Social Justice Review, v. 46 (1953), 170-172, 206-208.   L 176
A summary history of the seventy-five years of this Benedictine Abbey.

LEO XIII. De Opinionibus Quas Nomina Americanismi Nonnulli Indicant. American Ecclesiastical Review, v. 20 (1899), 399-409   L 177

LEONARD, LEWIS A. Life of Charles Carroll of Carrollton, N. Y. Moffat, Yard and Co. 1918. 313p. plates, 2 ports., coat of arms. L 178

LEONE, ALLESSANDRO. "Da una Lettera del P. Allesandro Leone," Lettere Edificanti Provincia Napolitana, ser. 8 n. 1 (1899), 64-66. L 179
Dated 'El Paso, 17 Dicembre, 1898." A description of life on the missions in Texas.

LEONE, ALLESSANDRO. "Lettra

XVIII," Lettere Edificanti Provincia Napolitana, ser 1 (1875), 45.
L 180
Dated "Santafe, Agosto, 1874."
A description of the conditions at Conejos and La Junta, Colo.
LEONE, ALLESSANDRO. 'El Paso (Texas). La Parrocchia dell' Immacolata," Lettere Edificanti Provincia Napolitana, ser. 8, n. 2 (1900), 138-141.
L 181
LEONE, ALLESSANDRO. 'El Paso (Texas). La Visita del Pastore," Lettere Edificanti Provincia Napolitana, ser. 8, n. 2 (1900), 141-144. L 182
LEOPOLD, . "Navajo Indian Missions in Arizona," Annals of the Propagation of the Faith, Baltimore, v. 69 (1906), 312-318. L 183
"LEOPOLDINE FOUNDATION AID FOR BISHOP LORAS," Central Blatt and Social Justice, v. 23 (1931), 383-384. L 184
LESLIE, SHANE. Henry Edward Manning. 2d ed. rev. London. Burns, Oates and Washbourne. 1921. xxiii, 515p. front., ports. L 185
LESOUSKY, ALPHONSUS. "Centenary of St. Mary's College, St. Mary's, Kentucky," Illinois Catholic Historical Review, v. 4 (1921), 154-171. L 186
"LETTRE D'UN PÈRE DE LA COMPAGNIE DE JESUS. FREDERICK CITY, AVRIL, 1862," Annales de la Propagation de la Foi, v. 35 (1863), 284-287. L 187
An unsigned account of missions in the northern cities.
"LETTER TO ARCHBISHOP CUSHING ON ST. BENEDICT CENTER," American Ecclesiastical Review, v. 127 (1952), 307-315. L 188
Latin text and official English translation of the letter from Rome.
"LETTERS CONCERNING SOME

MISSIONS OF THE MISSISSIPPI VALLEY, A.D. 1818-1827," American Catholic Historical Society of Philadelphia Records, v. 14 (1903), 141-216. L 189
Translations of letters from the Annales de la Propagation de la Foi, vv. 1 and 2. By DuBourg, Flaget, Odin, Rosati, Blanc.
"LETTERS TO AND BY CARROLL," American Catholic Historical Researches, v. 17 (1900), 1-16. L 190
LEUCKING, WILLIAM G. Reminiscences of Four Redemptorist Fathers. Ilchester, Md. Redemptorist Fathers Press. 1891. 266p. L 191
LEWANDOWSKA, SISTER M. THEODOSETTA. "The Polish Immigrant to Philadelphia to 1914," American Catholic Historical Society of Philadelphia Records, v. 65 (1954), 67-101, 131-141. L 192
LEWIS, CLIFFORD M. "French Jesuits in Western Pennsylvania," Woodstock Letters, v. 76 (1947), 130-158, 241-261. map. L 193
LEWIS, CLIFFORD M. "French Priests in Western Pennsylvania, 1739-1759," Mid-America, v. 18 (1947), 92-121.
L 194
LEWIS, CLIFFORD M. AND ALBERT J. LOOMIS. The Spanish Jesuit Missions in Virginia, 1570-1572. Chapel Hill. University of North Carolina Press. 312p. illus. maps. L 195
The story of the unsuccessful attempt to found a mission in the Chesapeake Bay area. The documents are given in the original and in translation.
LEWIS, THEOPHILUS. "Catholic Laymen's Union: Silver Anniversary," Interracial Review, v. 26 (1953), 204-206. L 196

A good general survey of
the history of the organization.

LIEBLANG, HENRY. "The
Church of Naperville," Illinois
Catholic Historical Review,
v. 5 (1922), 68-77.   L 197

LIEGEY, GABRIEL AND ERWIN
GEISMANN. "Early Jesuitica
in America," Thought, v. 28
(1953), 275-286.   L 198
A proposed union catalog of
the early Jesuitica in the
libraries of the United States.
This article lists the holdings
of Fordham University.

"LIFE SKETCH OF THE REV.
ZEPHYRIN ENGELHARDT,
O.F.M. (1851-1934)," Pro-
vincial Annals (Province of
Santa Barbara, O.F.M.), v.
6 (Apr., 1944), 3-7.   L 199

"LIFE SKETCH OF THE VERY
REV. JOSEPH JEREMIAS O'-
KEEFE, O.F.M.," Provincial
Annals (Province of Santa
Barbara, O.F.M.), v. 3
(Oct., 1940), 2-11.   L 200

LIGNE, PRINCE ALBER DE.
"Father Louis Hennepin,
Belgian," Minnesota History,
v. 11 (1930), 343-351. L 201

LIGUORI, SISTER M. "Mother
Mary Francis Siedliska in
America," Polish-American
Studies, v. 3 (1946), 30-34.
     L 202

LIGUORI, SISTER M. "Polish
Sisters in the Civil War,"
Polish American Studies, v.
7 (1950), 1-7.   L 203

LIGUORI, SISTER M. "Seventy-
five Years of Religious Growth,"
Polish American Studies, v. 7
(1953).   L 204

LIGUITTI, L. G. Survey of
Catholic Weakness. Des
Moines. N.C.R.L.C. 1948.
61p.   L 205

LILLY, EDWARD P. "A Major
Problem for Catholic American
Historians," Catholic Historical
Review, v. 24 (1939), 427-448.
     L 206

LINCOLN (DIOCESE) SYNOD,
1st, 1934. Statutes of the
diocese of Lincoln promulgated at the first diocesan
synod celebrated June 4, 1934
in the cathedral of the Immaculate Conception by Louis B.
Kucera bp. n.p., n.d.   121,
v. p.   L 207

LINDEMANN, GREGORY. The
Rise and Progress of the
Province of St. Joseph of the
Capuchin Order in the United
States. New York. Benziger.
1907. 333p. plates, port.
     L 208

LINDSAY, LIONEL."The Archives
of the Archbishop of Quebec,"
American Catholic Historical
Society of Philadelphia Records, v. 18 (1907), 8-43.
     L 209

LINDSAY, LIONEL (ed.) "Correspondence between Bishop
Conwell of Philadelphia and
Bishop Plessis of Quebec,
1821-1825," American Catholic Historical Society of
Philadelphia Records, v. 22
(1911), 268-285.   L 210

LINDSAY, LIONEL (tr. and ed.)
"Correspondence between
Bishop Plessis of Quebec,
Canada, and Bishop Flaget of
Bardstown, Ky., 1811-1833,"
American Catholic Historical
Society of Philadelphia Re-
cords, v. 18 (1907), 8-43.
     L 211

LINDSAY, LIONEL (tr. and ed.)
"Correspondence between the
Sees of Quebec and Baltimore,
1788-1847," American Catholic
Historical Society of Philadelphia Records, v. 18 (1907),
155-189, 282-305, 434-467.
     L 212

LINDSAY, LIONEL (ed.) "Letters from the Archdiocesan
Archives at Quebec," American Catholic Historical Society
of Philadelphia Records, v. 20
(1909), 406-430.   L 213
A series of letters from

Gibault to Briand, and one from Meurin to Briand giving interesting sidelights on the story of the Church in the Ohio Valley.

LINDSAY, LIONEL (tr. and ed.) "Pastoral Visitation of Bishop Plessis of Quebec, A.D. 1815," American Catholic Historical Society of Philadelphia Records, v. 15 (1904), 377-402. L 214

LINDSAY, LIONEL (ed.) "Some Correspondence Relating to the Dioceses of New Orleans and St. Louis, 1818-1843. From the Archiepiscopal Archives of Quebec," American Catholic Historical Society of Philadelphia Records, v. 19 (1908), 185-213 (New Orleans), 305-325 (St. Louis). L 215

LINDSAY, LIONEL (tr. and ed.) "Visitation of Detroit by Bishop Plessis of Quebec in 1816," American Catholic Historical Researches, v. 22 (1905), 222-232. L 216

LINEBERGER, MARK J. Critical Estimate of the Main Printed Sources for the Life and Labors of the Rev. Demitrius A. Gallatzin, 1770-1840. MA thesis. Catholic University. 1940. 59p. L 217

LINEHAN, PAUL H. "Holy Trinity Parish, Boston," United States Catholic Historical Society Records and Studies, v. 7 (1914), 132-144. L 218

LINEHAN, THOMAS. "Early Catholic Missions in Emmet County," Michigan History Magazine, v. 2 (1918), 327-329. L 219

LINK, MAURICE. Missionary Labors and Travels of Father Claude Jean Allouez, S. J.: 1658-1689. MA thesis. Loyola University (Chicago), 1937. L 220

LITHGOW, SISTER MARY BONAVENTURE. Missionary Rivalry among the Iroquois, Indiana, 1642-1775. MA thesis.

Villanova University. 1955. 89p. L 221

LITTLE, SISTER MARY BARTHOLOMEW. Development of the Catholic Religion in Northeast Missouri. MA thesis. Saint Louis University. 1946. 161p. L 222

LITTLE ROCK (DIOCESE) SYNOD 1. Synodus dioecesana Petriculana prima. Petriculae apud Cancellarium Dioecesanam. 1909. 151p. L 223

LITTLE ROCK, ARK., DIOCESAN HISTORICAL COMMISSION (ed.) The History of Catholicity in Arkansas. Little Rock. no pub. 1925. L 224

LITZ, FRANCIS A. Father Tabb. A Study of His Life and Works. Baltimore. Johns Hopkins Press. 1923. 363p. front. L 225

LOCHEMES, M. J. "Right Reverend J. J. Fox, D. D.," Salesianum, v. 10 (Apr., 1915), 1-8, port. L 226

LOCHEMES, SISTER M. FREDERICK. Robert Walsh, His Story. Washington. Catholic University of America. 1941. ix, 258p. L 227

[LOCKE, JESSE ALBERT] "The Early Years," The Epistle, v. 15 (1949), 94-97. L 228 Story of the beginnings of Saint Paul Guild.

LOCKWOOD, FRANCIS C. Story of the Spanish Missions of the Middle Southwest. Santa Ana, Calif. 1935. 78p. xxvpl. on 161. (incl. front.), double map. L 229

LOCKWOOD, FRANCIS C. With Padre Kino on the Trail. Tuscon. University of Arizona Press. 1934. 142p. illus. (incl. facsims.), maps. L 230

LOEHR, NORBERT P. Federal Relations with the Jesuit Osage Indian Mission, 1847-1870. MA thesis. Saint

Louis University. 1940. 124p.
L 231

LOMASNEY, PATRICK. "Marquette's Burial Site Located," Illinois Catholic Historical Review, v. 9 (1927), 348-362.
L 232

LONSWAY, JESSE W. The Episcopal Lineage of the Hierarchy in the United States, 1790-1948. New York. Pustet. 1948. 20p. pp. 6-15 tables. fold. table (in pocket). L 233

LOOMIS, JAMES. Within My Parish. Notes from the Notebook of a Deceased Parish Priest. Philadelphia. no pub. 1914. 191p. L 234

[LORAS, MATTHIAS.] "Bishop Loras' Account of Religion between the Mississippi and Missouri 1838-1854," American Catholic Historical Researches, v. 11 (1894), 160. L 235

[LORAS, MATTHIAS.] "Letters of Rt. Rev. Matthias Loras, First Bishop of Dubuque," Acta et Dicta, v. 1 (1907), 14-29. port. L 236

[LORAS, MATTHIAS.] "Documents," Acta et Dicta, v. 4 (1916), 275-293. L 237
Four letters of Loras written between 1829 and 1830--given in French and English translation.

[LORAS, MATTHIAS.] "Letters of Bishop Loras, 1832 and 1836," Acta et Dicta, v. 5 (1917), 111-119. L 238

LORD, DANIEL A. Played by Ear. Chicago: Loyola University Press, 1956, xii, 398p. L 239
The autobiography of a great Jesuit champion of Youth and the Sodality.

LORD, ROBERT H., JOHN E. SEXTON, AND EDWARD T. HARRINGTON. History of the Archdiocese of Boston in the Various States of Its Development, 1604-1943. New York. Sheed and Ward. 1944.

3v. front., plates, ports., map. L 240

LORD, ROBERT H. "The Organization of the Church in New England: Bishop Benedict Joseph Fenwick (1782-1846)," Catholic Historical Review, v. 22 (1936), 173-184. L 241

LORD, ROBERT H. "Religious Liberty in New England," United States Catholic Historical Society Records and Studies, v. 22 (1932), 7-31.
L 242

LORETTO, SISTER MARIE. "Visiting Nursing as Done by Sisters in the United States-- A Survey of the Field," Catholic Charities Review, v. 24 (1940), 41-44. L 243

LOS ANGELES AND SAN DIEGO (DIOCESE) SYNOD, 5th, 1927. Statuta dioecesis Angelorum et Sancti Dicaci lata ac promulgata a Joanne Joseph Cantwell ep. in synodo dioecesana quinta, die 6 mensis Decembris anni 1927 habita in ecclesia cathedrali S. Vibianae V. M. civitatis Angelorum in Calif. S. Ludovoci, typis B. Herder n. d. xxi, 53p.
L 244

LOUANT, ARMANT. "Le P. Louis Hennepin. Nouveaux jalons pour sa biographie," Revue d'Histoire Ecclésiastique, v. 45 (1950), 186-211.
L 245

LOUANT, A. "Une confirmation de l'identification du Père Louis Hennepin, "Revue d'Histoire Ecclésiastique, no. 4, 1957. L 246

LOUDEN, MICHAEL J. Catholic Albany. Albany. P. Donnelly. 1895. 358p. incl. front., plates, ports. L 247

LOUGHLIN, JAMES F. "The Higher and Lower Education of the American Priesthood," American Catholic Quarterly Review, v. 15 (1890), 101-

122.   L 248
LOUGHLIN, JAMES F. "The
School Controversy in the U-
nited States," American Ec-
clesiastical Review, v. 6
(1892), 119-122.   L 249
LOUGHRAN, E. WARD. "Did a
Priest Accompany Columbus in
1492?" Catholic Historical
Review, v. 16 (1930), 164-174.
                           L 250
LOUGHRAN, E. WARD. "The
First Vicar Apostolic of the
New World," American Ec-
clesiastical Review, v. 82
(1930), 1-14.   L 251
LOUGHRAN, SISTER MARY
CHRISTOPHER. The Develop-
ment of the Church in the City
of Fall River from the Begin-
ning until 1904. MA thesis.
Catholic University. n.d. 46p.
                           L 252
LOUIS, WILLIAM F. Diocesan
Archives. Washington. Catholic
University of America. 1941.
x, 101p.   L 253
LOUISVILLE (DIOCESE) SYNOD,
1st, 1850. Constitutiones
dioecesia ludovicopolitanae, quas
Martinus Joannes Spalding [ep.]
in synodo dioecesana prima
tulit et promulgavit. Cum
literis pastoralibus ad clerum.
Ed. altera. Ludovicopoli, J.F.
Brennan, 1857. xiii, 16p.
                           L 254
LOUISVILLE (DIOCESE) SYNOD,
2nd, 1858. Secunda synodus
dioecesis ludovicopolitanas,
habita ad ecclesiam Sancti
Joseph, in oppido bardensi:
die 1. Sept., A.D. 1858.
[17]-23p.   L 255
LOUISVILLE (DIOCESE) SYNOD,
3rd, 1862. Synodus tertia
dioecesana ludovicopolitana,
habita die 27 Augusti, 1862,
in ecclesia Sancti Joseph
bardensi. Ludovicopoli, Bradley et Gilbert, 1862. 1 p. 1.,
[25]-28p.   L 256
LOUISVILLE (DIOCESE) SYNOD,
4th, 1874. Synodus dioecesana

ludovicopolitana IV. in ecclesia
cathedrali, die XXI Julii,
A.R.S. MDCCCLXXIV. a
Gulielmo McCloskey [ep.]
Ludovicopoli, Bradley & Gil-
bert, 1874. 24p.   L 257
LOUISVILLE (DIOCESE) SYNOD,
4th-7th, 1874-1902. Synodi
dioecesanae ludovicopolitanae
IV., V., VI., VII., in
ecclesia cathedrali, die XXXI
Julii, 1874, die III. Jan.,
1889, die XIX Dec., 1895, die
XIX Dec., 1902, a Gulielmo
Georgio McCloskey habitae.
Ludovicopoli, 1903. 48p.
                           L 258
LOUY, SISTER MARY MERCEDES.
The Sisters of Notre Dame,
Covington, Kentucky. MA
thesis. Catholic University.
1949. 74p.   L 259
LOVE, THOMAS J. "The Evolu-
tion of St. Joseph's College,"
American Catholic Historical
Society of Philadelphia Records,
v. 52 (1941), 161-173.
                           L 260
LOWMAN, SISTER MARY
MARCIAN. James Andrew
Corcoran: editor, theologian,
scholar (1820-1889). Ph.D.
dissertation. Saint Louis Uni-
versity. 1958. xii, 487p.
                           L 261
LOWMAN, SISTER MARY
MARCIAN. "James Andrew
Corcoran: Editor, Theologian,
Scholar (1820-1889)," American
Catholic Historical Society of
Philadelphia Records, v. 70
(1959), 32-57.   L 262
Story of one of the contro-
versial priests of the Dio-
cese of Charleston, South
Carolina.
LOYOLA, SISTER. "Bishop
Benedict J. Fenwick and Anti-
Catholicism in New England,
1829-1845," United States
Catholic Historical Society Re-
cords and Studies, v. 27
(1937), 99-256.   L 263
LOYOLA, SISTER MARY. The

American Occupation of New
Mexico, 1821-1852. Albuquerque. University of New Mexico. 1939. 166p. Publica-
tion in History, University of
New Mexico, v. 8. Also
New Mexico Historical Review,
v. 14 (1939), 34-75, 143-
199, 230-286.　　　　L 264

LUCEY, JOHN M. The Catholic
Church in Arkansas. Little
Rock, Ark. No pub. 1906.
55p.　　　　　　　　L 265

LUCEY, JOHN M. "The Catholic
Church in Arkansas," Arkansas
Historical Association Publica-
tions, v. 2 (1908), 424-461.
　　　　　　　　　　　L 266

LUCEY, JOHN M. Souvenir of a
Silver Jubilee. Little Rock,
Ark. no pub. 1892. 32p.
　　　　　　　　　　　L 267

LUCEY, MICHAEL HENRY.
"Efforts to Regain State Support
for Catholic Schools: Founding
of New York's First Parochial
School," Catholic World, v.
93 (1911), 596-609.　L 268

LUCEY, WILLIAM LEO. "American Catholics a Century Ago,"
American Catholic Historical
Society Records, v. 61 (1950),
202-212.　　　　　　 L 269

LUCEY, WILLIAM LEO. The
Catholic Church in Maine.
Francistown, New Hampshire:
Marshall Jones Co., 1957.
xiv, 372p.　　　　　 L 270

LUCEY, WILLIAM L. "Catholic
Magazines: 1865-1880," American Catholic Historical Society
of Philadelphia Records, v. 63
(1952), 21-36.　　　 L 271

LUCEY, WILLIAM L. "Catholic
Magazines: 1880-1890," A-
merican Catholic Historical
Society of Philadelphia Records,
v. 63 (1952), 65-109. L 272

LUCEY, WILLIAM. "Check
List of 19th Century American
Serials, Dinand Library, Holy
Cross College," American
Catholic Historical Society of
Philadelphia Records, v. 65

(1954), 56-60.　　　 L 273

LUCEY, WILLIAM. "The Dio-
cese of Burlington, Vermont:
1853," American Catholic
Historical Society of Philadelphia Records, v. 64 (Sept.,
1953), 123-154.　　　L 274
A well documented sketch of
the history of the Church
in Vermont up to 1853 and
the happenings of 1853 on
the arrival of Bishop Louis
de Goesbriand, first Bishop
of Burlington.

LUCEY, WILLIAM LEO. Edward
Kavanagh: Catholic Statesman,
Diplomat from Maine, 1795-
1844. Francetown, N.H.
Marshall Jones Co. 1946.
viii, 270p. incl. geneal.
table.　　　　　　　　L 275

LUCEY, WILLIAM L. "Forgotten
Source on John Bapst, S.J.,"
Historical Bulletin. v. 34
(1956), 67-74.　　　　L 276
Points out the value of Mary
Agnes Tincker's House of
Yorke as a source for an
account of the Ellsworth
affair.

LUCEY, WILLIAM LEO.
"Madawaska on the River St.
John: New England's Last
Frontier," American Catholic
Historical Society of Philadel-
phia Records, v. 60 (1949),
147-164.　　　　　　　L 277

LUCEY, WILLIAM (comp.)
"Maine in 1854: Letters on
State Politics and Know-
Nothingism," American Cath-
olic Historical Society of
Philadelphia Records, v. 65
(1954), 176-186.　　　L 278

LUCEY, WILLIAM. "The Position of Catholics in Vermont:
1853," American Catholic
Historical Society of Philadelphia Records, v. 64 (1953),
213-235.　　　　　　　L 279
Good description of the difficulties with Nativism,
documented from newspapers
of the time.

LUCEY, WILLIAM LEO. 'Record of an American Priest: Michael Earls, S.J., 1873-1937," American Ecclesiastical Review, v. 137 (1957), 145-155, 217-229, 297-307, 414-422.   L 280
A sketch of this "literary-minded member" of the faculty" of the College of the Holy Cross, Worcester, Mass.

LUCEY, WILLIAM L. "Some Catholic Converts," American Catholic Historical Society of Philadelphia, v. 67 (1956), 67-87.   L 281
Short biographical sketches of Dr. Henry Bowen Clark, Greene, Josue Maria Young, Mary Agnes Tincker, Jon Joseph A'Becket, Charles Eugene Woodman.

LUCEY, WILLIAM. "Some Research Problems in the History of the Catholic Church in New England," American Catholic Historical Society of Philadelphia Records, v. 69 (1958), 9-19.   L 282

LUDWIG, JOSEPH. "The Story of Peter Carabin, Proto-Priest of Northwestern Ohio," Northwestern Ohio Quarterly, v. 22 (1950), 184-201.   L 283
A well documented study of this pioneer of the Ohio valley, who was ordained at Cincinnati in 1830 and served at Monroe until 1843 when he went to Wisconsin for a brief stay. He died 1873.

LUDWIG, SISTER M. MILETA. A Chapter in Franciscan History: the Sisters of the Third Order of Saint Francis of Perpetual Adoration, 1849-1949. New York. Bookman Associates, 1950. 455p.
                                L 284

"LUDWIG I AND THE CREATION OF ST. VINCENT ABBEY," Central Blatt and Social Justice, v. 19 (1926), 163.
                                L 285

LUEBERMANN, F. B. Address-Kalender der Hl. Dreifahltigkeits Gemeinde zu Evansville, f.d.j. St. Meinrads. 1883. L 286

LUGAN, ALPHONSE. Le Catholicisme aux Etats-Unis. Paris. Librairie Letouzey. 1930. 247p.   L 287

LUIGI M. GENTILE," Lettere Edificanti Provincia Napolitana, (1908), 325-328.   L 288

LUMMIS, CHARLES FLETCHER. The Land of Poco Tiempo. New York. Scribners. 1893. xii, 310p. illus., plates.
                                L 289

LUNCEFORD, A. M. 'Epitaphs from the Cemetery of the First Roman Catholic Church in Georgia," Georgia Historical Quarterly, v. 42 (1958), 217-221.   L 290

LYDON, P. J. "Notes on the History of the Diocese of Duluth," Acta et Dicta, v. 5 (1918), 238-288.   L 291

LYNAHAN, W. A. The Chinese Mission of San Francisco," The Missionary, (1936), 127-129.   L 292

LYNCH, HELEN M. In the Shadow of Our Lady of the Cenacle, 1892-1942. New York. Paulist Press. 1941. xiii, 249p. plates, ports.
                                L 293

LYNCH, J.S.M. A Page of Church History in New York. St. John's Church, Utica, N. Y. no pl. no pub. 1897.
                                L 294

LYNCH, SISTER MARY CLAIRE. Jesuit Missionary Activities in North America from 1572-1773. MA thesis. Marquette University. 1934.   L 295

LYNCH (PATRICK N.) "Lettre de Mgr. P-N Lynch, évêque de Charleston à M.M. les Membres des Conseils Centraux de l'Oeuvre de la Propagation de la Foi, 17 juin, 1867," Annales de la Propagation de la Foi, v. 40

(1868), 81-90.   L 296
LYONS, JOHN A. Historical
Sketches of Old St. Theresa's
in Meade County, Kentucky.
Louisville. The Author (747
Harrison Ave., Louisville, Ky.)
100p.   L 297
LYONS, JOHN A. Necrology of
the Diocesan Clergy of the
Archdiocese of Louisville and
the Diocese of Owensboro.
Louisville. Publishers Print-
ing Co. 1943. 64p. ports.
                              L 298
LYONS, JOSEPH A. Silver
Jubilee of Notre Dame (Uni-
versity), June 23rd, 1869.
Chicago. E.B. Myers and
Co.   L 299
LYONS, SISTER LETITIA MARY.
Francis Norbert Blanchet and
the Founding of the Oregon
Missions (1833-1857), Wash-
ington. Catholic University.
1940. xx, 200p.   L 300
LYONS, W. F. Brigadier General
Thomas Francis Meagher. New
York. Sadlier. 1870. vi, 357p.
front. (port.)   L 301

        - M -
M., S. L. "The Stack-O'Hara
Case," American Catholic
Quarterly Review, v. 5
(1880), 166-177.   M 1
M., V. "Catholic Secondary
Education in Philadelphia,"
American Catholic Historical
Society of Philadelphia Records,
v. 59 (1948),157-189, 259-278;
v. 60 (1949), 17-37, 71-78.
variant title.   M 2
MAAS, OTTO. Missiones de
Neuvo Mejico. Madrid. Imps.
Hijos de T. Minnesa de Los
Rios. 1929. lvi, 252p. M 3
MAAS, OTTO. Viajes Mission-
eros Franciscanos a la Con-
quista del Neuvo Mexico.
Sevilla. Impr. de San Antonio.
1915. 208p. map.   M 4
McADAMS, EDWARD P. "White
and Carroll," Woodstock
Letters, v. 78 (1949), 47-

59.   M 5
McALLISTER, ANNA SHANNON.
Ellen Ewing, Wife of General
Sherman. New York.
Benziger. 1936. xiv, 379p.
front., plate, ports., facsims.
                              M 6
McALLISTER, ANNA SHANNON.
Flame in the Wilderness.
Life and Letters of Mother
Angela Gillespie, C.S.C.,
1824-1887. Paterson, N.J.
St. Anthony Guild Press.
1944. xiv, 358p. front.
(port.), plates.   M 7
McALLISTER, ANNA SHANNON.
In Winter We Flourish. New
York. Longmans, Green and
Co. 1939. xi, 398p. front.,
plate, ports., facsims. M 8
The life of Sarah Worthing-
ton King Peter, outstanding
Catholic laywoman of Cin-
cinnati in the mid-century.
McANDREWS, DUNSTAN. Father
Joseph Kundek, 1810-1857.
A Missionary Priest of the Dio-
cese of Vincennes. St. Mein-
rad. Grail. 1955. 74p.
                              M 9
McARDLE, SISTER MARY
AURELIA. California's Pio-
neer Sister of Mercy, Mother
Mary Baptist Russell (1829-
1898). Fresno. Academy
Library Guild. 1954. 204p.
                              M 10
McARDLE, MARY AURELIA.
California's Pioneer Sister of
Mercy: Mother Mary Baptist
Russell (1829-1898). MA
thesis. University of San
Francisco. 1953. 186p.
                              M 11
McATEE, F. "Reminiscences of
an Army Chaplain in the Civil
War," Woodstock Letters, v.
43 (1915), 71-77.   M 12
McAULIFFE, HAROLD J.
Father Tim. Milwaukee.
Bruce. 1944. xiv, 162p.
front., plates, ports.,
facsims.   M 13
McAULIFFE, HAROLD J. "Father

Timothy Dempsey," Missouri Historical Review, v. 36 (1942), 320-333. M 14

McAULIFFE, SISTER MARY MICHAELINE. History of St. John's Hospital, Springfield, Missouri. MA thesis. Saint Louis University. 1947. 116p. M 15

McAVOY, MARY C. "Catholic Origins in Massachusetts," Catholic World, v. 132 (1930), 174-182. M 16

McAVOY, MARY C. "Humility was His Strength," Columbia, v. 13 (Nov., 1933), 8, 26. port. M 17
A biographical sketch of Bishop John Cheverus, Boston (1808-1823).

McAVOY, THOMAS T. "The Abbé Rivet at Vincennes (1795-1804)," Mid-America, v. 18 (1947), 24-33. M 18

McAVOY, THOMAS T. "Activism vs. Catholic Scholarship," Ave Maria, v. 65 (1947), 167-169. M 19

McAVOY, THOMAS T. "After Fifty Years," Ave Maria, v. 54 (1941), 327-329. M 20

McAVOY, THOMAS T. "An American Catholic Tradition," Ave Maria, v. 66 (1947), 46-49. M 21

McAVOY, THOMAS T. "This 'American' Catholicism," Catholic World, v. 190 (1959), 117-123. M 22
A good general survey of the Catholic Church in the United States.

McAVOY, THOMAS T. "American Catholics and the Second World War," Review of Politics, v. 6 (1944), 131-150. M 23
A general article.

McAVOY, THOMAS T. "The American Priest Discovers American History," American Ecclesiastical Review, v. 131 (1954), 180-185. M 24

McAVOY, THOMAS T. "Americanism and Frontier Catholicism," Review of Politics, v. 5 (1943), 275-301. M 25

McAVOY, THOMAS T. "Americanism, Fact and Fiction," Catholic Historical Review, v. 31 (1945), 133-153. M 26

McAVOY, THOMAS T. "'Americanism' Reviewed by Abbé Felix Klein," American Ecclesiastical Review, v. 122 (1950), 355-363. M 27

McAVOY, THOMAS T. (tr. and ed.) "Bishop Bruté's Report to Rome in 1836," Catholic Historical Review, v. 29 (1943), 177-233, map. M 28

McAVOY, THOMAS T. (ed.) "Bishop Flaget's Pastoral to the People of Detroit," Catholic Historical Review, v. 30 (1944), 28-40. M 29
French only.

McAVOY, THOMAS T. "Bishop John Lancaster Spalding and the Catholic Minority (1877-1908)," Review of Politics, v. 12 (1950), 3-19. M 30

McAVOY, THOMAS T. "Catholic Archives and Manuscript Collections," American Archivist, v. 24 (1961), 409-414. M 31

McAVOY, THOMAS T. The Catholic Church in Indiana, 1789-1834. New York. Columbia University Press. 1940. 226p. M 32

McAVOY, THOMAS T. "Catholic Education in Indiana," Indiana History Bulletin, v. 23 (1946), 55-61. M 33

McAVOY, THOMAS T. "Catholic Liberal Arts College and American Studies," Catholic Educational Review, v. 54 (1956), 295-311. M 34
A short history of the development and a study of the present setup with emphasis on the story at Notre Dame.

McAVOY, THOMAS T. "The Catholic Minority in the United States, 1789-1821," United States Catholic Historical Society Records and Studies, v. 39-40 (1952), 33-50. M 35

McAVOY, T. T. "Catholicism and the American Way of Life," America, v. 98 (Nov. 9, 1957), 162-163. M 36

McAVOY, THOMAS T. "Father Badin Comes to Notre Dame," Indiana Magazine of History, v. 29 (1933), 7-16. M 37

McAVOY, THOMAS T. "The Formation of the Catholic Minority in the United States, 1820-1860," Review of Politics, v. 10 (1948), 13-34. M 38

McAVOY, THOMAS T. The Great Crisis in American Catholic History, 1895-1900. Chicago: Regnery, 1957. xi, 402p. M 39
    A scholarly study of the problem of "ecclesiastical Americanism."

McAVOY, THOMAS T. "Hero of American Catholicism," Ave Maria, v. 91 (Feb. 20, 1960), 5-7. M 40

McAVOY, THOMAS T. "John F. O'Hara, C.S.C., and Notre Dame," American Catholic Historical Society of Philadelphia Records, v. 64 (1953), 3-22. M 41
    A chapter in the biographical issue on Archbishop O'Hara.

McAVOY, THOMAS T. "The Le Bras Approach to the History of the Diocese of Fort Wayne, Indiana," Indiana Magazine of History, v. 52 (1956), 369-382. M 42
    Explanation of an interesting method of organizing church history.

McAVOY, THOMAS T. "Manuscript Collections among Catholics," Catholic Historical Review, v. 37 (October, 1951) 281-295. M 43
    Sketch of James Farnham Edwards' work collecting materials on the history of the Catholic Church

in the United States for the archives of the University of Notre Dame.

McAVOY, THOMAS F. "The Old French Frontier in the Central Lakes Region," American Catholic Historical Society of Philadelphia Records, v. 65 (1954), 230-239. M 44

McAVOY, THOMAS T. "The Philosophers and American Catholic Education," Catholic Educational Review, v. 47 (1949), 579-585. M 45

McAVOY, THOMAS T. "The Role of History in the Catholic Liberal College," Catholic Educational Review, v. 48 (1950), 505-515. M 46

McAVOY, THOMAS T., ed. Roman Catholicism and the American Way of Life. Notre Dame, Ind. University of Notre Dame Press, 1960. viii, 248p. M 47
    Nineteen essays of varying quality.

McAVOY, THOMAS TIMOTHY. The War Letters of Father Peter Paul Cooney of the Congregation of the Holy Cross. MA thesis. University of Notre Dame. 1930. 83p. M 48

McAVOY, THOMAS T. "Where is the Catholic Vote?" Ave Maria, v. 83 (June 16, 1956), 12-16. illus. M 49
    A brief discussion of the problem of how Catholics vote, further substantiating the fact that religion is not the dominating influence in the choice of party or candidates by American Catholics.

McBEATH, JAMES JOSEPH. The Irish Empresarios in Texas. MA thesis. Catholic University. 1953. 96p. M 50

McBREEN, SISTER EILEEN MARIE. The Visit of the Most Reverend Cajetan Bedini (?) to Cincinnati in 1833. MA thesis. University of Notre Dame. 1937. vii, 105p. M 51

McBRIDE, SARA. "Beginnings of Catholicity in Des Moines," Iowa Catholic Historical Review, v. 3 (1931), 14-24. M 52

MacCAFFREY, JAMES. History of the Catholic Church in the Nineteenth Century. 2d ed. rev. St. Louis. Herder. 1910. 2v. M 53

McCAFFREY, PATRICK ROMAEUS. From Dusk to Dawn; A History of the Sisters of Saint Joseph of Newark, N.J. New York. Benziger. 1932. xi, 300p. front., plates, ports. M 54

McCAFFREY, THOMAS F. History of the Apostolate of the Catholic Church to the Deaf in the Archdiocese of New York. MA thesis. Fordham University. 1956. iv, 68p. M 55

McCALEB, WALTER F. The Spanish Missions of Texas. San Antonio. Naylor. 1954. 135p. M 56

McCALLEN, WILLIAM J. "Sunday Landmark Notabilia of Our Society," American Catholic Historical Society of Philadelphia Records, v. 23 (1913), 1-12. M 57

McCALLEN, WILLIAM J. "Temporary Schism over the Election of Father William Elling," American Catholic Historical Society of Philadelphia Records, v. 23 (1913), 193-216. M 58

McCANN, JAMES G. Bishop John England Pioneer American Catholic Spokesman on Church-State Relations. MA thesis. Loyola University (Chicago). 1958. 140p. M 59

McCANN, JOHN E. "History of Catholicity in Northampton County, Pennsylvania...1737-1920," American Catholic Historical Society of Philadelphia Records, v. 31 (1920),

339-348; v. 32 (1921), 61-92. M 60

McCANN, SISTER MARY AGNES. Archbishop Purcell and the Archdiocese of Cincinnati. Washington. Catholic University. 1918. 108p. M 61

McCANN, SISTER MARY AGNES. Centennial Story. Mt. St. Joseph, Ohio. 1929. M 62

McCANN, SISTER MARY AGNES. The History of Mother Seton's Daughters. The Sisters of Charity of Cincinnati, Ohio, 1809-1923. New York. Longmans, Green and Co. 1917-1923. 3 v. front., plates, ports., facsims. M 63

McCANN, SISTER MARY AGNES. "The Most Reverend John Baptist Purcell, D. D., Archbishop of Cincinnati (1800-1883)," Catholic Historical Review, v. 6 (1920), 172-199. M 64

McCANN, SISTER MARY AGNES. "Religious Orders of Women of the United States," Catholic Historical Review, v. 7 (1921), 318-331. M 65

McCARRICK, JOHN J. Jr. The National War Labor Board. MA thesis. St. John's University, N.Y., 1939. mss. pp. M 66
Especially for relation of principles to Rerum Novarum and for attitude of the Catholic Bishops.

McCARTHY, CHARLES FLORENCE. The Historical Development of Episcopal Nominations in the United States, 1784-1884. MA thesis. Catholic University. 1927. 72p. M 67

McCARTHY, CHARLES FLORENCE. "Historical Development of Episcopal Nominations in the Catholic Church of the United States, 1784-1884," American Catholic Historical Society of Philadelphia Records, v. 38 (1927),

297-354.   M 68
McCARTHY, FRANCIS F. The
History of Mission San José,
California, 1797-1835. Fresno,
Calif. Academy Library Guild,
1958. 285p.   M 69
McCARTHY, JAY DAVID. Orestes
Brownson - a Catholic Voice
on the Civil War. MA thesis.
University of Notre Dame.
1956. 108p.   M 70
McCARTHY, J. J. "The Jesuits
Relinquish Selma," American
Catholic Historical Society of
Philadelphia Records, v. 46
(1935), 49-57.   M 71
McCARTHY, JOHN MAURICE.
Catholics and the Temperance
Movement in New England, 1830-
1870. MA thesis. Boston
College. 1960. 94p.   M 72
McCARTHY, SISTER MARY
HELEN. History of the Sisters
of Mercy of Belmont, North
Carolina, 1869-1933. MA
thesis. Catholic University.
1934. 122p.   M 73
McCARTHY, P. F. "Bishop
James O'Connor in Omaha,"
American Catholic Historical
Society of Philadelphia Re-
cords, v. 3 (1891), 121-128.
port.   M 74
McCLOSKEY, MICHAEL B.
Formative Years of the Mis-
sionary College of Santa Cruz
of Queretaro, 1683-1733.
Washington. Academy of
American Franciscan History.
1955. 128p.   M 75
McCOLGAN, DANIEL T. "The
Catholic Home Bureau of New
York Celebrates Its Golden
Jubilee," Catholic Charities
Review, v. 33 (1949), 237-
240.   M 76
McCOLGAN, DANIEL T. "The
Society of St. Vincent de Paul
and the First White House
Conference on the Care of
Dependent Children (1909),"
Catholic Charities Review, v.
33 (1949), 100-104, 129-133.
                                M 77

McCONVILLE, SISTER M. ST.
PATRICK. Political Nativism
in the State of Maryland,
1830-1860. Washington.
Catholic University of Ameri-
ca. 1928. vi, 133p.   M 78
McCORMICK, ANNE O'HARE.
St. Agnes Church, Cleveland,
Ohio. Cleveland. Martin
Print. Co. c 1920. 48p.
                                M 79
McCORMICK, JOHN D. "Catholicity in New Jersey," A-
merican Catholic Historical
Researches, v. 14 (1897),
44-46.   M 80
McCORMICK, LEO J. Church-
State Relationships in Education in Maryland. Washington. Catholic University.
1942. xiii, 294p. incl.
tables.   M 81
McCORMICK, PATRICK J. "The
University and the Review,"
American Ecclesiastical Re-
view, v. 121 (1949), 257-
260.   M 82
Relations between the A-
merican Ecclesiastical Re-
view and the Catholic Uni-
versity of America.
McCOY, JOHN J. History of
the Catholic Church in the Dio-
cese of Springfield. Boston.
Hurd and Everts Co. 1900.
                                M 83
McCRAY, SISTER MARY
GERTRUDE. Evidences of
Catholic Interest in Social
Welfare in the United States
between 1830 and 1850.
MA thesis. University of
Notre Dame. 1937. iv, 75p.
                                M 84
McCULLOUGH, SISTER MARIE.
Contributions of the Ursulines
to Education in the Archdiocese
of New York. MA thesis.
Fordham University. 1939.
iii, 60p.   M 85
McDERMOTT, JOHN FRANCIS
(ed.) Old Cahokia. A Nar-
rative and Documents Illustra-
ting the First Century of Its

History. St. Louis. St. Louis Historical Documents Foundation. 1949. 355p. front., plates, facsims, map. on end papers. M 86

McDERMOTT, JOHN FRANCIS. "Private Schools in St. Louis, 1809-1821," Mid-America, v. 11 (1940), 96-119. M 87

McDERMOTT, PATRICK N. "Our Colonial Bishop," American Ecclesiastical Review, v. 49 (1913), 552-559. M 88

McDEVITT, MATTHEW. Joseph McKenna, Associate Justice of the United States. Washington. Catholic University. 1946. x, 250p. M 89

McDEVITT, V. EDMOND. The First California's Chaplain. Fresno, California: Academy Library Guild, 1956. 259p. M 90

McDEVITT, WILLIAM. "My Old Plantation Days with Father Tabb," Catholic World, v. 169 (1949), 424-429. M 91

McDONALD, D. "State of the Local Catholic Press," Commonweal, v. 51 (1950), 459-461. M 92

MacDONALD, FERGUS. The Catholic Church and the Secret Societies in the United States. MA thesis. Catholic University. 1946. 256p. M 93

MacDONALD, FERGUS. The Catholic Church and Secret Societies in the United States. New York. United States Catholic Historical Society. 1946. 220p. Monograph series. v. 22. M 94

McDONALD, SISTER GRACE. "The Benedictine Sisters and the St. Cloud Hospital," Minnesota History, v. 33 (1953), 291-297. M 95

McDONALD, SISTER GRACE. "Canon Vivaldi's Missionary Activities," Iowa Catholic Historical Review, v. 4 (1932), 32-45. M 96

McDONALD, SISTER GRACE (tr.

and ed.) "Documents. The Long Prairie Mission. A Letter of Canon Vivaldi," Acta et Dicta, v. 6 (1933), 114-131. M 97

McDONALD, SISTER GRACE. "Father Francis Pierz, Missionary," Minnesota History, v. 10 (1929), 107-125. M 98

McDONALD, SISTER GRACE. "A Finishing School of the 1880's" St. Benedict's Academy (St. Joseph, Minnesota)," Minnesota History, v. 27 (1946), 96-106. illus. M 99

McDONALD, SISTER GRACE. "Pioneer Teachers. The Benedictine Sisters at St. Cloud," Minnesota History, v. 35 (1957), 263-271. M 100

MACDONALD, ISABEL. The Truth about the Activities of Father Sebastian Rasle among the Abenaki Indians. 1934. ii, 111p. M 101

McDONALD, JOSEPH B. "Catholicity in North Dakota," Acta et Dicta, v. 1 (1908), 210-218. M 102

McDONALD, SISTER M. JUSTILLE. History of the Irish in Wisconsin in the Nineteenth Century. Washington. Catholic University. 1954. ix, 324p. M 103

McDONALD, LLOYD P. The Seminary Movement in the United States. Projects, Foundations, and Early Developments 1784-1833. Washington. Catholic University. 1927. v. 69p. M 104

McDONALD, WILLIAM E. "The Pious Fund of the Californias," Catholic Historical Review, v. 19 (1934), 427-436. M 105

McELRONE, HUGH P. "Bishop Lynch," Catholic World, v. 35 (1882), 160-168. M 106

McELROY, JOHN. "An Account of the Re-establishment of the

Society in the United
States," Woodstock Letters,
v. 16 (1887), 161-168. M 107
McELROY, JOHN. "Chaplains
for the Mexican War, 1846,"
Woodstock Letters, v. 15
(1886), 198-202, v. 16 (1887),
33-39, 225-229, v. 17 (1888),
3-12, 149-163. M 108
McENIRY, SISTER BLANCHE
MARIE. American Catholics
in the War with Mexico. Wash-
ington. Catholic University.
1937. xi, 178p. M 109
McENIRY, SISTER BLANCHE
MARIE. Woman of Decision.
New York. McMullen. 1953.
243p. front. (port.) M 110
A biography of Mother Mary
Xavier Mehegan, foundress
of the Sisters of Charity
of Saint Elizabeth Convent,
New Jersey.
McENTEE, SISTER MARY
VERONICA. The Sisters of
Mercy of Harrisburg, 1869-
1939. Philadelphia, Dolphin
Press. 1939. xviii, 416p.
front., plates, ports. M 111
McEVOY, E. L. "Beginnings of
the Catholic Church in North-
west Iowa, with Special Refer-
ence to Emmetsburg and Palo
Alto County," Iowa Catholic
Historical Review, v. 8 (May,
1935), 15-37. M 112
McEVOY, M. F. "The Catholic
Social Welfare Bureau of Mil-
waukee," Salesianum, v. 31
(1936), 51-56. M 113
McFADDEN, JOHN W. "Notes
for a History of Catholicism
in Holmeburg and Northeast
Philadelphia," American Cath-
olic Historical Society of
Philadelphia Records, v. 40
(1929), 156-192. M 114
McFARLAND, P. F. "Early
Catholic Affairs in Utica, N.
Y.," United States Catholic
Historical Magazine, v. 4
(1891-1892), 64-69. M 115
McGANN, SISTER AGNES
GERALDINE. "The Know

Nothing Movement in Kentucky,"
American Catholic Historical
Society of Philadelphia Re-
cords, v. 49 (1938), 291-
329. M 116
McGANN, SISTER MARY
GERALDINE. Nativism in
Kentucky to 1860. Washington.
Catholic University. 1944.
xi, 172p. M 117
McGARITY, JOHN EDWARD.
Rev. Samuel Sutherland
Cooper, 1769-1843. MA
thesis. Catholic University.
1926. 42p. M 118
McGARITY, JOHN EDWARD,
"Samuel Sutherland Cooper,
1769-1843," American Catholic
Historical Society of Phila-
delphia Records, v. 37 (1926),
305-340. M 119
McGARRY, DANIEL D. "Educa-
tional Methods of the Francis-
cans in Spanish California,"
The Americas, v. 6 (1950),
335-358. M 120
McGEE, J. FOREST. "History
of the Beginnings of the Fran-
ciscan Province of St. John
the Baptist, Cincinnati," Pro-
vincial Chronicle (Province of
St. John the Baptist, O.F.M.),
v. 20 (1948), 217-249.
M 121
McGEE, J. F. "A Jubilee in
Giants," Provincial Chronicle
(Province of St. John Baptist,
O.F.M.), v. 21 (1949), 152-
158. M 122
[McGEE, JOHN FOREST.] "A
Living Story of the Faith in
the Oklahoma Panhandle,"
Provincial Chronicle (Province
of St. John Baptist, O.F.M.),
v. 20 (1948), 68-85. M 123
[McGEE, JOHN FOREST.] "One
Hundred Years Ago. The
Coming of the Friars to
Hamilton, Ohio," Provincial
Chronicle (Province of St.
John Baptist, O.F.M.), v. 21
(1949), 127-131. M 124
McGEE, JOHN FOREST. "The
Story of Clovis [N.M.] and

Its Missions," Provincial Chronicle (Province of St. John Baptist, O.F.M.), v. 21 (1949), 137-150, 221-249. M 125

McGEE, JOHN FOREST. "The Story of the Friars Minor in the 'Franciscan Diocese of Texas,' " Provincial Chronicle (St. John Baptist Province, O. F.M.), v. 21 (1949), 29-56. 90-113. M 126

McGEE, JOHN W. The Catholic Church in the Grand River Valley, 1833-1950. Grand Rapids, Michigan. 1950. xviii, 538p. M 127
Centered around the story of St. Andrew's Parish, the Cathedral Church of Grand Rapids. Brief sketches of other parishes and institutions.

McGEE, THOMAS D. The Catholic History of North America. Boston. Patrick Donohue, 1855. 239p. M 128

McGILL, ANNA BLANCHE. The Sisters of Charity of Nazareth. New York. Encyclopedia Press. 1917. xvi, 436p. front., plates, ports., facsims. M 129

McGINN, STEWART A. Rene Menard, 1605-1661. Rochester, N.Y. Herndl Print. 1934. 76p. M 130

McGLADE, J. Progressive Educators and the Catholic Church. Westminster, Md. Newman. 1953. 164p. M 131

McGLOGAN, DANIEL T. A Century of Charity. Milwaukee. Bruce, 1951. 2v. M 132
A well written and thoroughly documented study of the first one hundred years of the Society of St. Vincent De Paul in the United States.

McGLOIN, JOHN B. "Another Priest in Politics," Historical Bulletin, v. 16 (1938), 65-66. M 133
The story of the activities of Bishop Lynch of Charleston during the Civil War.

McGLOIN, JOHN B. "The California Church, 1840-1849; a Report on Religion," American Catholic Historical Society of Philadelphia Records, v. 60 (1949), 213-223. M 134

McGLOIN, JOHN B. "A California Gold Rush Padre: New Light on the 'Padre of Paradise Flat,' " California Historical Society Quarterly, v. 40 (1961), 49-67. M 135

McGLOIN, JOHN B. "Centennial in San Francisco," Woodstock Letters, v. 79 (1950), 11-26. M 136

McGLOIN, JOHN B. "A Century of Service in El Dorado," San Francisco Quarterly, v. 16 (1949), 12-15. M 137

McGLOIN, JOHN B. "The Coming of Archbishop Alemany to California," Historical Bulletin, v. 28 (1949), 5-6, 15. M 138

McGLOIN, JOHN B. "The Coming of Joseph Sadoc Alemany, O.P., Pioneer Prelate of El Dorado," Records of the American Catholic Historical Society of Philadelphia, v. 62 (1951), 203-212. M 139

McGLOIN, JOHN B. Eloquent Indian: The Life of James Bouchard, California Jesuit. Stanford. Stanford University Press. 1949. xvii, 380p. illus., ports. M 140

McGLOIN, JOHN B. "Father Peter Masten Dunne," Woodstock Letters, v. 86 (1957), 338-350, port. M 141

McGLOIN, JOHN B. "Francis Parkman and the Jesuits," Historical Bulletin, v. 25 (1947), 57-59. M 142

McGLOIN, JOHN B. "The Jesuit Arrival in San Francisco, 1849," California Historical Quarterly, v. 29 (1950), 139-148. M 143

McGLOIN, JOHN BERNARD. "Michael Accolti, Gold Rush

Padre and Founder of the Californian Jesuits," Archivum Historicum Societatis Jesu, v. 20 (1951), 306-315.　　M 144

McGLOIN, JOHN B. "A Priest in Politics," Historical Bulletin, v. 16 (1938), 25-26.
　　M 145

The story of the activities of Archbishop Hughes during the Civil War.

McGLOIN, JOHN B., ed. "Some Letters of Patrick Manogue, Gold Miner and Bishop of Nevada and California," American Catholic Historical Society of Philadelphia Records, v. 71 (1960), 3-13.　　M 146

Seven letters dated variously 1868-1884.

McGLOIN, JOHN B. "Survey: European Archival Resources for the Study of California Catholic History," Church History, v. 30 (1961), 103-105.　　M 147

McGLOIN, JOHN B. "Two Early Reports Concerning Roman Catholicism in Utah, 1876-1881," Utah Historical Quarterly, v. 29 (1961), 322-344.
　　M 148

McGLOIN, JOSEPH T. Backstage Missionary: Father Dan Lord. New York: Pageant. 1958. 134p.　　M 149

McGLOIN, JOSEPH. I'll Die Laughing. Milwaukee. Bruce. 1955. 178p.　　M 150

An informal, and at times facetious, autobiography of a young Jesuit priest who tired of reading about those who "leaped over the wall."

McGONIGLE, JAMES A. "Right Reverend John B. Miège, S.J., First Catholic Bishop of Kansas," Kansas Historical Collections, v. 9 (1905), 153-159.
　　M 151

McGOVERN, JAMES J. The Life and Writings of the Right Reverend John McMullen, D.D., First Bishop of Davenport,

Iowa. Chicago. Hoffman Bros. xxiii, 301p. front., (port), plates.　　M 152

McGOVERN, JOHN. "The Gallipolis Colony," American Catholic Historical Society of Philadelphia Records, v. 37 (1926), 29-72.　　M 153

McGOVERN, JOHN. Gallipolis Colony. MA thesis. Catholic University. 1925. 59p.
　　M 154

McGOVERN, PATRICK A. History of the Diocese of Cheyenne. Cheyenne. Printed by the Wyoming Labor Journal. 1941. 249p. front., ports.
　　M 155

McGOVERN, PATRICK A. "History of the Diocese of Cheyenne," St. Louis Catholic Historical Review, v. 5 (1924), 5-13.　　M 156

McGRANAGHAN, SISTER MARY OF ST. JOSEPH HUBERT. Materials for a History of the Philadelphia Province of the Sisters of the Good Shepherd of Angels, 1850-1950. MA thesis. Villanova University. 1953. 209p.
　　M 157

McGRATH, SISTER PAUL OF THE CROSS. Political Nativism in Texas, 1825-1860. Washington. Catholic University. 1930. viii, 209p.
　　M 158

McGRATTY, ARTHUR R. "The American Tour of the Relic of Francis Xavier," Woodstock Letters, v. 79 (1950), 97-122.　　M 159

McGRAW, DANIEL. "Appeal of the Catholics of Natchez, Mississippi, to Archbishop Carroll for a priest, 1816," American Catholic Historical Researches, v. 19 (1902), 64.　　M 160

McGREAL, MARY N. Role of a Teaching Sisterhood in American Education. Washington. Catholic University of

America Press. 1951. xv,
144p. maps, diagrams, tables.
M 161
Story of the Sisters of St.
Dominic of Sinsinawa.
McGURRIN, JAMES. Bourke
Cockran: A Free Lance in A-
merican Politics. New York.
Scribner's. 1948. xv, 361p.
ports. M 162
McHALE, SISTER MARY
LORETTA. Catholic Church
in the District of Columbia,
1866-1938. MA thesis. Cath-
olic University. 1938. 117p.
M 163
MACHEBOEUF, JOSEPH. "Ex-
trait d'une lettre de Mgr.
Macheboeuf, Vicaire Apos-
tolique du Colorado. Denver
2 février, 1886," Annales de
la Propagation de la Foi, v. 58
(1886), 237-242. M 164
[MACHEBOEUF, JOSEPH P.]
"Father Macheboeuf on the
Sandusky," Northwestern Ohio
Quarterly, v. 16 (1944), 45-
64. M 165
MACHEBOEUF, JOSEPH P.
"Letter dated Baltimore, May
23, 1868." Annals of the
Propagation of the Faith,
Baltimore, v. 29 (1868), 315-
319. M 166
MACHEBOEUF, JOSEPH P.
"Lettre de Mgr. Macheboeuf,
Vicaire Apostolique du Colorado
et Utah à MM. les Membres
des Conseils Centraux de
l'Oeuvre de la Propagation de la
Foi, Baltimore, le mai,
1868," Annales de la Propa-
gation de la Foi, v. 40 (1868),
475-481. M 167
McHUGH, SISTER ANTONIO.
"The Mendota Convent School,"
Acta et Dicta, v. 7 (1935),
47-55. M 168
McHUGH, GEORGE J. Political
Nativism in Saint Louis, 1840-
1857. MA thesis. Saint Louis
University. 1939. 172p.
M 169
McHUGH, H. Giant of the Western

Trail. New York: Benziger.
1958. 181p. illus. M 170
A Banner Book biography of
Father DeSmet.
McHUGH, SISTER M. ST.
JOACHIM. The Sisters,
Servants of the Immaculate
Heart of Mary (West Chester,
Pennsylvania) in the Diocese
of Harrisburg, 1866-1950. MA
thesis. Villanova University.
1953. 222p. M 171
McINNIS, SISTER PETER MARY.
Development of Catholic Edu-
cational Institutions through
the Sisters of the Holy Names
of Jesus and Mary in the
Seattle-Nesqually Diocese,
1880-1955. MA thesis.
Seattle University. 1955. v.
133p. M 172
McISAAC, CALIN H. Santa
Barbara Mission. Santa Bar-
bara. 1926. M 173
McINTOSH, SISTER MARIA
AUSTIN. The Organization of
the Confraternity of Christian
Doctrine in our Lady of Angels
Parish (Brooklyn), MA thesis.
St. John's University, N.Y.,
1941. mss. pp. M 174
McKENNA, BERNARD A. History
of the National Shrine. 1927-
1928. 2v. M 175
McKENNA, BERNARD A. The
Story of Holy Angels Parish,
Philadelphia, 1900-1950. Phila-
delphia. Jeffries and Manz.
1950. 305p. plate, ports.,
facsims. M 176
McKENNA, HORACE B. "Colored
Catholics in St. Mary's
County (Maryland)," Woodstock
Letters, v. 79 (1950), 55-78.
M 177
McKENNA, NORMAN. "The
Story of the A.C.T.U.," Cath-
olic World, v. 168 (1949),
453-459. M 178
McKENNA, STEPHEN. "Our
Lady's Bishop (Archbishop
William Gross--Savannah,
Georgia; Oregon)," Central
Blatt and Social Justice, v.

24 (1931), 53-55; 88-89, 129-132, 176-178, 212-214, 249-251, 286-287, 322-323.
M 179

McKEON, SISTER FRANCIS JOSEPH. Formation of the Catholic Total Abstinence Union of America. MA thesis. Catholic University. 1946. iii, 62, iv-xxvip.　　M 180

McKEOUGH, JAMES A. "Silver Anniversary of the Millet Cross," Woodstock Letters, v. 81 (1952), 135-150.　　M 181
Account of the observance of the twenty-fifth anniversary of the erection of the Cross at Fort Niagara, 1926 in honor of the French Jesuit missionary to the Indians who began his work in New York state in 1668.

MacKINNON, DONALD. "The Redemptorists and the Parish School," Social Justice Review, v. 50 (1957), 152-153.
M 182

McLAUGHLIN, J. FAIRFAX. "The Beginnings of Georgetown College," Catholic World, v. 46 (1888), 610-619.　　M 183

McLAUGHLIN, J. FAIRFAX. "Father George Fenwick, S.J.," United States Catholic Historical Magazine, v. 1 (1887), 392-406.　　M 184

McLAUGHLIN, SISTER RAYMOND. A History of State Legislation Affecting Private Elementary and Secondary Schools in the United States, 1870-1945. Washington. Catholic University. 1946. ix, 348p.　　M 185

MacLEOD, DONALD X. Devotion to the Blessed Virgin in North America. New York. 1866. 467p.　　M 186

MacLEOD, XAVIER DONALD. History of Roman Catholicism in North America. N.Y. Virtue and Yorston. 186(?). xxiii, 467p.　　M 187

McMAHON. The Sisters of St. Joseph of Carondelet, Arizona's Pioneer Religious Congregation, 1870-1890. MA thesis. Saint Louis University. 1952. 161p.
M 188

McMAHON, CHARLES A. "National Catholic Welfare Conference," Sign, v. 16 (1936), 91-93.　　M 189

McMAHON, FRANCIS E. "Orestes Brownson on Church and State," Theological Studies, v. 15 (1954), 175-228.
M 190
Well written and thoroughly documented study of the opinions of this controversial convert.

McMAHON, THOMAS J. "Our American Cardinals," United States Catholic Historical Society Records and Studies, v. 36 (1947), 1-16. ports.
M 191

McMASTER, RICHARD K. "Father Benedict Fenwick and the End of the Charleston Schism 1818-1820," St. Meinrad Essays, v. 12 (1959), 1-24.　　M 192

McMENAMIN, HUGH L. Pinnacled Glory of the West. Denver. 1912.　　M 193
Brochure issued for the dedication of the new cathedral in Denver; includes some information on the Church in Colorado.

McMENAMY, CLAIRE. "Our Lady of Guadalupe at Conejos, Colorado," Colorado Magazine, v. 17 (1940), 180-183.
M 194

McMURRY, VINCENT DE PAUL. The Catholic Church during the Reconstruction, 1865-1877. MA thesis. Catholic University. 1951. 254p.
M 195

McNAMARA, ROBERT. The American College in Rome. Rochester, New York. Christopher Press, 1957. 858p.
M 196

McNAMARA, ROBERT F. A Century of Grace: The History of St. Mary's Roman Catholic Parish, Corning, New York, 1848-1948. Corning, N.Y. St. Mary's Church. 1948. xviii, 283p. illus., ports. M 197

McNAMARA, ROBERT F. "Trusteeism in the Atlantic States," Catholic Historical Review, v. 30 (1944), 135-154. M 198

McNAMARA, WILLIAM. The Catholic Church on the Northern Indiana Frontier, 1789-1844. Washington. Catholic University. 1931. vii, 84p. M 199

McNAMEE, JOSEPH F. Sketches of the Pioneer Priest, Father Berry, Father Gallagher, Father Donnely, and other Priests and Incidents Connected with the History of Armagh Parish (Franklin Co., Mo.). Pacific, Mo. Plowman Press. 1928. 28p. illus., port. M 200

MacNEIL, NORMAN. "Historical Progress of the Church in Philadelphia," Catholic Historical Society of Philadelphia Records. v. 62 (1951), 15-21. M 201

McNEILL, C. J. "Fifty Years of Catholicity in Colorado," Ave Maria, v. 46 (1937), 225-227. M 202

McNULTY, AMBROSE. "Chapel of St. Paul, and Beginnings of the Catholic Church in Minnesota," Minnesota Historical Society Collections, v. 10, pt. 1 (1905), 233-245. M 203

McNULTY, AMBROSE. "The Chapel of St. Paul, the Cradle of the Church in Minnesota," Acta et Dicta, v. 1 (1907), 60-72. port. (Lucien Galtier). M 204

McNULTY, JOHN P. "Diocesan Priests in Florida's Beginnings," Catholic World, v. 162 (1946), 527-532. M 205

McQUADE, VINCENT A. The American Catholic Attitude on Child Labor Since 1891. Washington. Catholic University. 1938. ix, 205p. M 206

McROSKEY, RACINE. The Missions of California. San Francisco. Philopolis Press. 1914. 174p. incl. illus., plates, col. front., map. M 207

McSHERRY, WILLIAM. History of St. Aloysius Church of Littlestown, Pennsylvania. Gettysburg, Pa. J.E. Wible. 1893. 127p. M 208

McSHERRY, WILLIAM (comp.) Relatio Itineris in Marylandiam. Baltimore. Murphy. 1874. iv, 10-61, 62-128. M 209

McSORLEY, SISTER ANN NOREEN. Cultural Factors Due to French Catholic Influence in the Region around Detroit, 1608-1812. MA thesis. Marquette University. 1945. M 210

McSORLEY, JOSEPH. Father Hecker and His Friends. St. Louis. Herder. 1952. xv, 304p. illus. M 211

McSWEENEY, EDWARD F. "Judge William Gaston of North Carolina," United States Catholic Historical Society Records and Studies, v. 17 (1926), 172-188. M 212

McSWEENEY, EDWARD F. "A New York Pastor of the Latter Half of the Nineteenth Century," American Catholic Historical Society of Philadelphia Records, v. 19 (1908), 42-58. M 213

McSWEENY, EDWARD F.X. AND MARY M. MELINE. The Story of the Mountain. Emmitsburg, Md. Weekly Chronicle. 1911. 2v. fronts., ports., plates. M 214

McSWEENEY, THOMAS DENIS. Cathedral on California Street. Fresno. Academy of California Church History. 1952.

xi, 95p.   M 215
McSWEENEY, THOMAS D. St.
Mary's Cathedral: San Fran-
cisco's First Cathedral, 1854-
1885. MA thesis. University
of San Francisco. 1950.
105p. plates.   M 216
McTIGUE, SISTER MARY
XAVIER. History of Saint
Leo's Parish, Saint Louis, Mis-
souri, 1888-1950. MA thesis.
Saint Louis University. 1951.
134p.   M 217
McWILLIAMS, LeROY E. Parish
Priest. New York. McGraw
Hill. 1953. 250p. illus.
    M 218
Autobiography of Father Mc-
Williams, who was curate for
twenty years and pastor since
1938 of St. Michael's parish,
Jersey City, New Jersey.
Contains much information
on the daily life of the parish
priest, but the telling is not
enhanced by the attempt
at literary elegance.
MADAJ, M. J. "The Polish Im-
migrant and the Catholic
Church in America," Polish A-
merican Studies, v. 6 (1949),
1-8.   M 219
MADDEN, MARGARET. "Catholic
Women of Illinois," Illinois
Catholic Historical Review, v.
1 (1919), 286-293.   M 220
MADDEN, RICHARD CAIN.
Joseph Pierre Picot de Limöe-
lan de Cloriviere, 1768-1826.
MA thesis. Catholic Univer-
sity. 1938. 104p.   M 221
MADDOX, GAYNOR. "Joseph
Sadoc Alemany, O.P., Arch-
bishop of San Francisco," U-
nited States Catholic Historical
Society Records and Studies,
v. 8 (1915), 223-228. M 222
MADLEM, W. San Jose Mission.
San Antonio. Naylor. 1934.
23p. illus.   M 223
MADLON, DANIEL. "Father
Hoecken's Spiritual Grandchil-
dren and genealogies," South
Dakota Historical Collections,

v. 20 (1943), 232-265.
    M 224
MAES, CAMILLUS P. "Father
John Rivet, Missionary,"
American Ecclesiastical Re-
view, v. 35 (1906), 33-51,
113-123.   M 225
MAES, CAMILLUS P. "Flemish
Franciscan Missionaries in
North America (1674-1738),"
Catholic Historical Review,
v. 1 (1915), 13-16.   M 226
MAES, CAMILLUS P. "History
of the Catholic Church in
Monroe City and County,
Michigan," United States Cath-
olic Historical Magazine, v. 2
(1888), 113-152.   M 227
MAES, CAMILLUS. The Life of
Reverend Charles Nerinckx.
Cincinnati. Robert H. Clarke
and Co. 1880. xvii, 635p.
front. (port.)   M 228
MAGARET, HELENE. Fr. De
Smet: Pioneer Priest of the
Rockies. New York. Farrar
and Rinehart. 1940. 371p.
front. (port.)   M 229
MAGEVNEY, EUGENE. "An In-
teresting Myth. Letter dated
Marquette College, Milwaukee,
Wisconsin, November 26,
1902," Woodstock Letters, v.
31 (1902), 369-375. M 230
MAGRI, FRANCIS JOSEPH. The
Catholic Church in the City
and Diocese of Richmond.
Richmond. Whitter and Shep-
person. 1906. 150p. front.,
plates, ports.   M 231
MAGRI, FRANCIS JOSEPH.
"Catholicity in Virginia during
the Episcopate of Bishop Mc-
Gill (1850-1872)," Catholic
Historical Review, v. 2
(1917), 415-426.   M 232
MAGUIRE, J. J. "Religion in
the Catholic College," Commonweal, v. 67 (Jan. 31, 1958),
447-450.   M 233
MAGUIRE, N. T. "The Beginning and Progress of Catholicity in Washington, Wilkes
Co., Georgia," American Cath-

240

olic Historical Researches,
v. 11 (1894), 17-28.   M 234
MAGUIRE, WILLIAM P.A. Cath-
olic Secondary Education in
the Diocese of Brooklyn.
Washington. Catholic Univer-
sity. 1932. vii, 62p.   M 235
MAHAN, TERRANCE L. The
Fifth St. Ignatius Church in
San Francisco. MA thesis.
University of San Francisco.
1951. n.p.   M 236
MAHER, MARY GRATIA. Organi-
zation of Religious Instruction
in Catholic Colleges for
Women. Washington. Cath-
olic University. 1951. xi,
158p. tables.   M 237
MAHER, ZACHEUS JOSEPH.
"Black Robes and Brown in
California," Catholic World,
v. 101 (1915), 433-446.
                       M 238
MAHON, SISTER MIRIAM. Con-
tributions of the Sisters of
Charity to Catholic Education
in New Jersey. MA thesis.
Fordham University. 1936.
vi, 134p.   M 239
MAHON, P. J. AND J. M.
HAYES. Trials and triumphs
of the Catholic Church in A-
merica during Four Hundred
Years. Chicago. J. S. Hy-
land and Co. 1907. 2v. in 1.
front., ports., plates.
(1035p.)   M 240
MAHONEY, CHARLES J. The
Relation of the State to
Religious Education in Early
New York, 1633-1825. Wash-
ington. Catholic University.
1941. xiii, 225p.   M 241
MAHONY, DANIEL H. Historical
Sketches of Churches and In-
stitutions in Philadelphia. Phila-
delphia. D. Mahony. 1895.
                       M 242
MAHONY, THOMAS H. "A Legal
Inquiry on the Church-State
Problem in the U.S.A.," Cath-
olic Educational Review, v.
48 (1950), 75-95.   M 243
MAIGNEN, CHARLES. Etudes

sur l'Américanisme. Le
Père Hecker, Est-il un
Saint? Rome. Desclee.
Paris V. Retaux. 1899.
xxxi, 406p.   M 244
MAIGNEN, CHARLES. Father
Hecker: Is He a Saint? Lon-
don. Burns and Oates. 1898.
423p.   M 245
MAIGNEN, CHARLES. La
Vraie Situation du Catholicisme
aux Etats-Unis, et M. Ferdi-
nand Brunetière. Paris.
Lamuelle et Poisson. 1899.
19p.   M 246
MAINE, SISTER MARY
URSULA. A History of the
Missionary Servants of the
Most Blessed Trinity of Phila-
delphia. MA thesis. Villa-
nova University. 1953. 139p.
                       M 247
MAINE CATHOLIC HISTORICAL
MAGAZINE, v. 8 (1919),
71p. A collection of docu-
ments and other material re-
lating to the history of the
Church in Maine.   M 248
MAITRUGUES, J. B. "St.
Charles College, Grand
Coteau, La.," Woodstock
Letters, v. 5 (1876), 16-29.
                       M 249
MAIWORM, L. J. Dedication.
Sacred Heart Church and
School. (Chicago, Ill.) no
pl. no pub. 1927. plates,
ports.   M 250
MAKWIMIK, A. "The Second
Founder of the Polish Semi-
nary," Polish-American
Studies, v. 2 (1945), 29-33.
                       M 251
MALLET, EDMOND. "The Ori-
gin of the Flathead Mission of
the Rocky Mountains," Ameri-
can Catholic Historical Society
of Philadelphia Records, v. 2
(1886), 174-205.   M 252
MALLETT, EDMOND. "The
Origin of the Oregon Mission,"
United States Catholic Historical Magazine, v. 1 (1887),
7-20.   M 253

MALLON, EDWARD A. "American Catholic Historical Society of Philadelphia," American Catholic Historical Society of Philadelphia Records, v. 58 (1947), 245-255.   M 254

MALLON, EDWARD A. (ed.) "The First American Nuns. Biographic Notice of Mother Sainte Cecilia (Marie Anne Davis)," American Catholic Historical Society of Philadelphia Records, v. 60 (1949), 109-110.   M 255

MALLON, EDWARD A. (tr.) "The First American Nuns," American Catholic Historical Society of Philadelphia Records, v. 60 (1949), 56-57.   M 256

MALLON, EDWARD A. "Sisters of Charity, St. Joseph's Hospital (Philadelphia), 1859-1947," American Catholic Historical Society of Philadelphia Records, v. 68 (1947), 209-213.   M 257

MALLON, EDWARD A. "Some Catholic Anniversaries of 1949," American Catholic Historical Society of Philadelphia Records. v. 60 (1949), 118-121.   M 258

MALMARTEL, . "A Texas Missionary Trip," Annals of the Propagation of the Faith, Baltimore, v. 67 (1904), 131-138.   M 259

MALOOF, ALLEN. "Catholics of the Byzantine-Melkite Rite in the U.S.A.," Eastern Churches Quarterly, v. 9 (1951-52), 191-197, 261-265, 320-325, 359-365.   M 260

MALONEY, SISTER MARY XAVIER. Catholic Church in the District of Columbia, 1790-1886. MA thesis. Catholic University. 1938. 106p.   M 261

MALONEY, PAUL. "Celestine de la Hailandière," St. Meinrad Historical Essays, v. 3 (1934), 134-143.   M 262

MAN, ALBAN P. "The Church and the New York Draft Riots of 1863," Catholic Historical Society of Philadelphia Records, v. 62 (1951), 33-50.   M 263

MANCHESTER (DIOCESE) SYNOD, 1st, 1886. Constitutiones dioecesanae, a Dionysio Maria Bradley [ep.] in synodo dioecesana prima, habita in ecclesia cathedrali, Manchester, die IV mensis Novembris, 1886, latae et promulgatae. Manchester, N.H., Typis O. D. Kimball, 1886. 60p.   M 264

MANCI, V. L. "The Texas Cyclone. Letter dated Cuero, De Witt Co., Texas, November 30, 1875," Woodstock Letters, v. 5 (1876), 67-79.   M 265

MANDALARI, ALFONSO MARIA. "Altre Notizie Intorno all Missione," Lettere Edificanti Provincia Napolitana, (1911), 217-226.   M 266
A very good historical sketch of the New Mexico-Colorado Mission of the Neapolitan Jesuits.

[MANDALARI, ALFONSO MARIA.] "Extracts of a Letter from Pueblo, Colorado, dated Dec. 18th, 1877," Woodstock Letters, v. 7 (1878), 44-47.   M 267

MANHATTAN, AVRO. Dollar and the Vatican. London: Pioneer, 1956. 312p.   M 268

"MANHATTAN'S FRANCISCAN CENTENARY," Provincial Annals (Province of the Most Holy Name, O.F.M.), v. 4 (1943-1944), 226-233, 262-270, 360-369; v. 5 (1945-1946), 70-77, 123-128, 172-176.   M 269

MANLEY, D. "The Catholic Church and the Indians," Catholic World, v. 55 (1892), 473-481.   M 270

MANNIX, EDWARD J. The A-

merican Convert Movement.
New York. Devin-Adair Co.
1923. xiv, 150p. M 271

MANNIX, E. J. Psychology of
the American Convert Movement. MA thesis. Catholic
University. 1921. 125p.
M 272

MANNIX, MARGARET W. The
Contribution of Eusebia Francisco Kino, S. J., to the
Exploration and Civilization
of the American South-west.
MA thesis. Marquette University. 1941. M 273

MANNIX, MARY E. Memoirs of
Sister Louise. Boston. Angel
Guardian Press. 1907. 338p.
plates, ports. M 274

MANTHEY, SISTER ROSANA.
Missionary Activities among
the Menominee, 1846-1884.
MA thesis. Catholic University. 1955. 110p. M 275

MANUCY, ALBERT C. "Florida
in North Carolina Spanish
Records," Florida Historical
Quarterly, v. 25 (1947), 85-
87. M 276

MANZ, GEORGE JOSEPH (pub.)
The Catholic Church in the U-
nited States of North America.
Regensburg, Germany. 1864.
518p. M 277

[MARECHAL, AMBROSE.] "Diary
of Archbishop Marechal, 1818-
1825," American Catholic Historical Society of Philadelphia
Records, v. 11 (1900), 417-
454. M 278

MARECHAL, AMBROSE. "The
Diocese of Baltimore in 1818,"
Catholic Historical Review, v.
1 (1916), 437-453. M 279

MARECHAL, AMBROSE. "Letters
to Baron Hyde de Neuville Concerning the Two Large Paint-
ings and Bell Presented to the
Cathedral by the Sovereign of
France," Maryland History
Magazine, v. 34 (1940), 344-
348. M 280

MARGARET, HELENE. Giant in
the Wilderness. Milwaukee.

Bruce. 1952. vi, 200p.
M 281
A popularized biography of
Father Nerinckx, founder
of the Sisters of Loretto and
pioneer priest in Kentucky.

MARGUERITE-FELICIE, SISTER.
Revetues de Force. Worcester.
Caron Press. 1952. xvii,
213p. M 282
An account of the fifty years'
activity of the Daughters of
the Holy Ghost in America.

MARIA ALMA, SISTER. "Foundations of Catholic Sisterhoods
in the United States, 1850,"
American Catholic Historical
Society of Philadelphia Records, v. 52 (1941), 34-61,
174-184, 219-243; v. 53
(1942), 21-32, 96-110, 162-
178, 250-257; v. 54 (1943),
66-73, 135-146, 159-175.
M 283

MARIA ALMA, SISTER. "A
Sketch of the Work and His-
tory of the Sisters, Servants
of the Immaculate Heart of
Mary, 1845-1920," American
Catholic Historical Society of
Philadelphia Records, v. 31
(1920), 276-338. M 284

MARIA, DONA. "The Oldest
Parish Keeps Its Records,"
Columbia, v. 18 (June, 1939),
7, 21. illus. M 285

MARIANITE CENTENNIAL IN
LOUISIANA, 1848-1948. New
Orleans. Provincial House,
Holy Angels Academy. 1948.
330p. M 286

MARIE IGNATIUS, D. d. m.
"Notre Mission chez les
Japonais de San Francisco,"
Accle. Urundi. 19 (Accle-
Bruxelles 1950-51), 74-76.
M 287

MARIE KOSTKA, SISTER.
Sisters of St. Joseph of
Philadelphia. Westminster,
Md. 1950. xii, 380p. illus.
ports. M 288

MARIQUE, PIERRE. "Joseph
Picot Limöelan de la Clori-

243

viere," United States Catholic Historical Society Records and Studies, v. 8 (1915), 195-208. M 289

MARKLEY, WAYNE A. Father Gabriel Richard. His Life and Times. MA thesis. University of Detroit. 1935. 60p. M 290

MARKOE, LORENZO J. "The Founding of a Minnesota Parish," Messenger of the Sacred Heart, v. 35 (1900), 795-804. M 291

MARLING, JOSEPH M. "A Pioneer Priest of Western Missouri," American Ecclesiastical Review, v. 133 (1955), 361-369. M 292 Bernard Donnelly, who died in 1880.

MARQUETTE (DIOCESE). Statuta dioecesis marianopolitanae in Michigan. Detroiti, Ex typis J. Slater, 1863. 84p. M 293

MARQUETTE (DIOCESE) SYNOD, 2nd, 1905. Synodus dioecesana marianopol. et marquettensis secunda habita die 21 Julii anno domini 1905. A Friderico Eis, episcopo marianopol. et marquettensi. Techny, Ill. Printed by the Society of the Divine Work, 1906. 48p. M 294

"MARQUETTE COLLEGE," Woodstock Letters, v. 21 (1892), 55-62. M 295

MARRA, GUISEPPI. "Da Las Vegas," Lettere Edificanti Provincia Napolitana, (1905), 106-109. M 296

MARRA, GUISEPPI. "Dalla Nostra Missione," Lettere Edificanti Provincia Napolitana, (1911), 209-215. M 297 A letter dated "Las Vegas, Nuovo Messico, Stati Uniti d'America 2 Aprile, 1910," An historical sketch describing the work of Father Gasparri, the Revista Catolica, and the Schools of the New Mexico-Colorado Mission of the Neapolitan Jesuits, by the

acting superior of the mission. Next to Gasparri, Marra was the greatest of the members of the mission.

MARRA, GUISEPPI. "Lettera LXVIII," Lettere Edificanti Provincia Napolitana, ser. 6 (1889-1891), 162-163. M 298 Dated "Denver, Colo., Aprile, 1784." A summary of the question of a mission among the Moqui Indians.

MARRA, GUISEPPI. "Un Viaggio in America," Lettere Edificanti Provincia Napolitana, (1905), 95-106. M 299

MARRARO, HOWARD R. "The Closing of the American Diplomatic Mission to the Vatican and the Efforts to Revive It, 1868-1870," Catholic Historical Review, v. 33 (1948), 423-447. M 300

MARRARO, HOWARD R. "Italians in New York in the Eighteen-Fifties," New York History, v. 30 (1949), 181-203, 276-303. M 301

MARRARO, HOWARD A. "Italians in New York in the First Half of the Nineteenth Century," New York History, v. 26 (1945), 278-306. M 302

MARRARO, HOWARD A. "Rome and the Catholic Church in the Eighteenth-Century Magazines," Catholic Historical Review, v. 32 (1946), 157-189. M 303

MARSDEN, K. GERALD. "Father Marquette and the A.P.A.: An Incident in American Nativism," Catholic Historical Review, v. 46 (1960), 1-21. M 304 Controversy over placing of statue in National Capital.

MARSHALL, BRUCE. "The Church in America," Sign, v. 33 (1954), 11-13. M 305 A Scot looks at American Catholics and is much impressed by the outstanding devotion of the laity and the American nuns.

MARSHALL, CHARLES C. The Roman Catholic Church in the Modern State. New York. Dodd, Mead and Co. 1928. xiv, 350p. M 306

MARTIN, BERNARD LEE. Cincinnati in 1853, a Study in Bigotry. MA thesis. Xavier University (Cincinnati). 1950. 96p. M 307

MARTIN, D. B. "Father Allouez and the Fox River," Catholic World, v. 81 (1905), 192-207. M 308

MARTIN, ELLIS R. "St. Mary's of Sylvan," Michigan History, v. 40 (1959), 493-496. M 309
A Catholic church in Michigan in 1844.

MARTIN, FELIX. Life of Father Isaac Jogues. N. Y. Benziger 1885. 263p. M 310
Published originally in French 1873.

"MARTIN I. J. GRIFFIN," American Catholic Historical Researches, v. 24 (1907), 267-270. M 311

MARTIN, JOSEPH. "The Wisconsin Centennial and Catholic Contributions," Salesianum, v. 31 (1936), 107-112. M 312

MARTIN, SISTER M. AQUINATA. The Catholic Church on the Nebraska Frontier, 1854-1885. Washington. Catholic University. 1936. ix, 202p. M 313

MARTIN, SISTER MARY AQUINATA. Irish Catholic Colonization in the Diocese of Omaha, 1856-1890. MA thesis. University of Notre Dame. 1932. 117p. M 314

MARTIN, SISTER MARY STILLA. Some Missionary Activities of the Lake Superior Region of the United States. MA thesis. Marquette University. 1940. M 315

MARTIN, P. "Résumé des huit Années de la Mission Fondée par les Révérends Pères Bénédictins dans l'Etat de l'Indiana, Adressé par le R. P. Martin à Ses Supérieurs et Confrères de Notre Dame des Ermites en Suisse. Saint Meinrad (Indiana) le ler janvier 1861," Annales de la Propagation de la Foi, v. 33 (1861), 449-458. M 316

MARTIN, P. "Letter dated St. Meinrad (Ind.), Jan. 1, 1861," Annals of the Propagation of the Faith, Baltimore, v. 22 (1864), 351-357. M 317

MARTIN, PAUL REVERE. The First Cardinal of the West. Chicago. New World Pub. Co. 1934. 215p. illus., plate, ports. M 318

MARTINDALE, C. C. "The Paulist Anniversary," Dublin Review, v. 192 (1933), 221-232. M 319

MARTINEAU, ROLLIN. Colonization Project of Bishop Benedict Joseph Fenwick at Benedicat, Aroostook County, Maine. MA thesis. Catholic University. 1932. 38p. M 320

MARTINKUS, SISTER MARY SALESIA. Diplomatic Relations between the United States and the Vatican during the Civil War. MA thesis. Loyola University (Chicago). 1953. 64p. M 321

MARTIRE, HARRIETTE A. A History of Catholic Parochial Elementary Education in the Archdiocese of New York. Ph. D. thesis. Fordham University. 1955. iii, 357p. M 322

MARTY, MARTIN. Dr. Johann Martin Henni. New York. Benziger. 1888. vi, 321p. incl. front., illus. (incl. ports.) M 323

MARTY, MARTIN. "The Indian Problem and the Catholic Church," Catholic World, v. 48 (1889) 577-584. M 324

MARTY, MARTIN. Die katholische Kirche in den Vereinigten Staaten von Nord-Amerika dargestellt von einheimischen Schriftstellen. Regensburg. Marz. 1864. xvi, 518p. M 325

"MARTYROLOGIUM AMERICAN-UM," American Catholic Historical Researches, v. 23 (1906), 332. M 326

"MARTYROLOGIUM AMERICAN-UM," American Catholic Historical Researches, v. 27 (1907), 75-76. M 327

"MARTYRS OF THE COLORADO, 1781, AND THE IDENTIFICATION OF THE PLACE WHERE THEY DIED," United States Catholic Historical Magazine, v. 1 (1887), 319-328. M 328

MARX, JOSEPH AND BENJAMIN J. BLIED. "Joseph René Vilatte," Salesianum, v. 37 (1942), 1-8, 59-67, 113-120. variant title. M 329

MARX, JOSEPH AND BENJAMIN J. BLIED. "The Old Catholics in America," Salesianum, v. 36 (1941), 155-161. M 330

MARY AGNES, SISTER. A Souvenir of Mount St. Joseph's Ursuline Academy. "Maple Mount," Daviess County, Kentucky. Boston. Angel Guardian Press. 1907. 200p. front., plates, ports. M 331

MARY ALOYSIUS, SISTER. A Memoir. Mother Mary Chrysostom. New York. Kenedy. 1931. xiv, 152p. front., plates, ports., maps. M 332

MARY BARNABA, SISTER. A Diamond Crown for Christ the King. Glenn Riddle, Pa. Sisters of St. Francis, Convent of Our Lady of the Angels. 1930. xiv, 309p. front., plates, ports. M 333

MARY BONIFACE, SISTER. "The Establishment of the Catholic Hierarchy in the United States," American Catholic Historical Society of Philadelphia Records, v. 47 (1936), 281-291. M 334

MARY ELEANOR, MOTHER. "Mother Cornelia Connelly," Review for Religious, v. 15 (1956), 57-68. M 335
A brief, pious biographical sketch of the foundress of the Society of the Holy Child Jesus.

MARY ELEANOR, SISTER. On the King's Highway. New York. D. Appleton-Century Co. 1931. xi, 447p. illus. M 336

MARY FLORENCE, SISTER. The Sodality Movement in the United States, 1926-1936. St. Louis, Mo. The Queen's Work. 1939. 214p. incl. plate, maps. M 337

MARY IMMACULATA, SISTER. Our Kateri. New York. Benziger. 1937. xv, 129p. front. M 338

MARY JANET, SISTER. Catholic Secondary Education, a National Survey. Washington. N.C.W. C. 1949. xvi, 146p. illus. M 339

MARY KATHERINE, SISTER. The Duluth Catholic Public Schools. Washington. N.C.W. C. 1923. 47p. M 340

MARY LIGOURI, SISTER. "The Central-Verein, a Non-Institutional Social Control," American Catholic Sociological Review, v. 2 (1941), 153-158. M 341

MARY LOYOLA, SISTER. The American Occupation of New Mexico, 1821-1852. Albuquerque, N.M. University of New Mexico Press. 1939. viii, 166p. M 342

MARY LOYOLA, SISTER. "The American Occupation of New Mexico, 1821-1852," New Mexico Historical Review, v. 14 (1939), 34-75, 143-199, 230-286. M 343

MARY LUCY, SISTER. Origin, History and Present Activities of the Sisters of Notre Dame. MA thesis. University of

Notre Dame. 1926. n. p.
M 344

MARY MAUD, SISTER. History of the Catholic Church in the Diocese of Brooklyn. New York. Benziger. 1938. vii, 9-64p. incl. front. (port.) illus.
M 345

MARY ODILE, SISTER. The Life of the Very Reverend Monseignor William J. White. New York. Loughlin Bros. 1913. 171p. front., port.
M 346

MARY THECLA, MOTHER. Nojoshing. St. Francis, Wis. no pub. 1925.
M 347

MARY THEODORE, SISTER. Heralds of Christ the King. New York. Kenedy. 1939. xiv, 273p. front., plates, ports.
M 348

MARY THOMAS, SISTER. Apostle of the Valley. Fresno, Calif. Academy of California Church History. 1947. 137p. plates, ports., maps, facsims.
Daniel Francis Dade. M 349

MARY VERONICA, SISTER. Sisters of Mercy of Harrisburg. Philadelphia. Dolphin Press. 1939. 434p. M 350

MASON, EDWARD G. "Kaskaskia and Its Parish Records," Magazine of American History with Notes and Queries, v. 6 (1881), 151-182.
M 351

MASON, SISTER M. LIGOURI. Mother Magdalen Daemen, and Her Congregation Sisters of St. Francis. Buffalo, N.Y. Rauch and Stoeckl. 1935. 430p.
M 352

MASON, SISTER MARY PAUL. Church State Relationships in Education in Connecticut, 1633-1953. Washington. Catholic University. 1953. xxi, 324p.
M 353

"MASTER MIND IN THE FIELD OF NAVAHOANA," Social Justice Review, v. 42 (1949), 99.
M 354
Sketch of the life of Father

Bernard Haile, O.F.M., who spent fifty years among the Navaho; first publication 1910.

MASTERSON, PETER V. "The Rev. Edward Ignatius Devitt, S.J. (1840-1920)," American Catholic Historical Society of Philadelphia Records, v. 31 (1920), 261-275. M 355

MATHAESER, WILLIBALD. "Das Beneditenerkloster Atchison i. J. 1860," Central Blatt and Social Justice, v. 20 (1920), 357-358, 395-396, 410-411.
M 356

MATHAESER, P. WILLIBALD. Bonifaz Wimmer, O.S.B., und König Ludwig I von Bayern; Ihre Briefe als Beitrag zur Geschichte der katholischen Kirche und des Deutschtums in Vereinigten Staaten Nordamerikas. Munich. 1938. 200p.
M 357

MATHASER, WILLIBALD. "A Forgotten Benefactor of the Church in the U.S.," Central Blatt and Social Justice, v. 31 (1938), 277-279; (1939), 313-315, 348-351. M 358
An account of Rev. Joseph Ferdinand Müller of the Ludwig Missionsverein. The article includes information on the help given to the United States by this mission aid society.

MATHEW, FRANK J. Father Mathew. London. Cassell. 1890. 223p. M 359

MATIGNON, FRANCIS. "Boston's First Catholic Church. Letters of Matignon to Carroll," American Catholic Historical Society of Philadelphia Records, v. 15 (1904), 35-45. M 360

MATILDA, SISTER M. "Father Charles Nerinckx," Review for Religious, v. 16 (1957), 129-142. M 361
A brief biography of the founder of the Sisters of Loretto.

MATTHEWS, SISTER MARY
SEBASTIAN. The Sisters
of Saint Joseph of the Diocese
of Cleveland as a Teaching
Community. MA thesis. Uni-
versity of Notre Dame. 1933.
vi, 118p. diagrs.   M 362
MATTINGLY, SISTER RAMONA.
The Catholic Church on the
Kentucky Frontier, 1785-
1812. Washington. Catholic
University. 1937. viii, 235p.
fold. map.   M 363
MATTISON, RAY H. 'Indian
Missions and Missionaries on
the Upper Missouri to 1900,"
Nebraska History, v. 38
(1957), 127-154.   M 364
A general article on all
religions.
[MATZ, NICHOLAS C.] "Bischof
Matz über siene Stellung zu
Rev. Malone," Central Blatt
and Social Justice, v. 14
(1921), 264.   M 365
MATZ, NICHOLAS C. 'Estratti
du una Letter dell' Illmo, e
Revmo. Mons. N.C. Matz,
Vescovo di Denver, al Rev.
P. Provinciale," Lettere
Edificanti Provincia Napolitana,
ser. 8, n. 1 (1899), 69-72.
                           M 366
MAURY, REUBEN. Wars of the
Godly. New York. Robert M.
McBride. 1928. 318p.
plates.   M 367
Popular study of anti-Catholic
prejudice at the time of the
Al Smith campaign.
MAXWELL, JOSEPH. Fifty
Golden Years. Congregation of
the Holy Union of the Sacred
Hearts in the United States.
Paterson, N. J. St. Anthony
Guild Press. 1936. ix, 29p.
illus.   M 368
MAY, GEORGE S. (ed.) "The
Discovery of Father Marquette's
Grave at St. Ignace in 1877 as
Related by Father Edward
Jacker," Michigan History, v.
42 (1958), 267-287.   M 369
MAY, JOHN L. "A Great Ameri-

can Abbey," Priest, v. 13
(1957), 977-980.   M 370
A brief sketch of St.
John's Abbey, Collegeville,
Minnesota.
MAYNARD, THEODORE. The
Better Part. The Life of
Teresa Demjanvich. New
York. Macmillan. 1952.
276p.   M 371
The biography of a member
of the Sisters of Charity of
St. Elizabeth (New Jersey),
who remained in the Eastern
rite her entire life, 1901-
1927.
MAYNARD, THEODORE. A Fire
Was Lighted. The Life of
Rose Hawthorne Lathrop.
Milwaukee. Bruce. 1948. x,
443p. port.   M 372
MAYNARD, THEODORE. Orestes
Brownson, Yankee, Radical,
Catholic. New York. Mac-
millan. 1943. xvi, 456p.
front., port.   M 373
MAYNARD, THEODORE. Great
Catholics in American History.
New York. Doubleday, 1958.
261p.   M 374
Twenty-one biographical
sketches.
MAYNARD, THEODORE. The
Long Road of Father Serra.
New York. Appleton Century
Crofts. 1954. xvii, 297p.
                           M 375
MAYNARD, THEODORE. The
Reed and the Rock. New York.
Macmillan. 1942. xi, 273p.
front. (port.), plate, map.
                           M 376
A popular biography of the
first Bishop of Vincennes,
Simon Bruté (1834-1839).
MAYNARD, THEODORE. The
Story of American Catholicism.
New York. Macmillan. 1941.
xv, 694p.   M 377
MAYNARD, THEODORE. Too
Small a World: The Life of
Mother Cabrini. Milwaukee.
Bruce. 1945. xvi, 335p.
front., (port.)   M 378

MAYNARD, THEODORE. The
Spirit of American Cath-
olicism. New York. Appleton.
1953. 309p.   M 379
A series of essays on the
problems and work of the
Catholic Church in America.
Offers little of value and is
suspiciously close to hack
writing.
MAZELLA, CAMILLO. "Letter
dated Georgetown, 26 Avril,
1868," Etudes, v. 21 (1868),
134-135.   M 380
Describes the use of
churches as hospitals. Points
out that the Church of St.
Louis was not used, but a
building is erected as a
substitute.
MAZELLA, CAMILLO. "Lettera
LVIII," Lettere Edificanti Provincia Napolitana, ser. 1
(1875), 156.   M 381
Dated "Albuquerque Otobre,
1875." A general descrip-
tion of the work of the
Jesuits in the southwest by
the officially appointed
visitor to the New Mexico-
Colorado Mission.
MAZELLA, CAMILLO. "Lettera
LXI," Lettere Edificanti
Provincia Napolitana, ser. 2
(1876-1877), 163-165. Dated
"La Junta, Nuova Messice, 26
Luglio, 1878."   M 382
A report of his visit and
the question of a residence
or college in Denver.
MAZELLA, CAMILLO. "Lettera
LXIII," Lettere Edificanti
Provincia Napolitana, ser. 2
(1876-1877), 168-169. M 383
Dated "Las Vegas, 20 Agosto,
1878," Mentions the arrange-
ments with the Archbishop
of Santa Fe with regard to
the exercise of ecclesiastical
functions by the Jesuits. In
view of the later controversy
this is an important letter.
MAZELLA, CAMILLO. "Lettera
LXVI," Lettere Edificanti

Provincia Napolitana, ser. 2
(1876-1877), 172-174. M 384
MAZZUCHELLI, SAMUEL.
Memoirs Historical and
Edifying of a Missionary
Apostolic. Chicago. W. F.
Hall. 1915. xx, xxiii-xxxv,
375p. front. (port.), plate,
maps.   M 385
MEAD, SIDNEY E. 'Religion in
English America," The Amer-
icas, v. 14 (1958), 356-360.
  M 386
MEADE, SISTER AGNES DAVID.
Beginnings of the Sisters of
Saint Joseph in Boston. MA
thesis. Boston College. 1941.
ii, 57p.   M 387
MEAGER, GEORGE T. A
Century at St. Bernards.
Watertown, Wisconsin. The
Rectory. 1946. xii, 176p.
plate, ports.   M 388
MEAGHER, WALTER J. His-
tory of the College of Holy
Cross [Worcester, Mass.] Ph.
D. thesis. Fordham Univer-
sity. 1944. iv, 149p.
  M 389
MEAUX, VISCOUNT C. De. "A
Catholic Centennial in the
United States," Catholic World,
v. 51 (1890), 373-394.
  M 390
MEAUX, VISCOMTE De.
l'Eglise Catholique et la Liberté
aux Etats-Unis. Paris. Victor
Lecoffre. 1893. vi, 427p.
  M 391
MECHAM, J. LOYD. "The
Martyrdom of Father Juan de
Santa Maria," Catholic His-
torical Review, v. 6 (1920),
308-321.   M 392
MECHTILDE, MOTHER MARY.
Mother Mary Walburga,
S. H. C. J., 1837-1903.
Rosemount, Pa. Rosemount
College. 1949.   M 393
MECKEL, JOSEPH F. Geschichte
der St. Paul's Gemeinde.
Highland, Illinois, September,
1896. no pl. no pub. 242p.
plates, ports.   M 394

MECKLIN, JOHN MOFFATT.
The Ku Klux Klan: A Study
of the American Mind. New
York. Harcourt, Brace and
Co. 1924. 244p.   M 395
MEEHAN, THOMAS F. "Arch-
bishop Hughes and Mexico,"
United States Catholic His-
torical Society Records and
Studies, v. 19 (1929), 33-40.
                       M 396
MEEHAN, THOMAS F. "The
Batteries of Bigotry," Columbia,
v. 3 (Oct., 1923), 6, 21.
                       M 397
MEEHAN, THOMAS F. "Catholic
Navy Chaplains," United States
Catholic Historical Society
Records and Studies, v. 32
(1941), 104-110.   M 398
MEEHAN, THOMAS F. "Catholics
in the War with Mexico," U-
nited States Catholic Historical
Society Records and Studies,
v. 12 (1918), 39-65.   M 399
MEEHAN, THOMAS F. "Arch-
bishop Hughes and the Draft
Riots," Historical Records
and Studies. v. 1 pt. 2
(1900), 171-190.   M 400
MEEHAN, THOMAS F. "The
Centenary of American Catholic
Fiction," United States Catholic
Historical Society Records and
Studies, v. 19 (1929), 52-72.
                       M 401
A biographical sketch of Fr.
Charles Constantine Pisa and
his work--called the first A-
merican Catholic novelist;
born 1829; also criticism of
some early Catholic poetry.
A weak article.
MEEHAN, THOMAS F. "Early
Catholic Weeklies," United
States Catholic Historical
Society Records and Studies, v.
38 (1937), 237-255.   M 402
MEEHAN, THOMAS F. "The
First American Cardinal,"
Catholic World, v. 90 (1909),
807-815.   M 403
Cardinal McCloskey.
MEEHAN, THOMAS F. "The

First Catholic Daily," Ameri-
ca, v. 39 (1928), 155-156.
                       M 404
MEEHAN, THOMAS F. "First
Catholic Monthly Magazines,"
United States Catholic His-
torical Society Records and
Studies, v. 31 (1940), 137-
144.   M 405
MEEHAN, THOMAS F. "Jay's
Treaty and Tolerance,"
Columbia, v. 2 (June, 1922),
6-24.   M 406
MEEHAN, THOMAS F. "Lincoln
and American Catholics,"
Columbia, v. 2 (Feb., 1923),
5, 25.   M 407
MEEHAN, THOMAS F. "Lincoln's
Opinion of Catholics," United
States Catholic Historical
Society Records and Studies,
v. 16 (1924), 87-93.   M 408
MEEHAN, THOMAS F. "A
Link between East and West,"
Illinois Catholic Historical
Review, v. 2 (1920), 339-
347.   M 409
MEEHAN, THOMAS F. "Mission
Work among Colored Catholics,"
United States Catholic His-
torical Society Records and
Studies, v. 8 (1915), 116-
128.   M 410
MEEHAN, THOMAS F. "Our
First Native-born Priest,"
America, v. 52 (1934), 11.
                       M 411
MEEHAN, THOMAS F. "Pioneers
of the Catholic Press," A-
merica, v. 52 (1935), 549-
550.   M 412
MEEHAN, THOMAS F. Thomas
Maurice Mulry. New York.
Encyclopedia Press. 1917.
247p. front. (port.) M 413
MEEHAN, THOMAS F. "Two
Pioneer Russian Missionaries,"
United States Catholic Histori-
cal Society Records and
Studies, v. 19 (1929), 105-
109.   M 414
A brief account of Mother
Elizabeth Gallitzin, R.S.C.J.
of New York, who died

1843, and of Demetrius
Gallitzin.
MEEHAN, THOMAS F. "Very
Rev. Johann Stephen Raffeiner,
V.G.," United States Catholic
Historical Society Records and
Studies, v. 9 (1916), 161-
175. M 415
MEEHAN, THOMAS F. "When
the Layman Awoke," Columbia,
v. 1 (Oct., 1921), 10,
18. M 416
A study of Catholic lay action
in the United States before
the founding of the Knights of
Columbus.
MEHOK, CHARLES JOHN. William
Banks Rogers, S.J., Eighteenth
President of Saint Louis Uni-
versity, 1900-1908. MA
thesis. Saint Louis University.
1945. ii, 161p. M 417
MEHOK, WILLIAM J. "Survey
of Jesuit High Schools: Evalua-
tions: 1946-1952," Jesuit
Educational Quarterly, v. 14
(1952), 209-218. M 418
MEIER, JOSEPH H. "Miscellany:
The Official Catholic Direc-
tory," Catholic Historical Re-
view, v. 1 (1915), 299-304.
M 419
MEIGS, PEVERIL. Dominican Mis-
sion Frontier of Lower Califor-
nia. Berkeley. University of
California. 1935. vi, 231p.
incl. maps, plates, tables.
M 420
MEINBERG, CARL H. "The
Norse Church in Medieval A-
merica," Catholic Historical
Review, v. (1925), 179-
216. M 421
MEINDT, SISTER M. CONCESSA.
Père Gabriel Druillettes,
Missionary Extraordinary. MA
thesis. Duquesne University.
1950. iv, 53p. M 422
[MEITTINGER, GUSTAVE.] "A
German-American Army
Chaplain at Newport News in
the Civil War," Central Blatt
and Social Justice, v. 18
(1925), 413-416; v. 19 (1926),

52-55, 88-92, 161-163.
M 423
MÉLANCON, A. Liste des Mis-
sionnaires Jésuites, Nouvelle
France et Louisiane, Montréal.
no pub. 1929. M 424
MELINE, MARY M. "The
Beginnings of Mount St.
Mary's," Catholic World, v.
45 (1887), 690-697. M 425
MELLON, KNOX Jr. "Christian
Priber and the Jesuit Myth,"
South Carolina Historical
Magazine, v. 61 (1960), 75-
81. M 426
MELVILLE, ANNABELLE. Arch-
bishop John Carroll-Priest
and Patriot. Washington.
1953. 43p. port. M 427
A well written popular
brochure on the first Cath-
olic Bishop of the United
States.
MELVILLE, ANNABELLE M.
Elizabeth Bayley Seton, 1774-
1821. New York. Scribner.
1951. 428p. illus. M 428
A well documented life with
eight pages of bibliography.
MELVILLE, ANNABELLE M.
Jean Lefebvre de Cheverus,
1768-1826. Milwaukee. Bruce.
1959. xiv, 527p. M 429
Biography of the first Cath-
olic Bishop of Boston.
MELVILLE, ANNABELLE M.
John Carroll of Baltimore,
Founder of the American Cath-
olic Hierarchy. New York.
Scribners. 1955. ix, 338p.
M 430
An excellent and popularly
written character study of
the first Catholic bishop of
the United States.
MEMBER OF THE ORDER OF
MERCY. Catholic History of
Alabama and the Floridas.
New York. 1918. M 431
"MEMOIR CONCERNING THE
CHURCH OF LOUISIANA (1722-
1728), dated Nov. 21, 1728,"
American Catholic Historical
Researches, v. 22 (1905),

124-127.   M 432
MEMORIAL OF THE MOST REV-
EREND MICHAEL AUGUSTINE
CORRIGAN, THIRD ARCH-
BISHOP OF NEW YORK.
Joseph F. Mooney, comp. New
York. Cathedral Library As-
sociation. 1902. xii, 234p.
incl. front., plates, ports.
                           M 433
MEMORIAL VOLUME. A History
of the Third Plenary Council
of Baltimore, November 9 -
December 7, 1884. Baltimore.
John Murphy. 1885. 418p.
front., plates, ports.   M 434
MEMORIAL VOLUME OF THE
ONE HUNDREDTH ANNIVER-
SARY ... OF THE CHURCH
OF THE HOLY CROSS, BOS-
TON. Boston. New England
Catholic Historical Society.
1903. 137p. illus. (incl.
ports.)   M 435
MENG, JOHN J. "Abbé Bandol
in America," Catholic His-
torical Review, v. 20 (1934),
135-153.   M 436
MENG, JOHN J. "Cahenslyism:
the First Stage, 1883-1891,"
Catholic Historical Review,
v. 31 (1946), 389-413. M 437
MENG, JOHN J. "Cahenslyism:
the Second Chapter, 1891-
1910," Catholic Historical Re-
view, v. 32 (1946), 302-340.
                           M 438
MENG, JOHN J. "A Century of
American Catholicism as
Seen Through French Eyes,"
Catholic Historical Review,
v. 27 (1941), 39-68. M 439
MENG, JOHN J. "Growing
Pains in the American Church:
1890-1908," United States
Catholic Historical Society Records and Studies, v. 36
(1947), 17-67.   M 440
MENGARINI, GREGORY. "The
Rocky Mountains. Memoirs of
Fr. Gregory Mengarini," Wood-
stock Letters, v. 17 (1888),
298-309, v. 18 (1889), 25-43,
142-152.   M 441

MENTAG, JOHN V. Catholic
Spiritual Revivals, Parish Mis-
sions in the Midwest to 1865.
Ph.D. thesis. Loyola Univer-
sity (Chicago). 1957. 305p.
                           M 442
MERKLE, SISTER MARY WIN-
FRIED. Mother M. Bonaven-
ture (Eva Wagner) of the
School Sisters of Notre Dame
(1835-1908). MA thesis.
Saint Louis University. 1932.
120p.   M 443
MERRILL, WILLIAM S. The
Catholic Contributions to the
History of the Norse Discovery
of America. Catholic Histori-
cal Review. v. 14 (1928),
589-619.   M 444
MERRILL, WILLIAM STETSON.
"Claude Jean Allouez,---Jesuit
Pioneer Missionary," Illinois
Catholic Historical Review,
v. 5 (1922), 59-67.   M 445
MERRIMAN, ROBERT B. The
Rise of the Spanish Empire
in the Old World and the
New. New York. Macmillan.
1918-1934. 4 v. front.
(v. 4 facsim.), maps, geneal.
tables.   M 446
MERRITT, EDWARD PERCIVAL.
Sketches of the Three Earliest
Roman Catholic Priests in
Boston. Boston. The Author.
1923. 173-229p.   M 447
MESSMER, SEBASTIAN G. "The
Catholic Colonization Society,"
Salesianum, v. 7 (Apr., 1912),
36-44.   M 448
MESSMER, SEBASTIAN G. "The
Catholic Hospital Association,"
American Ecclesiastical Re-
view, v. 54 (1916), 385-
398.   M 449
MESSMER, SEBASTIAN G. "Chips
for a Kundig Block," Salesian-
um, v. 12 (July, 1917), 1-7,
(Jan., 1918), 1-26; v. 13
(Apr., 1918), 1-17, (July,
1918), 1-27; v. 14 (Oct.,
1918), 1-14, (Jan., 1919), 1-11,
(Apr., 1919), 1-23, (July,
1919), 1-28, (Oct., 1919),

1-14.   M 450

MESSMER, SEBASTIAN. "The Early Jesuit Missions in the Fox River Valley," Wisconsin Historical Society, Proceedings. 1899. 147-152.   M 451

MESSMER, SEBASTIAN G. "The Episcopal Ancestry of the Catholic Hierarchy in the United States," Catholic Historical Review, v. 2 (1917), 427-433.   M 452

MESSMER, SEBASTIAN G. "The Establishment of the Capuchin Order in the United States," United States Catholic Historical Society Records and Studies, v. 4 (1906), 54-91. illus., port., plate.   M 453

MESSMER, SEBASTIAN G. "The Reverend Florimond Joseph Bonduel, Wisconsin Pioneer Missionary," Salesianum, v. 19 (Apr., 1924), 1-16, (July, 1924), 1-21, (Oct., 1924), 1-26; v. 20 (Jan., 1925), 1-24.   M 454

MESSMER, SEBASTIAN G. "The Rev. Hercule Brassac," Catholic Historical Review, v. 3 (1918), 392-416.   M 455
Letters and excerpts of letters of Brassac to American Bishops 1818-1861. pp. 448-470.

MESSMER, SEBASTIAN G. "The Right of Instruction," American Ecclesiastical Review, v. 6 (1892), 104-118.   M 456

METZGER, CHARLES H. "Catholics in the Period of the American Revolution," American Catholic Historical Society of Philadelphia Records, v. 59 (1948), 195-219, 294-317.   M 457

METZGER, CHARLES H. "Chaplains in the American Revolution," Catholic Historical Review, v. 31 (1945), 31-79.   M 458

METZGER, CHARLES H. The Quebec Act. A Primary Cause of the American Revolution. New York. United States Catholic Historical Society. 1936. x, 223p.   M 459

METZGER, CHARLES H. "Sebastian Louis Meurin," Illinois Catholic Historical Review, v. 3 (1921), 241-259, 378-388; v. 4 (1921), 43-56.   M 460

METZGER, CHARLES H. "Some Catholic Tories in the American Revolution," Catholic Historical Review, v. 35 (1949), 276-300, v. 35 (1950), 408-427.   M 461

MICHAUD, M. History of the Catholic Church in New England. Boston. no pub. 1889. n.p.   M 462

"MICHIGAN. DETROIT COLLEGE. Letter dated Detroit, Mich., Oct. 5, 1890," Woodstock Letters, v. 19 (1890), 376-385.   M 463
An unsigned descriptive letter.

MICKLER, THOMAS ROGERO. The Catholic Church in the Southland. MA thesis. Georgetown University. 1923. 121p.   M 464

MIDDLETON, THOMAS COOKE. Catholic Periodicals Published in the United States...1809... 1892. Philadelphia. 1908. 24p.   M 465

MIDDLETON, THOMAS C. "The Church of St. Nicholas of Tolentine in Western Pennsylvania from 1820-1848," American Catholic Historical Researches, v. 3 (1887), 69-71.   M 466

MIDDLETON, THOMAS C. (ed.) "Documents Relating to the Appointment of Coadjutors of the Right Rev. John Carroll, First Bishop of Baltimore, of the Years 1793 and 1794," American Catholic Historical Researches, v. 5 (1888), 188-193.   M 467

MIDDLETON, THOMAS C. "An

Early Catholic Settlement
...St. James of Carthage,
N.Y., 1785-1818-1898," American Catholic Historical Society
of Philadelphia Records, v. 10
(1899), 17-77, 138-195.
M 468

MIDDLETON, THOMAS C. (ed.)
"The Gallitzin Memorandum
Book from 1804-1824," American Catholic Historical Society
of Philadelphia Records, v.
4 (1893), 1-36. M 469

MIDDLETON, THOMAS C. Historical Sketch of Villanova,
1842-1892. Villanova College,
Pa. no pl. no pub. 1893.
M 470

MIDDLETON, THOMAS C. "A
List of Catholic and Semi-
Catholic Periodicals Published
in the United States from the
Earliest Date down to the
Close of the Year 1892," American Catholic Historical
Society of Philadelphia Records, v. 4 (1893), 213-242,
v. 19 (19), 18-41. M 471

MIDDLETON, THOMAS C. "A
New Jersey Sea-Side Mission,"
American Catholic Historical
Society of Philadelphia Records,
v. 17 (1906), 67-85, 144-179.
M 472

MIDDLETON, THOMAS C. "St.
Augustine's Mortuary Chapel,
South Boston, and Its Founder
Rev. Philip Laricy, O.S.A.,"
American Catholic Historical
Researches, v. 3 (1887), 12-
18. M 473

MIDDLETON, THOMAS C. "Some
Memoirs of Our Lady's Shrine
at Chestnut Hill, Pa.," American Catholic Historical Society
of Philadelphia Records, v.
12 (1901), 11-40, 129-168.
257-293, 385-418. M 474

MIDDLETON, THOMAS C. "A
Typical Old-Time Country
Mission," American Catholic
Historical Society of Philadelphia Records, v. 19 (1908),
276-304, 361-384. M 475

The story of St. Paul's of
Mechanicville, N. Y.,
1829-1908.

MIDDLETON, THOMAS C. "The
Very Rev. T. J. Donoghoe,"
American Catholic Historical
Society of Philadelphia Records, v. 21 (1910), 69-90.
M 476

MIDEKE, SISTER MARY ALICIA.
Bishop Meerschaert, First
Bishop of Oklahoma, 1847-
1924. MA thesis. Catholic
University. 1950. 59p.
M 477

MIÉGE, JOHN B. "An Early
Episcopal Visitation of Colorado," Mid-America, v. 7
(1936), 266-271. M 478

MIÉGE, JOHN B. "Lettre de
Mgr. Jean-Baptiste Miége de
la Compa de Jésus, Vicaire
Apostolique de l'Est des
Montagnes-Rocheuses, au R.
P. Général de la Companie de
Jésus. St. Marie des Potowatomies, ler janvier, 1852,"
Annales de la Propagation de
la Foi, v. 24 (1852), 433-
436. M 479

MIHANOVICH, CLEMENT S.
"Catholic Population Trends in
America," American Ecclesiastical Review, v. 119 (1948),
12-18. M 480

MILDRED, SISTER M. M.
"James Alphonsus McMaster,
Pioneer Catholic Journalist
of the United States," American Catholic Historical Society
of Philadelphia Records, v.
46 (1935), 1-21. M 481

MILES, THOMAS. "St. Joseph's
College, from 1861-1868,"
Woodstock Letters, v. 26
(1897), 105-108. M 482
Bardstown, Ky.

[MILET, PETER.] "Father
Milet's Captivity among the
Oneida Indians, 1689-1694,"
United States Catholic Historical Magazine, v. 2 (1888),
183-198. M 483

MILHAVEN, J. G. "Sociological

Soundings of U. S. Catholicism," America, v. 93 (1955), 123-125. M 484

MILLER, LEO FRANCIS, ET AL. Monsignor Joseph Jessing (1836-1899), Founder of the Pontifical College Josephinium. Columbus, O. Carroll Press. 1936. xi, 413p. front., plates, ports., facsims., maps. M 485

MILLER, SISTER MARY JANET. General Education in the American Secondary School. Washington. Catholic University. 1952. xxiii, 165p. illus. M 486

MILLER, NORBERT H. Pioneer Capuchin Missionaries in the United States, 1784-1816. MA thesis. Catholic University. 1930. 94p. M 487

MILLER, NORBERT H. Pioneer Capuchin Missionaries in the United States, 1784-1816. New York. Joseph F. Wagner. 1932. Franciscan Studies, no. 10 (1932). M 488

MILLER, NORBERT H. "Pioneer Capuchin Missionaries in the United States," United States Catholic Historical Society Records and Studies, v. 21 (1932), 170-234. M 489

MILLER, W. T. "From Small Beginnings," Columbia, v. 17 (Sept., 1937), 18-19, 23. M 490

MILLS, HAZEL. "Father Jacobo Sedelmayr, S. J.," Arizona Historical Review, v. 7 (1936), 3-18. M 491

MILWAUKEE (DIOCESE) SYNOD, 1st, 1847. Constitutiones in synodo dioecesana milwauchiensi prima latae die 20 Junii 1847 et recensione a S. Sede clementissime facta die lma Augusti 1853 promulgatae a Joanne Martino Henni [ep.] Additis statutis recentioribus. Milwauchiae, P. V. Deuster, 1858. 10p. M 492

MILWAUKEE (ARCHDIOCESE) PROVINCIAL COUNCIL, 1st,

1886. Acta et decreta concilii provincialis milwaukiensis primi. A. D. MDCCCLXXXVI. Praeside Michaele Heiss, archiepiscopo Milwaukiensi. Milwaukiae, Hoffman fratres, 1888. 1p. 1., [3]-52p., 1 1. M 493

MILWAUKEE. Acta et Decreta Concilii Provincialis Milwaukiensis Primi, A.D. MDCCCLXXXVI. Praeside Illmo ac Rmo Michaele Heiss, Archiepiscopo Milwaukiensis. Milwaukee, Hoffmann Bros. 1888. 53p. M 494

MINAHAN, SISTER MARY CANISIUS. "James A. McMaster: a Pioneer Catholic Journalist," American Catholic Historical Society of Philadelphia Records, v. 47 (1936), 87-131. M 495

MINASI, ANTONIO. "Lettera XVIII," Lettere Edificanti Provincia Napolitana, ser. 2 (1876-1877), 76-78. M 496 Dated "Conejos, Colorado, Decembre, 1876." Contains some information on the Penitentes.

MINASI, ANTONIO. "Lettera XLV," Lettere Edificanti Provincia Napolitana, ser. 2 (1876-1877), 134-155. M 497 Dated "United States, Las Vegas, N. M., Maggio 1878." Mentions the founding of the Revista Catolica, and the trouble with Governor Axtell of New Mexico over the school charter.

MINASI, ANTONIO. "Lettera LXIX," Lettere Edificanti Provincia Napolitana, ser. 2 (1876-1877), 179-180. M 498 Dated "Las Vegas, N.M. 5 Gennaio, 1879." Contains a description of Las Vegas College.

MINDRUP, THOMAS. "Catholicism in Indiana before 1834," St. Meinrad Historical Essays, v. 3 (1934), 102-111. M 499

MINOGUE, ANNA C. Loretto Annals of the Century. New York. America Press. 1912. xii, 252p. front., plates, ports., facsims. M 500

(MINOGUE, ANNA C.) Pages from a Hundred Years of Dominican History. New York. Pustet. 1921. 291p. ports., illus. M 501

MINOGUE, ANNA C. The Story of Santa Maria Institute. Cincinnati. Santa Maria Institute. 1922. 174p. plates, ports. M 502

MINOTTI, GUISEPPI M. "Collegio di Denver," Lettere Edificanti Provincia Napolitana, (1911), 226-238. M 503
A letter to the Jesuit Provincial of Naples dated "Santa Cueva, Spagna, 4 Novembre, 1909." Gives a detailed account of the activities of the Jesuit College in Denver.

"MISCELLANEOUS EXCERPTS FROM THE BALTIMORE ARCHIVES," American Catholic Historical Society of Philadelphia Records, v. 21 (1910), 180-200. M 504

"MISCELLANY: THE STORY OF A FAILURE: The Ohio Valley Catholic Historical Society," Catholic Historical Review, v. 1 (1916), 435-438. M 505

"MISSION IN FELSENGEBIRGE, Die Katholischen Missionen, v. 21 (1884), 42-46, 154-156- M 506

"MISSION OF CINCINNATI, 1837," American Catholic Historical Researches, v. 8 (1891), 171-174. M 507

"MISSION OF THE UNITED STATES IN 1838," American Catholic Historical Researches, v. 10 (1891), 161-167. M 508

"MISSIONARY SERVANTS OF THE MOST BLESSED TRINITY," Catholic Charities Review, v. 6 (1922), 193-196. M 509

MISSIONARY SISTERS OF THE

HOLY GHOST. Fifty Years in the United States. Techny, Ill. Holy Ghost Convent. 1952. n.p. M 510

MISSIONE DELLA PROVINCIA TORINESE DELLA COMPAGNIE DI GESU NELLE MONTAGNE ROCCIOSE DELLA AMERICA SETTENTRIONALE LETTERE DEI P.P. MISSIONARI. Torino. Guilio Speirani E. Figli. 1887. 97p. M 511

"DIE MISSIONEN DER BENEDIKTINER IM INDIANER-TERRITORIUM." Die Katholischen Missionen, v. 21 (1893), p. 1 ff. M 512

MISSIONI DEI PADRI DELLA COMPAGNIA DI GESU DELLA PROVINCIA DI TORINO AMERICA SETTENTRIONALE. I. Missione Della California (Stati Unite) Torino. Derossi. 1898. 47p. M 513

II. MISSIONI [Ut supra] II. Missione Delle Montagne Rocciose (Stati Uniti) Oregon, Washington, Idaho, Montana, Wyoming. Torino [ut supra] 1898, 51p. M 514

MISSIONI CATTOLICHE IV Antiche Missioni Dei P.P. Della Compagnia Di Gesù Nell'America Settentrionale et Territorio degli Stati Uniti 1613. 1892. Torino. G. Derossi. 1898. 27p. M 515

(MISSIONS D'AMÉRIQUE). "Montagnes Rocheuses," Annales de la Propagation de la Foi, v. 41 (1869), 374-384. M 516
Sketch of six missions of the Jesuits of the Turin Province in the Rocky Mountains.

(MISSIONS D'AMÉRIQUE). "Montagnes Rocheuses," Annales de la Propagation de la Foi, v. 45 (1873), 350-370. M 517
Death of De Smet, and news of the Rocky Mountain missions.

(MISSIONS DES ETATS-UNIS.) "Consolations et Souffrances de

l'Eglise aux Etats-Unis Pendant la Guerre Civile," Annales de la Propagation de la Foi, v. 36 (1864), 458-467.   M 518

"MISSIONS IN MAINE FROM 1613 TO 1854," Catholic World, v. 22 (1876), 666-677.   M 519

"MISSIONS OF THE ROCKY MOUNTAINS IN 1881," Woodstock Letters, v. 11 (1882), 43-56.   M 520

"MISSOURI--THE FIRST MISSION FROM MARYLAND," Woodstock Letters, v. 14 (1885), 305-316.   M 521

MITCHELL, HUDSON. "Virgil Horace Barber," Woodstock Letters, v. 79 (1950), 297-334.   M 522

MITCHELL, JAMES H. Golden Jubilee of Bishop Loughlin. Brooklyn. 1891.   M 523

"MITTEILUNGEN ZUM LEBEN DES PIONEER-PRIESTERS J. FERNEDING." Central Blatt and Social Justice, v. 13 (1921), 344.   M 524

MOAL-IOSA (pseud.) Franciscan Missionary Sisters of the Sacred Heart in the United States, 1865-1926. Peekskill, N.Y. Mount St. Francis. 1927. xi, 228p. plates, ports.   M 525

MOBILE (DIOCESE) SYNOD, 1st, 1835. Decreta synodi mobiliensis primae, die 19a Januarii 1835. congregatae. Notre Dame, Indiana, University press, 1890. 1 p.1., 4 p. The synod was held at Spring Hill, p. [1].   M 526

MOBILE (DIOCESE) SYNOD, 1st, 1861. Statuta synodi mobiliensis primae, mense Novembris, anno domini 1861 celebrata. Montgomery, Ala., Montgomery advertiser book and job office, 1862. 1 p. 1., 16p.   M 527

MOBILE, ALA. (DIOCESE) SYNOD, 2nd, 1888. Synodus mobiliensis secunda, mense

Augusti A.D. 1888, celebrata, a Jeremia O'Sullivan, episcopo mobiliensi, Mobile, Ala., Daily register print., 1888. 1 p. 1., 30p.   M 528

MOBILE (DIOCESE) SYNOD, 3rd, 1921. Decrete synodi dioecesanae mobiliensis tertiae, die 24 mensis Junii 1921 in ecclesia Sancti Josephi apud Spring Hill habitae ab Eduardo Patritio Allen [ep.] Mobile, Patterson printing co. [n.d.] 59p.   M 529

MODE, PETER G. Sourcebook and Bibliographical Guide for American Church History. Menasha, Wisconsin. George Banta Pub. Co. 1921. xxiv, 735p.   M 530

MOEDER, JOHN M. Early Catholicity in Kansas and History of the Diocese of Wichita. Wichita. Diocesan Chancery Office. 1937. xii, 200p. illus.   M 531

MOFFAT, SISTER M. EULALIA TERESA. Charles Constantine Pise, 1801-1866. MA thesis. Catholic University. 1930. 65p.   M 532

MOFFATT, SISTER M. EULALIA TERESA. "Charles Constantine Pise, 1801-1866," United States Catholic Historical Society Records and Studies, v. 20 (1931), 64-98. M 533

MOLINA, RODERICK. "Father Atanasio Lopez, O.F.M. (1876-1944)," Americas, v. 1 (1945), 486-489.   M 534

MOLLITOR, SABINUS. "Franciscan Historical Bibliography," Franciscan Education Conference, v. 4 (1922), 158-167.   M 535

MOLYNEUX, ROBERT. "Letter to John Carroll dated Philadelphia, April 23, 1785," Woodstock Letters, v. 15 (1886), 192-193.   M 536

MOLYNEUX, ROBERT. "Letter to John Carroll dated Philadelphia, dated June 18, 1875,"

Woodstock Letters, v. 15
(1886), 193-194.   M 537
[MOLYNEUX, ROBERT.] "Letters from Rev. Robr. Molyneux
to Rev. John Carroll, 1784-
1805," from the Baltimore
Archives," American Catholic
Historical Researches, v. 29
(1912), 267-268.   M 538
MONAGHAN, JOAN MARIE. Catholic Poetry in America, 1943-
1953; Index to Intellectual History. MA thesis. Georgetown University. 1954. 102p.
M 539
MONDESIR, EDOUARD DE.
Souvenir d'Edouard de Mondésir. ed. by Gilbert Chinard.
Baltimore. Johns Hopkins
Press. 1942. 60p.   M 540
MONICA, SISTER. Cross in the
Wilderness, a Biography of
Pioneer Ohio. London. Longmans. 1930. 290p. front.,
plates, ports., facsims. M 541
A popular history of the
Brown County Ursulines
beginning 1845. A frustrating book, or how history
should not be written.
MONTENARELLI, GUISEPPI M.
"Lettera LXXCII," Lettere
Edificanti Provincia Napolitana,
ser. 3 (1879-1880), 183-
184.   M 542
Dated "Isleta 14 Aprile,
1882," Description of a mission given at Las Gruces
during February, 1882.
MONTGOMERY, FRANCIS E.
History of St. Mary's Industrial
School for Boys. MA thesis.
Catholic University. 1932.
69p.   M 543
MONTEREY-LOS ANGELES,
CALIF. (DIOCESE) SYNOD,
4th, 1889. Constitutiones latae
et promulgatae a Francisco
Mora, episcopo montereyensi
et angelorum, in synodo 4.
diocesana. Habita in ecclesia
Sti. Vincentii a Paulo, in
civitate Angelorum diebus 30
et 31, mensis Julii, A.D.,

1889. Los Angeles, Ex typographia California Catholic,
1889. 47 [1] p.   M 544
Book preceded by the first
19 p. of this same book.
Imperfect copy.
MONTEREY-FRESNO, CALIF.
(DIOCESE) SYNOD, 1st., 1929.
Statuta dioecesis montereyensis-
fresnensis a Ioanne Bernardo
MacGinley eiusdem dioecesis
episcopo in prima synodo
dioecesana diebus XXIX et
XXX mensis Octobris, anni
MCMXXIX habita in ecclesia
cathedrali Ss. Ioannis Baptistae
et Ioannis Evangelistae Fresni
in California lata et promulgata.
Fresni, Sumptibus Saint Columbia guild [n.d.] 96p. M 545
MONTGOMERY, ROSS GORDEN,
WALSON SMITH, AND JOHN
OTIS BREW. Franciscan
Awatovi. Reports of the
Awatovi Expedition, Peabody
Museum of America Archaeology and Ethnology, Harvard
University. Cambridge.
Peabody Museum. xxiv,
361p.   M 546
MOONEY, JOHN A. "Our Recent American Catholic
Congress and Its Significance,"
American Catholic Quarterly
Review, v. 15 (1890), 150-
169.   M 547
MOORE, SISTER ALICE JOSEPH.
"Catholic College Student
Retention in the United States,"
Catholic University of America Educational Research Monographs, v. 20 (1957), 1-
156.   M 548
A study of the factors contributing to the holding
power of Catholic women's
colleges.
MOORE, CLARA B. St. Mary's
Roman Catholic Church,
Clinton, N.Y. Utica. Dodge
Print. 31p. illus.   M 549
MOORE, EDMUND A. A Catholic Runs for President. New
York. Ronald. 1956.

220p.   M 550
An account of the campaign
of 1928.
MOORE, JOHN J. "California.
Letter dated Santa Clara Col-
lege, Santa Clara, California,
August 15, 1888," Woodstock
Letters, v. 17 (1888), 329-
335.   M 551
MOORE, PAUL D. A History
of the Catholic Church in
Grinell, Iowa. Grinell,
Iowa. Herald-Register. n.d.
54p. illus., plates, ads.
              M 552
MOORE, STEPHEN N. History
of Holy Trinity Parish, Bloom-
ington, Illinois.   M 553
MOOSMÜLLER, OSWALD. Boni-
faz Wimmer. New York.
Benziger. 1891. x, 263p.
incl. front. (port.), illus.
              M 554
MOOSMÜLLER, OSWALD. St.
Vincenz in Pennsylvanian. New
York. Pustet. 1871. ii, 384p.
illus., 201p. (mounted photo-
graphs and plans.)   M 555
MORAN, DENIS M. "Anti-Cath-
olicism in Early Maryland
Politics; the Puritan Influence,"
American Catholic Historical
Society of Philadelphia Re-
cords, v. 61 (1950), 139-
154, v. 61 (1950), 213-235.
variant title.   M 556
MORAN, MICHAEL. Writings of
Francis Patrick Kenrick, Arch-
bishop of Baltimore, 1797-
1866. MA thesis. Catholic
University. n.d. 40p. M 557
MORAN, MICHAEL. "The
Writings of Francis Patrick
Kenrick, Archbishop of Balti-
more (1797-1863)," American
Catholic Historical Society of
Philadelphia Records, v. 41
(1930), 230-261.   M 558
MOREAU, M.C. Les Prêtres
Français Émigrés aux États-
Unis. Paris. Charles
Doumol. 1856. 520p. M 559
MORFI, JUAN DE. Diario Auto-
grafo de Padre Morfi a las

Missiones de Texas y Nuevo
Mexico en 1777. Documentor
para la Historic de Mexico,
3d series, v. 1. 290 leaves.
              M 560
MORFI, JUAN AGUSTIN. His-
tory of Texas, 1673-1779.
Tr. and annot. by C.E.
Castaneda. Albuquerque.
Quivira Society. 1935. 2v.
iv plates (incl. facsims.),
fold map.   M 561
MORGAN, W. D. "Through
Penitente Land with a Leica
Camera," Photo-Era, v. 62
(1929), 65-73. illus., map.
              M 562
MORIARTY, D. W. "St.
Stephan's Mission, Wyoming,"
Illinois Catholic Historical
Review, v. 9 (1926), 18-20.
              M 563
MORILLO, A. "Indian Missions.
Nez Perce Mission. Extract
from a Letter to the Superior
of the Mission," Woodstock
Letters, v. 12 (1883), 56-
58.   M 564
MORILLO, A. "Indian Missions.
The Nez Perce. Letter
dated Lapwai, Idaho Territory,
Jany. 1883," Woodstock Let-
ters, v. 13 (1884), 14-16.
              M 565
MORILLO, A. "Rocky Mountain
Missions. Letter dated
Lapwai, Idaho, Ty., Jany.
2nd, 1883," Woodstock Letters,
v. 12 (1883), 330-332.
              M 566
MORONEY, T. B. "The Condi-
tion of Catholic Colored Mis-
sion Work in the United
States," American Ecclesias-
tical Review, v. 61 (1919),
640-648.   M 567
MORRIS, SISTER MARY MER-
CEDES. The Sisters of
Mercy of Oklahoma, 1884-
1944. MA thesis. Catholic
University. 1947. 71p.
              M 568
MORRIS, WILLIAM S. The
Seminary Movement in the

United States. Projects, Foundations and Early Development, 1833-1866. Washington. Catholic University. 1932. vii, 119p.   M 569

MORRISON, JOHN L. "American Catholics and the Crusade Against Evolution," American Catholic Historical Society of Philadelphia Records, v. 64 (1953), 59-71.   M 570
A well written and documented study of the activity of Catholics during the Evolution controversy of the 1920's.

MORROW, SISTER MARY CLAVER. Bishop A.M.A. Blanchet and the Oblates of Mary Immaculate. MA thesis. Seattle University. 1956. v, 94p.   M 571

MORTON, SISTER M. ROSANA. Catholic Action in the Civil War. MA thesis. Villanova University. 1940. 106p.   M 572

MOTHER M. OF OUR LADY OF THE GOOD SHEPHERD. "A Visit to Our Lady of the Way School for Girls," Catholic Charities, v. 40 (1956), 13-16.   M 573
A description of the school at Jamaica Plain, Mass.

MOTHER THERESE AND THE CARMEL OF ALLENTOWN. Allentown, Pennsylvania. Carmel of St. Therese. 1949. xxvii, 217p.   M 574

"MOUNT ST. MARY'S SEMINARY OF THE WEST (CINCINNATI)," American Ecclesiastical Review, v. 18 (1898), 561-578. M 575

MOUSEL, SISTER MARY EUNICE. They Have Taken Root. New York. Bookman's Assoc. 1954. 384p.   M 576
The third attempt to write a history of the Sisters of the Third Order of St. Francis of the Holy Family (Dubuque, Ia.)

MOYNIHAN, HUMPHREY. "Archbishop Ireland," Acta et Dicta, v. 6 (1933), 12-34.   M 577

MOYNIHAN, HUMPHREY. "Archbishop Ireland," Catholic World, v. 108 (1918), 194-205.   M 578

MOYNIHAN, HUMPHREY. "Archbishop Ireland's Colonies," Acta et Dicta, v. 6 (1934), 212-231.   M 579

MOYNIHAN, JAMES H. The Life of Archbishop John Ireland. New York. Harpers. 1953. xii, 411p. ports., plates.   M 580
A highly laudatory biography of the great Archbishop of St. Paul.

MUELLER, JOSEPH. "Letter to Bishop Henni, dated July 6, 1844," The Salesianum, v. 22 (1947), 2-3.   M 581
A protest against begging bishops.

[MUELLER, JOSEPH P.] "Fr. Francis Xavier Weninger, S. J.," Central Blatt and Social Justice, v. 20 (1927), 88-89, 135-137, 179-180, 250-251, 287-288.   M 582

MUG, SISTER MARY THEODOSIA (ed.) Journals and Letters of Mother Theodore Guérin. St. Mary of the Woods, Ind. Providence Press. 1937. xxviii, 452p.   M 583

[MUG], SISTER MARY THEODOSIA. Life and Letters of Sister Francis Xavier. St. Mary of the Woods. Providence Press. 1934.   M 584

MUG, MARY THEODOSIA. Life and Work of Mother Theodore Guérin. New York. Benziger. 1904. xxvi, 15-499p. M 585

MUGGLEBEE, RUTH. Father Coughlin of the Shrine of the Little Flower. Boston. L.C. Page and Co. 1933. xii, 321p. front., plates, ports.   M 586

MULCAHY, GEORGE. "Catholic Background in Lewisburg, Union County, Pennsylvania,"

American Catholic Historical Society of Philadelphia Records, v. 61 (1950), 98-100.   M 587

MULHANE, L. W. "The Second Church in Ohio. St. Luke's Danville, Knox Co., Columbus Diocese," American Catholic Historical Researches, v. 13 (1896), 126-134.   M 588

MULHERIN, SISTER MARY JEANE. The First Years of the Catholic Layman's Association of Georgia, 1916-1921. MA thesis. Catholic University. 1954. 125p.   M 589

MULKERINS, THOMAS M. The History of Holy Family Parish (Chicago). no pl. no pub. 1923? 964p. illus., plates, ports.   M 590

MULLANEY, THOMAS W. Four Score Years: A contribution to the History of the Catholic Germans in Rochester. Rochester, N.Y., 1916. 207p. plates, ports.   M 591

MULLANY, KATHERINE F. Catholic Pittsfield and Berkshire. Pittsfield, Mass. Sun Printing Co. 1897-1924. 2v. front., plates, ports., illus.   M 592

MULLEN, SISTER FRANCIS CHARLES. Catholic Attitudes Towards Woodrow Wilson. MA thesis. Boston College. 1960. 138p.   M 593

MULLER, SERAPHIN. "The Apostle of California," Thought, v. 9 (1934/35), 458-476.   M 594

MULLIN, FRANCIS A. "The Chronicle of New Melleray Abbey," Iowa Catholic Historical Review, v. 6 (Apr., 1933), 14-20; v. 7 (June, 1934), 23-30.   M 595

MULLIN, FRANCIS A. "Father DeSmet and the Pottawatamie Indian Mission," Iowa Journal of History and Politics, v. 23 (1935), 192-216.   M 596

MULRENAN, PATRICK. A Brief Historical Sketch of the Catholic Church on Long Island. New York. O'Shea. 1871. 130p.   M 597

MULRY, GEORGE A. "Pictures of Missionary Life in Charles County, Maryland," United States Catholic Historical Magazine, v. 4 (1891-1892), 269-289.   M 598

MULVANEY, BERNARD G. "Catholic Population Revealed in Catholic Baptisms," American Ecclesiastical Review, v. 111 (1955), 183-193.   M 599
    Another attempt at statistical studies.

MULVEY, SISTER MARY DORIS. French Catholic Missionaries in the Present United States (1604-1791). Washington. Catholic University. 1936. ix, 158p.   M 600

MUNDIE, CATHERINE ELIZABETH. Diocesan Organization of Parochial Schools: Studies in Catholic Educational History of the United States. Ph. D. thesis. Marquette University. 1936.   M 601

MUNICH, AUSTIN F. Beginnings of Roman Catholicism in Connecticut. New Haven. Yale. 1935. 31p.   M 602

MUNTSCH, ALBERT. "Catholic Settlement Work in St. Louis," Central Blatt and Social Justice, v. 4 (1911), 73-74.   M 603
    The story of Guardian Angel Settlement.

MURCHIE, ANDREW. "John England, American," St. Meinrad Essays, v. 10 (1952), 11-44.   M 604

MURDOCH, RICHARD K. Governor Cesedes and the Religious Problem in East Florida, 1786-1787," Florida Historical Quarterly, v. 26 (1948), 325-344.   M 605

MURPHY, SISTER ANN ST. JOSEPH. Andrew Carney, the Boston Philanthropist.

MA thesis. Boston College.
1958. ii, 84p.   M 606

MURPHY, EDMUND. "Asheville
until Now," Provincial Annals
(Province of the Most Holy
Name, O.F.M.), v. 4 (1943),
219-226, 257-262.   M 607

MURPHY, FRANCIS X. The
Centennial History of Saint
Alphonsus Parish. New York.
St. Alphonsus Church. 1947.
55p.   M 608

MURPHY, JOHN C. An Analysis
of the Attitudes of American
Catholics toward the Immigrant
and the Negro. Washington.
Catholic University. 1940.
x, 158p.   M 609

MURPHY, JOHN J. "The Diocese
of Kansas City [Missouri] and
Its Schools," Catholic School
Journal, v. 52 (1952), 113-
115, illus.   M 610

MURPHY, JOHN L. "The American Catholic," Catholic World,
v. 182 (1956), 331-335. M 611

MURPHY, JOSEPH L. "Reverend
Charles Nerinckx," American
Catholic Historical Society of
Philadelphia Records, v. 27
(1916), 127-132.   M 612

MURPHY, SISTER MARY ENICE.
History of the American Protective Association in Ohio.
MA thesis. Catholic University, 1939. 116p.   M 613

MURPHY, MIRIAM T. "Catholic
Missionary Work among the
Colored People of the United
States, 1766-1866," American
Catholic Historical Society of
Philadelphia Records, v. 35
(1924), 101-136.   M 614

MURPHY, MICHAEL J. "The
Cornell Plan of Bishop Bernard McQuaid," St. Meinrad
Essays, v. 12 (1959), 76-
87.   M 615
A plan for the care of Catholic students attending state
universities.

MURPHY, ROBERT JOSEPH.
"The Catholic Church in the
United States during the Civil
War Period (1852-1866),"
American Catholic Historical
Society of Philadelphia Re-
cords, v. 39 (1928), 271-
346.   M 616

MURRAY, JOHN O'KANE. A
Popular History of the Catholic
Church in the United States.
3d rev. ed. New York.
Sadlier. 1876.   M 617

MURRAY, OLIVER. "Francis-
cans in the English Colonies,"
Franciscan Educational Conference Annual Report, v. 18
(1936), 234-249.   M 618

MURRAY, R. "Catholic Col-
leges; and Impressions of a
Visitor to the United States,"
Tablet, v. 197 (Feb. 17,
1951), 128.   M 619

MURRAY, T. "What I Have
Seen in America," Columbia,
v. 32 (1952), 6.   M 620

MURRETT, JOHN C. The Story
of Father Price. New York.
McMullen. 1953. 116p.
          M 621
A short biography of this
missionary pioneer of North
Carolina and co-founder of
Maryknoll.

MURRETT, JOHN C. Tar Heel
Apostle. New York. Long-
mans, Green and Co. 1944.
260p. front. (port.), illus.
          M 622
Popular biography of Father
Thomas Price, Missionary
and co-founder of Maryknoll.

MURTHA, SISTER MARY
DAMIEN. The Truth Teller:
a study in Early American
Catholic Journalism. MA
thesis. Fordham University.
1950. vi, 67p.   M 623

MUSSER, BENJAMIN F. "Be-
loved Mendicant (Father Francis
Koch, O.F.M.)," Provincial
Annals (Province of the Most
Holy Name, O.F.M.), v. 2
(1941-1942), 161-168, 200-
209, 246-256, 309-315, 357-
365; v. 4 (1942-1943), 31-36,
80-85, 126-132, 174-178.

M 624
MUSSER, BENJAMIN F. "Franciscan Impress in the United States," American Catholic Historical Society of Philadelphia Records, v. 54 (1943), 242-255.
M 625
MUSSER, BENJAMIN F. "The Lion of Winsted (Father Leo da Saracena, O.F.M.)," Provincial Annals (Province of the Most Holy Name, O.F.M.), v. 7 (1946), 260-273, 341-349.
M 626
MYERS, GUSTAVUS. History of Bigotry in the United States. New York. Random House. 1943. viii, 504p.
M 627
MYERS, R. "Obstacles Facing a Cornhusker Missionary," Information, v. 72 (1958), 42-47.
M 628
A Catholic priest in Nebraska.
MYERSCOUGH, SISTER ANGELITA. Pierre Gibault, Missionary Priest. MA thesis. Saint Louis University. 1947. vii, 229p.
M 629
MYLAR, ISAAC L. Early Days at the Mission Juan Bautista. Warsonville, California. Evening. Pajaronian. 1929. 195p. illus. (incl. ports.)
M 630
MYSLIWIEC, JOHN STANISLAUS. History of the Catholic Poles of St. Louis. MA thesis. Saint Louis University. 1936. iii, 117p.
M 631

- N -

NADEAU, PAUL. "Indian Missions--Lake Huron, Letter dated Killarney, Manitouline Island, May 6, 1874," Woodstock Letters, v. 3 (1874), 208-213.
N 1
NAGLE, BROTHER ROGER. The Historical Growth and Developments of the Franciscan Brothers of Brooklyn (1858-1943). MA thesis. St. John's University, N.Y., 1943. mss.
N 2

NASH, JAMES. "Sketch of the Mission of St. Malachy's, Doe Run, Chester Co., Pa.," United States Catholic Historical Magazine, v. 1 (1887), 305-313.
N 3
NASH, MICHAEL. "Letters from a Chaplain in the War of 1861. Dated Staten Island, New York Bay, N. Y.," Woodstock Letters, v. 16 (1887), 20-30.
N 4
NASH, MICHAEL. "Letters from a Chaplain in the War of 1861. Dated Off Fort Pickens, Gulf of Mexico, Steamer Vanderbilt, June 24th, 1861," Woodstock Letters, v. 16 (1887), 144-156.
N 5
NASH, MICHAEL. "Letters from a Chaplain in the War of 1861," Woodstock Letters, v. 16 (1887), 238-259.
N 6
NASH, MICHAEL. "Letters from a Chaplain in the War of 1861. Dated Camp Brown, Santa Rosa Island, Florida, July 24th, 1861," Woodstock Letters, v. 17 (1888), 12-29.
N 7
NASH, MICHAEL. "Letters from a Chaplain in the War of 1861. Dated Camp Brown, Santa Rosa Island, Fla., Sept., 25th, 1861," Woodstock Letters, v. 17 (1888), 135-149.
N 8
NASH, MICHAEL. "Letters from a Chaplain in the War of 1861. Dated Camp Brown, Santa Rosa Island, Fla., October 5th, 1861," Woodstock Letters, v. 17 (1888), 269-287.
N 9
NASH, MICHAEL. "Letters from a Chaplain in the War of 1861. Dated Camp Brown, Santa Rosa Island, Fla., Oct., 25, 1861," Woodstock Letters, v. 18 (1889), 3-25.
N 10
NASH, MICHAEL. "Letters from a Chaplain in the War of 1861. Dated Battery Scott,

near Fort Pickens, Santa
Rosa Island, Fla., Dec. 15,
1861," Woodstock Letters,
v. 18 (1889), 319-330. N 11
NASH, MICHAEL. "Letters
from a Chaplain in the War
of 1861. Dated Camp Brown,
Santa Rosa Island, December
31, 1861," Woodstock Letters,
v. 18 (1889), 153-168. N 12
NASH, MICHAEL. "Letters
from a Chaplain in the War
of 1861. Letter dated Camp
Arnold, Santa Rosa Island,
Fla., January 18, 1862,"
Woodstock Letters, v. 19
(1890), 22-41. N 13
NASH, MICHAEL. "Letters
from a Chaplain in the War
of 1861. Dated Camp Lincoln,
Santa Rosa Island, Fla.,
February 12, 1862," Woodstock
Letters, v. 19 (1890), 154-
163. N 14
NASH, MICHAEL. 'Our Fathers
in Kentucky. An Historical
Note," Woodstock Letters, v.
22 (1893), 25-27. N 15
An attempt to clear up the
confusion over the move of
the Jesuits from Kentucky
to Fordham.
NASH, MICHAEL. 'Reminis-
cences of Father Michael Nash;'
Woodstock Letters, v. 26
(1897), 257-283. N 16
NASHVILLE, TENN. (DIOCESE),
SYNOD, 1st. 1905. Synodus
dioecesana nashvillensis prima,
habita in urbe nashvillensi,
die decima Februarii, 1905,
in ecclesia cathedrali Sanctae
Mariae sub titulo Deptem
Dolorum a Thoma Sebastiano
Byrne, D.D., episcopo nashvillensi. [n.p., n.d.] ix,
162 p., 1 l. N 17
NASHVILLE, (DIOCESE) SYNOD,
2nd, 1937. The second synod
of the diocese of Nashville
celebrated June eleventh 1937
in the pro-cathedral of the
Incarnation, Nashville ...
William L. Adrian [bp.] pre-

siding. [n.p., n.d.] 116p.
N 18
NASHVILLE, (DIOCESE),
SYNOD, 3rd, 1947. The
third synod of the diocese of
Nashville convoked September
16, 1947 in the church of St.
Mary of the Seven Dolors,
Nashville, William L. Adrian
[bp.] presiding. [n.p., n.d.]
120p. N 19
NATCHEZ (DIOCESE) SYNOD,
1st, 1858. Synodus dioecesana
natchetensis prima, habita a
Gulielmo Henrico Elder [ep.]
New Aureliae, Ex typis
Propagatoris catholici, 1858.
xiv, p. N 20
NATCHEZ (DIOCESE) SYNOD,
1862. Acta synodi dioecesanae
natchetensis anno 1862 celebratae. [n.p., n.d.] xii p.
N 21
NATCHEZ (DIOCESE) SYNOD,
2nd, 1869. Synodus dioecesana
natchitochensis secunda,
habita a Augusto Maria Martin
[ep.] habdomada prima Quad-
ragesimae, anno MDCCCLXIX.
Neo Aureliae, Ex typis Propagatoris Catholici, 1869.
48p. N 22
NATCHEZ (DIOCESE) SYNOD,
4th, 1874. Synodus dioecesana
natchetensis 4. habita diebus
19a, 20a, et 21a mensis
Januarii A.D. 1874, a Gulielmo
Henrico Elder [ep.] in monas-
terio cui nomen "St. Theresa's
ret reat," patrum Congregationis Ss. Redemptoris, apud
Chatawa, Mississippi. [n.p.,
n.d.] 26p. N 23
NATCHEZ (DIOCESE) SYNOD,
5th, 1886. Synodus dioecesana
natchetensis quinta habita,
diebus 16, 17, mensis Sept.,
A.D. 1886 a Francisco Janssens ... [n.p., n.d.] 25-57p.
N 24
NATCHEZ (DIOCESE) SYNOD,
6th, 1892. Synodus dioecesana
natchetensis sexta habita,
mense Aprilis A.D. 1892 a

Thoma Heslin [ep.] [n.p., n.d.] 59-67 p. (typed) N 25
NATCHEZ (DIOCESE) SYNOD, 7th, 1897. Synodus dioecesana natchetensis septima, habita fine Aprilis principioque mensis Maii, 1897. A Thoma Heslin [ep.] [n.p., n.d.] 69-76p. (typed) N 26
NATCHEZ (DIOCESE) SYNOD, 8th, 1922. Constitutiones dioeceseos natchetensis quae in synodo dioecesana octava die 14 Julii, 1922, habita in ecclesia parochiali Bay St. Louis a Ioanne Edwardo Gunn [ep.] 1922. Latae et promulgatae fuerunt. [New Orleans, S.W. Taylor, n.d.] 135p. N 27
NATCHEZ (DIOCESE) SYNOD, 9th, 1935. Acta synodi dioecesanae natchetensis nonae habitae diebus 9a, 10a et 11a Julii, 1935, Bay St. Louis, Miss. A Richardo Oliviero Gerow [ep.] 1935. [16]p. N 28
"N.C.W.C. Reports to Meeting of Bishops, November, 1952," Catholic Action, v. 34 (December, 1952), 8-16. N 29
NATIONAL CATHOLIC EDUCATIONAL ASSOC. Catholic Colleges of the United States of America at the Middle of the Twentieth Century. Compiled by Joames F. Whelan, S. J. New Orelans, La. Loyola University. 1952. xvii, 151p. N 30
NATIONAL CATHOLIC WELFARE COUNCIL. Legal Dept. Mode of Tenure. Washington, D.C. National Catholic Welfare Council, 1941. Supplement 1955. 51p. N 31
On the method of holding Roman Catholic Church property in the United States.
"NATIVE INDIAN VOCATIONS," Catholic World, v. 65 (1897), 343-355. N 32

NAUGHTON, GABRIEL. "Franciscan Beginnings in Bergen County (N.J.)," Provincial Annals (Province of the Most Holy Name, O.F.M.), v. 2 (1942), 110-116. N 33
NAVAHO SAGA. St. Michael's, Arizona. St. Michael's Mission. 1949. 56p. illus. N 34
An account of the first fifty years of the Franciscan Navaho missions. Popularly written, but based upon expert knowledge of Navaho history and culture. Well illustrated.
"NAVAHOANA" Social Justice Review, v. 37 (1945), 390-391. N 35
NEALE, LEONARD. "Letter to Father Marmaduke Stone, Stonyhurst College, England. Geo. Town, Oct. 19, 1801," Woodstock Letters, v. 12 (1883), 73-74. N 36
Inquiry regarding the reestablishment of the Society of Jesus, points out that the youngest ex-Jesuit in the United States is fifty-four years old.
NEALE, LEONARD. "Letter to Rev. Marmaduke Stone, Stonyhurst College, England. Geo. Town. Ap. 21, 1802," Woodstock Letters, v. 12 (1883), 75-76. N 37
NEALE, LEONARD. "Letter to Rev. Marmaduke Stone, Stonyhurst College, England. Geo. Town, June 30, 1802," Woodstock Letters, v. 12 (1883), 76-77. N 38
NEALE, LEONARD. "Letter to Rev. Marmaduke Stone, Stonyhurst College, England. Geo. Town. 1803," Woodstock Letters, v. 12 (1883), 77-79. N 39
NEALE, LEONARD. "Letter to Rev. Marmaduke Stone, Stonyhurst College, England. Geo. Town C. May 5, 1804," Wood-

stock Letters, v. 12 (1883), 79. N 40

NEALE, LEONARD. "Letter to Rev. Marmaduke Stone, Stonyhurst College, England. Geo. T. March 15, 1805," Woodstock Letters, v. 12 (1883), 80-81. N 41

NEALE, LEONARD. "Letter to Rev. Marmaduke Stone, Stonyhurst College, England. Geo. Town Feb. 16, 1808," Woodstock Letters, v. 12 (1883), 82-83. N 42

NEILL, THOMAS P. "The American Church at Mid-Century," The Priest, v. 4 (1950), 661-665. N 43

NEILL, THOMAS P. "Americanism," Historical Bulletin, v. 22 (1943-1944), 3-4, 33-34, 42-43. N 44

NEILL, THOMAS P. 'Religious Liberty in Colonial America," Sign, v. 31 (May, 1952), 15-18. N 45

[NEUMANN, JOHN.] 'Ein Schreiben Joh. Nep. Neumanns aus dem Jahre 1837," Central Blatt and Social Justice, v. 17 (1924), 163-164, 179-181. N 46

[NEUMANN, JOHN.] "A Hitherto Unknown Letter by Ven. John N. Neumann," Central Blatt and Social Justice, v. 27 (1934), 129-130, 176-178, 241. N 47

[NEUMANN, JOHN.] "Schreiben des Herrn Neumann, Missionars in der V. St. von Nord Amerika, an seinen Freund Herrn Dichtl in Prag," Central Blatt and Social Justice, v. 17 (1924), 200-201, 215. N 48

NÈVE, J. DE. "Extrait d'une Lettre de M. de Nève, Missionaire dans le Berrien County, Etat du Michigan à M. Van Dorpe, Curé de Waerschort (Flandre Orientale), St. Joseph 25 Avril, 1859," Annales de la Propagation de la Foi, v. 31 (1859), 446-455. N 49

NÈVE, J. DE. Letter dated St. Joseph (Mich.), April 25, 1859," Annals of the Propagation of the Faith, Baltimore, v. 20 (1859), 342-349. N 50

NEVILS, W. COLEMAN. A Moulder of Men. New York. Apostleship of Prayer. 1953. 248p. N 51
    A biography of Father John J. O'Rourke, S.J., who was a prominent figure in the training of the Jesuits of eastern United States.

NEW ORLEANS (DIOCESE). Lettre pastorale de Monseigneur l'évêque de la Nouvelle-Orleans, à l'occasion du synode diocesain, terminé le 29 avril, 1844. 16p. N 52

NEW ORLEANS (DIOCESE) SYNOD, 2nd, 1844. Synodus dioecesana Neo-Aurelianensis secunda, habita mense Aprili anno MDCCCXLIV. Neo Aureliae, H. Meridier, 1844. 22p. N 53

NEW ORLEANS (DIOCESE) COUNCIL, 1st, 1860. Concilium Neo-Aurelianense Provinciale Primum. Habitum Anno 1856. New Orleans. H. Meridier. 1857. 35p. N 54

NEW ORLEANS (DIOCESE) COUNCIL, 2nd, 1860. Concilium neo-aurelianense provinciale secundum, habitum anno 1860. Neo Aureliae, Ex typis Propagatoris catholici, 1864. 19p. N 55

NEW ORLEANS (DIOCESE) SYNOD, 4th, 1869. Synodus dioecesana neo-aurelianensis quarta, habita mense Januario anno MDCCCLXIX. Neo-Aureliae, Ex typis Propagatoris catholici, 1869. 32p. N 56

NEW ORLEANS (ECCLESIASTICAL PROVINCE) COUNCIL, 3rd. Concilium Neo-Aurelianense provinciale tertium

habitum mense Januario, A.D. 1873. Cui addita sunt in appendice duae constitutiones Vaticanae - Epistola encyclica Quanta cura - Syllabus - et Formula juramenti pro ordinandis ad subdianconatum sub titulo missionis. Neo-Aureliae, Ex typis Propagatoris Catholici, 1875. 1 p. 1., 68p. 1 1.
N 57

NEW ORLEANS (DIOCESE) SYNOD, 5th, 1889. Synodus dioecesana neo-aurelianensis quinta habita mense Maii anno MDCCCLXXXIX a Francisco Janssens [ep.] Neo Aureliae, Ex typis F. C. Philippe, 1889. 40p.
N 58

NEW ORLEANS (DIOCESE) SYNOD, 6th, 1922. Constitutiones dioeceseos Novae-Aureliae quae in synodo dioecesana sexta die 16 Februarii, 1922, habita in ecclesia metropolitana Sancti Ludovici a Ioanne Gulielmo Shaw [ep.] latae et promulgatae fuerunt. [New Orleans, S.W. Taylor] 1922. 103p.
N 59

NEW YORK (DIOCESE) SYNOD, 1st, 1842. Synodus dioecesana neo-eboracensis prima, habita anno MDCCCXLII. Neo Eboraci, Typis G. Mitchell, 1842. 22p.
N 60

NEW YORK (DIOCESE) COUNCIL, 1st, 1854. Concilium Neo-eboracense primum. Habitum anno MDCCCLIV. Neo Eboraci, Apud E. Dunigan, 1855. 32p.
N 61

NEW YORK (ECCLESIASTICAL PROVINCE) COUNCIL, 1861. Concilium provinciale. Neo-Eboracense III., mense Junii, anno MDCCCLXI. celebratum. Neo-Eboraci, Apud E. Dunigan et fratrem, 1862. 37p.
N 62

NEW YORK (DIOCESE) SYNOD, 3rd, 1868. Synodus Dioecesana Neo-Eboracensis Tertia, quae antecedentrum etiam complectitur Constitutiones, die 29, et die 30 Septembris, A.D. 1868 in ecclesia Metropolitana S. Patritii, Neo Eboraci, habita ab Illustrissimo et Reverendissimo Joanne McCloskey, Archiepiscopo Neo Eboracensi. New York. Catholic Publication Society. 1868. 23p.
N 63

NEW YORK (DIOCESE) SYNOD, 4th, 1882. Synodus dioecesana neo-eboracensis quarta, quae antecendentium etiam complectitur constitutiones, diebus VIII. et IX. Novembris, A.D. 1882, in ecclesia metropolitana S. Patritii, Neo-Eboraci habita a Joanne Cardinali McCloskey. Neo-Eboraci, Typis Societatis pro libris catholicis evulgandis, 1882. ix, 51p.
N 64

NEW YORK (DIOCESE) SYNOD 1-9. Synodorum archdioeceseos Neo-Eboracensis collectio. Neo-Eboraci. Typ. Bibliothecae Cathedralis. 1901. viii, 172p.
N 65

NEW YORK (DIOCESE) SYNOD 17. Acta et statuta synodi Neo-Eboracensis XVII [1951] xxi, 137p.
N 66

NEW YORK. (ECCLESIASTICAL PROVINCE). Acta et Decreta Concilii Provincialis New-Eboracensis IV. New York. Catholic Publication Soc. 1886.
N 67

NEWARK (DIOCESE) SYNOD, 1st, 1856. Statuta novarcensis dioeceseos a Jacobo Roosevelt Bayley [ep.] in synodo dioecesana prima habita mense Aug., 1856, in collegio Seton-Hall, Madison, N.J. lata et promulgata. Neo Eboraci, E. Dunigan, 1857. 52p.
N 68

NEWARK (DIOCESE) SYNOD, 1868. Statuta novarcensis dioeceseos a Jacobo Roosevelt Bayley [ep.] in synodo dioecesana prima, mense Aug.1856,

lata et promulgata, iterumque, cum nonullis mutationibus additionibusque, in dioecesana synodo, habita die 10 Julii, 1868, in collegio Seton Hall, South Orange, N.J., confirmata. Novarce, Typis Societatis pro libris catholicis evulgandis, Neo Eboraci, 1869. 95p.
N 69

NEWARK (DIOCESE) SYNOD, 3rd, 1878. Statuta dioecesis novarcensis quae post synodum Ium A.D. 1853, et Illum A.D. 1868, a Jacobo Roosevelt Bayley, Fe. Mf., celebratas, in synodo dioecesana tertia, diebus 8 et 9 Maji 1878 habita, tulit et promulgavit Michael Augustinus Corrigan [ep.] Neo-Eboraci Benziger, 1878. 161p. N 70

NEWARK (DIOCESE) SYNOD, 5th, 1886. Synodus dioecesana novarcensis quinta A.D. MDCCCLXXXVI celebrata a Michaele Venantio Wigger. Arlington, Neo-Caes, Typis Paedotrophii Ss. Cordis, 1887. 45p. N 71

NEWARK, N.J. (DIOCESE) SYNOD, 8th, 1896. Statuta dioecesis novarcensis quae post synodos antecedentes, in synodo dioecesana octava, die 26, Junii, 1896 habita, denuo renovavit, confirmavit et promulgavit Venantius Michael Wigger, episcopus novarcensis. Arlington, Neo-Caes., Typis Paedotrophii Ss. Cordis, 1897. 143p. N 72

NEWARK (DIOCESE) SYNOD, 16. Statuta archdioeceseos Novarcensis [Arlington. Catholic Protectory Press. 1941.] 137p. N 73

NEW YORK (STATE). State Historian. Ecclesiastical Records of the State of New York. Albany. J.B. Lyon. 1901-1916. 7v. N 74

NEWCOMB, REXFORD. The Old Mission Churches and Historic Houses of California. Lippincott. Philadelphia. 1925. vii, 329p. front., 217 illus., 24 line drawings. N 75

NEWHALL, NANCY. "Mission San Xavier del Bac," Arizona Highways, v. 30 (1954), 13-34. N 76

NICHOLS, M. LEONA. The Mantle of Elias: the Story of Fathers Blanchet and Demers in Early Oregon. Portland Binfords. 1941. 337p. N 77

NIEBERDING, VELMA. "St. Mary's of the Quapaws. Chronicles of Oklahoma, v. 31 (1953), 2-14. illus. N 78
A well documented story of the only Catholic school on the Old Quapaw reservation in Oklahoma (1893).

NIEBERDING, VELMA. "Very Reverend Urban de Hasque ... Pioneer Priest of Indian Territory," Chronicles of Oklahoma, v. 38 (1960), 35-42. N 79
Pastoral work in Oklahoma for fifty-four years, died in 1954.

NIEBERDING, VELMA. "Chief Splitlog and the Cayuga Mission Church," Chronicles of Oklahoma, v. 32 (1954), 18-28. plates, ports. N 80
The fascinating story of the Church of St. Matthias built by Chief Splitlog in the 1890's.

NIEBERDING, VELMA. "St. Agnes School of the Chactaws," Chronicles of Oklahoma, v. 23 (1955), 183-192. N 81
Founded 1897 by Father Wm. H. Ketcham at Antlers, Okla. Destroyed by a tornado 1945.

NIEDEMAYER, A. The Council in Baltimore (7th to 21st October, 1866): A Picture of American Life. Baltimore. Commercial Ptg. and Sta. Co. 1914. 54p. N 82

The original German edition
was issued in 1867. This
translation was directed by
George C. Perine.
"1950 General Session of the
Bishops of the United States,"
Catholic Action, v. 32 (1950),
7-16. N 83
NIX, JAMES T. "Introduction to
Study of Occupational Diseases
of Religious," Linacre Quarter-
ly, v. 24 (1957), 115-122.
N 84
NOBILIS, SISTER M. "First
Polish American Teaching
Nun," Polish American Studies,
v. 9 (1952), 78-85. N 85
Sister Mary Tita of the S.
S.N.D., b. 1850, d. 1922.
NOBILIS, SISTER M. "The First
Polish School in the United
States," Polish American
Studies, v. 4 (1947), 1-5.
N 86
NOBILIS, SISTER M. "The
Schools Sisters of Notre Dame
in Polish American Education,"
Polish American Studies, v.
12 (1955), 77-83. N 87
NOLAN, DANIEL. "Maurice
de St. Palais," St. Meinrad
Historical Essays, v. 3
(1934), 144-152. N 88
NOLAN, EDWARD J. "Certain
Churches in the West," Amer-
ican Catholic Historical
Society of Philadelphia Re-
cords, v. 5 (1894), 88-97.
N 89
NOLAN, HUGH J. "Cardinal
Doughterty: an Appreciation,"
American Catholic Historical
Society of Philadelphia Re-
cords, v. 62 (1951), 133-
141. N 90
NOLAN, HUGH J. "Fields in A-
merican Catholic History for
Polish Americans," Polish
American Studies, v. 7 (1950),
65-72. N 91
NOLAN, HUGH J."In Memoriam:
Richard J. Purcell," American
Catholic Historical Society of
Philadelphia Records, v. 61

(1950), 3-8. N 92
NOLAN, HUGH J. "Most Rev.
Dr. Paschal Robinson, O.F.
M.," American Catholic His-
torical Society of Philadelphia
Records, v. 59 (1948),
279-291. N 93
NOLAN, HUGH J. The Most
Reverend Francis Patrick
Kenrick, Third Bishop of
Philadelphia, 1830-1851.
Philadelphia. 1948. xix,
502p. N 94
NOLAN, HUGH J. "Philadelphia's
First Diocesan Synod, May
13-15, 1832," American Cath-
olic Historical Society of
Philadelphia Records, v. 54
(1943), 28-43. N 95
NOLAN, J. FRANCIS. "The
Liquor Problem and the
Jesuit Missions in New
France," Acta et Dicta, v. 3
(1911), 91-141. N 96
NOLAN, MARK. "Statistical
Survey of the II and III Orders
of St. Francis in North A-
merica," Franciscan Educa-
tional Conference Annual Re-
port, v. 18 (1936), 331-
358. N 97
NOLL, JOHN F. The Diocese
of Fort Wayne. Fragments
of History. v. 2 Fort Wayne.
The Author. 1941. N 98
NOLL, SISTER MARIE NOELINE.
History of St. Paul's Church
(Brooklyn). MA thesis. St.
John's University, N.Y. 1944.
mss. pp. N 99
NOONAN, CARROLL J. Nativism
in Connecticut, 1829-1860.
Washington. Catholic Univer-
sity. 1938. vi, 351p.
N 100
NOONAN, MATTHEW J. Catholic
Press Opinion of the Civil
War Period, 1860-1870. MA
thesis. Catholic University.
1944. 79p. N 101
NOONAN, MAURICE FRANCIS.
A Catholic Colony in Pennsyl-
vania: Loretto. MA thesis.
Catholic University. 1932.

269

47p. N 102

NOONAN, MICHAEL J. "25
Years a-Growing," The Mission
Call, v. 20 (1948), 260-262,
266, 285. N 103

NORTH, WILLIAM E. Catholic
Education in Southern California.
Washington. Catholic Univer-
sity. 1936. xiii, 227p.
N 104

(NORTH GUILFORD, CONN.)
"Monastery of Our Lady of
Grace, North Guilford, Conn.,"
Dominicana, v. 41 (1956),
27-32. N 105
An account of the destruction
by fire of this Dominican
monastery on Dec. 23,
1955.

NORTON, KATHERINE E. His-
tory of the Saint Ignace Mission
in Michigan from 1671 to
1706. MA thesis. University
of Detroit. 1934. ii, 37p.
N 106

NORTON, SISTER MARY AQUINAS.
Catholic Missionary Activities in
the Northwest, 1818-1864.
Washington. Catholic Univer-
sity. 1930. 154p. N 107
Pembina, 1818-1823, and
St. Joseph, 1848-1864.
Chippewa missions on Lake
Superior, 1835-1864. Fr.
Pierz among the Chippewa,
1852-1864.

NORTON, SISTER MARY AQUINAS.
"Catholic Missions and Missionaries among the Indians of
Dakota," North Dakota Historical Quarterly, v. 5 (1931),
149-165. N 108

NORTON, SISTER MARY AQUINAS.
"Missionary Activity in the
Northwest under the French
Regime, 1640-1740," Acta et
Dicta, v. 6 (1934), 141-160.
map. N 109

NORWORTH, HOWARD. Pathway
of the Padres. Los Angeles.
Shields Ways Pub. Co. 1951.
144p. illus., maps. N 110
Story of the founding of the
Franciscan mission in Cali-

fornia. Contains road maps
giving location of each mission. Primarily intended for
a guide book.

"NOTABLE EVENTS IN CATH-
OLIC AMERICAN HISTORY,"
American Catholic Historical
Researches, v. 19 (1902),
170-172. N 111

"NOTICE ON THE CHURCH IN
THE UNITED STATES," An-
nals of the Propagation of
the Faith, London, v. 11
(1850), 253-263, v. 12 (1851),
73-88, 311-326. N 112

"NOTICE SUR LES PREMIERS
ETABLISSEMENTS, LES
PROGRES ET L' ETAT ACTUEL
DU CATHOLICISME AUX
ETATS-UNIS," Annales de la
Propagation de la Foi, v. 22
(1850), 329-342, v. 23 (1851),
101-111, 409-433. N 113

NOTIZIE STORICHE E DES-
CRITTIVE DELLE MISSIONI
DELLA PROVINCIA TORINESE
DELLA COMPAGNIA DI GESÙ
NELL AMERICA DE NORD.
Torino. G. Derrossi. 1898.
xii. N 114

NOTT, SHARRARD. "Jesuit
Martyrs in Virginia," America,
v. 54 (1935), 131-132.
N 115

NOVAK, COSMAS. "A Survey of
Intercultural Education in
Catholic Elementary and
Secondary Schools of the United
States," American Catholic
Sociological Review, v. 10
(1949), 159-171. N 116

NOWLAND, SISTER MARY
JULICE. United States
Government Relations with the
Catholic Indian Missions of
the Trans-Mississippi West,
1803-1882. MA thesis. Saint
Louis University. 1940.
iv, 180p. N 117

NUESSE, CELESTINE JOSEPH.
The Social Thought of American Catholics, 1634-1829.
Washington. Catholic University. 1945. x, 315p. M 118

NUESSE, CELESTINE JOSEPH.
"Social Thought among Ameri-
can Catholics in the Colonial
Period," American Catholic
Sociological Review, v. 7
(1946), 43-52.   N 119
NUESSE, C. J. AND THOMAS
J. HARTE. Sociology of
the Parish. Milwaukee. Bruce.
1951.   N 120
NUTE, GRACE LEE. Caesars of
the Wilderness. New York.
D. Appleton-Century. 1943.
xvi, 386p. maps, ports.n 121
Biographical sketch of Des
Groseilliers and Radisson,
with a chapter on the
seventeenth century Jesuit-
Franciscan quarrel.
NUTE, GRACE LEE (ed.) "Docu-
ments: Father Skolla's Report
on His Indian Missions," Acta
et Dicta, v. 7 (1936), 216-
268.   N 122
NUTE, GRACE LEE (ed.) Documents Relating to the Northwest Missions, 1815-1827.
St. Paul. Minnesota Historical
Society. 1942. xix, 469p.
                        N 123
Documents relating to the
Indian mission of Red River,
chiefly concerning the efforts
of Archbishop Plessis of
Quebec to keep the mission
alive.
NUTE, GRACE LEE. "Father
Hennepin's Later Years,"
Minnesota History, v. 19
(1938), 393-398.   N 124

- O -

OBERMÜLLER, JOHANN M.
Erinnerungen aus dem Leben
und Werken des hochw. P.
Franz Xavier Weninger,
Buffalo, N. Y. Häfners.
1859. 51p.   O 1
OBLASSER, BONAVENTURE.
Mission San Xavier del Bac.
Topawa, Arizona. The Author.
1937. 32p. illus.   O 2
OBLASSER, BONAVENTURE.
"The Franciscans in the

Spanish Southwest," Francis-
can Educational Conference
Annual Report, v. 18 (1936),
98-123.   O 3
O'BOYLE, PATRICK A. "Fifty
Years of Child Care," Catholic
Charities Review, v. 33
(1949), 266-269.   O 4
O'BRIEN, ALBERT. "Francis-
can Schools in the United
States," in Catholics in A-
merica. Boston. Continental
Press. 1922.   O 5
O'BRIEN, DENIS R. "The
Centenary of Rev. Sylvester
Malone, Great Catholic and
Great Citizen," American
Irish Historical Society Journal,
v. 20 (1921), 179-192. O 6
O'BRIEN, E. J. Jesuits in
Spanish Florida. MA thesis.
Loyola University (Chicago).
1942.   O 7
O'BRIEN, ERIC AND MAYNARD
GEIGER. Padre Junipero
Serra and the California Mis-
sions. Santa Barbara, Calif.
Old Mission "Serra Shop."
1949. 65p. illus., maps.
                        O 8
O'BRIEN, F. WILLIAM.
"General Clark's Nomination
as Ambassador to the Vatican;
American Reaction," Catholic
Historical Review, v. 45
(1959), 421-429.   O 9
O'BRIEN, FRANK A. "The Dio-
cese of Detroit--What It Was
and What It Is," Michigan
Pioneer and Historical Col-
lections, v. 9 (1886), 128-
137.   O 10
O'BRIEN, GEORGE. "The
Irish in the American Melting
Pot," Studies, v. 35 (1946),
343-350.   O 11
O'BRIEN, JAMES J. Louisiana
and Mississippi Martyrs. New
York. Paulist Press. 1928.
                        O 12
O'BRIEN, JAMES J. "Our
Louisiana and Mississippi
Martyrs," Woodstock Letters,
v. 58 (1929), 24-38.   O 13

271

O' BRIEN, JAMES J. "Sketch of the Expulsion of the Society of Jesus from Louisiana," Louisiana Historical Society Publications, v. 9 (1916), 9-24. O 14

O' BRIEN, JOHN A. (ed.) Catholics and Scholarship. Huntington, Ind. Our Sunday Visitor. 1939. 256p. O 15

O' BRIEN, JOHN A. 'Religious Freedom in the American Colonies," Ave Maria, (1950), 39-43. O 16

O' BRIEN, JOSEPH LAWRENCE. John England. New York. Edward O'Toole Co. 1934. xiii, 222p. front. (port.). O 17

O' BRIEN, JOSEPH LAWRENCE. "John England (1786-1842). The Apostle of the Press," Catholic World, v. 137 (1933), 192-201. O 18

O' BRIEN, KENETH R. Nature of Support of Diocesan Priests in the United States of America. Washington. Catholic University. 1949. xvi, 162p. O 19

O' BRIEN, MOTHER MARY. Reverend Mother Hardy and Her Foundations to 1872. MA thesis. Catholic University. 1935. 79p. O 20

O' BRIEN, MICHAEL J. Pioneer Irish in New England. N. Y. Kenedy. 1937. xiv, 325p. O 21

O' BRIEN, W. D. "Fifty Years of Church Extension," Extension, v. 50 (Oct., 1955), 14-16. O 22
A brief appreciation of Extension's great work for the Church in the United States.

O' BROWN, EDWARD. Two Missionary Priests at Mackinac. The Parish Register of the Mission of Michilimackinac. Chicago. n. pub. 1889. n.p. O 23

O' CALLAGHAN, SISTER M. THEODOSIA. 'Echoes of Gallicanism in New France," Catholic Historical Review, v. 12 (1926), 16-58. O 24

O' CARANZA, FERNANDO. Establecimientos Franciscanos en el Misterioso Reino de Nuevo Mexico. Mexico, D.F. 1934. 199p. plates, port., facsims. O 25

O' CONNELL, GEORGE. "Santa Cruz and Its Martyr, Franciscan Father Andrew Quintana, O.S.F., Slain October 11, 1812," Messenger of the Sacred Heart, v. 26 (1889), 882-896. O 26

O' CONNELL, J. J. Catholicity in the Carolinas and Georgia: Leaves of History, 1820-1878. New York. Sadlier. 1879. xviii, 647p. incl. front. (port.) O 27

O' CONNELL, WILLIAM HENRY CARDINAL. Recollections of Seventy Years. Houghton Mifflin. 1934. ix, 395p. front., plates, ports. O 28

O' CONNOR, DOMINIC. Brief History of the Diocese of Baker City. 1906. O 29

O' CONNOR, DOMINIC. A Brief History of the Diocese of Baker City. Baker. 1930. O 30

O' CONNOR, BEDE. "Lettre du R. P. Bede O'Connor au Reverendissime Abbé Henri de Notre Dame des Ermites a Einsiedeln (Suisse), octobre, 1865," Annales de la Propagation de la Foi, v. 38 (1866), 381-393, 460-471. O 31

O' CONNOR, JACQUES. "Lettre de Mgr. O'Connor, Vicaire Apostolique du Nebraska a MM. les Membres des Conseils Centraux de l'Oeuvre de la Propagation de la Foi. Omaha 13 décembre, 1879," Annales de la Propagation de la Foi, v. 52 (1880), 201-232. O 32

O' CONNOR, JAMES. 'The

Flathead Indians," American Catholic Historical Society of Philadelphia Records, v. 3 (1888-1891). 85-110.   O 33

O' CONNOR, SISTER MARY PASCHALA. "Some Mazzuchellian 'Firsts,'" Salesianum, v. 49 (1954), 161-169.   O 34

[O' CONNOR, MICHAEL.] "Memorandum of the Visitation of the Diocese of Pittsburgh, A.D. 1846," American Catholic Historical Researches, v. 2 (1885), 27-32.   O 35

O' CONNOR, MICHAEL J. "A Catholic University and Its Founders," United States Catholic Historical Society Records and Studies, v. 7 (1914), 145-162.   O 36

O' CONNOR, STELLA. "The Charity Hospital at New Orleans: An Administration and Financial History, 1736-1941," Louisiana Historical Quarterly, v. 31 (1948), 1-109.   O 37

O' CONNOR, THOMAS F. "An Alleged Spanish Entrada into New York," Mid-America, v. 14 (1943), 130-138.   O 38

O' CONNOR, THOMAS F. "Bishop Macheboeuf," Colorado Magazine, v. 12 (1935), 130-138.   O 39

O' CONNOR, THOMAS F. "Catholic Archives of the United States," Catholic Historical Review, v. 31 (1946), 414-430.   O 40

O' CONNOR, THOMAS F. "The Catholic Tradition in Vermont," The Michaelman, v. 3 (Nov., 1937), 20-21, (Jan., 1938), 22-23, (Apr., 1938), 12-13, (June, 1938), 18-19.   O 41

O' CONNOR, THOMAS F. "Catholicism in the Fort Stanwix Country (1776-1876)," American Catholic Historical Society of Philadelphia Records, v. 60 (1949), 79-93.   O 42

O' CONNOR, THOMAS F. "Century of Catholicism in the Oregon Country," United States Catholic Historical Society Records and Studies, v. 34 (1938), 29-48.   O 43

O' CONNOR, THOMAS F. "The Church in Mid-America. A Selective Bibliography," Historical Bulletin, v. 13 (1935), 30-32; 50-52; 70-74; v. 14 (1935), 11-12.   O 44

O' CONNOR, THOMAS F. (ed.) "Documents. Letters of John Grassi to Simon Bruté de Remur, 1812-1832," Mid-America, v. 4 (1933), 245-265.   O 45

O' CONNOR, THOMAS F. (ed.) "Documents. Narratives of a Missionary Journey to New Mexico in 1867," Mid-America, v. 8 (1937), 63-67.   O 46

O' CONNOR, THOMAS F. "Father Gabriel Richard," Historical Bulletin, v. 13 (1935), 12-13.   O 47

O' CONNOR, THOMAS F. "The Founding of Mount Saint Mary's College, 1808-1835," Maryland Historical Magazine, v. 43 (1948), 197-209. O 48

O' CONNOR, THOMAS F. "Gilbert Garraghan, S.J., Historian," Historical Bulletin, v. 21 (1943), 53-54, 66-67. O 49

(O' CONNOR, THOMAS F.) "In Memoriam: Thomas F. O'-Connor," Records of the American Catholic Historical Society of Philadelphia, v. 61 (1950), 199-201.   O 50

O' CONNOR, THOMAS F. "John E. Rothensteiner," Catholic Historical Review, v. 22 (1937), 432-434.   O 51

O' CONNOR, THOMAS F. (ed.) "Joseph Rosati, C.M., Apostolic Delegate to Haiti, 1842-- Two letters to Bishop John Hughes," The Americas, v. 1 (1945), 491-494.   O 52

O' CONNOR, THOMAS F. "A Kentucky Contribution to Religion on the Frontier," Kentucky Historical Society Register, v. 34 (1936), 131-

138.   O 53
  Sisters of Loretto.

O' CONNOR, THOMAS F. "A
Kentucky Sesquicentennial,"
America, v. 53 (1935), 607-
609.   O 54

O' CONNOR, THOMAS F. "A
Major Contribution to the History of the American Church,"
Catholic Historical Review,
v. 30 (1945), 427-449.   O 55

O' CONNOR, THOMAS F. "The
Onandaga Mission," Mid-America, v. 6 (1935), 10-29. O 56

O' CONNOR, THOMAS F. "Pierre
DeSmet: Frontier Missionary,"
Mid-America, v. 6 (1935),
191-196.   O 57

O' CONNOR, THOMAS F. "Religious
Toleration in New York, 1664-
1770," New York History, v.
17 (1936), 391-410.   O 58

O' CONNOR, THOMAS F. "Trends
and Portends in American Catholic Historiography," Catholic
Historical Review, v. 29
(1947), 3-11.   O 59

O' CONNOR, THOMAS F. "Vincennes, 1834-1934," Historical
Bulletin, v. 12 (1934), 63-
65.   O 60

O' CONNOR, THOMAS F. "William Howlett, Pioneer Missionary and Historian," Mid-
America, v. 9 (1938), 37-
50, 103-106.   O 61

O' CONNOR, THOMAS F. "Writings on United States Catholic
History, A Selective Bibliography," The Americas, v. 1
(1945), 480-485, v. 2 (1946),
482-488, v. 3 (1947), 508-
513, v. 4 (1948), 501-509,
v. 5 (1949), 462-473, v. 6
(1950), 451-466.   O 62

O' DANIEL, VICTOR F. An A-
merican Apostle. The Very
Reverend Mathew Anthony O'-
Brien, O.P. Washington. The
Dominicana. 1923. xvi, 341p.
incl. front., plates, ports.
         O 63

O' DANIEL, VICTOR F. (tr. and
ed.) "Bishop Flaget's Report

of the Diocese of Bardstown
to Pope Pius VII, April 10,
1815," Catholic Historical Review, v. 1 (1915), 305-319.
         O 64

O' DANIEL, VICTOR F. "The
Centenary of Ohio's Oldest
Catholic Church," Catholic
Historical Review, v. 4 (1919),
18-37.   O 65

O' DANIEL, VICTOR. "Concanen's
Election to the See of New
York 1808-1810," Catholic Historical Review, v. 2 (1916),
19-46.   O 66

O' DANIEL, VICTOR F. The
Dominican Province of Saint
Joseph, Historico-Biographical
Studies. New York. National
Headquarters of the Holy Name
Society. 1942. xii, 517p.
         O 67

O' DANIEL, VICTOR F. Dominicans in Early Florida. New
York. United States Catholic
Historical Society. 1930. xiii,
230p.   O 68

O' DANIEL, VICTOR F. The
Father of the Church in Tennessee, Richard Pius Miles,
O.P. New York. Sold by
Frederick Pustet. 1926.
xiv, 607p. front., plates,
ports.   O 69

O' DANIEL, VICTOR F. A
Light of the Church in Kentucky, Samuel Thomas Wilson,
O.P. Washington. The
Dominican. 1932. xiv, 333p.
front., illus. (map), plates,
ports.   O 70

O' DANIEL, VICTOR F. "A long
Misunderstood Episode in A-
merican History," Catholic Historical Review, v. 6 (1920),
15-45, 66-80.   O 71
  A re-evaluation of the
  Dominican-Badin and Nerinckx
  controversy.

O' DANIEL, VICTOR F. "The
Rev. John Ceslas Fenwick, O.
P. (1759-1815)," Catholic Historical Review, v. 1 (1915),
17-29.   O 71a

O' DANIEL, VICTOR F. The Right Reverend Edward Dominic Fenwick, O.P. Washington. The Dominicana. 1920. xiv, 473p. front. (port.), plates. O 71b

O' DANIEL, VICTOR F. "The Right Rev. Richard Luke Concanen, O.P.," Catholic Historical Review, v. 1 (1916), 400-421. O 72

O' DANIEL, VICTOR F. "The Right Rev. Juan de Las Cabezas de Altamirano," Catholic Historical Review, v. 2 (1917), 400-414. O 73

O' DANIEL, VICTOR F. Very Rev. Charles Hyacinth McKenna, O.P., P.G. New York. Holy Name Bureau. 1917. xiv, 409p. O 74

O' DEA, THOMAS F. American Catholic Dilemma: An Inquiry into the Intellectual Life. New York: Sheed and Ward. 1958. xv, 173p. O 75

O' DEA, THOMAS F. "The Catholic Immigrant and the American Scene," Thought, v. 31 (1956), 251-270. O 76

ODIN, JEAN-MARIE. "Extrait d'une Lettre de Mgr. Odin, Évêque de Galveston à M. Duplay, Supérieur du Grand-Séminaire à Lyon. Galveston le 12 juillet, 1858," Annales de la Propagation de la Foi, v. 31 (1859), 442-445. O 77

[ODIN, J.M.] "Missionary Life in Texas Fifty Years Ago," United States Catholic Historical Magazine, v. 4 (1891-1892), 210-219. O 78

ODIVE, FR. "Bishop Schinner's First Confirmation Tour to the Indians of Yellow River," Salesianum, v. 6 (1911), 17-25. O 79

O' DONNELL, GEORGE E. "John F. O'Hara, C.S.C., Archbishop of Philadelphia (1951-   )," American Catholic Historical Society of Philadelphia Records, v. 64 (1953), 37-

42. O 80
A chapter in the biographical issue of the Records.

O' DONNELL, GEORGE E. St. Charles Seminary, Overbrook. [Philadelphia. Jeffries & Manz. 1943-53.] 2v. published by American Catholic Historical Society of Philadelphia. O 81

O' DONNELL, JAMES H. History of the Diocese of Hartford. Boston. D.H. Hurd. 1900. vii, 473p. illus., plates, ports. O 82

O' DONNELL, JOHN HUGH. "The Catholic Church in Northern Indiana," Catholic Historical Review, v. 25 (1939), 135-145. O 83

O' DONNELL, JOHN HUGH. The Catholic Hierarchy of the United States. Washington. Catholic University. 1922. 222p. O 84

O' DONNELL, THOMAS J. "For Bread and Wine," Woodstock Letters, v. 80 (1951), 99-142. O 85
The story of the Healy family.

O' DONOHUE, SISTER MARY AQUINAS. Sisters of Mercy in Texas, 1875-1945. MA thesis. Catholic University. 1948. 80p. O 86

O' DRISCOLL, SISTER M. FELICITY. Political Nativism in Buffalo, 1830-1860. MA thesis. Catholic University. 1936. 53p. O 87

O' DRISCOLL, SISTER M. FELICITY. "Political Nativism in Buffalo, 1830-1860," American Catholic Historical Society of Philadelphia Records, v. 48 (1937), 247-319. O 88

O' DWYER, GEORGE FRANCIS. "Ann Glover, First Martyr to the Faith in New England," United States Catholic Historical Society Records and Studies, v. 15 (1921), 70-78. O 89

O' DWYER, GEORGE F. Irish Genesis of Lowell. Lowell.

American Irish Historical
Society. 1921. O 90
O' DWYER, GEORGE F.
"Lowell's First Catholic
Schools," United States Catholic Historical Society Records
and Studies, v. 21 (1932),
235-238. O 91
OECHSLE, PLACIDUS. Historical Sketch of the Congregation
of Our Lady of Perpetual Help
at Altus, Arkansas. Golden
Jubilee, 1930. no pl. no
pub. 1930? unpaged. illus.
O 92
OFFICIAL CATHOLIC DIREC-
TORY. New York. Kenedy.
Published under various titles
and by different publishers
since 1817 this directory contains the names and addresses
of the priests of the United
States, together with information on the territory, past
prelates and statistics of the
various dioceses. Also a list
of the religious orders. While
not a definitive source it is
an excellent guide. See also
N 149. O 93
O' FLAHERTY, PATRICK D.
History of St. Brigid's Parish
in the City of New York under
the Administration of the Rev.
Patrick F. McSweeney, 1877-
1907. MA thesis. Fordham
University. 1952. 126p.
O 94
O' FLAHERTY, PATRICK W.
"Growth of the Catholic Church
in the United States," United
States Catholic Historical
Society Records and Studies,
v. 33 (1941), 31-41. O 95
[O' FLYNN, SISTER M. AGNES.]
A Souvenir of Mount St.
Joseph's Ursuline Academy "
"Maple Mount," Davis County,
Kentucky. Boston. Angel
Guardian Press. 200p. illus.,
ports. O 96
OGDENSBURG (DIOCESE) SYNOD,
1st., 1875. Statuta dioeceseos
ogdensburgensis quae in synodo

ogdensburgensi I, A. D.
1875, lata ac promulgata
fuere ab Edgaro P. Wadhams
[ep.] Troy, N.Y., T. J.
Hurley. 1875. xii, 79p.
O 97
OGDENSBURG (DIOCESE) SYNOD,
2nd, 1886. Statuta dioeceseos
ogdensburgensis quae in synodo
ogdensburgensi II., A. D.
1886, lata ac promulgata
fuere ab Edgaro P. Wadhams
[ep.] Troy, N.Y., T.J.
Hurley, 1886. xiii, 112p.
O 98
OGDENSBURG (DIOCESE) SYNOD,
8th, 1904. Statuta dioecesis
ogdensburgensis quae in synodo
ogdensburgensi VIII A.D. 1904
lata ac promulgata fuere a
Henrico Gabriels, episogdens-
burgensi, Ogdensburg, Republican & journal company,
1905. xiv, 111p. O 99
OGDENSBURG (DIOCESE) SYNOD,
13th, 1928. Statuta dioecesis
ogdensburgensis quae in
synodo ogdensburgensi XIII.
A.D. 1928 lata ac promulgata
fuere a Josepho Henrico Conroy [ep.] Ogdensburg, Ogdensburg advance co., 1928. xiv,
115p. O 100
OGER, H. M. L'église Catholique
aux Etats-Unis. Liège. La
Pensée Catholique. 1948.
19p. O 101
O' GORMAN, J. J. "Early American (Catholic) Hospital,"
Catholic World, v. 131 (1930),
290-298. O 102
O' GORMAN, JOHN J. "The
Franciscans in New Mexico,"
American Ecclesiastical Review, v. 79 (1928), 153-
173. O 103
O' GORMAN, JOHN J. "The
Franciscans in New Mexico
in the Sixteenth Century,"
American Ecclesiastical Re-
view, v. 81 (1929), 244-269.
O 104
O' GORMAN, THOMAS. The
Educational Policy of Arch-

bishop Ireland," Educational Review, v. 3 (1892), 462-471. O 105

O' GORMAN, THOMAS. A History of the Roman Catholic Church in the United States. New York. Christian Literature Co. 1895. xviii, 515p. O 106

O' GORMAN, THOMAS. The Medieval American Church. Catholic University Bulletin, v. 1 (1895), 415-427. O 107

O' GRADY, JOHN. Catholic Charities in the United States. Washington. National Conference of Catholic Charities. 1937. xxvi, 475p. O 108

O' GRADY, JOHN. Directory of Catholic Charities in the United States. Washington. National Conference of Catholic Charities. 1922. lv, 365p. O 109

O' HAGAN, THOMAS. "In the Footsteps of Texas Missionaries," Catholic World, v. 71 (1900), 340-351. O 110

O' HANLON, JOHN. Life and Scenery in Missouri. Reminiscences of a Missionary Priest. Dublin. J. Duffy and Co. 1890. xii, 292p. O 111

O' HANLON, JOHN CANON. "The Two Kenricks," American Catholic Historical Society of Philadelphia Records, v. 17 (1892), 382-406. O 112

O' HARA, EDWIN V. "Catholic Pioneers of the Oregon Country," Catholic Historical Review, v. 3 (1917), 187-201. O 113

O' HARA, EDWIN. "De Smet in the Oregon Country," Catholic World, v. 89 (1909), 317-331. O 114

O' HARA, EDWIN V. "De Smet in the Oregon Country," Oregon Historical Society Quarterly, v. 10 (1910), 239-262. O 115

O' HARA, EDWIN V. "Father De Smet in the Ecclesiastical Province of St. Paul," Acta et Dicta, v. 3 (1914), 290-305. O 116

O' HARA, EDWIN V. Pioneer Catholic History of Oregon. Portland, O. Glass and Prudhomme. 1911. 236p. incl. front., illus., port., maps. O 117

O' HARA, GEORGE. "Notes on Catholicity on Long Island," United States Catholic Historical Magazine, v. 4 (1891-1892), 203-205. O 118

O' HARA, GERALD P. "The Catholic Philopatrian Institute of Philadelphia, 1850-1890," Records of the American Catholic Historical Society of Philadelphia, v. 62 (1951), 23-32. O 119

O' HARA, JOHN P. Catholics in the Development of the Northwest. Portland. 1925. O 120

O' HARA, JOSEPH M. Chester's Century of Catholicism, 1842-1942. Philadelphia. Reilly. 1942. 221p. front. O 121

O' HARE, PATRICK F. Historical Sketch of the Church of St. Anthony of Padua, Brooklyn, New York. Benziger. 1897. O 122

O' HERN, JOHN F. "The Paulists' Diamond Jubilee," American Ecclesiastical Review, v. 88 (1933), 275. O 123

O' KEANE, JOSEPHINE. "Church in the Valley: St. Mary's Mission (Montana)," Ave Maria, v. 73 (Feb. 3, 1951), 148-152. O 124

O' KEEFE, SISTER FRANCIS OF ST. AUGUSTINE. "Letter to Rev. Th. Flynn, S.J., dated Ursuline Convent, New Orleans, June 17th, 1887," United States Catholic Historical Society Records and Studies, v. 4 (1906), 218-231. O 125

O' KEEFE, HENRY E. "Very Rev. Augustine F. Hewit, C. S. P.," American Catholic

277

Quarterly Review, v. 28 (1903), 535-542.   O 126

O' KEEFE, SISTER M. CALLISTA. Development of Catholic Education in the Diocese of Wilmington. MA thesis. Villanova University. 1929. 46p. O 127

OKLAHOMA (DIOCESE) SYNOD 1. Statuta dioeceseos Oklahomensis. Oklahoma. St. Joseph's Orphanage Press. n.d. [1913] xv, 143p.   O 128

OLSZYK, EDMUND G. The Polish Population in America. MA thesis. Marquette University. 1939.   O 129

OMAHA, NEB. (DIOCESE) SYNOD, 1st. 1887. Synodus dioecesana prima habita in ecclesia cathedrali ad S. Philumenae, in urbe Omaha, praeside Jacobo O'Connor, D. D., die I et 2 Martii 1887. Philadelphiae, Ex typographia Hardy et Mahony [n.d.] vii, 52p.   O 130

OMAHA (DIOCESE) SYNOD, 4th, 1934. Synodus dioecesana omahensis quarta die XIV Junii A.D. 1934 in ecclesia Sancti Joannis Omahae habita a Josepho Francisco Rummel [ep.] Omaha, Burkley envelope and printing co., 1934. 177p.   O 131

OWENSBORO (DIOCESE) SYNOD, 1st, 1943. The first synod of the diocese of Owensboro. St. Stephen's cathedral, Owensboro, Kentucky, Feb. 22nd, 1943. 85p.   O 132

O' MALLEY, AUSTIN. "Catholic Collegiate Education in the United States," Catholic World, v. 67 (1890), 289-304. O 133

O' MALLEY, FRANCIS JOSEPH. A Literary Addendum: Willa Cather's Archbishop Latour in Reality - John Baptist Lamy ... MA thesis. University of Notre Dame. 1933. 240p. map.   O 134

ONAHAN, MARY JOSEPHINE. "Sketch of Catholicity in Chicago," United States Catholic Historical Magazine, v. 4 (1891-1892), 91-96.   O 135

ONAHAN, WILLIAM J. "The Catholic Movement in Western Colonization--Colonization in Nebraska," American Catholic Quarterly Review, v. 6 (1881), 434-444.   O 136

ONAHAN, WILLIAM J. "Catholic Progress in Chicago," Illinois Catholic Historical Review, v. 1 (1918), 176-183.   O 137

ONAHAN, WILLIAM J. "A Chapter of Catholic Colonization," Acta et Dicta, v. 5 (1917), 67-77.   O 138

ONAHAN, WILLIAM J. "Irish Settlements in Illinois," Catholic World, v. 33 (1881), 157-162.   O 139

"ONE HUNDRED YEARS IN PHILADELPHIA: A CHAPTER FROM THE FORTHCOMING HISTORY OF THE CONGREGATION OF THE SISTERS OF ST. JOSEPH OF PHILADELPHIA," American Catholic Historical Society of Philadelphia Records, v. 58 (1947), 1-21.   O 140

ONG, WALTER J. American Catholic Crossroads: Religious-Secular Encounters in the Modern World. New York: Macmillan, 1959. xi, 160p.   O 141

ONG, W. J. "American Catholicism and America," Thought, v. 27 (1952), 521-541.   O 142

ONG, WALTER J. Frontiers of American Catholicism. New York: Macmillan, 1957. viii, 125p.   O 143
  Essays on ideology and culture.

O' NEILL, JAMES M. The Catholic in Secular Education. New York. Longmans, 1956. 172p.   O 144
  A discussion of the problems of the Catholic scholar in secular schools.

O' NEILL, JAMES M. Catholicism and American Freedom. New York. Harper. 1952. xii, 287p.   O 145
A scholarly and complete answer to Blanshard.

O'' NEILL, JAMES MILTON. "Church and State in the United States," United States Catholic Historical Society Records and Studies, v. 37 (1948), 22-87.   O 146

O'' NEILL, SISTER MARY ROSE-LINE. History of the Contribution of the Sisters of the Holy Names of Jesus and Mary to the Cause of Education in Florida. MA thesis. Fordham University. 1941. iii, 84p.   O 147

OPDNEAKER, THEODORE A. Saint Mary's Parish Centennial, 1849-1949. no pl. no pub. 1949? unpaged. illus.   O 148
St. Mary's, Perth Amboy, N.J.

ORE, LUIS JERONIMO DE. The Martyrs of Florida (1513-1616). Tr. by Maynard Geiger. New York. J.F. Wagner. 1937. xx, 145p.   O 149

O' REILLY, EDWARD C. Looking Back Fifty Years. Baraboo, Wis. The Author. 1949. x, 117p. plate, port.   O 150

O' REILLY, ISABEL M. (ed.) "An Interesting Correspondence," American Catholic Historical Society of Philadelphia Records, v. 14 (1903), 299-382, 439-514, v. 15 (1904), 83-112.   O 151
Bishop Cheverus.

O' REILLY, JOHN J. "The Centenary of the Diocese of Philadelphia--1908," American Catholic Historical Society of Philadelphia Records, v. 69 (1958), 3-8.   O 152

ORF, S.J. Chronicle of St. Peter's Parish, Jefferson City, Mo. Golden Jubilee, 1896. no pl. no pub. 1896? 59p. plates, ports, map.   O 153

"ORIGIN AND PROGRESS OF THE MISSION OF KENTUCKY," Catholic World, v. 21 (1875), 825-835.   O 154

"ORIGIN, DEVELOPMENT, AND POLICY OF THE CENTRAL VEREIN," Central Blatt and Social Justice, v. 2 (1909), 6-10.   O 155

O' ROURKE, JAMES J. Parish Registers. Washington. Catholic University. 1934. vii, 109p.   O 156

O' ROURKE, SISTER MARGHER-ITA MARIA. "History of the Cathedral Free Circulating Library of New York City (1887-1905)," Catholic Library World, v. 25 (1954), 115-119.   O 157
The library circulated 2,775,666 books during this time.

O' ROURKE, THOMAS P. The Franciscan Missions in Texas (1690-1793). Washington. Catholic University. 1927. iv, 107p.   O 158

O' RYAN, WILLIAM, AND T.H. MALONE. History of the Catholic Church in Colorado. Denver. Kelly. 1889.   O 158a

O' SHEA, JOHN J. The Two Kenricks. Philadelphia. J.J. McVey. 1904. xiv, 495p. 3 ports., incl. front. O 159

OSBORNE, WILLIAM. "Slavery's Sequel: a Freeman's Odyssey," Jubilee, v. 3 (Sept., 1955), 10-23.   O 160
On the beginnings of the work of the Church among the Negroes of the United States.

OSSENDORF, SISTER HENRITA. "Religious Community Life in the United States," Benedictine Review, v. 8 (1953), 27-29.   O 161
A summary report on the first National Congress of Religious held at the University of Notre Dame in

1952.
[OSTER, ANATOLE.] "My First
Mass in Graceville," Acta
et Dicta, v. 1 (1908), 192-
196.   O 162
OSTER, A. "Personal Reminis-
cence of Bishop Cretin," Acta
et Dicta, v. 1 (1907), 73-88.
                              O 163
OSTERMANN, L. "The Fran-
ciscans in the Wilds and
Wastes of Navajo Country,"
St. Anthony's Messenger, v.
8 (1899).   O 164
OSUCH, JOSEPH. "Patriarch of
the American Jesuits," Polish
American Studies, v. 18
(July-Dec. 1960), 92-100.
                              O 165
     Francis Dzierozynski, b.
     1779, to America 1822,
     d. 1850.
O' SULLIVAN, DONAL. "St.
Francis Cabrini," Studies, v.
35 (1946), 351-356.   O 166
O' SULLIVAN, DONAL. "Ter-
centenary of a Martyr. Saint
Isaac Jogues, S.J., Martyred
12 October, 1646," Studies,
v. 36 (1947), 49-56.   O 167
O' SULLIVAN, ST. JOHN. Little
Chapters About San Juan
Capistrano. 18th ed. San
Juan Capistrano, Calif. no
pub. 1912. 32p. incl. illus.,
ports.   O 168
OTT, E. R. (ed.) "Documents.
Selections from the Diary and
Gazette of Father Pierre
Portier, S.J. (1708-1781),"
Mid-America, v. 6 (1936),
199-207, 260-265.   O 169
OTT, SISTER MARY OF THE
SACRED HEART. The Know
Nothings in Alabama, 1854-1860.
MA thesis. Catholic Univer-
sity. 1945. 91p.   O 170
OTT, MICHAEL. "Benedictine
Education in the United States,"
Catholic Educational Review,
v. 2 (1911), 499-507.   O 171
OTTO, N.J. Die Mariengemeinde
zu Buffalo Grove, Illinois.
Techny, Ill. S.V.D. 1912.

125p. plates (ports.)
                              O 172
"OUR CONVENTS: THE URSU-
LINES," Metropolitan Magazine, v. 4 (1856), 87-92.
                              O 173
OUR HERITAGE. ONE HUN-
DRED YEARS OF FAITH. no
place. no pub. 1953. 44p.
illus., ports., statistics,
maps.   O 174
     The Centennial booklet of
     the Diocese of Springfield
     Illinois, 1853-1953.
OUR NEGRO AND INDIAN MIS-
SIONS. Baltimore. Com-
mission for the Catholic Mis-
sions among the Colored Peo-
ple and the Indians, 1886-
1925. Washington, 1925- .
                              O 175
"OUR TENTH BIRTHDAY"
Provincial Annals (Province
of the Most Holy Name, O.
F.M.), v. 7 (1947), 2.
                              O 176
"OUR UNKNOWN HEROES,"
Social Justice Review, v.
41 (1949), 352-353.   O 177
OURSLER, FULTON AND WILL.
Father Flanagan of Boys'
Town. Garden City. Double-
day. 1949. xvi, 302p.
illus., ports.   O 178
OWEN, ALLISON. "The Catholic
Martime Club of New Orleans,"
Catholic Charities Review, v.
35 (1949), 45-47.   O 179
OWENS, JOSEPH A. "Father
Choo Choo," Columbia, v. 40
(July 1960), 12-13, 45.
illus.   O 180
     Father Kieran A. Cassion,
     O.F.M., and his apostolate
     to railroad workers.
OWENS, SISTER M. LILLIANA.
"Across the Century in the
Chicago Catholic Church,
1843-1943," Illinois State
Historical Journal, v. 37
(Mar. 1941), 86-89.   O 181
OWENS, SISTER M. LILLIANA.
"The American Douai: The
National Pontifical Seminary

of Our Lady of Guadalupe,"
American Catholic Historical
Society of Philadelphia Re-
cords, v. 58 (1947), 22-
39.   O 182
OWENS, SISTER M. LILLIANA.
Carlos M. Pinto, S.J. El
Paso. Revista Catolica Press.
1951. 228p. illus.   O 183
A sketch of the life of the
Apostle of El Paso. In-
cludes much scattered infor-
mation on the story of the
Church of the Southwest.
OWENS, SISTER M. LILLIANA.
"Clerics of St. Viator," His-
torical Bulletin, v. 23 (1945),
37-38.   O 184
OWENS, M. LILLIANA. "Coming
of the Sisters of Loretto to
Denver and the Founding of St.
Mary's Academy," Colorado
Magazine, v. 16 (1939), 231-
235.   O 185
OWENS, SISTER M. LILLIANA.
"Denver's Pioneer Academy,"
Colorado Magazine, v. 14
(1937), 85-92.   O 186
OWENS, SISTER M. LILLIANA.
"The Early Work of the Loret-
tines in Southeastern Kansas,"
Kansas Historical Quarterly
v. 15 (1947), 263-276. illus.
                          O 187
OWENS, SISTER LILLIANA.
Florissant Heroines. Floris-
sant, Mo. King Publishing
Co. 1960. 45p. illus. O 188
Mother Philippine Duchesne
and the Sisters of Loretto at
the Foot of the Cross.
OWENS, SISTER M. LILLIANA.
"Frances Xavier Cabrini,
Foundress of Queen of Heaven
Institute," Colorado Magazine,
v. 22 (1945), 171-178. O 189
OWENS, SISTER M. LILLIANA.
"Growth of the Lorettines in
Missouri," American Catholic
Historical Society of Phila-
delphia Records, v. 71
(Sept.-Dec. 1960), 93-112.
                          O 190
OWENS, SISTER M. LILLIANA.

"The Guiding Light of the
Osages," Catholic Educational
Review, v. 39 (1941), 414-
420.   O 191
Mother Bridget Heyden.
OWENS, SISTER M. LILLIANA.
"Historical Sketch of the
Bernalillo Public High School,
1891-1945," American Cath-
olic Historical Society of
Philadelphia Records, v. 57
(1946), 73-87.   O 192
OWENS, SISTER MARY LILLIANA.
A History of the Sisters of
Loretto in the Trans-Missis-
sippi West. Ph.D. disserta-
tion Saint Louis University.
1925. xv, 621p.   O 193
OWENS, SISTER M. LILLIANA.
Jesuit Beginnings in New
Mexico, 1867-1882. El Paso,
Texas. Revista Catolica
Press. 1950. illus., ports.
plates.   O 194
OWENS, SISTER M. LILLIANA.
"Joseph Projectus Macheboeuf,"
New Mexico Historical Review,
v. 12 (1937), 193-203.
                          O 195
OWENS, SISTER M. LILLIANA.
"Loretto and Her Sesquicen-
tennial," Social Justice Review,
v. 54 (July-Aug., 1961),
133-136.   O 196
OWENS, SISTER M. LILLIANA.
"Loretto Foundations in
Louisiana and Arkansas,"
Louisiana History, v. 2
(Spring, 1961).   O 197
OWENS, SISTER M. LILLIANA.
Most Reverend Anthony J.
Schuler, S.J., D.D. El Paso,
Texas. Revista Catolica.
1953. xxiii, 584p. illus.
                          O 198
A profusely illustrated
biography of the first bishop
of El Paso. The book con-
tains information on the
story of the Church in Texas,
but is marred by inconse-
quential footnotes and ir-
relevant matter.
OWENS, SISTER M. LILLIANA.

"Our Lady of Light Academy,"
New Mexico Historical Review,
v. 13 (1938), 129-145. O 199
OWENS, SISTER LILLIANA. "The
Pioneer Days of the Loret-
tines in Missouri, 1823-1841,"
American Catholic Historical
Society of Philadelphia Records,
v. 70 (1960), 67-87. O 200
OWENS, SISTER M. LILLIANA.
"A Pioneer Educator," Catholic
Educational Review, v. 38
(1940), 419-424. O 201
Biographical sketch of Sister
Pancratia Bonfils and her
work in Colorado, born
1853, to Colorado 1868,
died 1915.

- P -

P., L.B. "Indian Education: An
Impending Calamity to the
Catholic Indians of Montana,"
American Ecclesiastical Review,
Supplementary Issue, October,
1892. 20p. P 1
PACELLI, CARLO. "Some
Considerations on the Catholic
Church and Catholics in the
United States," Il Dritto Ec-
clesiastico, (Oct.-Dec. 1953).
P 2
PAGANI, HUMBERT P. 200
Years of Catholicism in
Indiana, Indianapolis. H.P.
Pagani. (1934). 39p. incl.
front., illus., ports. P 3
PAHOREZKI, SISTER M.
SEVINA. The Social and
Political Activities of William
James Onahan. Washington.
Catholic University. 1942.
x, 249p. P 4
PALLADINO, LAWRENCE B.
Anthony Ravalli. Memoir.
Helena. 1884. P 5
PALLADINO, LAWRENCE B.
"The Catholic Church in
Montana," Woodstock Letters,
v. 9 (1880), 95-106. P 6
PALLADINO, LAWRENCE B.
Indian and White in the North-
west. A History of Catholicity
in Montana (1831-1891). rev.

ed. Lancaster, Pa. Wicker-
sham Printing Co. 1922. xx,
514p. front., illus., plates,
ports. P 7
PALM, SISTER MARY BORGIA.
The Jesuit Missions of the
Illinois Country, 1673-1763.
Cleveland. no pub. 1933.
138p. map. P 8
PALM, SISTER MARY BORGIA.
"Kaskakia. Indian Mission
Village," Mid-America, v. 5
(1933), 14-25. P 9
PALMIERI, AURELIO. Il
Grave Problema Religioso-
Italiano Negle Stati Uniti.
Firenze. Libreria editrice
Florentina. 1921. 68p.
P 10
PALOU, FRANCISCA. The
Expedition into California of
the Venerable Fray Junipero
Serra ... 1769. San Fran-
cisco. Nueva California
Press. 1934. 124p. front.
(port.) fold, map, facsims.
P 11
PALOU, FRAY FRANCISCO.
Historical Memoirs of New
California. tr. and ed. by
Herbert Bolton. Berkeley.
University of California Press.
1926. 4v. fronts, plates,
ports., maps, facsims. P 12
PALOU, FRANCISCO. Junipero
Serra. Santa Barbara. W.
D. Cogan. 1934. xv, 48p.
front., illus., facsim. P 13
PALOU, FRANCISCO. Francis-
co Palou's Life and Apostolic
Labors of the Venerable
Father Junipero Serra. Pasa-
dena. G.S. James. 1913.
xxiv, 338p. incl. illus.,facsim.
fold. map. P 14
PANTANELLA, DOMENICO.
"Lettera LV," Lettere Edificanti
Provincia Napolitana, ser. 4
(1882-1883), 125-126, P 15
Dated "Morrison, Colo.,
10 Ottobre, 1884." On the
question of a college in
Denver.
PANTANELLA, DOMENICO.

"Lettera LXIX," Lettere Edificanti Provincia Napolitana, ser. 4 (1882-1883), 168-169.　　　P 16
　Dated "College of the Sacred Heart, Colorado, N.M. [sic.] 3 Ottobre, 1885," A general letter on the college at Morrison and the possibilities of a school in Denver.

PARE, GEORGE. The Catholic Church in Detroit. Gabriel Richard Press. 1951. xv, 717p. plates, ports, maps on end papers.　　　P 17
　An excellent history of the Church in Detroit, concentrating on early Detroit. Considered one of the finest productions in church history in recent years.

PARE, GEORGE. "St. Joseph Mission," Mississippi Valley Historical Review, v. 17 (1930), 24-54.　　　P 18

PARGELLIS, STANLEY. "Father Gabriel Richard," Michigan History, v. 43 (1959), 155-172.　　　P 19
　Popular.

PARISEAU, A.A. History of the Society of Mary in Texas. MA thesis. Loyola University (Chicago). 1939.　　　P 20

PARISH, . "Father Mazzuchelli," The Palimpsest, v. 1 (1920), 101-110.　　　P 21

PARISOT, P. F. Reminiscences of a Texas Missionary. San Antonio. Johnson Bros. Printing Co. 1899. 227p. front. (port.)　　　P 22

PARISOT, P. F. AND C. J. SMITH (comp.) History of the Catholic Church in the Diocese of San Antonio, Texas. San Antonio. Carrico and Bowen. 1897. 218p. incl. ads, illus.　　　P 23

PARK, ROBERT E. The Immigrant Press and Its Control. New York. Harper and Bros. 1922. xix, 487p. illus. (maps), tables, diagr.　　　P 24

PARKE, Catholic Missions in Virginia. Richmond. 1850.　　　P 25

PARKMAN, FRANCIS. The Jesuits in North America in the Seventeenth Century. Boston. Little Brown and Co. 1867. lxxxix, 463p. map.　　　P 26

"PAROCHIAL STATISTICS OF THE UKRANIAN CATHOLIC EXARCHY IN THE UNITED STATES OF AMERICA," The Ark, v. 11 (1956), 5-8.　　　P 27

PAROKI, L. "Indian Missions. Letter dated Yakima, Ellensburgh, June 11, 1882," Woodstock Letters, v. 12 (1883), 53-56.　　　P 28

PARRINGTON, VERNON L. The Main Currents in American Thought. New York. Harcourt, Brace and Co. 1939. 3v.　　　P 29

"PARROCCHIA DEL SACRO CUORE IN DENVER," Lettere Edificanti Provincia Napolitana, ser. 8, n. 1 (1899), 55-58.　　　P 30
　On the question of the ownership of the property and the necessity of an Italian parish in Denver.

PARSONS, KITTY. The Story of the Church of Our Lady of Good Voyage, Gloucester, Mass. N. Montpelier, Vt. Driftwood Press. 1945. 30p. illus.　　　P 31

PARSONS, ROBERT A. "Catholic Education in Philadelphia," America, v. 45 (1927), 278-279.　　　P 32

PARSONS, ROBERT A. "Father Henry Harrison," Woodstock Letters, v. 82 (1953), 118-140.　　　P 33
　A well documented biography of this Jesuit of colonial Maryland who was also known as a missionary to the Indians of New York and who died in 1700.

PARSONS, WILFRID. "Brownson, Hecker, and Hewit," Catholic World, v. 153 (1941), 396-408. P 34

PARSONS, WILFRID. "The Catholic Church in America in 1819," Catholic Historical Review, v. 5 (1920), 301-310. P 35

PARSONS, WILFRID. Early Catholic Americana. New York. Macmillan. 1939. xxv, 282p. P 36

PARSONS, WILFRID. "Early Catholic Publishers of Philadelphia," Catholic Historical Review, v. 24 (1938), 141-152. P 37

PARSONS, WILFRID. "Father Anthony Kohlman, S.J. (1771-1824)," Catholic Historical Review, v. 4 (1918), 38-51. P 38

PARSONS, WILFRID. The First Freedom. Considerations on Church and State in the United States. New York. Declan X. McMullen. 1948. xii, 178p. P 39

PARSONS, WILFRID. "The Paulist Fathers, 1853-1933," America, v. 48 (1933), 379-381. P 40

PARSONS, WILFRID. "Researches in Early Catholic Americana," Papers of the Bibliographical Society of America, v.33 (1939), 55-68. P 41

PARTOLL, ALBERT J. ed. Mengarini's Narrative of the Rockies, Memoirs of Old Oregon, 1841-1850, and St. Mary's Mission. Missoula. 1938. P 42

"PASTORS OF CONEWAGO, 1750-1880," American Catholic Historical Society of Philadelphia Records, v. 60 (1949), 144-146. P 43

PATERSON, CHARLES E. "Notes on Old Cahokia," Illinois State Historical Society Journal, v. 42 (1949), 7-29, 193-208, 313-343. P 44

PATERSON (DIOCESE) SYNOD 1. Synodal statutes of the diocese of Paterson. Paterson. St. John Baptist Cathedral. n.d. P 45

"PATRIARCH DES NORDWES-TERN ÜBER DIE DEUTSCHEN EINWANDERER," Central Blatt and Social Justice, v. 16 (1923), 161. P 46

PATRICE, SISTER M. "Art Education in Catholic Schools," Catholic School Journal, v. 52 (1952), 5-7, 107-111. P 47
Contains a good summary of the present status of the teaching of art in the Catholic secondary schools.

PATEE, RICARDO. El Catolicismo en Estados Unidos. Mexico. Editorial Jus. 1945. ii, 541p. P 48

PATTERSON, HARVEY. "Old Missions of San Antonio, Texas," St. Anthony Messenger, v. 1933/34, 643-645. P 49

PATTERSON, SISTER MARY HYACINTH. The Life of a Jesuit Missioner in France. MA thesis. Marquette University. 1934. P 50

PAUL. Paulist Fathers in Tennessee, 1900-1950. Memphis, Tenn. Wimmer Bros. 43p. P 51

PAUL, PETER J. "Some Facts in the Early Missionary History of the Northwest: The Legend of Marcus Whitman," American Catholic Historical Society of Philadelphia Records, v. 40 (1929), 97-122. P 52

PAULHUBER, FRANZ XAVER. Bilder des Amerika. Missions-Lebens in zwölf aus lesenen in Nord Amerika gehalten Predigten. Freycing. 1864. P 53

PAULHUBER, FRANZ XAVER. "Letter of the Rev. Francis Xaver Paulhuber to Archbishop Reisach, Milwaukee, July 22, 1855," Salesianum,

v. 39 (1944), 171-177.   P 54
PAULHUBER, FRANZ XAVER.
"Letter of Rev. Francis X.
Paulhuber to Archbishop
Reisach, President of the
Ludwig Missionsverein, Hei-
deck, Bavaria, April 11,
1859," Salesianum, v. 40
(1945), 124.   P 55
PAULHUBER, FRANZ XAVER.
"Letter to Archbishop Reisach,
President of the Ludwig Mis-
sionsverein, Heideck, Bavaria,
April 11, 1859," Salesianum,
v. 40 (1945), 123.   P 56
PAULHUBER, FRANZ XAVER.
"Mittheilungen des Missionärs
V.X. Paulhuber über seinen
Aufenthalt in usereem Lande,"
Central Blatt and Social Jus-
tice, v. 10 (1917), 44-46, 74-
76, 133-136, 163-165, 236-
238, 266-268, (1918), 327-328,
356-358.   P 57
PAULMANN, FREDERICK H.
Catholic Beginnings in the
Town of New Rochelle: the
Mission Period. MA thesis.
Fordham University. 1952.
iv, 93p.   P 58
PAULMANN, FREDERICK H. "Cath-
olic Beginnings in the Town of
New Rochelle," United States
Historical Society Records and
Studies, v. 51 (1953), 71-93.
     P 59
PAULWELYN, CYRIL. "The
Beginnings and Growth of the
Catholic Church in the State
of Montana," Acta et Dicta,
v. 5 (1918), 230-237.   P 60
PAULWELYN, C. The Beginning
and Growth of the Catholic
Church in the State of Montana.
Butte. 1918.   P 62
PAX, GEORGE. "Andenken an den
Hochwürdigen Johannes Nicolaus
Mertz, einen der ersten
deutschen Priester in den Ver-
einigten Staaten," Pastoral Blatt
(St. Louis), v. 1 (1866-1867),
103-106, 142-147.   P 62
PAYNE, RAYMOND. "Annals of
the Leopoldine Association,"

Catholic Historical Review, v.
1 (1915-1916), 51-63, 175-
191.   P 63
A list of items in the
"Berichte der Leopoldine
Stiftung im Kaiserthum
Oesterreich" dealing with
the Church in America.
PAYNE, RAYMOND. Leopoldine
Association and Its Work in
Ohio, 1829-1840. MA thesis.
Catholic University. 1916.
72p.   P 64
PERROTTA, CHRISTOPHER.
Catholic Care of the Italian
Immigrant in the United States.
MA thesis. Catholic Univer-
sity. 1925. 100p.   P 65
PEKARI, MATTHEW A. "The
German Catholics of the U.S.
of America," American Cath-
olic Historical Society of
Philadelphia Records, v. 36
(1925), 305-358.   P 66
PEKARLI, MATTHEW A. Ger-
man Catholics in the United
States of America. MA thesis.
Catholic University. 1925.
68p.   P 67
PELLENTZ, JAMES. "Pennsyl-
vania, 1785-1786," Woodstock
Letters, v. 15 (1886), 190-
193.   P 68
PELOQUIN, PIERRE J. Notre
Dame de Chicago, 1887-1937.
Chicago. Fathers of the
Blessed Sacrament. 1937.
164p. illus., ports., facsims.
     P 69
"PENN." "Father Barbelin," A-
merican Catholic Historical
Researches, v. 26 (1911),
205-210.   P 70
"PENNSYLVANIA. SOME HIS-
TORICAL DOCUMENTS,"
Woodstock Letters, v. 15
(1886), 48-61.   P 71
PEORIA, ILL. (DIOCESE) SYNOD,
3rd, 1915. Constitutiones
dioecesis peoriensis quae in
synodo dioecesana tertia die I,
mensis Decembris, A.D. 1915
habita in ecclesia cathedrali
Sanctae Mariae Peoriae, Illinois,

ab Edmundo M. Dunne, S.T. D. episcopo peoriensi latae et promulgatae fuerunt. Bloomington, Ill., Typis Pantagraph printing and stationary co., 1915. xvi, 72p.   P 72

PERBAL, A. "Le Père Jésuite Sébastian Rasle agent de la France chez les Abenakis," RHM (Paris) 1939, 527-539.   P 73

PERE THÉODORE DE THEUX DE LA COMPAGNIE DE JESUS ET LA MISSION BELGE DU MISSOURI. Roulers. 1913.   P 74
The only printed English account of de Theux is in DeSmet, Western Missions and Missionaries, pp. 474-485.

PEREZOINA, SISTER ISABELLA. "Aus dem Anfangen der Ursulinen Niederlassung in St. Louis," Central Blatt and Social Justice, v. 17 (1925), 376-377, 395.   P 75

PERKINS, WILLIAM RUFUS. History of the Trappist Abbey of New Melleray, Iowa City. The University. 1892. iv, 79p.   P 76

PEROTTI, LEONARD DAVID. "Jeffersonville Parish Celebrates Centennial," Provincial Annals (Province of the Most Holy Name, O.F.M.), v. 4 (1944), 197-204.   P 77

PERRICHON, ABBE J. Vie de Mgr. Dubuis, L'Apôtre de Texas. Lyon. Librairie Vitte. 1900.   P 78

PERRIG, E.M. "Dakota. Letter dated St. Francis Mission, Feb. 15th, 1887," Woodstock Letters, v. 16 (1887), 173-175.   P 79

PERRIG, E.M. "Dakota. St. Francis Mission. Rosebud Agency, Oct. 25th, 1886," Woodstock Letters, v. 15 (1886), 316-318.   P 80

PERRY, SISTER MARY DOROTHEA. A History of the Educational Work of the Sisters of the Holy Names of Jesus and Mary in California from 1868 to 1920. MA thesis. Catholic University. 1957.   P 81

PERSONÉ, CARLO. "Lettera XLVII," Lettere Edificanti Provincia Napolitana, ser. 4 (1882-1883), 111-112.   P 82

PERSONÉ, CARLO. "Lettera XLIX," Lettere Edificanti Provincia Napolitana, ser. 4 (1882-1883), 115-116.   P 83

PERSONÉ, SALVATORE. "Da Trinidad (Colo.)," Lettere Edificanti Provincia Napolitana ser. 9, n. 2 (1902), 362-366.   P 84
Two letters to the Jesuit Provincial at Naples dated "27 Marzo, 1901, 26 Dicembre, 1901." Description of a mission given in Tucson, Arizona by Father Modesto Isaguirre.

PERSONÉ, SALVATORE. "Da Varie Lettere del P. Salvatore Persone," Lettere Edificanti Provincia Napolitana, ser. 8, n. 1 (1899), 83-99.   P 85

PERSONÉ, SALVATORE. "Lettera III," Lettere Edificanti Provincia Napolitana ser. 1 (1875), 2-4.   P 86
Dated "Conejos (Colorado) Febr. 1874." A description of Conejos and the San Luis Valley, with a history of the Mission at Conejos.

PERSONÉ, SALVATORE. "Lettera XV," Lettere Edificanti Provincia Napolitana, ser. 1 (1875), 38-40.   P 87
Dated "Conejos, N.S. de Guadalupe, Augosto, 1874." A description of the observance of the Feast of Corpus Christi, burial customs, and the Penitentes.

PERSONÉ, SALVATORE. "Lettera XLI," Lettere Edificanti Provincia Napolitana, ser. 1 (1875), 111-114.   P 88

Dated "Guadalupe-Conejos
Marzo, 1875." A description
of a mission given at Trinidad, Colorado.
PERSONÉ, SALVATORE. "Lettera
LI," Lettere Edificanti Pro-
vincia Napolitana, ser. 2
(1876-1877), 140-144. P 89
Dated "Las Vegas, 24
Maggio, 1878." On troubles
connected with the establish-
ment of Las Vegas College,
and the formation of a corpor-
ation to hold property.
PERSONÉ, SALVATORE. "Lettera
L," Lettere Edificanti Pro-
vincia Napolitana, ser. 4
(1882-1883), 116-118. P 90
Dated "Albuquerque (Nuovo
Messico), 20 Gemnaio,
1884." A description of
the work of the Jesuits in
Albuquerque.
PERSONÉ, SALVATORE. "Texas.
Letter dated Isleta, Texas,
January 17th, 1884," Woodstock
Letters, v. 13 (1884), 123-
124. P 91
PERSONÉ, SALVATORE. "Trinidad
(Colorado)," Lettere Edificanti
Provincia Napolitana, ser. 9,
n. 1 (1901), 119-126. P 92
PERSONÉ, SALVATORE. "Trinidad
(Colorado). Una Missioncella
nel Saguache," Lettere Edificanti
Provincia Napolitana, ser. 8,
n. 2 (1900), 133-137. P 93
PERSONS, BILLIE. "Secular
Life in the San Antonio Mis-
sions," Southwestern Historical
Quarterly, v. 62 (1958), 45-
62. P 94
[PERSONS, ROBERT.] "The
Jesuit Father Person's Judg-
ment about Transferring
English Catholics to the
Northern Parts of America, for
Inhabiting Those Parts and Con-
verting Those Barbarous People
to Christianity," American
Catholic Historical Researches,
v. 18 (1901), 15-17. P 95
PETER, P. "Cluny, in Southern
Illinois, A One-Time Bene-

dictine Priory," Central Blatt
and Social Justice, v. 19
(1927), 377-379, 414-416;
v. 20 (1927), 54-56, 89-91,
137-139, 180-181, 251-252,
287-288. P 96
PETER, SARAH. Memoirs of
the Life of Mrs. Sarah Peter.
ed. by Margaret Rivers King.
Cincinnati. R.H. Clarke and
Co. 1889. 2v. P 97
PETERS, SISTER MARY
PETRINA. Pioneer German
Catholics of Iowa, 1833-
1860. MA thesis. Catholic
University. 1941. 95p.
P 98
PETERSON, SVEND. "The Little
Rock Against the Big Rock,"
Arkansas Historical Quarterly,
v. 2 (1943), 164-170. P 99
Brief sketch of the activities
of Bishop Edward Fitzgerald
of Little Rock, Arkansas, at
the Vatican Council.
PETIT, . "The Natchez Indians
in 1730. Letter of Rev. Fr.
Petit, S.J., to Rev. Fr.
Davougour, S.J., Procurator
General of the Missions in
North America, dated New
Orleans, July 12, 1730,"
Woodstock Letters, v. 3 (1874),
163-172, v. 4 (1875), 21-29,
150-160, v. 5 (1876), 3-16.
P 100
PETIT, BENJAMIN MARIE. The
Trail of Death. Letters of
Benjamin Marie Petit. ed.
by Irving McKee. Indianapolis.
Indiana Historical Society.
1941. 141p. P 101
"PETITION OF INDIANS OF
MAINE TO BISHOP CARROLL
FOR A PRIEST, 1791," A-
merican Catholic Historical
Researches, v. 16 (1899),
115-116. P 102
PEYTON, PAULINE LANCASTER.
"Pierre Gibault, Priest and
Patriot," American Catholic
Historical Society of Phila-
delphia Records, v. 12
(1901), 452-498. P 103

PFAB, CHARLES B. American Hospital Chaplains during the Civil War, 1861-1865. MA thesis. Catholic University. 1955. P 104

PFALLER, LOUIS L. "Abbot and Bishop Wehrle: a Benedictine on the Old Frontier," American Benedictine Review, v. 12 (December, 1961), 461-484. P 105
A series of letters dated variously 1886-1894, dealing with the Dakota Territory.

PFALLER, LOUIS L. Catholic Missionaries and the Fort Berthold Indians before 1889. MA thesis. Loyola University (Chicago). 1950. 153p. P 106

PFAU, RALPH SYLVESTER. History of Catholic Secondary Education in the Diocese of Indianapolis. MA thesis. Fordham University. 1934. iii, 109p. P 107

PFEIL, N. "St. Mary's Theological Seminary, Cleveland, Ohio," American Ecclesiastical Review, v. 19 (1898), 272-282. P 108

PHELAN, JOHN G. A History of the Rise and Progress of Catholicism in Wallingford. 40p. front. P 109

PHELAN, THOMAS P. Catholics in Colonial Days. New York. Kenedy. 1935. xviii, 292p. front. (port.) P 110

PHELAN, THOMAS P. Thomas Dongan, Colonial Governor of New York, 1683-1688. New York. Kenedy. 1933. xv, 154p. front. (port.) P 111

PHELAN, THOMAS P. 'Rt. Rev. John England, First Bishop of Charleston," American Irish Historical Society Journal, v. 14 (1914), 115-126. P 112

PHILADELPHIA (DIOCESE) SYNOD, 1st, 1832. Acta synodi dioecesanae philadelphiensis primae, habita in ecclesia cathedrali S. Mariae, Philadel-

phiae, A.D. MDCCCXXXII, mense Maii, a Francisco Patricio Kenrick ... Philadelphiae, E. Cummiskey, ed. - ex typis F. Pierson, 1832. 16p. P 113

PHILADELPHIA (DIOCESE) SYNOD, 1857. Constitutiones dioecesanae in synodis philadelphiensibus, annis, 1832. 1842, 1847, 1853, et 1855 latae et promulgatae Philadelphiae, Ex typis J.B. Chandler, 1855. 62p. P 114
Includes the 6th synod held in 1857.

"PHILADELPHIA PARISH," Jubilee, v. 3 (1955), Sept., 24-30. Story of the Negro parish of St. Elizabeth in Philadelphia. P 115

PHILIBERT, HELENE, et. al. St. Matthew's of Washington. 1840-1940. Baltimore. A. Hoen and Co. 1940. vii, 154p. plates, ports. P 116

PHILLIPS, PHILIP. "On the Religious Proscription of Catholics," American Jewish Archives, v. 11 (1959), 176-183. P 117

"PIERRE HUET DE LA VALINIÈRE, PRIEST, ON LAKE CHAMPLAIN, 1790-1791," Moorsfield Antiquarian, v. 1 (1938), 239-255. P 118

PIERZ, FRANZ. Die Indianer in Nord-America. St. Louis. Mo. Franz Saler. 1855. 130p. P 119

PIERZ, FRANZ. "The Indians of North America," Social Justice Review, v. 40 (1947), 24-27, 59-62, 130-132, 167-170, 207-209, 243-245, 278-282, (1948), 316-318, 353-355, 388-390; v. 41 (1948), 24-27, 60-64, 97-100, 132-134, 168-170. P 120

PIERZ, FRANZ. "Letters of Father Franz Pierz, Pioneer Missioner," Central Blatt and Social Justice, v. 26 (1934), 320-323, 356-359, 394-396;

v. 27 (1934-1935), 18-19, 54-56, 90-92, 132, 178-179, 212-214, 285-286, 320-322. P 121

PIETTE, CHARLES J.G.M. "The Diaries of Early California, 1769-1784," Americas, v. 2 (1946), 409-422. P 122

PIETTE, CHARLES J.G.M. Evocation de Junipero Serra. Washington. Academy of American Franciscan History. 1946. 439p. P 123

PIETTE, CHARLES J.G.M. "The Missions of Colonial New Mexico," Americas, v. 4 (1947), 243-254. P 124

PIETTE, CHARLES J.G.M. (tr. and ed.) "A Real Cedula in Favor of the Entrada of the Dominican Fathers into New Mexico," Americas, v. 4. (1947), 255-256. P 125

PIETTE, CHARLES J.G.M. Le Secret de Junipero Serra, Fondateur de la Californie-Nouvelle, 1769-1784. Washington. Academy of American Franciscan History. 1949. 2v. 480p. P 126

PIETTE, CHARLES J.G.M. "Two Unknown Manuscripts Belonging to Early California (Crespi and Serra)," Americas, v. 3 (1946), 91-101. P 127

PIETTE, CHARLES, J.G.M. (ed.) "An Unpublished Diary of Fray Juan Crespi, O.F.M.," Americas, v. 3 (1946), 102-114, 234-243, (1947), 368-381. Spanish only. P 128

PIKE, J. J. History of St. Charles Church and Centenary of the Congregation, 1806-1906, St. Mary, Ky. no pub. 1907. 120p. ports., illus. P 129

PINE, SISTER MARY PAULINE. A Glory of Maryland. Philadelphia. Salesian Press, Don Bosco Institute. 88p. P 130 Leonard Neale.

PINTO, CARLOS M. "Lettera IV," Lettere Edificanti Provincia Napolitana, ser. 1 (1875), 5-7. P 131

Dated "Pueblo Febr., 1874," A description of the beginnings of the Jesuit parish in Pueblo.

PINTO, CAROLOS M. "Lettera XXVI," Lettere Edificanti Provincia Napolitana, ser. 1 (1875), 71-72. P 132 Dated "Pueblo, Novembre, 1874." On the difficulties of the mission work in Colorado.

PINTO, CARLOS M. "Lettera XX," Lettere Edificanti Provincia Napolitana, ser. 2 (1876-1877), 79-80. P 133 Dated "Trinidad, Decembre, 1876." On the work of the Jesuits in Trinidad, Colorado.

PINTO, CARLO M. "Lettera L," Lettere Edificanti Provincia Napolitana, ser. 2 (1876-1877), 139. P 134

PIOTRZKOWSKI, JAMES. Benedictines in Rural Colonization. MA thesis. Catholic University. 1934. 107p. P 135

PIRET, ANDREW J. "Father Piret Lands in New York, 1846," Mid-America, v. 37 (1955), 229-235. P 136 Introduction and editing by Alexis A. Praus, taken from Piret's Journal.

PIRON, PAUL. Isaac Jogues. Apôtre et martyr des Paux-Rouges, 1607-1646. Namur. Grands Lace. 1946. 176p. P 137

PITTSBURGH (DIOCESE) SYNOD, 1846. Statuta Dioecesis Pittsburgensis lata in Dioecesana habita A.D. 1844 et in aliis synodis A.D. 1846 et A.D. 1854 emendata. Pittsburgh. George Quigley, 1854. 26p. P 138

PITTSBURGH (DIOCESE) SYNOD. Statuta Dioecesis Pittsburgensis lata in Synodo Dioecesana habita A.D. 1844 cum decretis in aliis Synodis A.D. 1846, 1854, 1858, 1869 promulgatis.

Pittsburgh. James Porter. 1870.
43p. P 139
PITTSBURG, PA. (DIOCESE)
SYNOD, 1st to 6th, 1844 to
1893. Statuta dioeceseos pittsburgensis in synodis dioecesanis,
habitis annis Domini 1844, 1846,
1856, 1858, 1869, lata, et
prout nunc prostant promulgata
in synodo dioecesana sexta,
diebus 7, 8 et 9 Februarii,
1893 habita, a Richardo Phelan,
episcopo pittsburgensi, Pitts-
burgi, 1893. 1 p.l., iii, 81p.
P 140
PITTSBURG, PA. (DIOCESE)
SYNOD, 7th, 1896. Statuta
synodi septimae pittsburgensis
habitae die 15ta Aprilis 1896.
[4]p. P 141
Caption title.
PITTSBURG, PA. (DIOCESE)
SYNOD, 8th, 1899. Decreta
synodi octavae pittsburgensis,
habitae die 13tia Octobris
1899. [n.p.,n.d.] [4]p. P 142
Caption title.
PITTSBURG, PA. (DIOCESE)
SYNOD, 9th, 1902. Decreta
synodi nonae pittsburgensis
habitae 30mo Octobris 1902.
[n.p., n.d.] [4]p. P 143
PITTSBURG, (DIOCESE) SYNOD,
10th, 1905. Statuta dioeceseos
pittsburgensis in synodis
dioecesanis lata, et prout nunc
prostant promulgata in synodo
dioecesana decima die 10
mensis Oct., A.D. 1905 habita,
a Regis Canevin [ep.] [n.p.]
1906. 100p. P 144
PLAISSANCE, ALOYSIUS. "Benedictine Monks in Alabama,
1876-1956," Alabama Review,
v. 11 (1958), 56-63. P 145
PLAISSANCE, ALOYSIUS. "Dom
Pierre Joseph Didier, Pioneer
Benedictine Missionary in the
United States," American
Benedictine Review, v. 3
(1952), 23-26. P 146
PLAISSANCE, ALOYSIUS.
"Ethan Allen's Daughter, First
United States Nun," American

Benedictine Review, v. 8
(1957), 144-152. P 147
PLANTE, GEORGE ROBERT.
The Franco-American Parish
in New England. MA thesis.
Fordham University. 1940.
iii, 128p. P 148
[PLASSMANN] Very Rev. Thomas
Plassmann, 1879-1959. Pro-
vincial Annals (Province of
the Most Holy Name, O.F.M.),
v. 16 (1959), 97-102. P 149
On the faculty of St. Bona-
venture College for 45
years.
PLASSMANN, THOMAS. "Reminis-
cences of the Late Archbishop
(Paschal) Robinson," Provin-
cial Annals (Province of the
Most Holy Name, O.F.M.),
v. 9 (1949), 77-84. P 150
PLASSMANN, THOMAS. "In
Memoriam: Adalbert Callahan,
O.F.M.," Provincial Annals
(Province of the Most Holy
Name, O.F.M.), v. 9 (1949),
154. P 151
PLASSMANN, THOMAS. "There
Were Giants in Those Days,"
Provincial Annals (Province
of the Most Holy Name, O.
F.M.), v. 14 (1959), 92-
96. P 152
Recollections of O.F.M.'s
at turn of century, Paterson,
N.J.
PLASSMEYER, THEODORE.
"Propaganda Foiled: A contri-
bution to the Study of Prejudice
and Intolerance," Social Jus-
tice Review, v. 42 (1949),
312-314, 348-350, 385-389;
v. 43 (1949-1950), 25-29, 61-
64, 96-100, 132-135, 168-
170, 204-206, 238-242, 276-
278. P 153
PLASSMEYER, THEODOSIUS.
"The Church in Early Iowa
City, 1864-1865," Iowa Catholic Historical Review, v. 9
(Jan., 1936), 21-37. P 154
PLESSIS, JOSEPH-OCTAVE.
Journal des Visites Pastorales
de 1815 et 1816, ed. by Henri

Têtu. Québec. Imprimerie
Franciscaine Missionnaire.
1903. P 155
PLUMPE, J. C. "Father Jessing
(1836-1899)," Central Blatt
and Social Justice, v. 30
(1937), 17-19, 53-55, 71,
88-91. P 156
POLLOCK, SISTER MARY
AZRAELIA. Story of St.
Boniface's German Catholic
Parish as Related by Rev. F.
J. Simonik, World Missionary,
in His Journal for 1890-1891.
MA thesis. Seattle University.
1955. ii, 37p. P 157
POHLKAMP, DIOMEDE. "Father
Bonaventure Hammer, O.F.M.,"
Provincial Chronicle (St.
John Baptist Province, O.F.
M.), v. 9 (1927), 45-50.
P 158
POHLKAMP, DIOMEDE. The
First Franciscan Missionary
in Kentucky. St. Anthony
Hospital, Louisville, Ky. no
pub. 1944. 21p. P 159
Charles Whelan.
POHLKAMP, DIOMEDE. "First
Franciscan Pastor of Hamilton,
Ohio," Provincial Chronicle
(St. John Baptist Province,
O.F.M.), v. 6 (1934),
21-23. P 160
POHLKAMP, DIOMEDE. "A
Franciscan Artist of Kentucky.
Johann Schmitt, 1825-1898,"
Franciscan Studies, v. 28
(1947), 147-170. P 161
POHLKAMP, DIOMEDE. "Life
and Times of Father William
Unterthiner, O.F.M., 1809-
1857," Provincial Chronicle
(St. John Baptist Province,
O.F.M.), v. 15 (1943), 3-15,
57-73. P 162
POHLKAMP, DIOMEDE. "Spanish
Franciscans in the Southeast,"
Franciscan Educational Confer-
ence Annual Report, v. 18
(1936), 124-150. maps, plate.
P 163
POINT, NICHOLAS. "Recollec-
tions of the Rocky Mountains,"

Woodstock Letters, v. 11
(1882), 298-321; v. 12 (1883),
3-22, 133-153, 262-268; v.
13 (1884), 3-13. P 164
POLD, F.B. "Erinnerungen an
das Missionsleben in Nebraska,"
Die Katholischen Missionen,
v. 17 (1889), 137-142, 165-
170, 191-194. P 165
"POLISH MISSIONARY WORK IN
THE UNITED STATES,"
Woodstock Letters, v. 38
(1909), 350-364. P 166
POLNAISE, A. "Parkman and
the Martyrs," Commonweal,
v. 12 (1930), 546-548.
P 167
PONZIGLIONE, PAUL MARY.
"The Arapahoe Indians. Letter
dated St. Stephen's Mission,
Lander, Wyoming, April 14th,
1890," Woodstock Letters, v.
19 (1890), 312-316.] P 168
PONZIGLIONE, PAUL MARY.
"The Arapahoes in Wyoming.
Letter dated St. Stephen's
Mission, Spokane Reservation,
December 23, 1890," Wood-
stock Letters, v. 20 (1891),
220-224. P 169
PONZIGLIONE, PAUL MARY.
"The Arapahoes in Wyoming.
Letter dated St. Stephen's
Missions, Fremont Co.,
Wyoming, Aug. 29, 1891,"
Woodstock Letters, v. 20
(1891), 385-388. P 170
PONZIGLIONE, PAUL MARY.
"History of the Society's Work
in Southeastern Kansas,"
Woodstock Letters, v. 13
(1884), 19-32. P 171
PONZIGLIONE, PAUL MARY.
"Indian Traditions. Among the
Osage," Woodstock Letters, v.
18 (1889), 68-76. P 172
PONZIGLIONE, PAUL MARY.
"Indian Missions. Letter
dated St. Francis' Institute,
Osage Mission, Neosho Co.,
Kansas, July 1, 1878," Wood-
stock Letters, v. 7 (1878),
184-187. P 173
PONZIGLIONE, PAUL MARY.

"Indian Missions. Letter dated Neosho County, Kansas, December 15th, 1878," Woodstock Letters, v. 8 (1879), 80-86. P 174

PONZIGLIONE, PAUL MARY. "Indian Missions. Letter dated Residence of St. Francis de Hieronymo, Osage Mission, Kansas, July 17th, 1879," Woodstock Letters, v. 8 (1879), 158-163. P 175

PONZIGLIONE, PAUL MARY. "Indian Missions. Letter dated Osage Mission, Kansas, December 31st, 1879," Woodstock Letters, v. 9 (1880), 118-124. P 176

PONZIGLIONE, PAUL MARY. "Indian Mission. Letter dated Osage Mission, Kansas, June 30th, 1880," Woodstock Letters, v. 9 (1880), 213-220. P 177

PONZIGLIONE, PAUL MARY. "Kansas. Letter dated Osage Mission, Neosho County, Kansas, Dec. 31st, 1880," Woodstock Letters, v. 10 (1881), 133-137. P 178

PONZIGLIONE, PAUL MARY. "Kansas. Letter dated Osage Mission, Neosho Co., Kansas, July 7th, 1881," Woodstock Letters, v. 10 (1881), 286-292. P 179

PONZIGLIONE, PAUL MARY. "Kansas. Letter dated Osage Mission, Neosho Co., Kansas, Dec. 31, 1881," Woodstock Letters, v. 11 (1882), 163-169. P 180

PONZIGLIONE, PAUL MARY. "Kansas. Letter dated Osage Mission, Neosho Co., Kansas, July 1st, 1882," Woodstock Letters, v. 11 (1882), 279-286. P 181

PONZIGLIONE, PAUL MARY. "Kansas. Letter dated Osage Mission, Neosho Co., Kansas, December 31, 1882," Woodstock Letters, v. 12 (1883), 112-117. P 182

PONZIGLIONE, PAUL MARY. "Kansas. Letter dated Osage Mission, Neosho Co., Kansas, July 2, 1883," Woodstock Letters, v. 12 (1883), 292-298. P 183

PONZIGLIONE, PAUL MARY. "Kansas. St. Francis' Institution. Osage Mission, Neosho Co., Kansas. January 1st, 1884," Woodstock Letters, v. 13 (1884), 142-149. P 184

PONZIGLIONE, PAUL MARY. "Kansas. Letter dated Osage Mission, Kansas, June 6th, 1884," Woodstock Letters, v. 13 (1884), 309-320. P 185

PONZIGLIONE, PAUL MARY. "Kansas. Letter dated Osage Mission, Neosho County, Dec. 31st, 1884," Woodstock Letters, v. 14 (1885), 230-242. P 186

PONZIGLIONE, PAUL MARY. "Letter dated Osage Mission, Neosho Co., Kansas, December 31st, 1877," Woodstock Letters, v. 7 (1878), 99-105. P 187

PONZIGLIONE, PAUL MARY. "Letter from Fr. Ponziglione to Very Rev. Fr. O'Neil, Dated Osage Mission, Neosho Co., Kansas, Dec. 31, 1871," Woodstock Letters, v. 1 (1872), 111-121. P 188

PONZIGLIONE, PAUL MARY. "New Catholic Stations in Kansas from Two Letters of Fr. Ponziglione," Woodstock Letters, v. 2 (1873), 149-156. P 189

PONZIGLIONE, PAUL MARY. "Origin of the Osage Mission (Written, 1869)," Woodstock Letters, v. 6 (1877), 141-147. P 190

PONZIGLIONE, PAUL MARY. "Osage Mission. Letter dated Osage Mission, Neosho Co., Kansas, December 30th, 1876," Woodstock Letters, v. 6 (1877), 100-105. P 191

PONZIGLIONE, PAUL MARY.
"Osage Mission. Letter dated
Osage Mission, Neosho Co.,
Kansas, Dec. 31, 1873,"
Woodstock Letters, v. 3 (1874),
126-132.   P 192
PONZIGLIONE, PAUL MARY.
"Osage Mission. Letter dated
Osage Mission, Neosho County,
Kansas, July 1st, 1874,"
Woodstock Letters, v. 4
(1875), 64-71.   P 193
PONZIGLIONE, PAUL MARY.
"Osage Mission. Letter dated
Osage Mission, Neosho County,
Kansas, December 1st, 1874,"
Woodstock Letters, v. 4
(1875), 160-166.   P 194
PONZIGLIONE, PAUL MARY.
"Osage Mission. Letter dated
St. Francis' Institution, Osage
Mission, Neosho Co., Kansas,
July 13, 1875," Woodstock
Letters, v. 5 (1876), 54-59.
                            P 195
PONZIGLIONE, PAUL MARY.
"Osage Mission. Letter dated
Residence of St. Francis of
Hieronymo, Osage Mission,
Neosho County, Kansas,"
Woodstock Letters, v. 5
(1876), 144-148.   P 196
PONZIGLIONE, PAUL MARY.
"Osage Mission. Letter dated
St. Francis' Institution, Osage
Mission, Neosho Co., Kansas,"
July 1st, 1876," Woodstock
Letters, v. 5 (1876), 223-
229.   P 197
PONZIGLIONE, PAUL MARY.
"Osage Mission. Letter dated
Neosho Co., Kansas, July
1st, 1877," Woodstock Letters,
v. 6 (1877), 194-199. P 198
PONZIGLIONE, PAUL MARY.
"Osage Mission during the
Civil War," St. Louis Catholic
Historical Review, v. 4
(1922), 219-229.   P 199
PONZIGLIONE, PAUL MARY.
"Plan of a Reduction for Our
North American Indians, With
a Letter from Fr. Ponziglione.
Letter dated St. Ignatius Col-

lege, Chicago, Ill., March
29, 1896," Woodstock Letters,
v. 25 (1896), 353-361.
                            P 200
PONZIGLIONE, PAUL MARY.
"Recollections of Father
Van Quickenborne, and the
Osage Mission. Letter dated
St. Ignatius College, Chicago,
Ill., May 28, 1894," Wood-
stock Letters, v. 24 (1895),
37-42.   P 201
PONZIGLIONE, PAUL MARY.
"St. Stephen's Mission.
Letter dated Shoshone Reser-
vation, Wyoming Ter., Sept.
20th, 1886," Woodstock Letters,
v. 15 (1886), 278-284.
                            P 202
POOLE, JOHN FRANCIS. The
Know Nothing Movement in
Brooklyn. MA thesis. Cath-
olic University. 1935. 101p.
                            P 203
POPP, SISTER CLARISSA.
History of the Sisters of St.
Francis of the Diocese of
Pittsburgh, Pennsylvania,
1868-1938. Mt. Alverna,
Millvale, Pa. Sisters of St.
Francis. 1939. xiv, 308p.
illus.   P 204
PORTEOUS, LAURA L. (tr.
and ed.) "Marriage Contracts
of the Spanish Period in
Louisiana," Lousiana Historical
Quarterly, v. 10 (1927), 385-
397.   P 205
PORTLAND, ORE. (DIOCESE)
COUNCIL, 1881. Acta et
decreta concilii provincialis
oregonopolitani secundi, cele-
brati anno MDCCCLXXXI,
diebus 16, 17, 18 Aug. [n.p.,
n.d.] [27]-49p.   P 206
PORTLAND, M. (DIOCESE)
SYNOD, 1st, 1886. Synodus
dioecesana portlandensis prima
habita die 25 Augusti A.D.
1886 in ecclesia cathedrali
portlandiae a Jacobo Augustino
Healy [ep.] Ex typis Collegii
Woodstock, 1886. 32p.
                            P 207

PORTLAND, M. (DIOCESE) SYNOD, 2nd, 1904. Acta et decreta secundae synodi dioecesis portlandensi, Gulielmo O'Connell episcopo, habitae anno 1904. Romae, typis vaticanis, 1905. xiv, 70p. P 208

PORTLAND, OR. (DIOCESE) SYNOD, 3rd, 1935. Synodus dioecesana portlandensis in Oregon tertia, celebrata die 14 mensis Iunii Anno Domini 1935, praeside Eduardo D. Howard abp. [Portland, Sentinel printery, n.d.] 58, [2]p. P 209

POSITIO OF THE HISTORICAL SECTION OF THE SACRED CONGREGATION OF RITES ON THE INTRODUCTION OF THE CAUSE FOR BEATIFICATION AND CANONIZATION AND ON THE VIRTUES OF THE SERVANT OF GOD KATHERINE TEKAKWITHA, THE LILY OF THE MOHAWKS. ed. by Robert E. Holland, S.J. New York. Fordham University Press. 1940. P 210

POST, ALBERT. Popular Freethought in America, 1825-1850. New York. Columbia University Press. 1943. 258p. P 211

POST, J. "The Rocky Mountains. Letter dated St. Ignatius, Montana, Feb. 23rd, 1888," Woodstock Letters, v. 17 (1888), 194-195. P 212

"POTTOWATTOMY INDIANS, THE MISSION OF OUR FATHERS AMONG THEM FROM 1846 TO THE PRESENT TIME," Woodstock Letters, v. 6 (1877), 3-18, 73-84. P 213

POULIOT. LÉON. "L'église de l' Orégon, Fondation Canadienne," La Bulletin des Recherches Historiques, v. 48 (Jan. 1942). P 214

POULIOT, LÉON. Le Père Nicolas Point 1799-1868, collaborateur du P. de Smet ..." Rapport de la Société Canadienne de l'Histoire de l' Église Catholique. v. 1936/37, 20-30. P 215

POULIOT, LÉON. "Trois Lettres du P. Marquette," Le Bulletin des Recherches Historiques. Quebec. 1937, 152-157. P 216 Dated 1665, 1666, 1667.

POWDERLY, TERENCE V. The Path I Trod. An Autobiography of Terence V. Powderly. ed. by Harry J. Carman et al. New York. Columbia University Press. 1940. xiv, 460p. front. (port.), illus. P 217

POWDERLY, TERENCE V. Thirty Years of Labor, 1859-1869. Columbus. Excelsior Publishing House. 1890. 693p. front. (port.), plate. P 218

POWELL, FREDERICK CECIL. A Guide Book. Or Microcosmographia religiosa, Describing the Life and Work of St. John's House, Arlington Heights, Massachusetts, and Other Convents of the Order of St. Anne. Boston. St. Anne's House. 1923. xv, 317p. incl. front., illus., fold. map. P 219

POWELL, JAMES M. The Political and Religious Contribution of Charles Carroll of Carrollton. MA thesis. Xavier University (Cincinnati). 1955. 94p. P 220

POWER, EDWARD JOHN. "Brownson's Attitude Towards Catholic Education," American Catholic Historical Society of Philadelphia Records, v. 63 (1952), 110-128. P 221

POWER, EDWARD J. "The Formative Years of Catholic Colleges Founded before 1850 and Still in Existence as Colleges or Universities," American Catholic Historical Society of Philadelphia Re-

cords, v. 65 (1954), 24-39.
P 222
The first installment includes
Georgetown, and Mount St.
Mary's, eventually ten are
to be treated.

POWER, EDWARD J. "Formative
Years of Catholic Colleges
Founded before 1850 and Still
in Existence as Colleges and
Universities," American Catholic Historical Society of Philadelphia Records, v. 65 (1954),
240-252; v. 66 (1955), 19-34.
P 223

POWER, EDWARD J. "Is the
Catholic College Academically
Respectable?" Homiletic and
Pastoral Review, v. 56 (1956),
734-741.
P 224

POWER, EDWARD J. "Orestes
A. Brownson," Records of the
American Catholic Historical
Society of Philadelphia, v. 62
(1951), 72-94.
P 225

POWER, EDWARD J. "Orestes
Brownson on Catholic Schools,"
Homiletic and Pastoral Review,
v. 55 (1955), 563-570. P 226

POWERS, B. B. Missions of
California. San Francisco.
n. p. 1897. n. p. P 227

POWERS, GEORGE C. The
Maryknoll Movement. MA
thesis. Catholic University.
1925. 142p. P 228

POWERS, GEORGE C. The
Maryknoll Movement. New
York. Catholic Foreign Mission Society. 1926. xix,
167p. front., plates, ports.,
maps. P 229

POWERS, JAMES M. Memoirs.
The Seminary of Montezuma.
Erie: 205 9th St. 1953. xiii,
225p. P 230
Documents and writings of
the Most Reverend John Mark
Gannon, Chairman of the
Bishop's Committee for Monte-
zuma Seminary and his Epis-
copal Associates.

POWERS, JOSEPH LEO. The
Knights of Labor and the

Church's Attitude on Secret
Societies. MA thesis. University of Notre Dame. 1943.
iv, 103p. P 231

POWERS, LAURA B. The Story
of the Old Missions of California. San Francisco. W.
Doxey. 1893. 106p. front.,
illus., plates. P 232

POWERS, WILLIAM J. P. The
Beginnings of English Catholic
Emigration to the New World.
MA thesis. Catholic Univer-
sity. 1928. 55p. P 233

POWERS, WILLIAM F. "A
Minister and Three Jesuits in
New Netherlands," St. Meinrad
Essays, v. 12 (1959), 1-12.
P 234
Joannes Megapolensis and
Fathers Jogues, Bressani,
and LeMoyne.

POWLESON, LUKE. "History of
St. Francis Mission, Cowlitz,
Washington. Provincial Annals O.F.M., (California).
v. 1 (1939), 12-16. P 235

PRANDO, P. "From the Same
to His Superior. Letter dated
Black Rock Camp," Woodstock
Letters, v.12 (1883), 326-330.
P 236
On Indian marriage customs.

PRANDO, P.P. "Indian Mis-
sions. Montana Territory.
Letter dated St. Peter's Mission, M.T., January 31st,
1881," Woodstock Letters, v.
10 (1881), 144-148. P 237

PRANDO, P. "Indian Missions
of the Rocky Mountains. Letter dated Mission of St. Peter,
July 28, 1881," Woodstock Letters, v. 12 (1883), 34-37.
P 238

PRANDO, P. "Indian Missions.
Mission of the Rocky Mountains. Letter (fall, 1881),"
Woodstock Letters, v. 12
(1883), 37-43. P 239

PRANDO, P. "Letter from
Father Prando," Woodstock
Letters, v. 12 (1883), 317-
326. P 240

PRANDO, P. 'Rocky Mountain Missions. Letter dated St. Peter's Mission," Woodstock Letters, v. 12 (1883), 305-316. P 241

PREMOLI, ORAZIO M. Contemporary Church History (1900-1925). London. Burns, Oates and Washbourne. 1932. xvi, 407p. P 242

PRENDERGAST, WILLIAM A. 'The Apostle of Wall Street: Thomas F. Woodlock," Catholic World, v. 169 (1949), 446-450. P 243

PRESTON, THOMAS F. "American Catholicity," American Catholic Quarterly Review, v. 16 (1891), 396-408. P 244

PRETA, LUDOVICO. Storia delle Missioni Franciscane in California. San Francisco. Castagno, Bright and Gold. 1915. P 245

PRIESTLEY, HERBERT INGRAM. Franciscan Exploration in California. Glendale, Calif. Arthur H. Clark Co. 1946. 189p. P 246

PRIESTLEY, HERBERT INGRAM (ed.) The Luna Papers. Deland. Florida State Historical Society. 1928. 2v. port., facsims. P 247

PRINDEVILLE, SISTER MARY J. History of Catholic Education in the Diocese of Green Bay. MA thesis. Catholic University. 1953. 114p. P 248

PRINGLE, HENRY. The Life and Times of William Howard Taft. A Biography. New York. Farrar and Rinehart. 1939. fronts., plates, ports., facsims. P 249

PRINGLE, HENRY. Theodore Roosevelt. A Biography. New York. Harcourt, Brace and Co. 1931. x, 627p. front., plates, ports. P 250

PRIOR, FRANK HART. Father Gibault's Connection with the Winning of the West. MA thesis. Catholic University. 1920. 37p. P 251

PRITCHETT, JOHN PERRY. "Catholic Pioneers in the Northwest," United States Catholic Historical Society Records and Studies, v. 38 (1949), 23-96. P 252

PROGRESS OF THE CATHOLIC CHURCH IN AMERICA AND THE GREAT COLUMBIAN CONGRESS OF 1893. 5th ed. Chicago. J.S. Hyland and Co. 1897. 2v. front., illus., plates. P 253

PROHON, EDOUARD P. LE. 'Memorial of the Rt. Rev. William Tyler, First Bishop of Hartford, Connecticut," American Catholic Historical Researches, v. 12 (1895), 2-10. P 254

PROVIDENCE (DIOCESE) SYNOD, 1878. Constitutiones dioecesanae in synodo Providentiae A.D. 1878 habita, latae et promulgatae. Providentiae, Press co., 1878. 12p. P 255

PROVIDENCE (DIOCESE) SYNOD, 3rd, 1887. Acta et decreta synodi dioecesanae providentiensis tertiae habitae in ecclesia cathedrali a Matthaeo Harkins [ep.] die 21 Decembris, 1887. Ex typis Collegii Woodstockiensis 1888. 64p. P 256

"PROVINCE OF THE ASSUMPTION OF THE B.V.M. IN BRIEF RETROSPECT," Chronicle (Assumption B.V.M. Province O.F.M.), v. 1 (1943), 8-15. P 257

PROVOST, HONORIUS. 'Un Chapitre d'Histoire Religieuse dans le Maine," Le Revue du l'Université Laval, v. 2 (1948), 853-860. P 258

[PUCCI, JOSEPH J.] The Yakima Valley Catholic Centennial (1847-1947). Moxee City, Washington. Holy Rosary Rectory. 88p. P 259

PUCKETT, FIDELIA MILLER. 'Ramon Ortiz: Priest and

Patriot," New Mexico Historical Review, v. 25 (1950), 265-295. P 260

PUEBLO (DIOCESE) SYNOD 1. Statutes of the diocese of Pueblo. Pueblo Cathedral of the Sacred Heart. n.d. [1948] xv, 160p. P 261

PURCELL, EDMUND S. Life of Cardinal Manning, Archbishop of Westminster. New York. Macmillan. 1896. 2v. 3 port. (incl. front.) P 262

PURCELL, RICHARD J. "The American Cardinals," American Catholic Historical Society of Philadelphia Records, v. 57 (1946), 137-144. P 263

PURCELL, RICHARD J. "Archbishop Ireland: An Appreciation," American Catholic Historical Society of Philadelphia Records, v. 60 (1949), 95-105. P 264

PURCELL, SISTER MARY DANIEL. Contributions to Education of the Catholic School of the Scranton Diocese. Ph.D. thesis. Fordham University. 1935. xii, 358p. tables, maps. P 265

PURCELL, RICHARD J. "Daniel Carroll, Framer of the Constitution," American Catholic Historical Society of Philadelphia Records, v. 52 (1941), 65-87, 136-160. P 266

PURCELL, RICHARD J. "Education and Irish Schoolmasters in Maryland's National Period," Catholic Educational Review, v. 32 (1934), 198-207. P 267

PURCELL, RICHARD J. "Education and Irish Teachers in Colonial Maryland," Catholic Educational Review, v. 32 (1934), 143-153. P 268

PURCELL, RICHARD J. "Father John Thayer," Studies, v. 31 (1942), 171-184. P 269

PURCELL, RICHARD J. "The Irish Immigrant, the Famine and the Irish-American," Irish Ecclesiastical Record, v. 69 (1947), 849-869. P 270

PURCELL, RICHARD J. "John A. Ryan: 1869-1945," Studies, v. 35 (1946), 153-171. P 271

PURCELL, RICHARD J. "Justice Joseph McKenna," American Catholic Historical Society of Philadelphia Records, v. 56 (1945), 177-233. P 272

PURCELL, RICHARD J. "Missionaries from All Hallows (Dublin) to the United States, 1842-1865," American Catholic Historical Society of Philadelphia Records, v. 53 (1942), 204-249. P 273

PURCELL, RICHARD J. "Mr. Justice Pierce Butler," Catholic Educational Review, v. 42 (1944), 193-215, 327-341, 420-432. P 274

PURCELL, RICHARD J. "New York Commissioners of Emigration and Irish Immigrants, 1847-1860," Studies, v. 37 (1948), 29-42. P 275

RUSCH, EDMUND. "Louis Marie Fink: First Bishop of Leavenworth," Benedictine Review, v. 5 (1950), 5-8. P 276

PUTZ, LOUIS J. Catholic Church, U.S.A. Chicago. Fides. 1956. xxiii, 451p. P 277
This book contains a series of brief articles on various phases of the history and the present state of the Church in the United States. Not a scholarly production.

- Q -

QUIGLEY, SISTER MARY JACQUELINE. James Cardinal Gibbons, Champion of Labor. MA thesis. Villanova University. 1951. 81p. Q 1

QUINLAN, JOHN B. "Florida. Letter dated Church of St. Louis, Tampa, Fla., July 6, 1890," Woodstock Letters, v. 19 (1890), 316-318. Q 2
On the work of the Jesuits in Florida.

QUINLAN, JOHN B. "Galveston,

Texas. Letter," Woodstock Letters, v. 16 (1887), 282-283. Q 3
A description of the parish of the Sacred Heart.

QUINLAN, JOHN B. "Macon, Georgia. Letter dated St. Stanislaus, Vineville, Feast of St. Michael, 1887," Woodstock Letters, v. 16 (1887), 299-302. Q 4

QUINLAN, SARA-ALICE K. In Harvest Fields by Sunset Shores. San Francisco. Gilmartin Co. 1926. xii, 317, xiii p. plates, ports. Q 5
Story of the Sisters of Notre Dame de Namur on the Pacific coast, 1851-1926.

QUINN, DENIS. Heroes and Heroines of Memphis (1873-1879). Providence, R.I. E.L. Freeman and Sons. 1887. xii, 306p. illus. Q 6

QUIRK, JOHN F. "Father Ferdinand Farmer. An Apostolic Missionary in Three States," Woodstock Letters, v. 44 (1915), 55-67. Q 7

QUIRK, JOHN F. "Father Ferdinand Farmer. An Apostolic Missionary in Three States," United States Catholic Historical Society Records and Studies, v. 6 pt. 2 (1912), 235-248. Q 8

- R -

R., E. "Indian Missions--Lake Superior. Letter dated Fort William, Lake Superior, October 24th, 1875," Woodstock Letters, v. 5 (1876), 59-64. R 1

RADKE, THEODORE J. "The Padre Follows His Flock," Sign, v. 33 (1954), 9-12. R 2
A sketch of Father Pepe Morales, one of the twenty-three priests loaned to the United States to work among the Braceros.

RAHILL, PETER J. "An Episcopal Contribution to History,"

Mid-America, v. 37 (1955), 48-55. R 3
An account of the holdings of Bishop FitzSimon of Amarillo on the history of the Church in the Southwest, with particular emphasis on Texas.

RAHILL, PETER J. "Archives of the Archdiocese of Boston," American Archivist, v. 22 (1959), 427-432. R 4

RAHILL, PETER J. The Catholic Indian Missions and Grant's Peace Policy, 1870-1884. Washington. Catholic University. 1953. xx, 396p. R 5
An excellent account of the founding and early years of the Catholic Indian Bureau.

RAHILL, PETER J. St. Alphonsus' Parish in Millwood, Missouri. MA thesis. Saint Louis University. 1947. vii, 131p. R 6

RAINER, JOSEPH. Dr. Joseph Salzmanns Leben und Werken. St. Louis. Herder. 1876. xi, 292p. front. (port.), plates. R 7

RAINER, JOSEPH (ed.) "Letters of the Late Archbishop Michael Heiss," Salesianum, v. 9 (Apr., 1914), 8-14, (July, 1914), 15-28; v. 10 (Oct., 1914), 16-25, (Jan., 1915), 14-27, (Apr., 1915), 17-26, (July, 1915), 10-20; v. 10 (Oct., 1915), 17-23; v. 11 (Jan., 1916), 6-12, (Apr. 1916), 18-24, (July, 1916), 14-23; v. 12 (Oct., 1916),1-9, (Jan., 1917), 1-17, (July, 1917), 8-17; v. 13 (Oct.,1917) 39-45, (Jan., 1918), 27-33, (Apr., 1918), 18-27, (July, 1918), 28-34; v. 14 (Oct., 1918), 17-22, (Jan. 1919), 12-19, (Apr., 1919), 24-33, (July, 1919), 29-39; v. 15 (Oct., 1919), 15-18. R 8
A series of letters written by the second Archbishop of

Milwaukee, Michael Heiss (1881-1890) between the years 1843-1889 which give considerable information on the story of the Church in Wisconsin.

RAINER, JOSEPH. A Noble Priest: Joseph Salzmann. Milwaukee. Olinger and Schwartz. 1903. 254p. front. (port.)　　　R 9

RAINER, JOSEPH (ed.) 'Reminiscences of the late Archbishop Michael Heiss," Salesianum, v. 5 (Jan. 1910), 15-18, (Apr., 1910), 7-10, (July, 1910), 9-14; v. 6 (Oct., 1910), 9-13, (Jan., 1911), 13-17, (Apr., 1911), 10-15, (July, 1911), 12-16; v. 7 (Oct., 1911), 9-14, (Jan., 1912), 10-15, (Apr., 1912), 14-20, (July, 1912), 12-20, port.; v. 8 (Oct., 1912), 8-17, (Jan., 1913), 11-16, (Apr., 1913), 15-19, (July, 1913), 11-18; v. 9 (Oct., 1913), 13-18, (July, 1914), 20-32.　　　R 10

RALEIGH (DIOCESE) SYNOD 1. First synod of the diocese of Raleigh. Raleigh. Sacred Heart Cathedral. n.d.　R 11

RAMEUR, E. "The Progress of the Church in the United States," Catholic World, v. 1 (1865), 1-19.　　　R 12

RAMONA, SISTER M. "Ecclesiastical Status of New Mexico, 1680-1875," Catholic Historical Review, v. 16 (1928), 525-568.　　　R 13

RANKIN, DANIEL S. "An American Catholic Historian," Sign, v. 16 (1936), 210-212. port.　　　R 14
　A good biographical sketch of Martin I.J. Griffin who was born 1842, died 1911, and was for years the editor of the American Catholic Historical Researches.

RAPPAGLIOSI. "Extraits d'une Lettre du R.P. Rappagliosi de la Compagnie de Jésus, Mis-

sionnaire aux Montagnes-Rocheuses," Annales de la Propagation de la Foi, v. 49 (1877), 285-292.　　　R 15

[RAPPAGLIOSI]. Memorie del P. Filippo Rappagliosi D C D G Missionario Apostolico nelle Montagne Rocciose. Roma. Bernardo Morine. 1879.　　　R 16
　B. 1841, to America 1873, died 1878.

RAUSCH, JEROME W. The Crosier Story. Onamia, Minn. Crosier Press, 1960. 384p.　　　R 17
　Birth and growth of the American Province.

RAVEL, GABRIEL I. "Lettera XLIV," Lettere Edificanti Provincia Napolitana, ser. 2 (1876-1877), 169-171. R 18

RAVOUX, AUGUSTINE. The Labors of Mgr. A. Ravoux among the Sioux or Dakota Indians. St. Paul? no pub. 1897?　　　R 19

RAVOUX, AUGUSTINE. "Lettre de M. l'Abbé Ravoux, Vicaire Général à Mgr. Grace, Evêque de Saint Paul (Minnesota), Saint Paul le 29 décembre, 1862," Annales de la Propagation de la Foi, v. 35 (1863), 239-251.　　　R 20
　Describes the conversion of thirty-three of the thirty-eight Indians condemned to death at Mankato.

RAVOUX, AUGUSTINE. Reminiscences, Memoirs, Lectures. St. Paul. Brown, Tracy and Co. 1890. x, 223p. 3 port. (incl. front.)　　　R 21

RAY, SISTER M. AUGUSTINA. American Opinion of Roman Catholicism in the Eighteenth Century. New York. Columbia University Press. 1936. 457p. illus.　　　R 22

RAY, SAMUEL H. "A Neglected Chapter in Florida History," Historical Bulletin, v. 6 (1927), 1-4.　　　R 23

RAYMOND, ALLEN. Waterfront
Priest. New York. Henry
Holt. 1955. 269p.   R 24
A good biographical study of
Father John Corridan and
his work on the docks of
New York City.
RAYMOND, M. Burnt Out Incense.
New York. P.J. Kenedy and
Sons. 1949. xviii, 457p.
                          R 25
RAYMOND, M. The Man Who Got
Even with God; the Life of an
American Trappist. Milwaukee.
Bruce. 1941. xiii, 170p.
                          R 26
RAYMOND, M. The Less Trav-
elled Road. Milwaukee. Bruce.
1953. vii, 250p.   R 27
Memoir of Mary Frederic
Dunne, O.C.S.O., first A-
merican Trappist Abbot at
Gethsemani, Kentucky.
RAYNOR, SISTER MIRIAM. The
Development of the Catholic
Church in the Lake Erie
Region to 1850. MA thesis.
Marquette University. 1941.
                          R 28
READ, NEWBURY FROST (ed.)
The Story of St. Mary's:
The Society of the Free Church
of St. Mary the Virgin, New
York City, 1868-1931. New
York. Published for the
Board of Trustees. 1931.
281p. illus.   R 29
READHEAD, MARJORIE M.
Religious Intolerance in the
Massachusetts Bay Colony.
MA thesis. University of
Detroit. 1932. ix, 93p. R 30
REARDON, JAMES M. The
Basilica of St. Mary of Min-
neapolis, A Historical and
Descriptive Sketch. St. Paul.
no pub. 1932. 144p. illus.,
incl. plates, ports.   R 31
REARDON, JAMES M. "The
Beginning of the Catholic
Total Abstinence Movement in
Minnesota," Acta et Dicta, v.
1 (1908), 199-209, v. 2
(1909), 44-93. variant title.

R 32
REARDON, JAMES MICHAEL.
Catholic Church in the Dio-
cese of St. Paul from Earliest
Origin to Centennial Achieve-
ment. St. Paul. North Cen-
tral Publishing Co. 1952.
726p. illus. pl.   R 33
REARDON, JAMES M. "The
Church of St. Mary in St.
Paul," Acta et Dicta, v. 6
(1934), 232-257, v. 7 (1935),
24-46.   R 34
REARDON, JAMES M. George
Anthony Belcourt, Pioneer
Catholic Missionary of the
Northwest, 1803-1874, St.
Paul. North Central Pub. Co.
1955. xiii, 223p.   R 35
REARDON, MAURICE E. (ed.)
Mosaic of a Bishop. An
Autobiographical Appreciation
of His Grace, The Most Rev-
erend John T. McNicholas, O.
P. Cincinnati. St. Gregory's
Seminary, 1957. xii, 365p.
                          R 36
REARDON, TIMOTHY J. "A
Century of Catholic Progress,"
United States Catholic His-
torical Society Records and
Studies, v. 16 (1924), 78-
86.   R 37
REARDON, TIMOTHY J. "St.
Peter's Sesquicentennial Cele-
bration," United States Catholic
Historical Society Records and
Studies, v. 26 (1936), 7-37.
                          R 38
REDDEN, JOHN. "The Begin-
nings of Catholic Education in
Maine," Catholic Educational
Review, v. 37 (1939), 509-
516.   R 39
REDDEN, JOHN D. History and
Development of the Parochial
Schools in the Diocese of Man-
chester, New Hampshire.
Ph.D. thesis. Fordham Uni-
versity. 1935. iii, 196p.
                          R 40
REDMOND, MARY LOUISE.
"The Work of the Grey Nuns
in Buffalo," Catholic Educa-

tional Review, v. 1 (1911), 402-412. R 41

REED, JOHN C. "Catholic Refugee Families in St. Louis, 1948-1954," American Catholic Sociological Review, v. 15 (1954), 323-331. tables. R 42

REGAN, EMMETT T. 100 Years. The History of the Church of the Holy Name, Chicago. Chicago. The Cathedral of the Holy Name. 1949. unpaged. illus., plates. R 43
Describes the conversion of thirty-three of the thirty-eight Indians condemned to death at Mankato.

'REGISTER OF THE BAPTISMS AND INTERMENTS WHICH TOOK PLACE AT FORT DUQUESNE DURING THE YEARS 1753-1754, 1755 and 1756," American Catholic Historical Researches, v. 1 (1884-1885), 60-75, 102-20, 138-153; v. (1885), 18-126. R 44

REGNET, HENRY H. "The Buffalo Mission (1869-1907)," Social Justice Review, v. 52 (1960), 384-386. R 45
German Jesuit Mission.

REID, RICHARD. "Senator Walsh of Georgia," Columbia, v. 14 (Dec. 1934), 10, 25. R 46

REILAND, J. J. The New Church of the Sacred Heart, Parkston, South Dakota. 1905. no pl. no pub. 1905? 16p. front. R 47

REILLY, A. J. "Poet, Patriot and Fighter," Columbia, v. 24 (Aug., 1944), 1, 12, 14. R 48

REILLY, DANIEL F. The School Controversy (1891-1893), Washington. Catholic University. 1944. x, 302p. R 49

REILLY, EDWARD M. 'Education in the Archdiocese of Philadelphia," Catholic School Journal, v. 49 (1949), 111-116. illus. R 50

REILLY, GEORGE. A Century of Catholicism. History of the Church of the Immaculate Conception, Montclair, New Jersey. Newark, N.J. Washington Irving Pub. Co., 1957. 136p. R 51

REILLY, GEORGE L.A. Sacred Heart in Bloomfield. Diamond Jubilee History of the Parish, 1878-1953. Bloomfield, N.J. Sacred Heart Church. 1953. 224p. R 52

REILLY, L. W. "An Army Chaplain in the Civil War," American Ecclesiastical Review, v. 11 (1871), 26-33, 111-122. R 53
Story of Father William Corby, C.S.C., chaplain of the 88th New York Infantry (the Irish Brigade) for three years.

REILLY, L.W. 'The Education of Catholic Deaf-Mutes in the United States," American Ecclesiastical Review, v. 14 (1896), 289-311. R 54

REILLY, L.W. "Why There is No Indian Priest," American Ecclesiastical Review, v. 4 (1890), 267-280. R 55

REILLY, LOUIS W. "Blackrobes and Red Men," Columbia, v. 6 (July, 1926), 26-27, 40-41. R 56

REILLY, LOUIS W.'The Molokai of America," Columbia, v. 6 (Aug., 1926), 7, 38. R 57

REILY, JOHN T. (comp.) Collections and Recollections in the Life and Times of Cardinal Gibbons. Martinsburg, W.Va. and McSherrystown, Pa. The Author. 1890-1904. 10v. in 7. variant title. R 58

REILY, JOHN TIMON. Conewago, A Collection of Catholic Local History. Martinsburg, W. Va. Herald Print. 1885. 220p. illus. (incl. ports.), photos. R 59

REINDORF, REGINALD C. (tr. and ed.) "Documents: The Founding of Missions at La

Junta de los Rios," Mid-America, v. 9 (1938), 107-131. R 60

REINDERS, ROBERT C. "The Louisiana American Party and the Catholic Church," Mid-America, v. 40 (1958), 218-228. R 61

REINERT, PAUL C. "Catholic Educators and Public Education," Association of American Colleges Bulletin, v. 38 (1952), 446-448. R 62

REINHARD, EDWARD G. "American Catholics and Scientific Research," Catholic University of America Bulletin, v. 24 (1957), 1-2, 9. R 63
A very good survey of the need of such activity in Catholic schools.

REITER, ERNST A. Schematismus der Katholischen Deutschen Geistlichkeit in der Ver. Staaten Nord-Amerika's. New York. Frederick Pustet. 1869. R 64

REITER, ROMAULD. St. Joseph's Centennial. The Author. Utica. N. Y. 1941. 40p. plates, ports., facsims. R 65

'RELIGION IN NEW YORK," Catholic World, v. 3 (1866), 381-389. R 66

REMIGIA, SISTER M. "The Polish Immigrant in Detroit to 1914," Polish-American Studies, v. 2 (1945), 4-11. R 67

'REMINISCENCES OF A KENOSHA PIONEER," Central Blatt and Social Justice, v. 29 (1936), 90-92, 126-127. R 68

RENSHAW, HENRY. "The Ursuline Nuns in America," Louisiana Historical Society Publications, v. 2, pt. 4 (1901), 25. R 69

REPETTI, SISTER JULIE ST. TERESA. The Association of Catholic Trade Unionists: Catholicism in the American Labor Movement. MA thesis. Villanova University. 1950. 83p. R 70

REPETTI, W. C. "Catholic Schools in Colonial Maryland," Woodstock Letters, v. 81 (1952), 123-134. R 71

REPETTI, WILLIAM C. (ed.) "Letters of James Pye Neale," Woodstock Letters, v. 82 (1953), 238-270. R 72
Information gathered from 130 letters of James Pye Neale to his mother, gives interesting glimpses of the Jesuits of the Maryland Province. James Pye Neale was born 1840, joined the Society of Jesus 1859, left the Order in 1893.

REPPLIER, AGNES. Père Marquette. Garden City. Doubleday Doran and Co. 1929. 298p. col. front. R 73

REPPLIER, AGNES. Junipero Serra, Pioneer Colonist of California. Garden City. Doubleday, Doran and Co. 1933. vi, 312p. R 74

RESCH, PETER ANTHONY. A Hundred Years of Educational Foundations by the Brothers of Mary in America, 1849-1949. Kirkwood, Mo. Maryhurst Press. 1949. 32p. R 75

RESCH, PETER ANTHONY. Shadows Cast Before: The Early Chapters of the History of the Society of Mary in the Saint Louis Country. Kirkwood, Mo. Maryhurst Press. 1948. 158p. front. R 76

'RESIDENCE OF ST. MARY'S, BOSTON, MASS., 1868-1876," Woodstock Letters, v. 6 (1877), 31-52. R 77

'RESTORATION OF THE JESUITS," American Catholic Historical Researches, v. 8 (1891), 25-26. R 78

'REUSS, FRANCIS X. Biographical Cyclopaedia of the Catholic Hierarchy of the United States, 1784-1898. Milwaukee. M. H. Wiltzius and Co. 1898. R 79

REUSS, FRANCIS X. "Catholic Chronicles of Lancaster County, Pa.," American Catholic Historical Society of Philadelphia Records, v. 9 (1898), 212-222. R 80

REUSS, FRANCIS X. "Catholic Chronicles of Lancaster County, Pennsylvania," American Catholic Historical Society of Philadelphia Records, v. 18 (1907), 354-361. R 81

REUSS, FRANCIS X. "Catholic Chronicles of Pennsylvania," American Catholic Historical Society of Philadelphia Records, v. 14 (1903), 41-49. R 82

REUSS, FRANCIS X. "A Contribution of the History of St. Peter's Church, Columbia, Lancaster Co., Pa.," American Catholic Historical Society of Philadelphia Records, v. 16 (1905), 187-201. R 83

REUSS, FRANCIS X. "Memoir of the Rt. Rev. James Zilliox, O.S.B., D.D.," American Catholic Historical Society of Philadelphia Records, v. 11 (1900), 129-155, 257-280. port. R 84

REUSS, FRANCIS X. (ed.) "Original Documents Relating to the Civil War (1863-1867)," American Catholic Historical Society of Philadelphia Records, v. 11 (1900), 312-320. R 85

REUSS, FRANCIS X. "St. Peter's Church, Columbia, Lancaster Co., Pa.," American Catholic Historical Society of Philadelphia Records, v. 4 (1893), 90-125. R 86

REUSS, FRANCIS X. "A Short Sketch of Old St. Gregory's Church and Parish in (West) Philadelphia," American Catholic Historical Society of Philadelphia Records, v. 90 (1899), 78-89. R 87

REUSS, FRANCIS X. "Sketch of the Life of Rev. Joseph Ignatius Balfe, D.D.," American Catholic Historical Society of Philadelphia Records, v. 9 (1898), 35-63. R 88

REUSS, FRANCIS X. "Some Notes in the Life of the V. Rev. Charles Ignatius Hamilton Carter, V.G.," American Catholic Historical Society of Philadelphia Records, v. 9 (1898), 399-421. R 89

REUSS, FRANCIS X. "Some Recollections of Rev. Patrick Rafferty," American Catholic Historical Society of Philadelphia Records, v. 8 (1897), 394-398. R 90

'REV. DEMETRIUS AUGUSTIN GALLITZIN AND THE CATHOLIC SETTLEMENTS IN PENNSYLVANIA," Catholic World, v. 2 (1865), 145-158. R 91

REVILLE, JOHN C. "John Cardinal Farley," United States Catholic Historical Society Records and Studies, v. 13 (1919), 140-151. port. R 92

REY, AGAPITO. "Missionary Aspects of the Founding of New Mexico," New Mexico Historical Review, v. 23 (1948), 22-31. R 93

REYNOLDS, EDWARD D. Jesuits for the Negro. New York. America Press. 1949. 232p. R 94

REYNOLDS, MIRIAM LOUISE. Printed Materials Useful to Scholars of Catholic Northwest History. MA thesis. Portland University. 1953. 95p. R 95

REYNOLDS, ROBERT L. "The French Era," Jubilee, v. 3 (Nov. 1955), 24-43. R 96
An illustrated article on the contribution of the French to the development of the Church in the United States.

REYNOLDS, ROBERT L. "The Ultimate Courage of Jean de Brébeuf," American Heritage, X (1959), 54-59, 102-106,

303

illus. R 97

REYNOLDS, ROBERT L. "Worcester: New Diocese," Jubilee, III (Feb.,1956), 6-17. R 98
An interesting illustrated account of the early years of the diocese of Worcester, Massachusetts.

REZEK, ANTOINE I. History of the Diocese of Sault Ste. Marie and Marquette. Houghton, Mich. The Author. 1907. 2v. front., illus. (incl ports., maps, facsims.) R 99

REZEK, A. J. "The Leopoldine Society," Acta et Dicta, v. 3 (1914), 305-320. R 100

ROMMALD, THEINDORFF. Die St. George Pfarrei zu Hermann, Mo. no pl. no pub. no date. 19p. illus., ports. R 101

RICE, BERNADINE. "The Irish in Texas," American Irish Historical Society Journal, v. 30 (1932), 60-70. R 102
A general account, includes a bibliography.

RICE, MADELEINE HOOKE. American Catholic Opinion in the Slavery Controversy. New York. Columbia University Press. 1944. 177p. R 103

RICE, SISTER MARY OF SAINT DENIS. Materials for a History of the Sisters of Good Shepherd in Detroit, 1833-1933. MA thesis. University of Detroit. 1934. iii, 83p. R 104

RICHARD, OTTO. Souvenir of Golden Jubilee of Sacred Heart Parish, Indianapolis, Ind., 1925. no pl. no pub. 1925? R 105

RICHARDS, JOSEPH HAVENS. A Loyal Life. A Biography of Henry Livingston Richards. St. Louis. Herder. 1913. ix, 397p. front., ports. R 106

RICHARDSON, EUDORA RAMSAY. "Giles Brent, Catholic Pioneer of Virginia," Thought, v. 6 (1932), 650-664. R 107

RICHARDSON, J.P. "Sister Alfred and the Mayo Clinic," Ave Maria, v. 87 (June 14, 1958), 5-7, 23; illus. R 108

RICHMOND (DIOCESE). Richardus Vincentius episcopus richmondensis. Omnibus nostrae dioeceseos sacerdotibus ... [n.p., n.d.] 16p. R 109

RICHMOND (DIOCESE) SYNOD, 1856. Statuta Synodi Richmondensis primae mense Octobris Anno Domini 1856 celebratae. Baltimore. John Murphy. 1857. 39p. R 110

RICHMOND (DIOCESE) SYNOD, 2nd, 1886. Acta et statuta synodi richmondensis secundae mense Aug. A.D. 1886 celebratae. Baltimorae. J. Murphy, 1886. 77p. R 111

RIDDELL, ALEXANDER. The Rise of Ecclesiastical Control in Quebec. New York. Columbia University Press. 1916. R 112

RIDDELL, WILLIAM RENWICK. "The First British Bishop of Quebec and the Catholics of Kaskaskia," Illinois Historical Society Journal, v. 23 (1930), 205-208. R 113

RIDDELL, WILLIAM RENWICK. "Pastoral Letters from the Bishop of Quebec to the Inhabitants of Detroit," Michigan History Magazine, v. 15 (1931), 42-51. R 114

RIDDER, CHARLES H. "The United States Catholic Press Exhibit at Vatican City, 1936," United States Catholic Historical Society Records and Studies, v. 27 (1937), 28-151. R 115

RIEMAECKER, M. de. Joseph et Charles De La Croix. Gent. n.p. 1894. R 116
Charles, b. 1792, to Louisiana 1878. Worked among Osage in Missouri, died 1869.

"RT. REV. JULIAN BENOIT," Illinois Catholic Historical Review, v. 7 (1925), 309-

322.   R 117
RILEY, ARTHUR J. Catholicism
in New England to 1788. Wash-
ington. Catholic University.
1936. ix, 479p.   R 118
RILEY, SISTER MARY PATRICK.
"Religious Vacation Schools in
the Diocese of Leavenworth,
1929-1945," Benedictine Review,
v. 4 (1949), 38-41.   R 119
RINES, EDWARD F. Old His-
toric Churches of America:
Their Romantic History and
Their Traditions. New York.
Macmillan. 1936. vii, 733p.
                        R 120
Among Catholic edifices in-
cluded are the Alamo (Texas),
Mission Santa Barbara
(Calif.), the Cathedral at
Bardstown, and St. Francis
Xavier Church at New Town,
Md.
RING, NANCY M. "The First
Sioux Mission," Mid-America,
v. 3 (1932), 344-351.   R 121
RING, NANCY M. "The Religious
Affiliations of Our Presidential
Assassins," Mid-America. v. 5
(1934), 89-104, 147-156. R 122
RIORDAN, JOSEPH W. The First
Half Century of St. Ignatius
Church and College. San
Francisco. H.S. Crocker.
1905. 389p. front., plates,
ports., facsims.   R 123
RIORDAN, MICHAEL J. "The
Archdiocese and Province of
Baltimore," in v. 2 of The
Catholic Church in the United
States of America. New York.
Catholic Editing Co. 1912.
                        R 124
RIORDAN, MICHAEL J. Cathedral
Records from the Beginning of
Catholicism in Baltimore to
the Present Time. Baltimore.
Catholic Mirror Press. 114,
43p. illus., incl. ports.
                        R 125
RIORDAN, P. J. "The Pope's
Letter to the American Bishops
on the School Question," Amer-
ican Catholic Quarterly Review,

v. 18 (1893), 642-649.
                        R 126
RIORDAN, WILLIAM. "Growth
of the Church in Fillmore
County, Minn.," Acta et Dicta,
v. 1 (1908), 197-198. R 127
RIOS, EDUARDO E. Life of
Fray Antonio Margil, O.F.M.
Washington, D.C. Academy
of Franciscan History, 1959.
xiii, 159p.   R 128
Translated and revised by
Benedict Leutenegger.
RITA, SISTER M. "Catholicism
in Colonial Maryland," Amer-
ican Catholic Historical Society
of Philadelphia Records, v. 51
(1940), 65-83.   R 129
RITA, SISTER M. A Story of
Fifty Years, from the Annals
of the Congregation of the
Sisters of the Holy Cross,
1865-1905. Notre Dame, Ind.
Ave. Maria Press. 1905.
                        R 130
ROBAUT, A. "Rocky Mountains.
Letter dated Spokane Falls,
Washington Territory, October
1st, 1883," Woodstock Letters,
v. 13 (1884), 151-157. R 131
ROBERTSON, JAMES A. "Notes
on Early Church Government in
Spanish Florida," Catholic His-
torical Review, v. 17 (1931),
151-174.   R 132
ROBINSON, WILLIAM DAVIS.
"Spanish Friars in the Oregon
Country, 1810-1811," Washington Historical Quarterly, v.
10 (1919), 141-149.   R 133
ROCHE, DOUGLAS. "Catholics
and the YMCA," Ave Maria,
v. 87 (June 21, 1958), 5-8.
                        R 134
ROCHE, JAMES J. Life of
John Boyle O'Reilly, together
with His Complete Poems and
Speeches. New York. Cassell.
1891. xix, 790p. front., plates,
facsims.   R 135
ROCHE, THOMAS B. The Re-
demptorists in Pittsburgh, Pa.
100 Years. Pittsburgh. no

pub. 1939. R 136
ROCHEMONTEIX, CAMILLE DE.
Les Jésuites et la Nouvelle
France au XVIIIᵉ Siècle. Paris.
Picard. 1906. 2v. R 137
ROCHEMONTEIX, CAMILLE DE.
Les Jésuites et la Nouvelle
France au XVIIᵉ Siècle. Paris.
Letouzey. 1895-1896. 3v.
R 138
ROCHESTER, N.Y. (DIOCESE)
SYNOD, 1st, 1875. Acta &
statuta synodi dioecesanae
roffensis primae, habitae diebus
13 & 14 Octobris, A.D. 1875.
Roffae, Ex typis Union and
advertiser company, 1875. 36p.
R 139
ROCHESTER, N.Y. (DIOCESE)
SYNOD, 2nd, 1887. Statuta
dioecesana a Bernardo J. Mc-
Quaid, episcopo roffensi, in
synodo roffensi secunda, 14a
Junii, A.D. 1887, lata et
promulgata. Roffae, Ex typis:
Union and advertiser, 1887.
91p. R 140
ROCHESTER (DIOCESE) SYNOD
3. Acta synodi Roffensis
tertiae Rochester. P. Smith
Ptg. Co. 1914. xxviii, 168p.
R 141
ROCHESTER (DIOCESE) SYNOD,
5th, 1934. Synodus roffensis
quinta quam die XII mensis
decembris anno Domini 1934
in ecclesia cathedrali S.
Patritii rucupis Eduardus Mooney
abp. celebravit. [n.p., n.d.]
xiii, 81, [2]p. R 142
ROCKFORD (DIOCESE) SYNOD,
1st, 1916. Synodus dioecesana
rockfordensis prima, die
quarta Aprilis, 1916 in civitate
rockfordansi habita a Petro
Jacobo Muldoon [ep.] Chicagine,
Mayer et Miller socii, 1916.
128p. R 143
RODRIGUEZ, ARNOLD L. "New
Mexico in Transition," New
Mexico Historical Review, v. 24
(1949), 184-222; 267-299.
R 144
RODRIGUEZ, ARNOLD L. New

Mexico in Transition, 1830-
1860. MA thesis. Catholic
University. 1948. 100p.
R 145
RODRIGUEZ, J.I. "Father
Felix Varela, Vicar General
of New York from 1837-
1853," American Catholic
Quarterly Review, v. 8
(1883), 463-466. R 146
ROEMER, THEODORE. The
Catholic Church in the United
States. St. Louis. Herder.
1950. viii, 444p. maps.
R 147
ROEMER, THEODORE. "The
Centenary of the Ludwig Mis-
sionsverein: 1838-1938,"
Catholic Historical Review,
v. 25 (1939), 53-58. R 148
ROEMER, THEODORE. "Initial
Difficulties of a Century in
the Schools," Historical Bul-
letin, v. 25 (1947), 79-80,
88-91. R 149
ROEMER, THEODORE. "The
Leopoldine Foundation and the
Church in the United States,
1829-1839," United States
Catholic Historical Society
Monograph Series, v. 13
(1933), 145-211. R 150
ROEMER, THEODORE. The Ludwig Missionsverein and the
Catholic Church in the United
States, 1838-1918. Washington. Catholic University.
1933. Also published as
Franciscan Studies, 12 (1933),
viii, 161p. R 151
ROEMER, THEODORE. "Munich
and Green Bay," Salesianum,
v. 35 (1940), 76-83. R 152
ROEMER, THEODORE. "Munich
and LaCrosse," Salesianum,
v. 35 (1940), 11-19. R 153
ROEMER, THEODORE. "Munich
and Milwaukee," Salesianum,
v. 29 (Apr., 1934), 14-22.
R 154
ROEMER, THEODORE (tr. and
ed.) Pioneer Capuchin Letters. New York. J.F.
Wagner. xii, 160p. Francis-

can Studies, v. 16.   R 155
ROEMER, THEODORE. "The
Present Provinces of the Three
Franciscan Families," Francis-
can Educational Conference
Annual Report, v. 18 (1936),
250-273. map, table.   R 156
ROEMER, THEODORE. Saint
Joseph in Appleton. Appleton.
Banta. 1943. xiii, 306p.
R 157
ROEMER, THEODORE. "Some
Aspects of a Benedictine Cen-
tury," Historical Bulletin, v.
25 (1947), 29-30, 39-40.
R 158
ROEMER, THEODORE. Ten
Decades of Alms. St. Louis.
Herder. 1942. vii, 322p.
R 159
ROETS, EMMANUEL. Historical
Sketch of St. Labre's Catholic
Indian Mission. Northern
Cheyenne Indians, Montana.
Detroit, Mich. no pub.
1927.   R 160
ROGERS, PATRICK. Father
Theobald Mathew. Apostle of
Temperance. New York. Long-
mans, Green and Co. 1945.
xxiii, 166p. front., plates,
ports.   R 161
ROIRDAN, D. J. "University
of St. Mary of the Lake,"
Illinois Catholic Historical Re-
view, v. 2 (1919), 135-160.
illus.   R 162
ROLAND, THOMAS F. "The Order
of Saint Augustine in the United
States of America, 1796-1946,"
American Catholic Historical
Society of Philadelphia Records,
v. 58 (1947), 40-61.   R 163
ROMAN, FRANK B. "Polish A-
merican Religious Bodies: A
Select Annotated Bibliography,"
Polish American Studies, v. 13
(1957), 41-43, 107-113.R 164
Catholic Clergy, sisterhoods,
parishes, schools, mostly
from Polish language publica-
tions.
ROMERO, CECIL V. (tr. and ed.)
"Apologia of Presbyter Antonio

Martinez (Taos, 1838),"
New Mexico Historical Review,
v. 3 (1928), 325-346. R 165
ROMIG, WALTER. The Book of
Catholic Authors. Grosse
Pointe, Michigan. Romig,
1957. 302p.   R 166
Rommald, T. See R 102.
RONINGER, MOTHER STELLA
MARIS. Contributions of the
Missionary Sisters of the
Sacred Heart to Education in
Italy and the United States.
MA thesis. Fordham Univer-
sity. 1938.   iii, 78p.R 167
ROONEY, EDMUND T. "A
Priest in Jail," Ave Maria, v.
184 (Sept. 1, 1956), 8-12,
20. illus.   R 168
A biographical appreciation
of Father Cronan J. Murphy
at Cook County Jail, Chicago,
Ill.
ROONEY, JAMES A. "Early
Times in the Diocese of Hart-
ford, Conn., 1829-1874,"
Catholic Historical Review, v.
1 (1915), 148-163.   R 169
ROONEY, JOHN JEROME.
"Bishop Watterson," Catholic
World, v. 69 (1899), 407-
411.   R 170
ROONEY, MIRIAM THERESA.
"Fifty Years Ago," New Scholas-
ticism, v. 19 (1954), 353-
368.   R 171
ROONEY, SISTER NELLIE. A
History of the Catholic Church
in the Pan-handle Plains Area
of Texas from 1875 to 1916.
MA thesis. Catholic Univer-
sity. 1954. 172p. maps.
R 172
ROSALIA, SISTER M. Hidden
Fields. A Brief Sketch of
the Life of Mother M. Deme-
trias, Foundress and First
Superior General of the Mis-
sion Helpers of the Sacred
Heart. Westminster, Md.
Newman. 1948. viii. 55p.
R 173
ROSALITA, SISTER M. Achieve-
ment of a Century. Detroit.

Evans-Winter-Hobbs. 1948.
299p. illus. lithographed.
R 174
ROSALITA, SISTER M. Education
in Detroit Prior to 1850.
Lansing, Mich. Historical
Commission. 1928. 364p.
illus., ports., facsims. R 175
ROSALITA, SISTER M. "Four
Women Lay Apostles of the Old
Northwest," United States His-
torical Society Records and
Studies, v. 31 (1940), 119-
136. R 176
ROSALITA, SISTER M. "Gabriel
Richard, American," Michigan
History Magazine, v. 27
(1943), 603-610. port.
R 177
ROSALITA, SISTER M. No
Greater Service. The History
of the Congregation of the
Sisters, Servants of the Im-
maculate Heart of Mary, Mon-
roe, Michigan, 1845-1945.
Monroe, Mich. St. Mary's
Academy. 1948. xx, 863p.
illus., ports., facsims.
R 178
ROSALITA, SISTER M. "The
Springfield Indian School Cor-
respondence," Michigan History
Magazine, v. 14 (1930), 94-
149. R 179
[ROSATI, JOSEPH]. "Diary,
1822-1824," St. Louis Catholic
Historical Review, v. 3
(1921), 311-369, v. 4 (1921-
1922), 76-108, 165-184, 245-
271, v. 5 (1922), 60-88.
R 180
ROSATI, JOSEPH. Life of the
Very Rev. Felix de Andreis.
St. Louis. Herder. 1900. xiii,
308p. front. (port.) R 181
ROSE, SISTER M. EILEEN. "Holy
Cross in Its Hundredth Year,"
Catholic Charities Review, v.
25 (1941), 190-192. R 182
Centenary of the Sisters of the
Holy Cross.
ROSEN, PETER. The Catholic
Church and Secret Societies.
Milwaukee. Hautkamp and Can-

non. 1902. 329p. front.
(port.), illus. R 183
ROSEN, PETER. Reply to My
Critics. Dubuque, Iowa Cath-
olic Print Co. 1903. 28p.
R 184
ROSER, JOHN B. Review of
Catholic Life in the United
States with Special Reference
to Franciscan Missions in the
Eastern States. St. Bonaven-
ture, N. Y. no pub. 1926.
R 185
ROSILDA, SISTER M. "Religious
Vocations Among Women,"
Catholic Educational Review,
v. 53 (1955), 296-305.
R 186
A comparative study of
schools and places they
come from.
ROSS, MARY. "Restoration of
the Spanish Missions in Georgia.
1598-1616," Georgia Historical
Quarterly, v. 10 (1926), 171-
199. R 187
[ROSSETER, JOHN]. "Letters
of Fr. John Rosseter, O.S.A.
to Bishop Carroll 1799-1808,"
American Catholic Historical
Society of Philadelphia Records,
v. 43 (1932), 360-382, v. 44
(1943), 70-96, 170-191, 238-
261. R 188
ROSSI, JEREMIAH. "The Rocky
Mountains. Letter from the
Mission of the Sacred Heart,
Dec. 5th, 1887," Woodstock
Letters, v. 17 (1888), 73-81.
R 189
ROSSI, LOUIS. Six ans en
Amérique--Californie et Orégon.
2d ed. Paris. E. Dentur.
1863. iv, 322p. maps.
R 190
ROTH, BENEDICT, AND FRANCIS
R. SADLIER. Brief History
of the Churches of the Diocese
of St. Augustine, Florida.
St. Leo, Fla. Abbey Press.
1923-1940. 10 parts. R 191
ROTH, EDWARD. "Memoir of
the Very Rev. Patrick Reilly,
V.G.," American Catholic His-

torical Society of Philadelphia Records, v. 5 (1894), 7-18.   R 192

ROTHAN, EMMETT. An Austrian Observer of the Catholic Church in the United States in 1842: Canon Joseph Salzbacher. MA thesis. Catholic University. 1940.   R 193

ROTHAN, EMMET H. The German Catholic Immigrant in the United States, 1830-1860. Washington. Catholic University in America. 1946. vii, 172p.   R 194

ROTHENSTEINER, JOHN. "Archbishop Eccleston of Baltimore and the Visitandine's Foundation at Kaskaskia," Illinois Catholic Historical Review, v. 1 (1919), 500-509.   R 195

ROTHENSTEINER, JOHN. "Archbishop Peter Richard Kenrick and the Vatican Council," Illinois Catholic Historical Review, v. 11 (1928), 3-26.   R 196

ROTHENSTEINER, JOHN (ed.) "Bishop England's Correspondence with Bishop Rosati," Illinois Catholic Historical Review, v. 9 (1926), 260-273, (1927), 363-371; v. 10 (1927), 59-61.   R 197

ROTHENSTEINER, JOHN. "Catholic Germans in the Making of America," Central Blatt and Social Justice, v. 17 (1925), 374-376.   R 198

ROTHENSTEINER, JOHN E. "The Champion of the Catholic Indian Schools," Central Blatt and Social Justice, v. 17 (1924), 161-163.   R 199
Msgr. Joseph Andrew Stephans.

ROTHENSTEINER, JOHN E. Chronicles of an Old Missouri Parish. St. Louis. Amerika Print. 1917. 87p. illus. Historical sketches of St. Michael's Fredericktown, Mo.   R 200

ROTHENSTEINER, JOHN E. Chronicles of an Old Missouri Parish. Cape Girardeau, Mo. no pub. 1928. 119p. illus., ports.   R 201

ROTHENSTEINER, JOHN E. "Early Missionary Efforts among the Indians in the Diocese of St. Louis," St. Louis Catholic Historical Review, v. 2 (1920), 57-96.   R 202

ROTHENSTEINER, JOHN E. "Father Charles Nerinckx and His Relations to the Diocese of St. Louis," St. Louis Catholic Historical Review, v. 1 (1918), 157-175.   R 203

ROTHENSTEINER, JOHN. "First Years of Bishop Kenrick's Administration, of St. Louis Diocese," St. Louis Catholic Historical Review, v. 5 (1923), 205-229.   R 204

ROTHENSTEINER, JOHN. "The Flathead and Nez Perce Delegation to St. Louis 1831-1839," St. Louis Catholic Historical Review, v. 2 (1920), 183-197.   R 205

ROTHENSTEINER, JOHN. "Historical Antecedents of the Diocese of St. Louis," Illinois Catholic Historical Review, v. 4 (1922), 243-254.   R 206

ROTHENSTEINER, JOHN. "His torical Sketch of Catholic New Madrid," St. Louis Catholic Historical Review, v. 4 (1922), 113-129, 206-218.   R 207

ROTHENSTEINER, JOHN E. History of the Archdiocese of St. Louis. St. Louis. Herder. 1928. 2v. front., plates, ports., maps, facsims.   R 208

ROTHENSTEINER, JOHN. "Interesting Facts Concerning Chicago's First Four Bishops," Illinois Catholic Historical Review, v. 9 (1926), 151-161.   R 209

ROTHENSTEINER, JOHN (ed.) "Kaskaskia--Fr. Benedict Roux," Illinois Catholic Historical Review, v. 1 (1918),

198-213. R 210

ROTHENSTEINER, JOHN E. Die literarische Wirksamkeit der Deutsch-Katholiken Amerikas. St. Louis. The Author. 1922. v, 58p. R 211

ROTHENSTEINER, JOHN E. "The Missouri Priest One Hundred Years Ago," Missouri Historical Review, v. 21 (1927), 562-569. R 212

ROTHENSTEINER, JOHN E. "The Northeastern Part of the Diocese of St. Louis under Bishop Rosati," Illinois Catholic Historical Review, v. 2 (1919-1920), 175-195, 269-285, 396-416; v. 3 (1920-1921), 61-72, 126-145, 284-302, 389-403; v. 4 (1921-1922), 34-42, 135-153. R 213

ROTHENSTEINER, JOHN E. "Paul de Saint Pierre, the First German-American Priest of the West," Catholic Historical Review, v. 5 (1920), 195-222. R 214

ROTHENSTEINER, JOHN E. Remembrance of the Diamond Jubilee (1925) of the German St. Vincent's Orphan Society, with a Historical Sketch. St. Louis. St. Vincent's Orphan Society. 1925. 319p. illus. R 215

ROTHENSTEINER, JOHN E. A Sketch of Catholic Journalism in St. Louis. R 216

ROTHENSTEINER, JOHN E. "The Sulpicians in the Illinois Country," Illinois Catholic Historical Review, v. 8 (1926), 233-249. R 217

ROWE, HENRY K. The History of Religion in the United States. New York. Macmillan. 1924. viii, 213p. R 218

ROWE, KENNETH W. Mathew Carey. A Study in American Economic Development. Baltimore. Johns Hopkins Press. 1933. 140p. R 219

ROWE, WILLIAM. "St. Joseph's Church, Brandywine, Delaware,"

American Catholic Historical Researches, v. 6 (1889), 139-142. R 220

ROWLAND, KATE MASON. Life and Correspondence of Charles Carroll of Carrollton, 1737-1832, with His Correspondence and Public Papers. New York. G.P. Putnam's Sons. 1898. 2v. fronts., plates, ports., geneal. tables. R 221

ROYER, FANCHON. The Franciscans Came First. Patterson, N.J. St. Anthony Guild Press. 1951. 206p. illus. maps. R 222

Portraits of nine Franciscan missionaries to New Spain--to Central America, Mexico, California, and the Gulf coast.

ROYS, RALPH L. AND MARGARET W. HARRISON. "Sylvanus Griswold Morley, 1883-1948," American Antiquity, v. 14 (1949), 215-221. R 223

ROZIER, FIRMIN A. "Rev. James Maxwell, Missionary at St. Genevieve," United States Catholic Historical Magazine, v. 1 (1887), 283. R 224

RUANE, JOSEPH W. The Beginnings of the Society of St. Sulpice in the United States (1791-1829). Washington. Catholic University. 1935. x, 266p. illus. (plan). R 225

RUPP, AUGUST (tr. and ed.) "A Picture of New Mexico in 1681," United States Catholic Historical Society Records and Studies, v. 9 (1916), 191-199. R 226

RUPPEL, GEORGE. "Early Days of the University of Dayton: Excerpts from the Chronicles of Nazareth," Ohio State Archaeological and Historical Quarterly, v. 63 (1954), 378-387. R 227

The Chronicles are a history of the early years of the School begun 1850, written by Brother John A. Brueck.

RUSH, ALFRED C. "Diplomatic Relations: The United States and the Papal States," American Ecclesiastical Review, v. 126 (1952), 12-27.   R 228

RUSH, ALFRED C. The Supply of Clergy in Louisiana, 1763-1805. MA thesis. Catholic University. 1938. 111p.
          R 229

RUSKOWSKI, LEO F. French Emigré Priests in the United States (1791-1815). Washington. Catholic University. 1940. ix, 150p.   R 230

RUSS, WILLIAM A. "Anti-Catholic Agitation during Reconstruction," American Catholic Historical Society of Philadelphia Records, v. 45 (1934), 312-321.   R 231

RUSSELL, CHARLES RUSSELL, BARON. Diary of a Visit to the United States of America in the Year 1883. ed. by Charles G. Herbermann. New York. United States Catholic Historical Society. 1910. 235p. front., plates, ports.   R 232

RUSSELL, MATTHEW. The Life of Mother Mary Baptist Russell Sister of Mercy. Fresno, Calif. Academy of California Church History. 1952. 194p.
          R 233

RUSSELL, WILLIAM H. "The Catholic Evidence Guild in the United States," Lumen Vitae, v. 3 (1948), 300-315. R 234

RUSSELL, W. H. "John M. Cooper--Pioneer," Catholic Educational Review, v. 47 (1949), 435-441.   R 235

RUSSELL, WILLIAM T. Maryland: The Land of Sanctuary. Baltimore. J.H. Furst Co. 1907. xxxvii, 621p. front., ports.   R 236

RUSSO, N. "The Origin and Progress of Our Italian Mission in New York." Letter dated 303 Elizabeth St., New York, Jan. 29, 1896," Woodstock Letters, v. 25 (1896), 135-143.   R 237

RUSSWORM, NORBERT. Rev. Paul J. Volk. St. Bernard, Ala. Abbey Book Shop. 1937. iv, 147p.   R 238

RUTKOWSKI, SISTER M. NEO-MISIA. "A Polish Pioneer Jesuit in America," Polish American Studies, v. 3 (1946), 98-103.   R 239
          Francis Dzierozynski.

RYAN, CARL J. "Ghosts of Trusteeism," Homiletic and Pastoral Review, v. 57 (1957), 705-714.   R 240

RYAN, DANIEL J. American Catholic World War I Records. Washington. Catholic University. 1941. vii, 473p. incl. illus. (incl facsim.), plates, forms.   R 241

RYAN, EDWARD A. "Cardinal Gibbons after Thirty Years," Theological Studies, v. 14 (1953), 430-442.   R 242
          An extensive review of Ellis's Gibbons.

RYAN, EDWARD A. "An Historical Sketch of St. Aloysius' Parish, Littlestown, Pennsylvania," Woodstock Letters, v. 71 (1942), 290-298.
          R 243

RYAN, EDWARD A. "Pages from the Story of an Ancient Parish," Woodstock Letters, v. 76 (1947), 321-341.
          Leonardtown, Md. R 244

RYAN, EDWIN. "Diocesan Organization in the Spanish Colonies," Catholic Historical Review, v. 2 (1915), 146-156, v. 4 (1917), 170-186, v. 5 (1919), 3-18.   R 245

RYAN, J. F. "Bishop Kozlowski," Salesianum, v. 9 (Jan., 1914), 1-11. port. R 246

RYAN, J. F. "The Franciscan Missions of California," Illinois Catholic Historical Review, v. 9 (1926), 134-150.
          R 247

RYAN, JOHN A. The Catholic Church and the Citizen. New York. Macmillan. 1928. 94p. R 248

RYAN, JOHN A. "The Significance of the Supreme Court Decision in the Oregon School Case," Catholic Educational Review, v. 23 (1925), 585-588. R 249

RYAN, JOHN A. Social Doctrine in Action. A Personal History. New York. Harper and Bros. 1941. vii, 297p. front. (port.) R 250

RYAN, JOHN CONWAY. Mr. Theodore Basselin and His Foundation. MA thesis. Catholic University. 1926. 38p. R 251

RYAN, JOHN J. Chronicle and Sketch of the Church of St. Ignatius of Loyola, Baltimore, 1856-1906. Baltimore. A. Hoen and Co. 1907. 79p. ports. R 252

RYAN, JOHN J. "St. John's College, Frederick, Half a Century Ago," Woodstock Letters, v. 30 (1901), 231-246. R 253

RYAN, JOHN J. "The Story of the 'Wizard Clip' or 'Clip Ghost,' " Woodstock Letters, v. 36 (1907), 92-99. R 254

RYAN, JOSEPH P. "American Contributions to the Catholic Missionary Effort in China in the Twentieth Century," Catholic Historical Review, v. 31 (1945), 171-180. R 255

RYAN, JOSEPH PAUL. "Travel Literature as Source Material for American Catholic History," Illinois Catholic Historical Review, v. 10 (1928), 179-238, 301-363. R 256

RYAN, LEO RAYMOND. Old St. Peter's, the Mother Church of Catholic New York (1785-1935). Ph.D. thesis. Fordham University. 1936. xiii, 282p. (printed). R 257

RYAN, LEO RAYMOND. Old St. Peter's, the Mother Church of Catholic New York (1785-1935). New York. United States Catholic Historical Society. 1935. xiii, 282p. plates. R 258

RYAN, SISTER MARIA ALMA. Catholic Education ... to 1850. Ph.D. thesis. Villanova University. 1924. 278p. R 259

RYAN, SISTER MARY TIMOTHY. History of Sancta Maria in Ripa, St. Louis, Missouri, 1901-1924. MA thesis. Saint Louis University. 1941. 126p. R 260

RYAN, MICHAEL J. "Old St. Mary's--A National Shrine," American Catholic Historical Society of Philadelphia Records, v. 38 (1927), 158-167. R 261

RYAN, P. J. "Most Rev. Peter Richard Kenrick, D.D.," American Catholic Quarterly Review, v. 21 (1896), 425-428. R 262

RYAN, PAUL E. History of the Diocese of Covington. Covington, Ky. Diocese of Covington. 1954. 1054p. R 263

RYAN, STEPHEN. "Early Lazarist Missions and Missionaries," United States Catholic Historical Magazine, v. 1 (1887), 233-257, 366-387. R 264

RYAN, T. E. Burrville, R. I., and the Catholic Church. no. pl. The Author. 1925. R 265

RYAN, THOMAS R. "Brownson on Salvation and the Church," American Ecclesiastical Review, v. 117 (1947), 117-124. R 266

RYAN, THOMAS R. "Brownson's Technique in Apologetics," American Ecclesiastical Review, v. 118 (1948), 12-22. R 267

RYDER, JOHN H. "West Coast Russian Mission," Woodstock Letters, v. 81 (1952), 107-121. R 268

Brief sketch of the work among the Russians on the Pacific coast, centered principally around the activity of St. Andrew's Mission, Los Angeles.

- S -

SACRAMENTO, CALIF. (DIOCESE) SYNOD, 1887. Synodus dioecesana sacramentensis A.D. MDCCCLXXXVII. habita. Sancti Francisci Typis, P.J. Thomas, 1887. 18p.   S 1

SACRAMENTO (DIOCESE) SYNOD, 2nd, 1929. Statuta dioecesis sacramentensis lata ac promulgata in synodo dioecesana secunda die 18 mensis Decembris, 1929, habita a Roberto J. Armstrong [bp.] Sacramento, The Tribune printing co. [n.d.] 38p.   S 2

SAGINAW (DIOCESE) SYNOD, 1st, 1945. Synodus dioecesana saginavensis prima in ecclesia cathedrali Sanctae Mariae Virginis die 22 mensis Martii A. D. 1945 celebrata, praeside Guillelmo Murphy [ep.] [n.p. n.d.] 18p.   S 3

ST. AUGUSTINE, FLA. (DIOCESE) SYNOD, 2nd, 1889. [Decreta] Contains decrees 1-15. 3 p. 1., [7]-13p.   S 4

SAINT AUGUSTINE (DIOCESE) SYNOD, 3rd, 1902. Synodus dioecesana III Sancti Augustini die decima Decembris, A.D. 1902 in ecclesia cathedrali Sti. Augustini habita a Gulielmo Joanne Kenny, D.D., episcopo Sti. Augustini. St. Augustine, Fla. Record [n.d.] 30p., 1 1.   S 5

ST. AUGUSTIN DE TRANCHE-PAIN, MERE. Relation du Voyage des Premières Ursulines à la Nouvelle Orléans et leur établissement en cette ville. N.Y. Isle de Manate. Cramoisy de Jean Marie Shea. 1859. 62p.   S 6

(ST. AUGUSTINE, FLA. ST. AUGUSTINE CATHEDRAL). History of Nuestra Senora de la Leche Buen Parto, and Saint Augustine. St. Augustine. Cathedral Parish of St. Augustine. 1937. 64p. illus. (incl. ports.)   S 7

(ST. AUGUSTINE, FLA. ST. AUGUSTINE CATHEDRAL). Roman Catholic Records, St. Augustine Parish: White Baptisms, 1784-1792. Tallahassee, Florida. State Library Board. 1941. viii, 162p.   S 8

(ST. CHARLES SEMINARY, OVERBROOK, PA.) "Index of Historical Pamphlets in the Library of St. Charles Seminary, Overbrook, Pa.," American Catholic Historical Society of Philadelphia Records, v. 13 (1902), 60-119.   S 9
Cover a wide variety of subjects.

SAINT CLOUD (DIOCESE) SYNOD, 1924. Synodal decrees of the diocese of Saint Cloud, promulgated in diocesan synod held June 10, 1924, by the Right Reverend Joseph F. Busch, D.C., bishop of St. Cloud. [n.p., 1924] 37p.   S 10

SAINT CLOUD (DIOCESE) SYNOD, 1929. Additions and amendments to the synodal decrees of the diocese of St. Cloud, promulgated in the diocesan synod held June 20, 1929. [8]p.   S 11

ST. CLOUD (DIOCESE) SYNOD, 3rd, 1939. Synodal decrees of the diocese of Saint Cloud, promulgated in the third diocesan synod held June 22, 1939. By Joseph F. Busch [bp.] [n.p., n.d.] 56p.   S 12

"ST. DAVID'S," Jubilee, v. 4 (1956), 22-29.   S 13
The illustrated story of a private elementary school

run by Catholic laymen
and offering New York boys
a unique education.
ST. HENRY, SISTER M. "Nativism in Pennsylvania with Particular Regard to Its Effects on
Politics and Education," Amer-
ican Catholic Historical Society
of Philadelphia Records, v. 47
(1936), 5-47.   S 14
"ST. JOHN'S CHURCH AND
RESIDENCE, FREDERICK, MD.,"
Woodstock Letters, v. 5 (1876),
29-36, 99-114, 174-188. S 15
A historical sketch.
ST. JOSEPH, MO. (DIOCESE)
SYNOD, 1879. Statuta a
Joanne Josepho Hogan [ep.]
in synodo dioecesana, in
cathedrali diebus 11 ac 12 Feb.
A.D. 1879 habita, lata et
promulgata. Sti. Josephi, Mo.,
J.H. McGuire, 1879. 41p.
                                 S 16
ST. JOSEPH, MO. (DIOCESE)
SYNOD, 3rd, 1930. Statuta
dioecesana quae in synodo
tertia S. Joseph, die 27a
Jan., 1930, habita in ecclesia
cathedrali S. Joseph a Francis-
co Gilfillan [ep.] lata et pro-
mulgata fuerunt. Sancti Joseph,
Apud Cancellariam Dioecesanam,
1930.   S 17
(ST. JOSEPH, N.Y. ST. JOSEPH
SEMINARY). Souvenir of the
Blessing of the Corner Stone
of the New Seminary of St.
Joseph, N.Y. New York.
Cathedral Library Association.
1891. 117p. illus.   S 18
"ST. JOSEPH'S APACHE MIS-
SION, MESCALERO, NEW
MEXICO," Provincial Annals
(Province of Santa Barbara,
O.F.M.) v. 2 (Oct., 1939),
15-18.   S 19
"ST. JOSEPH'S CHURCH, YORK-
VILLE, NEW YORK CITY,"
Woodstock Letters, v. 15
(1886), 62-65.   S 20
Begun 1872.
(ST. JOSEPH'S COLLEGE, PHIL-
ADELPHIA). Crimson and

Grey. Centennial Edition. St.
Joseph's College, Philadelphia,
Pennsylvania. 1951. illus.
                                 S 21
(ST. LEO, FLA. ST. LEO AB-
BEY). Silver Jubilee of Ab-
bey and Abbot of St. Leo,
Florida, 1927. [St. Leo, Fla.
St. Leo Abbey]. 1927? 111p.
illus., plates, ports. S 22
ST. LOUIS (DIOCESE) SYNOD,
1839. [Statuta] [n.p., n.d.]
24p.   S 23
ST. LOUIS (DIOCESE) SYNOD,
1850. Statuta lata et pro-
mulgata a Petro Ricardo Ken-
rich [ep.] in synodo dioecesana
Aug., 1850 habita. S. Ludo-
vici, R. Phillips, 1850. 19p.
                                 S 24
ST. LOUIS (ECCLESIASTICAL
PROVINCE) COUNCIL, 1st.
Acta et decreta concilii pro-
vincialis primi, mensi Octobri,
A.D., 1855, Sancti Ludovici,
habiti. S. Ludovici, Apud G.
Knapp & Co., 1858. 16p.
                                 S 25
ST. LOUIS (ECCLESIASTICAL
PROVINCE) COUNCIL, 2nd,
1858. Concilium provinciale
secundum. Mense Septembris,
A.D. 1858. Sancti Ludovici,
habitum. S. Ludovici, G.
Knapp & Co., 1859. 16p.
                                 S 26
ST. LOUIS (DIOCESE) SYNOD,
3rd, 1896. Synodus dioecesana
Sti. Ludovici tertia, habita die
8 Sept. A.D. 1896 a Joanne
Josepho Kain [ep.] Sti. Ludo-
vici, Apud Cancellariam dioe-
cesanam, 1897. 179p. S 27
ST. LOUIS, MO. (DIOCESE)
SYNOD, 5th, 1905. Synodus
dioecesana Sancti Ludovici
quinta, habita die tertia Octobris
anno Domini, 1905, praesedente
Joanne Josepho Glennon, arch-
iepiscopo S. Ludovici. S.
Ludovici, Cancellaria dioecesana
1905. 19p.   S 28
ST. LOUIS, MO. (ARCHDIOCESE)
SYNOD, 6th, 1908. Synodus

dioecesana Sancti Ludovici sexta, habita die vicesima sexta Junii, Anno Domini, 1908, praesidente Joanne Josepho Glennon, archiepiscopo S. Ludovici. S. Ludovici, Cancellania dioecesana, 1908. 28p. S 29

ST. LOUIS, (DIOCESE) SYNOD, 7th, 1929. Synodus dioecesana Sancti Ludovici septima habita die 10 mensis Iunii A.D. 1929 praesidente Ioanne Iosepho Glennon [abp.] Sancti Ludovici, Apud Cancellariam dioecesanam [n.d.] xiii, 126p. S 30

ST. LOUIS, MO. (DIOCESE) SYNOD 7th, 1960. Synodus Diocesana Sancti Ludovici nona habita die vigensima prima Novembris A.D. 1960 ... praesidente Josepho Elmero Ritter. n.p., n.d. xxxv,112p. S 31

"ST. MARY'S CHURCH AND RESIDENCE, ALEXANDRIA, VIRGINIA," Woodstock Letters, v. 13 (1884), 344-356; v. 14 (1885), 97-112, 243-257. S 32

(ST. MARY'S, ELK CO., PA.) History of the Development of Catholicity in St. Mary's, Elk Co., Pa., 1869-1919. no pl. no pub. 1919? 35p. plates, ports. S 33

(ST. MARY'S COLLEGE. ST. MARY'S, KANS.) Historical Sketch and Pictorial. St. Mary's, Kans. no pub. 1913. 36p. front., plates, ports. S 34

ST. PATRICK CHURCH COMPLETES A CENTURY. Provincial Annals, O.F.M. (New York), [Buffalo], v. 13 (1956), 5-8. illus. S 35

ST. PAUL (DIOCESE) SYNOD, 1st, 1861. Decreta primae synodi dioecesanae, die 10 Junii, A.D. 1861, Sti. Pauli de Minnesota habitae [n.p., n. d.] 16p. S 36

ST. PAUL (DIOCESE) SYNOD, 2nd, 1863. Decreta secundae synodi dioecesanae, die 24

Septembris, A.D. 1863, Sti. Pauli de Minnesota habitae. [n.p., n.d.] [17]-25p. S 37

ST. PAUL (DIOCESE SYNOD, 3rd, 1873. Decreta tertiae synodi dioecesanae, die 14 Julii, A.D., 1873, Sti. Pauli de Minnesota habitae [n.p., n.d.] [31]-36p., 1 1. S 38

ST. PAUL (DIOCESE) SYNOD, 4th, 1875. Decreta quartae synodi dioecesanae, die 24a mensis Augusti, A.D. 1875, Sti. Pauli de Minnesota habitae. [n.p., n.d.] 8p. S 39

ST. PAUL (DIOCESE) SYNOD, 4th, 1875. Decreta quartae synodi dioecesanae, die 24a mensis Augusti, A.D. 1875, Sti. Pauli de Minnesota habitae. [n.p., n.d.] 23p. Decrees of the 5th synod, 1877: p. [9]-23. S 40

"ST. PETER'S PARISH ROSWELL, NEW MEXICO," Provincial Chronicle (St. John Baptist Province, O.F.M.), v. 6 (1934), 69-72. S 41

ST. ROMULAD, SEVEN HERMITS OF. "The Camaldolese Come to America," American Benedictine Review, v. 12 (Mar. 1961), 40-54. S 42
An interview at The Hermitage of the Immaculate Heart of Mary, Lucia Ranch, Big Sur, California.

SALES, LUIS. Observations on California, 1772-1790. Los Angeles. Glen Dawson, 1956. xiii, 218p. S 43
An account by an early Dominican missionary.

(SALMON, .) "Father Salmon, Missionary in Kentucky, Describes to Bishop Carroll His Journey from Baltimore and the Condition of the Church and Character of the People of the State--1799," American Catholic Historical Researches, v. 28 (1911), 105-107. S 44

SALPOINTE, JOHN BAPTIST.
"The Church in Arizona. Letter of J. B. Salpointe, Vicar
Apostolic of Arizona, to John
Gilmary Shea. Tucson, Ari-
zona, October 1, 1874," Amer-
ican Catholic Historical Society
of Philadelphia Records, v.
60 (1949), 224-227.   S 45
SALPOINTE, JOHN BAPTIST.
"Etats-Unis. Vicariat Apos-
tolique de l'Arizona," Annales
de la Propagation de la Foi,
v. 43 (1871), 265-274.   S 46
SALPOINTE, JOHN BAPTIST.
Soldiers of the Cross. Ban-
ning, Calif. St. Boniface
Industrial School. 1898.
299p.   S 47
SALT LAKE CITY (DIOCESE)
SYNOD 1. Statuta dioecesis
Lacus Salsi. Bronx, N.Y.
N.Y. Catholic Protectory.
[1929] vii, 41p.   S 48
SALTER, J.M. "Our College at
Augusta, Georgia. Letter
dated Sacred Heart College,
Augusta, Georgia, December
9, 1905," Woodstock Letters,
v. 34 (1905), 381-385.   S 49
(SALVATORIAN COLLEGE. ST.
NAZIANZ, WIS.) Diamond
Jubilee ... St. Nazianz, Wis.
The Salvatorian College,
1929. no pl. no pub. 1929?
80p. incl. illus., plates,
ports., facsim.   S 50
[SALZBACHER, J.] "Eine
frühe Nachtricht über Teutopolis,
Illinois," Central Blatt and
Social Justice, v. 11 (1918),
183-184.   S 51
[SALZBACHER, J.] "Das kath-
olische Deutschtum Cincinnatis
im Jahre 1842," Central Blatt
and Social Justice, v. 10
(1918), 325-326.   S 52
SALZBACHER, JOSEPH. Meine
Reise Nach Nord Amerika in
Jahre 1842. Wien. Wimmer
Schmidt and Leo. 1845. vii,
479p. fold. map.   S 53
[SALZBACHER, J.] "Nicholas
Mertz, eine vergessener

deutscher Missionär," Central
Blatt and Social Justice,
v. 11 (1918), 186.   S 54
SALZMANN, JOSEPH. "(Letters
to the Ludwig Missionverein
of Munich)." Salesianum,
1942-1953. passim.   S 55
In 1942 Father Peter Leo
Johnson began the editing
and publishing of the Salzmann correspondence; the
series appeared in the
quarterly issues of the
Salesianum. Many letters
were published; while the
individual letters generally
are not of sufficient importance to merit separate entry, the correspondence
taken as a whole makes a
significant contribution to
the knowledge of the conditions of the Church in Wisconsin at the beginning of the
Civil War. The last of the
series appeared in the
Salesianum, v. 68 (January,
1953).
SAMPSELD, BROWNE, "Phila-
delphia's Labor Priest," The
Priest, v. 11 (1955), 1011-
1014.   S 56
Biographical sketch of Fr.
Dennis J. Comey, S.J.
SAN ANTONIO (DIOCESE) SYNOD,
1st, 1879. Statuta dioeceseos
San Antonianae quae in synodo
dioecesana prima V. et VI.
calendas Maii, 1879, tulit et
promulgavit Antonius Dominicus
Pellicer, D.D. [n.p. n.d.]
24p.   S 57
SAN ANTONIO, TEXAS (DIO-
CESE) SYNOD, 2nd, 1906.
Synodo dioecesana Sti. Antonii
secunda, habita die 19 Julii,
anno Domini 1906, a Joanne
Antonio Forest, Sti Antonii
episcopo. [n.p., n.d.] 31p.
                           S 58
SAN ANTONIO (DIOCESE) SYNOD,
4th, 1930. Synodus dioe-
cesana Sancti Antonii quarta
celebrata die 23 Aprilis Anni

316

Domini 1930 in ecclesia cathedrali Sancto Ferdinando dedicata a ... Arthuro Hieronymo Drossaerts [abp.] San Antonio, Cancellaria archidioecesana [1930] 46p. S 59

SAN FRANCISCO (DIOCESE) SYNOD, 1862. Synodus dioecesana Sancti Francisci, habita mense Julii MDCCCLXII. Sancti Francisci, Towne et Bacon, 1862. 16p. S 60

SAN FRANCISCO (ECCLESIASTICAL PROVINCE) COUNCIL, 1874. Concilii provincialis S. Francisci I. in ecclesia metropolitana Sancti Francisci A.D. MDCCCLXXIV. habiti, et a Sede Apostolica, recogniti, Acta et decreta. Sancti Francisci, Ex typographia Thomas et soc., 1875. 90p., 1 1.
  S 61

SAN FRANCISCO (ECCLESIASTICAL PROVINCE) COUNCIL, 2d, 1882. Concilii Provincialis S. Francisci II. In Ecclesia Metropolitana Sancti Francisci A.D. MDCCCLXXXII. Habita, Eta Sede Apostolica Recogniti. Acta et Decreta. San Francisco. P.J. Thomas, 1883. 36p. S 62

SAN FRANCISCO (ARCHDIOCESE) SYNOD, 2nd, 1936. Statuta archidioecesis Sancti Francisci lata ac promulgata a Joanne Joseph Mitty [abp.] in synodo dioecesana secunda, die 14 mensis Octobris Anno 1936 habita in ecclesia cathedrali Sanctae Mariae civitatis Sancti Francisci in California. San Francisco, The Monitor publ. co., [n.d.] 156p. S 63

SAN LUIS REY CELEBRATES A SILVER JUBILEE. Provincial Annals (Santa Barbara Province, v. 17 O.F.M.), 1954-55), 93-111. S 64

"SAN XAVIER DEL BAC. ARIZONA," Woodstock Letters, v. 10 (1881), 157-170. S 65

SANDBERG, H.W. Drums of Destiny--Katherine Tekakwitha. St. Meinrad, Ind. Grail Press. 1915. 98p. S 66

SANDERLIN, GEORGE. "The Wide World of Francesca Cabrini," Ave Maria, v. 78 (Oct. 17, 1953), 15, 17-19. port. S 67
  A popular biographical sketch.

SANNING, AMBROSE. "The First Missionaries of the New World," American Catholic Historical Society of Philadelphia Records, v. 10 (1899), 309-327. S 68

SANSONE, AUGUST. "Potawatomi Mission of Indiana," St. Meinrad Historical Essays, v. 1 (1928), 48-57. S 69

[SANTA BARBARA] History of the Mission Towers [Santa Barbara] Finally Revealed. Provincial Annals (Santa Barbara Province, O.F.M.) 13 (1951), 86-91. illus.
  S 70

SANTA FE (DIOCESE). Constituciones eclesiásticas para la diocesis de Santa Fe, N. M. publicadas por el Ilmo. Sr. opispo D. Juan B. Lamy. Albuquerque, N.M., Imprenta del Rio Grande, 1874. 35p., 1 1. S 71

SANTA FE, N.M. (DIOCESE) SYNODS 1-3. Constitutiones syndorum dioecesanarum Sanctae Fider Novi Mexici primae secundae et tertiae. Las Vegas. Revista Catolica, 1893. 63p. S 72

SARGENT, DANIEL. All the Day Long. New York. Longmans, Green and Co. 1941. x, 259p. front., plates, ports.
  S 73
  A popular life of Bishop James A. Walsh, co-founder of Maryknoll.

SERGENT, DANIEL. Catherine Tekakwitha. New York. Longmans, Green and Co. 1936. vii, 246p. front. (port.)

S 74
SARGENT, DANIEL. Our Land
and Our Lady. New York.
Longmans, Green and Co.
1939. v, 263p. S 75
SARGENT, DANIEL. Mitri, The
Story of Prince Demetrius
Augustine Gallitzin. New York.
Longmans, Green and Co.
1945. 327p. S 76
SARGENT, KATE. "Catholicism
in Massachusetts," The Forum,
v. 74 (1925), 521-532, 730-
742. S 77
SATOLLI, FRANCIS. Loyalty to
Church and State. 2d ed.
Baltimore. John Murphy and
Co. 1895. 315p. S 78
(SATOLI, FRANCIS). "Der
päpstliche Delegat Satoli über
die deutschen Katholischen
Americas," Central Blatt and
Social Justice, v. 11 (1918),
47-49. S 79
SAULT SAINT MARIE, MICH.
(DIOCESE). Statuta dioecesis
Sanctae Mariae. Cincinnati,
Typis C. Clark, 1856. 97p.
S 80
SAUM, GEORGE. "Father
Roman Weinzapfel," St. Mein-
rad Historical Essays, v. 1
(1928), 38-47. S 81
SAUNDERS, CHARLES F., AND
J. SMEATON CHASE. The
California Padres and Their
Missions. Boston. Houghton
Mifflin. 1915. xi, 417p.
col. front., illus., plates,
map. S 82
SAUNDERS, CHARLES F., AND
ST. JOHN O'SULLIVAN.
Capistrano Nights. New York.
McBride. 1930. xi, 202p.
front., illus. (incl. map),
plates. S 83
SAVAGE, ALMA H. Dogsled
Apostles. N.Y. Sheed.
1942. 231p. Alaska. S 84
SAVAGE, SISTER M. LUCIDA.
The Congregation of Saint
Joseph of Carondolet. A Brief
Account of Its Origin and Its
Work in the United States

(1650-1922). Washington.
Catholic University. 1923.
xviii, 334p. front., plates,
ports. S 85
SAVAGE, SISTER M. LUCIDA.
"A Statistical Survey of the
Church in the United States--
1841," American Catholic
Historical Society of Philadelphia Records, v. 38
(1927), 193-206. S 86
SAVANNAH (DIOCESE). Pastoral
letter on the temporalities
of the church, in the diocese
of Savannah. Augustin Verot
bishop of Savannah and ad-
ministrator apostolic of
Florida. [n.p., n.d.] 36p.
Decrees of the 4th (1868) and
5th (1868!) diocesan synods:
p. 35-36. S 87
SAVANNAH, GA. (DIOCESE),
SYNOD, 6th, 1879. Statuta
dioecesis savannensis a Gulielmo
H. Gross, S. Th. D.,
episcopo savannensi, in synodo
dioecesana sexta, mense Septembris A.D. 1879, lata et
promulgata. [n.p., n.d.]
54p. S 88
SAVANNAH, GA. (DIOCESE)
SYNOD, 8th, 1900. Constitutiones dioecesanae savannensis,
quas in synodo dioecesana
octava, die XII Julii, A.D.
1900. Confirmavit et auxit
Benjamin Joseph Keiley, episcopus savannensis. Neo
Eboraci, Typis C.A. Searing,
1900. 47, v p. S 89
SAVANNAH-ATLANTA (DIOCESE)
SYNOD, 1939? Statuta dio
ecesis savannensis-atlantensis
necnon facultates sacerdotibus
concessae. Savannah,
Chancery Office, 1939. 54
[3]p. S 90
SAVEY, RAYMOND NORBERT.
The Use of Psalms by American Catholics. MA thesis.
University of Notre Dame.
1956. S 91
SAVS, MATHIAS. "The Catholic
Church in Wright County,

Minn.," Acta et Dicta, v. 4 (1916), 219-242. S 92

SCANLAN, ARTHUR J. St. Joseph's Seminary, Dunwoodie, New York, 1896-1921, with an account of the Other Seminaries of New York. New York. United States Catholic Historical Society. 1922. xv, 237p. front., plates, ports. S 93

SCANLAN, CHARLES M. "Little Sisters of the Poor, Milwaukee," Salesianum, v. 32 (1937), 107-111. S 94

SCANLAN, LAWRENCE. "Lettre de Monseigneur Scanlan, Vicaire Apostolique à MM. les Directeurs de l'Oeuvre de la Propagation de la Foi. Park City (Utah), le 10 octobre 1886," Annales de la Propagation de la Foi, v. 59 (1887), 24-27. S 95

SCANLAN, LAWRENCE. 'Rapport de M. Lawrence Scanlan, curé de Salt Lake City, à MM. les Membres de Conseils Centraux de l'Oeuvre de la Propagation de la Foi, 13 novembre, 1876," Annales de la Propagation de la Foi, v. 49 (1877), 292-295. S 96

SCANLAN, PETER LAWRENCE. Centennial History of St. Gabriel's Parish, Prairie du Chien, Wisconsin, 1836-1936. no pl. no pub. 1936. 61p. S 97

SCANLAN, PETER LAWRENCE. "Pioneer Priests at Prairie du Chien," Wisconsin Magazine of History, v. 13 (1929), 97-106. illus. S 98

SCANLAN, PETER LAWRENCE. Prairie du Chien and Centennial History of St. Gabriel's Parish, Prairie du Chien, Wisconsin. Prairie du Chien. Printed Privately. 1937. 258p. S 99

SCANNELL-O'NEILL, D.J. Distinguished Converts to Rome in America. St. Louis. Herder. 1907. S 100

SCHABART, JOSEPH A. "The Ludwig-Missionsverein," Catholic Historical Review, v. 8 (1922), 23-41. S 101

SCHAEFER, CATHERINE. "A Chronology of Missions and Churches in Illinois from 1675 to 1844," Illinois Catholic Historical Review, v. 1 (1918), 103-109. S 102

SCHAEFER, FRANCIS J. "Bibliography on the Kensington Rune Stone," Catholic Historical Review, v. 6 (1920), 387-391. S 103

SCHAEFER, FRANCIS J. Golden Jubilee of St. Mary's Parish, Sleepy Eye, Minnesota. 1926. New Ulm. no pub. 1926. 151p. plates, ports. S 104

SCHAEFER, FRANCIS J. "Hennepin, the Discoverer of the Falls of St. Anthony," Acta et Dicta, v. 6 (1933), 54-85, 161-186. S 105

SCHAEFER, FRANCIS J. "The History of the Diocese of St. Paul," Acta et Dicta, v. 4 (1915), 32-71. S 106

SCHAEFER, FRANCIS J. "The Kensington Rune Stone," Acta et Dicta, v. 2 (1910), 206-210. illus. S 107

SCHAEFER, FRANCIS J. "Parish of the Most Holy Redeemer, St. Paul, Minn., for Catholics of Italian Descent," Acta et Dicta, v. 2 (1910), 241-255. S 108

SCHAEFERS, WILLIAM. 'Growth of Episcopal Sees in America," American Ecclesiastical Review, v. 107 (1942), 367-371. S 109

SCHAEFFER, CLAUDE. "The First Jesuit Mission to the Flathead, 1840-1850; A Study in Culture Conflicts," Pacific Northwest Quarterly, v. 18 (1937), 227-250. S 110

SCHAGEMANN, JOSEPH J. "The Catholic Maternity Guild Apostolate," American Ecclesiastical Review, v. 127 (1952),

264-269. S 111
SCHARPER, PHILIP, ed. American Catholics: A Protestant-Jewish View. New York. Sheed and Ward, 1959. viii, 235p. S 112
SCHARPER, PHILIP. "American Catholics and American Culture," Critic, v. 29 (1960), 7-9. S 113
SCHANZER, GEORGE O. "A Russian Visit to the Spanish Franciscans in California, 1836," Americas, v. 9 (1950), 453-458. S 114
Description of the visit of the Orthodox priest John Veniaminov.
SCHAUINGER, J. HERMAN. Cathedrals in the Wilderness. Milwaukee. Bruce. 1952. xiii, 334p. S 115
The biography of Bishop Flaget of Bardstown. Unfortunately set in a depressing format and difficult to read, but well worth the effort.
SCHAUINGER, J. HERMAN. "The Domestic Life of William Gaston, Catholic Jurist," Catholic Historical Review, v. 30 (1945), 394-426. S 116
SCHAUINGER, JOSEPH HERMAN. "A Great Southern Catholic," United States Catholic Historical Society Records and Studies, v. 32 (1941), 83-93. S 117
A short biographical sketch of Judge William Gaston of North Carolina.
SCHAUINGER, J. HERMAN. "Kentucky: Cradle of Catholicism in the Old West," Ave Maria, v. 94 (Nov. 4, 1961), 5-10. ports. (Badin, Carroll, Flaget, Nerinckx). S 118
SCHAUINGER, J. HERMAN. "William Gaston and the Supreme Court of North Carolina," North Carolina Historical Review, v. 21 (1944), 97-117. S 119

SCHAUINGER, J. HERMAN. William Gaston, Carolinian. Milwaukee. Bruce. 1949. ix, 242p. illus., ports. S 120
SCHEIBL, H. J. "Catholics in the History of Texas," America, v. 48 (1933), 526-527. S 121
SCHENKELBERG, SISTER M. MATILDA. Fort Atkinson and the Catholic Frontier of Iowa: the Evolution of a Catholic Indian Mission into a Parish Unit, 1842-1942. MA thesis. Catholic University. 1947. 82p. S 122
SCHEPER, FRANCIS. "German Pioneers of the Faith," Social Justice Review, v. 47 (1955), 386-388 (Rev. John Bernard Weikamp, O.F.M.); v. 48 (1955), 26-27 (Fr. Innocent Wapelhorst, O.F.M.), 217-219 (Fr. Francis X. Obermuller); 250-251 (Dr. John Henni in Ohio); 288-289 (Rev. Martin Fox), 324-326 (Rev. Peter Kreusch, and Msgr. C. H. Linnenkamp); 360-362, 396-398, 433-434 (Fr. Francis X. Pierz); v. 49 (1956), 26-27, 59-62 (Fr. Ambrose Oschwald). S 123
SCHIAVO, GIOVANNI. Italian American History. New York. Vigo Press. 1947- . v. 2 S 124
SCHIER, SISTER M. ANGELA. The History of Indian Missions in North Dakota, 1874-1938. MA thesis. Catholic University. 1938. 97p. S 125
SCHIFFINI, BIAGIANTONIO. "Lettera LXV," Lettere Edificanti Provincia Napolitana, ser. 4 (1882-1883), 159-160. S 126
SCHIFFINI, BIAGIANTONIO. "Lettere del P. Biagiantonio Schiffini al R.P. Provinciale," Lettere Edificanti Provincia Napolitana, ser. 8, n. 1 (1899), 53-55. S 127
SCHIFFINI, BIAGIO. "Da Denver

Colorado," Lettere Edificanti Provincia Napolitana, ser. 9, n. 1 (1901), 109-111. S 128

SCHIFFINI, BIAGIO. "Collegio del Sacro Cuore in Denver, Ministere Parrocchiali," Lettere Edificanti Provincia Napolitana, ser. 8, n. 2 (1900), 114-119. S 129

SCHLAERTH, WILLIAM. "Simon Le Moyne, S.J., and the Early Jesuits of the Syracuse Area," Woodstock Letters, v. 77 (1948), 265-287. S 130

SCHIAFLY, JAMES J. "Birth of Kansas City's Pioneer Church," Missouri Historical Review, v. 44 (1950), 364-372. plates (sketch). S 131

SCHLARMANN, JOSEPH H. Souvenir of the Cathedral Fire. Belleville, Illinois, 1912. no pl. no pub. 1912? 56p. plates, ports. S 132

SCHLARMANN, JOSEPH H. "The Jesuit Epic in Mid-America," Catholic Historical Review, v. 25 (1939), 1-27. S 133

SCHLECTER, N. L. "Missouri: A Short History of Osage County," Woodstock Letters, v. 13 (1884), 357-361. v. 14 (1885), 22-28. S 134

SCHLESINGER, ARTHUR M. A Critical Period in American Religion, 1875-1900. Boston. Massachusetts Historical Society Proceedings. 1932. S 135

SCHLESINGER, ARTHUR M., JR. Orestes Brownson. A Pilgrim's Progress. Boston. Little Brown and Co. 1939. 320p. front. (port.) S 136

SCHLICHER, J. J. "History of St. Nazianz," Wisconsin Magazine of History, v. 31 (1947), 84-91. S 137

SCHMAL, DESMOND A. "The Ruthenian Question in the United States," American Ecclesiastical Review, v. 97 (1937), 448-461. S 138

SCHMECKEBIER, LAURENCE F. History of the Know-Nothing Party in Maryland. Baltimore. Johns Hopkins Press. 1899. 125p. S 139

SCHMIDT, MOTHER JEROME. "Congregation of St. Gertrude the Great," Benedictine Review, v. 4 (1949), 50-52. S 140

SCHMIEDELER, EDGAR. A Better Rural Life. New York. Joseph F. Wagner. 1938. xi, 304p. S 141

SCHMITT, ED. Bibliographie der Benedictiner-Schriftsteller der Vereinigten Staaten Nord Amerikas. (Amerika) [Brünn. 1893?]. 66p. S 142

SCHMITT, E.J.P. Catalogue of Franciscan Missionaries in Texas (1528-1859). Austin, Texas. no pub. 1901. S 143

SCHMITT, EDM. J.P. Lose Blätter aus der Geschichte der deutschen St. Marien Gemeinde von New Albany, Indiana. Cincinnati. S. Rosenthal and Co. 1890. 228p. illus., ports. S 144

SCHMITT, MOTHER M. JEROME. "The Benedictine Sister Today," American Benedictine Review, v. 11 (1960), 249-261. S 145 An interview with Mother Schmitt.

SCHMITZ, JOSEPH W. "Beginnings of the Society of Mary in Texas, 1852-1866," Mid-America, v. 14 (1943), 3-28. S 146

SCHNEE, KARL. "Fond Memories of Seminary Life in Obernberg," Provincial Annals (Province of the Most Holy Name, O.F.M.), v. 8 (1948), 371-374. S 147

SCHNEPP, GERALD J. Leakage from a Catholic Parish. Washington. Catholic University. 1942. xii, 408p. incl tables. diagrs. S 148

SCHNEPP, GERALD, AND ROBERTS, LOUIS A. "Residential Propinquity and Mate Selection on a Parish Basis,"

American Journal of Sociology, v. 58 (1952), 45-50. S 149
Shows that the parish fails to act as a cohesive force in the promotion of mate selection.

SCHOENBERG, WILFRED P. Father Dave, David Plante Mc-Astocker, S.J. Milwaukee. Bruce. 1960. 123p. S 150

SCHOENBERG, WILFRED P. "Historic St. Peter's Mission," Montana, v. 11 (Jan. 1961), 68-87. illus., ports. S 151

SHOENBERG, WILFRED P. Jesuit Mission Presses in the Pacific Northwest. Portland. Champoeg Press. 1957. 76p. illus. S 152

SCHOENBERG, WILFRED P. Jesuits in Montana. Portland. 1960. S 153

SCHOENBERG, WILFRED P. Jesuits in Oregon, 1844-1959. Portland, Ore. The Oregon-Jesuit, 1959. 64p. illus. S 154

SCHOENER, GEORGE. Solemn Dedication of New St. Cecilia's Church, Rochester. Beaver Co., Pa., 1906. no pl. no pub. 1906? S 155

SCHOLES, FRANCE V. "Church and State in New Mexico, 1610-1650," New Mexico Historical Review, v. 10 (1935), 9-76, 145-178, 283-294, 297-349; v. 11 (1936), 41-77. S 156

SCHOLES, FRANCE V. Church and State in New Mexico. Albuquerque. Publications in History, University of New Mexico Press. 1939. 206p. S 157

SCHOLES, FRANCE V. "Documents for the History of the New Mexican Missions in the Seventeenth Century," New Mexico Historical Review, v. 4 (1929), 45-58, 195-201. S 158

SCHOLES, FRANCE V. "Problems in the Early Ecclesiastical History of New Mexico," New Mexico Historical Review, v. 7 (1932), 32-74. S 159

SCHOLES, FRANCE V. "The Supply Service of the New Mexico Missions in the Seventeenth Century," New Mexico Historical Review, v. 5 (1930), 93-115, 186-210, 386-404. S 160

SCHOLES, FRANCE V., AND LANSING B. BLOOM. "Friar Personnel and Mission Chronology, 1598-1639," New Mexico Historical Review, v. 19 (1944), 319-336; v. 20 (1945), 58-82. S 161

"SCHOOL FOR FARMERS," Jubilee, v. 4 (Sept., 1956), 42-45. S 162
An excellent illustrated article about the only Catholic agricultural school in America--located in West Virginia and under the administration of the Salesian Fathers.

SCHRIEBER, ALBERT. Mesquite Does Bloom. San Antonio. Standard Print. 1942. 124p. S 163
Golden Jubilee of St. Mary's, Windhorst, Texas (1892-1942).

SCHRIEBER, JOACHIM. Father James Power and the Reading Colony, from Reading, Pa. to Conception, Mo. MA thesis. Catholic University. 1954. 92p. S 164

SCHROEDER, ALBERT H. "Fray Marcos de Niza, Coronado and the Yavapai," New Mexico Historical Review, v. 30 (1955), 265-296; v. 31 (1956), 24-37. S 165

SCHROEDER, JOS. "Leo XIII and the Encyclical 'Longinqua'," American Catholic Quarterly Review, v. 20 (1895), 369-388. S 166

SCHROEDER, SISTER M. CAROL. The Catholic Church in the Diocese of Vincennes, 1847-1877. Washington. Catholic

University. 1946. vii, 227p. S 167

SCHROLL, SISTER AGNES CLAIR. "John Lancaster Spalding and Quadragesimo Anno," American Benedictine Review, v. 7 (1956-57), 248-262. S 168

SCHROLL, SISTER AGNES CLAIRE. The Social Thought of John Lancaster Spalding. Washington. Catholic University. 1944. xxii, 299p. S 169

SCHROTT, LAMBERT. Pioneer German Catholics in the American Colonies, 1734-1784. MA thesis. Catholic University. 1932. 177p. S 170

SCHROTT, LAMBERT. Pioneer German Catholics in the American Colonies (1734-1784). New York. United States Catholic Historical Society. 1933. xviii, 211p. S 171

SCHROTT, LAMBERT. "Some New Notes on Father Theodore Schneider, S.J. ... (1741-1764)," American Catholic Historical Society of Philadelphia Records, v. 45 (1924), 179-185. S 172

SCHUCKMAN, SISTER MARY GERTRUDE. The Place of Catholic Culture in the Development of Early Indiana. MA thesis. Marquette University. 1952. S 173

SCHULER, SISTER MARGUERITE. The Mission Life of Father Martin Kundig. MA thesis. University of Notre Dame. 1940. 4, 158p. S 174

SCHULLER, SISTER MARY VIATORA. History of Catholic Orphan Homes in the United States, 1727 to 1884. MA thesis. Loyola University (Chicago). 1954. 415p. S 175

[SCHULTE, AUGUSTINE J.] ? The Philadelphia Theological Seminary of St. Charles Borromeo. Philadelphia. Printed for His Grace, Most Rev. Edmund J. Prendergast. 1917. S 176

SCHULTE, MARIE LOUIS. "Catholic Press Reaction to the Custer Disaster," Mid-America, v. 37 (1955), 205-214. S 177

Includes a general description of the attitudes of Catholics toward the Indians.

SCHULTE, PAUL C. The Catholic Heritage of Saint Louis. A History of the Old Cathedral Parish. St. Louis, Mo. St. Louis. Printed by the Catholic Herald. 1934. 274p. front., plates, facsims. S 178

SCHUMACHER, LEO CARL. German Catholic Settlements in the Leopoldine Letters, 1870-1913. MA thesis. Catholic University. 1932. 67p. S 179

SCHUMERTH, HAROLD JOHN. A History of the Green Bay Diocese Apostolate. MA thesis. University of Notre Dame. 1943. vi, 72p. S 180

SCHUSTER, SISTER MARY FAITH. "Elizabeth Ann Seton: Person and Symbol," Benedictine Review, v. 15 (1960), 38-43. S 181

Popular sketch.

SCHUSTER, SISTER M. TERESA. "Documents: Letters from the Dakota Frontier, I," American Benedictine Review, v. 11 (1960), 302-326, v. 12 (1961), 97-130. S 182

From Sister M. Mathilda Cattani to relatives. Letters dated variously 1882-87, mostly from Fort Yates.

SCHUTHUIS, ROSE M.D. Pioneer Bishops of Indiana. [Vincennes (?), Ind.] 1950. 47p. illus., ports. S 183

Includes sketches of Bruté, Hailandiere, Bazin, St. Palais.

SCHUYLER, H. C. "The Apostle

of the Abanakis: Father Sebastian Rale, S.J. (1657-1724)," Catholic Historical Review, v. 1 (1915), 164-174. S 184

SCHUYLER, H. C. "The Apostle of the Abanakis--Father Sebastian Rale," American Catholic Historical Society of Philadelphia Records, v. 18 (1907), 121-154, 306-353. S 185

SCHUYLER, HENRY C. "Rt. Rev. Msgr. Hugh T. Henry... An Appreciation," American Catholic Historical Society of Philadelphia Records, v. 57 (1946), 103-106. S 186

SCHUYLER, H. C. "The Sisters of the I.H.M.," American Catholic Historical Society of Philadelphia Records, v. 33 (1922), 338-353. S 187

SCHUYLER, HENRY C. Sebastian Rale: Jesuit Missionary in Maine, 1694-1724. MA thesis. Catholic University. 1905. 93p. S 188

SCHUYLER, JOSEPH B. "Religious Behavior in a Northern Parish: A Study of Motivating Values," American Catholic Sociological Review, v. 19 (1958), 134-144. S 189

SCHUYLER, J. B. "Status of American Catholicism," America, v. 93 (1955), May 14, 196. S 190

SCHUYLER, WILLIAM BISHOP. "The Beginnings of the Perkionen Valley Missions," American Catholic Historical Society of Philadelphia Records, v. 61 (1950), 101-109. S 191

SCHUYLER, WILLIAM BISHOP. Historical Sketch of St. Aloysius' Parish, Pottstown, Pa. Norstown, Pa. Time Print. 1906. 64p. illus., ports. S 192

SCHUYLER, WILLIAM BISHOP. "Memoirs of the Rev. Augustin Baily, S.J.," American Catholic Historical Society of Philadelphia Records, v. 20 (1909), 209-249. S 193

SCHUYLER, WILLIAM BISHOP. The Pioneer Catholic Church of Chester County, St. Agnes, West Chester, Pennsylvania, 1793-1943. Philadelphia. Peter Reilly Co. 1944. xii, 283p. front., plates, ports., maps. S 194

SCHWARZ, JOHN H. "The Parish Priest in America," Homiletic and Pastoral Review, v. 53 (1952), 18-25, 124-128. S 195
An analysis of, and solutions for some of the problems facing the parish priest in our country today.

SCHWINN, BONAVENTURE. "Report on American Culture," American Benedictine Review, v. 5 (1954), 101-104. S 196
A review of Catholicism in America.

SCHWITALLA, ALPHONSE M. "Graduate Study in Catholic Colleges and Universities," North Central Educational Association Bulletin, v. 30 (1933), 92-122. S 197

SCHWITALLA, ALPHONSE M. "The Medical Apostolate of the American Assistancy," Woodstock Letters, v. 83 (1954), 227-300. S 198
An excellent historical survey and evaluation of the work of the Jesuit Universities of the United States in the field of medicine.

SCISCO, LOUIS D. Political Nativism in New York State. New York. Columbia Univ. Press. 1921. 259p. S 199
Also as Studies in History, Economics and Public Law, v. 13, n. 2.

SCRANTON (DIOCESE) SYNOD, 1, 1949. First synod of the diocese of Scranton. Scranton. St. Peter's Cathedral. XXXI [1949] 142p. S 200

SCRIBNER, ROBERT L. "Father

John B. Tabb," Virginia Cavalcade, v. 6 (Summer, 1956). S 201

SEARY, JOHN LEO. The Society of Jesus in the United States, 1773-1814. MA thesis. Catholic University. 1927. 47p. S 202

SEATTLE (DIOCESE)SYNOD, 1st, 1883. Acta et statuta synodi dioecesis Nesqualiensis I. habitae diebus 24, 25, et 26 mensis Oct., A.D. 1883. Tulalip, W.T., Ex typis Stae. Annae missionis, 1884. 21p. S 203

SEATTLE, WASH. (DIOCESE) SYNOD, 4th, 1898. Synodus dioecesana nesqualliensis quarta. Quae antecedentium etiam compleatitur constitutiones, diebus VIII et IX Augusti, A.D. 1898. In Collegio Sti. Martini, Woodland, in statu washingtonensi, habita. Ab Eduardo Joanne O'Dea, episcopo nesqualliensi. Portlandi, Oregon, Ex typis Glass & Prudhomme, 1898. xx p., 1 1. 109p. S 204

[SEATTLE UNIVERSITY], Seattle, Washington. Seattle University, Fifty Golden Years, 1898-1948. Seattle. The University. 1948. S 205

SEBASTYANSKI, LADISLAUS. "Nebraska. Labors among the Poles and Bohemians. Letter dated Kelso P.O., Howard Co., Nebr., December 8th, 1885," Woodstock Letters, v. 15 (1886), 75-76. S 206

"SECOND PLENARY COUNCIL OF BALTIMORE AND ECCLESIASTICAL DISCIPLINE IN THE UNITED STATES," Catholic World, v. 9 (1869), 397-511. S 207

SEDGWICK, HENRY D. Father Hecker. Boston. Small, Maynard and Co. 1900. 157p. front. (port.) S 208

SEGALE, SISTER BLANDINA. At the End of the Santa Fe

Trail. Milwaukee. Bruce. 1948. xi, 298p. illus., ports. S 209

SEGHERS, CHARLES. Life and Labors of Most Rev. F.N. Blanchet with Funeral Sermons by Most Rev. Charles Seghers. Portland. no pub. 1883. n.p. S 210

SEGREST, STELLA A. "History of St. Anne's Church of Philadelphia, Pa.," American Catholic Historical Society of Philadelphia Records, v.11 (1900), 295-302. S 211

SEIZ, SISTER MARY ANTHONY. Dominican Contribution to the Catholic Youth Movement in the United States. Ph.D. thesis. Fordham University. 1945. iv, 262p. S 212

SELIG, SISTER M. LUCY JOSEPHINE. Know-Nothing Party in Florida, 1852-1860. MA thesis. Catholic University. 1944. 49p. S 213

SELISKAR, JOHN. "The Reverend Francis Pirec, Indian Missionary," Acta et Dicta, v. 3 (1911), 66-90. S 214

[SELLERS, A.I.] "A Letter Describing the Native American Riots in Philadelphia in 1844," American Catholic Historical Society of Philadelphia Records, v. 64 (1953), 246-247. S 215

SELNER, JOHN C. "Father James Gillis, C.S.P.," American Ecclesiastical Review, v. 137 (1957), 31-38. S 216
An appreciation of this great Paulist and editor of the Catholic World.

SEMPLE, HENRY C. (ed.) The Ursulines in New Orleans and Our Lady of Prompt Succor, A Record of Two Centuries, 1729-1925. New York. P.J. Kenedy and Sons. 1925. xiii, 319p. front., plates, ports., facsims. S 217

SENA, JOSE D. "The Chapel of Don Antonio Jose Ortiz," New

325

Mexico Historical Review, v. 13 (1938), 347-351. S 218

SENA, JOSE D. 'Reminiscence of the Santa Fe Cathedral," Provincial Chronicle (St. John Baptist Province, O.F.M.), v. 10 (1938), 56-64. S 219

SENER, SAMUEL M. "The Catholic Church at Lancaster, Pennsylvania," American Catholic Historical Society of Philadelphia Records, v. 5 (1894), 305-338. illus., port. (Bernard Keenan). S 220

SENER, S.M. "Eventful Career of the Reverend John Baptiste Cause," United States Catholic Historical Magazine, v. 4 (1891-1892), 199-202. S 221

SENER, S.M. 'Historical Sketch of the Ancient Parish of St. Mary's, Lancaster, Pa.," United States Catholic Historical Magazine, v. 1 (1887), 42-53, additional historical notes pp. 215-219. S 222

SENER, S.M. "Some Lancaster Catholics and Other Notes," United States Catholic Historical Magazine, v. 2 (1888), 49-54. S 223

SENER, S.M. "Very Rev. Bernard Keenan, V.G.," United States Catholic Historical Magazine, v. 4 (1891-1892), 430-439.S 224

"SEQUEL TO A TEXAS STORY," Provincial Annals (Province of the Most Holy Name, O.F.M.) v. 7 (1947), 167-171. S 225
    The Franciscans in Texas during the Civil War.

SERRA, JUNIPERO. Diary of Fray Junipero Serra, O.F.M. North Providence, R.I. The Franciscan Missionaries of Mary. 1936. 64p. S 226

"SESQUICENTENNIAL OF MISSION SAN LUIS REY," Provincial Annals (Province of Santa Barbara, O.F.M.), v. 11 (1948), 1-5. S 227

SETON, ROBERT. Memories of Many Years (1839-1922). London. J. Long. 1923. 320p.

incl. front. (port.) S 228

SETON, THERESA. "Bishop Neumann: Apostle of Zeal," Ave Maria, v. 55 (1942), 231-236. S 229

SEVENTY-FIFTH ANNIVERSARY, FIFTY YEARS IN AMERICA. Society of the Divine Word. (Techny, Ill.) Mission Press, Society of the Divine Word. 1950. 56p. illus., ports. S 230

SEVIER, CHRISTIAN. History of the Albany Cathedral of the Immaculate Conception, 1852-1927. Albany. Cathedral of Immaculate Conception. 1927. 482p. plates, ports. S 231

SEWALL, CHARLES. "Letter to His Brother, Fr. Nicholas Sewall, St. Thomas Manor, Nov. 21st, 1803," Woodstock Letters, v. 12 (1883), 83-84. S 232

SEWALL, CHARLES. "Letter to His Brother Nicholas Sewall, St. Thomas Manor, Feb. 5th, 1805," Woodstock Letters, v. 12 (1883), 85-86. S 233

SEXTON, JOHN E., AND ARTHUR J. RILEY. History of St. John's Seminary, Brighton. Boston. Roman Catholic Archbishop of Boston. 1945. 320p. incl. front., illus. (incl. ports.) S 234

SHAHAN, THOMAS J. "Archbishop Spalding and the Catholic University," Catholic Educational Review, v. 7 (1914), 138-144. S 235

SHAHAN, THOMAS J. "The Catholic Church in Connecticut," United States Catholic Historical Magazine, v. 3 (1890), 16-25. S 236

SHAHAN, THOMAS J. 'Early Catholics in Connecticut," United States Catholic Historical Magazine, v. 2 (1888), 274-294. S 237

SHAHAN, T. J. "Further Notes on Pope-Day," United States Catholic Historical Magazine,

v. 2 (1888), 214-216. S 238
SHAHAN, THOMAS J. "L'Histoire de l'Eglise Catholique aux Etats-Unis," Revue d'Histoire Ecclésiastique, v. 1 (1900), 679-689. S 239
SHANAHAN, EMMET A. Minnesota's Forgotten Martyr. Crookston, Minn. Diocese of Crookston. 1949. 35p.S 240
Jean Pierre Aulneau.
SHANLEY, JOHN. "The Beginnings of Catholicism in North Dakota," Acta et Dicta, v. 1 (1907), 54-59. S 241
SHANNON, JAMES P. "Bishop Ireland's Connemara Experiment," Minnesota History, v. 35 (1957), 205-213, illus.
S 242
SHANNON, JAMES P. "Catholic Boarding Schools on the Western Frontier," Minnesota History, v. 35 (1956), 133-139. S 243
SHANNON, JAMES P. Catholic Colonization on the Western Frontier. New Haven, Connecticut. Yale University Press, 1957. 302p. S 244
An excellent study of the efforts of Archbishop Ireland to draw Catholic settlers to the frontier in Minnesota.
SHARKEY, SISTER M. AGNES. The New Jersey Sisters of Charity. New York. Longmans, Green and Co. 1933. 3v. front., plates, ports., fold, map, facsims. S 245
SHARP, J. K. "How the Baltimore Catechism Originated," American Ecclesiastical Review, v. 81 (1929), 573-586.
S 246
SHARP, JOHN K. "How Many Catholics in Pre-Diocesan Brooklyn?" United States Catholic Historical Society Records and Studies, v. 36 (1947), 97-101. S 247
SHARP, JOHN K. Priests and Parishes of the Diocese of Brooklyn, 1820-1844. Man-

hasset, L.I., N.Y. The Author. 1944. 255p. illus., incl. ports., map, facsim.
S 248
SHAUGHNESSY, GERALD. Has the Immigrant Kept the Faith? New York. Macmillan. 1925. 299p. incl. table. S 249
SHAW, J. G. Edwin Vincent O'Hara, American Prelate. New York. Farrar, Strauss and Cudahy, 1957. viii, 274p.
S 250
SHAW, THOMAS A. The Story of the La Salle Mission. Chicago, Ill. M.A. Donohue and Co. c1907. 2v. plates, ports. S 251
SHEA, JOHN GILMARY. "American Hierarchy in Its Threefold Source," American Catholic Quarterly Review, v. 8 (1883), 296-316. S 252
SHEA, JOHN GILMARY. "Anti-Catholic Issue in the Late Election," American Catholic Quarterly Review, v. 6 (1881), 36-50. S 253
SHEA, JOHN GILMARY. Archbishop Hughes. New York. Houghton Mifflin. 1889.
S 254
SHEA, JOHN GILMARY. "Bancroft's False Charges against the Catholics of 1776," United States Catholic Historical Magazine, v. 2 (1888), 328-330. S 255
SHEA, JOHN GILMARY. "Capuchin Missions in Maine," Historical Magazine, v. 8 (1860), 177, 301. S 256
SHEA, JOHN GILMARY. "Catholic Church in American History," American Catholic Quarterly Review, v. 1 (1876), 148-173. S 257
SHEA, JOHN GILMARY. Catholic Church in New York City. New York. Lawrence G. Golding and Co. 1878. 748p.
S 258
SHEA, JOHN GILMARY. "The Catholic Church in the United

States in the Recent Translation of Alzog," American Catholic Quarterly Review, v. 4 (1879), 138-142. S 259

SHEA, JOHN GILMARY. "Catholic Free Schools in the United States, Their Necessity, Condition, and Future," American Catholic Quarterly Review, v. 9 (1884), 713-724. S 260

SHEA, JOHN GILMARY. Catholic Gems. New York. Office of Catholic Publications. 1893. S 261

SHEA, JOHN GILMARY. "A Century of Catholicity in the United States," Ave Maria, v. 29 (1889), 433-438. S 262

SHEA, JOHN GILMARY. "Coming Plenary Council of Baltimore," American Catholic Quarterly Review, v. 9 (1884), 340-357. S 263

SHEA, JOHN GILMARY. "Consecration of the Philadelphia Cathedral," American Catholic Quarterly Review, v. 15 (1890), 422-433. S 264

SHEA, JOHN GILMARY. "Converts--Their Influence and Work in This Country," American Catholic Quarterly Review, v. 8 (1883), 525. S 265

SHEA, JOHN GILMARY. The Cross and the Flag. New York. Catholic Historical League of America. 1899. xx, 1013, 28, xvip. illus., plates, ports. S 266

SHEA, JOHN GILMARY. Defenders of Our Faith. New York. Office of Catholic Publications. c1891. xii, 43-47, 49-417, xi, 133p. front., illus., plates, ports. S 267

SHEA, JOHN GILMARY. Discovery and Exploration of the Mississippi Valley. New York. Redfield. 1852. lxxx, 267p. front. (facsim), fold. map. S 268

SHEA, JOHN GILMARY. "Earliest Discussion of the Catholic Question in New England--Sequenot and Burnett, 1727," American Catholic Quarterly Review, v. 6 (1881), 216-228. S 269

SHEA, JOHN GILMARY. "Early Catholicity in Indiana," Ave Maria, v. 18 (1882), 301-304. S 270

SHEA, JOHN GILMARY. "Early Franciscan Missions in This Country," American Catholic Quarterly Review, v. 7 (1882), 121-136. S 271

SHEA, JOHN GILMARY. Hierarchy of the Catholic Church in the United States. New York. Office of Catholic Publications. 1886. S 272

SHEA, JOHN GILMARY. The History of the Catholic Church in the United States. New York. John G. Shea. 1886-1892. 4v. front. (v. 2), illus. (incl. facsims.) plates, ports., maps. S 273

SHEA, JOHN GILMARY. History of the Catholic Missions among the Indian Tribes of the United States, 1529-1845. New York. D. Dunigan and Bros. 1855. 514p. illus. (facsims.) ports. S 274

SHEA, JOHN GILMARY. "Jansenists, Old Catholics, and Their Friends in America," American Catholic Quarterly Review, v. 14 (1889), 533-541. S 275

SHEA, JOHN GILMARY. "Jesuits, Recollects, and the Indians," Wisconsin Historical Society Collections, v. 4 (1857), 236-298. S 276

SHEA, JOHN GILMARY. (tr. and ed.) "Journal of an Embassy from Canada to the United Colonies of New England in 1650, by Father Gabriel Druillets, S.J.," New York Historical Society Collections, 2d ser., v. 3, pt. 1 (1857), 303-328. S 277

SHEA, JOHN GILMARY. Life and Times of the Most Rev.

John Carroll. New York. J.G. Shea. 1888. 695p. front., illus. (incl. facsims.), ports. S 278

SHEA, JOHN GILMARY. "Log Chapel on the Rappahannock, Erected A.D. 1570," Catholic World, v. 20 (1875), 847-856. S 279

SHEA, JOHN GILMARY. Memorial of the First Centenary of Georgetown College, D.C., Comprising a History of Georgetown University. Washington. Published for the College by P.F. Collier. New York. 1891. xv, 480p. illus., plates, ports. S 280

SHEA, JOHN GILMARY. "Notes on the Early History of the Catholic Church in New England," Historical Magazine, 2d ser., v. 5 (1869), 313-317, 391-394; v. 6 (1869), 41-47 S 281

SHEA, JOHN GILMARY. "Pastoral Letter of the Third Plenary Council of Baltimore," American Catholic Quarterly Review, v. 10 (1885), 1-17. S 282

SHEA, JOHN GILMARY. "Pioneer of the West--Rev. Charles Nerinckx," American Catholic Quarterly Review, v. 5 (1880), 486-508. S 283

SHEA, JOHN GILMARY. "Pope Day in America," United States Catholic Historical Magazine, v. 2 (1888), 1-7. S 284

SHEA, JOHN GILMARY. "Progress of the Church in the United States from the First Provincial Council to the Third Plenary Council of Baltimore," American Catholic Quarterly Review, v. 9 (1884), 471-497. S 285

SHEA, JOHN GILMARY. "Proposed American Catholic University," American Catholic Quarterly Review, v. 10 (1885), 312-325. S 286

SHEA, JOHN DAWSON GILMARY. "St. James--The First Church

in Brooklyn," United States Catholic Historical Magazine, v. 1 (1887), 298-303. S 287

SHEA, JOHN GILMARY. "Sir John James of Crishall, Essex, Bart., The Benefactor of the Pennsylvania Missions," United States Catholic Historical Magazine, v. 2 (1888), 85-92. S 288

SHEA, JOHN GILMARY. "Ven. Anthony Margil of Jesus, of the Order of St. Francis, Apostle of Texas and Guatemala," Ave Maria, v.21 (1885), 105-108, 128-131. S 289

SHEA, JOHN GILMARY. "Ven. John Nepomucene, C.SS.R.," Ave Maria, v. 30 (1890), 181-183. S 290

SHEA, JOHN GILMARY. World's Columbian Catholic Congress, 1893. Chicago. 1893. 208p. S 291

SHEA, MICHAEL J. Century of Catholicism in Western Massachusetts. Springfield, Mass. Mirror Press. 1931. cxxxii, 350p. illus., map. S 292

SHEARER, DONALD. Ignatius Cardinal Persico, O.M.C., 1823-1895. MA thesis. Catholic University. 1931. 94p. S 293

SHEARER, DONALD C. "Ignatius Cardinal Persico, O.M. Cap. (1823-1895)," United States Catholic Historical Society Records and Studies, v. 21 (1932), 54-137. S 294

SHEARER, DONALD C. Pontificia Americana: A Documentary History of the Catholic Church in the United States, 1784-1884. Washington. 1933. S 295

SHEEDY, MORGAN M. "The Catholic Parochial Schools of the United States," in Report of the Commissioner of Education for 1903, pp. 1079-1101. S 296

SHEEDY, MORGAN M. "The Catholic Total Abstinence Union of America," American Ecclesiastical Review, v. 12 (1872), 183-192. S 297

SHEEHY, MAURICE S. "Rev. Francis A. Mullin, Ph.D.; In Memoriam," American Ecclesiastical Review, v. 116 (1947), 171-173. S 298

SHEEHY, MAURICE S. "Monsignor John M. Cooper--Scientist, Scholar, Priest," Catholic University of America Bulletin, v. 17 (1949), 7-9. S 299

SHEEN, FULTON J. America Was Once a Foreign Mission," World Mission, v. 7 (May 1956), 3-10. S 300

SHEERIN, JOHN B. "The Development of the Catholic Magazine in the History of American Journalism," United States Catholic Historical Society Records and Studies, v. 51 (1953), 5-13. S 301

SHELLEY, THOMAS J. "Orestes Brownson and Archbishop Hughes," St. Meinrad Essays, v. 12 (1959), 25-39. S 302

"SHEPHERDS OF THE NORTH," Provincial Annals (Province of the Most Holy Name, O.F.M.), v. 2 (1941-1942), 250-260, 279-285, 324-334; v. 3 (1942-1943), 21-30, 76-81, 115-119, 153-160, 209-214, 256-265. S 303
The Story of St. Stephen's, Groghan, N.Y.

SHERIDAN, PHILIP HENRY. Personal Memoirs ed. by Michael V. Sheridan. New York. D. Appleton and Co. 1902. 2v. front., illus., port., maps, facsim. S 304

SHERIDAN, SISTER MARY BENIGNUS. Bishop Odin and the New Era of the Catholic Church in Texas, 1840-60. Ph.D. dissertation. Saint Louis University. 1938. 392p. S 305

SHERWOOD, GRACE H. "The Oblate Sisters of Providence," America, v. 42 (1929), 179-181. S 306

SHERWOOD, GRACE. The Oblate's Hundred and One Years. New York. Macmillan. 1931. xi, 288p. plate, ports. S 307

SHIELDS, CURRIN V. Democracy and Catholicism in America. New York. McGraw Hill, 1958. ix, 310p. S 308
A non-Catholic states the Catholic positions in political theory.

SHIELDS, JOHN L. "Catholic Church in Northumberland County," Northumberland County Historical Society Proceedings, v. 7 (1935), 90-108. S 309

SHIELDS, MOTHER MARY EUSTACE. The Catholic Herald in Philadelphia, 1833-1863. MA thesis. Catholic University. 1941. 109p. S 310

SHIELDS, THOMAS EDWARD. "The Sisters' College," Catholic Educational Review, v. 3 (1912), 1-12. 6 plates. S 311

SHIELS, W. EUGENE. "The Jesuits in Ohio in the Eighteenth Century," Mid-America, v. 7 (1936), 27-47. S 312

SHIPMAN, PAUL R. "Establishment of the Visitation Nuns in the West," American Catholic Quarterly Review, v. 11 (1886), 31-57. S 313

SHORT, JOSEPH CARLTON. "Jacques Marquette, S.J., Catechist," La Revue de l'Université Laval, v. 3 (1949), 436-443. S 314

"SHORT HISTORY OF THE MISSION OF OUR LADY OF LORETTO, NEW YORK," Woodstock Letters, v. 46 (1917), 172-187. S 315

SHUSTER, GEORGE W. The Catholic Spirit in America. New York. L. MacVeagh, Dial Press. 1927. xi, 365p. S 316

SIALM, PLACIDUS. "La Mission des Sioux," Revue Mis-

sionnaire, 1935, 23-26. S 317
SIEKANIEC, LADISLAUS J. "The
Poles in the Diocese of Supe-
rior, Wisconsin," Polish-Amer-
ican Studies, v. 15 (1958),
10-17. S 318
SIEKANIEC, LADISLAUS J. "The
Poles of Ashland, Wisconsin:
1884-1888," Polish American
Studies, v. 6 (1949), 14-
17. S 319
SIEVERS, HARRY J. "The Cath-
olic Indian School issue and the
Presidential Election of 1892,"
Catholic Historical Review,
v. 38 (1952), 129-155. S 320
SILCOX, CLARIS E. AND GALEN
M. FISHER. Catholics, Jews, and
Protestants. A Study of Re-
lationships in the United States
and Canada. New York.
Harper and Bros. c1934. xvi,
369p. S 321
SILVER IS MINE. Wilmington,
Del. Monastery of the Visita-
tion. 1953. 117p. S 322
History of St. Joseph's
Monastery of the Visitation
in Wilmington, Del., 1853-
1953.
"SILVER JUBILEE OF SAN JOSE
PAPAGO MISSION, TUCSON,"
Provincial Annals (Province
of Santa Barbara, O.F.M.),
v. 11 (1949), 145-147. S 323
SIMMONS, SISTER MARY
AGNEZE. "William Gaston:
His Political and Constitutional
Contributions to North Carolina,"
American Catholic Historical
Society of Philadelphia Records,
v. 50 (1939), 173-219. S 324
SIMONITSCH, ROLAND GERARD.
Religious Instruction in Catholic
Colleges for Men. Washington.
Catholic University. 1952. xvi,
327p. tables. paper. S 325
SINGOWAN, GUILLAUME. "Ex-
trait d'une Lettre de Singowan,
Chef d'une Tribu de Potowato-
mies, à M. le Président du
Conseil Central de Paris.
Dowagiac. 19 juin, 1863," An-
nales de la Propagation de la

Foi, v. 35 (1863), 485-487.
S 326
SIOUX CITY, IOWA (DIOCESE)
SYNOD, 1st, 1902. Acta
synodi Sioupolitanae primae,
die 22a mensis Augusti A.D.
1902, in ecclesia Sancti
Josephi in civitate Le Mars
habitae. A Philippo Josepho
Garrigan, episcopo Sioupolitano.
[n.p., n.d.] x p. S 327
SIOUX CITY (DIOCESE) SYNOD,
2nd, 1909. Synodus dioecesana
sioupolitana secunda, die sexta
mensis Jan., 1909 in ecclesia
cathedrali Epiphaniae Sioupolitana habita a Philippo Josepho
Garrigan [ep.] Philadelphia,
The Dolphin press, 1909. iv,
95p. S 328
SIOUX CITY, IOWA (DIOCESE)
SYNOD, 3rd, 1912? Synodus
dioecesana sioupolitana tertia.
[n.p., n.d.] 12p. S 329
SIOUX CITY (DIOCESE) SYNOD,
4th, 1931. Statuta dioecesana
facta et promulgata in quarta
synodo in ecclesia cathedrali
Epiphaniae dioecesis Sioupolitanae habita, die 24 mensis
Nov., 1931 ab Edmundo Heslan
[ep.] Ex Cancellaria dioecesana,
1931. xxi, 104p. S 330
SIOUX FALLS (DIOCESE) SYNOD
3, 1949. Synodus diocesana
Siouxormensis tertia ab ...
Guilelmo O Brady Episcopo
Siouxormensis die XXVII
mensis Januarii 1949 habita.
[Sioux Falls, 1949.] 112p.
S 331
"SIR JOHN JAMES FUND," Amer-
ican Catholic Historical Re-
searches, v. 8 (1891), 113-
120. S 332
SISTERS OF CHARITY. Sacred
Heart Chapel at the National
Leprosarium, Carville,
Louisiana. Prov. Chron. (Cin-
cinnati), v. 31 (1959), 305-
310. illus. S 333
SISTERS ADORERS OF THE
MOST PRECIOUS BLOOD.
Congregation of Sisters Ador-

ers of the Most Precious
Blood, Province of Ruma.
Techny, Ill. Printed by the
Mission Press. 1938. xviii,
159p. front., illus., plates.
S 334

(SISTERS ADORERS OF THE
MOST PRECIOUS BLOOD),
Diamond Jubilee, 1876-1951.
(1951). 33p. ports., plates.
S 335
Contains a brief history of
the Province of Ruma, Illinois.

SISTERS OF CHARITY OF THE
B.V.M., DUBUQUE, IA. In
the Early Days--Pages from
the Annals of the Sisters of
Charity of the B.V.M. St.
Louis. Herder. 1912. 367p.
front., plates, ports. S 336

SISTERS OF CHARITY OF THE
INCARNATE WORD. Houston,
Texas. Brief History of the
Sisters of Charity of the In-
carnate Word of the Diocese of
Galveston, 1866-1941. Galves-
ton. no pub. 1941. 47p.
port. S 337

SISTERS OF DIVINE PROVIDENCE.
Memoirs of Fifty Years. San
Antonio. Sisters of Divine
Providence. 1916. S 338

"SISTERS OF MERCY," Illinois
Catholic Historical Review,
v. 3 (1921), 339-370. S 339

SISTERS OF MERCY. Manchester,
N.H. Life of Rev. Mother
Xavier Warde. Boston. Marlier
and Co. 1902. 287p. S 340

SISTERS OF MERCY. Manchester,
N.H. Mother Mary Gonzaga.
Magnificat. 1921. S 341

SISTERS OF MERCY. Pittsburgh
Memoirs of the Pittsburgh.
Sisters of Mercy ... 1843-
1917. New York. Devin
Adair. 1918. xii, 467p.
front., plates, ports. S 342

SISTERS OF MERCY. Providence,
R.I. Seventy-Five Years in
the Passing. Providence, R.I.
St. Xavier's Convent. 1926.
S 343

SISTERS OF MERCY OF CHARLES

TON. "A Southern Teaching
Order," American Catholic
Historical Society of Philadelphia Records, v. 15 (1904),
249-265. S 344

SISTERS OF NOTRE DAME,
CINCINNATI. "Letters Bear-
ing on the Foundation of the
Sisters of Notre Dame de
Namur in America," American
Catholic Historical Society of
Philadelphia Records, v. 11
(1900), 320-337. S 345

SISTERS OF NOTRE DAME DE
NAMUR. American Founda-
tions of the Sisters of Notre
Dame de Namur. Philadelphia.
Dolphin Press. 1928. 690p.
incl. illus., plates, front.
(port.) S 346

SISTERS OF NOTRE DAME DE
NAMUR (comp.) A Brief
History of the Catholic Church
in the United States. New
York. Schwartz, Kirwin and
Fauss. 1910. viii, 97p.
4 maps. S 347

SISTERS OF NOTRE DAME DE
NAMUR. Trinity College.
Washington. The College.
1927. S 348

"SISTERS OF PROVIDENCE IN
INDIANA," Catholic Educational
Review, v. 1 (1917), 137-
145. S 349

(SISTERS OF OUR LADY OF
PERPETUAL HELP). 50th
Anniversary of Foundation of
the Congregation of Franciscan
Sisters of Our Lady of Perpetual Help, Saint Louis, Missouri, 1901-1951. St. Louis.
1951. 80p. incl. ads., ports.
S 350

(SISTERS OF SAINT FRANCIS,
OLDENBURG, INDIANA).
"Sisters of St. Francis Cen-
tenary (Oldenburg, Indiana),"
American-German Review, v.
17 (1951), 27-28. S 351

SISTERS OF ST. JOSEPH OF
ROCHESTER. By a Sister of
St. Joseph. (Rochester? New
York). 1950. vii, 163p.

illus., port.   S 352
SISTERS OF THE BLESSED
SACRAMENT FOR INDIANS
AND COLORED PEOPLE.
Golden Jubilee. Cornwell
Heights, Pa. no pub. 1941.
126p. incl. illus., ports.
                                 S 353
SISTERS OF THE BLESSED
SACRAMENT. Navajo Adven-
ture. Cornwell Heights. 195?
54p.   S 354
50 year jubilee.
SISTERS OF THE DIVINE SAVIOR.
These Fifty Years ... 1888-
1938. Milwaukee. St. Mary's
Convent. 1938. xix, 84p.
                                 S 355
SISTERS OF THE HOLY CROSS.
Pioneers and Builders. Ham-
mond, Ind. Print. by W.B.
Conkey and Co. 1941. x, 215p.
ports.   S 356
SISTERS OF THE HOLY CROSS.
Story of Fifty Years ... 1855-
1905. Notre Dame, Ind. Ave
Maria. n.d. 214p. illus.
                                 S 357
SISTERS OF THE HOLY NAMES
OF JESUS AND MARY.
Gleanings of Fifty Years. Port-
land, O. Press of Glass and
Prudhomme Co. 1909. xvi,
230p. plates, ports.   S 358
SISTERS OF THE I.H.M.   New
York. Kenedy. 1921. xv,
503p. front., plates, ports.
                                 S 359
SISTERS OF THE ORDER OF ST.
DOMINIC. San Rafael, Calif.
The Dominicans of San Rafael.
San Rafael. Dominican Con-
vent of San Rafael. 1941.
108p. front., illus. (coat of
arms), plates, ports.,
facsim.   S 360
SISTERS OF THE PRECIOUS
BLOOD. Dayton, Ohio. Not
with Silver and Gold. Dayton,
O. Sisters of the Precious
Blood. xii, 464p.   S 361
"SISTERS OF THE THIRD ORDER
OF ST. FRANCIS, 1855-1928,"
American Catholic Historical

Society of Philadelphia Re-
cords, v. 40 (1929), 38-64,
123-155, 226-248, 347-381;
v. 41 (1930), 27-68. S 362
SISTERS OF THE THIRD ORDER
OF ST. FRANCIS OF PEN-
ANCE AND CHARITY, TIF-
FIN, OHIO, 1869-1942. By
a member of the community.
Paterson, N.J. St. Anthony
Guild Press. 1942. xiv,
126p. incl. front., illus.,
(incl. ports.)   S 363
SISTERS OF THE THIRD ORDER
OF SAINT FRANCIS OF THE
PERPETUAL ADORATION.
The Origin and Development
through Seventy Years of the
Congregation of the Sisters of
the Third Order of Saint
Francis of the Perpetual
Adoration, La Crosse, Wis.,
1849-1919. La Crosse, Wis.
St. Rose Convent. 1920.
287p.   S 364
SISTERS OF THE THIRD ORDER
REGULAR OF ST. FRANCIS.
Oldenburg, Ind. Historical
Sketch of the Convent and
Academy of St. Francis in
Oldenburg, Ind., and of the
Work of Their Community in
the U.S. Oldenburg, Ind.
The Community. 1901. 289p.
plates, ports.   S 365
SISTERS OF THE VISITATION.
St. Louis. Centennial Sou-
venir. Academy of the Visita-
tion. St. Louis. Francis de
Sales Press. 1933. 33p.
front., illus., plates. S 366
SISTERS OF THE VISITATION.
Wilmington, Del. Life and
Characteristics of Right Rev-
erend Alfred A. Curtis, D.D.
Second Bishop of Wilmington.
New York. P.J. Kenedy and
Sons, 1913. xiv, 446p. front.
illus. (facsim.), plates, ports.
                                 S 367
SISTERS OF THE VISITATION
AT HOLY MARY, BROOKLYN,
Jubilee Gems of the Visitation
Order. New York. Christian

Press. 1905. 365p.
S 368
SISTERS, SERVANTS OF THE
IMMACULATE HEART OF
MARY. A Retrospect. Three
Score Years and Ten. New
York. Benziger. 1916. 190p.
front., plates.   S 369
SKEABECK, ANDREW. "Most
Reverend William Gross: Mis-
sionary Bishop of the South,"
American Catholic Historical
Society of Philadelphia Re-
cords, v. 65 (1954), 11-23,
102-115, 142-157.   S 370
An excellent and well docu-
mented biographical sketch
of the fifth bishop of Savan-
nah, Georgia (1873-1885)
who later became fourth
bishop of Portland in Oregon
(1885-1898).
SKELTON, ISABEL. The Life of
Thomas D'Arcy McGee.
Gardenvale, Canada. Garden
City Press. 1925. vi, 554p.
front., plates, ports.   S 371
"SKETCH OF CATHOLICITY IN
PENNSYLVANIA PRIOR TO
1800," Catholic Record, v. 12
(1876-1877), 321-328.   S 372
"SKETCH OF ST. MARY'S CITY.
ANCIENT CAPITAL OF
MARYLAND," Woodstock Let-
ters, v. 14 (1885), 360-370.
S 373
"SKETCH OF THE NEZ PERCES
INDIANS," Woodstock Letters,
v.9 (1880), 43-50, 109-118,
191-199, v. 10 (1881), 71-
77.   S 374
"SKETCH OF THE WORK AND
HISTORY OF THE SISTERS,
SERVANTS OF THE IMMACU-
LATE HEART OF MARY,
1845-1920," American Catholic
Historical Society of Philadel-
phia Records, v. 31 (1920),
276-338.   S 375
SKILLIN, EDWARD S. "The
Catholic as American Citizen,"
American Benedictine Review,
v. 5 (1954), 104-112. S 376
A study in political philosophy.

SKINNER, THOMAS LAWRENCE.
The Redemptorists in the
West. St. Louis. Redemp-
torists Fathers. 1933. xiii,
514p. port. (front.) S 377
SLATER, FLETCHER D.
"Men of Boys' Town," Colum-
bia, v. 20 (1941), 2-3, 17,
illus.   S 378
SLAUGHTER, LINDA W. "Leaves
from a Northwestern History,"
North Dakota Historical
Society Collections, v. 1
(1906), 200-292.   S 379
SLEDZ, LADISLAUS S. The
Beginnings of Catholicity in
Minnesota. MA thesis. Cath-
olic University. 1923. 38p.
S 380
SLOMINSKA, SISTER M. DON-
ATA. "Rev. John Pitass,
Pioneer Priest of Buffalo,"
Polish American Studies, v.
17 (Jan.-June, 1960), 28-41.
S 381
Born 1844, Buffalo 1873,
died 1913.
SMELTZER, SISTER MARY
JOSEPHINE. "St. Mary-of-
the-Woods," Sign, v. 20
(1940), 167-168.   S 382
SMET, PIERRE JEAN DE.
Cinquante Nouvelles Lettres
du R.P. de Smet. Paris,
Tournai. H. Casterman.
1858. ix, 502p.   S 383
SMET, PIERRE JEAN DE.
"Extrait d'une lettre du R.P.
de Smet, Missionnaire de la
Compagnie de Jésus à MM.
les Membres des Conseils
Centraux de Lyon et de Paris.
Université de St. Louis. 24
Février, 1852," Annales de la
Propagation de la Foi, v. 24
(1852), 416-423.   S 384
SMET, PIERRE JEAN DE. "Let-
ter dated St. Louis University,
Nov. 1, 1859," Annals of the
Propagation of the Faith,
Baltimore, v. 21 (1860), 223-
235.   S 385
SMET, PIERRE JEAN DE. "Let-
ter dated St. Louis University,

334

Feb. 2d, 1870," American Catholic Historical Researches, v. 7 (1890), 41-42.　　S 386
A very short autobiography with a bibliography of his writings.

SMET, PIERRE JEAN DE. "Letter dated St. Louis Univ., Feb. 2, 1870," Historical Magazine, ser. 3, v. 3 (1874-1875), 25-26.　　S 387

SMET, PIERRE JEAN DE. "Letter to Madame Sophie Parmentier, Dated St. Louis University, Feb. 6, 1847," United States Catholic Historical Society Records and Studies, v. 4 (1906), 268-279.　　S 388

SMET, PIERRE JEAN DE. "Letter to Madame Sophie Parmentier, dated St. Louis University, Jan. 9, 1866," United States Catholic Historical Society Records and Studies, v. 4 (1906), 277-282.　　S 389

SMET, PIERRE JEAN DE. "Letter to Madame Sophie Parmentier, dated St. Louis University, Feb. 5, 1866," United States Catholic Historical Society Records and Studies, v. 4 (1906), 282-283.　S 390

SMET, PIERRE JEAN DE. "Letter to Madame Sophie Parmentier, dated St. Louis University, Nov. 1, 1867," United States Catholic Historical Society Records and Studies, v. 4 (1906), 283-284.　S 391
A series of four letters dealing with the Indian missions.

SMET, PIERRE JEAN DE. "Lettre du R.P. de Smet de la Compagnie de Jésus à MM. les Membres des Conseils Centraux de Lyon et Paris. Université de St. Louis, 16 janvier, 1852," Annales de la Propagation de la Foi, v. 24 (1852), 236-242.　　S 392
A report of the heroic death of Fr. Hoeken.

SMET, PIERRE JEAN DE. "Lettre du Père de Smet de la Compagnie de Jésus au T.-R. P. Général de la Même Compagnie. Université Saint-Louis, 1er novembre, 1859," Annales de la Propagation de la Foi, v. 32 (1860), 279-295.　　S 393

SMET, PIERRE JEAN DE. Lettres Choisies du Révérend Père Pierre-Jean de Smet, 1849-1857. 3d ed. Bruxelles. M. Closson. 1875. viii, 405p. front. (port.)　S 394

SMET, PIERRE JEAN DE. Lettres Choisies du Révérend Père Pierre Jean de Smet. 2e série. 1855-1861. 3d ed. Bruxelles. F. Haenen. 1876.　　S 395

SMET, PIERRE JEAN DE. Lettres Choisies du Révérend Père Pierre-Jean de Smet. 3e série. Bruxelles. M. Closson. 1877. xi, 416p.　　S 396

SMET, PIERRE JEAN DE. Life, Letters, and Travels of Father Pierre Jean de Smet. ed. by Chittenden and Richardson. New York. F.P. Harper. 1905. 4v. front., plates, ports., fold. map in pocket. facsims.　　S 397

SMET, PIERRE JEAN DE. New Indian Sketches. New York. Sadler. 1865. 175p. incl. front.　　S 398
Includes life of the heroic Louise Sighouin.

SMET, PIERRE JEAN DE. "Personal Letters of the Rev. P. J. de Smet, S.J.," United States Catholic Historical Society Records and Studies, v. 4 (1904), 265-284, v. 5 (1909), 119-147, 463-489.　　S 399

SMET, PIERRE JEAN DE. Voyages aux Montagnes Rocheuses et séjour Chez les Tribus Indiens de l'Orégon. Nouv. ed. rev. Bruxelles. V.

Devaux. 1873. xxxv, 408p. front. (port.), pl. fold. map. S 400

SMET, PIERRE JEAN DE. Voyages dans l'Amérique Septentrionale, Orégon. 3e ed. Bruxelles. M. Closson. 1874. vi, 406p. front. (port.) fold, map. S 401

SMET, PIERRE JEAN DE. Western Missions and Missionaries. New York. J.B. Kirker. 1863. 532p. incl. front. (port.) S 402

SMITH, ELLEN HART. Charles Carroll of Carrollton. Cambridge. Harvard University. Press. 1942. x, 430p. front., plates, ports. S 403

SMITH, FRANCES H. The Mission of San Antonio de Padua. Palo Alto, Calif. Stanford University Press. 1932. ix, 108p. front., illus., maps, plans. S 404

SMITH, FRANCES READ. "Mission of Nuestra Señora de la Soledad," California Historical Society Quarterly, v. 23 (1944), 1-18, illus. S 405

SMITH, HELEN GRACE. "Sketch of the Life of Mother Katherine Drexel," American Catholic Historical Society of Philadelphia Records. v. 67 (1956), 51-60. S 406
A popular appreciation of this great American.

SMITH, HELEN GRACE. "A Woman of the Drexels," Sign, v. 13 (1933), 77-80. illus. S 407
A biography of Mother Katherine Drexel.

SMITH, HOWARD S. "Archbishop Keane of Dubuque," Ave Maria, v. 83 (Apr. 21, 1956), 12-13, 28, port. S 408

SMITH, JOHN S. St. Anthony's, 1837-1953. Davenport. St. Anthony's Rectory. 1953. 99p. S 409
The story of the first Church in Davenport, Iowa.

SMITH, JOHN T. "Archbishop Ireland," Dublin Review, v. 168 (1921), 23-40. S 410

SMITH, JOHN TALBOT. The Catholic Church in New York. New York. Hall and Locke Co. 1908. 2v. front., illus., plates, ports. S 411

SMITH, JOHN TALBOT. "Edgar P. Wadhams," United States Catholic Historical Magazine, v. 4 (1891-1892), 337-370. S 412

SMITH, JOHN TALBOT. "First Three American Cardinals: McCloskey, Farley, Gibbons," Dublin Review, v. 169 (1921), 45-59. S 413

SMITH, JOHN TALBOT. A History of the Diocese of Ogdensburg. New York. John W. Lovell Co. 1885. 354p. illus., 2 ports. (incl. front.) S 414

SMITH, LEO R. "John F. O'-Hara, C.S.C., Bishop of Buffalo (1945-1951)," American Catholic Historical Society of Philadelphia Records, v. 64 (1953), 29-33. S 415
A chapter in the biography of Archbishop O'Hara as published in the March issue of the Records.

SMITH, M. History of the Catholic Church in New York. New York. no pub. 1905. n.p. S 416

SMITH, SISTER MARIE BARAT. History of St. Emma's Military Academy and St. Francis de Sales High School. MA thesis. Catholic University. 1949. 68p. S 417

SMITH, MARK J. "Notes of Jesuit Activity in American History," Woodstock Letters, v. 69 (1940), 40-59. S 418

SMITH, MARY CONSTANCE. Our Pastors in Calvary. St. Louis. Blackwell Wielandy Co. 1924. 174p. front., plate., ports. S 419
Biographical sketches of

parish priests of St. Louis, 1854-1924.

SMITH, MARY CONSTANCE. A Sheaf of Golden Years, 1856-1906. 191p. port., plates. S 420
The Sisters of Mercy in St. Louis, Mo.

SMITH, SISTER MARY ESTHER. Missionary Work of Father Francisco Palou, O.F.M. MA thesis. Catholic University. 1934. 210p. S 421

SMITH, ROBERT F. 'Rocky Mountains. Letter dated Spokane Falls, W.T., April 15th, 1886," Woodstock Letters, v. 15 (1886), 196-198. S 422

SMITH, ROBERT. 'Rocky Mountains. Among the Kootenais. Letter dated Spokane Falls, June 4, 1886," Woodstock Letters, v. 15 (1886), 265-268. S 423

SMITH, ROBERT J. "The Rocky Mountains. Letter From Spokane Falls, W.T., Sept. 20th, 1877," Woodstock Letters, v. 17 (1888), 82-85. S 424

SMITH, SARA TRAINER. "Notes on Saterlee Military Hospital, West Philadelphia, Penna.," American Catholic Historical Society of Philadelphia Records, v. 8 (1897), 399-449. S 425

SMITH, SARA TRAINER. "Philadelphia's First Nun," American Catholic Historical Society of Philadelphia Records, v. 5 (1894), 417-522. S 426

SMITH, SEBASTIAN B. Notes on the Second Plenary Council of Baltimore. New York. O'Shea. 1874. xvi, 480p. S 427

SMITH, WALTER G., AND HELEN GRACE. Fidelis of the Cross (James Kent Stone). New York. G.P. Putnam's Sons. 1926. xvi, 467p. front., plates, ports. S 428

SMYTH, EUGENE. The Missions of California. Chicago. A.

Belford and Co. 1899. 27 1., illus., 14 plates (incl. front.) S 429

SNEE, J.M. "POAU v. Freedom of Religion," America, v. 98 (Mar. 22, 1958), 714. S 430

SNYDER, JAMES L. 'Duquesne University, 1878-1953," Catholic Educational Review, v. 50 (1952), 649-665. S 431

SOCIETY OF THE SISTERS OF THE HOLY NAMES OF JESUS AND MARY. OREGON. Gleanings of Fifty Years ... 1859-1909. Portland. no pub. 1909. xvi, 230p. front., plates, ports. S 432

SOER, A. 'Idaho Territory. Letter dated St. Joseph's Lapwai, June 30th, 1888," Woodstock Letters, v. 17 (1888), 356-361. S 433

SOER, A. "The Rocky Mountains. Letter from St. Joseph's Mission, August 22nd, 1887," Woodstock Letters, v. 17 (1888), 85-88. S 434

SOHN, EUGENE J. History of the Society of Mary in the St. Louis Area. MA thesis. Saint Louis University. 1945. 123p. S 435

SOLIS, JOSE DE. "Diary of a Visit of Inspection of the Texas Missions Made by Fray Gaspar Jose de Solis, in the Year 1767-1768," tr. by Margaret K. Kress, Southwest Historical Quarterly, v. 35 (1931), 28-72. S 436

"SOME CORRESPONDENCE RELATING TO THE DIOCESE OF NEW ORLEANS AND ST. LOUIS 1818-1843. FROM THE ARCHIEPISCOPAL ARCHIVES OF QUEBEC," American Catholic Historical Society of Philadelphia Records, v. 19 (1908), 185-213 (New Orleans), 305-325 (St. Louis). S 437

"SOME NOTES ON THE 'CATHOLIC MISCELLANY,' " Amer-

ican Catholic Historical
Society of Philadelphia Re-
cords, v. 56 (1945), 54-66.
S 438
"SOME OF THE SOURCES FOR
CATHOLIC HISTORY OF
ILLINOIS," Illinois Catholic
Historical Review, v. 1 (1919),
520-528. S 439
A bibliography of letters in
Jesuit Relations, of books,
and letters and reports in
the Annals of the Leopolding
Association.
SOMMERHAUSER, W. J. "The
Jesuit Parish of Mankato,"
Woodstock Letters, v. 57
(1928), 213-221, 400-411.
S 440
SOPKO, SISTER MARY CARNATH.
Religious Issues in Ohio Poli-
tics. 1875. MA thesis.
Xavier University (Cincinnati)
1953. 102p. S 441
SORRENTINO, GUISEPPE.
Dalle Montagne Rocciose al
Rio Bravo. Napoli. Casa
Ed. Federico and Ardia. 194.
307p. map. S 442
A history of the New Mexico-
Colorado Mission of the
Jesuit Province of Naples as
told by a former member of
the mission. Undocumented
and incomplete, but contains
much information.
"SOUTHERN CATHOLICS AND
INTEGRATION," Sign. v. 35
(1956), 13-27. S 443
A special and impartial sur-
vey which is very informa-
tive.
SOUVAY, CHARLES L. The
Cathedrals of St. Louis: An
Historical Sketch. no pl.
no pub. n.d. 41p. illus.,
plates. S 444
SOUVAY, CHARLES L. "Cen-
tennial of the Church in St.
Louis," Catholic Historical
Review, v. 4 (1918), 52-
75. S 445
SOUVAY, CHARLES L. "DuBourg
and the Biblical Society (New

Orleans, 1813)," St. Louis
Catholic Historical Review, v.
2 (1920), 18-25. S 446
SOUVAY, CHARLES L. "Epis-
copal Visitation to the Diocese
of New Orleans, 1827-1828,"
St. Louis Catholic Historical
Review, v. 1 (1919), 215-
230. S 447
SOUVAY, CHARLES L. "The
Lazarists in Illinois," Illinois
Catholic Historical Review, v.
1 (1919), 303-319. S 448
SOUVAY, CHARLES L. "Rosati's
Elevation to the See of St.
Louis," Catholic Historical
Review, v. 3 (1917), 165-
186. S 449
SOUVAY, CHARLES L. "Rosati's
Election to the Coadjutorship
of New Orleans," Catholic
Historical Review, v. 3 (1917),
3-21. S 450
SOUVAY, CHARLES L. "Rum-
maging through Old Parish
Records: An Historical Sketch
of the Church of Lafayette,
Louisiana, 1821-1921," St.
Louis Catholic Historical Re-
view, v. 3 (1921), 242-294.
S 451
SOUVAY, CHARLES L. "The
Society of St. Vincent de
Paul as an Agency of Recon-
struction," Catholic Historical
Review, v. 7 (1922), 441-457.
S 452
SOUVENIR OF THE SILVER
JUBILEE IN THE EPISCOPACY
OF HIS GRACE THE MOST
REV. PATRICK AUGUSTINE
FEEHAN, ARCHBISHOP OF
CHICAGO, NOV. 1, 1890.
Chicago. no pub. 1891. 371p.
S 453
SPALDING, HENRY S. Catholic
Colonial Maryland. A Sketch.
Milwaukee. Bruce. 1931. xv,
243p. front., illus., plates,
ports. S 454
SPALDING, HENRY S. "English-
Maryland Catholics in Kentucky,"
Month, v. 157 (1931), 128-
132. S 455

SPALDING, HENRY S. "Life
of James Marquette," Illinois
Catholic Historical Review, v.
9 (1926), 3-17, 109-133,
(1927), 223-246.   S 456
SPALDING, HENRY S. "The
Priest's House--a Relic of
Early Catholicity in Kentucky,"
Illinois Catholic Historical Re-
view, v. 9 (1927), 372-376.
                          S 457
SPALDING, JOHN L. The Life
of the Most Reverend M.J.
Spalding. New York. Catholic
Publication Society. 1873.
468p. front. (port.)   S 458
SPALDING, JOHN L. "Position of
Catholics in the United States,"
Dublin Review, v. 88 (1881),
97-116.   S 459
SPALDING, JOHN L. "The Reli-
gious Mission of the Irish
People and Catholic Coloniza-
tion. New York. Catholic
Publication Society. 1880.
339p.   S 460
SPALDING, M.J., AND BONA-
VENTURE HAMMER. Aussage
aus der Geschichte der Diocese
Louisville. Louisville. Geo.
D. Deuser. 1884-1885. 2v.
                          S 461
SPALDING, MARTIN J. Sketches
of the Life and Times and
Character of Benedict Joseph
Flaget. Louisville. Webb and
Levering. 1852. xvi, 405p.
front., port.   S 462
SPECHT, JOSEPH. "An Eight
Days' Mission among the Chip-
pewas and Whites at Odanah,
Wisconsin. Letter dated Holy
Cross Mission, Wilwenikong,
Ont., Dec. 6, 1902," Woodstock
Letters, v. 31 (1902), 363-
368.   S 463
SPECHT, JOSEPH. "Three Weeks'
Missionary Labors among the
Chippewas and Whites of
Northern Wisconsin," Wood-
stock Letters, v. 33 (1904), 198-
209.   S 464
SPECHT, JOSEPH. "Two Weeks
Mission Labors among the Chip-

pewas of Wisconsin and Min-
nesota. Letter dated Holy
Cross Mission, Wilwenikong,
Ont. July 21, 1908," Wood-
stock Letters, v. 37 (1908),
376-386.   S 465
SPELLISSY, MARY ANGELA.
"Sketch of the Life of Philip
Francis Scanlan (1794-1800),"
American Catholic Historical
Society of Philadelphia Re-
cords, v. 11 (1900), 385-
416. port.   S 466
SPELMAN, SISTER M. CAJETAN.
The Church on the Kentucky
Frontier ... MA thesis. Uni-
versity of Notre Dame. 1945.
viii, 111p.   S 467
SPENCE, HARTZELL. "The
Story of Religions in America:
Roman Catholics," Look, v. 21
(1957), 116-129, illus.
                          S 468
SPERRY, WILLARD L. Religion
in America. New York. Mac-
millan. 1946. viii, 317p.
                          S 469
SPIERS, EDWARD F. The Central Catholic High School: a
Survey of Their History and
Status in the United States.
Washington. Catholic University. 1951. xv, 216p. illus.,
maps, tables.   S 470
SPILLANE, EDWARD. "Bibliog-
raphy of John Gilmary Shea,"
United States Catholic Historical Society Records and
Studies, v. 6 (1913), 249-
274.   S 471
SPILLANE, EDWARD P. Life
and Letters of Henry Van Renn-
sselaer, Priest of the Society
of Jesus. New York. Ford-
ham University Press. 1908.
vii, 293p. plates, ports.
                          S 472
SPITZER, ALLEN. "The Cultural
Organization of Catholicism,"
American Catholic Sociological
Review, v. 19 (1958), 2-12.
                          S 473
SPOKANE (DIOCESE) SYNOD,
1st, 1939. Statuta dioecesis

spokanensis lata ac promulgata a Carolo D. White [ep.] in synodo dioecesana spokanensi prima, die 13 Aprilis, A.D. 1939, celebrata in ecclesia cathedrali Nostrae Dominae de Lourdes apud Spokane, Washington. Seattle, Metropolitan press printing co. [n.d.] 124p.
S 474

SPRINGFIELD, ILL. (DIOCESE). Pastoral instruction, of the bishop of Alton, to the clergy, secular and regular, and to all whom it may concern, of his diocese. Alton, Ill., Perrin & Smith, 1879. 55p.
S 475

SPRINGFIELD, ILL. (DIOCESE) SYNOD, 1st, 1889. Synodus dioecesana altonensis prima, ecclesia in cathedrali Ss. Petri et Pauli Altoni, die 27. Februarii, 1889, habita, in qua constitutiones chicagienses necnon Neoeboracenses, tenuissimis quidem additamentis et modificationibus, adoptatae fuerunt. S. Ludovici, Typis "Amerika," 1889. xii, 56p.
S 476

SPRINGFIELD, MASS. (DIOCESE) SYNOD, 1st, 1874. Constitutiones dioecesanae a Patritio Thoma O'Reilly [ep.] in synodo dioecesana prima, habita Campifonte A.D. 1874. Latae et promulgatae. Worcester, C. Hamilton, 1881. vi, 65p.
S 477

[SPRINGFIELD URSULINES]. Half a Century's Record of the Springfield Ursulines. By a member of the Community. Springfield, Ill. 1909. S 478

(SPRINGHILL COLLEGE, MOBILE, ALA.) Springhill College, Ala. 1830-1905. Mobile. no pub. 1906. S 479

STANDARDT, SISTER MARY COLETTE. The Early Development of Social and Economic Nativism in San Francisco and the Mining Regions of Califor-

nia, 1848-1856. MA thesis. Catholic University. 1949. 90p. S 480

STANDER, GOLDA G. "Jesuit Educational Institutions in the City of New York (1683-1860)," United States Catholic Historical Society Records and Studies, v. 14 (1934), 209-275. S 481

STANDERWICK, DE SALES. "After Fifty Years," The Lamp, v. 47 (1949), 300-308. S 482

STANG, URBAN J. History of Conciliar Legislation in the Province of Cincinnati, 1852-1861. MA thesis. Catholic University. 1940. 111p.
S 483

STANLEY, CROCCHIOLA. Socorro, The Oasis. World Press. c1950. 221p. ports., plates. S 484
Contains the story of the old mission at Socorro, New Mexico.

STANTON, T. A Century of Growth, Or the History of the Church in Western Maryland. Baltimore. no pub. 1891. 2v. S 485

"STATUTES RELATING TO FLORIDA IN THE DIOCESAN SYNOD ... JUNE, 1684," United States Catholic Historical Magazine, v. 1 (1887), 287-297. S 486

STAUF, H. MARGARET. The Anti-Catholic Movement in Missouri: Post Civil War Period. MA thesis. Saint Louis University. 1936. 83p.
S 487

STECK, FRANCIS BORGIA. "Christopher Columbus and the Franciscans," Americas, v. 3 (1947), 319-341. S 488

STECK, FRANCIS BORGIA. "Death of Our Foremost Franciscan Historian," Fortnightly Review, v. 41 (1934), 127-128. S 489

STECK, FRANCIS B. Essays Re-

340

lating to the Jolliet-Marquette
Expedition, 1673. Quincy, Ill.
The Author. 1953. 2v. mimeo.
S 490

STECK, FRANCIS BORGIA.
"Father Marquette's Place in
American History," Americas,
v. 5 (1949), 411-438. S 491

STECK, FRANCIS BORGIA. Fore-
runners of Captain de Leon's
Expedition to Texas, 1670-
1675. Austin, Texas. Texas
Catholic Historical Society.
1932. Preliminary Studies, v.
2, n. 3. S 492

STECK, FRANCIS BORGIA. "Fray
Junipero Serra and the Military
Heads of California," Fortnightly Review, v. 28 (1921),
451-453, v. 29 (1922), 8-9,
29-32, 49-51, 70-72, 87-91.
S 493

STECK, FRANCIS BORGIA. "Interesting Incidents in the
Catholic History of the Southwest," Fortnightly Review
v. 40 (1933), 121-122. S 494

STECK, FRANCIS BORGIA. The
Jolliet-Marquette Expedition,
1763. Washington. Catholic
University. 1927. S 495

STECK, FRANCIS BORGIA.
"Junipero Serra, Pioneer and
Missionary," Fortnightly Review,
v. 38 (1931), 97-99. S 496

STECK, FRANCIS BORGIA. "The
Real Author of the 'Recit,' "
Americas, v. 4 (1948),
474-500. S 497

STECK, FRANCIS BORGIA.
"Remarks on the History of
Florida," Historical Bulletin,
v. 6 (1927), 37-39. S 498

STECK, FRANCIS BORGIA.
A Tentative Guide to Historical
Materials on the Spanish Border-
lands. Philadelphia. American
Catholic Historical Society.
1943. 106p. S 499

STECK, FRANCIS BORGIA. "The
Texas K. of C. History
Project," Fortnightly Review, v.
39 (1932), 63-64. S 500

STECK, FRANCIS BORGIA. "A

Tribute to the Apostle of Wisconsin, Father Claude Al-
louez," Fortnightly Review,
v. 38 (1931), 251-252.
S 501

STECKEL, ALFRED. "The
Catholic Church in Wisconsin,"
American Catholic Historical
Society of Philadelphia Re-
cords, v. 7 (1896), 225-
233; v. 8 (1897), 20-27.
S 502

STECKEL, ALFRED. "German
Roman Catholic Central
Society of the United States
of North America," American
Catholic Historical Society of
Philadelphia Records, v. 6
(1895), 252-265. S 503

STEELE, VINCENT EARL.
The Society of Mary in Cali-
fornia, 1884-1956. MA
thesis. University of San
Francisco. 1958. iii, 172p.
S 504

[STEINAUER, FIDELIS]. "Ein
Jahr unter der Menominie,
Indianen von Keschina, Wisconsin," Die Katholische Missionen, v. 21 (1893), 147-
151. S 505

STEINHAUER, ARTHUR H. A
History of Parochial Elementary Education in the Diocese
of Trenton, N. J. Ph.D. thesis.
Fordham University. 1945.
vi, 274p. S 506

STEPHENSON, GEORGE M.
"Nativism in the Forties and
Fifties, with Special Refer-
ence to the Mississippi Valley,"
Mississippi Valley Historical
Review, v. 9 (1922), 185-
202. S 507

STOCK, LEO F. "Catholic Historical Activities in the United
States," Fortnightly Review, v.
36 (1928), 151-153. S 508

STOCK, LEO F. "Catholic Participation in the Diplomacy of
the Southern Confederacy,"
Catholic Historical Review, v.
16 (1930), 1-18. S 509

STOCK, LEO F. (ed.) Consular

Relations between the United
States and the Papal States:
Instructions and Despatches.
Washington. American Catholic
Historical Association. 1945.
xxxix, 467p. S 510
STOCK, LEO F. "The Papal
Consuls of Philadelphia," Amer-
ican Catholic Historical Society
of Philadelphia Records, v. 55
(1944), 178-189. S 511
STOCK, LEO F. United States
Ministers to the Papal States,
Instructions and Dispatches,
1848-1868. Washington. A-
merican Catholic Historical As-
sociation. 1933. xxxix, 456p.
S 512
STOCK, LEO F. "Was the Papal
Consulate in the United States
Officially Ended?" Catholic
Historical Review, v. 30
(1944), 165-170. S 513
STODDARD, JOHN L. Rebuilding
a Lost Faith. 4th ed. New
York. P.J. Kenedy and Sons.
1924. vii, 222p. S 514
STOKES, GEORGE STEWART.
Agnes Repplier, Lady of Let-
ters. Philadelphia. University
of Pennsylvania Press. 1949.
xiii, 274p. ports. S 515
STONE, JAMES KENT. An
Awakening and What Followed.
Notre Dame, Ind. Ave Maria
Press. 1920. S 516
STONE, JAMES KENT. The In-
vitation Heeded. London.
Burns and Oates. 1869. 341p.
S 517
These two volumes comprise
the autobiography of the
famous convert and Passionist
missionary, Father Fidelis
of the Cross.
STONER, V. R. "Diocese of Tuc-
son," Extension, v. 27 (1932),
23. illus. S 518
STONER, VICTOR R. "Fray
Pedro de Arriquibar, Chaplain
of the Royal Fort at Tucson,"
Arizona and the West, v. 1
(1959), 71-79. S 519
STORER, MRS. BELLAMY. "Arch-

bishop Ireland and the Hat,"
Dublin Review, v. 168 (1921),
203-208. S 520
STORER, BELLAMY. Letter of
Bellamy Storer to the Presi-
dent and the Members of His
Cabinet, November, 1906.
S 521
STORER, MARIA LONGWORTH.
In Memoriam: Bellamy
Storer. Boston. Merrymount
Press. 1923. 119p. ports.
S 522
STOREY, SISTER MARY ALEX-
ANDER. Catholic Social Teach-
As Reflected in the Michi-
gan Catholics during the Depres-
sion Decade, 1929-1939. MA
thesis. University of Detroit.
1940. 68p. S 523
"STORY OF CLOVIS AND ITS
MISSIONS," Provincial
Chronicle (Province of St.
John Baptist, O.F.M.), v.
21 (1949), 137-150, 187, 221-
242. S 524
STORY OF ST. JOHN'S UNIVER-
SITY. New York. The Uni-
versity. 1945. S 525
STORY OF ST. JOSEPH'S PROTO-
CATHEDRAL AND ITS PAINT-
INGS. Bardstown, Ky. no
pub. c1930. 15p. photos,
illus. S 526
STRANGE, BARNARD. "Francis
Silas Chatard," St. Meinrad
Historical Essays, v. 3
(1934), 153-163. S 527
STRATEMEIER, GEORGE B.
Thomas Cornwaleys. Com-
missioner and Counsellor of
Maryland. Washington. Cath-
olic University. 1922. x,
139p. S 528
STREIT, ROBERT ... Biblioteca
Missionum. Munster i.w.
Aachen. 1916- . 10v, vv.
2, 3. S 529
STRITCH, ALFRED G. Nativism
in Cincinnati, 1830-1860.
MA thesis. Catholic Univer-
sity. 1935. 59p. S 530
STRITCH, ALFRED G. "Political
Nativism in Cincinnati, 1830-

1860," American Catholic Historical Society of Philadelphia Records, v. 48 (1937), 227-278.   S 531

STRITCH, ALFRED G. "Trusteeism in the Old Northwest, 1800-1850," Catholic Historical Review, v. 30 (1944), 155-164.   S 532

STUART, ANNA M. "Catholic Writers of Iowa," Iowa Catholic Historical Review, v. 4 (Apr., 1932), 3-31; v. 6 (Apr., 1933), 21-27; v. 7 (June, 1934), 41-46; v. 9 (Jan., 1936), 38-41.   S 533

STUART, ANNA M. "History of the Catholic Press of Iowa," Iowa Catholic Historical Review, v. 5 (Oct., 1932), 11-38.   S 534

STUART, MARY MAURICITA. The Religious Convictions of Theodore Roosevelt and His Relations with Catholics and the Catholic Church. MA thesis. University of San Francisco. 1959. v, 128p.   S 535

STUBBER, SISTER MARY CARINA. History of the Franciscan Sisters of Perpetual Adoration of La Crosse under the Administration of Mother Ludovica Keller, 1882-1928. MA thesis. Catholic University. 1943. 75p.
                                  S 536

STUDER, SISTER MARY MIRA. History of the Foundations of the School Sisters of St. Francis. MA thesis. Marquette University. 1937.   S 537

STUDY, GUY. "The Restoration of the Holy Family Church, Cahokia, Illinois," Missouri Historical Society Bulletin, v. 5 (1949), 257-265.   S 538

STURGES, WALTER KNIGHT. "A Bishop and His Architect: The Story of the Building of Baltimore Cathedral," Liturgical Arts, v. 17 (1949), 53-64.
                                  S 539

STUTZ, JOSEF. Mariahilf Kirche. Loretto, Rush County, Kansas,

1932. no pl. no pub. 1932. 24p. plates   S 540

STYLES, WILLIAM A. L. "Pioneer American Nuns," Ave Maria, v. 55 (1942), 167-170.   S 541

STYLES, WILLIAM A. L. "Pioneer Nuns of New England," Magnificat, v. 56 (1935), 282-288.   S 542

STYLES, WILLIAM A. L. "Religious First Facts," Ave Maria, v. 56 (1942), 752-755. Also Catholic Mind, v. 41 (1943), 40-44.   S 543
A popular presentation of various firsts in the story of the Church in North America.

SUAREZ, RALEIGH A. "Religion in Rural Louisiana, 1850-1860," Louisiana Historical Quarterly, v. 38 (1955), 55-63.   S 544
A general article, contains little information on the Catholic Church.

SUELLENTROP, C. "A Pioneer German Catholic Settlement in Tennessee," Central Blatt and Social Justice, v. 25 (1932), 204-205.   S 545

SUGRANES, EUGENE. The Old San Gabriel Mission. San Gabriel, Calif. no pub. 1909. 104p. illus. (incl ports.) facsim.   S 546

SULLIVAN, A.A. "Minor Seminary Conferences at the Catholic University of America, Retrospect and Prospect," National Catholic Educational Association Bulletin, v. 50 (1953), 119-122.   S 547

SULLIVAN, DANIEL C. History of Catholic Elementary Education in the Archdiocese of Newark, New Jersey. Ph.D. thesis. Fordham University. 1942. iv, 342p.   S 548

SULLIVAN, ELLA C. AND ALFRED E. LOGIE. The Story of the Old Spanish Missions of the Southwest. Chicago. Lyons and Carnahan. c1927.

v, 217p. front., illus. S 549
SULLIVAN, M. Catholic Church
of New England. Portland
[Me] no pub. 1895. n.p.
S 550
SULLIVAN, SISTER MARY
CHRISTINA. "Some Non-
Permanent Foundations of
Religious Orders and Congrega-
tions of Women in the United
States (1793-1850)," United
States Catholic Historical
Society Records and Studies,
v. 31 (1940), 7-118. S 551
SULLIVAN, SISTER MARY
DOROTHY. The Catholic Church
among the Blackfeet Indians in
the United States. MA thesis.
University of Notre Dame. 1939.
iii, 118p. S 552
SULLIVAN, SISTER M. XAVERIA.
The History of Catholic Second-
ary Education in the Archdio-
cese of Boston. Washington.
Catholic University. 1946.
xiii, 183p. incl. tables,
diagrs. S 553
SULLIVAN, RICHARD. Notre
Dame, the Story of a Univer-
sity. New York. Holt. 1951.
242p. S 554
A publicity brochure rather
than a scholarly history.
"'SUNDAY HOUSES' OF GER-
MAN SETTLERS," Central
Blatt and Social Justice, v.
21 (1929), 54-55. S 555
SUREN, VICTOR T. "Our
Leader Called by God," Social
Justice Review, v. 44 (1952),
352-354. S 556
A short biographical
obituary of Frederick P.
Kenkel, founder and director
of the Central Bureau of St.
Louis, Catholic Social Pio-
neer, Apologist, Historian,
and Apostle of Charity,
1863-1952.
SWASTEK, JOSEPH. "The Poles
in South Bend in 1914," Polish-
American Studies, v. 2 (1945),
79-88. S 557
SWEENEY, ELIZABETH ANN.

"Catholic Church at Central
City," Colorado Magazine, v.
19 (1941), 181-186. S 558
SWEET, WILLIAM WARREN.
The Story of Religion in A-
merica. rev. ed. New York.
Harper and Bros. 1939.
vi, 656p. S 559
SWEET, WILLIAM WARREN.
Religion in Colonial America.
New York. Charles Scribner's
Sons. 1942. xiii, 267p.
S 560
SWEETMAN, JOHN. "The Sweet-
man Catholic Colony of Currie,
Minnesota, a Memoir," Acta
et Dicta, v. 3 (1912), 39-
65. S 561
SWISHER, CARL B. Roger B.
Taney. New York. Macmillan.
1935. x, 608p. front., illus.
(facsim.) plate, ports.
S 562
SYLVAIN, ROBERT. "Relations
d'Alexis de Tocqueville avec
les Catholiques américains,"
La Revue de l'Université
Laval, v. 11 (1957), 471-
486. S 563
SYRACUSE (DIOCESE) SYNOD,
1st, 1887. Synodus dioecesana
syracusana prima, die XIV.
Septembris, A.D. 1887, in
ecclesia Sanctae Mariae in
coelos Assumpta, Syracusis
habita a Patritius A. Ludden
[ep.] Neo Eboraci, Typis
Societatis pro libris catholicis
evulgandis, 1887. 113p.
S 564
SYRACUSE, N.Y. (DIOCESE)
SYNOD, 2nd, 1890. Synodus
dioecesana syracusana secunda,
die XXX. Septembris, A.D.
1890, in ecclesia cathedrali
Sancti Joannis Evangelistae,
Syracusis habita, a Patritio A.
Ludden, D.D., episcopo syracusano. Syracusis, in statu
Neo Eboracensi, 1890. 12p.
S 565
SYRACUSE (DIOCESE) SYNOD,
3rd, 1893. Synodus dioecesana
syracusana tertia, die VI.

Novembris A.D. 1893, in
ecclesia cathedrali Sancti Joannis Evangelistae, Syracusis
habita a Patritio A. Ludden,
D.D., episcopo syracusano.
Syracusis, in statu Neo Eboracensi, 1893.   11p.   S 566
SYRACUSE (DIOCESE) SYNOD,
4th, 1896. Synodus dioecesana
syracusana quarta, die XXII
Octobris A.D. 1896, in ecclesia cathedrali Sancti Joannis
Evangelistae, Syracusis habita,
a Patritio A. Ludden, D.D.,
episcopo syracusano. Syracusis,
in statu Neo Eboracensi, 1896.
11p.   S 567
SYRACUSE (DIOCESE) SYNOD,
5th, 1899. Synodus dioecesana
syracusana quinta, die XVIII
Octobris A.D. 1899, in ecclesia
cathedrali Sancti Joannis Evangelistae, Syracusis habita, a
Patritio A. Ludden, D.D.,
episcopo syracusano. Syracusis,
in statu Neo Eboracensi, 1899.
1 p.l., 39-55p.   S 568
SYRACUSE, N.Y. (DIOCESE)
SYNOD, 6th, 1902. Synodus
dioecesana syracusana sexta,
die XVI Octobris A.D. 1902,
in ecclesia cathedrali Sancti
Joannis Evangelistae, Syracusis
habita, ab ... Patritio A. Ludden, D.D., episcopo syracusano.
Syracusis, in statu Neo Eboracensi, 1902. 8p.   S 569
SYRACUSE (DIOCESE) SYNOD,
7th, 1905. Synodus dioecesana
syracusana septima, die XVII
Octobris A.D. 1905 in ecclesia
cathedrali Immaculatae Conceptionis, Syracusis habita, a
Patritio A. Ludden [ep.] Syracusis, 1905. 7p.   S 570
SYRACUSE, N.Y. (DIOCESE)
SYNOD, 8th, 1908. Synodus
dioecesana syracusana octava,
die XIII Octobris A.D. 1908,
in ecclesia cathedrali Immaculatae Conceptionis, Syracusis
habita, a Patritio A. Ludden,
D.D., episcopo syracusano.
Syracusis, in statu Neo Ebora-

censi, 1908. [8]p.   S 571
SYRACUSE, N.Y. (DIOCESE)
SYNOD, 9th, 1911. Synodus
dioecesana syracusana nona,
die IX Maii A.D., 1911, in
ecclesia cathedrali Immaculatae Conceptionis, Syracusis
habita, a Patritio A. Ludden,
D. D., episcopo syracusano.
Syracusis, in statu Neo Eboracensi, 1911. [8]p.   S 572
SYRACUSE, N.Y. (DIOCESE)
SYNOD, 10th, 1914. Synodus
dioecesana syracusana decima,
die I Septembris A.D. 1914,
in ecclesia cathedrali Immaculatae Conceptionis, Syracusis
habita, a Joanne Grimes, D.
D., episcopo syracusano.
Syracusis, in statu Neo Eboracensi, 1914. 12p.   S 573
SYRACUSE (DIOCESE) SYNOD,
11th, 1921. Synodus dioe-
cesana syracusensis undecima,
die 8 Septembris A.D. 1921 in
ecclesia cathedrali Immaculatae
Conceptionis Syracusis habita a
Joanne Grimes, D.D., episcopo
syracusensi. Rochester, N.Y.
Typis J.P. Smith printing co.,
1922. xix, 66p.   S 574
SYRACUSE (DIOCESE) SYNOD,
12th, 1942. Synodus dioe-
cesana syracusana duodecima
quam die XV mensis Decem-
bris Anno Domini 1942 in ecclesia cathedrali Immaculatae
Conceptionis Syracusis habita
a Gualtero Andrea Foery,
D.D. Syracuse, Peerless
press [n.d.] xxi, 52p. S 575

- T -
TAAFFE, THOMAS G. A His-
tory of St. John's College,
Fordham. New York. Catholic
Publication Society. 1891. viii,
154p. plates, ports.   T 1
TABB, JOHN B. Letters - Grave
and Gay, and Other Prose.
Edited with introduction and
notes by Francis E. Litz.
Washington. Catholic Univer-
sity. 1950. xix, 266p.

illus. T 2

TAC, PABLO. "Indian Life and Customs at Mission San Luis Rey," translated and edited by Minna and Gordon Hewes. The Americas, v. 9 (July, 1952), 87-106. T 3

TALBOT, FRANCIS X. "Blessed Isaac Jogues," United States Catholic Historical Society Records and Studies, v. 19 (1929), 21-32. T 4

TALBOT, FRANCIS XAVIER. Jesuit Education in Philadelphia. Philadelphia. St. Joseph's College. 1927. xvii, 146p. incl front., plates, ports. T 5

TALBOT, FRANCIS X. "The Huron Sodality in 1653," Woodstock Letters, v. 82 (1953), 335-360. T 6
A well written and thoroughly documented story of the first Sodality in what is now continental Canada and the United States.

TALBOT, FRANCIS XAVIER. Richard Henry Tierney, Priest of the Society of Jesus. New York. America Press. 1930, 200p. front. (port.) T 7

TALBOT, FRANCIS XAVIER. Saint Among Savages. New York. Harper Brothers. 1935. ix, 466p. front. (port.), map, facsim. T 8

TALBOT, FRANCIS XAVIER. Saint Among the Hurons. New York. Harper Brothers. 1949. 351p. T 9

TALBOT, FRANCIS XAVIER. "The Three Martyrs of the United States," Catholic World, v. 163 (1946), 506-513. T 10
An article on the third centenary of the martyrdom of Sts. Isaac Jogues, Rene Goupil, and John Lalande.

TALBOT, FRANCIS XAVIER. "The Torture Trial of St. Isaac Jogues," United States Catholic Historical Society Records and Studies, v. 23

(1933), 7-86. T 11

TAMBOLA, SISTER M. DAMIEN. James F. Edwards, Pioneer Archivist of Catholic Church History of America. MA thesis. University of Notre Dame. 1958. 156p. T 12

TANGNEY, M. C. Development of Catholic Institutions in Chicago during the Incumbencies of Bishop Quarter and Bishop Van De Velde, 1844-1853. MA thesis. Loyola University (Chicago) 1935. T 13

TANSEY, ANNE. "Saint Among the Skyscrapers," Ave Maria, v. 71 (1950), 559-563. T 14

TANSILL, CHARLES C. "Pope Benedict XV's Peace Efforts," United States Historical Society Records and Studies, v. 34 (1945), 1-19. T 15

TARDIVEL, JULES P. La Situation Religieuse aux Etats-Unis. Illusions et Réalité. Lille. Desclee, De Brouwer et Cie. 1900. viii, 302p. T 16

TATA, YVONNE. "The National Laywomen's Retreat Movement," Ave Maria, v. 72 (1950), 429-431. T 17

TAYLOR, DANIEL CRANE. John L. Stoddard. New York. P.J. Kenedy and Sons. 1935. ix, 325p. front., plates, ports. T 18

TAYLOR, SISTER MARY JOHN FRANCIS. St. Francis Xavier Mission, 1838-1880, Cowlitz Prairie, Washington. MA thesis. Seattle University. 1948. vi, 91p. T 19

TEGEDER, VINCENT. "Abbot Smith Letters and American Benedictines," American Benedictine Review, v. 6 (1955), 24-38. T 20
A study of the help given by the Roman agent of the American Benedictines.

TEGEDER, VINCENT; "The Benedictines in Frontier Minnesota," Minnesota History, v. 32 (1951), 34-43. T 21

TEGEDER, VINCENT. "Pioneering
Monks," Minnesota History,
v. 32 (1951), 34-43; v. 33
(1952), 59-69- illus.   T 22

TELL, HUGO. Diamond Jubilee
Souvenir of the Immaculate
Conception Parish, New Munich,
Minn. 1861-1936. no pl. no
pub. 1936? 32p. plates, ports.
                            T 23

TELLER, RAYMOND J. "The
Conewago Historian: John T.
Reilly (1956-1924)," Records
of the American Catholic Historical Society of Philadelphia,
v. 62 (1951), 124-132.   T 24
Also includes a tentative
bibliography of Reilly's
works.

TELLER, RAYMOND J. "The
Geiger House, Salem County,
New Jersey," American Catholic Historical Society of Philadelphia Records, v. 68 (1957),
121-125.   T 25
Scene of early Catholicism
in New Jersey.

TENISON, EVA M. Louise
Imogen Guiney. London. Macmillan. 1923. xxvii, 348p.
front. (port.), facsims. T 26

TENNELLY, J.B. (tr. and ed.)
"Documents. Father Pierz,
Missionary and Colonizer,"
Acta et Dicta, v. 7 (1935),
104-118.   T 27

M. TERSITA, SISTER. "Mother
Dolores," Review for Religious,
v. 15 (1956), 238-246.   T 28
A brief, pious biographical
sketch of the foundress of
the Sisters of the Holy
Family.

"TEXAS. DIOCESE SAN ANTONIO.
MISSION DER DEUTSCHEN
BESCHUHTEN KARMELITER
IN TEXAS," Die Katholischen
Missionen, v. 23 (1895), 114-
116.   T 29

"TEXAS MISSIONS IN 1785.
DOCUMENT. [REPORT OF
FATHER PRESIDENT OF THE
MISSION, 1785]," Mid-America,
v. 11 (1945), 38-58.   T 30

"THATIGKEIT DER VOLKSMIS-
SIONÄRE UNTER DEN DEUT-
SCHSPRÄCHIGEN KATHOLIKEN
AMERICAS," Central Blatt
and Social Justice, v. 14
(1921), 187-189.   T 31

THAUREN, JOHANNES. Ein
Gnadenstrom zur Neuen Welt
und Seine Quelle. Wein.
Moedling Missiondrukerei St.
Gabriel. 1940.   T 32
Story of the Leopoldinung
Stiftung.

THAYER, JOHN. "Letter of
Rev. John Thayer to Bishop
Carroll," American Catholic
Historical Researches, v. 28
(1911), 24-25.   T 33

THEBAUD, AUGUSTUS J. Three
Quarters of a Century (1807-
1882). A Retrospect. ed. by
Charles G. Herbermann. New
York. United States Catholic
Historical Society. 1904, 1912-
1913. 3v.   T 34

THIE, JOSEPH A. "German
Catholic Activity in the United
States Seventy Years Ago,"
American Catholic Historical
Society of Philadelphia Records,
v. 20 (1909), 89-121.   T 35

THIELE, A.J. Geschichte der
St. Aloysius--Gemeinde,
Chicago, 1909. no pl. no
pub. 1909? 73p. plates,
ports.   T 36

THILL, JOHN M. A Chronicle of
St. Joseph Congregation of
Prescott, Wis. Silver Jubilee,
1912-1937. no pl. no pub.
1937? 48p. plates, ports.
                            T 37

THEOBALD, STEPHEN L. "Catholic Missionary Work among
the Colored People of the U-
nited States (1776-1866), A-
merican Catholic Historical
Society of Philadelphia Records, v. 35 (1924), 324-
344.   T 38

THOMAS, SISTER EVANGELINE.
Footprints on the Frontier.
Westminster, Md. Newman,
1948. xiv, 400p. illus.,

ports., facsim.   T 39
A scholarly history of the
Sisters of St. Joseph of
Concordia, Kansas.

THOMAS, SISTER EVANGELINE.
Nativism in the Old Northwest,
1850-1860. Washington. Catholic University. 1936. vii,
270p.   T 40

THOMAS, SISTER EVANGELINE.
"The Rev. Louis Dumortier,
S.J., Itinerant Missionary to
Central Kansas, 1859-1867,"
Kansas Historical Quarterly,
v. 20 (1952), 252-270.   T 41

THOMAS, JOHN L. The Amer-
ican Catholic Family. Engle-
wood Cliffs, N.J. Prentice
Hall, 1956. xii, 471p.
                           T 42

THOMAS, JOHN L. "Out-group
Marriage Patterns of Some
Selected Ethnic Groups," American Catholic Sociological Review, v. 15 (1954), 6-18.
                           T 43

THOMAS, J. L. "Some Observations on Mixed Marriages in
the United States," Lumen, v.
6 (1951), 173-186.   T 44
Includes bibliography and
tables.

THOMAS, JOHN L. "The Urban
Impact on Catholic Families,"
American Catholic Sociological
Review, v. 10 (1949), 258-
267.   T 45

THOMAS, SISTER MARIAN
JOSEPHINE. Abbé Jean-
Baptiste Abraham Brouillet,
First Vicar General of the Dio-
cese of Seattle. MA thesis.
Seattle University. 1950. 261p.
                           T 46

THOMAS, SISTER M. URSULA.
The Catholic Church on the
Oklahoma Frontier, 1824-1907.
Ph.D. dissertation. Saint
Louis University. 1938.   347p.
                           T 47

THOMAS, SISTER URSULA. "The
Catholic Church on the Oklahoma Frontier," Mid-America,
v. 9 (1938), 170-207.   T 48

THOMAS, SISTER URSULA.
"Sources for the Study of
Oklahoma Catholic Missions.
A Critical Bibliography,"
Chronicles of Oklahoma, v. 16
(1938), 346-377.   T 49

THOMAS, P.J. Founding the
Missions of California. San
Francisco. no pl. no pub.
1882.   T 50

THOMAS, PATRICK J. Our
Centennial Memoir. San Francisco. P.J. Thomas. 1877.
192p.   T 51

THOME, SISTER MARY GEROLD.
Development of the Catholic
Church among the Chippewa
Indians of Wisconsin. MA
thesis. Catholic University.
1942. 99p.   T 52

THOMPSON, BERNARD. "The
Leopoldine Society," St. Meinrad Historical Essays, v. 1
(1929), 201-225.   T 53

THOMPSON, JOSEPH. "The
Franciscans in New Spain,
1522-1600," Franciscan Educational Conference Annual Report, v. 18 (1936), 54-97.
                           T 54

THOMPSON, JOSEPH J. "An
American Martyrology," Illinois
Catholic Historical Review, v.
4 (1921), 57-73,   T 55

THOMPSON, JOSEPH J. Arch-
diocese of Chicago--Antece-
dents and Development.
Chicago. Archdiocesan Chancery. 1920. 700p. illus.
                           T 56

THOMPSON, JOSEPH J. "The
Cahokia Mission Property,"
Illinois Catholic Historical
Review, v. 5 (1923), 195-
218, v. 6 (1924), 99-136.
                           T 57

THOMPSON, JOSEPH J. "The
Catholic Church in Illinois in
the Transition Period," Illinois
Catholic Historical Review, v.
1 (1919), 320-338.   T 58

THOMPSON, JOSEPH J. "The
Catholic Clergy of Illinois,"
Illinois Catholic Historical Re-

view, v. 7 (1924), 155-163. **T 59**

THOMPSON, JOSEPH J. "Catholic Statesmen of Illinois," Illinois Catholic Historical Review, v. 3 (1920), 196-216. ports. **T 60**

THOMPSON, JOSEPH J. "The Development of the Church, 1844-1919," Illinois Catholic Historical Review, v. 1 (1919), 424-435. ports. **T 61**

THOMPSON, JOSEPH J. (ed.) The Diocese of Springfield in Illinois. Springfield. Hartman Printing Co. 1928. 888p. illus. **T 62**

THOMPSON, JOSEPH J. "The First Catholics in and about Chicago," Illinois Catholic Historical Review, v. 2 (1921), 227-240. **T 63**

THOMPSON, JOSEPH J. "First Chicago Church Records," Illinois Catholic Historical Review, v. 3 (1921), 404-436, v. 4 (1921), 6-21. **T 64**

THOMPSON, JOSEPH J. "Illinois' First Citizen--Pierre Gibault," Illinois Catholic Historical Review, v. 1 (1918-1919), 79-94, 234-248, 380-387, 484-494; v. 4 (1921), 197-214, 296-300; v. 5 (1922), 154-159, 226-245; v. 8 (1925), 3-29, 99-106. **T 65**

THOMPSON, JOSEPH J. "Illinois Missions," Illinois Catholic Historical Review, v. 1 (1918), 38-63, 185-197. **T 66**

THOMPSON, JOSEPH J. "The Illinois Part of the Diocese of Vincennes," Illinois Catholic Historical Review, v. 4 (1922), 255-265, 381-397; v. 5 (1922), 41-51, 137-143. **T 67**

THOMPSON, MARY P. "The Catholic Church in New Hampshire," Catholic World, v. 52 (1890), 171-185. **T 68**

THOMPSON, T.P. The St. Louis Cathedral of New Orleans. New Orleans. no pl. no pub.

1918. **T 69**

THORNING, J.F. "The Pope's First Consul General in the United States," Thought, v. 7 (1933), 636-645. **T 70**

THORNING, JOSEPH F. Religious Liberty in Transition. Washington. Catholic University. 1931. 252p. **T 71**

THORNTON, FRANCIS A. (ed.) The Notable Catholic Institutions of St. Louis and Vicinity. St. Louis. Finkenbiner-Reed Pub. Co. 1911. 334p. incl. ads, illus., plates, ports. **T 72**

THRAPP, RUSSELL. "Early Religious Beginnings in Illinois," Illinois State Historical Society Journal, v. 4 (1911), 303-317. **T 73**

THWAITES, RUEBEN G. (ed.) Early Western Travels, 1748-1846. Cleveland. Burrows Bros. 1904-1907. 32v. front., illus., plates, ports., maps, plan, facsims. **T 74**

THWAITES, RUEBEN G. Father Marquette. New York. D. Appleton and Co. 1902. xv, 244p. front. (port.) plates, maps, facsim. **T 75**

THWAITES, RUEBEN GOLD. Jesuit Relations and Allied Documents. Cleveland. Burrows Brothers Co. 1896-1901. 73v. **T 76**

TIBESAR, ANTONINE (ed.) Publication: Documentary Series v. 4: Writings of the Presidentes of the California Missions, Ser. 1. 4v. v. 1 (Writings of Junípero Serra). Washington, D.C. Academy of American Franciscan History. 1956. **T 77**

TIERNEY, JOHN J. "St. Charles College: Foundation and Early Years," Maryland Historical Magazine, v. 43 (1948), 294-311. **T 78**

TIERNEY, RICHARD H. "Father Andrew White, S.J., and The Indians," United States Catholic

Historical Society Records and Studies, v. 15 (1921), 89-103. T 79

TIFFANY, GEORGE E. "The Catholic Church and the Changing Frontier," United States Catholic Historical Society Records and Studies, v. 35 (1946), 73-144. T 80

[TIMON, JOHN] "The Church in Texas, Bishop Timon's Account of His Visitation in 1840-1841," American Catholic Historical Researches, v. 14 (1897), 187-189. T 81

TIMON, JEAN. "Extrait d'une Lettre de Mgr. Timon, Evêque de Buffalo à MM. les Directeurs de l'Oeuvre de la Propagation de la Foi. Buffalo 21 novembre, 1854," Annales de la Propagation de la Foi, v. 27 (1855), 315-318. T 82

TIMON, JOHN. Missions in Western New York and Church History of the Diocese of Buffalo. Buffalo. Catholic Sentinel Print. 1862. vi, 258p. T 83

TIMOURAN, ARA. "Catholic Exploration of the Far West, 1794-1835," American Catholic Historical Society of Philadelphia Records, v. 48 (1937), 329-387, v. 49 (1938), 50-66, 135-170. T 84
Short accounts of Catholic explorers' work in the West.

TIMPE, GEORGE. "Concerning St. Joseph's Parish, St. Louis, in 1849," Central Blatt and Social Justice, v. 27 (1935), 358-360. T 85

TIMPE, GEORGE. "An Emigrant's Letter of 1838," Central Blatt and Social Justice, v. 29 (1937), 385-387. T 86

TIMPE, GEORGE. "German Periodicals as Sources for American Church History," Central Blatt and Social Justice, v. 29 (1936), 54-56. T 87

TIMPE, GEORGE (ed.) Katholisches Deutschtum in den Vereinigten Staaten von Amerika. Ein Querschnitt. Freiburg in Breisgau. Herder. 1937. xii, 247p. illus., incl. ports., facsims. T 88

TIMPE, GEORGE. "Der Wahrheitsfreund (Friend of Truth)," Central Blatt and Social Justice, v. 30 (1927), 277-279, 312-314. T 89

TISSOT, . "Extraits de plusieurs Lettres du P. Tissot, de la Compagnie de Jésus, à son Frère. Camp Mary, près Washington, 12 Juillet, 1861. 2 février, 1862," Annales de la Propagation de la Foi, v. 35 (1863), 278-284. T 90

TITTEL, CLARENCE. Golden Jubilee of Holy Family Parish, Kansas City, Missouri. Provincial Chronicles, O.F.M. (Cincinnati), v. 28 (1956), 127-130. illus. T 91

TOLEDO, O (DIOCESE) SYNOD 1. Acta et decreta synodi dioecesanae Toletanae primae. Toleti. Cancellana Curia Dioecesanae. 1941. 274p. n.d. T 92

TOMASSINI, FRANCESCO SAV. "Lettera LXXVIII," Lettere Edificanti Provincia Napolitana, ser. 3 (1879-1880), 184. T 93

TOMASSINI, FRANCIS X. "Colorado. Letter dated St. Ignatius Church, Pueblo, Colorado, January 19th, 1884," Woodstock Letters, v. 13 (1884), 50-53. T 94
On the destruction by fire of St. Patrick's Church 1882, and dedication of the new building 1883.

TOMASSINI, PASQUALE. "Lettera VI," Lettere Edificanti Provincia Napolitana, ser. 1 (1875), 9-11. T 95

TOMASSINI, PASQUALE. "Lettera XXIV," Lettere Edificanti Provincia Napolitana, ser. 1 (1875), 68-69. T 96

TOMASSINI, PASQUALE. "Lettera

VII," Lettere Edificanti Provincia Napolitana, ser. 2 (1876-1877), 30-31. T 97

TOMASSINI, PASQUALE. "Lettera X," Lettere Edificanti Provincia Napolitana, ser. 3 (1879-1880), 23-27. T 98

TOMASSINI, PASQUALE. "Lettera VIII," Lettere Edificanti Provincia Napolitana, ser. 4 (1882-1883), 25-30. T 99

TOMASSINI, PASQUALE. "Lettera XXIII," Lettere Edificanti Provincia Napolitana, ser. 4 (1882-1883), 60-61. T 100
Dated "Conejos, Colo., 1 Marze, 1883," This letter mentions the idea of a "Unione Catolica"--an organization which he was to use with great effectiveness.

TOMASSINI, PASQUALE. "Lettera XVII," Lettere Edificanti Provincia Napolitana, ser. 6 (1889-1891), 37-39. T 101

TONNE, ARTHUR. Story of Chaplain Capaun. Emporia, Kansas. Didde Pub. 1954. 256p. T 102
A biography of this heroic priest of the Diocese of Wichita, who gave his life serving his fellow man in Korea.

TOOHY, WILLIAM J. "The Holy See and the American Civil War," St. Meinrad Essays, v. 12 (1959), 41-52. T 103

TOOMEY, JOHN D. "Priest Poet, and Hero," Columbia, v. 17 (Jan., 1938), 10. T 104
A commemoration of the anniversary of Father Abram Ryan.

TORCHIANA, HENRY A. The Story of Mission Santa Cruz. San Francisco. P. Elder and Co. 1933. xix, 460p. plates, ports., maps, plan, facsims. T 105

TORREN Y NICOLAU, D. FRANCISCO. Bosqueja Historico del Insigne Franciscano, V.P.F.

Junípero Serra, Fundador, y Apostol de la California Septentrional. Spain. no pub. 1913. T 106

TORRIELLI, ANDREW J. Italian Opinion of America as Revealed by Italian Travelers, 1850-1900. Cambridge. Harvard University Press. 1941. vi, 330p. T 107

TOULEMONT, (ed.) "L'Apostolate Catholique aux Etats-Unis pendant la Guerre," Etudes, v. 8 (1863), 862-887. T 108
Five letters from Jesuit Army chaplains during the Civil War.

TOURSCHER, FRANCIS E. "Catholic Historical Scholarship in the United States," Catholic Historical Review, v. 13 (1927), 470-479. T 109

TOURSCHER, FRANCIS E. "Fr. Thomas Cooke Middleton, D. D., O.S.A., 1842-1923," American Catholic Historical Society of Philadelphia Records. v. 35 (1924), 20-32. T 110

TOURSCHER, FRANCIS E. The Hogan Schism and Trustee Troubles in St. Mary's Church, Philadelphia, 1820-1829. Philadelphia. Peter Reilly Co. 1930. xxii, 234p. map. T 111

TOURSCHER, FRANCIS E. (tr. and ed.) The Kenrick-Frenaye Correspondence, 1830-1862. Philadelphia. Wickersham Printing Co. 1920. 500p. T 112
A selection of about 300 letters from the Cathedral archives in Philadelphia. The first fifty-nine letters comprise the Kenrick-Frenaye correspondence. Other letters include some 198 from Brother Peter Richard who became Archbishop of St. Louis. The Frenaye letters are important because of his

position as an intimate
friend of the Archbishop of
Philadelphia and financer
to three of the prelates of
that See. Good index.
TOURSCHER, FRANCIS E.
(comp.) "List of the Augustinian Friars, Members of the
Province of St. Thomas of
Villanova, Who Have Departed
This Life since the Foundation
of the Province in 1796," A-
merican Catholic Historical
Society of Philadelphia Records,
v. 47 (1946), 227-248. T 113
TOURSCHER, FRANCIS E. "Old
St. Augustine's in Philadelphia--
Its Foundation and Its Missions,"
American Catholic Historical
Society of Philadelphia Records. v. 44 (1933), 289-
310; v. 45 (1934), 33-50, 97-
118, 201-211, 257-274; v. 47
(1936), 48-65.   T 114
TOURSCHER, FRANCIS E. Old
St. Augustine's in Philadelphia,
with Some Records of the
Work of the Austin Friars in
the United States. Peter
Reilly Co. 1937. vi, 261p.
                         T 115
TOURSCHER, FRANCIS E. "Saint
Basil's, Dushore, Pennsylvania,
during One Hundred Years, 1838-
1938," American Catholic His-
torical Society of Philadelphia
Records, v. 49 (1938), 27-
49.   T 116
TOURSCHER, FRANCIS E.
"Sketch of the Life of Mother
Cornelia Connelly," American
Catholic Historical Society of
Philadelphia Records, v. 31
(1920), 1-42.   T 117
TOURSCHER, FRANCIS E. "Work
of the Sisters during the
Epidemic of Influenza, October,
1918," American Catholic His-
torical Society of Philadelphia
Records, v. 30 (1919), 25-
63, 135-176, 193-226.   T 118
TRAHEY, JAMES J. The
Brothers of Holy Cross, Notre
Dame, Ind. 2d ed. Notre Dame,

Ind. University Press. 1907.
168p. front., illus. (incl.
ports.)   T 119
TRAUDT, BERNARD G. "Arch-
bishop Messmer," Salesianum,
v. 12 (Apr., 1917), 1-10.
ports.   T 120
TRAUDT, BERNARD G. (tr.
and ed.) "Some Early Let-
ters to Archbishop Henni,"
Salesianum, v. 22 (1927),
1-11, (Apr., 1927), 20-
26, (July, 1927), 1-6. T 121
TRAVELERS ON THE WAY OF
PEACE. v. no pl. no pub.
1955. unpaged. illus. T 122
A well written and illustrated
history of the seventy-five
years of the Benedictine
community of Sacred Heart
Convent, Yankton, South
Dakota.
"TRAVELLER'S ACCOUNTS OF
CATHOLICS IN THE UNITED
STATES," American Catholic
Historical Researches, v. 7
(1890), 9-16.   T 123
TREACY, GERALD C. "Evils of
Trusteeism," United States
Catholic Historical Society
Records and Studies, v. 8
(1915), 136-156.   T 124
TREACY, GERALD C. "Father
John Bapst, S.J., and the
'Ellsworth Outrage,' " United
States Catholic Historical
Society Records and Studies,
v. 14 (1920), 7-19.   T 125
TREACY, JEREMIAH F. "Docu-
ments. First Catholic Mis-
sions in Nebraska," Mid-
America, v. 3 (1932), 269-
275.   T 126
TREACY, WILLIAM P. "A
Biographical Sketch of Father
Robert Molyneux, S.J." Amer-
ican Catholic Quarterly Review,
v. 11 (1876), 140-153. T 127
TREACY, WILLIAM P. "His-
torical Points Connected with
Newtown Manor and Church,"
Woodstock Letters, v. 13
(1884), 69-70, 97-119, 265-
296; v. 14 (1885), 61-79;

v. 15 (1886), 7-33.　　T 128
TREACY, WILLIAM P.　Old
Catholic Maryland and Its
Early Jesuit Missions.
Swedesboro, N.J. no pub.
1889. 183p.　　　　　T 129
TREMONTI, JOSEPH B. "The
Status of Catholic Junior Col-
leges," Catholic Educational Re-
view, v. 49 (1951), 28-39,
91-105, 175-185, 306-313.
　　　　　　　　　　　T 130
TRENTON (DIOCESE) SYNOD,
2nd, 1896. Statuta dioeceseos
trentonensis, quae in synodo
dioecesana secunda, die 25
mensis Junii A.D. 1896, in ecclesia cathedrali Beatae Mariae
Virgini dicata, Trentonii habita,
sanxit et promulgavit Jacobus
Augustinus McFaul [ep.] Trentonii, Typis "True American,"
1897. v. 162p.　　　　T 131
TREUTLEIN, THEODORE E.
"Father Gottfried Bernhardt
Middendorff, S.J. Pioneer of
Tucson," New Mexico His-
torical Review, v. 32 (1957),
310-318.　　　　　　　T 132
　Born 1723, he was thirty-
　three years old when he
　came to Tucson.
TREUTLEIN, THEODORE E.
(trans.) "The Relation of
Philipp Segesser," Mid-Ameri-
ca, v. 16 (1945), 139-187,
257-260.　　　　　　　T 133
"TRIAL OF JOHN URY," Ameri-
can Catholic Historical Re-
searches, v. 16 (1899), 1-53.
　　　　　　　　　　　T 134
TROCKUR, EMMANUEL. "Back-
ground of the Indian Missions,"
Provincial Chronicle (Province
of St. John Baptist, O.F.M.),
v. 11 (1939), 3-16.　　T 135
TROCKUR, EMMANUEL. "Fifty
Years among the Navahos,"
The Indian Sentinel, v. 28
(1948), 131-133.　　　T 136
TROCKUR, EMMANUEL. "Fran-
ciscan Missions among the
Navajo Indians," Provincial
Chronicle (Province of St.

John Baptist, O.F.M.), v. 12
(1940), 18-26, 64-75, 145-
163; v. 13 (1941), 63-90,
133-152; v. 14 (1942), 37-
57, 122-140; v. 16 (1944),
17-31.　　　　　　　　T 137
TROESCH, HELEN (ed.) "The
First Convent in Illinois.
Reminiscences of Sister Mary
Josephine Barber," Illinois
Catholic Historical Review,
v. 1 (1919), 352-371. T 138
TROMBY, VITO M. "Lettera
XVII," Lettere Edificanti Pro-
vincia Napolitana, ser. 1
(1875), 43-45.　　　　T 139
TROMBY, VITO M. "Lettera
LII," Lettere Edificanti Pro-
vincia Napolitana, ser. 2
(1876-1877), 144.　　T 140
　Dated 'Albuquerque, Nuovo
　Messico, 2 Giugno, 1878."
　Mentions the opening of a
　Jesuit novitiate at Albuquer-
　que.
TROMBY, VITO M. "Lettera
XXXIX. Cenni Biographica
del P. Donato M. Gasparri,"
Lettere Edificanti Provincia
Napolitana, ser. 4 (1882-
1883), 88-92.　　　　T 141
TROMBY, VITO M. "Lettera
XXVIII. Cenni Biographici del
P. Rafaele Bianchi," Lettere
Edificanti Provincia Napolitana,
ser. 4 (1882-1883), 70-71.
　　　　　　　　　　　T 142
TROMBY, VITO M. "Lettera
XXXVI. Cenni Biographici del
P. Vito Carrozzini," Lettere
Edificanti Provincia Napolitana,
ser. 4 (1882-1883), 81-82.
　　　　　　　　　　　T 143
TROMPTER, SISTER IRENE.
"Benedictine Sisters in Capu-
lin," Benedictine Review, v. 4
(1949), 55-59.　　　　T 144
TRUJILLO, MIGUEL H. "The
First Christian Martyr of the
Southwest," New Mexico
Quarterly, v. 4 (1934), 292-
298.　　　　　　　　　T 145
TRUMAN, BENJAMIN C. Mis-
sions of California. Los

VALENTINO, ARCANGELO M.
"Da Trinidad," Lettere Edifi-
canti Provincia Napolitana,
(1905), 109-117.   V 3
VALENTINO, ARCANGELO M.
"Missione del N. Messico e
Colorado," Lettere Edificanti
Provincia Napolitana, (1908),
120-125.   V 4
VALENTINO, ARCANGELO M.
"Sullo Stesso Argmento,"
Lettere Edificanti Provincia
Napolitana, (1912-1914), 183-
188.   V 5
VALENTUKONIS, SISTER MARY
ALOYSIUS. Lithuanians in the
Archdiocese of Boston. MA
thesis. Boston College. 1957.
v, 61p.   V 6
VALLETTE, MARC F. "Brief
Sketch of the Seminary of St.
Charles Borromeo," United
States Catholic Historical
Magazine, v. 1 (1887), 21-
27.   V 7
VALLETTE, MARC F. "The
Diocese of Brooklyn," United
States Catholic Historical
Magazine, v. 4 (1891-1892),
46-51.   V 8
VALLETTE, MARC F. (ed.)
"Father Fenwick's First Visits
to Ohio," United States Catholic
Historical Magazine, v. 4
(1891-1892), 220-222.   V 9
VALLETTE, MARC F. "John
Gilmary Shea," Catholic World,
v. 55 (1892), 55-62.   V 10
VALLETTE, MARC F. "The
Vicariate of Arizona Forty
Years Ago," American Catholic
Quarterly Review, v. 44
(1919), 616-633.   V 11
VAN DE VELDE, JAMES OLIVER.
"Aus Bishchof Van de Velde's
Tagebuch," Central Blatt and
Social Justice, v. 15 (1922),
313-314.   V 12
VAN DE VELDE, JAMES OLIVER.
"Autobiographical Sketch,"
Illinois Catholic Historical Re-
view, v. 9 (1926), 56-70.
          V 13
VAN DE VELDE, JAMES OLIVER.

"Letters of Father James O.
Vandevelde," Woodstock Letters,
v. 10 (1881), 53-65, 121-
132, 198-204.   V 14
VAN DER DONCKT, CYRIL.
"Founders of the Church in
Idaho," American Ecclesiastical Review, v. 32 (1905), 1-19,
123-134, 280-291.   V 15
VAN DER HEYDEN, J. "Monsig-
nor Adrian J. Croquet, Indian
Missionary," American Cath-
olic Historical Society of
Philadelphia Records, v. 16
(1905), 121-161, 268-295,
456-462; v. 17 (1906), 86-
110, 220-242, 267-288. V 16
VAN DER HEYDEN, J. "An
Oregon and Idaho Missionary,
Father L. Verhaag," Ameri-
can Catholic Historical Society
of Philadelphia Records, v.
31 (1920), 229-242.   V 17
VAN FLEET, J.A. Old and
New Mackinac. Ann Arbor.
Mich. Courier Steam Print-
ing House. 1870. iv, 176p.
          V 18
VAN MIERT, LOUIS (ed.)
"Some Historical Documents
Concerning the Mission of
Maryland, 1807-1820. With
Biographical Sketches and
Notes by Father Louis Van
Miert, S.J.," Woodstock
Letters, v. 30 (1901), 333-
352.   V 19
VAN QUICKENBORNE, CHARLES
F. "An unpublished Letter
dated Georgetown, 16 Januarii,
1818," Woodstock Letters, v.
30 (1901), 82-94.   V 20
VAN REE, L. "The Spokane
Indians. Sketch of the Work
of Our Fathers," Woodstock
Letters, v. 18 (1899), 354-
364.   V 21
VAN RENSSELAER, HENRY.
"Sketch of the Catholic Church
in Montana," American Cath-
olic Quarterly Review, v. 12
(1887), 492-507.   V 22
VAN WELL, SISTER MARY
STANISLAUS. The Educational

Aspects of the Missions in the Southwest. Milwaukee, Wis. Marquette University Press. 1942. 161p. V 23

"VANISHED BISHOPRIC OF OHIO. DOCUMENTS RELATIVE TO APPOINTMENT OF A BISHOP FOR SCIOTO COLONY," Catholic Historical Review, v. 2 (1917), 195-204. V 24

VARELA, FELIX. "Felix Varela (1788-1853)," American Catholic Historical Society of Philadelphia Records, v. 38 (1927), 15-46. V 25

VASTA, ACHILLES. "The Arapahoes and Their Amusements. Letter dated St. Stephen's Mission, Wyoming, April 26, 1892," Woodstock Letters, v. 21 (1892), 185-189. V 26

VASTA, ACHILLES. "Baptism among the Arapahoes. Letter dated St. Stephen's Mission, Fremont Co., Wyoming, February 8, 1893," Woodstock Letters, v. 22 (1893), 227-230. V 27

"VATER KUNDIG, EIN APOSTEL DER NACHSTENLIEBE," Central Blatt and Social Justice, v. 15 (1922), 161. V 28

VEALE, JAMES. History of the Catholic Church in Florida. V 29

VELARDE, LUIS. "Padre Luis Velarde's Relacion of Primeria Alta, 1716," New Mexico Historical Review, v. 6 (1931), 111-157. V 30

VELLE, LINUS J., LA. Some Materials for a United States History of Catholic Schools. MA thesis. Catholic University. 1927. 66p. V 31

VENEGAS, MIGUEL. Juan Maria de Salvatierra of the Company of Jesus. tr. by Marguerite Eyer Wilbur. Cleveland. Arthur H. Clarke Co. 1929. 350p. incl. front. (port.), plates, ports., maps, facsims. V 32

VENISSE, JOSEPH. "Lettre de M. Joseph Venisse, de la Congrégation de Picpus, à son frère. Californie 18 septembre, 1851," Annales de la Propagation de la Foi, v. 24 (1852), 405-415. V 33

VERE, AUBREY DE. Heroines of Charity. New York. Sadlier. n.d. 260p. illus. V 34

"VERGESSENER PIONIERPRIESTER DER DIOZESE ALTON-BELLEVILLE," Central Blatt and Social Justice, v. 11 (1918), 360. V 35
Brief biographical sketch of Father Arnold Prinkers, O.S.F., who died 1872.

"VEREINIGTEN STAATEN. NEW ORLEANS," Die Katholishen Missionen, v. 7 (1878), 86-88. V 36
A list of priests, Brothers, and Sisters who died in the care of the sick in the 1878 epidemic in New Orleans.

VÉROT, AUGUSTIN. "Lettre de Mgr. Vérot, Evêque de Savanah, Administrateur Apostolique de la Floride, aux Conseils Centraux de la Propagation de la Foi. Saint Augustin (Floride) 28 janvier, 1863," Annales de la Propagation de la Foi, v. 35 (1863), 290-292. V 37
An account of the death of Fr. Silvain Huming, martyr of charity during an epidemic at Key West.

VÉROT, AUGUSTIN. "Letter en date du 25 Mai," Annales de la Propagation de la Foi, v. 37 (1865), 395-405. V 38

VERRETTE, ADRIEN. Paroisse Saint Charles-Borromee, Dover, New Hampshire, 1893-1933. Manchester, N.H. Ateliers Typographiques de l'Avenir National. 1933. 383p. illus. V 39

VERWYST, CHRYSOSTOM. "The Chippewas, Their History

Religious Idea, Missionaries, and Needs," Salesianum, v. 6 (1910), 19-24. V 40
VERWYST, CHRYSOSTOM. Life and Labors of the Rt. Rev. Frederick Baraga, First Bishop of Marquette. New York. Benziger. 1900. xv, 476p. front., plates, ports., facsim. V 41
VERWYST, CHRYSOSTOM. Missionary Labors of Fathers Marquette, Menard, and Allouez in the Lake Superior Region. Milwaukee. Hoffmann. 1886. 262p. V 42
VERWYST, CHRYSOSTOM. "A Short Account of the Fond du Lac Indian Mission," Acta et Dicta, v. 3 (1914), 236-252. V 43
VILLANIS, FELIX. Anni Istorici Del Progresso Del Catholicismo Negli Stati Uniti Di America E Segnatamente Nella Diocese Di Nuova York. Roma. S.C. de Propaganda Fide. 1851. 62p. V 44
VINCENNES (DIOCESE) SYNOD, 1st, 1844. Synodus dioecesana vincennensis prima habita anno 1844. Louisville, B.J. Webb, 1844. 16p. V 45
VINCENNES (DIOCESE) SYNODS 1-5, 1844-1891. Acta et decreta quinque synodorum dioeceseos vincennopolitanae, 1844-1891. Indianapoli, Carlon & Hollenbeck, 1891. 18, 17, 12, 22, 10p. V 46
[VINCENT DE PAUL, FR.] "Some Account of What Befell Father Vincent de Paul, Religious of La Trappe, With Observations, Made by Him When in America...," American Catholic Historical Researches, v. 22 (1905), 360-367. port. V 47
VISCHER, EDWARD. Missions of Upper California. San Francisco. 1872. V 48
VISSANI, CHARLES A. (tr. and ed.) "Summary of the Cath-

olic Religion in the English Colonies in America," United States Catholic Historical Magazine, v. 2 (1888), 206-212. V 49
A report from Propaganda archives, apparently by the agent of the English Bishops at Rome prior to the appointment of Briand to Quebec in 1766.
VIVALDI, FRANÇOIS DE. "Extrait d'une Lettre du Chanoine de Vivaldi, Missionaire Apostolique, aux Conseils Centraux de l'Oeuvre de la Propagation de la Foi. Longue-Prairie le 5 juin, 1852," Annales de la Propagation de la Foi, v. 24 (1852), 437-443. V 50
An account of missionary work among the Winnebagos.
VIVAS, G. E. "Our Spanish-speaking U. S. Catholics," America, v. 91 (May 15, 1954), 187-188. V 51
[VIVER, .] "Jesuit Missions to the Illinois, 1750," American Catholic Historical Researches, v. 11 (1894), 177-181. V 52
VOELKER, FREDERIC E. "Cahokia's 250 Years of History," Missouri Historical Society Bulletin, v. 5 (1949), 333-336. V 53
VOGEL, CLAUDE L. The Capuchins in French Louisiana, (1722-1766). Washington. Catholic University. 1935. xxiv, 201p. illus., (map), facsim. V 54
VOGEL, CLAUDE. "The Capuchins in Lower Louisiana," Franciscan Educational Conference Annual Report, v. 18 (1936), 198-233. V 55
VOGEL, E. M. "The Ursulines in America," American Catholic Historical Society of Philadelphia Records, v. 1 (1884-1886), 214-243. V 56
VOGT, BERARD. Cradle of the Catholic Church in Northern

New Jersey. rev. ed. Echo Lake, N.J. 1935. 18p. plate. V 57

VOGT, BERARD. Souvenir of the Diamond Jubilee of St. Vincent de Paul's Church, Belfort, N.Y., 1919. no pl. no pub. 1919? V 58

VOGT, BERARD. Souvenir of the Silver Jubilee of St. John the Baptist Church, Vandalia, New York. 1925. no pl. no pub. 1925? V 59

VOIGT, GILBERT P. "Hawthorne and the Roman Catholic Church," New England Quarterly, v. 19 (1946), 394-395. V 60

VOLLENWIEDER, ROY W. "Springhill College: The Early Days," Alabama Review, v. 17 (1954), 127-135. V 61
Some interesting information on the life at this Jesuit school near Mobile, Alabama in the 1830s.

VOLLMAR, EDWARD R. The Catholic Church in America: an Historical Bibliography. New Brunswick, N.J. Scarecrow Press, 1956. xxvii, 354p. V 62

VOLLMAR, E.R. "The Colorado Bible Case," American Ecclesiastical Review, v. 138 (1958), 190-195. V 63

VOLLMAR, EDWARD R. "Donato Gasparri, New Mexico-Colorado Mission Founder," Mid-America, v. 9 (1938), 96-102. V 64

VOLLMAR, E. R. "First Jesuit School in New Mexico," New Mexico Historical Review, v. 27 (1952), 296-299. V 65

VOLLMAR, EDWARD R. History of the Jesuit Colleges of New Mexico and Colorado, 1867-1919. MA thesis. Saint Louis University. 1939. 168p. V 66

VOLLMAR, E.R. (ed. and tr.) "Missionary Life in Colorado," Mid-America, v. 35 (1953), 175-180. V 67
A letter of Fr. Rafael

Baldasarre dated Conejos, Colo., Nov. 12, 1874, describing the conditions of the mission in the San Luis Valley. First published in the Cartas de Poyanne.

VOLLMAR, E.R. "Proposed Jesuit Colleges at Conejos and Pueblo," Colorado Magazine, v. 30 (1953), 77-78. V 68
Two plans to open colleges in Colorado in the 1870's, both of which failed to materialize.

VOLLMAR, E.R. (tr. and ed), "Religious Processions and Penitente Activities at Conejos, 1874," Colorado Magazine, v. 31 (1954), 172-179. V 69
A letter to Salvador Personé dated Conejos, Colo., Aug., 1874, in which he describes the Corpus Christi Procession, funeral customs, and some of the activities of the penitentes.

VOLLMAR, E.R. "Writings in United States Church History," Historical Bulletin, v. 30 (1952), 213-218; v. 31 (1953), 198-205; v. 32 (1954), 210-222; v. 33 (1955), 216-224; v. 34 (1956), 222-228; Manuscripta, v. 1 (1957), 81-88. V 70
An annual bibliography of the writings on the history of the Catholic Church in the United States.

VOLLMAR, E.R. "Writings on the History of Religion in the United States," Manuscripta, v. 2 (1958), 74-83; v. 3 (1959), 90-97; v. 4 (1960), 90-97; v. 5 (1961), 78-87; v. 6 (1962). V 71
An annotated listing of writings on the history of the various denominations.

VORNHOLT, J.B. "Only Half a Century Since the Sodhouse Church," Central Blatt and

Social Justice, v. 24
(1931), 251.   V 72
VOSS, SISTER RITA. The His-
tory of the Providence Hospital
School of Nursing, Washington,
D. C. Washington. Catholic
University. 1940. vii, 42p.
incl. tables.   V 73

- W -

WADE, MASON. "The French
Parish and Survivance in Nine-
teenth Century New England,"
Catholic Historical Review, v.
36 (1950), 163-189.   W 1
WADE, MASON. "Some Aspects
of the Relation of French
Canada with the United States,"
Canadian Historical Associa-
tion Report, v. (1944), 16-
39.   W 2
WAGER, ELLIOT. "The Catholic
Messenger of Davenport," Ave
Maria, v. 83 (Feb. 18, 1956),
8-10, 20-24.   W 3
    A brief sketch of one of the
    best Catholic papers in the
    United States.
WAGGETT, GEORGE M. Oblates
of Mary Immaculate in the
Pacific Northwest, 1847-1878.
MA thesis. Catholic Univer-
sity. 1944. 104p.   W 4
WAGGETT, GEORGE M. "The
Oblates of Mary Immaculate in
the Pacific Northwest, of the
United States," Etudes Oblates,
v. 6 (Ottawa 1947), 7-88.
                                W 5
WAGGETT, GEORGE M. "The
Oblates of Mary Immaculate
in the Pacific Northwest,
1847-1878," American Catholic
Historical Society of Philadel-
phia Records, (1953), 72-93,
166-182, 199-212.   W 6
WAHLEN, JOSEPH J. "Henry J.
Spaunhorst. A Catholic
Leader," Central Blatt and
Social Justice, v. 22 (1930),
248-250, 284-286, 356-357.
                                W 7
WAHLGREN, ERIK. The Kensing-
ton Stone: A Mystery Solved.

Madison Wis. University of
Wisconsin, 1958. xii, 228p.
                                W 8
WAIBL, J.E. St. Roman's
Catholic Church, Jonesboro,
Ark., 1905. no pl. no pub.
1905?   W 9
WAIBLE, ALBERT H. "Venerable
John Nepomucene Neumann,"
American Catholic Historical
Society of Philadelphia Re-
cords, v. 52 (1941), 25-33.
                                W 10
WAKIN, EDWARD. "National
Center of Catholic Culture,"
Sign, v. 41 (Oct., 1961),
33-35. illus.   W 11
    Catholic University.
WAKIN, EDWARD. "St. John's:
Midwest Campus for the Whole
Man," Sign, v. 41 (1961), 32-
35, 79.   W 12
    St. John's University,
    Collegeville, Minnesota.
WALBURG, ANTHONY H. Ques-
tion of Nationality in Its Rela-
tion to the Catholic Church in
the United States. Cincinnati.
Herder. 1889. 62p. W 13
WALKER, FINTAN G. The
Catholic Church in the Meeting
of Two Frontiers. Southern
Illinois County (1763-1793).
Washington. Catholic Univer-
sity of America. 1935. xiv,
170p.   W 13a
WALKER, FINTAN G. "Some
Correspondence of an Eighteenth
Century Bishop with His Mis-
sionaries, 1767-1778," Catholic
Historical Review, v. 27
(1941), 186-209.   W 13b
    Letters exchanged between
    Fathers Maurin and Gibault
    and Bishop Briand of Quebec.
WALKER, JAMES BERNARD.
"The College Idea in the His-
tory of the Dominican Province
of St. Joseph," Catholic His-
torical Review, v. 23 (1938),
312-330.   W 14
WALKER, THERON J. First
Hundred Years of the Catholic
Church in Robertson County,

359

Tennessee. Centennial of St. Michael's Church, 1942. no pl. no pub. 1942? 24 p. illus., ports., ads. W 15

WALL, JOHN PATRICK. The Settlement and Progress of the Catholic Church in New Brunswick, N.J. New Brunswick, N.J. Catholic Record Press. 1907. 12p. illus. (incl. ports.) W 16

WALLACE, W.S. "Pierre-Georges Roy and the Bulletin des Recherches Historiques," Canadian Historical Review, v. 25 (1944), 29-32. W 17

WALSH, ELIZABETH P. "A Connecticut Yankee of Our Lady's Court," Catholic World, v. 169 (1949), 91-97. W 18
A short biographical sketch of William Thomas Walsh by his daughter.

WALSH, GERALD GROVELAND. "Church and State in the United States," United States Catholic Historical Society Records and Studies, v. 37 (1948), 3-12. W 19

WALSH, GRACE. The Catholic Church in Lynchburg, 1829-1936. Lynchburg, Va. Coleman and Bradley. 1936. 39p. W 20

WALSH, HENRY L. Hallowed Were the Gold Dust Trails. Santa Clara, Calif. University of Santa Clara Press. 1946. xii, 559p. incl. front., illus. (maps), plates, ports. W 21
An account of the pioneer priests of northern California in the decades following the discovery of gold in this region, now comprised in the Diocese of Sacramento. Popularly written, but based on a wide variety of archival material.

WALSH, JAMES J. The American Jesuits. New York. Macmillan. 1934. ix, 336p. W 22

WALSH, JAMES J. "Fr. Hudson of the Ave Maria," Catholic World, v. 139 (1934), 31-39.

W 23
WALSH, JAMES J. "The First Prayer in America," Columbia, v. 13 (Aug., 1933), 10, 20. W 24
A popular article on the Kensington rune stone.

WALSH, JAMES J. "John Gilmary Shea," American Catholic Quarterly Review, v. 38 (1913), 185-203. W 25

WALSH, JAMES J. "Murphy, America's Greatest Surgeon," Columbia, v. 3 (Feb., 1924), 5, 21. port. W 26

WALSH, JAMES J. Our American Cardinals. New York. Parish of St. Mary-of-the-Woods. St. Mary-of-the-Woods, Ind. Providence Press. 1937. 46p. illus., ports., facsims. W 27

WALSH, JAMES J. Our American Cardinals. New York. Appleton. 1926. xvii, 352p. ports. W 28

WALSH, JAMES J. (comp.) These Splendid Sisters. New York. J.H. Sears. 1927. 252p. W 29

WALSH, LAURENCE E. Father David S. Phelan versus the American Protective Association in Saint Louis. MA thesis. Saint Louis University. 1949. vii, 133p. W 30

WALSH, LOUIS S. Origin of the Catholic Church in Salem. Boston. 1890. 151p. W 31

WALSH, MARIE T. The Mission Bells of California. San Francisco. Herr Wagner. 1934, xii, 327p. front., plates, ports. W 32

WALSH, MARIE T. "The Mission of the Passes," Santa Ines. Los Angeles. Times-Mirror Press. 1930. 122p. plates, ports., plan, facsims. (incl. music). W 33

WALSH, M. KATHLEEN. "The Origins of Ecclesiastical Jurisdiction in New Spain (1492-1545)," American Catholic His-

torical Society of Philadel-
phia Records, v. 42 (1931),
101-154. W 34
WALSH, SISTER M. VERONA. The
Educational Contributions of
Archbishop Ireland. MA thesis.
University of Notre Dame. 1934.
127p. W 35
WALSH, MATTHEW J. "The
Beginning of Notre Dame," U-
nited States Catholic Historical
Society Records and Studies, v.
11 (1917), 15-30. W 36
WALSH, MATTHEW J. "Notre
Dame. Antecedents and Devel-
opment," Illinois Catholic His-
torical Review, v. 4 (1922),
270-277. W 37
WALSH, RICHARD. Father
Hecker and the Catholic Press.
MA thesis. Catholic Univer-
sity. 1945. 138p. W 38
WALSH, RICHARD H. "Père
Marquette--Padre Kino--Father
De Smet," American Catholic
Historical Society of Philadel-
phia Records, v. 57 (1946),
169-178. W 39
WALSH, RICHARD J. "The His-
tory of St. Teresa's Parish,
Philadelphia," American Cath-
olic Historical Society of Phil-
adelphia Records, v. 67 (1956),
105-119. W 40
WALSH, WILLIAM. Life of the
Most Rev. Peter Richard Ken-
rick, Archbishop of St. Louis.
St. Louis. Catholic Publishing
Co. 1891. 65p. plates, ports.
W 41
WALSH, WILLIAM JOSEPH. Anti-
Catholic Legislation in the
Colonies. MA thesis. Cath-
olic University. 1922. 37p.
W 42
WALTER, FRANK AND VIRGINIA
DONEGHY (comps.), Jesuit
Relations and Other Americana
in the Library of James F.
Bell. Minneapolis, Minn. Uni-
versity of Minnesota Press.
1950. xii, 419p. W 43
WALWORTH, CLARENCE A.
The Oxford Movement in A-

merica. New York. Catholic
Book Exchange. 1895. iv,
175p. front., illus. (incl.
ports.), plate. W 44
WALWORTH, C.A. "Reminis-
cences of Edgar P. Wadhams,
First Bishop of Ogdensburg,"
Catholic World, v. 55 (1892),
317-328, 482-495, 662-676,
826-844, v. 56 (1893), 104-
115, 241-255, 407-416.
W 45
WALWORTH, ELLEN H. The
Life and Times of Kateri
Tekakwitha. Buffalo. P. Paul
and Bro. 1891. xii, 314p.
front. (port.), plates, maps.
W 46
WALWORTH, ELLEN H. Life
and Sketches of Father Wal-
worth; With Notes and Letters.
Albany. B.J. Lyon. 1907.
vi, 370p. front., illus.
(facsim.), ports. W 47
WAMMERS, SISTER MARY
CHARLOTTE. Sisters of
Mercy in the Archdiocese of
Cincinnati. MA thesis. Catholic University. 1944. 122p.
W 48
WAND, AUGUSTINE C. "Pioneer
Bishop of the Prairies: John
Baptist Miége, S.J.," Bene-
dictine Review, v. 4 (1949),
5-11, 46-50. W 49
WAND, AUGUSTIN C. "Some
New Lights on Louis Hennepin,
Recollect," Historical Bulletin,
v. 51 (1953), 195-197. W 50
Incidental bits of informa-
tion that help for a clearer
understanding of the per-
sonality of Hennepin. The
material for the article
was taken from two letters
published originally in the
Revue d'Historique Ecclés-
iastique for 1950.
WARD, FELIX. The Passionists.
New York. Benziger. 1923.
478p. front., plate, ports.
W 51
WARD, JUSTINE. Thomas
Edward Shields: Biologist,

361

Psychologist, Educator. New York. Charles Scribner's Sons. 1947. xv, 309p. W 52

WARD, JUSTINE. William Pardow of the Company of Jesus. New York. Longmans. 1915. xiv, 274p. front., ports. W 53

WARD, LEO R. (ed.) The American Apostolate. Westminster, Md. Newman. 1951. 285p. W 54

A selection of essays by various experts on Catholic activity in social action.

WARD, LEO R. "American Bishops' 1952 Statement," Ave Maria, v. 77 (Jan. 17, 1953), 71-74. W 55

A general summary and evaluation.

WARD, LEO. Catholic Life in the United States of America. St. Louis. B. Herder. 1959. 263p. W 56

Accounts of contemporary lay movements.

WARD, LEO R. New Life in Catholic Schools. St. Louis. B. Herder. 1958. 198p. W 57

WARD, LOUIS B. Father Charles E. Coughlin; An Authorized Biography. Detroit, Mich. Tower Publications Inc. 1933. xv, 352p. front. (port), illus. (facsims), plan, maps. W 58

WARING, GEORGE. Catholic Chaplains in the World War. New York. Ordinariate, Army and Navy Chaplains. 1924. xxxv, 359p. incl. ports., diagr. W 59

WARNER, LOUIS H. Archbishop Lamy, An Epoch Maker. Santa Fe. Santa Fe New Mexican Publishing Co. 1936. 316p. W 60

WARTIME CORRESPONDENCE BETWEEN PRESIDENT ROOSE-VELT AND POPE PIUS XII. New York. Macmillan. 1947. xiii, 127p. W 61

"WAS DIE LEOPOLDINENSTIFTUNG

IN JAHRE 1837 FÜR ROCHES-TER THAT," Central Blatt and Social Justice, v. 18 (1925), 91-92. W 62

(WASHINGTON, D.C. GONZAGA COLLEGE). An Historical Sketch, 1821-1921. Washington. no pl. no pub. 1922. W 63

(WASHINGTON, D. C. ST. DOMINIC'S). "Centenary of the Foundation of Saint Dominic's Parish, Washington, D.C., 1852-1952," Dominicana, v. 37 (1952), 408-412. W 64

WATRIN, P.F. "Memoir on the Louisiana Missions by Father Francis Watrin, S.J.," American Catholic Historical Researches, v. 17 (1900), 89-93. W 65

WATTS, HENRY C. "Conewago, Our First Shrine to the Sacred Heart," United States Catholic Historical Society Records and Studies, v. 2 (1932), 138-169. W 66

WAUGH, EVELYN. "American Epoch in the Catholic Church," Life, v. 27 (1949), 134-138. W 67

WAUGH, J. N. 'Return of the Franciscans," America, v. 46 (1931), 62-63. W 68

WAUGH, MRS. JULIA. Castroville and Henry Castro. San Antonio. Standard Printing Co. 1934. 97p. front. (port.) W 69

WAWRO, DESIDERIUS. "Modern Franciscan Libraries," Franciscan Educational Conference Annual Report, v. 28 (1946), 395-416. W 70

WAYMAN, DOROTHY G. Cardinal O'Connell of Boston. New York. Farrar, Strauss. 1955. vii, 307p. W 71

WEADOCK, THOMAS A.E. "A Catholic Priest in Congress," United States Catholic Historical Society Records and Studies, v. 4 (1891-1892), 11-30. W 72

An account of Fr. Richard's political activity in the United States House of Representatives as an elected delegate from Michigan in 1813.

WEADOCK, THOMAS A.E. "Père Marquette, The Missionary Explorer," United States Catholic Historical Magazine, v. 4 (1891-1892), 371-395. W 73

WEBB, B. J. "Catholicity in Kentucky--The Elder Family of Maryland and Kentucky," American Catholic Quarterly Review, v. 5 (1880), 653-665. W 74

WEBB, B.J. "Catholicity in Kentucky--Grace Newton Simpson," American Catholic Quarterly Review, v. 6 (1881), 609-616. W 75

WEBB, BENJAMIN J. The Centenary of Catholicity in Kentucky. Louisville. CA Rogers. 1884. v, 594p. front., ports. W 76

WEBB, EDITH. "Agriculture in the Days of the Early California Padres," Americas, v. 4 (1948), 325-344. W 77

WEBB, EDITH. "Pigments Used by the Mission Indians of California," Americas, v. 2 (1945), 137-150. W 78

WEBER, FRANCIS J. A Historical Sketch of Pioneer Catholicism in the Californias, Missions and Missionaries. Van Nuys, California Historical Publications. 1961. 56p. W 79

WEBER, N.A. "The Rise of the National Catholic Churches in the United States," Catholic Historical Review, v. 1 (1916), 422-434. W 80
Mostly concerned with early German parishes.

WEBER, RALPH E. The Life of Reverend John A. Zahm, C.S.C. Ph.D. thesis. University of Notre Dame. 1956. 492p. maps. W 81

WEBER, WILLIAM. St. John the

Baptist's Parish Jubilee. Eighty-fifth Anniversary of the Parish, and Twenty-fifth Anniversary of the Church. Johnsburg, Illinois, 1842-1927, 1902-1927. no pl. no pub. 1927? 32p. plates, ports. W 82

WEBSTER, MOTHER ANNE KATHRYN. The Correspondence Between Bishop Joseph Rosati and Blessed Philippine Duchesne. MA thesis. Saint Louis University. 1950. iv, 414p. W 83

WEHRLE, VINCENT. "Parishes in a Northwestern Diocese," American Ecclesiastical Review, v. 63 (1920), 388-391. W 84

WEIBEL, GEORGE F. "Beginning and Progress of Catholicity in Spokane," Gonzaga Magazine, v. 3 (1911-1912), 65-71, 112-120, 167-175, 231-239, 288-294, 345-354, 397-406, 448-457, 518-528. W 85

WEIBEL, GEORGE. "Father Cataldo," Gonzaga Quarterly (Gonzaga Univ.), v. 16 (1928), 74-109. W 86

WEIBEL, GEORGE F. "Fifty Years of Peaceful Conquest," Gonzaga Magazine, v. 5 (1913-1914), 18-25, 70-78, 125-133, 179-187, 232-241, 293-303, 344-356, 407-418, 455-464, 520-532. W 87

WEIBEL, J. E. Vierzig Jahre Missionar in Arkansas. Lucerne. Raber. 1927. 320p. W 88

WEIDLE, CATHERINE E. The Parish of Cahokia, Illinois, 1699-1949. MA thesis. Saint Louis University. 1949. vi, 139p. W 89

WEIGEL, GUSTAVE. "American Catholic Intellectualism--a Theologian's Reflections," Review of Politics, v. 19 (1957), 275-307. W 90
The theologian should get closer to reality.

WEISENHORN, C.M. "A Missionary Trip in South Dakota. Letter dated St. Louis University," Woodstock Letters, v. 49 (1920), 151-163.　　　　W 91

WEISER, FRANZ X. Ein Apostel der Neuen Welt. Wien. Verlag "Fahre Mariens," 1937. 167p.
　　　　W 92

WEISER, FRANZ. Der Gesandte des Grossen Geistes. Wien. Habbel. 1936.　　　W 93
Popular biography of De Smet.

WEISS, ARTHUR A. "Jesuit Mission Years in New York State, 1654-1879," Woodstock Letters, v. 75 (1946), 7-25, 124-139.
　　　　W 94

WEITZMAN, LOUIS G. 100 Years of Catholic Charities in the District of Columbia. Washington. Catholic University. 1931. vii, 161p.　　W 95

WELD, LAENAS GIFFORD. "Joliet and Marquette in Iowa," Iowa Journal of History and Politics, v. 1 (1930), 3-16.　　W 96

WELFLE, FREDERICK E. "Menendez and the Massacre at Fort Caroline," Historical Bulletin, v. 8 (1929), 1-3, 14.　　　　W 97

WELTY, FREDERICK (ed.) "A Bad Boy at 'The Mountain,' " American Catholic Historical Society of Philadelphia Records, v. 59 (1948), 45-62.
　　　　W 98
Reminiscences of John W. McFallen, late of Holmesburg, Pa., concerning his school days at Mt. St. Mary's College, Emmitsburg, Maryland.

WELTY, FREDERICK. "A Review and a Challenge," American Catholic Historical Society of Philadelphia Records, v. 60 (1949), 53-55.　　W 99
A review of Dieter Cunz's The Maryland Germans.

WENINGER, FRANCIS XAVIER. "Account of the Miracles Admitted by the Congregation

of Rites for the Canonization of St. Peter Claver," Woodstock Letters, v. 17 (1888), 106-109.　　W 100

WENINGER, FRANCIS XAVIER. Erinnerungen aus meinen Leben in Europa und Amerika durch achtzig jahre, 1805-1885. Columbus, Ohio. J.J. Jessing. 1886. 2v.　W 101

WENINGER, FRANCIS XAVIER. "Father Weninger's Testimony Regarding the Intercession of St. Peter Claver," Central Blatt and Social Justice, v. 19 (1926), 199-200.　W 102

WENINGER, FRANCIS XAVIER. "Father Weninger on the Pacific Coast," Woodstock Letters, v. 1 (1872), 181-188, v. 2 (1873), 31-41, 142-146, 218-230, v. 3 (1874), 112-126, 200.　　　W 103

WENINGER, FRANCIS XAVIER. "Fr. Weninger's Trip from Oregon to San Francisco in 1869," Social Justice Review, v. 36 (1943), 129.　　W 104

WENINGER, FRANCIS XAVIER. "Relation du R.P. Weninger de la Compagnie de Jésus sur les Missions qu'il a données dans les Etats-Unis," Annales de la Propagation de la Foi, v. 33 (1861), 458-470.
　　　　W 105

[WESTCOTT, THOMPSON]. "Catholic Historical Notes Relating to Philadelphia, 1826-1833," American Catholic Historical Researches, v. 13 (1896), 135-145.　　　W 106

WESTCOTT, THOMPSON. "Memoir of Very Rev. Michael Hurley, D.D., O.S.A.," American Catholic Historical Society of Philadelphia Records, v. 1 (1884-1886), 165-212.　　　　W 107

WESTERMEIER, THERESE S. "Saint Walburga in America," The American German Review, v. 18 (1952), 19, 31. W 108
An account of the foundation

and progress of the convent farm conducted by the German refugee nuns near Boulder, Colorado.

WESTERN JESUIT, v. (1949), December. This issue is devoted to the Centennial of the Jesuits in California. W 109

WHALEN, WALTER WILLIAM. Catholic Church in Civil War Diplomacy. MA thesis. Xavier University (Cincinnati). 1951. 99p. W 110

WHALEN, WILLIS L. The Pioneer Period of the Catholic Church in Portland, Oregon, 1851-1881. MA thesis. Portland University. 1950. iv, 155p. W 111

WHALEN, W. L. "Stick from Above: Father Blanchet, the Indians in the Oregon Country and the Catholic Ladder," Homiletic and Pastoral Review, v. 44 (1946), 427-431. W 112

WHEELER, FERDINAND C. "Scranton University. The Beginnings and First Year," Woodstock Letters, v. 73 (1944), 106-120. W 113

WHEELING (DIOCESE) SYNOD, 1873. Statuta a Richardo Vinc. Whelan [ep.] in synodo dioecesana, in cathedrali, 28 ac 29 Oct., an. 1873, habita, lata et promulgata. Wheeling, J.F. Carroll, 1873. xiiip. W 114

WHEELING (DIOCESE) SYNOD, 4th, 1882. Synodus dioecesana wheelingensis quarta, quae antecedentium etiam complectitur constitutiones; diebus 9 et 10 Aug., 1882 habita a Joanna Joseph Kain [ep.] Wheelingii, J.F. Carroll, 1882. 49, 22p. 1 1. W 115

WHEELING (DIOCESE) SYNOD, 5th, 1886. Synodus dioecesana wheelingensis quinta. Diebus 7 et 8 Aug. A.D. 1888 habita a Joanne Josepho Kain [ep.] Wheelingii, J.F. Carroll, 1888.

16p., 1 1. W 116

[WHELAN, CHARLES]. "Early Church in Delaware--Trials of a Pastor," American Catholic Historical Researches, v. 26 (1911), 193-196. W 117

WHITE, ANDREW. "An Account of the Colony of the Lord Baron of Baltimore, 1633," in Narratives of Early Maryland, 1633-1684. New York. 1910. 1-10. W 118

WHITE, ANDREW. "A Brief Relation of the Voyage into Maryland," in Narratives of Early Maryland, 1633-1684. New York. 1910. 25-45. W 119

WHITE, ANDREW. Relatio Itineris in Marylandiam. Baltimore. Maryland Historical Society. 1874. W 120

WHITE, ANDREW. "A Relation of the Colony of the Lord Baron of Baltimore in Maryland, near Virginia; a Narrative of the Voyage to Maryland," Woodstock Letters, v. 1 (1872), 12-24, 71-80, 145-155; v. 2 (1873), 1-13. W 121

WHITE, CHARLES I. Mother Seton, Mother of Many Daughters. Garden City, N. Y. Doubleday and Co. 1949. xx, 300p. W 122

WHITE, JAMES ADDISON. The Era of Good Intentions--a Survey of American Catholics Writing between the Years 1880 and 1915. Ph.D. thesis. University of Notre Dame. 1957. W 123

WHITE, JAMES A. The Founding of Cliff Haven. Early Years of the Catholic Summer School of America. New York. United States Catholic Historical Society. 1950. x, 105p. W 124

WHITE, SISTER MARY EMMANUEL. Archbishop Peter Richard Kenrick and the Civil War. MA thesis. Saint Louis

University. 1948. iii, 114p.
W 125

WHITE, SISTER M. TERESA.
"Reminiscences," American
Catholic Historical Society of
Philadelphia Records, v. 12
(1901), 61-66.   W 126

[WHITFIELD, JAMES.] "Archbishop Whitfield's Report to
the Propaganda," American
Catholic Historical Researches,
v. 19 (1902), 107.   W 127

WHITMAN, JOHN H.A. The
Influence of Know-Nothingism in
the Pivotal States in 1860.
MA thesis. University of Notre
Dame. 1927. 38p.   W 128

WIDMAN, S. "Das ehemalige
Collegium Americanum zu
Münster in Westfalen," Central
Blatt and Social Justice, v. 17
(1924), 89-97.   W 129

WIDMAN, C.M. "Grand Coteau
College in War Times, 1860-
1866," Woodstock Letters, v.
30 (1901), 34-49.   W 130

WIDMAN, C.M. "Outlines of His-
tory--St. Charles' Church,
Grand Coteau, La.," American
Catholic Historical Society
of Philadelphia Records, v. 9
(1898), 343-351.   W 131

WIDMAN, C.M. "Springhill Col-
lege (1830-1898)," Woodstock
Letters, v. 27 (1898), 267-276.
W 132

"WIE DER EHRW. JOH. NEP.
NEUMANN NACH AMERICA
KAM," Central Blatt and Social
Justice, v. 17 (1924), 91-92,
107, 198-200, 266-268. W 133

WIECHMANN, . Diamond Jubilee
of St. Wendelin's Parish,
Luxemburg, Minnesota, 1859-
1934. no pl. no pub. 1934.
42p. plates (ports.)   W 134

WIGGER, PETER. History of
Holy Cross Parish. St. Louis.
Printed by Hlas Printing Co.
1936.   W 135

WIGHT, WILLARD E. "The Bishop
of Natchez and the Confederate
Chaplaincy," Mid-America, v.
39 (1957), 67-72.   W 136

A study of William Henry
Elder's efforts to supply
Catholic chaplains for the
Confederacy.

WIGHT, WILLARD E. "Bishop
Verot and the Civil War,"
Catholic Historical Review, v.
47 (1961), 153-163.   W 137

WIGHT, WILLARD E. ed. "Letters from the Diocese of Little
Rock, 1861-1865," Arkansas
Historical Quarterly, v. 18
(1959), 366-374.   W 138
Helps to provide understanding of Catholic attitudes during the Civil War.

WIGHT, WILLARD E. (ed.)
"Some War Letters of the
Bishop of Mobile, 1861-1865,"
Mid-America, v. 43 (1961),
61-68.   W 139
John Quinlan 2d Bishop of
Mobile.

WIGHT, WILLARD E. "Some
Wartime Letters of Bishop
Lynch (1861-1864)," Catholic
Historical Review, v. 43
(1957), 20-37.   W 140
Presents an interesting pic-
ture of this great Catholic
friend of the Confederacy.

WIGHT, WILLARD E., ed. "War
Letters of the Bishop of
Richmond (John McGill),"
Virginia Magazine of History
and Biography, v. 67 (1959),
259-270.   W 141
A Catholic Bishop views the
war.

WILBERFORCE, R. "Church in
America; an English View,"
Catholic Mind, v. 29 (1931),
555-561.   W 142

WILKEN, ROBERT L. Anselm
Weber, O.F.M. Missionary
to the Navaho, 1898-1921.
Milwaukee. Bruce. 1955.
xiv, 255p.   W 143

WILKEN, ROBERT (comp.)
Crosses on the Delta. Buras,
La. Compiler. 1940. 64p.
plates, maps.   W 144

WILKEN, ROBERT. A Historical
Sketch of the Holy Family

Church and Parish, Oldenburg,
Indiana, 1837-1937. Oldenburg,
Ind. no pub. 1937. W 145

WILL, ALLEN SINCLAIR. "America's Debt to Cardinal Gibbons,"
Columbia, v. 2 (July, 1923),
17, 23. W 146

WILL, ALLEN SINCLAIR. Life
of Cardinal Gibbons, Archbishop
of Baltimore. New York. E.
P. Dutton Co. 1922. xiii, 414p.
front., plates, ports., facsim.
W 147

WILLCOX, JOSEPH. "Biography of
Rev. Patrick Kenny, 1763-1840,"
American Catholic Historical
Society of Philadelphia Records,
v. 7 (1896), 27-79. W 147a

WILLGING, EUGENE. "The
Catholic College and University Library: A Second Survey," Catholic Educational
Review, v. 51 (Nov., 1953),
577-591. W 148
A continuation of the survey
first published in the C.E.
R. April, 1951.

WILLGING, EUGENE P. "The
Catholic Directories," Catholic
Historical Review, v. 20
(1934), 281-284. W 149
Lists the biographical
sketches in the Directories
1843-1867.

WILLGING, EUGENE, AND HERTA
HATSFIELD. "Catholic Serials
in the Nineteenth Century in
the United States," American
Catholic Historical Society of
Philadelphia, v. 65 (1954),
158-175; v. 66 (1955), 156-
173, 222-238; v. 67 (1956),
31-50, 120-132; v. 68 (1957),
106-120; v. 69 (1958), 98-118;
v. 70 (1959), 18-31; v. 71
(1960), 40-58, 109-120.
W 150
A bibliographical survey and
union list.

WILLGING, EUGENE P. Index to
American Catholic Pamphlets.
St. Paul, Minn. Catholic Library Service. 1937; 1939-
1942; 1942-1946; 1946-1948;

1948-1950. variant title,
variant publisher. W 151
A classified index containing items of historical use.
Since 1946 entitled: Index
to Catholic Pamphlets in the
English Language.

WILLIAM, SISTER CHARLES A.
The Know-Nothing Party in
Missouri, 1855-1860. MA
thesis. Catholic University.
1945. 71p. W 152

WILLIAMS, MARGARET. A
Second Sowing. The Life of
Mary Aloysia Hardey. New
York. Sheed and Ward. 1942.
495p. illus., port. W 153

WILLIAMS, MICHAEL. American
Catholics in the War. New
York. Macmillan. 1921. x,
467p. W 154
A record of the activities
of Catholics in World War I.
Contains some valuable
material on the early history of the National Catholic
Welfare Conference.

WILLIAMS, MICHAEL. Catholicism and the Modern Mind.
New York. L. MacVeagh.
Dial Press. 1928. 348p.
W 155

WILLIAMS, MICHAEL. "A
Powerhouse of Prayer," Columbia, v. 7 (June, 1928), 20-
22, 40. illus. W 156
A popular article on Gethsemani, Kentucky.

WILLIAMS, MICHAEL. The Present Position of Catholics in
the United States. New York.
Calvert. 1928. 47p. W 157

WILLIAMS, MICHAEL. The
Shadow of the Pope. New York.
McGraw-Hill Book Co. 1932.
xi, 329p. front., illus.,
plates, facsims. W 158
Of value for the study of
anti-Catholicism, especially
in relation to the presidential campaign of 1928 and
the Ku Klux Klan.

WILLINGER, ALOYSIUS. "Diocese in the Sun," Extension,

A biographical sketch of one of the most important figures in the promotion of higher education for nuns.

WITTE, CYRIL MARCEL. A History of St. Mary's Industrial School for Boys of the City of Baltimore, 1866-1950. Ph.D. thesis. University of Notre Dame. 1955. 306, xxxiiip. W 178

WITTE, RAYMOND P. Twenty-five Years of Crusading: a History of the National Catholic Rural Life Conference. Ph.D. dissertation. Saint Louis University. 1946. vi, 385p. W 179

WITTE, RAYMOND PHILIP.Twenty-five Years of Crusading: a History of the National Catholic Rural Life Conference. Des Moines, Iowa. National Catholic Rural Life Conference. 1948. xviii, 274p. W 180

WITTKE, CARL. "The Catholic Historical Review--Forty Years," Catholic Historical Review, v. 42 (1956), 1-14. W 181

WITTKE, CARL We Who Built America. The Saga of the Immigrant. New York. Prentice Hall, Inc. 1939. xviii, 547p. W 182

WLODKOWSKI, SISTER M. SYMPHOROSE. Political Nativism in Cleveland, Ohio to the Civil War. MA thesis. Catholic University. 1938. 65p. W 183

WOBIDO, LEO P. "Father Daniel Lord," Woodstock Letters, v. 84 (1955), 261-270. port. W 184

Obituary of the Priest of the Sodality by an intimate friend and fellow laborer.

WOLANIN, ALPHONSE S. Polonica in English. Annotated Catalogue of the Archives and Museum of the Polish Roman Catholic Union. Chicago. Polish Roman Catholic Union of America. 1945.

186p. W 185

WOLANIN, ALPHONSE S. "Some Recent Publications Relative to Polish-American History," Polish-American Studies, v. 2 (1945), 118-120; v. 3 (1946), 110-113; v. 4 (1947), 41-44, 106-109; v. 5 (1948), 37-41. W 186

WOLF, SISTER MARY MILDRED. The Pioneer Sisterhoods of the Pacific Northwest. MA thesis. Portland University. 1945. 92p. W 187

WOLFF, BERNICE LOUISE. The Sodality Movement in the United States, 1926-1936. MA thesis. Saint Louis University. 1936. 175p. W 188

WOLFF, GEORGE D. "Our Parochial School System--The Progress It has Made and Is Making," American Catholic Quarterly Review, v. 17 (1892), 867-872. W 189

WOOD, THOMAS O. The Catholic Attitude toward the Social Settlement Movement, 1886-1914. MA thesis. University of Notre Dame. 1959. W 190

WOODS, HENRY. "California. Letter dated Santa Clara College, Santa Clara, 15th July, 1885," Woodstock Letters, v. 14 (1885), 371-374. W 191

WOODS, HENRY. "California Mission of the Soc. of Jesus. Founded by the Province of Turin, Italy," Woodstock Letters, v. 13 (1884), 157-164. W 192

WOODS, WILL. "Cardinalatial See of the West," Ave Maria, v. 77 (Feb. 7, 1953), 167-171. W 193

A description of the Diocese of Los Angeles.

WOTTLE, CLEMENTIN. "The Church and the Hopi Indians," Provincial Chronicles (Cincinnati), 321-330. port. of Wottle. W 194

"WOUNDED KNEE, EIN EHRENTAG FÜR ZWEI KATHOLISCHE MIS-

SIONÄRE," Central Blatt and Social Justice, v. 10 (1917), 265-266. W 195

WRIGHT, JOHN J. "The Church and American Society," Catholic Mind, v. 58 (1960), 484-492. W 196
A Catholic bishop describes American Catholicism.

WRIGHT, JOHN L. "Father Michael's Boys' Town," Ave Maria, v. 86 (Oct. 12, 1957), 13-17, illus. W 197
For the Colored, near Montgomery, Alabama.

WRIGHT, LOUIS B. Religion and Empire. The Alliance between Piety and Commerce in English Expansion, 1558-1625. Chapel Hill. Univ. of North Carolina Press. 1943. ix, 190p.
W 198

WRIGHT, SISTER MARY KATHLEEN. Fifty Years of the Sisters of Mercy in San Francisco, 1904-1954. MA thesis. Catholic University. 1955.
W 199

WRIGHT, RALPH. "Something New for Historians. Letters of the Notre Dame Archives Reveal New Facts About Catholic America," Catholic Educational Review, v. 47 (1949), 380-383. W 200

WRIGHT, RALPH B. California Missions. Los Angeles. Sterling Press. 1950. 96p. illus., ports., map. W 201

WUEST, JOHN B. "Archbishop James F. Wood of Philadelphia and the Bavarian Preface to the History of Our Province," Provincial Chronicle (St. John Baptist Province, O.F.M.), v. 6 (1934), 108-115. W 202

WUEST, JOHN B. "Father Francis Huber. First Franciscan in Cincinnati," Provincial Chronicle (St. John Baptist Province, O.F.M.), v. 12 (1940), 3-16, 130-135.
W 203

WUEST, JOHN B. One Hundred

Years of St. Boniface Parish, Louisville, Kentucky. Louisville. Geo. G. Fetter Co. 1937. 157p. illus. (incl. ports.) W 204

WUEST, JOSEPH (comp.) History of the Redemptorists at Annapolis, Md., from 1853-1903, with a Short History of the Preceding Hundred and Fifty Years of Catholicity in the Capital of Maryland. Ilchester, Md. College Press. 1904. xxiii, 253p. plates, ports. W 205

WUEST, JOSEPH. "Register of the Clergy Laboring in the Archdiocese of New York from Early Missionary Times," United States Catholic Historical Society Records and Studies, v. 11 (1917), 98-112. W 206

WURZEL, ARNOLD A. Fray Francisco Hidalgo, a Pioneer Missionary in Texas. MA thesis. Loyola University. Chicago. 1954. 126p.
W 207

WUTHENAU, A. Von. "Spanish Military Chapels in Santa Fe and the Records of Our Lady of Light," New Mexico Historical Review, v. 10 (1935), 175-194. W 208

WYLLYS, RUFUS KING. "Kino of Primeria Alta," Arizona Historical Review, v. 5 (1932), 5-32, 95-134, 205-225, 308, 326. W 209

WYLLYS, RUFUS KING (tr. and ed.). "Padre Luis Velarde's Relacion of Primeria Alta, 1716," New Mexico Historical Review, v. 6 (1931), 111-157.
W 210

WYLLYS, RUFUS KING. "Short Bibliography of Works in English on the Spanish Missions of the Southwest," Arizona Historical Review, v. 4 (1932), 58-61. W 211

WYLLYS, RUFUS KING. "Spanish Missions of the Southwest,"

Arizona Historical Review, v. 6 (1935), 27-37. W 212

WYNNE, JOHN J. "A Great American Name," Columbia, v. 1 (May, 1922), 11. W 213 John Carroll.

WYNNE, JOHN J. "Jesuit Martyrs of America," Columbia, v. 4 (Feb., 1925), 16. W 214

WYNNE, JOHN J. The Jesuit Martyrs of North America. New York. Universal Knowledge Foundation. 1925. xi, 246p. ports., maps. W 215

WYNNE, JOHN J. "The Lily of the Mohawks," Columbia, v. 2 (July, 1923), 14, 19, 26, port. W 216

WYNNE, JOHN J. "Mohawk Martyr Missionaries," New York History, v. 13 (1932), 59-74. W 217

- X -

XAVIER, SISTER MARY. Father Jaillet, Saddlebag Priest of the Nueces. Austin, Texas. Von Boeckmann-Johnes Co. 1949. X 1

- Y -

YANITELLI, VICTOR R. "Gerald Groveland Walsh: in Appreciation," Thought, v. 27 (1952), 341-349. Y 1
Father Walsh was editor of Thought during the first ten years of its university existence.

YAUCS, LOUIS H. The History of Fifty Years, 1868-1918. no pl. no pub. unpaged. n.d. Y 2

YEAGER, SISTER M. HILDE-GARDE. The Life of James Roosevelt Bayley, First Bishop of Newark and Eighth Archbishop of Baltimore. Washington. Catholic University. 1947. xi, 512p. Y 3

YEAKEL, SISTER MARY AGNES. The Nineteenth Century Educational Contribution of the

Sisters of Charity of Saint Vincent de Paul in Virginia. Baltimore. Johns Hopkins Press. 1939. 115p. Y 4

YEALY, FRANCIS J. Sainte Genevieve: The Story of Missouri's Oldest Settlement. St. Genevieve, Mo. Bi-centennial Historical Committee. 1935. ii, 150p. front., illus. (facsims), plates, ports., map. Y 5

YOUNG, CECILIA MARY. "Annals of the Society for the Propagation of the Faith," Illinois Catholic Historical Review, v. 1 (1918), 214-224. Y 6
A selection of documents relating to the early Illinois Church, published in the Annals 1818-

YOUNG, SISTER LUCY MARIE. The Literary Aspects of the Letters, Journals and Sketches of Father De Smet, S.J. MA thesis. University of Notre Dame, 1933. 116p. Y 7

YZENDOORN, REGINALD. History of the Catholic Mission in the Hawaiian Islands. Honolulu Star Bulletin. 1937. 254p. Y 8

YZERMANS, VINCENT A. "Blessed Pius X and the United States," American Catholic Historical Society of Philadelphia Records, v. 65 (1954), 3-10. Y 9

YZERMANS, VINCENT A. "Church of Mary in the United States," American Ecclesiastical Review, v. 132 (1955), 169-180. Y 10
An interesting study of the Churches dedicated under the titles of Mary, gives numbers by dioceses and number by title.

- Z -

Z. "TEXAS, SEQUIN. LETTER,"

Woodstock Letters, v. 13 (1884), 125-129. Z 1

ZABEL, ORVILLE H. God and Caesar in Nebraska. Lincoln, University of Nebraska. 1955. x, 198p. Z 2
A study of the legal relationship of Church and State in this western state 1854-1954.

ZACHAREWICZ, SISTER MARY MISAELA. "Attitude of the Catholic Press toward the League of Nations," American Catholic Historical Society of Philadelphia Records, v. 67 (1956), 3-30, 88-104. Z 3

ZAHN, GORDON C. "The Content of Protestant Tensions: Fears of Catholic Aims and Methods," American Catholic Sociological Review, v. 18 (1957), 205-212. Z 4

ZAISER, ARTHUR J. Diamond Jubilee, 1840-1915. St. Joseph's Church, Fort Madison, Iowa. Techny, Ill. Mission Press. 1915. 126p. plates. Z 5

ZAND, HELEN STANKIEWICA. "Polish Folkways in America," Polish-American Studies, v. 6 (1949), 33-41. Z 6

ZAPLOTNIK, J. L. (ed.) "Documents. Rev. Lawrence Lautisher in Minnesota," Acta et Dicta, v. 6 (1934), 258-287. Z 7

ZAPLOTNIK, J.L. 'Rev. George Gostenchnik, a Pioneer Missionary," American Catholic Historical Society of Philadelphia Records, v. 53 (1942), 33. Z 8

ZAPLOTNIK, J. L. "The Very Rev. John Ev. Mosetizh, Vicar General of Pittsburgh, Pa.," Catholic Historical Review, v. 2 (1917), 202-209. Z 9

ZARDETTE. "Maryland, die Wiege des Katholizismus und der Freiheit Nord-Amerikas," Frankfurter Zeitgemässe

Broschüren. Neue Folge. Band II (Frankfurt) pp. 111-141. Z 10

ZAWART, ANSCAR. The Capuchins, 1528-1928. Washington. Capuchin College. 1928. Z 11

ZENS, SISTER M. SERENA. "The Educational Work of the Catholic Church among the Indians of South Dakota from the Beginning to 1935," South Dakota Historical Collections, v. 20 (1940), 299-356. Z 12

ZEPHYRIN [ENGELHARDT?]. "Franciscan School at Santa Fe, New Mexico, in 1717," American Catholic Historical Researches, v. 20 (1903), 35-37. Z 13

ZERWEKH, SISTER EDWARD MARY. John Baptist Salpointe, Historian of the Kingdom, First Vicar Apostolic of Arizona, 1868-1884, Second Archbishop of Santa Fe, 1885-1894. MA thesis. University of San Francisco. 1956. 114p. Z 14

ZIMMER, PETER. Leben und Wirken des hochw. P. Franz Seelos. N.Y. Benziger. 1887. n.p. Z 15

ZIMMERMANN, ATHANSIUS. Die Universitaten in den Vereinigten Staaten Amerikas. Freiburg in Breisgau. Herder. 1896. viii, 116p. Z 16

ZIMPFER, GEORGE. The History of the Roman Catholic Parish of SS. Peter and Paul. Williamsville, N.Y., 1936. no pl. no pub. 1936? 64p. plates, ports., facsim. Z 17

ZIRBES, LOUIS N. "The Diocesan Rural Life Bureau," Salesianum, v. 31 (1936), 116-121. Z 18

ZOLLMANN, CARL. American Church Law. 2d ed. St. Paul. West Publishing Co. 1933. xv, 675p. Z 19

ZOOK, MARY. "Lay Teachers in Catholic Schools," Ave Maria,

v. 184 (Oct., 27, 1956), 16-19. Z 20

ZUBILLAGA, FELIX. La Florida, la Mission Jesuitica (1566-1572), y La Colonizacion Española. Rome. Biblioteca Instituti Historica S.J. 1941. xiv, 473p. Z 21

ZUBILLAGA, FELIX (ed.) Monumenta Antiquae Floridae (1566-1572). Roma. Monumenta Historical Soc. Jesu. 1946. xxxvi, 692p. Z 22

ZÜRICHER, FRANZ. Katholische Studien. II Heft. Die Benediktiner in America. Würzburg. Leo Woerl'sche. 1875. 37p. Z 23

ZUGMUNTA, SISTER M. "A Half-Century on American Soil," Polish-American Studies, v. 2 (1945), 24-28. Z 24

ZUR ERRINNERUNG AN DAS SILBER JUBILÄUM DER AMERIKA, 1897. no pl. no pub. 1897? 135, 22p. illus. Z 25

"ZUR GESCHICHTE DER ST. JOHANNES GEMEINDE ZU JOHNSBURG, ILL.," Central Blatt and Social Justice, v. 16 (1923), 53-54. Z 26

ZURBONSEN, A. "Catholic Bishops of the Diocese of Alton, Ill.," Illinois Historical Society Journal, v. 10 (1917), 127-137. Z 27

ZURBONSEN, A. "Fifty Years in American Hospital Service," Illinois Catholic Historical Review, v. 8 (1925), 143-154, 275-280; v. 9 (1926), 71-83, (1927), 277-288. variant title. Z 28
The story of the Hospital Sisters of St. Francis of Springfield, Illinois.

ZURBONSEN, A. Golden Jubilee, St. Mary's Congregation of Quincy, Illinois, 1917. no pl. no pub. 1917? 48p. plates, ports. Z 29

ZURBONSEN, A. In Memoriam-- Clerical Beadroll of the Dio-

cese of Alton. Quincy. Jost and Kiefer. 1918. 152p. incl. illus. (ports.) Z 30

ZWIERLEIN, FREDERICK. "The American College in Rome, Criticism and Supplement," Social Justice Review, v. 50 (1957), 164-167, 200-206. Z 31

ZWIERLEIN, FREDERICK J. "Americanism, Some Roots of Controversy," Social Justice Review, v. 52 (1959), 47-49. Z 32

ZWIERLEIN, FREDERICK J. "Bishop McQuaid of Rochester," Dublin Review, v. 165 (1919), 261-289. Z 33

ZWIERLEIN, FREDERICK J. "Catholic Beginnings in the Diocese of Rochester," Catholic Historical Review, v. 1 (1915), 282-298. Z 34

ZWIERLEIN, FREDERICK J. "The Catholic Contribution to Liberty in the United States," United States Catholic Historical Society Records and Studies, v. 15 (1921), 112-136. Z 35

ZWIERLEIN, FREDERICK J. "Henry George and American Catholicism," Social Justice Review, v. 35 (1942), 39-40, 75-76. Z 36

ZWIERLEIN, FREDERICK J. "Know Nothingism in Rochester, New York," United States Catholic Historical Society Records and Studies, v. 14 (1920), 20-69. Z 37

ZWIERLEIN, FREDERICK J. (ed.) Letters of Archbishop Corrigan to Bishop McQuaid and Allied Documents. Rochester, N.Y. Art Print Shop. 1946. 218p. Z 38

ZWIERLEIN, FREDERICK J. Life and Letters of Bishop McQuaid. Rochester, N.Y. Art Print Shop. 1925-1927. 3v. front., plates, ports., maps. Z 39

ZWIERLEIN, FREDERICK J.

"Les Nominations Episcopales aux Premiers Temps de l'Episcopat Américain," Melanges d'Histoire Offerts à Charles Moeller. Louvain. 1913. v. 2 pp. 527-555.   Z 40

ZWIERLEIN, FREDERICK J. "One Hundred Years of Catholicism in Rochester," Rochester Historical Society Publications, v. 13 (1934), 189-276.   Z 41

ZWIERLEIN, FREDERICK J. "Our Colonial Bishop," American Ecclesiastical Review, v. 49 (1913), 697-701.   Z 42

ZWIERLEIN, FREDERICK J. Religion in New Netherlands, 1623-1664, Rochester, N.Y. J.P. Smith Printing Co. 1910. vii, 365p. front. (map).
                                         Z 43

ZWIERLEIN, FREDERICK J. 'Rochester's Catholic Pioneers,' United States Catholic Historical Society Records and Studies, v. 16 (1924), 66-77.
                                         Z 44

ZWIERLEIN, FREDERICK J. 'Rome's Condemnation of Georgism," Social Justice Review, v. 34 (1942), 331-333.
                                         Z 45

ZWIERLEIN, FREDERICK J. "A Source of American No-Popery," St. Louis Fortnightly Review, v. 40 (1933), 269-273.   Z 46
Points out the importance of the writings of Filmer and Sidney.

ZWIERLEIN, FREDERICK J. Theodore Roosevelt and Catholics, 1882-1919. Rochester, N.Y. Art Print Shop. 1956. xii, 392p.   Z 47

ZWIERLEIN, FREDERICK. Theodore Roosevelt and Catholics. St. Louis, Missouri. Central Bureau of the Central Verein, 1956. xiii, 302p.
                                         Z 48

ZWIERLEIN, FREDERICK J. 'Theodore Roosevelt and Catholics," Social Justice Review, v. 48 (1955), 60-64, 96-99, 150-155.   Z 49

ZWINGE, JOSEPH. "Jesuit Farms in Maryland," Woodstock Letters, v. 39 (1910), 374-382; v. 40 (1911), 65-77, 180-199; v. 41 (1912), 85-97, 195-222, 275-291; v. 42 (1913), 1-13, 137-150, 336-352; v. 43 (1914), 83-89, 194-200.
                                         Z 50

ZWINGE, JOSEPH. "Our Fathers and the Colonization of Maryland," Woodstock Letters, v. 36 (1907), 78-92.   Z 51

Dominicans in, A 53, M 420, S 43

Mission property, H 98

Mission secularization, G 97

Missions, Franciscan, A 68, B 12, B 132, B 141, B 174, B 410, C 59, C 60, C 234, C 236, C 254, C 260, C 328, C 369, D 12, D 25, D 158, E 29, E 99, E 101-118, F 78, F 112, F 197, F 200, G 10, G 26, G 96-98, G 105, G 111, G 118, G 120-123, G 179, H 31, H 98, H 103, H 106, H 197, H 234, H 360, H 367, J 6-8, J 25-28, J 51, J 115, K 88, K 124, K 210, L 229, M 69, M 120, M 172, M 630, N 75, N 110, O 168, P 11-14, P 122, P 123, P 227, P 232, P 245, P 246, R 247, S 64, S 82, S 83, S 227, S 228, S 404, S 405, S 429, S 546, S 549, T 3, T 50, T 54, T 105, T 106, T 146, V 48, W 32, W 77-79, W 201.

Society of Jesus in, B 123, C 235, D 287, D 288, G 26, J 51, M 513, W 109, W 191, W 192

Callahan, A. F 20, P 151

Callaghan, J., C 12

Camaldolese, C 23, S 42

Cambria Co., Pa., W 171

Campbell, J., G 369

Campion College, D 8

Cana Movement, C 227

Cancer, Luis, D 301

Canisius College (Buffalo), L 96

Canisius High School (Buffalo), H 140

Canton, Ohio, G 233

Capuchins, B 220, H 2, J 45, L 119, L 120, L 208, M 453, M 487-489, V 54, V 55, Z 11

Capulin, Colo., T 144

Carabin, Peter, L 282

Carbon, Centre, Pa., L 154

Cardinals, biog., F 90, M 190, P 263, W 27, W 28

Carey, Mathew, B 21, C 41, D 185, G 295, R 219

Carey, Ohio, H 17

Carlisle, Pa., G 28, G 29

Carmelites, Allenton, M 574

Iowa, C 45

Port Tobacco, Md., H 104, H 240, K 63

Carney, Andrew, M 606

Carolina, O 27

Caroline, Mother, D 308

Carroll, Charles, B 304, C 50, G 407, L 178, P 220, R 221, S 403

Carroll, Daniel, C 363, G 101, G 367, L 84, P 267

Carroll, John, A 92, B 420, D 122, D 126, E 68, G 372, G 387, G 405, G 410, H 111, L 190, M 5, M 427, M 430, P 102, S 278, W 213, Z 42

Carroll Co., Ia., G 268

Carter, C.I.H., F 158, R 89

Carthage, N.Y., M 468

Carthusians, Vt., G 168

Cartier, Fr., D 268

Carville, La., S 333

Cassion, K. A., O 180

Castañeda, C.E., K 128

Castro-ville, W 69

Catala, Magin, E 100

Cataldo, Joseph, W 86

Catechetics, C 261-263

Catechisms, F 247

Catherine de Ricci, Mother, J 30

Catholic Authors, H 247, R 166

Catholic Charities, B 206, B 340, O 108, O 109

Catholic Colonization Society, M 448

Catholic Daily Tribune, G 99

Catholic Directories, W 149

Catholic Evidence Guild, H 393, R 234

Catholic Historical Review, W 181

Catholic Historical Societies, G 365

Catholic Hospital Association, C 115, C 116, M 449

Catholic Hour, H 124

Catholic Interracial Council, G 87

Catholic Ladder, W 112

Catholic Laymen's Association (Georgia), M 589

378

Catholic Laymen's Union, L 196
Catholic Medical Mission Board,
  G 31
Catholic Medical Missionaries,
  G 203
Catholic Messenger, W 3
Catholic Minority, M 30, M 35,
  M 38
Catholic School Journal, F 62
Catholic Seaman's Institute,
  K 164
Catholic Sentinal (Portland, Ore.)
  H 142
Catholic Serials, W 150
Catholic Signers of the Constitu-
  tion, C 363
Catholic Telegraph, C 284
Catholic Telegraph Register,
  V 1
Catholic Theater, H 198
Catholic Total Abstinence
  League, B 235, R 32
Catholic Total Abstinence Union,
  G 253, S 297
Catholic Trade Unionists, R 70
Catholic University. A 26-28,
  B 81, B 422, B 424, B 519,
  C 65, D 149, E 78, E 81,
  G 376, H 275, K 178, O 36,
  S 235, S 286, W 11
Catholic Vote, F 62, M 49
Catholic Worker, A 88
Cause, J. B., S 221
Cebul, John, B 273
Cecil Co., Md., D 127
Cedar Rapids, Ia., G 340
Cenacle Nuns, L 293
Centers for Youth, G 30
Central City, Colo., S 558
Central Verein, B 6, B 389,
  G 144, M 341, O 155, S 503
Calloner, Richard, B 520
Chaplains, D 296, G 286, G 142,
  G 143, M 398; see also
  individual wars.
Charles Co., Md., M 598
Charleston, S.C., F 251, H 330
Charlestown, Mass., B 202,
  D 99, D 100
Charlestown, W. Va., L 153
Chartrand, Joseph, L 58
Chatard, F. S., S 527
Chattanooga, Tenn., F 144
Chazelle, Pierre, C 414, C 417

Cheraw, S.C., L 76
Chestnut Hill, Pa., M 474
Cheverus, John, G 405, M 17,
  M 429, O 151
Cheyenne, Wyo. (eccl. div.),
  M 156
Chicago, Ill. (eccl. div.), E 130,
  T 56
Chicago, Ill., B 201, B 459,
  B 463, C 21, D 35, G 43,
  G 46, G 49, G 52, G 55,
  H 22, H 63, H 299, K 11,
  M 590, O 135, O 137, P 69,
  R 43, T 13, T 36, T 63,
  T 64
Child Labor, M 205
Christian Brothers, A 30, A 82,
  B 402, D 197, E 154, G 137,
  H 66, L 2, L 14
Church Property, H 176, N 31
Cicognani, A.G., A 72
Cincinnati, Ohio (eccl. div.),
  C 283, L 45, L 52, S 483,
Cincinnati, Ohio, J 52, K 85,
  M 507
Civil War, B 251, B 254, B 256,
  M 380, R 86, S 302, T 107,
  V 38, W 29, W 130
  Catholic Press, B 253
  Catholics, B 257, D 46, D
    230, F 235, G 204, M 518,
    M 572, N 101, W 110,
    W 138
  Chaplains, A 86, C 152, C
    325, D 181, F 147, G 95,
    K 131, K 132, M 12, M
    423, N 4-14, R 53, T 90,
    T 108
  Elder, Bp. (Natchez), W 136
  Hughes, Archb. (New York),
    A 78, H 360, W 136
  Kenrick, Archb. (St. Louis),
    W 125
  Lynch, Bp. (Charleston),
    W 140
  Mc Gill, Bp. (Richmond),
    W 141
  Northern Bishops, B 245
  Quinlan, Bp. (Mobile),
    W 139
  Sisters during, B 98,
    C 138, E 164, H 190, L
    203
  Southern Bishops, B 246

Verot, Bp. (Savannah), W 137
Clay, Henry, F 138
Clerics of St. Viator, O 184
Cleveland, Ohio (eccl. div.),
  H 334, H 336, H 337, H 406,
  J 17
Cleveland, Ohio, H 335, M 79
Cliff Haven, W 124
Clinton Co., Ill., B 93, F 80
Clinton Co., Iowa, D 282
Clinton, N.Y., M 549
Cloriviere, J.P.L., M 289
Clovis, N.M., M 125, S 524
Cockran, Bourke, M 161
College of the Holy Cross
  (Worcester, Mass.), M 389
Colorado, E 149, E 151, G 153,
  G 154, H 93, J 105, L 103,
  L 180, M 166, M 202, M 266,
  M 297, M 478, O 158a,
  S 209, S 442, V 63, V 66-
  69
Colorado Bible Case, V 63
Columban Congress, P 254, S
  291
Columbus, Christopher, S 488
Columbus, Ohio (eccl. div.),
  H 83
Columbus, Ohio, L 115
Comey, D.J., S 56
Commonweal, G 245
Concanen, H 384, O 66, O 72
Conception, Mo., B 167, C 400-
  402
Conejos, Colo., B 27, B 28,
  M 194, P 86-88.
Conewago, Pa., C 278, H 110,
  P 43, R 59, W 66
Confirmation, Colonial, H 383
Congregation of Notre Dame,
  B 13, B 14
Congregation of Our Lady of
  Perpetual Help (Altus, Ark.),
  O 92
Congregation of St. Catherine
  of Sienna (Racine, Wis.), K
  189
Congregation of St. Gertrude the
  Great, S 140
Congregation of St. Paul, A 67
Congregation of the Grey Nuns,
  K 36
Congregation of the Sisters of
  the Holy Cross, R 130

Congregation of the Holy Union
  of the Sacred Hearts, M 368
Congregation of the Mission
  D 246
Congregation of the Sisters of the
  Third Order of St. Francis of
  the Perpetual Adoration, C 277
  see also Sisters ...
Connecticut, D 273, G 351, G
  407, H 122, M 353, M 602,
  S 236, S 237
Connelly, Cornelia, E 33, M 335,
  T 157
Connersville, Ind., H 126
Conquistadora, La., C 170, C
  171, C 173, C 174, E 153
Converts, C 428, D 23, G 156,
  G 229, L 281, M 271, M 272
  S 100, S 265
Conway, James, G 38
Conwell, Bp. H., G 309, L 210
Cooney, P.P., M 48
Cooper, J.M., R 237, S 229
Cooper, S.S., F 159, G 329,
  M 118, M 119
Copley, Thomas, B 151, D 232
Corby, Wm., R 53
Corcoran, J.A., L 261, L 262
Cornell Plan, M 615
Corning, N.Y., M 197
Cornwaleys, Thomas, S 528
Corridan, John, R 24
Corrigan, M.A., M 433, Z 38
Cosgrove, Henry, G 157
Coshocton Co., Ohio, K 125
Cote des Allemands, La., H 302
Caughlin, C.E., M 586, W 59
Council Bluffs, Ia., C 77
Covington, Ky. (eccl. div.),
  R 263
Covington, Ky., A 84, B 444
Cowlitz, Wash., P 236
Creighton University, D 238,
  O 36
Crespi, Juan, C 369, P 128
Cretin, Joseph, H 254, I 23,
  O 163
Croix, Charles, B 1
Croquet, A.J., V 16
Crosier Story, R 17
Cullen, Thomas, E 52
Cumberland, Md., D 174
Curran, J.J., C 233
Custer, G.A., S 177

Hidalgo, Francisco, W 207
Hieronymo, Mother, K 54
Highland, Ill., B 290, M 394
Historiography, G 365, G 380,
    G 382, G 390, G 395, G 399,
    L 140, L 206, M 42, M 530,
    O 59
Hoban, M.J., H 102
Hobi, Isidore, H 119
Hoecken, H 246, M 223, S 392,
    W 160
Hoffman, E.T.A., D 24
Hogan, William, D 268
Hogan schism, L 210, T 111
Hohenlohe, Prince, L 158
Holy Family Sisters of San
    Francisco, K 32
Holy Ghost, devotion, F 64
Hospital Sisters of the Third
    Order of St. Francis, C 316
Howlett, William, xxxvii, O 61
Huber, Francis, W 203
Hudson, D. F., W 26
Huebner, Fr., B 189
Hughes, John, A 78, B 212,
    B 356, B 413, B 414, B 426,
    C 306, F 51, H 88, H 361,
    H 368, H 369, M 145, M
    396, M 400, S 254, S 302
Hughes, T.A., xxxvii, xxxviii
Huming, Silvain, V 37
Hurley, Michael, W 107
Huron Mission, D 279, E 49
Husslein, Joseph, H 290
Hyland, A.R., B 311

Idaho, D 139, H 225, S 431,
    V 14
Illinois, B 97, B 190, B 191,
    B 193, C 223, C 225, C 270,
    D 230, F 2, G 54, G 237,
    H 147, H 366, I 4, L 66-68,
    M 220, O 139, P 8, P 96,
    R 217, S 102, S 439, S 448,
    T 58-61, T 66, T 67, T 73,
    T 138, V 52, W 13a, Y 6
Immaculate Conception Academy,
    San Francisco, Cal., B 407
Immigration, C 360, K 64,
    M 609, O 76
Inama, Adelbert, L 157
Incarnate Word Sisters in Texas,
    H 320
Indian Clergy, E 12, E 138,

N 32, R 55
Indian Mission Bureau, Catholic,
    B 484-486
Indian Missions, A 103, B 8,
    B 9, B 47, B 49-51, B 55
    B 62, B 73, B 94, B 168,
    B 337, B 377, B 443, B 489,
    C 25, C 51, C 67, C 68, C
    82, C 183, C 194, C 251,
    C 289, C 393, D 11, D 17,
    D 18, D 66, D 152, D 153,
    D 166, D 167, D 176, D 198,
    D 215, D 278, D 283, D 291,
    E 13, E 20, E 36, E 40,
    E 51, E 53, E 136, E 138,
    F 119, F 124, F 125, F 166,
    F 214, F 227-229, G 8, G 11,
    G 23, G 27, G 65, G 73, G
    75, G 82, G 83, G 199, G 221,
    G 236, G 242-244, G 276, G
    352, G 359-361, H 87, H 102,
    H 191, H 213, H 214, H 241,
    H 250, H 363, I 12-14, J-1,
    J 16, J 21, J 25-28, J 68,
    J 72, J 74, J 124, J 128-
    130, K 25, K 42, K 50,
    K 201, K 217, L 51, L 61,
    L 108, L 183, L 229, L 231,
    M 252, M 253, M 275, M 298,
    M 351, M 364, N 1, N 34,
    N 35, N 78-81, N 106-109,
    N 117, N 122, N 123, O 23,
    O 30-32, O 56, O 79, O 164,
    O 175, O 191, P 8, P 9,
    P 28, P 79, P 80, P 102,
    P 106, P 120, P 212, P 213,
    R 1, R 5, R 202, S 19, S 69,
    S 109, S 125, S 383-401,
    S 463-465, S 552, T 52, V
    21, V 26, V 27, V 40, V 43,
    W 194, W 195.
Indiana, B 228, L 221, M 32,
    M 33, M 199, M 270, M 499,
    O 83, P 3, S 173, S 183,
    S 270
Indianapolis, Ind. (eccl. div.),
    P 107
Indianapolis, Ind., H 3, R 105
Indian's Lament, D 253, J 58,
    R 205
Industrial conflict, A 9
Infallibility, B 291
Inglesi affair, H 301
Institute of St. Catherine de

386

Northampton Co., Pa., M 60
Northumberland Co., S 309
Notre Dame College (Maryland), C 24
Notre Dame University, C 276, H 328, S 554

Obernberg, N.Y., S 147
Oblates of Mary Immaculate, W 5, W 6
Oblate Sisters of Providence, S 306
O'Brien, F.A., C 141, H 18
O'Brien, M.A., O 63
O'Callaghan, E.B., G 416
O'Callaghan, Jeremiah, C 3
O'Connell, James Cardinal, C 198, W 71
O'Connor, James, H 118, M 74
O'Connor, T.F., xxxvi, xxxvii, O 50
Odilia, Mary, B 226
Odin, J.M., C 154, S 305
Official Catholic Directory, M 419
Ogdensburg, N.Y. (eccl. Div.) J 105, S 414
O'Hanlon, John, C 272
O'Hara, E.V., G 177, S 250
O'Hara, John F., J 57, M 41
Ohio, A 95, K 94, L 146, L 138, M 541, O 65, S 312, V 9, V 24
Ohio Valley Catholic Historical Society, M 505
O'Keefe, J.J., L 200
O'Kelley, P., J 86
Oklahoma, H 86, H 322, L 64, M 123, N 78, N 80, T 47-49
Old Catholics, M 330
Old Laguna, N.M., L 28
Old Northwest, B 507
Oldenburg, Ind., D 148, U 1, W 145
Omaha, Nebr. (eccl. div.), M 314
Omaha, Nebr., F 129, M 74
Onahan, W.J., P 4
O'Neill, John, L 57
Opelousas, La., C 259
Open Pulpit Controversy, H 100, H 101
Orange, N.J., C 39

Order of St. Augustine, R 163
Oregon, B 16, B 113, B 214, B 231-234, D 84, D 183, D 292, D 293, F 171, H 228, J 124, L 59, M 251, O 43, O 113-115, P 164, P 214, P 215, R 133, R 190, S 154.
Oregon School Case, R 249
O'Reilly, J.B., F 89, R 135
Orphan Homes, S 175
Ortiz, Ramon, P 260
O'Rourke, J.J., N 51
Ostanberger, G.H., H 312
Oswald, A., L 131
Owensboro, Ky., L 297
Oxford Movement, W 44

Padilla, Juan de, B 44, C 179, C 180, F 182, H 202
Paducah, Ky., D 221
Palou, G 107, S 421
Panna Maria, Texas, D 303
Pardow, William, F 109, W 53
Parish Missions, A 110
Parish Priest, S 195
Parkman, Francis, B 378, M 142
Parkston, S.D., R 47
Parsons, Wilfrid, L 7
Passionist Fathers, G 195, H 201, W 51
Paul, Fr., of Greymoor, F 253, G 25
Paulhuber, F.X., L 168
Pauline, Mother, J 44
Paulists, G 166, M 319, O 123, P 40, P 51
Pax, Alesander, H 316
Pena Diary, F 203
Penitentes, A 18, A 109, B 66, C 175, F 172, F 206, H 137 H 138, K 98, L 104, M 496, M 562, V 69
Penn, William, G 334, K 161
Pennsylvania, A 13, A 14, B 230, C 133, C 134, C 288, F 86, G 23, H 90, H 376, L 117, L 193, L 194, M 466, P 68, S 372, T 56
Peoria, Ill. (eccl. div.), G 41
Perkionen Valley, S 191
Persone, Salvador, F 34
Persico, Ignatius Cardinal, S 293, S 294

391

Perth Amboy, N.J., O 148
Peter, S.W.K., M 8, P 97
Petersburg, Va., B 18
Petit, Nicholas, F 31, H 327
Philadelphia, Pa. (eccl. div.)
  F 7, K 114-116, N 95, O 152
Philadelphia, A 83, B 169,
  B 367, F 155, F 164, G 287,
  G 297, G 300-305, G 307-
  309, G 311, G 315, G 316,
  G 324, G 331, G 332, H 99,
  J 10-14, K 149, L 25, L 27,
  L 150, M 2, M 114, M 176,
  M 200, M 242, M 256, O 119,
  P 32, R 50, R 87, S 211,
  S 426, T 111-114, W 40,
  W 107
Phoenix, Ariz., H 238
Picot de Limoelan Cloriviere, J.
  P., M 221, M 289
Pierz, Francis, B 394, F 254,
  K 80, K 81, M 98, T 27
Pinet, P.F., G 349
Pinto, C.M., O 183
Pio Nono College, Milwaukee,
  Wis., B 237
Pioneer Laymen, C 32
Pioneer Priests, C 33
Pirec, Francis, S 214
Piret, Fr., P 136
Pise, C.C., M 401, M 532,
  M 533
Pitass, John, S 381
Pittsburgh, Pa. (eccl. div.),
  L 31, L 33-35, L 40, L 60
  O 35
Pittsburgh, Pa., C 126, C 314,
  L 43, R 136
Pittsfield, Mass., M 592
Pius Fund, D 242, M 104
Pius X, D 22
Plessis de Mornacy, L.F.,
  B 429
Pocahontas Co., Ia., F 18
Poets, F 47
Point, Nicholas, B 11, P 215
Point Pleasant, J 103
Polish influence, A 13, A 14, A
  64, A 70, B 308, D 304, H 26,
  H 64, K 26, K 199, L 192,
  M 219, M 251, M 631, N 85-
  87, N 91, O 129, R 67, R 164,
  S 318, S 319, S 557, W 185
  W 186, Z 6

Pollock, Oliver, J 29
Ponziglione, P.M., B 375, G 248,
  H 209
Pontificia American, C 88
Poor Clares, B 339, W 166
Pope's Stone, K 156
Porras, Martin de, B 170
Portland, Ore., W 111
Portier, Pierre, E 47, O 169
Pottstown, Pa., S 192
Powderly, R.V., B 427, B 428
Power, James, S 164
Prairie du Chien, Wis., B 305,
  S 97-99
Prairie du Rocher, Ill., E 141
Prefontaine, F.X., B 320
Pramonstratentions, K 147,
  K 148
Prescott, Wis., T 37
Presidents, USA, R 122
Priber, Christian, M 426
Price, Thomas, B 546, M 621,
  M 622
Prinkers, Arnold, V 35
Propaganda, Congregation of,
  C 346
Propagation, Society of the, F 234,
  H 189
Prosser, Wash., D 30
Prost, Joseph, K 182, K 183
Providence, R.I., B 376
Providence Hospital, Washington,
  D.C., V 73
Provincetown, Mass., B 403
Purcell, J.B., D 136, H 208,
  M 61, M 64
Purcell, R.J., xxxvi, N 92
Pueblo, Colo., B 461, G 128,
  M 267, P 131, P 132

Quabache, D 278
Quapaw, Okla., L 77
Quarter, William, R 209
Quebec Act, K 129, M 459
Quebec-United States relations,
  L 78, L 210-212, L 214,
  L 215, R 113, R 114, S 437
Quebec Archives, L 209, L 213
Queen's Work, G 32
Quesnay, see Mercier
Quincy, Ill., B 443, Z 29
Quinlan, J., W 139
Quintano, Andrew, O 26

Sisters of Charity of the B. V.
M., C 21, D 226, F 169
Sisters of Charity of the Incar-
nate Word, F 81 (San
Antonio).
Sisters of Divine Providence,
C 18
Sisters of Loretto, A 67, B 61,
D 239, M 500, O 53, O 185-
190, O 193, O 196, O 197,
O 199, O 200
Sisters of Mercy, A 67, F 50
(Bishop England), B 180
(Mississippi), B 545 (Camden,
N.J.), C 57, C 288, (Phila-
delphia), C 351 (Maryland),
C 373 (Nebraska), D 157
(Cincinnati), F 120 (Buffalo),
G 94, H 162, H 163, H 287,
(Cedar Rapids, Ia.), L 174,
(St. Louis, Mo), M 111
(Harrisburg, Pa.), M 350
(Harrisburg, Pa.), M 568
(Oklahoma), O 86, (Texas),
S 420 (St. Louis, Mo.), W 48,
(Cincinnati), W 199 (San
Francisco, Cal.)
Sisters of Notre Dame, M 344,
F 73 (Columbia, Ohio), L 258
(Covington, Ky.)
Sisters of Notre Dame de Namur,
G 266, Q 5
Sisters of Providence, G 200
Sisters of Providence of Saint
Mary of the Woods, B 406
Sisters of St. Dominic of Sin-
sinawa, M 161
Sisters of St. Dominic of the
Congregation of St. Thomas
Aquinas, Seattle, Wash.,
F 142
Sisters of St. Felix, K 6
Sisters of St. Francis, H 233,
M 333 (Oldenburg, Ind.),
P 205 (Pittsburgh, Pa.),
Z 28 (Springfield, Ill.)
Sisters of St. Francis of Assisi,
Milwaukee, Wis., H 60
Sisters of St. Francis of the
Holy Family, G 182
Sisters of St. Joseph, A 71,
C 253, C 361 (Minnesota),
H 242 (Carondolet), H 249
(Carondolet), H 390 (Caron-

dolet), M 54 (Newark, N.J.)
M 288 (Philadelphia), M 362
(Cleveland), M 387 (Boston),
O 140 (Philadelphia), S 85
(Carondolet), T 39 (Concordia).
Sisters of the Blessed Sacrament
for Indians and Colored People,
A 67
Sisters of the Divine Compas-
sion, A 67
Sisters of the Good Shepherd,
B 184 (Oregon), M 157
(Philadelphia), R 104 (Detroit).
Sisters of the Holy Cross, A 1,
E 32, R 182
Sisters of the Holy Names, M 171,
O 147, P 81 (California),
S 432 (Oregon)
Sisters of the Humility of Mary,
A 67
Sisters of the Immaculate Heart
of Mary, S 187, S 375
Sisters of the Third Order of St.
Dominic of the Congregation
of the Most Holy Rosary,
B 286
Sisters of the Third Order of St.
Francis of Perpetual Adora-
tion, L 284
Sisters of the Third Order of St.
Francis of the Holy Family,
M 576
Sisters of the Visitation, D 39,
K 186, S 313
Sisters, Servants of the Immacu-
late Heart of Mary, K 16
(Scranton), M 170 (West
Chester, Pa.), M 284, R 178
Slavery, A 49, C 55, R 103
Sleepy Eye, Minn., S 104
Smet, P.J. De, C 137, C 338,
D 27-29, D 137, D 207, D 208,
D 210, D 233, E 19, G 57,
H 246, H 329, L 80, M 170,
M 229, M 596, O 57, O 114-
116, W 39, W 93, Y 7
Smith, "Father," D 133, G 294
Smith, A.E., F 104, G 234
Smith, Charles, D 112
Smith, Clement, H 255
Smyth, Clement, H 146
Social Justice, A 3
Social Problems, A 4, A 7
Social Relations, F 75-77

72
80
82
87 —
95 —
98 —
102 —
106 —
114
119
(127) ×
+128
129
(131)
(133)
135
136
140
(145)
(146)
(151)

(311)
(154)
(337)
(763)
(351)
171
(362)
172
(320)
181
(184)
(190)
(91)
(197)
(199)
202
204
(208)
(209)
(213)
213
(220)
(228)
(233)
(250)
(253)
(271)
(274)

2141
337

373